Mario Vargas Llosa was born in 1936 in Peru. He has established an international reputation as one of Latin America's most important novelists. His works include *The War of the End of the World* (1985), *The Real Life of Alejandro Mayta* (1986), *Captain Pantoja and the Special Service* (1987), *Who Killed Palomino Molero?* (1988), *The Storyteller* (1989), *In Praise of the Stepmother* (1991), *A Writer's Reality* (1992) and a study of Flaubert, *The Perpetual Orgy* (1987). Faber and Faber also publish his earlier novels *The Time of the Hero*, *The Green House*, *Conversation in The Cathedral* and *Aunt Julia and the Scriptwriter* in paperback.

by the same author

THE TIME OF THE HERO
THE GREEN HOUSE
CONVERSATION IN THE CATHEDRAL
AUNT JULIA AND THE SCRIPTWRITER
THE WAR OF THE END OF THE WORLD
THE REAL LIFE OF ALEJANDRO MAYTA
CAPTAIN PANTOJA AND THE SPECIAL SERVICE
THE PERPETUAL ORGY
WHO KILLED PALOMINO MOLERO?
THE STORYTELLER
IN PRAISE OF THE STEPMOTHER
THE CUBS AND OTHER STORIES
A WRITER'S REALITY

A FISH
IN THE WATER

A Memoir

MARIO VARGAS LLOSA

Translated by
Helen Lane

faber and faber

First published in the USA by Farrar, Straus and Giroux, Inc.
Published simultaneously in Canada by HarperCollins *Canada* Ltd
First published in Great Britain in 1994
by Faber and Faber Limited
3 Queen Square London WC1N 3AU
This paperback edition first published in 1995

Originally published in Spanish as *El pez en el agua*
Spanish edition supervised by
Maria del Carmen Ghezzi and Alex Zisman

Printed in England by Clays Ltd, St Ives plc

All rights reserved

© Mario Vargas Llosa, 1993
English translation © Farrar, Straus and Giroux, Inc., 1994

Helen Lane is hereby identified as translator of this work
in accordance with Section 77 of the Copyright,
Designs and Patents Act 1988.

*This book is sold subject to the condition that it shall not, by way of trade
or otherwise, be lent, resold, hired out or otherwise circulated without the
publisher's prior consent in any form of binding or cover other than that
in which it is published and without a similar condition including
this condition being imposed on the subsequent purchaser.*

A CIP record for this book is
available from the British Library

ISBN 0–571–17512–0

2 4 6 8 10 9 7 5 3 1

This book is dedicated to
Frederick Cooper Llosa
Miguel Cruchaga Belaunde
Luis Miró Quesada Garland
Fernando de Szyszlo

with whom everything began

and to my friends
of the Freedom Movement

Contents

Primitive Christians also knew very explicitly that the world is ruled by demons and that anyone who becomes involved in politics, that is to say, anyone who agrees to use power and violence as means, has sealed a pact with the devil, so that it is no longer true that in his activity the good produces only good and the bad bad, but that the contrary frequently happens. Anyone who does not see this is a child, politically speaking.

—MAX WEBER, *Politics as a Vocation* (1919)

A Fish in the Water

ONE

~~~~~~~~~~~

The Man Who Was
My Papa

M Y mama took me by the arm and led me out into the street by the service entrance of the prefecture. We walked along toward the Eguiguren embankment. It was the final days of 1946 or the first days of 1947, but exams at the Salesian school were already over, I had finished the fifth grade, and summer in Piura, with its white light and asphyxiating heat, had already come.

"You already know it, of course," my mama said, without her voice trembling. "Isn't that so?"

"Know what?"

"That your papa isn't dead. Isn't that so?"

"Of course. Of course."

But I didn't know that, or even remotely suspect it, and it was as if the world had left me paralyzed with surprise. My papa, alive? And where had he been all the time I thought he was dead? It was a long story that up until that day—the most important day in my life till then and, perhaps, in my later life, too—had been carefully hidden from me by my mother, my grandfather and grandmother, my great-aunt Elvira—Mamaé—and my aunts and uncles, that vast family with which I spent my childhood, first in Cochabamba and then, once my grandfather Pedro was appointed mayor of this city, here in Piura. An episode in a cruel and vulgar serial, which—I gradually discovered this later, as I went about reconstructing it with facts from here and there and imaginary additions in places where it turned out to be impossible to fill in the blanks—had made my mother's family (my only family, in fact) terribly ashamed and ruined my mother's life when she was still little more than an adolescent.

A story that had begun thirteen years before, more than two thousand kilometers away from this Eguiguren embankment, the scene of the great revelation. My mother was nineteen years old. She had gone to Tacna with my granny Carmen—who came from Tacna—from Arequipa, where the family lived, to attend the wedding of a relative, on March 10, 1934, when, in what must have been a jerry-built, very recently constructed airport in that provincial city, someone introduced her to the man who operated the radio transmitter for Panagra, the company that would later become Pan American Airlines: his name was Ernesto J. Vargas. He was twenty-nine years old and very good-looking. My mother was very taken with him, from that moment on and for the rest of her life. And he must have fallen in love at first sight, too, because when, after a few weeks' vacation in Tacna, she went back to Arequipa, he wrote her a number of letters and even made a trip there, to say goodbye to her when Panagra transferred him to Ecuador. On that very brief visit of his to Arequipa they became officially engaged. The engagement was carried on by letter; they didn't see each other again until a year later, when my father—whom Panagra had just transferred once more, this time to Lima—appeared in Arequipa again for the wedding. They were married on June 4, 1935, in the house on the Bulevar Parra where my grandparents lived, beautifully decorated for the occasion. In the photograph that survived (they showed it to me many years later), Dorita can be seen posing in her white dress with a long train and a transparent veil, wearing an expression not at all radiant, but solemn, rather, and in her big dark eyes a somber shadow of curiosity as to what the future would bring her.

What it brought her was disaster. After the wedding, they immediately journeyed to Lima, where my father worked for Panagra. They lived in a little house on the Calle Alfonso Ugarte, in Miraflores. From the very first, he gave evidence of what the Llosa family was to call, euphemistically, Ernesto's strange-mindedness. Dorita was subjected to a prison routine, forbidden to visit friends of hers, in particular her relatives, and forced to remain permanently at home. Her only outings were made in the company of my father and consisted of going to a movie theater or visiting his older brother, César, and his wife Orieli, who also lived in Miraflores. Jealous scenes followed one upon the other on the slightest pretext, and sometimes without any pretext at all, and they could lead to violence.

Many years later, when I already had gray hair and it was possible for me to talk with her about the five and a half months that her marriage lasted, my mother was still putting forward the family's explanation for its failure: Ernesto's bad disposition and his fiendish fits of jealousy. And casting part of the blame on herself, too, perhaps, since she had been such a pampered young girl, for whom life in Arequipa had been so easy, so comfortable, had not prepared her for that difficult test: having to leave overnight to go live in another city with such a dominating person, so different from all those around her.

But the real reason for the failure of their marriage was not my father's jealousy or his bad disposition, but the national disease that gets called by other names, the one that infests every stratum and every family in the country and leaves them all with a bad aftertaste of hatred, poisoning the lives of Peruvians in the form of resentment and social complexes. Because Ernesto J. Vargas, despite his white skin, his light blue eyes and his handsome appearance, belonged—or always felt that he belonged, which amounts to the same thing—to a family socially inferior to his wife's. The adventures, misadventures, and deviltry of my paternal grandfather, Marcelino, had gradually impoverished and brought the Vargas family down in the world till they reached that ambiguous margin where those who are middle-class begin to be taken for what those of a higher status call "the people," and in a position where Peruvians who believe that they are *blancos* (whites) begin to feel that they are *cholos*, that is to say mestizos, half-breeds of mixed Spanish and Indian blood, that is to say poor and despised. In particolored Peruvian society, and perhaps in all societies which have many races and extreme inequalities, *blanco* and *cholo* are terms that refer to other things besides race or ethnic group: they situate a person socially and economically, and many times these factors are the ones that determine his or her classification. This latter is flexible and can change, depending on circumstances and the vicissitudes of individual destinies. One is always *blanco* or *cholo* in relation to someone else, because one is always better or worse situated than others, or one is more or less poor or important, or possessed of more or less Occidental or mestizo or Indian or African or Asiatic features than others, and all this crude nomenclature that decides a good part of any one person's fate is maintained by virtue of an effervescent structure of prejudices and sentiments—disdain, scorn, envy, bitterness, admiration, emulation—which, many times, beneath ideologies, values, and contempt for values, is the deep-seated explanation for the conflicts and frustrations of Peruvian life. It is a grave error, when discussing racial and social prejudices in Peru, to believe that they act only from the top down; parallel to the contempt that the white shows toward the mestizo, the Indian, and the black, there exists the bitterness of the mestizo against the white and the Indian and the black, and of each one of these latter three against all the others, feelings—or perhaps it would be more accurate to speak of impulses or passions—that lie concealed behind political, professional, cultural, and personal rivalries, in accordance with a process which cannot even be called hypocritical, since it is rarely rational and seldom openly revealed. In the majority of cases it is unconscious, stemming from an ego that is hidden and blind to reason; it is taken in with one's mother's milk and begins to be shaped from the time of the Peruvian's first birth-cry and babblings as a baby.

That was probably true of my father. More intimately and decisively than by his bad disposition or his jealousy, his life with my mother was ruined by the sensation, which never left him, that she came from a world of names that meant something—those Arequipa families that boasted of their Spanish forebears, of their good manners, of the purity of the Spanish they spoke—that is to say, families from a world superior to that of his own, impoverished and brought to ruin by politics.

My paternal grandfather, Marcelino Vargas, had been born in Chancay, a town not far from Lima, and learned the métier of radio operator, which he was to teach my father in the brief calm interludes of his frenzied existence. But the passion of his life was politics. He entered Lima through the Cocharcas gate with Piérola guerrilla fighters on March 17, 1895, when he was a young lad. And later on he was a faithful follower of the charismatic liberal leader Augusto Durán, at the latter's side throughout all his political vicissitudes, living for that reason a life of continual ups and downs, the prefect of Huánuco one day and deported to Ecuador the next, and many a time a jailbird and an outlaw. This life on the run forced my grandmother Zenobia Maldonado—whose photographs show her with an implacable expression—to perform all sorts of miracles in order to feed her five children, whom she brought up and educated practically all by herself (she had eight children, but three of them died shortly after they were born). My father used to say, in a voice full of emotion, that she had no compunction about whipping him and his brothers till she drew blood when they misbehaved.

They must have lived in great poverty, for my father studied at a public secondary school—the Colegio Guadalupe—which he left at the age of thirteen so as to contribute to his family's support. He worked as an apprentice in an Italian shoemaker's shop, and then, thanks to the rudiments of radiotelegraphy that Don Marcelino taught him, in the post office as a radio operator. In 1925 my grandmother Zenobia died and that same year my father was in Pisco, working as a tele- grapher. One day with a friend he bought a ticket in the Lima lottery that won first prize: a hundred thousand soles! With his share, fifty thousand, a fortune in those days, he went off to Buenos Aires (which, in the affluent Argentina of the 1920s, was to Latin America what Paris was to Europe), where he led a dissipated life that made his fortune dwindle very quickly. With what little he had left, he was prudent enough to complete his studies in radiotelephony, at Trans Radio, from which he received a professional diploma. A year later he won a competitive examination as a junior operator in the Argentine merchant marine, where he remained for five years, plying all the seas in the world. (There existed from this period a photograph of him, very handsome, in a navy-blue uniform, that stood on my night table during my entire childhood in Cochabamba, and apparently I kissed it when I went to bed, saying good night to "my beloved papa who's in heaven.")

He returned to Peru around 1932 or 1933, having been hired by Panagra as a flight operator. He spent more than a year in those little pioneer airplanes flying through the unexplored Peruvian skies until, in 1934, he was assigned to the Tacna airport, where that meeting of March 1934, thanks to which I came into the world, took place.

His transient and varied life did not free my father from the tortuous rancors and complexes that constitute the psychology of Peruvians. In some way or other and for some complicated reason, my mother's family came to represent for him what he had never had, or what his family had lost—the stability of a middle-class home and fireside, the strong network of relations with other families like his own, the ref- erence point of a tradition and a certain social distinction—and, as a consequence, he conceived an enmity toward that family that came to the surface on the slightest pretext and turned into insults against "the Llosas" in his fits of rage. In all truth, these feelings had almost no basis in fact in those years—the mid-1930s. The Llosa family, which for some generations after the arrival in Arequipa of the first of their lineage—the field marshal Don Juan de la Llosa y Llaguno— had been well-off and possessed of aristocratic airs, had gradually come down in the world until, in my grandfather's generation, it was a middle-class Arequipa family of modest means. It was true, nonetheless, that the family had solid ties to the little world of "society" and was firmly established. This latter fact was, in all likelihood, what that rootless being without a family and without a past, my father, was never able to forgive my mother for. My grandfather Marcelino, after Doña Zenobia's death, had put the finishing touch on his adventurous life by doing something that filled my progenitor with shame: going off to live with an Indian woman who braided her hair and wore wide skirts, in a little village in the central Andes, where he reached the end of his life, a nonagenarian with countless offspring, having worked as a stationmaster for the national railway system. Not even the Llosas gave rise to such invective as that inspired in my father by Don Marcelino, on the rare occasions when he mentioned him. His name was taboo in my father's house, as was everything else related to him. (And, no doubt for that reason, I always harbored a secret liking for the grandfather I had never known.)

My mother became pregnant with me shortly after marrying. She spent the first months of her pregnancy by herself in Lima, with the occasional company of her sister-in-law Orieli. Domestic quarrels followed one upon the other and life was very hard for my mother, yet her passionate love for my father never flagged. One day, Granny Carmen sent word from Arequipa that she would come to Lima to be at my mother's side during her lying-in. My father had been entrusted by Panagra with the job of going to La Paz to open the company office there. As though it were the most natural thing in the world he said to his wife: "Go have the baby in Arequipa instead." And he arranged everything in such a way that my mother hadn't the least suspicion of what he was plotting to do. On that morning in November 1935, he said goodbye like an affectionate husband to his wife, who was five months pregnant.

He never phoned her again or wrote to her or gave any signs of life till eleven years later, that is to say, till very shortly before that afternoon when, on the Eguiguren embankment of Piura, my mother revealed to me that the father whom up until that moment I had believed was in heaven was still on this earth, alive and wagging his tail.

"You're not telling me a fib, Mama?"

"Do you think I'd lie to you about a thing like that?"

"Is he really and truly alive?"

"Yes."

"Am I going to see him? Am I going to meet him? Where is he, then?"

"Here in Piura. You're going to meet him right now."

When at last we were able to talk about it, many years after that afternoon and many years after my father had died, my mother's voice still trembled and her eyes filled with tears, remembering how upset she was in those days, in Arequipa, when, in the face of the sudden total silence of her husband—no telephone calls, no letter, no message informing her of his whereabouts in Bolivia—she began to suspect that she had been abandoned and that, given his famous bad disposition, she would no doubt never see him again or have any news of him. "The worst of the whole thing," she says, "was the gossip. What people made up: the rumors, the lies, the whispering campaigns. I was so ashamed! I didn't dare set foot outside the house. When someone came to visit my parents, I shut myself up in my room and turned the key." Luckily, Grandpa Pedro, Granny Carmen, Mamaé and all her brothers had behaved very well, cosseting her, protecting her, and making her feel that, even though she had been abandoned by her husband, she would always have a home and family.

I was born on the second floor of the house on the Bulevar Parra, where my grandparents lived, early on the morning of March 28, 1936, after a long and painful labor. My grandfather sent a telegram to my father, by way of Panagra, giving him the news of my arrival in the world. He did not answer, and he also failed to answer a letter that my mother wrote telling him that I had been baptized with the name of Mario. Since they didn't know whether he hadn't replied because he didn't want to or because the messages hadn't reached him, my grandparents asked a relative who lived in Lima, Dr. Manuel Bustamante de la Fuente, to look him up at Panagra. The doctor went to speak with him at the airport, to which my father had returned after several months' stay in Bolivia. His reaction was to demand a divorce.

My mother consented, and it was granted, on the grounds of mutual incompatibility, through the intermediary of lawyers, without the former spouses having to see each other face to face.

This first year of my life, the only one I spent in the city where I was born and about which I remember nothing, was a hellish year for my mother as well as for my grandparents and the rest of the family —a typical middle-class family of Arequipa, in all that expression implies as regards their conservatism, their traditionalism, and their narrow outlook on life—who shared the shame of their abandoned daughter, now the mother of a fatherless child. In Arequipa society, prejudiced and afraid of its own shadow, the mystery of what had happened to Dorita caused talk. My mother didn't venture outside the house, except to go to church, and devoted herself to caring for the newborn baby, unfailingly aided by my grandmother and my Mamaé, who made this first-born baby of the new generation their pampered pet.

A year after I was born, my grandfather signed a ten-year contract with the Said family to go off to cultivate landed properties—the Saipina hacienda—that they had just acquired in Bolivia, near Santa Cruz, where the Saids wanted to introduce cotton growing, a crop that my grandfather had successfully cultivated in Camaná. Although I was never told as much, I could never rid myself of the idea that that unfortunate story of their elder daughter, and the enormous trouble caused them by my mother's abandonment and divorce, had driven my grandfather to accept a job that got the family out of Arequipa, never to return. "It was a great relief to me to go to another country, to another city, where people would leave me in peace," my mother says in reference to that move.

The Llosa family moved to Cochabamba, at that time a more livable city than the tiny, isolated little town of Santa Cruz, and settled in an enormous house on the Calle Ladislao Cabrera, in which my entire early childhood was spent. I remember it as a paradise. It had an entry hall with a tall curved roof that sent back the echo of people's voices, and a patio with trees where, with my cousins Nancy and Gladys and my school chums from La Salle, we reenacted the Tarzan films and the serials we saw on Sundays, after the Mass held at school, and at the matinees at the Cine Rex. Around the front patio was a pillared terrace with sun awnings and rocking chairs where Grandpa Pedro, when he was not out at the hacienda, used to take his afternoon nap, swaying back and forth, with snores that used to make me and my two cousins almost die laughing. There were two other patios, one paved with tiles and the other with beaten earth, where the laundry and the servants' quarters were located, along with pens in which there were always hens and, at one time, a baby goat brought from Saipina which my grandmother finally adopted. One of the first terrors of my childhood was that kid, which when it worked itself loose from its tether used to attack everything that got in its way, causing a great hubbub in the house. At another period I also had a chatterbox of a parrot that imitated the loud fits of stamping my feet that frequently came over me and screeched, in exactly the same way as I did: "Graaanny! Graaanny!"

The house was huge, but we all had our own places in it, with our own rooms: my grandma and grandpa, Mamaé, my mama and I, my Aunt Laura and my Uncle Juan and their daughters Nancy and Gladys, Uncle Lucho and Uncle George, and Uncle Pedro, who was studying medicine in Chile but who came to spend his vacations with us. Besides all of them, there were the cook and the servants, who never numbered less than three.

In that house I was pampered and spoiled to extremes that made a little monster out of me. The pampering was thanks to the fact that I was the grandparents' first grandchild and the aunts' and uncles' first grandnephew, and also because I was the son of poor Dorita, a fatherless little boy. Not having a papa, or rather, having a papa who was in heaven, wasn't anything that tormented me; on the contrary, it conferred on me a privileged status, and the lack of a real father had been compensated by any number of surrogates: my grandpa and my uncles Juan, Lucho, Jorge, and Pedro.

My wild pranks made my mama enroll me at La Salle when I was five, a year before the one recommended by the order's brothers. I learned to read shortly thereafter, in Brother Justiniano's class, and this—the most important thing that happened to me before that afternoon on the Eguiguren embankment—calmed down my tempestuous behavior, for the reading of books for children—*Billikens, Penecas*—and all sorts of little stories and tales of adventure became an exhilarating pastime that kept me quiet for hours and hours. But reading did not keep me from playing games, and I was capable more than once of inviting my whole class to have tea at my house, excesses that Granny Carmen and Mamaé, whom I hope, if God and heaven exist, have been adequately rewarded, would tolerate without a word of protest, carefully preparing slices of buttered bread, cold drinks, and coffee with milk for this swarm of children.

The entire year was one big party. It included outings to Cala-Cala, going to the main square to eat Salta-style meat pies on the days when there were open-air military band concerts, going to the movies, and playing at friends' houses—but there were two holidays that stood out, for the excitement and the happiness they brought me: Carnival and Christmas. For Carnival, we filled balloons with water beforehand—it was the custom—and when the day arrived, my cousins Nancy and Gladys and I bombarded the people passing by on the street and stole peeks, bedazzled, at our uncles and aunts as they dressed in fantastic costumes to go to masked balls. The preparations for Christmas were meticulous. Granny and Mama sowed wheat seeds in special containers for the Nativity scene, a laborious structure brought to life with little plaster figures of shepherds and animals that the family had brought from Arequipa (or that had perhaps been brought from Tacna by Granny). Decorating the tree was a fantastic ceremony. But nothing was as exciting as writing to the Baby Jesus—who had not yet been replaced by Santa Claus—little letters about the presents that I wanted him to bring on the twenty-fourth of December. And getting into bed that night, trembling with eagerness, with my eyes half-closed, wanting and at the same time not wanting to see the Baby Jesus steal into my room with the presents—books, many books—that he would leave at the foot of the bed and that I would discover the next day, my chest bursting with excitement.

While I was in Bolivia, up until the end of 1945, I believed that the Baby Jesus brought toys, and that storks brought babies from heaven, and not one of what my confessors called bad thoughts ever crossed my mind; they made their appearance later, when I was living in Lima. I was a mischievous child and a crybaby, but as innocent as a lily. And devoutly religious. I remember the occasion of my first communion as a great event: the preparatory classes given us every afternoon beforehand by Brother Agustín, the principal of La Salle, in the chapel of the school, and the moving ceremony—with me dressed in white for the occasion and the entire family present—in which I received the host from the hands of the bishop of Cochabamba, an imposing figure enveloped in royal purple vestments whose hand I hastened to kiss when I met him on the street or when he appeared at the house on Ladislao Cabrera (which was the Peruvian consulate as well, a post my grandfather had assumed *ad honorem*). And I remember as well the breakfast with hot chocolate and sweets made of almonds and candied fruit which they gave to those of us who had celebrated our first communion, and our families, in the patio of the school.

From Cochabamba I remember the Salta-style meat pies and the Sunday lunches, with the whole family present—Uncle Lucho was already married to Aunt Olga, no doubt, and Uncle Jorge to Aunt Gaby—and the enormous family dining table, where everyone always reminisced about Peru, or perhaps I should say about Arequipa, and where we all hoped that when it came time for dessert there would appear the *sopaipillas*, delicious fritters dipped in honey, and the *guargüeros*, pineapple and coconut sweets, desserts typical of Tacna and Moquegua, that Granny and Mamaé made with magic hands. I remember the Urioste and Beverley swimming pools to which Uncle Lucho took me, in which I learned to swim, the sport I liked best as a youngster and the only one in which I managed to acquire a certain skill. And I also remember, with the greatest affection, the little stories and the books that I read with mystical concentration and absorption, totally immersed in their world of illusion—the stories of Genevieve of Brabant and William Tell, of King Arthur and Cagliostro, of Robin Hood and the hunchback Lagardère, of Sandokán and Captain Nemo, and, above all, the series about Guillermo, a mischievous little boy my age, about whom each book in the series recounted an adventure which I tried to repeat afterward in the garden of the house. And I remember my first scribblings as a storyteller, which were usually in the form of little verses, or prolongations and amended versions of the stories I read, for which the family praised me. Grandfather was fond of poetry—my great-grandfather Belisario had been a poet and had had a novel published—and he taught me to memorize verses by Campoamor or Rubén Darío, and both he and my mother (who kept on her night table a copy of Pablo Neruda's *Veinte poemas de amor y una canción desesperada*, Twenty Love Poems and a Song of Despair, which she forbade me to read) congratulated me on those preliterate ventures as charming signs of my poetic gifts.

Despite her being so young, my mother did not have—nor did she want—suitors. Shortly after arriving in Cochabamba she began to work as an assistant accountant in the branch office of the Grace Line and her work and her son occupied her entire life. The explanation was that she couldn't even think of marrying again since she was already married in God's eyes, the only kind of marriage that counted, something she doubtless believed wholeheartedly, since she is the most Catholic of Catholics in that firmly Catholic family that the Llosas were—and still are, I believe. But, even more deep-seated than the religious reason for her remaining indifferent to those suitors who flocked about her after her divorce, was the fact that, despite what had happened, she was still in love with my father, with a total and unyielding passion, which she hid from all those around her, until, when the family went back to Peru, the Ernesto J. Vargas who had disappeared appeared again, to enter her life and mine once more, like a whirlwind.

"My papa is here in Piura?"

It was like one of those storybook fantasies, so captivating and exciting that they seemed true, but only as long as the time it took to read them. Was this one too going to vanish all of a sudden, like the ones in books the minute I closed them?

"Yes, in the Hotel de Turistas."

"And when am I going to see him?"

"Right now. But don't tell Grandpa and Grandma. They don't know he's here."

From a distance, even the bad memories of Cochabamba seem like good ones. There were two bad ones: my tonsillectomy and the Great Dane in the garage of a German, Señor Beckmann, located across the street from our house on Ladislao Cabrera. They tricked me into going to Dr. Sáenz Peña's office, telling me that it was just another visit like the other ones I made for my frequent fevers and sore throats, and once we got there they sat me down in the lap of a male nurse who imprisoned me in his arms, as Dr. Sáenz Peña opened my mouth and sprayed a little ether in it, with a squirt gun that looked like the one that my uncles took with them to festivities in the streets at Carnival time. Afterward, as I was convalescing under the pampering care of Granny Carmen and Auntie Mamaé, I was allowed to eat lots of ice cream. (Apparently, during that operation under local anesthesia, I screamed and wriggled about, interfering with the removal of my tonsils by the surgeon, who botched the operation and failed to remove bits of them. They grew larger and larger and today they are again the same size as they were then.)

Señor Beckmann's Great Dane fascinated and terrified me. He kept it tied up and its barking deafened me in my nightmares. At one time Jorge, the youngest of my uncles, kept his car in that garage and I would go there with him, secretly relishing the idea of what might happen if Señor Beckmann's Great Dane got loose. One night it flung itself on us. We took off at a run. The animal chased us, caught up with us as we reached the street, and tore the seat of my trousers. The bite it gave me was superficial, but the excitement and the dramatic versions of it that I gave my schoolmates lasted for weeks.

And one day it happened that "Uncle José Luis," the Peruvian ambassador to La Paz and a relative of my grandfather Pedro's, was elected president of the Republic, in far-off Peru. The news electrified the whole family, in which Uncle José Luis was looked upon as a revered celebrity. He had come to Cochabamba and been at our house a number of times, and I shared the family's admiration for this important relative who was so well-spoken, wore a bow tie, a hat with a ribbon-bound brim, and walked with his short legs spread wide apart, just like Charlie Chaplin—because on each of those visits to Cochabamba he had left a bit of spending money in my pocket when he said goodbye to me.

Once he had entered office, Uncle José Luis offered to appoint my grandfather to the post either of Peruvian consul in Arica or of prefect of Piura. My grandpa, whose ten-year contract with the Saids had just ended, chose Piura. He departed almost immediately, leaving the rest of the family with the task of clearing out our things from the house. We stayed there until almost the end of 1945, so that my cousins Nancy and Gladys and I could take our year-end exams. I have a vague idea of those last months in Bolivia, of the interminable succession of visitors who came to say goodbye to the Llosas, who in many ways were now a Cochabamba family: Uncle Lucho had married Aunt Olga, who, although Chilean by birth, was Bolivian by family background and heartfelt loyalties, and Uncle Jorge was married to Aunt Gaby, who was Bolivian on both sides of her family. Moreover, our family had grown in Cochabamba. Family legend has it that I tried to see the arrival in this world of the first daughter, Wanda, born to Uncle Lucho and Aunt Olga, by spying on her birth from one of the tall trees in the front patio, from which Uncle Lucho hauled me down by one of my ears. But that must not be true, since I don't remember it, or if it's true, I didn't manage to find out very much, because, as I've already said, I left Bolivia convinced that children are ordered from heaven and brought into the world by storks. In any event, I was not able to spy on the appearance on this earth of the second daughter born to Uncle Lucho and Aunt Olga, my cousin Patricia, for she was born in the hospital—the family was resigning itself to modern ways —barely forty days before the return of the tribe to Peru.

I have a very vivid impression of the Cochabamba railway station, the morning we took the train. There were many people who had come to say goodbye to us and some of them were weeping. But I wasn't, nor were my friends from La Salle who had come to give me one last farewell hug: Romero, Ballivián, Artero, Gumucio, and my closest friend of all, the son of the town photographer, Mario Zapata. We were grownups—nine or ten years old—and grownup men don't cry. But Señora Carlota and other ladies, and the cook and the house-maids, were crying, and, holding fast to Granny Carmen, the gardener, Saturnino, an old Indian, wearing sandals and a cap with earflaps, was weeping too. I can still see him running alongside the train window and waving goodbye as the train pulled out of the station.

The whole family went back to Peru, but Uncle Jorge and Aunt Gaby, and Uncle Juan and Aunt Laura, went to live in Lima, which was a great disappointment to me, since it meant being separated from Nancy and Gladys, the cousins I had grown up with. They had been like two sisters to me and their absence was hard to bear during the first months in Piura.

The only ones who made that journey from Cochabamba to Piura—a long, unforgettable one in many stages, by train, boat, car, and plane—were my grandmother, Auntie Mamaé, myself, and two members added to the family through the kindness of Granny Carmen: Joaquín and Orlando. Joaquín was a youngster only a little older than I was, whom Grandfather Pedro had met on the Saipina hacienda, with no parents, relatives, or identity papers. Feeling sorry for him, he took him to Cochabamba, where he had shared the life of the house servants. He grew up with us, and my grandmother couldn't bear the thought of leaving him behind, so he came to form part of the family entourage. Orlando, a boy a little younger, was the son of a cook from Santa Cruz named Clemencia, whom I remember as being tall and good-looking, and with hair she always wore loose. One day she got pregnant and the family was unable to find out who the father was. After giving birth, she disappeared, abandoning the newborn baby boy at our house. Attempts to discover her whereabouts came to nothing. Granny Carmen, who had grown fond of the child, brought him with her to Peru.

Throughout that entire journey, crossing the Altiplano by train, or Lake Titicaca on a little steamer that plied between Huaqui and Puno, my one thought was: "I'm going to see Peru, I'm going to get to know Peru." In Arequipa—where I had been once before, with my mother and my grandmother, for the Eucharistic Congress of 1940—we again stayed at Uncle Eduardo's, and his cook Inocencia again made me those reddish, very hot, highly spiced fresh shrimp stews that I dearly loved. But the highlight of the trip was the discovery of the sea, on reaching the top of "Skull Hill" and catching sight of the beaches of Camaná. I was so excited that the driver of the car that was taking us to Lima stopped so that I could dive into the Pacific. (The experience was a disaster because a crab pinched my foot.)

That was my first contact with the landscape of the Peruvian coast, with its endless empty expanses, tinged gray, blue, or red depending on the position of the sun, and its solitary beaches, with the ocher and gray spurs of the cordillera appearing and disappearing amid the sand dunes. A landscape that would always remain with me as my most persistent image of Peru when I went abroad.

We stayed a week or two in Lima, where Uncle Alejandro and Aunt Jesús put us up, and the only thing I remember about that stay is the little tree-lined streets of Miraflores, where they lived, and the roaring ocean waves at La Herradura, where Uncle Pepe and Uncle Hernán took me.

We went by plane north to Talara, for it was summer and my grandfather, thanks to his post as prefect of the *departamento*, had a little house there, made available to him during the vacation season by the International Petroleum Company. Grandfather met us at the airport of Talara and handed me a postcard showing the façade of the Salesian elementary school in Piura, where they had already registered me for the fifth grade. Of those vacations in Talara I remember friendly Juan Taboada, the chief steward of the club owned by International Petroleum, a head of a labor union and a leader of the APRA (Alianza Popular Revolucionaria Americana: American Popular Revolutionary Alliance) party. He also worked in the vacation house and took a liking to me; he took me to see soccer matches and, when they showed films for underaged children, to performances at an open-air movie theater whose screen was the white wall of the parish church. I spent the entire summer immersed in the International Petroleum swimming pool, reading little stories, climbing the cliffs close by and spying in fascination on the mysterious goings and comings of the crabs on the beach. But, to tell the truth, feeling lonely and sad, far from my cousins Nancy and Gladys and my Cochabamba friends, whom I began to miss a great deal. In Talara, on March 28, 1946, I turned ten.

My first encounter with the Salesian school and my new classmates was not at all pleasant. All of them were a year or two older than I was, but they seemed even bigger because they used dirty words and spoke of nasty things that those of us at La Salle, in Cochabamba, didn't even know existed. I came back home every afternoon to the big house that was a perquisite of the post of prefect, to complain to Uncle Lucho, scandalized by the obscene words I had heard and furious because my schoolmates made fun of my highland accent and my rabbit's teeth. But little by little I began making friends—Manolo and Ricardo Artadi, Borrao Garcés, plump little Javier Silva, Chapirito Seminario—thanks to whom I gradually adapted myself to the customs and the people of that city which was to leave such a profound mark on my life.

Shortly after entering the school, the brothers Artadi and Jorge Salmón, one afternoon when we were taking a dip in the already ebbing waters of the Piura—at the time a river in flood—revealed to me the real origin of babies and the meaning of that unutterable dirty word: *fuck.* It was a traumatic revelation, although I am certain that this time I silently mulled the subject over in my mind and did not go to tell Uncle Lucho about the repugnance I felt on imagining men who turned into animals, with stiff penises, mounted on top of the poor women who had to tolerate being gored. That my mother had been able to endure such an attack so that I could come into the world filled me with disgust, and made me feel that, by finding out about it, I had sullied myself and sullied my relationship with my mother and somehow sullied life itself. To me, the world had suddenly become dirty. The explanations of the priest who was my confessor, the one person whom I dared consult about this deeply distressing subject, must not have brought me any peace of mind, since the matter tormented me day and night and a long time went by before I resigned myself to accepting that that was what life was like, that men and women did together the filthy things summed up in the verb *fuck* and that there was no other way for the human species to continue to exist and for me to have been born.

The job as prefect of Piura was the last steady one my grandfather Pedro ever had. I believe that during the years that the family lived there, until Odría's military coup in 1948, which brought down José Luis Bustamante y Rivero, it was quite happy. Grandpa's salary must have been very modest, but Uncle Lucho, who was working at the Romero Company, and my mother, who had found a job in the Piura branch of the Grace Line, contributed to meeting the household expenses. The prefecture had two patios and several mucky garrets where bats nested. My friends and I explored the garrets on our hands and knees, in hopes of catching one of those winged rats and making it smoke, since we held firmly to the belief that a bat in whose mouth anyone managed to place a cigarette could be killed off with a few puffs, since it was an avid smoker.

The Piura of those days was a very small and happy place, with prosperous and good-humored hacienda owners—the Seminarios, the Checas, the Hilbcks, the Romeros, the Artázars, the Garcías—with whom my grandparents and my aunts and uncles established ties of friendship that were to last throughout their lives. We went on outings to the pretty little beach at Yacila, or to Paita, where bathing in the ocean always involved the risk of being attacked by stingrays (I remember one lunch, at the Artadi house, when my grandfather and Uncle Lucho, who had gone swimming at low tide, got stung by a ray and how a fat black woman cured them, right there on the beach, by heating their feet with her brazier and squeezing lemon juice on their wounds), or to Colán, at that time just a handful of little wooden houses built on pylons amid the vastness of that gorgeous sandy beach full of sparrow hawks and seagulls.

At the Yapatera hacienda, belonging to the Checas, I rode horseback for the first time and heard England spoken of in a rather mythical way, since my friend James MacDonald's father was British, and both he and his wife—Pepita Checa—revered that country, which they had more or less reproduced in those arid reaches of the highlands of Piura (at their house at the hacienda five o'clock tea was served and the conversation was in English).

That year in Piura that was to end on the Eguiguren embankment with the revelation concerning my father lingers in my memory like a jigsaw puzzle: vivid, isolated, exciting images. The young Civil Guard who kept watch over the back door of the prefecture and made Domitila, one of the housemaids, fall in love with him by serenading her with the song *Muñequita linda*, in a voice filled with exaggeratedly heartfelt feeling, and the excursions with a bunch of my schoolmates along the dry riverbed and the sand pits of Castilla and Catacaos to watch the prehistoric iguanas or see the donkeys fornicating, hidden among the carob trees. The dips in the swimming pool of the Club Grau, our efforts to sneak into the films for grownups at the Variedades movie theater and the Municipal, and the expeditions, which filled us with excitement and guilt-ridden consciences, to spy from the shadows on that green house, the Casa Verde, built in the open countryside separating Castilla from Catacaos, concerning which myths redolent of sin circulated. The word *puta*, whore, filled me at one and the same time with horror and fascination. Going to post myself in the vicinity of that building, so as to see the wicked women who lived there and their night visitors, was an irresistible temptation, though I knew full well that I was committing a mortal sin and I would be obliged to go to confession afterward to reveal it.

And the stamps that I began to collect, spurred on by the collection that my Grandpa Pedro had—a collection of rare postage stamps, triangular, multicolored, from exotic countries and in exotic languages, that my great-grandfather Belisario had collected and the two volumes of which were one of the treasures that the Llosa family had lugged all over the world—which he allowed me to look through if I'd been a good boy. The parish priest of the Plaza Merino, Father García, an aged, grouchy man from Spain, was also a stamp collector and I used to come to exchange duplicate stamps with him, in bargaining sessions that sometimes ended with one of those fits of rage of his that my friends and I took great delight in arousing. The other family keepsake was the Opera Book that Granny Carmen had inherited from her parents, a lovely old illustrated volume with red and gold backings, which contained the plots of all the great Italian operas and some of their main arias, and which I spent hours reading and rereading.

The gusty winds of local politics in Piura—where the political forces were more in equilibrium than they were in the rest of the country— touched me only in a confused way. The bad guys were the members of the APRA party, who had betrayed "Uncle José Luis" and were making life impossible for him there in Lima; the leader of APRA, Víctor Raúl de la Torre, had attacked my grandfather in a speech, there in Piura in the Plaza de Armas, the main square, accusing him of being a "prefect who was against the APRA." (I went in secret to have a look at that APRA demonstration, despite my family's having forbidden me to do so, and I discovered my schoolmate Javier Silva Ruete, whose father was a dyed-in-the-wool Aprista, waving a placard bigger than he was that read: "Maestro, young people acclaim you.") But despite all the evils that the APRA embodied, there were, in Piura, a few decent Apristas, friends of my grandparents and my aunts and uncles, men like Jaime's father, Dr. Máximo Silva, Dr. Guillermo Gulman, and Dr. Iparraguirre, our family dentist, with whose son we organized evening theatrical performances in the entry hall of his house.

The mortal enemies of the Apristas were the Urristas of the Unión Revolucionaria (the Revolutionary Union), headed by the Piuran Luis A. Florez, whose bastion was the district of La Mangachería, celebrated for its *chicherías*, which sold the cheap fermented *chicha* that is the drink of the poor, along with its *picanterías*, where highly spiced dishes were served, and its music. Legend had it that General Sánchez Cerro—the dictator who was the founder of the UR, the Unión Revolucionaria, and who was murdered by an Aprista on April 30, 1933—had been born in La Mangachería and because of that all the people of the district were Urristas, and all the huts made of adobe and wild cane in this district of dirt streets and *churres* and *piajenos* (the words for children and donkeys in Piuran slang) displayed on their walls a faded image of Sánchez Cerro. Besides the Urristas, there were the Socialists, whose leader, Luciano Castillo, was also a Piuran. The street fights between Apristas, Urristas, and Socialists were frequent, and I was aware of it because in those days—when a street demonstration often turned into fisticuffs—I wasn't allowed to go out of the house and more police came to guard the prefecture, which at times did not prevent the Aprista hoodlums, once their demonstration was over, to creep as close as they could to throw stones at our windows.

I felt very proud to be the grandson of somebody so important: the prefect. I went with Grandpa to certain public functions—inaugurations, the parade on national holidays, ceremonies at the Grau barracks—and was puffed up with pride when I saw him presiding over the meetings, receiving the salutes of the military, or delivering speeches. With all the lunches and public ceremonies he had to attend, Grandfather Pedro had found an excuse for the avocation he had always had and which he encouraged in his oldest grandson: composing poems. He did so with the greatest of ease, on the slightest pretext, and when it came his turn to speak, at banquets and official functions, he often read verses written for the occasion.

Only thirty or forty years later did I learn about the two things that were to decide my future life and that occurred in that year of 1946. The first of them was a letter that my mother received one day from Orieli, my father's sister-in-law. She had read in the newspapers that my grandfather was prefect of Piura and presumed that Dorita was with him. What had her life been like? Had she remarried? And how was Ernesto's young son? She had written the letter following instructions from my father, who, driving in his car to his office, had heard on the radio news of the appointment of Don Pedro J. Llosa Bustamante as prefect of Piura.

The second was a trip of a few weeks that my mama had made to Lima, in August, for a minor operation. She telephoned Orieli, who invited her to come have tea with her. On entering the little house in Magdalena del Mar where Orieli and Uncle César lived, she spied my father, in the living room. She fell into a faint. They had to pick her up off the floor, stretch her out in an armchair, bring her to with smelling salts. Seeing him for a moment was enough for those five and a half hellish months of her marriage and her abandonment and

the eleven years of silence on the part of Ernesto J. Vargas to be erased
from her memory.

No one in the family learned about that meeting or about the secret
reconciliation or the epistolary conspiracy that went on for several
months, setting up the ambush that had already begun to take place
that afternoon, on the Eguiguren embankment, beneath the bright
sun of early summer. Why didn't my mother tell her parents and her
brothers that she had seen my father? Why didn't she tell them what
she was going to do? Was it because she knew that they would have
tried to dissuade her and would have predicted what awaited her?

Gamboling about with happiness, believing and not believing what
I had just heard, I hardly listened to my mother as we headed for the
Hotel de Turistas, while she repeated to me that if we ran into my
grandparents, or Auntie Mamaé or Uncle Lucho or Aunt Olga, I was
not to say a word about what she had just revealed to me. In my
excitement, it never entered my mind to ask her the reason for all the
mystery, why it had to be kept a secret that my papa was alive and
had come to Piura and that within a few minutes I was going to meet
him. What would he be like? What would he be like?

We went inside the Hotel de Turistas and, the moment we crossed
the threshold of a little reception room that was on the left, a man
dressed in a beige suit and wearing a green tie with little white raised
dots got up out of his chair and came toward us. "Is this my son?" I
heard him say. He leaned down, put his arms around me, and kissed
me. I was disconcerted and didn't know what to do. My face was frozen
in a false smile. My consternation was due to the difference between
this flesh-and-blood papa, gray at the temples and with such sparse
hair, and the handsome young man in a merchant marine uniform
whose photo was standing on my night table. I had something of the
feeling that it was a con game: this papa didn't look like the one I had
thought was dead.

But I didn't have time to think about that, for the man was saying
that we should come have a ride around Piura in his car. He spoke
to my mama with a familiarity that I didn't much care for and that
made me just a little jealous. We went out onto the main square, full
of scorching sunlight and people as it was on Sundays, when there were
open-air band concerts, and climbed into a blue Ford, with him and

my mother in the front seat and me in the back. As we were leaving, a classmate of mine, Espinoza, slender and swarthy-skinned, came by on the sidewalk and was sauntering over to the car in his easygoing way when the car took off and all the two of us could do was wave goodbye to each other.

We drove around the downtown area for a while and all of a sudden the man who was my papa said that we should go see the countryside, the outskirts of town. Why didn't we go out to Kilometer 50, where there was that little place where we could have a cold drink? I knew that highway marker very well. It was a long-standing custom for us to escort travelers headed for Lima that far, as we had done during the national holidays, when Uncle Jorge, Aunt Gaby, Aunt Laura, and my cousins Nancy and Gladys (and their newborn baby sister, Lucy) had come and spent a few days' vacation. (Getting together with my cousins once again had been great fun and we had once more played together a lot, although aware, this time, that I was a little boy and they were little girls, and that it was unthinkable, for example, to do things that we had done together back in Bolivia, like sleeping and taking baths together.) The dunes that surround Piura, with their stretches of quicksand, their clumps of carob trees, and their herds of goats, and the mirages of ponds and springs that can be glimpsed there in the afternoons when the red ball of the sun on the horizon tinges the white and gold sands with a light the color of blood, make up a landscape that always impressed me, and that I have never tired of looking at. When I contemplated it, my imagination would run away with me. It was the ideal setting for epic deeds, by cavalrymen and adventurers, by princes who rescued damsels held prisoner or by brave men who fought like lions and routed evildoers. Every time we went along this highway on an outing or to bid someone goodbye, I allowed my imagination to take wing as that burning-hot, deserted landscape went past through the window alongside me. But I am certain that this time I didn't see anything of what was going on outside the car, on tenterhooks as I was, with all my senses on the alert for what that man and my mama were saying, sotto voce at times, exchanging glances that infuriated me. What were they hinting at to each other underneath what I could hear? They were talking something over and pretending not to be. But I was well aware of that, because I was far from being a dummy. What was it that I was aware of? What were they hiding from me?

And on arriving at Kilometer 50, after having cold drinks, the man who was my papa said that, now that we had gone that far, why not go on to Chiclayo? Was I acquainted with Chiclayo? No, I wasn't. Well then, let's go to Chiclayo, so that Marito can get to know the city of rice with duck.

I grew more and more ill at ease and spent the four or five hours' journey along that unpaved stretch of road, full of ruts and potholes and long lines of trucks on the steep grade up to Olmos, with my mind filled with suspicions, convinced that the whole scheme had been worked out long before, behind my back, with my mama's complicity. They were trying to trick me as though I were a little kid, when I realized very clearly that I was being deceived. When it got dark, I stretched out on the back seat, pretending to be asleep. But I was wide awake, my head and my soul focused on what they were whispering.

At one moment during the night, I protested: "Grandma and Grandpa are going to be scared when they see that we haven't come back, Mama."

"We'll call them from Chiclayo," the man who was my papa volunteered.

We arrived at Chiclayo just at first light and there was nothing to eat at the hotel, but I didn't care, because I wasn't hungry. They were, though, and bought crackers, which I didn't touch. They left me in a room by myself and locked themselves in the one next door. I spent what was left of that night with my eyes open and my heart pounding with fear, trying to hear a voice, a sound from the adjoining room, dying with jealousy, feeling that I was the victim of a monstrous act of betrayal. At times I found myself retching in disgust, overcome by an infinite loathing, imagining that my mama might be in there doing those filthy things with that stranger that men and women did together to have children.

In the morning after breakfast, as soon as we got into the blue Ford, he said what I knew very well he was going to say:

"We're going to Lima, Mario."

"And what are my grandparents going to say?" I stammered. "Mamaé, Uncle Lucho."

"What are they going to say?" he answered. "Shouldn't a son be with his father? Shóuldn't he live with his father? What do you think? How does that strike you?"

He said this in a quiet voice that I heard him use for the first time, with a cutting tone, emphasizing every syllable, which was soon to instill more fear in me than the sermons on hell given us by Brother Agustín when he was preparing us for first communion, there in Cochabamba.

TWO

The Plaza San Martín

Aᴛ the end of July 1987, I found myself in the far north of Peru, on a half-deserted beach, where, years before, a young man from Piura and his wife had built several bungalows with the idea of renting them to tourists. Isolated, rustic, squeezed in between empty stretches of sand, rock cliffs, and the foamy waves of the Pacific, Punta Sal is one of the most beautiful sites in Peru. It has the air of a place outside time and history with its flocks of seabirds—gannets, pelicans, gulls, cormorants, little ducks, and albatrosses, which the locals call *tijeretas*—parading in orderly formations from the bright dawns to the blood-red twilights. The fishermen of this remote stretch of the Peruvian coast use rafts still made in exactly the same way as in pre-Hispanic times, simple and light: two or three tree trunks tied together and a pole that serves as both an oar and a rudder, with which the fisherman propels the craft along in sweeping gyres, as if tracing circles in the water. The sight of those rafts had greatly impressed me the first time I visited Punta Sal, since no doubt they were craft identical to the raft from Tumbes that, according to the chronicles of the Conquest, was found by Francisco Pizarro and his comrades, four centuries ago and not far from here, and taken to be the first concrete proof that the stories of a golden empire that had made them venture forth from Panama to these shores were a reality.

I was in Punta Sal with Patricia and my children, to spend the national holiday week there, far from winter in Lima. We had returned to Peru not long before from London, where, for some time now, we were in the habit of spending three months or so every year, and I had intended to take advantage of the stay in Punta Sal to correct the proofs of my latest novel, *El hablador* (*The Storyteller*), between dips in the ocean and to practice, from morning to night, the solitary vice: reading, constantly reading.

I had turned fifty-one in March. Everything seemed to indicate that my life, an unsettled one since the day I was born, would go by more calmly from now on: spent between Lima and London, and devoted exclusively to writing, with a stint of university teaching every so often somewhere in the United States. Now and again I scribble in my memo books a few work plans for the immediate future, ones that I never carry out altogether. When I reached fifty, I had dreamed up the following five-year plan:

1) A play about a little old Quixote-like man who, in the Lima of the 1950s, embarks on a crusade to save the city's colonial-era balconies threatened with demolition.

2) A novel, something between a detective story and a fictional fantasy, about cataclysms, human sacrifices, and political crimes in a village in the Andes.

3) An essay on the gestation of Victor Hugo's *Les Misérables*.

4) A comedy about a businessman who, in a suite in the Savoy Hotel in London, meets his best friend from his school days, whom he has thought dead, but who has now turned into a good-looking woman, thanks to hormones and surgery; and

5) A historical novel inspired by Flora Tristan, the Franco-Peruvian revolutionary, ideologist, and feminist, who lived in the first third of the nineteenth century.

In the same memorandum book I had also jotted down, as less urgent projects, learning that devilishly difficult language, German; living for a while in Berlin; trying yet again to get through books that had always defeated me—such as *Finnegans Wake* and *The Death of Virgil*; going down the Amazon from Pucallpa to Belém do Pará in Brazil; and bringing out a revised edition of all my novels. Other vague projects of a less publishable nature also figured on the list. The one thing that wasn't even hinted at anywhere in these notes was the activity that, through the caprice of the wheel of fortune, was about to monopolize my life for the next three years: politics.

I didn't have the least inkling that that would be so, on that 28th of July, at noon, when we prepared to listen, on my friend Freddy Cooper's little portable radio, to the speech that the president of the Republic delivers in person to Congress on the national holiday. Alan

García had been in office for two years and was still very popular. To me, his politics seemed like a time bomb. Populism had been a catastrophic failure in Allende's Chile and in Siles Suazo's Bolivia. Why would it go over well in Peru? Subsidizing consumption, in a country like Peru that depends on imports for a large share of its food and its industrial components, brings with it a deceptive bonanza that lasts only as long as the country has reserves of foreign currency available to allow the flow of incoming goods to be maintained. This was how things had gone so far, thanks to a massive expenditure of foreign currency reserves, which had increased owing to the government's decision to spend only 10 percent of the money earned by exports in servicing the country's foreign debt. But this policy was beginning to give signs of having been run into the ground. The country's reserves were being depleted; because of its confrontation with the International Monetary Fund and the World Bank—the bêtes noires of the speeches delivered by President García—Peru had seen all the doors of the international financial system slam shut; the printing of paper money with no backing so as to cover the fiscal deficit was making inflation worse; the dollar, maintained at an artificially low price, was increasingly discouraging exports on the one hand and encouraging speculation on the other: the best deal for a businessman was to get an import license that allowed him to pay for what he ordered from abroad with cheap dollars (there were any number of rates of exchange for the dollar, depending on the "social necessity" of the product). The traffickers in contraband goods saw to it that the products thus imported—sugar, rice, medicine—passed through Peru as fast as if over hot coals and went on to Colombia, Chile, or Ecuador, where their prices were not controlled. The system had enriched a handful of people but had plunged the rest of the country's population into poverty that was increasing by the day.

The president did not appear worried. Or so it seemed to me at least, a few days earlier, during the only interview I had with him while he was in power. When I arrived from London, at the end of June, he sent one of his aides-de-camp to welcome me back, and as protocol required, I went to the Presidential Palace to thank him for the courtesy. He received me personally and we talked together for about an hour and a half. Standing in front of a blackboard, he explained to me his goals for the current year and showed me a hand-made bazooka, put together by Sendero Luminoso—Shining Path, the Maoist guerrilla movement—with which terrorists had fired a projectile on the palace from Rímac. He was young, self-assured, and likable. I had seen him only once before, during the election campaign, at the home of a mutual friend—Manuel Checa Solari, the auctioneer and art collector—who was bent on our having lunch together. The impression García gave me then was that of a young man of limitless ambition capable of anything if it would bring him to power. For that reason, a few days after that first meeting, I said on two television interviews conducted by the journalists Jaime Bayly and César Hildebrandt that I would vote not for him but for the candidate of the PPC (the Partido Popular Cristiano: the Christian Popular Party), Luis Bedoya Reyes. Despite that fact, and despite an open letter that I wrote to him when he had been in power for exactly a year, condemning him for the massacre of the rioters in the Lima prisons in June of 1986,* he did not seem to bear me any ill will that morning at the Presidential Palace, for his attitude toward me was warm and friendly. At the beginning of his term in office he had sent word to me to ask if I would accept the ambassadorship to Spain, and now, even though he knew how critical I was of his policies, the conversation could not have been more cordial. I remember having said to him, jokingly, that it was a shame that having had the chance to be the Felipe González of Peru he was determined to be our Salvador Allende, or, worse still, our Fidel Castro. Wasn't the world headed in other directions?

Naturally, among all the things I heard from him that morning concerning his immediate political plans, the most important subject of all didn't come up—a measure that at the time he had already cooked up with a group of intimates, and that Peruvians first heard of by way of that speech on the 28th that Freddy and I heard, with García's voice broken and crackling on that ancient radio beneath the burning-hot sun of Punta Sal: his decision to "nationalize and bring under government control" all banks, insurance companies, and financial institutions in Peru.

"Eighteen years ago I learned in the daily papers that Velasco had

---

* "Una montaña de cadáveres: carta abierta a Alan García," *El Comercio*, Lima, June 23, 1986; reprinted in *Contra viento y marea*, III (Barcelona: Seix Barral, 1990), pp. 389–93.

taken my country estate away from me," a gentleman already well along in years, in a bathing suit and with an artificial hand hidden by a leather glove, exclaimed. "And now, from this little radio I learn that Alan García has just taken my insurance company away from me. That's quite something, wouldn't you say, my friend?"

He rose to his feet and dived into the ocean. Not all the vacationers in Punta Sal took the news in the same debonair spirit. They were professionals, executives, and a few businessmen associated with the threatened companies, and to one degree or another they were aware that the measure was going to go against their interests. They all remembered the years of the dictatorship (1968–80) and the massive nationalizations—at the beginning of Velasco's regime there had been seven public enterprises and at the end of it close to two hundred—which had turned the poor country that Peru was then into the poverty-stricken one it is today. At dinner that night in Punta Sal, a lady at the next table was lamenting her fate: her husband, one of the many Peruvians who had emigrated, had just left a good position in Venezuela to come back to Lima—to take over the management of a bank! Would the family have to take to the world's highways and byways yet again in search of work?

It was not difficult to imagine what was going to happen. The owners would be paid in worthless bonds, as had happened to those whose holdings had been expropriated in the days of the military dictatorship. But those proprietors would suffer less than the rest of the Peruvians. They were quite well off and, ever since General Velasco's plundering had begun, many had taken precautions by sending their money abroad. It was those who had no protection at all—workers and employees in banks, insurance agencies, and financial firms—who would become part of the public sector. Those thousands of families did not have accounts abroad, and no way to head off the people of the party in power, who would march in and take possession of the prey they coveted. From now on, the latter were the ones who would occupy the key posts, political influence would be the determining factor when it came to promotions and being named to important posts, and in no time the same corruption would take over in these companies as in the rest of the public sector.

"Once more in its history Peru has taken yet another step backward toward barbarism," I remember saying to Patricia the next morning, as we were going for a run along the beach toward the little village of Punta Sal, escorted by a flock of gannets. The nationalizations that had been announced would bring more poverty, discouragement, parasitism, and bribery to Peruvian life. And furthermore, in either the long run or the short, they would fatally damage the democratic system that Peru had recovered in 1980, after twelve years under military rule.

"Why all the fuss," I have often been asked, "over a few nationalizations? President Mitterrand nationalized the banks, and even though the measure was a failure and the Socialists had to reverse course, was French democracy ever endangered?" People who follow that line of argument have no understanding that one of the characteristics of underdevelopment is the total identity of the government and the state. In France, Sweden, or England, a public enterprise maintains a certain autonomy in relation to those who hold political power: it belongs to the state; and its administration, its personnel, and its functioning are more or less safe from the abuse of governmental power. But in an underdeveloped country, exactly as in a totalitarian one, the government *is* the state and those in power oversee it as though it were their own private property, or, rather, their spoils. Public enterprises are useful for providing cushy jobs for the protégés of those in power, for feeding the people under their patronage, and for making shady deals. Such enterprises soon turn into bureaucratic swarms paralyzed by the corruption and inefficiency introduced into them by politics. There is no danger that they will go broke; almost always they are monopolies protected against competition and their life is guaranteed indefinitely thanks to subsidies, that is to say, the taxpayer's money.* Peruvians have seen this process repeated, ever since the days of the "socialist, libertarian, and participatory revolution" of General Velasco, in all the nationalized companies—petroleum, electricity, mines, sugar refineries, et cetera—and now, as in a recurrent nightmare, the whole story was going to be repeated with the banks, insurance companies, and financial firms that Alan García's democratic socialism was getting ready to gobble up.

Moreover, the nationalization of the financial system involved an aggravating political factor. It was about to place absolute control over

---

* In 1988, the deficit of public enterprises in Peru amounted to $2,500,000,000, the equivalent of all the foreign currency brought in that year by exports.

all credit in the hands of an ambitious leader capable of lying with-out the least scruple—not very long before, in late November 1984, Velasco had given his word, at CADE, the Conferencia Anual de Ejecutivos, that he would never nationalize the banks. Once he had taken them over, all the business enterprises in the country, beginning with the radio stations, the television networks, and the press, would be at the mercy of the government. There was no need to be possessed of the gift of prophecy to realize that in the future funds for the news media would have their price: subservience. General Velasco had placed the daily papers and television channels under state control so as to wrest them away "from the oligarchy" and place them in the hands "of the organized people." Through this, during the dictatorship, the communications media in Peru fell to levels of indescribable ser-vility and contemptibility. Being more clever, Alan García was going to obtain total control of information through credits and publicity, in the meanwhile maintaining the appearance, in the Mexican fashion, that the media were independent.

The allusion to Mexico is not gratuitous. The system of the Mexican PRI (Partido Revolucionario Institucional: Institutional Revolutionary Party)—a party dictatorship that keeps up democratic appearances by dint of tolerating elections, a "critical" press, and a civilian govern-ment—has traditionally been a temptation for Latin American dic-tators. But none of them has been able to duplicate the model, an authentic creation of Mexican culture and history, because one of the requisites of its "success" is something that none of its emulators can resign himself to: the ritual sacrifice, every certain number of years, of the president, in order that the party may continue in power. General Velasco dreamed of a Mexican-style regime—for himself alone. And it was a commonplace of public opinion that President García had dreams of perpetuating his presidency indefinitely. Sometime before that July 28, 1987, one of his faithful congressmen, Héctor Marisca, passing himself off as an independent, had formally proposed a con-stitutional amendment allowing the president to be reelected, a change that aroused vehement protest. The control of government funds by the executive branch was a decisive step toward the perpetuation in power of the APRA, to which one of Alan García's appointees, the minister of energy and mines, Wilfredo Huayta, had promised "fifty years in power."

"And the worst of it is," I said to Patricia, panting as I was about to finish the four-kilometer run, "that this proposal is going to be supported by 99 percent of Peruvians."

Is anyone in the world fond of bankers? Aren't they the symbol of affluence, of selfish capitalism, of imperialism, of everything to which the ideology of the Third World attributes the wretchedness and the backwardness of our countries? Alan García had found the ideal scapegoat to explain to the Peruvian people why his program did not produce the fruits that he had promised: it was all the fault of the financial oligarchies that made use of banks to take their dollars out of Peru and used the money of those with savings accounts to make loans under the table to the companies they controlled. Now, with the financial system in the hands of the people, all that was going to change.

Almost the moment I returned to Lima, a few days later, I wrote an article, "Hacia el Perú totalitario" ("Toward a Totalitarian Peru") that appeared in *El Comercio* on August 2,* outlining the reasons for my opposition to the measure and urging Peruvians to oppose it by any and every legal means if they wanted the democratic system to survive. I did so in order to put my reaction to it on record, even though I was convinced that my effort would be useless, and that, with the exception of a few protests, the measure would be passed by Congress with the approval of the majority of my compatriots.

But that was not how things turned out. At the same time that my article appeared, the employees of banks and of other threatened companies took to the streets, in Lima, in Arequipa, in Piura, participating in marches and small-scale meetings that surprised everyone, me first of all. In order to support them, along with four close friends with whom for years Patricia and I had gone out to have dinner and talk together once a week—three architects, Luis Miró Quesada, Frederick Cooper, and Miguel Cruchaga, and the painter Fernando de Szyszlo—we decided to draft a manifesto as quickly as possible, for which we were sure we could collect some hundred signatures. The text, affirming in part that "the concentration of political and economic power in the hands of the party in power may well mean the end of freedom of expression and, should worst come to worst, of democracy,"

---

* *Contra viento y marea*, III, pp. 417–20.

was given to me to read on television and published under my name in the newspapers of August 5 with the heading "Against the Totalitarian Threat."

What happened in the next few days unexpectedly turned my life upside down. My house was flooded with letters, phone calls, and visits of individuals who were in entire accord with the manifesto and brought piles of signatures that they had spontaneously collected. Lists of the names of hundreds of new supporters appeared every day in the press not controlled by the government. Even people from the provinces sought me out, asking how they could help. I was stunned. General Velasco had nationalized hundreds of companies without anyone's lifting a finger; on the contrary, he had the support of a large percentage of public opinion, which saw in these measures an act of social justice and the hope for a change. In Peru, as in the rest of Latin America, statism, the pillar of Third World ideology, had become the ruling doctrine not only of the left but also of vast sectors of the center and the right, to such a degree that Belaunde Terry's conservative government (1980–85), elected at the end of the military dictatorship, had not dared to privatize a single one of the companies nationalized by Velasco (with the exception of the communications media, returned to their owners immediately after Belaunde Terry took power). But in those feverish days of August 1987 it appeared that significant sectors of Peruvian society had become disenchanted with the statist formula.

Alan García, nervous over the protest moves, decided to "bring the masses out into the streets." He traveled through the north of the country, the traditional citadel of the APRA party, vituperating imperialism and bankers and voicing threats against those of us who were protesting. His party, a revolutionary one half a century before, had little by little, over the course of the years, turned into a bureaucratic and opportunistic party, and followed his lead with obvious reluctance. It had first attained power in 1985, after it had been in existence for sixty years, with a very clever electoral campaign, presenting a moderate social-democratic image, and the majority of the party leaders seemed to be quite satisfied to be enjoying the prerogatives of power. The business of going about making a revolution at this point seemed to set about as well with many Apristas as a kick in the belly. But the

APRA, whose doctrine of state control is socialist, owes its hierarchical structure to fascism—its founder, Haya de la Torre, called the Jefe Máximo, the Maximum Leader, had imitated the organization, the stage effects, and the shortcut methods of Italian fascism—and for the sake of discipline, although without a great deal of enthusiasm, followed Alan García when he called for revolutionary mobilizations. Those, on the other hand, who supported him with sincere and irrepressible enthusiasm were the Socialists and Communists of the coalition of the IU (Izquierda Unida: United Left). Whether moderates or extremists, they could not believe their eyes. The APRA, their old enemy, was putting their very own program into effect. Were the good old days of General Velasco, when they had very nearly managed to seize power, being brought back to life, then? Socialists and Communists immediately adopted as their own the fight for nationalization. Their leader at the time, Alfonso Barrantes, appeared on television to read a speech in favor of the nationalization law, and the senators and representatives of the United Left became its most unyielding defenders in Congress.

Felipe Thorndike and Freddy Cooper turned up at my house one night at the beginning of the second week in August, all excited and in a conspiratorial mood. They had had meetings with groups of independents and had come to propose to me that we call for a public demonstration, at which I would be the main speaker. The idea was to show that if the Apristas and the Communists could take to the streets in defense of statism, we could too, to impugn their policy in the name of freedom. I accepted their proposal, and that night I had the first of a series of arguments with Patricia that were to go on for a year.

"If you go up onto that platform you'll end up going into politics, and literature can go to hell. And your family along with it. Can it be that you don't know what it means to go into politics in this country?"

"I headed the protest against nationalization. I can't back down now. It's just one demonstration, just one speech. That doesn't mean devoting one's life to politics!"

"Then there'll be another and another and you'll end up being a candidate for president. Are you going to leave your books, the quiet, comfortable life you're living now, to go into politics in Peru? Don't you know how they're going to pay you back? Have you forgotten Uchuraccay?"*

"I'm not going to go into politics or give up literature or be a candidate for any office. I'm going to speak at this one demonstration so that it will at least be clear to everyone that not all of us Peruvians are letting ourselves be taken in by Señor Alan García."

"Don't you know what kind of thugs you're picking as enemies? I've noticed you don't answer the phone anymore."

Because, ever since the day our manifesto came out, the anonymous calls had started. They came in the daytime or at night. In order to be able to get some sleep we had to disconnect the phone. The voices sounded like different ones each time, so that I came to think that every Aprista's idea of fun, once he had a drink under his belt, was to call my house to threaten us. These calls went on for almost the entire three years this account covers. They finally became a part of the family routine. When the calls stopped, a sort of vacuum, a nostalgia even, lingered on in the house.

The demonstration—we called it A Meeting for Freedom—was set for August 21 in the classic place for rallies in Lima: the Plaza San Martín. The organizing of it was in the hands of independents who had never been political militants or had any experience in this sort of contention, people like the university professor Luis Bustamante Belaunde or the business leader Miguel Vega Alvear, with whom we were to become fast friends. Among the political novices that all of us were, the exception perhaps was Miguel Cruchaga, Belaunde Terry's nephew, who as a young man had been a member of the AP (Acción Popular: Popular Action) party. But he had kept his distance from active militancy for some time. My friendship with the tall, gentlemanly, grave Miguel was of long standing, but it had become a very intimate one after my return to Peru, after nearly sixteen years in Europe, in 1974, on the eve of the capture of the news media by the dictatorship. We always used to talk politics whenever we were together, and each time, somewhat cast over with sickly melancholy,

---

* In January 1983, eight journalists were killed in Uchuraccay, a remote village in the Andes. Vargas Llosa was one of the members of a commission appointed by Belaunde Terry's government to investigate the killings. This was the only government position that Vargas Llosa had held. He wrote the commission's report and came under fierce attack in the press. (*Trans. note*)

we wondered why everything in Peru always tended to get worse, why we were wasting opportunities and persisting so perversely toward working for our ruin and our downfall. And each time, too, in a very vague way, we outlined projects to do something, at some time or other. That intellectual game took on, all of a sudden, in the fever and boiling fury of those August days, a disconcerting reality. Because of this background and because of his enthusiasm, Miguel took on the job of coordinating the arrangements for the protest rally. These were intense and exhausting days which, from a distance, seem to me to be the most generously motivated and the most exciting ones of those years. I had asked the shareholders of the threatened companies and the opposition parties—Popular Action and the Christian Popular Party—to remain on the sidelines, so as to make the event clearly a matter of principle, of Peruvians who were not taking to the streets to defend personal or political interests but to defend values that seemed to us to be endangered by nationalization.

So many people mobilized to help us—collecting money, printing pamphlets and placards, preparing pennants, lending their homes for meetings, offering transportation for the demonstrators, and going out to paint slogans and drive through the streets in vehicles with loudspeakers—that from the very beginning I had the premonition that the Meeting for Freedom would be a success. Since my place was a madhouse, on the evening of August 21 I hid out for a few hours at the home of Carlos and Maggie Ferreyros, two friends, to prepare the first political speech of my life. (Carlos was kidnapped shortly thereafter, by the MRTA [Movimiento Revolucionario Túpac Amaru: Túpac Amaru Revolutionary Movement] and held in captivity for six months, in a tiny cellar without ventilation.)

But, despite the favorable signs, not even the most optimistic person among us could have predicted the extraordinary number of people who packed the Plaza San Martín elbow to elbow that night and overflowed the neighboring streets. When I went up onto the speakers' platform I felt a mixture of boundless joy and terror: tens of thousands of people—130,000, according to the review *Sí*[*]—were waving flags and singing out in chorus at the top of their lungs the "Hymn to Freedom," the words and music of which had been written for the

[*] Lima, August 24, 1987.

occasion by Augusto Polo Campos, a very popular composer. Something must have changed in Peru when a crowd like that fervently applauded on hearing me say that economic freedom was inseparable from political freedom, that private property and a market economy were the only guarantee of development, and that we Peruvians would not allow our democratic system to be "Mexicanized" or the APRA to be turned into the Trojan Horse of Communism in Peru.

The story has it that that night, on seeing on the little TV screen the magnitude of the Meeting for Freedom, Alan García, in a fit of rage, smashed the set to smithereens. What is certain is that the immense demonstration had enormous consequences. It was a decisive factor in making it evident that the nationalization law, though already passed in Congress, could never be put into effect, and the law was later annulled. It was a death blow to Alan García's ambition to stay in office for an unlimited time. It opened the doors of Peruvian political life to liberal thought that up until then had lacked a public presence, since all of our modern history had been, practically speaking, a monopoly of the ideological populism of conservatives and socialists of various tendencies. It gave the initiative back to the opposition parties, Popular Action and the Christian Popular Party, which, following their defeat in 1985, had appeared to be invisible, and laid the foundations for what would become the Frente Democrático (Democratic Front)[*] and, as Patricia feared, for my candidacy for the presidency.

Buoyed up by our success in the Plaza San Martín, we immediately organized two other meetings, in Arequipa, on August 26, and in Piura, on September 2. Both of them were also attended by thousands. In Arequipa there was violence; we were attacked by Aprista counterdemonstrators—the famous buffaloes or bullies and armed hoodlums of the party—and by a Maoist faction of the United Left, the Patria Roja (Red Fatherland). They set off explosives and, armed with clubs, stones, and stink bombs, attacked just as I was beginning to speak, so as to start a stampede. The young people in charge of maintaining order on the outer edge of the Plaza, organized by Fernando Cháves Belaunde, resisted the attack, but several of them were injured. "You see? You see?" Patricia grumbled; she and María Ame-

---

[*] The Frente Democrático, after joining with Acción Popular (AP) and the Partido Popular Cristiano (PPC), was often also called La Alianza (the Alliance). (Trans. note)

lia, Freddy Cooper's wife, had been obliged to dive underneath a policeman's riot shield that night in order to escape a hail of bottles. "What I predicted has already started happening." But the truth of the matter was that, despite her opposition in principle, she too worked morning and night organizing the meetings and was in the front row at all three of them.

It was the country's middle classes who filled those three plazas. Not the rich, since in the indescribably wretched country that bad governments have turned Peru into there would not be enough of them to fill a theater and perhaps not even a living room. And not the poor, the peasants or the inhabitants of the shantytowns that were euphemistically called "young towns," who listened to the debate pitting state ownership against a market economy, collectivism against free enterprise, from afar, as if it were no concern of theirs. These middle classes—office workers, professionals, technicians, tradesmen, state employees, housewives, students—had seen their lot worsen by the day. For three decades they had watched their standard of living decline and their hopes come to nothing under each succeeding government. Under the first administration of Belaunde Terry (1963–68), whose reformism had aroused great expectations. Under the military dictatorship and its repressive socialist policy, which had impoverished, ravished, and corrupted Peruvian society as no other previous government ever had. Under the second administration of Belaunde Terry, who had won by an overwhelming majority, and who did not remedy a single one of the disasters of the previous regime and left behind him an overt inflationary process. And under Alan García, who—in those days this was barely beginning to be perceived—would beat all records in the history of Peru for inefficient administration, bequeathing to his successor, in 1990, a country in ruins, in which real salaries had been reduced by half, paychecks by a third, and in which national production had fallen to the levels of thirty years before. Stunned, lurching in bewilderment from the political right to the left, overcome by fear and at times by desperation, these middle classes had rarely mobilized in Peru outside of election campaign periods. But they had done so this time, nonetheless, with an instinctive certainty that if the nationalization of banks, insurance companies, and financial firms came about, the situation would be worse still and Peru would be even farther away from being that decent, reliable country, with jobs and opportunities, that they longed for.

The recurrent theme of my three speeches had been that the way out of poverty does not lie in redistributing the little wealth that exists but in creating more. And in order to do that markets must be opened up, competition and individual initiative encouraged, private property not be fought against but extended to the greatest number, our economy and our psychology taken out of the grip of the state, and the handout mentality that expects everything from the state replaced by a modern outlook that entrusts the responsibility for economic life to civil society and the market.

"I see it but I don't believe it," my friend Felipe Thorndike said to me. "You talk about private property and popular capitalism, and instead of lynching you they applaud you. What's happening in Peru?"

That is how the story of my candidacy began. From that time on, whenever I've been asked why I was ready to give up my vocation as a writer and enter politics I've answered: "For a moral reason. Because circumstances placed me in a position of leadership at a critical moment in the life of my country. Because it appeared that the opportunity was at hand to accomplish, with the support of a majority of Peruvians, the liberal reforms which, ever since the early 1970s, I had been defending in articles and polemical exchanges as being necessary in order to save Peru."

But someone who knows me as well as I know myself, or perhaps even better, Patricia, doesn't see it that way. "The moral obligation wasn't the decisive factor," she says. "It was the adventure, the illusion of living an experience full of excitement and risk. Of writing the great novel in real life."

This may well hit the nail on the head. It is true that if the presidency of Peru had not been, as I said jokingly to a journalist, "the most dangerous job in the world," I might never have been a candidate. If the decadence, the impoverishment, the terrorism, and the multiple crises of Peruvian society had not made it an almost impossible challenge to govern such a country, it would never have entered my head to accept such a task. I have always believed that writing novels has been, in my case, a way of living the many lives—the many adventures—that I would like to have had myself and therefore I can't discard

the possibility that, in those dark depths where the most secret moti-
vations of our acts are plotted, it was the temptation of adventure,
rather than some sort of altruism, that induced me to enter professional
politics.

But if it is true that the temptation of adventure played a role, so
did another one, either major or minor, which, in an attempt to be
as far from grandiloquent as possible, I shall call a moral commitment.

I shall try to explain something that is not easy to put into words
without lapsing into platitudes or into sentimental simplemindedness.
Although I was born in Peru ("through an accident of geography,"
as the head of the Peruvian Army, General Nicolás de Bari Hermoza,
put it, thinking that he was insulting me),* my vocation is that of a
cosmopolitan and an expatriate who has always detested nationalism,
which strikes me as one of the human aberrations that has made the
most blood flow, and I also know that patriotism, as Dr. Johnson said,
can be the last refuge of a scoundrel. I have lived a good part of my
life abroad and I have never felt like a total stranger anywhere. Despite
this, the relations I have with the country where I was born are more
intimate and long-lasting than those I have with any other, including
the ones in which I have come to feel completely at home: England,
France, or Spain. I don't know why this is, but in any case it is not
on account of a question of principle. But what happens in Peru affects
me more—makes me happier or irritates me more—than what happens elsewhere, and in a way that I would be unable to justify rationally,
I feel that between me and Peruvians of any race, language, and social
status, for better or for worse—especially for worse—there is something
that ties me to them in a seemingly invincible way. I don't know
whether this is related to the stormy past that is our heritage, to the
violent and miserable present of our country, to its uncertain future,
ucial experiences of my adolescence in Piura and Lima,
my childhood, there in Bolivia, where, as tends to
ates, in my grandparents' and my mother's household,
u, the fact of being Peruvian, as the most precious gift
ever bestowed on our family.

* On July 8, 1992, in a ceremony that took place at the Rafael Hoyos Rubio barracks,
in Rímac, in which all the leaders of the Peruvian Army supported the coup d'état
of April 5 perpetrated by Alberto Fujimori, who until then had been the constitutional
president.

Perhaps saying that I love my country is not true. I often loathe it, and hundreds of times since I was young I have promised myself to live a long way from Peru forever and not write anything more about it and forget its aberrations. But the fact is that it is continually on my mind, and whether I am living in it or residing abroad as an expatriate, to me it is a constant torment. I cannot free myself from it; when it doesn't exasperate me, it saddens me, and often both at once. It has grieved me most of all ever since I have had ample evidence that it manages to interest the rest of the world only because of its natural cataclysms, its record rates of inflation, the activities of its drug traffickers, its terrorist massacres, or the villainies of those who govern it. And to know that it is spoken of, outside its borders, when it is spoken of at all, as a horrible, caricatural country that is dying by the inch because of the inability of Peruvians to govern themselves with a minimum of common sense. I remember having thought, when I read George Orwell's essay "The Lion and the Unicorn," in which he says that England is a good country of good folk with "the wrong people in control," how well that definition applied to Peru. For among us are decent people capable of accomplishing, for example, what the Spaniards have in Spain in the last ten years; but such people have rarely gone into politics, an area that in Peru has almost always been in dishonest and mediocre hands.

In June of 1912, the historian José de la Riva Agüero made a journey on muleback from Cuzco to Huancayo, following one of the highroads of the Inca empire, and left as testimony of the experience a beautiful book, *Paisajes peruanos* (*Peruvian Landscapes*), in which he evokes, in sculptural prose, the geography of the Andes and the historic epic deeds to which those brave territories, Cuzco, Apurímac, Ayacucho, and Junín, were witness. On reaching the great plain of Quinua, outside Ayacucho, the scene of the battle that put the final stamp on the emancipation of Peru, a somber reflection causes him to halt. A strange battle for liberation that one—in which the royalist band of the Viceroy La Serna was made up exclusively of Peruvian soldiers and the emancipating army was two-thirds Colombian and Argentine. This paradox sends him into an acid consideration concerning the failure as a republic of his country, which, ninety years after the battle that made it a sovereign nation, is a laughable shadow of what it was in its pre-Hispanic stage, and in the three colonial centuries, of the most prosperous viceroyalty of all the Spanish possessions. Who is responsible? The "poor colonial aristocracy," the "poor stupid Lima nobility, incapable of any sort of idea and of any effort"? Or "the military leaders" with "vulgar appetites," "greedy for gold and avid for command," whose "befuddled intelligences" and "depraved hearts" were incapable of serving their country, and when someone managed to do so, "all his rivals plotted to destroy him"? Or, perhaps, those "Creole bourgeois" possessed of "sordid and Phoenician selfishness" who "were ashamed later on in Europe, with the basest instincts for social climbing, of their condition as Peruvians, to which they owed everything they were and had"?

Peru had gone on ruining itself and was now more backward and perhaps with worse social iniquities than when it inspired in Riva Agüero this gloomy meditation. Ever since I read it, in 1955, for an edition being prepared by my professor and mentor, Porras Barrenechea, the pessimism that permeates it struck me as being the same one that very often paralyzed me with regard to Peru. And until those days in August 1987, that historical failure seemed to me to be a sort of sign of a country which, at some moment in its trajectory, "fucked itself all up" (this had been the obsessive rhetorical device I had deliberately hammered away at in my novel *Conversation in The Cathedral*, in which I had tried to represent Peruvian frustration) and had never discovered how to get over it without continuing to sink deeper and deeper into error.

Several times in my life, before the events of August 1987, I had lost all hope in Peru. Hope of what? When I was younger, hope that, skipping intermediate steps in one leap, it would become a prosperous, modern, cultivated country, and that I would live to see that day. Later on, the hope that, before I died, Peru would have at least begun to cease being poor, backward, and violent. There are no doubt many bad things about our era, but there is one very good one, without precedent in history. Countries today can *choose* to be prosperous. One of the most damaging myths of our time is that poor countries live in poverty because of a conspiracy of the rich countries, who arrange things so as to keep them underdeveloped, in order to exploit them. There is no better philosophy than that for keeping them in a state of backwardness for all time to come. Because *today* that theory is false. In the past, to be sure, prosperity depended almost exclusively on geography and power. But the internationalization of modern life—of markets, of technology, of capital—permits any country, even the smallest one with the fewest resources, if it opens out to the world and organizes its economy on a competitive basis, to achieve rapid growth. In the last two decades, by practicing, through its dictatorships or its civilian administrations, populism, exclusively economic nationalism, and government intervention in the economy, Latin America chose instead to go backward. And through its military dictatorship and Alan García, Peru pursued, farther than other countries, policies that lead to economic disaster. Up until those days of the campaign against the nationalization of the financial system, I had the impression that, though deeply divided on many subjects, among Peruvians there was a sort of consensus in favor of populism. The political powers that be disagreed as to the amount of intervention that was desirable, but all of them appeared to accept, as an axiom, that without it neither progress nor social justice would be possible. The modernization of Peru seemed to me to have been put off till pigs had wings.

In the public debate I had with my adversary, on June 3, 1990, the agricultural engineer Alberto Fujimori gibed: "It seems that you would like to make Peru a Switzerland, Doctor Vargas." Aspiring to see Peru "become a Switzerland" had come to be, for a considerable portion of my compatriots, a grotesque goal, whereas for others, those who would prefer to turn it into a Cuba or a North Korea, it was something intolerable, not to mention impossible.

One of the best essays of the historian Jorge Basadre is entitled "La promesa de la vida peruana" ("The Promise of Peruvian Life"), published in 1945. Its central idea is pathetic and splendid: there is an unfulfilled promise throughout the whole of the history of the Republic of Peru, an ambition, an ideal, a vague necessity that never managed to take shape, but that since emancipation was always there, buried and alive, amid the tumult of civil wars, the devastation wrought by military rule, and the eloquent oratory of the debates that took place on political speakers' platforms. A hope forever reborn and forever frustrated from saving us, someday, from the barbarism we had been brought to by our persistent inability to do what we ought to do.

But on the night of August 21, 1987, standing before that deliriously enthusiastic crowd in the Plaza San Martín, and then later in the Plaza de Armas of Arequipa, and on the Avenida Grau of the Piura of my childhood, I had the impression—the certainty—that hundreds of thousands, perhaps millions, of Peruvians had suddenly decided to do what was necessary to make our country "a Switzerland" someday— a country without people who were poor or illiterate, a country of cultivated, prosperous, and free citizens—and to make the promise at last become a part of history, thanks to a liberal reform of our incipient democracy.

THREE

Lima the Horrible

T H E Lima–San Miguel streetcar went along the Avenida Salaverry, in front of the little house in La Magdalena where we came to live in those final days of 1946 or early 1947. The house still exists, faded and shabby, and even now, when I pass that way, I feel sharp pangs of anxiety. The year and a little more that I lived in it was the most agonizing one in my life. It was a two-story house. Downstairs there was a little living room, a dining room, a kitchen, and across a little patio, the maid's room. And upstairs, the bathroom and my bedroom and my parents', separated from mine by a short staircase landing.

From the moment we arrived, I felt excluded from the relationship between my mama and my papa, a man who, as the days went by, seemed to keep his distance from me. It infuriated me that they shut themselves up in their bedroom during the day, and on one pretext or another I kept going to knock on the door, until my father upbraided me, warning me not to do it again. His cold way of speaking and the steely look in his eyes is what I remember best of those first days in Lima, a city I detested from the very first moment. I was lonely, I missed my grandparents, Auntie Mamaé, Uncle Lucho, my friends from Piura. And I was bored, shut up in the house, not knowing what to do to occupy myself. Shortly after we arrived, my father and mother enrolled me in the sixth grade of the La Salle primary school, but classes didn't begin until April and it was only January. Was I going to spend the summer shut up inside the house, seeing the clanging San Miguel streetcar go by every so often?

Around the corner, in a little house identical to ours, Uncle César lived with Aunt Orieli and their sons Eduardo, Pepe, and Jorge. The first two were a little older than I was and Jorge was my age. My uncle and aunt were affectionate toward me and did their best to make me feel a part of the family, taking me one night to a Chinese restaurant on the Calle Capón—the first time I'd ever tasted Chino-Peruvian food—and my cousins took me with them to soccer games. I remember very vividly the visit to the old stadium on the Calle José Díaz, sitting in the cheap seats, watching the classic Alianza Lima–Universitario de Deportes match. Eduardo and Jorge were fans of the Alianza and Pepe of the U, and like him, I too became a rooter for this top-notch team, and soon I had, in my room, photographs of its star players: the spectacular goalie Garagate, the guard and captain Da Silva, the blond Toto Terry, "the Arrow," and above all the very famous Lolo Fernández, the great center forward, the gentleman of the field and a scorer. My cousins had a *barrio*, a gang of friends from the neighborhood with whom they got together in front of their house to talk and kick a soccer ball around and make shots at the goal, and they would call to me to come play with them. But I never managed to belong to their *barrio*, in part because, unlike my cousins, who could go outside on the street anytime and have their friends over to their house, this was forbidden me. And partly because, although Uncle César and Aunt Orieli, as well as Eduardo, Pepe, and Jorge, always made gestures to me to come closer, I kept my distance. Because they were the family of that man who was my father, not *my* family.

After we'd been in La Magdalena for only a short while, I burst out crying one night at dinnertime. When my father asked what was the matter, I told him I missed my grandparents and that I wanted to go back to Piura. That was the first time he had a fight with me, without hitting me, but raising his voice in a way that scared me, and looking at me with a fixed stare that from that night on I learned to associate with his fits of rage. Up until then I had been jealous of him, because he had stolen my mama from me, but from that day on I began to be afraid of him. He sent me up to bed and a little while later, having already climbed into bed, I heard him reproaching my mother for having brought me up as a flighty little boy, and making extremely cruel remarks about the Llosa family.

From then on, every time we were alone, I began to torment my mother for having brought me to live with him, and demand that we escape together to Piura. She tried to calm me down, told me to be patient, to do my best to win my papa's affection, for he found me hostile and resented this. I shouted back at her that that man didn't matter to me, that I didn't love him and never would, because the people I loved were my aunts and uncles and my grandfather and grandmother. Those scenes exasperated her and made her cry.

Across from our house, on the Avenida Salaverry, there was a bookstore in a garage. It sold books and magazines for children and I spent every bit of my pocket money buying *Penecas*, *Billikens*, and an *El Gráfico*, an Argentine sports magazine with nice illustrations in color along with whatever books I could, by Salgari, Karl May, and above all Jules Verne; Verne's *Michael Strogoff, or The Courier of the Czar* and *Around the World in Eighty Days* had set me to dreaming of exotic countries and lives that were out of the ordinary. I never had enough pocket money to buy everything I wanted to, and the bookstore owner, a little man with a beard and all bent over, sometimes lent me a magazine or a book of adventures, on condition that I bring it back all in one piece within twenty-four hours. In those first long and gloomy months in Lima, in 1947, reading was my escape from that loneliness I suddenly found myself lost in, after having lived surrounded by relatives and friends, accustomed to their pleasing me in every possible way and looking on my bad behavior as if it were a joke. In those months I grew used to fantasizing and to dreaming, to seeking in my imagination, which those magazines and little storybooks aroused, an alternative life to the one I had, imprisoned and solitary. If I already had had the seeds of a storyteller within me, they began to take firm root in this stage, and if I didn't have them, they must have been planted then and there and begun to send out their first shoots.

Worse than not ever going out and spending hours on end in my room was a new sensation, an experience that during those months took possession of me and from then on was my companion: fear. Fear that that man would come home from the office with that paleness, those dark circles under his eyes, and that little swollen vein in his forehead that foretold a storm brewing, and would start insulting my mama, making her account to him for all the things she'd done in the last ten years, asking her what lewd behavior she'd gone in for while he was separated from her, and cursing out all the Llosas, one by one, grandparents, aunts and uncles, all of whom he shat on— yes, shat on—even though they were relatives of that poor weakling who was the president of the Republic, on whom, naturally, he shat as well. I felt panicked. My legs trembled. I wanted to shrink to nothing, to disappear. And when, overexcited by his own fit of rage, he sometimes flung himself at my mother to hit her, I wanted to die for real, because even dying seemed preferable to the fear I felt.

He gave me a beating too, every so often. The first time was on a Sunday, as Mass let out at the parish church in La Magdalena. For some reason I was being punished and was not to leave the house, but I had supposed that the punishment did not include missing Mass, and with my mama's permission, I went to church. As I came out, amid the crowd of people, I saw the blue Ford, at the foot of the steps. And I saw him, standing motionless in the street, waiting for me. By the look on his face, I knew what was going to happen. Or perhaps I didn't, for it was toward the very beginning and I still didn't know him. I may have imagined that, as my uncles had sometimes done when they couldn't stand my misbehavior any longer, he would cuff me on the head or pull my ears and five minutes later the whole thing would be forgotten. Without a word, he gave me such a hard slap on the face that it threw me to the ground; he hit me again and then pushed me into the car, where he began to say those terrible dirty words that made me suffer as much as his blows. And, once we got back home, as he forced me to beg his pardon, he went on beating me, as he warned me that he was going to straighten me out, to make a little man of me, because he wouldn't allow his son to be the sissy the Llosas had raised.

Then, along with the terror, he made me feel hatred. The word is cruel and it seemed so to me too, at that time, and all of a sudden, at night, when, huddled in my bed, hearing him shout at my mother and insult her, I wanted all the misfortunes in the world to happen to him—for Uncle Juan, Uncle Lucho, Uncle Pedro, and Uncle Jorge to ambush him and give him a thrashing someday, for instance. I was overcome with fear, because hating one's own father was surely a mortal sin, for which God would punish me. At La Salle, there was confession every morning and I frequently made confession; my conscience was always sullied by that fault, hating my father and wanting him to die so that my mama and I could again have the life we'd had before. I approached the confessional with my face burning with shame for having to repeat the same sin every time.

Neither in Bolivia nor in Piura had I been very pious, one of those sanctimonious little prigs that abounded among my schoolmates at La Salle and at the Salesian Brothers' school, but in this first period in Lima I came close to being one, even though for bad reasons, since that was a discreet way of resisting my papa. He made fun of the religious hypocrites that the Llosas were, of that pantywaist habit they had inculcated in me of crossing myself when I passed in front of a church and of that custom of Catholics to kneel before those men in skirts: priests. He said that in order for him to be on good terms with God he didn't need intermediaries, and needed even less lazy, para-sitical ones in women's skirts. But even though he ragged us a lot about how devout my mama and I were, he didn't forbid us to go to Mass, perhaps because he suspected that, even though she obeyed his every order and prohibition, she would not have respected that one: her faith in God and in the Catholic Church was stronger than the passion she felt for him. Although who knows? My mother's love for my father, as masochistic and tortured as it always seemed to me, had that excessive and transgressive nature of great love-passions that do not hesitate to defy heaven and even pay the price of going to hell in order to prevail. At any event, he allowed us to go to Mass and sometimes—I suppose it was because of his inordinate jealousy—he went with us himself. He remained standing throughout the entire Mass, without crossing himself or kneeling during the consecration. I, on the other hand, did so, and prayed with fervor, joining my hands and half-closing my eyes. And I took communion as often as I could. These demonstrations were a way of opposing his authority and, per-haps, of annoying him.

But it was also a matter of something more indirect and barely conscious, because the fear that I had of him was too great for me to risk deliberately provoking those storming rages that turned into the nightmare of my childhood. My manifestations of rebellion, if they can be called that, were remote and cowardly; they were contrived in my imagination, safe from his gaze, when, in my bed, in the dark, I invented evil deeds against him, or acted them out with attitudes and gestures imperceptible to anyone but myself. For example, not kissing him ever again after the afternoon I first met him, in the Hotel de Turistas in Piura. In the little house in La Magdalena, I kissed my mama and merely said good night to him and ran upstairs to bed, frightened of my daring in the beginning, afraid he'd call me back, rivet his motionless gaze on me and with his knife-sharp voice ask me why I hadn't kissed him as well. But he didn't, doubtless because the block was as filled with stubborn pride as the chip that had come off it.

We lived in constant tension. I had the presentiment that something dreadful was about to happen at any moment, a terrible catastrophe, that in one of his fits of rage he was going to kill my mama or me or both of us. It was the most abnormal house in the world. There was never a single visitor, we never ever went out to visit anybody. We didn't even go to Uncle César and Aunt Orieli's, because my father abhorred social life. When we were alone and I began to throw it up to my mama that the reason she had become reconciled with him was so that we'd die of fear, she tried to persuade me that my papa wasn't so bad. He had his virtues. He never drank a drop of alcohol, he didn't smoke, he never went out on the town, he was so polite and such a hard worker. Weren't those great virtues? I told her that it would have been better if he got dead drunk, if he liked to live it up, because that way he'd be a more normal man, and she and I could go out together and I could have friends and invite them to my house and go to play at theirs.

After a few months in La Magdalena, the relationship with my cousins Eduardo, Pepe, and Jorge came to an abrupt end, after a family quarrel that was to keep my papa and his brother César apart for many years. I don't remember the details, but I do remember that Uncle César came to the house with his three sons and invited me to go see a soccer match. My papa wasn't home, and having learned to be prudent, I told my uncle that I didn't dare go without having first asked my father for his permission. But Uncle César said he'd explain about the match later. When we got back, after dark, my father was waiting for us in the street outside Uncle César's front door. And Aunt Orieli was at the window, with an alarmed expression, as if to warn us of something. I still remember the terrible set-to, the way my father screamed at poor Uncle César, who drew back in bewilderment, trying to explain, and my own terror, as my father kicked me all the way home.

When he beat me, I went off the deep end, and terror many times made me humble myself before him and beg his pardon with my hands joined. But that didn't calm him down. And he went on hitting me, screaming and threatening to put me in the army as a private as soon as I was old enough to be a recruit, so that I'd be set on the right path. When the whole scene was over and done with, and he could lock me in my room, it was not the blows, but rage and disgust with myself for having been so afraid of him and having humbled myself before him in that way, that made me spend a sleepless night, weeping in silence.

From that day on I was forbidden to go back to my Uncle César and Aunt Orieli's and to be with my cousins. I was completely alone until the summer of 1947 was over and I'd turned eleven. With the classes at La Salle, things became better. For several hours a day I was outside the house. The blue bus from the school picked me up on the corner, at seven-thirty in the morning, brought me back at noon, picked me up again at one-thirty, and brought me back to La Magdalena at five. The trip along the long Avenida Brasil to Breña, picking up schoolboys and leaving them off, was a liberation from being shut up at home and I was overjoyed. Brother Leoncio, our sixth-grade teacher, a ruddy-faced Frenchman of around sixty, rather bad-tempered, with rumpled white hair, a thick lock of which kept constantly falling over his forehead and which he tossed back with equine movements of his head, made us learn poems by Fray Luis de León by heart. I soon got over the inevitable embarrassment of being a newcomer in a class of boys who had been together for several years now, and I made good friends at La Salle. Some lasted longer than the three years that I was a pupil there, among them José Miguel Oviedo, my desk mate, who later on would be the first literary critic to write a book about me.

But despite these friends, and a few good teachers as well, my memory of the years at La Salle was clouded by the presence of my father, whose overwhelming shadow grew larger and larger, dogged my footsteps, and appeared to intrude on all my activities and spoil them. Real life at school is one of games and rites; it is not lived during classes but before and after them, in corners where friends get together, in private houses when they seek each other out and meet to plan the matinees or the parties they'll all go to or the pranks they'll play; parallel to classes, these make up the profound education of a boy, the enchanting adventure of childhood. I had had that in Bolivia and in

Piura and now that I no longer had it, my existence was one of nostalgia for that period, full of envy toward those schoolmates at La Salle— like Perro Martínez, or Perales, or Vieja Zanelli, or Flaco Ramos— who could stay after classes to play soccer on the school field, visit each other's houses, and go to the serials at the neighborhood movie theaters even though it wasn't Sunday. I had to go back home once the day's classes were over and shut myself up in my room to do my homework. And when it occurred to one of the boys at school to invite me to have tea or go to his house on Sunday after Mass, to have lunch and go to the matinee, I had to invent all sorts of excuses, because how was I going to dare to ask my father for permission to do things like that?

I went back to La Magdalena and pleaded with my mother to give me my dinner early so that I might be in bed before he got home and thereby manage not to see him until the next day. Often, when I was still not finished eating, I would hear the blue Ford braking outside the door, and go scurrying upstairs and dive into bed with all my clothes on, covering even my head with the sheet. I kept hoping that they were eating or listening on Radio Central to Teresita Arce's program, "La Chola Purificación Chauca" ("The Mestiza Purification Chauca"), which made him roar with laughter, so that I could get out of bed on tiptoe and put my pajamas on.

To think that Uncle Juan, Aunt Laura, and my cousins Nancy and Gladys, and my Uncle Jorge and Aunt Gaby, and Uncle Pedro lived in Lima and that we couldn't go see them because of my papa's antipathy for the Llosa family embittered me as much as being subjected to his authority. My mama tried to make me understand, with reasons I didn't even hear: "He's the way he is, we have to please him if we want to lead a joyful life in peace and quiet." Why did he forbid us to see my aunts and uncles, my cousins? When he wasn't around, when I was alone with my mother, I regained my sense of security and again felt free to engage in the impertinent behavior that, before, my grandparents and Mamaé had indulgently tolerated. My scenes demanding that we run away together to a place where he could never find us must have made her life much more difficult. One day, in desperation, I even went so far as to threaten that, if we didn't leave, I would tell my papa that in Piura the Spaniard whose name was Azcárate, the one who tried to buy me off by taking me to see a boxing championship bout, had visited her in the prefect's house. She began to cry and I felt like a miserable wretch.

Until one day we made our escape. I don't remember which one of the fights—although using that word to describe those scenes in which he shouted, insulted, and lashed out while my mother wept or listened to him without a word is an exaggeration—made her decide to take the great step. Perhaps it was that episode that lingers in my memory as one of the worst of all. It was at night and we were coming home from somewhere, in the blue Ford. My mama was recounting something and suddenly mentioned a lady from Arequipa named Elsa. "Elsa?" he asked. "Elsa who?" I started to tremble. "Yes, that Elsa," my mother stammered and tried to change the subject. "The number-one whore in person," he hissed. He fell silent for some time and suddenly I heard my mother cry out. He had pinched her so hard on the leg that a large purple bruise formed immediately. She showed it to me later, saying that she couldn't stand any more. "Let's leave, Mama, let's leave once and for all, let's run away."

We waited until he'd left for the office, and taking with us only a few things that we could carry by hand, we went by taxi to Miraflores, to the Avenida 28 de Julio, where Uncle Jorge and Aunt Gaby lived, and also Uncle Pedro, still a bachelor, who was finishing his medical training that year. It was exciting to see my aunts and uncles again and to be in this neighborhood that was so pretty, with tree-lined streets and little houses that had well-cared-for gardens. Above all, it was marvelous to feel that I was with my family once more, far from that man, and to know that I would never again hear him or see him or feel afraid. Uncle Jorge and Aunt Gaby's house was small, and they had two children, Silvia and Jorgito, who were still hardly older than toddlers, but we all fit in somehow—I slept in an armchair—and my happiness knew no bounds. What would happen to us now? My mama and my aunt and uncle held long conversations which I was not allowed to participate in. In any event, I didn't have words enough to thank God, the Virgin, and that Lord of Limpias to whom Granny Carmen was so devoted, for having freed us from that man.

A few days later, when classes were over, just as I was about to climb into the La Salle school bus that took the pupils to San Isidro and Miraflores, my heart sank: there he was. "Don't be afraid," he said to me. "I'm not going to do anything to you. Come with me." I noticed that he looked very pale and had big dark circles under his eyes, as though he hadn't had any sleep for days. In the car, talking to me in a friendly way, he explained that we'd go pick up my clothes and my mama's and that then he'd take me to Miraflores. I was certain that that affable manner was a hidden trap and that the moment we arrived at the house on the Avenida Salaverry he would beat me. But he didn't. He had already packed part of our clothes in suitcases and I had to help him put the rest in some sacks and, when those gave out, in a blue blanket, which we tied together by the corners. As we were doing that, I, with my soul hanging by a thread, constantly fearing that at any moment he would regret allowing me to leave, noted, in surprise, that he had removed many of the photos that my mama kept on her night table, thereby eliminating her and me, and that he had stuck pins in others. When we had finally finished packing everything, we brought it all down to the blue Ford and took off. I couldn't believe that it would be so easy, that he would act in such an understanding way. In Miraflores, in front of Uncle Jorge and Aunt Gaby's, he wouldn't let me call the maid to unload the things. He left them outside, on the tree-lined sidewalk, and the blanket came undone and clothes and various objects spilled out over the lawn. My aunt and uncle remarked afterward that with a spectacle like that, the whole neighborhood had had an eyeful of the family's dirty linen.

A few days later, when I came back for lunch, I noticed something strange about the expression on the faces of Uncle Jorge and Aunt Gaby. What had happened? Where was my mama? They passed the news on to me tactfully, as was their habit, aware that it would be a tremendous disappointment for me. My mama and papa had made up and my mama had gone back to him. And that afternoon, when I got out of school, instead of going to Miraflores, I too was to go to the Avenida Salaverry. My world came tumbling down. How could she do such a thing? Was my mama too betraying me?

At the time I was unable to understand it, only suffer it, and I emerged from each of these escapes of ours and my parents' later reconciliations more embittered, feeling that life was full of sudden shocks, without any compensation. Why did my mother make up with him every time, knowing full well that, after having calmed down for a few days or weeks, he would begin his physical violence and his insults once again, on the slightest pretext? She did so because, despite everything, she loved him with that obstinacy that was one of the traits of her character (one that I would inherit from her) and because he was the husband that God had given her—and a woman like her could have only one husband till the end of time, even though he mistreated her and even though she had a vague semi-definite divorce decree—and also because, despite her having worked for Grace Lines in Cochabamba and in Piura, my mother had been brought up to have a husband, to be a housewife, and so she felt incapable of earning a living for herself and for her son with her own earnings alone. She did it because she felt ashamed that she and I were continuing to be supported by my grandparents, who weren't all that well off—Grandpa had never been able to put money aside with that tribe on his back—or else we would one day come to be supported by my aunt and uncle, who were trying their best to make their way financially in Lima. I know that now, but when I was eleven or twelve years old I didn't know it, and even if I had, I wouldn't have understood. The only thing I knew and understood was that, every time my mother and father took up with each other again, I had to go back to being imprisoned, to loneliness and fear, and this was gradually filling my heart with bitterness toward my mother as well, with whom, from that time on, I was never again as close as I had been before I met my father.

Between 1947 and 1949 we made our escape a number of times, at least half a dozen, always to the house of Uncle Jorge and Aunt Gaby or to Juan and Laura's, also in Miraflores, and each time, within a few days, the much-feared reconciliation came about. With the distance of the years, how comical those escapes, hidden refuges, tearful receptions, those makeshift beds set up for us in the living rooms or dining rooms of my aunts and uncles seem. There was always that lugging of suitcases and sacks, the goings and comings, the very embarrassing explanations at La Salle, to the Brothers and to my schoolmates, of why, all of a sudden, I would be taking the Miraflores school bus instead of the La Magdalena one and then, after a while, the La Magdalena bus once more. Had I moved from one house to another again, or hadn't I? Because nobody moved back and forth from one house to another every so often the way we did.

One day—it was summer, so it must have been shortly after our arrival in Lima—my papa took me alone with him in the car and we picked up two boys on a street corner. He introduced me to them:

"They're your brothers." The older one, a year younger than I was, was named Enrique, and the other one, two years younger, Ernesto. The latter had blond hair and such light blue eyes that anybody would have taken him for a little gringo. All three of us were embarrassed and didn't know what to do. My papa took us to the beach at Agua Dulce, rented an awning, sat down in the shade, and sent us to play in the sand and take a dip in the ocean. Little by little we began to feel closer to each other. They were students at the Colegio San Andrés and spoke English. Wasn't San Andrés a Protestant school? I didn't dare ask them. Afterward, when we were alone, my mama told me that, after separating from her, my papa had married a German lady and that Enrique and Ernesto were the sons of that marriage. But that he had separated from his gringa wife some years before, because she too had a testy temperament and couldn't stand his bad moods. I didn't see my brothers again for quite some time. Until, during one of those periodic escapes—this time we had taken refuge at Aunt Lala and Uncle Juan's—my papa came to La Salle for me when school let out. Like the time before, he made me get into the blue Ford. He looked very stern and I was terrified. "The Llosas are plotting to send you abroad," he said to me. "Taking advantage of their family ties with the president. They're going to have me to contend with and we'll see who wins." Instead of going to La Magdalena, we went to Jesús María, where he stopped in front of a group of little red brick houses, made me get out of the car, knocked, and we went in. There were my brothers. And their mama, a blond lady, who offered me a cup of tea. "You stay here until I arrange matters," my papa said. And he went away.

I was there for two days, without going to school, convinced that I would never see my mama again. He had kidnapped me and this would be my house from then on. They had given me one of my brothers' beds and the two of them shared the other one. At night they heard me crying and got up, turned the light on, and tried to console me. But I went on crying, until the lady of the house also appeared and tried to calm me down. Two days later my papa came to get me. There had been another reconciliation and my mama was waiting for me in the little house in La Magdalena. Then she told me that, in fact, she had thought of asking the president for a job in a Peruvian consulate somewhere abroad, and that my papa had found out. Wasn't the fact that he had kidnapped me a proof that he loved me? When my mama tried to convince me that he loved me or that I should love him, since, in spite of everything, he was my papa, I felt even more bitter toward her than I did because of their periodic making up with each other.

I believe I saw my brothers only a couple of times more in that year, and always for only a few hours. The following year, they left with their mother for Los Angeles, where she and Ernesto—who goes by the name of Ernie now, since he's an American citizen and a prosperous attorney—still live. Enrique began to suffer from leukemia when he was in school and suffered a painful death. He came back to Lima for a few days, shortly before he died. I went to see him and could scarcely recognize, in that fragile little figure racked with disease, the handsome, sporting boy of the photographs that he used to send to Lima and that my papa sometimes showed us.

During the time he kept me confined at the gringa's (as my mother and I called her), my papa had turned up without warning at my Uncle Juan's. He didn't come in. He told the maid that he wanted to talk with my uncle and that he would wait for him in the car. My father had not been on speaking terms with anybody in the family ever since that long-ago day when he abandoned my mother at the Arequipa airport, at the end of 1935. Uncle Juan told me some time later about their meeting, straight out of a movie. My father was sitting at the wheel of the blue Ford waiting for him and when Uncle Juan got in, he warned him: "I'm armed and ready for anything." So as not to leave any doubt in my uncle's mind, he showed him the revolver he was carrying in his pocket. He said that if the Llosas, taking advantage of their relationship with the president, tried to send me abroad, he would take reprisals against the family. Then he railed against the upbringing they had given me, spoiling me and drumming it into my head that I should hate him and fostering in me fancy-pants ideas like saying that when I was grown up I'd be a bullfighter and a poet; his name was at stake and he wouldn't have a son who was a pansy. Following this semi-hysterical peroration, in which Uncle Juan couldn't get so much as a word in edgewise, he noted that as long as the Llosas refused to give him any guarantees that my mother wouldn't go off abroad with me, the family wouldn't see my face again. And he drove off.

That revolver he showed Uncle Juan was an emblematic object of my childhood and adolescence, the symbol of the relationship I had with my father as long as I lived with him. I heard him shoot it, one night, in the little house in La Perla, but I don't know if I ever managed to see the revolver with my own eyes. It is quite true that I saw it constantly, in my nightmares and in my moments of terror, and every time I heard my father shout and threaten my mama, it seemed to me that, in all truth, what he said he was going to do, he really and truly would do: take out that revolver, shoot five times, and kill her and then me.

These abortive escapes nonetheless eventuated in my having a counterweight to the life I led on the Avenida Salaverry, and, later, in La Perla: being able to spend the weekends in Miraflores, with my aunts and uncles. This came about after one of the times we ran away; in the course of the reconciliation, my mother managed to get my papa to allow me, when Saturday classes were over, to go directly from La Salle to Aunt Lala and Uncle Juan's. I went back home on Mondays, after the morning classes. That day and a half a week, in Miraflores, far from his prying eyes, living the normal life of other youngsters my age, became the most important thing in my life, the objective fondly imagined all week long, and that Saturday afternoon and Sunday in Miraflores an experience that filled me with courage and happy images, enabling me to resist the horrendous five remaining days.

I couldn't go to Miraflores every weekend, only when I got the grades E (excellent) or O (highest in class) on my report card. If my grades were D (unsatisfactory) or M (bad), I had to go back home to spend the weekend shut up inside. And then there were, besides, the punishments that I received for some other reason, and which, once my father discovered that what I hoped for most in the world was to spend those weekends a long way away from him, consisted of: "This week you're not going to Miraflores." For the most part, though, the years 1948 and 1949 and the summer of 1950 were divided up for me like this: Mondays to Fridays in La Magdalena or in La Perla, then Saturdays and Sundays in the Diego Ferré *barrio* of Miraflores.

A *barrio* was a parallel family, a group of youngsters of the same age with whom one talked of sports or played soccer—*fútbol*—or a version of it on a smaller scale—*fulbito*. With whom one went swimming at the pool and bodysurfing at the beaches of Miraflores—the

Club Regatas or La Herradura—and took walks around the park after eleven o'clock Mass, went to the matinee at the Leuro or Ricardo Palma movie theater, and finally went for a stroll through the Salazar gardens. And with whom, as one grew older, one learned to smoke, dance, and make girls fall in love—the ones who, little by little, got permission from their families to come stand in the doorways of the houses to talk to the boys and organize, on Saturday nights, parties in which, dancing a bolero—preferably "Me gustas," by Leo Marino— the boys fell for the girls and announced to them that they were *templados* (in love). The girls would say, "I'm going to think it over," or "All right," or "I don't want to have a boyfriend yet because my mama won't let me." If the answer was "All right," one now had a girlfriend. One could dance cheek to cheek with her at parties, go to the Sunday matinee together, and kiss each other in the dark. And also, walk hand in hand after having an ice cream at the Crem Rica on the Avenida Larco, and ask her to go with you to see the sun set on the ocean from the Salazar gardens while you made a wish. Aunt Lala and Uncle Juan lived in a little white two-story house, in the heart of one of the most famous districts in Miraflores, and Nancy and Gladys belonged to the youngest generation of the *barrio*, which also had its old-timers, who were fifteen, eighteen, or twenty years old, and thanks to my cousins I joined it. I owe all my good memories between the ages of eleven and fourteen to my *barrio*. It was called the Happy Barrio at one time, but it changed its name when the newspapers began to call the Jirón Huatica de La Victoria (the street where the prostitutes were) by that name, and it became the Diego Ferré or the Colón *barrio*, because our main hangout was at the intersection of those two streets.

Gladys and I had our birthdays on the same day, and Aunt Lala and Uncle Juan gave a party with boys and girls of the *barrio* on March 28, 1948. I remember my surprise when I came in and saw that there were couples dancing and that my two cousins also knew how to dance. And that the birthday party was being held not to play games but to put records on, to hear music, and to serve as a "mixer" for the boys and girls. All my aunts and uncles were there and they introduced me to some youngsters with whom I would be great friends later on— Tico, Coco, Luchín, Mario, Luquen, Víctor, Emilio, el Chino—and they even made me ask Teresita to dance. I was dying of embarrassment and felt like a robot, not knowing what to do with my hands and feet. But afterward I danced with my cousins and other girls and from that day on I began to dream romantic dreams of being in love with Teresita. She was my first sweetheart. Inge was the second, and Helena the third. I made a very formal declaration of love to the three of them. We boys rehearsed the declaration beforehand, among ourselves, and each of them suggested words or gestures so that all would not be lost when one fell for a girl. Some of them preferred to declare their love at the movies, taking advantage of the darkness at the matinee and making the declaration coincide with some romantic moment of the film, which they presumed had a contagious effect. I tried that method, once, with Maritza, a very pretty girl with dark black hair and very pale skin, and the result was farcical. Because when, after hesitating for a long time, I dared to murmur in her ear the time-hallowed words—"I like you a whole lot; I'm in love with you. Would you be my girl?"—she turned to look at me, weeping like a Mary Magdalene. Totally absorbed in the film, she had barely heard me and asked: "What's that? What did you say?" Incapable of taking up again where I had left off, all I managed to do was to stammer what a sad movie it was, wasn't it?

But I made my declarations to Tere, Inge, and Helena in an orthodox way, dancing a bolero at a Saturday night party, and I wrote love poems to all three of them that I never showed them. I dreamed about them all week, counting how many days were left before I saw them again and praying that there would be a party that Saturday so that I might dance cheek to cheek with my sweetheart. At the Sunday matinee I grabbed their hand in the dark, but didn't dare kiss them. I only kissed them when we played spin the bottle, or forfeits, when my friends from the *barrio*, who knew that we were sweethearts, sent us away as a punishment if we lost at the game, to give each other three, four, and even ten kisses. But they were kisses on the cheek and that, according to Luchín, the one who wanted to be considered a grownup, didn't count, because a kiss on the cheek wasn't a smacker. Smackers were given on the mouth. But at that time couples from Miraflores twelve or thirteen years old were still more or less innocent little archangels and not many of them dared give each other real smackers. I, naturally, didn't dare. I fell in love the way calves fall in love with the moon—a pretty expression that we used to use to define boys who were enamored of a girl—but I was abnormally timid with the girls from Miraflores.

Spending the weekend in Miraflores was an adventure in freedom, the possibility of a thousand entertaining and exciting things. To go to the Club Terrazas to play *fulbito* or have a swim in the pool, from which great swimmers had come. Among all sports—I liked all of them—the one I was best at was swimming. I came to master the crawl quite well and one of my frustrations was not having been able to train in the academy directed by Walter Ledgard, the Sorcerer, as did some Miraflores boys my age who later became international champions, Ismael Merino or Rabbit Villarán for instance. I was never a very good soccer player, but my enthusiasm compensated for my lack of skill and one of the happiest days of my life was the Sunday when Toto Terry, a star from our *barrio*, took me to the National Stadium and had me play with the youngsters of the Universitario de Deportes against those of the Deportivo Municipal. Wasn't going out onto that enormous field, wearing the uniform of the top team, the best thing that could happen to anyone in the world? And didn't the fact that Toto Terry, the blond "Arrow" of the U, was from our *barrio* prove that ours was the best one in Miraflores? That was demonstrated in a series of "Olympic Games" we organized on several consecutive weekends, in which we competed with the *barrio* of the Calle San Martín in cycling, field and track, *fulbito*, and swimming races.

Carnival was the best time in the year. We went out during the day to squirt water on people, and in the afternoons, disguised as pirates, to the masked balls. There were three children's balls that weren't to be missed: the one at the park in Barranco, the one at the Club Terrazas, and the one at the Lawn Tennis Club. We brought paper streamers and squirt guns full of ether, and the group from the *barrio*, all dressed in identical costumes, was a large, joyful one. For one of those carnivals Dámaso Pérez Prado came with his orchestra. The mambo, recently invented in the Caribbean, was all the rage in Lima too, and contestants had even been invited to a national mambo championship in the Plaza de Acho, but the archbishop, Monsignor Guevara, forbade it, threatening to excommunicate the participants. The arrival of Pérez Prado filled the Córpac airport, and there too I was with my friends, running behind the convertible with the top down that was taking the composer of "El ruletero" and of "Mambo número cinco," greeting people right and left, to the Hotel Bolívar. Aunt Lala and Uncle Juan laughed as they watched me, almost the minute I reached the house on Diego Ferré, on Saturdays at noon, begin practicing mambo steps, all by myself, on the stairs and through the rooms, in preparation for that night's party.

Teresita and Inge were transitory sweethearts, for just a few weeks, something halfway between a children's game and puppy love, what Gide calls the harmless caracoles of love. But Helena was a serious and steady long-time sweetheart, an expression that meant a relationship of several months or perhaps even a year. She was a close friend of Nancy's, and her classmate at the Colegio La Reparación. She lived in one of a group of little ocher-colored townhouses with a common entrance, in Grimaldo del Solar, a place some distance away from Diego Ferré, in which there was also a *barrio*. If a stranger came to make the girls of one's own neighborhood fall in love with him it was not looked upon with favor; it constituted a violation of one's territory. But I was very much in love with Helena, and as soon as I reached Miraflores, I ran to the townhouse in Grimaldo del Solar to see her, if only from afar, in the window of her house. I went with Luchín and my namesake Mario, who had received declarations of love from Ilse and Lucy, neighbors of Helena's. If luck was with us, we could talk with them for a moment in the doorway of their houses. But the kids in that neighborhood moved closer to hurl insults or throw stones at us, and on one of those afternoons we were obliged to come to blows with them, because they tried to kick us out of their turf.

Helena was blond, with bright blue eyes, very pretty teeth, and a very joyful laugh. I missed her a lot in the desolation and loneliness of La Perla, in that isolated little house in the middle of a vast stretch of open countryside to which we moved in 1948. My father, besides working for the International News Service, bought lots, built houses, and then sold them; for several years that was an important source of income for him. I say this with some hesitation because his economic situation, like a fair part of his life, was a mystery to me. Did he earn good money? Did he save much of it? He lived an extremely abstemious life. He never went out to a restaurant, much less, needless to say, to those cabarets—the Cabaña, the Embassy, or the Bolívar Grill—to which my aunt and uncle sometimes went to dance on Saturday nights. In all likelihood he and my mama went to the movies once in a while, but I do not recall their ever doing that either, or perhaps they did so on the weekends that I spent in Miraflores. From Monday to Friday he came home from the office between seven and eight, and after dinner he sat down to listen to the radio, for an hour or two, before going to bed. I think that the programs of Teresita Arce's comic series, "La Chola Purificación Chauca," on Radio Central, ones he always laughed at, were the only diversion in that house. And my mama and I laughed too, in unison with our lord and master. He himself had built the little house in La Perla, with the help of a construction foreman.

La Perla, at the end of the 1940s, was a gigantic empty lot. Only on the Avenida de Las Palmeras and on the Avenida Progreso were there any buildings. The rest of the area, between that square of streets and the steep cliff overlooking the sea, consisted of blocks and blocks laid out as straight as a string, with street lighting and sidewalks but not a single house. Ours was one of the first in that district and in the year and a half or two that we were there, we lived in a wilderness. Toward Bellavista, a few blocks away, there was a settlement with one of those grocery stores that in Peru are still called *chinos*—Chinamen's stores—and at the other end, close to the sea, the police station. My mama was afraid of being left alone there all day long, because of the isolation of the place. And one night, in fact, footsteps were heard on the roof and my father went out to find the thief. I woke up hearing shouting and it was then that I heard the two shots in the air of the mythical revolver, which he fired so as to scare the intruder off. At the time Mamaé was already living with us, for I remember the little old lady's frightened face, as she stood in her nightdress in the cold hallway with black and white tiles that separated our rooms.

If in the little house on the Avenida Salaverry I lacked friends, in La Perla I lived the life of a fungus. I went to and from La Salle in the little interurban Lima–Callao minibus that I took on the Avenida Progreso, and got off at the Avenida Venezuela, from where it was several blocks' walk to the school. They enrolled me as a half-boarder, so that I had my lunch at La Salle. When I got back home to La Perla, at around five, since there was still lots of time before my father came home from work, I used to go out to the vacant lots and kick a soccer ball around as far as the police station and the cliff and come back home again, and that was my daily diversion. I'm lying: the important diversion was to think about Helena and write letters and love poems to her. To write poems was another of the secret ways of resisting my father, since I knew how much it irritated him that I wrote verses, something he associated with eccentricity, bohemia, and what could horrify him most: being queer. I suppose that, for him, if it was necessary to write verses, something that remained completely unproved—in the house there was not a single book, either of poetry or of prose, outside of the ones that belonged to me, and I never saw him read anything else but the newspaper—it was most probably women who wrote them. That men should do such a thing discon- certed him, struck him as an extravagant way of wasting time, a pastime incompatible with wearing trousers and having balls.

For I read many verses and learned them by heart—Bécquer, Cho- cano, Amado Nervo, Juan de Dios Pesa, Zorrilla—and wrote them, before and after doing my homework, and sometimes I dared read them, on weekends, to Aunt Lala, Uncle Juan, or Uncle Jorge. But never to Helena, the inspiration and the ideal addressee of these rhe- torical effusions. The fact that my papa could give me a dressing-down if he discovered me writing poems surrounded the writing of poetry with a dangerous aura, and that, of course, made it all the more exciting to me. My aunts and uncles were delighted that I was going out with Helenita, and the day that my mama met her, at Aunt Lala's, she was very much taken by her too: what a pretty little girl and how likable. I would often hear her regret, years later, that having been able to marry someone like Helenita, her son had instead committed all the follies he had.

Helena was my sweetheart until I entered the Leoncio Prado Military Academy, in the third year of secondary school, a few days after my fourteenth birthday. And she was also my last sweetheart—in the decorous, serious, and purely sentimental connotations of the word in that milieu in those days. (What came after that, in the amorous domain, was more complicated and less mentionable.) And because of how deeply in love with Helena I was, I dared to falsify my report card one day. My teacher in the second year of secondary school at La Salle was a layman, Cañón Paredes, with whom I always got along badly. And on one of those weekends he handed me my report card with an ignominious D for "unsatisfactory." And so I would have to go back home to La Perla. But the idea of not going to Miraflores, of not seeing Helena for another week, was intolerable and I left for my aunt and uncle's. Once there, I changed the D to an O for highest in class, believing that my cheating would pass unnoticed. Cañón Paredes discovered it, days later, and without a word to me had the principal summon my father to the school.

What happened then still fills me with shame when even without warning my unconscious brings those images back to life. After recess, standing in line to go back into the classrooms, I saw my father appear in the distance, accompanied by Brother Agustín, the principal. My father approached the line and I realized that he knew everything and that I was going to pay the price. He gave me a terrific slap on the face that silenced and electrified the dozens of boys. Then, grabbing me by one ear, he dragged me to the principal's office, where he began to beat me, in front of Brother Agustín, who tried to calm him down. I imagine that thanks to that beating the principal took pity on me and didn't expel me from the school, as my misdeed deserved. My punishment was to be forbidden to go to Miraflores for several weeks.

In October 1948, the military coup of General Odría brought down the democratic government and Uncle José Luis went into exile. My father celebrated the coup as a personal victory: the Llosas could no longer boast of having a relative who was the president of Peru. I cannot recall having ever heard talk of politics after our arrival in Lima, either in my parents' house or at my aunts and uncles', except for an isolated phrase or two in passing against the Apristas, whom all those around me seemed to regard as scoundrels (on this subject my father agreed with the Llosas). But the fall of Bustamante and the rise to power of General Odría became the object of my father's triumphant monologues celebrating the event, delivered straight to my mother's wistful face, and in those same days I heard her wonder how she could send a note "to poor José Luis and María Jesús [whom the military had banished to Argentina] without your papa finding out."

Grandpa Pedro resigned as prefect of Piura on the same day as the military coup, bundled up his tribe—Grandmother Carmen, Mamaé, Joaquín, and Orlando—and brought them to Lima. Uncle Lucho and Aunt Olga stayed in Piura. That post as prefect was the last steady job my grandfather ever had. There would then begin for him, still robust and lucid at the age of seventy-five, a long *via crucis*, the slow immersion in the mediocrity of routine and poverty that he never grew weary of fighting, seeking work right and left, sometimes securing, temporarily, an audit or a liquidation with which he was entrusted by a bank, or minor matters to take up with administrative agencies, which filled him with hope, got him up out of bed at dawn to get ready in a great hurry and wait impatiently for it to be time to leave for "his job" (although this might well consist merely of standing in line in some ministry to secure the official seal of some bureaucrat). Miserable and mechanical, those little jobs made him feel alive and relieved him of the torture that it was for him to live on the small monthly sums that his children slipped him. Later on—I know that it was as a protest by his body against the tremendous injustice of not finding a job when he was still able to work, of feeling condemned to a useless and parasitic life—when he had his first cerebral hemorrhage and could no longer manage to secure even those temporary assignments, the inactivity little by little drove him mad. He rushed out onto the streets, walking from one place to another, very fast, inventing tasks for himself. And my uncles tried to find some sort of work for him to do, some sort of minor business transaction for him to carry out for them, so he wouldn't feel like a useless old man.

Grandfather Pedro wasn't the sort to take his grandchildren in his arms and devour them with kisses. Children bothered him and, at times, in Bolivia, in Piura, and then later in the little houses in Lima where he lived, when his grandchildren and great-grandchildren made a great racket, he ordered them to cut it out. But he was the kindest and most generous man I have ever known and I often have recourse to the memory of him when I feel overcome with despair for the species and inclined to believe that, all things considered, humanity is nothing but trash. Not even in the very last stage of his life, a penniless old age, did he lose the moral composure that he had always had, and that, through his prolonged existence, led him to respect unfailingly certain values and rules of behavior that stemmed from a religion and principles that in his case were never frivolous or me-chanical. They determined all the important acts of his life. If he had not assumed the burden of supporting all those abandoned creatures that my Granny Carmen took in, and adopting them—adopting us, since he was my real father during the first ten years of my life, who reared me and fed me—perhaps he wouldn't have reached old age pitifully poverty-stricken. But neither would he have reached that point if he had stolen, or coldly calculated his life, if he had been less decent in everything he did. I believe that his great concern in life was to go about things in such a way that Granny Carmen would not learn that what is evil and filthy is also part of existence. He was only partially successful, of course, even though his children helped him in this endeavor, but he managed to spare her many sufferings and bring her considerable relief from others that he was unable to prevent. He devoted his life to this goal and Granny Carmen knew it, and therefore in their marriage they were the happiest that a couple can be in this life, where so often the word *happiness* seems obscene.

They nicknamed my grandfather "Gringo" when he was young, apparently because he had blond hair. I, for my part, as far back as I can remember, see him with sparse white hair, a ruddy face, and that big nose that is a trait shared by the Llosa family, as is walking with our feet splayed apart. He knew many poems by heart, some written by others and some his own, which he taught me to memorize. That I should write verses as a small boy amused him, and that later on articles of mine should appear in the newspapers made him highly enthusiastic, and that I should reach the point of having books of mine published filled him with satisfaction. Although I am certain that it must also have alarmed him, as it did my Granny Carmen, who told me so, that my first novel, *La ciudad y los perros* (*The Time of the Hero*), which I sent them from Spain as soon as it came out, was full of dirty words. Because he was always a gentleman and gentlemen never say—much less write—dirty words.

In 1956, when Manuel Prado won the elections and took office, the brand-new minister of the interior, Jorge Fernández Stoll, summoned my grandfather to his office and asked if he would agree to be the prefect of Arequipa. I never saw my grandfather so happy. He was going to work, to stop depending on his children. He would go back to Arequipa, his beloved homeland. With great care he wrote a speech for the ceremony of taking office and read it to us, in the little dining room of the house on the Calle Porta. We applauded it. He smiled. But the minister didn't call him back or return his calls, and only much later informed him that the APRA, an ally of Prado's, had vetoed the appointment because he was related to Bustamante y Rivero. It was a very hard blow, but I never heard him blame it on anyone.

When he gave up the prefecture of Piura, he and Granny Carmen came to live in an apartment on the Avenida Dos de Mayo, in Mira-flores. It was a small place and they were quite uncomfortable there. Shortly thereafter, Auntie Mamaé moved in with us, in La Perla. I don't know how my father came to agree that someone who was as vital a representative of the family that he detested should become part of his household. Perhaps what decided him was knowing that in this way my mother would have company during the long hours that he spent at the office. Mamaé stayed with us as long as we lived in La Perla.

Her real name was Elvira, and she was a cousin of Granny Carmen's. She had been left an orphan as a small child, and in the Tacna of the end of the nineteenth century she had been adopted by my great-grandparents, who brought her up like a sister to their daughter Carmen. When still an adolescent, she was engaged to a Chilean officer. As the wedding day approached—family legend has it that her bridal gown had already been made and the wedding announcements sent out—something happened, she found out about something, and broke the engagement. From that time on, until her death at the age of a hundred and four, she remained a spinster and never again became engaged. She never separated from my granny, whom she followed to Arequipa when the latter married, and then to Bolivia, to Piura, and to Lima. She brought up my mother and all my uncles, who called her Auntie Mamaé. And she also brought up my cousins and me, and even held my children and theirs in her arms. The secret of why she broke off with her fiancé—what dramatic episode made her choose spinsterhood forever after—she and Granny Carmen, the only ones who knew the details, took to their graves with them. Mamaé was always a tutelary shadow in the family, the second mama of everyone, the one who stayed up all night keeping watch over anyone who was ill and acted as babysitter and chaperone, the one who took care of the house when everyone was gone, the one who never protested or complained and the one who loved and pampered all of us. Her diversions were listening to the radio when the others did, rereading the books of her youth as long as her eyes held out, and, of course, praying and arriving punctually for Sunday Mass.

She was a great deal of company to my mother, there in La Perla, a great happiness to me to have her in the house, and also someone whose presence toned down to some degree my father's fits of fury.

Every once in a while, amid those attacks accompanied by insults and blows, Mamaé would come out, a tiny little thing, dragging her feet, with her hands placed together, to implore him: "Ernesto, I beg you," "Ernesto, in the name of what you hold most dear," and he would usually make an effort and calm down.

At the end of 1948, when we had already taken the final examinations of the first year of secondary school—around the beginning or the middle of December—something happened to me at La Salle that had a delayed but decisive effect on my relations with God. These had been those of a boy who believed and practiced everything that he had been taught insofar as religion was concerned, and for whom the existence of God and the true nature of Catholicism were so evident that not even the shadow of a doubt in this respect had ever entered his head. The fact that my father made fun of the pious believers that my mother and I were only served to confirm that certainty. Wasn't it only to be expected that someone who seemed to me to be the very embodiment of cruelty, the evildoer personified, should be an unbeliever and an apostate?

I do not remember that the Brothers at La Salle overwhelmed us with catechism classes and exercises in piety. We had a course in religion—the one given us by Brother Agustín, in the second year of secondary school, was as entertaining as his lessons in universal history, and it impelled me to buy a Bible for myself—together with Sunday Mass and a few retreats during the year, but nothing that resembled those schools that were renowned for the rigor of their religious instruction, such as La Inmaculada or La Recoleta. Every so often the Brothers made us fill out questionnaires to check to see if we had felt the call of God, and I always answered no, that my vocation was to be a sailor. And in all truth, I never experienced, as some of my schoolmates did, religious crises and fears. I remember what a surprise it was, in my *barrio*, to see one of my friends suddenly burst into tears and sobs one night, and when Luchín and I, who were trying to calm him down, asked him what was the matter, to hear him stammer that he was weeping over how greatly men offended God.

I couldn't go get my report card, at the end of that year in 1948, for some reason or other. I went the following day. The school was empty of pupils. They handed me my report card in the principal's office and I was just leaving when Brother Leoncio, who had been our teacher the year before, appeared, cheerful and smiling. He asked me about my grades and my vacation plans. Despite his reputation as a little old grouch, who used to rap our heads with his knuckles when we behaved badly, we all loved Brother Leoncio for his picturesque appearance, his ruddy face, his unruly forelock, and his Spanish full of Gallicisms. He devoured me with questions, without giving me an opening so as to say goodbye, and all of a sudden he told me that he wanted to show me something and to come with him. He took me to the top floor of the school, where the Brothers had their rooms, a place where we students never went. He opened a door and there was his room: a small one with a bed, a clothes closet, a little worktable, and religious prints and photographs on the walls. I noticed that he was very excited, talking very fast about sin, the devil, or something like that, as he poked around in this clothes closet. I began to feel uncomfortable. Finally he took out a pile of magazines and handed them to me. The first one I opened was called *Vea* and was full of pictures of naked women. I felt tremendous surprise, mingled with embarrassment. I didn't dare raise my head, or answer, for still speaking in a rush and tripping over his words, Brother Leoncio had come closer to me, asking me if I was acquainted with those magazines, if my friends and I bought them and leafed through them by ourselves. And, all of a sudden, I felt his hand on my trousers fly. He was trying to open it at the same time as, clumsily, with his hand on top of my trousers, he rubbed my penis. I remember his congested face, his tremulous voice, a thread of saliva dangling from his mouth. I wasn't afraid of him, as I was of my papa. I began to shout "Let me go! Let me go!" at the top of my lungs and in an instant Brother Leoncio's face turned from beet-red to deathly pale. He opened the door for me and murmured something like "But why are you afraid?" I ran down to the street.

Poor Brother Leoncio! How embarrassed he too must have been after that episode. The next year, the last one in which I attended La Salle, when he met me in the patio his eyes avoided mine and his face showed signs of how ashamed he felt.

From that time on, I gradually stopped being interested in religion and in God. I went on attending Mass, going to confession and taking communion, and even saying prayers at night, but in a more and more mechanical way, not participating in what I was doing, and during the obligatory daily Mass at school, thinking of something else, until one day I realized that my faith was gone. I had turned into an unbeliever. I didn't dare tell anyone, but when I was by myself, I told myself, without shame or fear. Only in 1950, when I entered the Leoncio Prado Military Academy, did I dare defy the people around me with the curt remark "I'm not a believer; I'm an atheist."

That episode with Brother Leoncio, besides making me gradually lose interest in religion, augmented the disgust I'd felt for sex ever since that afternoon down by the Piura River when my friends revealed to me how babies were made and how they came into the world. It was a disgust I hid very well, since both at La Salle and in my *barrio* talking about fucking was a sign of virility, a way of ceasing to be a child and becoming a man, something I wanted as much as my pals and perhaps even more than they did. But even though I too talked of fucking and boasted of having spied on a girl as she was undressing and having masturbated, things like that repelled me. And when, on occasion, in order not to make myself look bad, I engaged in them— like one afternoon, when I climbed down the cliff with half a dozen boys from the *barrio* to hold a masturbating contest along the beach at Miraflores, which the astronautical Luquen won—I had a lingering feeling of disgust for days afterward.

For me, then, falling in love had absolutely nothing to do with sex: what I felt for Helena was a diaphanous, disincarnate, intense, and pure sentiment. It consisted of daydreaming a great deal about her and fantasizing that we had gotten married and were traveling about in gorgeous places, of writing verses to her and imagining impassioned heroic situations, in which I saved her from dangers, rescued her from enemies, wrought vengeance on her attackers. She rewarded me with a kiss. A kiss without tonguing: we had had a discussion on the subject with the boys in the *barrio*, and I defended the position that one could not kiss one's sweetheart with a tongue kiss; only girls you might be able to score with, vulgar show-offs, lower-class chicks. Tongue kissing was like pawing, and who outside of the worst of degenerates was going to paw a decent girl?

But if sex revolted me, I shared, on the other hand, the passion of my friends from the *barrio* for being well dressed and shod and, if it had been possible, going around in the Ray-Ban sunglasses that made boys irresistible to girls. My papa never bought me clothes, but my uncles gave me the suits that had grown too small for them or were going out of style, and a tailor on the Calle Manco Cápac turned them inside out and altered them to fit me, so that I always went around well dressed. The problem was that, when the tailor turned the suits inside out, it left a visible seam down the right side of the jacket, where the handkerchief pocket had been, and I insisted each time to the tailor that he make an invisible darn to hide any trace of that pocket that might make people suspect that my suit was a hand-me-down turned inside out.

As for pocket money, Uncle Jorge and Uncle Juan, and sometimes Uncle Pedro—who after graduating had left to work in the North, as a doctor on the San Jacinto hacienda—gave me five, and then ten soles every Sunday, and with that amount I had more than enough for the matinee, the Viceroy cigarettes we bought one at a time, or to have a glass of *capitán*—a mixture of vermouth and pisco brandy— with the boys in the *barrio* before the parties on Saturday nights, at which only nonalcoholic refreshments were served. In the beginning, my papa also gave me some pocket money, but ever since I first began to go to Miraflores and receive a bit of money from my uncles, I discreetly refused to accept any from my father, saying goodbye to him very quickly on Saturday morning before he gave it to me: another of my overly subtle ways of opposing him, an idea conceived by my cowardice. He must have understood, because from around that time on, the beginning of 1948, he never gave me another centavo.

But despite these demonstrations of economic pride, in 1949 I dared—it was the one time I ever did anything like it—to ask him to have my teeth straightened. Because they stuck out, they had bothered me a lot at school, where I was called Rabbit and teased about them. I don't believe that it had mattered all that much to me before, but once I began to go to parties, to keep company with girls and to have a sweetheart, getting braces to straighten my teeth as several of my friends had done became a passionately embraced ambition. And, suddenly, the possibility came within reach. One of my friends in the *barrio*, Coco, was the son of a dental technician, whose specialty was none other than those braces to line up the upper and lower teeth. I talked to Coco and he to his papa, who arranged for the kindly Dr. Lañas, the dentist he worked for, to give me an appointment at his office on the Jirón de la Unión, in the downtown district of Lima, and examine me. He would fit me with braces without charging me for his work; the only thing I would have to pay for was the material. My pride and my vanity battled it out for many days before I took that great step, which, at heart, I considered to be an abject surrender. But vanity won out—my voice must have trembled—and I ended up asking to be fitted with the braces.

My father said that was fine with him, that he would talk to Dr. Lañas, and perhaps he did. But before Dr. Lañas began the treatment, something happened, one or another of those domestic tempests or running away again with my mother to my aunt and uncle's house, and, once the crisis subsided and family unity was restored, my father didn't say anything more to me about the subject nor did I remind him of it. I was left with my rabbit's teeth, and the following year, when I entered the Leoncio Prado Military Academy, it no longer mattered to me if I was buck-toothed.

FOUR

The Democratic Front

AFTER the Meetings for Freedom, in August and September 1987, I left for Europe, on October 2, as I was in the habit of doing every year during this period. But unlike other years, this time I took along, deep within me, despite Patricia's outbursts and her apocalyptic prophecies, the disease of politics. Before leaving Lima, in a televised program thanking those who had supported me in the mobilizations against nationalization, I said that I was returning "to my study and my books," but nobody believed me, beginning with my wife. I didn't believe it either.

In the two months that I was in Europe, as I was attending the premiere of my work *La chunga*, in a theater in Madrid, or was scribbling the drafts of my novel *Elogio de la madrastra* (*In Praise of the Stepmother*) under the skylighted cupola of the Reading Room of the British Museum (just a step away from the little cubicle in which Marx had written a good part of *Das Kapital*) my mind often wandered from the fantasies of *La chunga*'s male characters or from the erotic rites of Don Rigoberto and Doña Lucrecia to what was happening in Peru.

My friends—the old ones and the new ones, from the days of the mobilization—met periodically in my absence to make plans and to hold discussions with the party leaders. Every Sunday Miguel Cruchaga wrote me detailed and euphoric reports which, invariably, sent my wife into a rage or off to get a Valium. From the very first public opinion polls I appeared as a popular figure, with nearly a third of the electorate declaring their intention to vote for me in case I became a candidate—the highest percentage among the presumed candidates for the presidency in the 1990 election, still a long way away. But what made Miguel happiest was the fact that the pressure of public opinion in favor of a great democratic alliance, under my leadership, seemed irresistible to him. It was a subject that Miguel and I had toyed with, in our conversations concerning Peru, as a remote ideal. All of a sudden, it had become a real possibility, one that depended on my decision.

It was true. Ever since the rally in the Plaza San Martín, and because of its great success, in the newspapers, on the radio, on television, and all over Peru people began to speak of the need for an alliance of the democratic forces of opposition to confront the APRA and the United Left in the 1990 elections. As a matter of fact, the militants of Popular Action and the Christian Popular Party had become one with the independents in the main square that night. And in Piura and Arequipa as well. During all three demonstrations I brought those parties and their leaders to applaud because of their opposition to the government's nationalization plan.

This opposition had been immediate in the case of the Christian Popular Party and somewhat lukewarm at first in that of Popular Action. Its leader, ex-President Belaunde, present in Congress on the day of the announcement, made a cautious statement, fearing perhaps that nationalization would have strong backing. But over the next few days, in accord with the reaction of broad sectors of the populace, his pronouncements became increasingly more critical and his supporters had assembled en masse in the Plaza San Martín.

In the weeks that followed the Meetings for Freedom, the pressure from the non-Aprista news media and from the public in general, urging in letters, phone calls, and statements for the press that our mobilization solidify into an alliance with an eye to 1990, was enormous, and it continued while I was in Europe. Miguel Cruchaga and my friends agreed that I should take the initiative to make that plan a reality, although they disagreed as to the timing. Freddy thought it premature for me to return to Lima immediately. He feared that, in the three years ahead before the change of presidencies, my bright new public image would fade. But if I were going to be active in politics it was indispensable to travel a great deal in the interior of the country, where people scarcely knew who I was. So, after shuffling any number of formulas, in discussions by telephone that cost us an arm and a leg, we decided that I would return to Peru at the beginning of December, by way of Iquitos.

The choice of the capital of the Peruvian region of Amazonia as the gateway for my return to Peru was not by chance. During the fight against nationalization, at the time of the rallies in Lima, Arequipa, and Piura, we had arranged for a fourth one in Loreto, from which I had received requests to hold one. The APRA and the government then unleashed against me, in Iquitos, an extraordinary campaign, and, strictly speaking, a literary one. It consisted of denouncing me on radio stations and on the state television channel as a maligner of the women of Loreto, because of my novel *Pantaleón y las visitadoras* (*Captain Pantoja and the Special Service*), set in Iquitos, from which they reproduced whole paragraphs and pages that were distributed in leaflet form or were read aloud on the radio and TV, so that the aim of the novel appeared to be to call all the women of Loreto "visitors of the evening" and to describe their ardent sexual exploits. There was a parade of mothers dressed in mourning and the APRA called upon all the pregnant women in the city to lie down on the landing strip so as to prevent a landing of the plane in which I, "the pornographic slanderer who is endeavoring to sully the soil of Loreto" (I am quoting one of the tracts), would arrive. To cap the climax, it so happened that on the one opposition radio station in Loreto, the likable reporter who defended me (in language that resembled that of Sinchi, a character in my novel) believed that the best way to do so was by making an impassioned apologia in favor of prostitution, to which he devoted several programs. All this made us fear a fiasco or, perhaps, a grotesque witches' Sabbath, and we gave up our plans for that rally.

But now that I was returning to Peru with far-reaching political intentions, it was best to confront the bull of Loreto from the very start and know what to expect. Miguel Cruchaga and Freddy Cooper went to the jungle to prepare for my arrival. I came by plane alone, via Miami, since Patricia, as a sign of protest against these first signs of proselytism, refused to come with me. A small but cordial crowd welcomed me at the Iquitos airport, and on the following day, December 13, in the auditorium of the Colegio San Agustín, filled to capacity, I spoke of my relationship to Amazonia and of how much my novels, in particular *Pantaleón y las visitadoras*, owed to that region. The women of Loreto, who constituted the great majority of my listeners, gave proof of better humor than my adversaries, laughing at my anecdotes concerning that fictitious work (and, two and a half years later, voting overwhelmingly for me in the general elections, since it was in Loreto that I won the most impressive plurality in the country).

The stop-off in Loreto took place without incident, in a warm and friendly atmosphere, and the only unforeseen event was Freddy Cooper's fit of rage, on getting up at midnight in the Hotel de Turistas where we spent the night and discovering that the bodyguards responsible for our safety had all gone off to the brothel.

As soon as I arrived in Lima, on the 14th of December, I set to work creating that Frente Democrático (Democratic Front)* which the reporters rebaptized with the dreadful contraction Fredemo (which Belaunde and I always refused to use).

I went to visit, separately, the leaders of Popular Action and the Christian Popular Party, and both Fernando Belaunde and Luis Bedoya Reyes proved favorable to the idea of the Front. We held many meetings, full of circumlocutions and veiled tensions, in order to clear away the obstacles conspiring against the alliance. Bedoya was much more enthusiastic about the idea than Belaunde, for the latter had to confront the stubborn opposition of many of his friends and fellow party members, bent on his being, once again, the candidate for president and insistent that Popular Action alone should present the opposition candidate. With his superb tact, Belaunde evaded and discouraged these pressures, little by little, but it was a joyless exercise, for he doubtless feared that, with the realization that their leader was about to enter winter quarters—at the time he was, after all, in his middle seventies—his party, so closely linked to him personally, would fall to pieces.

Finally, after many months of negotiations in which, very often, I felt asphyxiated by his byzantine maneuvers, we agreed to set up a tripartite commission charged with the task of setting up the bases of the alliance. Three delegates represented AP on it, three the PPC, and three others the "independents," whose representatives acknowledged me as their leader and for whom we chose a name that stood for

* Also widely known as La Alianza (The Alliance). (*Trans. note*)

something that as yet did not exist: the Movimiento Libertad (Freedom Movement). The three delegates whom I designated to represent the Freedom Movement—Miguel Cruchaga, Luis Bustamante, and Miguel Vega Alvear—would later constitute, with Freddy Cooper and me, the first executive committee of that movement, Libertad, that we were beginning to create, at top speed, in those final days of 1987 and the beginning ones of 1988, at the same time that we were organizing the Democratic Front.

I have been endlessly criticized for this alliance with two traditional parties that had already been in power (for a good part of Belaunde Terry's two terms as president, Bedoya Reyes had been his ally). This alliance, critics maintain, took away the freshness and the newness of my candidacy and made it appear to be a machination of the old bosses of the Peruvian right—who had lost prestige after the negative balance sheet of Belaunde's second term as president—with the aim of returning to power through a third person. "How could the Peruvian people believe in the 'great change' that you offered," they've asked me, "if you went along arm in arm with those who governed the country between 1980 and 1985 without changing a single thing that was going badly in Peru? When you joined up with Belaunde and Bedoya, you committed suicide."

I was aware from the beginning of the risks that such an alliance meant, but I decided to run them for two reasons. The first: because so many reforms were needed in Peru that, in order to see them through, a broad popular base was required. AP and the PPC had influence in significant sectors and both parties had impeccable democratic credentials in their favor. If we present ourselves to the voters as separate parties, at the polls, I told myself, the splitting of the votes for the center and the right will make either the United Left or APRA the winner. The negative image of "old pols" can be effaced with a plan for deep-seated reforms that would not have anything to do with the populism of AP or the conservatism of the PPC, but would be associated, rather, with a radical liberalism never before put forward in Peru. These are the ideas that will give freshness and newness to the Front.

Moreover, I was afraid that three years would not be enough, in a country with the complicated problems of Peru—vast zones affected by terrorism, roads in terrible condition or nonexistent, an almost total lack of means of communication—for a new organization of inexperienced people such as Libertad to set up branches in all the provinces and districts in order to compete with the APRA, which in addition to its good organization could also count this time on all the apparatus of the state as part of its electoral machine, and to put up a fight against a left that had been battle-hardened in a number of electoral contests. However discredited they might be, I calculated, AP and the PPC can count on a national infrastructure, indispensable for winning the election.

Both calculations were quite wrong. It is true that my friends and I, fighting with the allies at times like cats and dogs, with Popular Action especially, were able to see to it that the Front's program for governing was reformist and radical. But when election day came, this carried less weight in the popular sectors than the presence among us of names and faces that had lost all credibility in view of their past political activities. And, what was more, it was ingenuous on my part to believe that Peruvians would vote for ideas. They voted the way people do in an underdeveloped democracy, and sometimes in the mature ones as well—on the basis of images, myths, heart throbs, or on account of obscure feelings and resentments with no particular connection to processes of reason.

The other supposition was even more erroneous. Neither Popular Action nor the Christian Popular Party had a solid *national* organization. The latter had never had one. A small party, largely middle-class, about all it could count on outside of Lima was a few committees in the capital cities of *departamentos* and provinces and very few followers. And Popular Action, despite having won two presidential elections and having been in its best periods a mass party, never reached the point of having the disciplined, efficient organization that the APRA had. It was always an alluvial party that sedimented around its leader during elections and then scattered. But following its reverse in 1985—its presidential candidate, Dr. Javier Alva Orlandini, obtained just over 6 percent of the vote—it had lost its impetus and begun to fall apart. Its committees, where such existed, were made up of former bureaucrats, held in bad repute sometimes because of abuses or poor management in their assigned jobs, many of whom appeared to want the Front to win so that they could go back to their old ways.

In the end, the results were precisely the opposite of what I had foreseen. The infrastructures of the allies never amalgamated during the campaign and, on the contrary, in many places in the interior the two parties devoted their energies to fighting each other, because of personal rivalries and petty greed, and sometimes, as in Piura, exchanging savage press releases via the radio and the newspapers that couldn't have pleased their adversaries more. Despite our deficiencies as far as organization was concerned, and they were serious ones, Libertad may well have been, among the forces of the Front—in addition to AP and the PPC, it was joined by SODE (Solidaridad y Democracia: Solidarity and Democracy), a small group of executives and professionals—the one that managed to set up the most widespread network of committees in the country (though not for long).

The alliance with AP and the PPC was not the principal reason for my defeat in the elections. A number of factors brought it about, and doubtless a great deal of the responsibility for my failure was my own, for having focused the entire campaign on the defense of a program for government, for disregarding the exclusively political aspects of the situation, for giving signs of intransigence and maintaining, from beginning to end, an openness in my proposals that made me vulnerable to the attacks and the maneuvers to discredit me and that frightened off many of my initial supporters. But the alliance thanks to which the AP and the PPC had governed the country between 1980 and 1985 contributed to the fact that popular confidence in the Front—which lasted throughout nearly the entire campaign—was precarious and, at a certain juncture, vanished altogether.

All through this period of close to three years I met with Belaunde and Bedoya at intervals of two or three times a month, alternating in the beginning the places where we met so as to dodge the pack of reporters, and then later on at my house for the most part. Our meetings took place in the morning, around ten o'clock. Bedoya invariably arrived late, which irritated Belaunde, a most punctual man and always eager for the meetings to end promptly so that he could be off to the Club Regatas to swim and play badminton (he sometimes came with his slippers and racquet).

It is hard to imagine two people—two politicians—so completely different. Belaunde had been born in an aristocratic family, though not a wealthy one, and had reached the winter of his life heaped with honors: two presidential victories and an image as an upright, democratic statesman that not even his bitterest adversaries denied him. Bedoya, who was somewhat younger, born in Callao in 1919, and whose origins were much humbler—he came from a lower-middle-class family—had had a long way to go in order to carve out a career for himself, as an attorney. His political career had had a brief apogee—he had been a magnificent mayor of the capital, from 1964 to 1966, during Belaunde's first term, and had been reelected from 1967 to 1969, but after that nothing had enabled him to shake off the labels of "reactionary," "defender of the oligarchy," and "man of the extreme right" that the left had pinned on him, and he was defeated both times he ran for president (in 1980 and 1985). Those labels, along with his not being a very good speaker and sometimes acting too hastily, contributed to the fact that Peruvians were never going to allow him to head the government of the country. It was an error for which we paid dearly, especially in the 1985 election, for his administration would surely have been less populist than Alan García's, been more aggressive against terrorism and, without the slightest doubt, more honest.

Of the two of them, the one who was eloquent and brilliant, elegant and charming, was Belaunde. Bedoya, on the other hand, could be far off the mark and long-winded, with his long courtroom-style soliloquies that infuriated Belaunde, a man constitutionally allergic to anything abstract and totally uninterested in ideologies and doctrines. (The ideology of Popular Action consisted of an elementary form of populism—a great many public works projects—inspired by Roosevelt's New Deal, that president being the model of a statesman for Belaunde; of nationalistic slogans like "the conquest of Peru by Peruvians"; and of romantic allusions to the empire of the Incas and the cooperative and communal work of the pre-Hispanic people of the Andes.) But of the two, Bedoya proved to be more flexible and ready to make concessions for the sake of the alliance, and the one who, once we had arrived at an agreement, fulfilled it to the letter. Belaunde always acted—keeping up, I readily grant, the proper formalities at all times—as if the Democratic Front were Popular Action, and the Christian Popular Party and Libertad two mere bit players. Beneath his most elegant manners there was a certain vanity about him, not a little stubbornness, and a touch of the caudillo—the political boss accustomed to doing and undoing whatever he pleased in his party without anybody ever daring to contradict him. Very courageous, a public speaker with a splendid nineteenth-century rhetorical style, a man of melodramatic gestures—fighting a duel, for instance—he had been one of the moving forces of the Democratic Front in 1945, which won José Luis Bustamante y Rivero the presidency, and he had suddenly attracted attention in the last years of General Odría's dictatorship (1948–56) as a reformist leader, determined to make social changes and modernize Peru. His winning of the presidency in 1963 stirred up enormous hope. But his administration did not accomplish very much, in large part because of the APRA and the faction supporting Odría (which, acting as allies in Congress, where they had a majority, blocked all of Belaunde's projects, beginning with agrarian reform) and in part because of his indecision and his bad choices of collaborators. Velasco's military coup sent him into exile in Argentina, from which he went to the United States, where he lived all during the days of the dictatorship, very modestly, teaching. In his second term, unlike the first, he was not overthrown by the military, but that was perhaps his one merit: surviving until the next election. For in every other respect—and above all in his economic policy—he was a failure. During his first two years he entrusted the premiership and the portfolio of minister of finance to Manuel Ulloa, an intelligent and likable man, extremely loyal to him but frivolous to the point of irresponsibility. He did not rectify any of the catastrophic measures taken by the dictatorship, such as the socialization of land and the nationalization of the most important companies in the country. He dangerously increased the national debt, failed to confront terrorism resolutely when it was still in its germinating stage, was unable to control the corruption that contaminated people in his own administration, and allowed inflation to rage unchecked.

I had voted for Belaunde every time he was a candidate, and even though I was aware of his shortcomings, I defended his second term as president, since it seemed to me that after twelve years of dictatorship, the reconstruction of democracy was the first priority and could best be attained if Popular Action remained in power. And also because those who attacked it—the APRA and the United Left—represented even worse choices. And, above all else, because there is, in the person of Belaunde, in addition to his wide reading of good books and his good manners, a profound decency, along with two qualities that I have always admired in him, inasmuch as they are not often found in Peruvian politicians: a genuine belief in democracy* and absolute honesty. He is one of the few presidents in our history who left the Presidential Palace poorer than when he entered it. But mine was qualified support, not exempt at times from criticism of his administration, of which, moreover, I was never a part. With just one exception, I refused all the posts he offered me: the embassies in London and in Washington, the Ministry of Education and that of Foreign Relations and, finally, the office of prime minister. The exception was the unremunerated, month-long appointment, the memory of which gave Patricia and me nightmares, as one of the members of the commission investigating the killing of eight journalists in a remote region of the Andes, Uchuraccay,† for which I had been mercilessly attacked and for which I was about to be taken to court.

In the middle of Belaunde's second term, I was unexpectedly summoned one night to the Presidential Palace. He is a reserved man who, even when he talks a great deal, never reveals his most intimate thoughts. But on that occasion—we had two or three meetings on the same subject in the next few months—he spoke to me in a much more explicit way than usual, with some emotion, and allowed me to catch a glimpse of certain matters that were tormenting him. He was deeply distressed at those experts to whom he had given carte blanche to manage the country's economy. And what had been the result? He was certain that history would not remember them, but he for his part would not be forgotten. He was indignant that certain ministers had hired advisers whose salaries were paid in dollars when the entire country had been asked to make sacrifices. And there was melancholy and a sort of bitterness in his tone of voice and in his silences. His immediate preoccupation was the 1985 election. Popular Action wouldn't stand a chance of winning, nor would the Christian Popular Party, since Bedoya, without detracting from his personal merits, lacked drawing power at the polls. This could mean the triumph of the APRA, with Alan García in the presidency. The consequences for the country would be frightful. In the years that followed, I would always remem-

* He was to demonstrate his democratic convictions once again, when he was past eighty, from April 5, 1992, on, following the "self-coup" by Alberto Fujimori, coming out publicly to wage a tenacious fight against the dictatorship.
† See "Sangre y mugre de Uchuraccay," in Contra viento y marea, III, pp. 85–226.

ber, because of the confirmation that time brought, the prophecy Belaunde made that night: "Peru has no idea what that young man may be capable of if he comes to power." His idea was that this could be avoided if I were the candidate of AP and the PPC. He thought that my candidacy would attract the independent vote. He answered my arguments that I was no good at politics (a prophecy that time would also confirm) with flattering phrases and with a kindliness—I would use the term affection, if this word were not so at odds with his sober, not at all emotional personality—that he never failed to show me even in the tensest moments of the life of the Democratic Front (as at the time of my resignation, in mid-1989, because of the dispute over municipal elections). That project of Belaunde's never went any farther, in large part because of my own lack of interest, but also because it found no echo either in AP or in the PPC, which wanted to present their own candidates in the 1985 election.

Bedoya, a witty man and with some ironic gibe or other always on the tip of his tongue, said that Belaunde was "a master at taking the syringe out of his backside." And in fact there was no way of pinning down anything with Belaunde or even discussing it when a subject wasn't to his liking or didn't seem worthwhile to him. In such cases he always managed to take off on another tangent, telling anecdotes about his travels—he had been all over Peru, from top to bottom, on foot, on horseback, in a canoe, and had an encyclopedic knowledge of the country's geography—or about his two terms in office, without leaving anyone room to get a word in edgewise to interrupt him. And then, suddenly, he would look at his watch, get to his feet, and without further ado—"Well, just look how late it's gotten"—bid us goodbye and disappear. One night I also saw him inflict these same clever evasive maneuvers that he used with Bedoya and me on three Aprista leaders high up in the administration hierarchy—the prime minister, Armando Villaneuva, the president of the Congress, Alva Castro, and the senator and historical relic of the party, Luis Alberto Sánchez— who had asked to talk with the leaders of the Democratic Front in view of a possible political truce. We met at the home of Jorge Grieve, in San Isidro, on September 12, 1988. But the Apristas didn't even have the chance to propose such a thing to us, because Belaunde kept them silent all evening long, relating details of his first term in office, reminiscing about his travels and about well-known figures long since dead, cracking jokes and telling anecdotes, until in discouragement and, I suppose, driven half out of their minds, the Apristas gave up and left.

What we practically never talked about with Belaunde and with Bedoya, throughout those three years, was what the policy of the Front would be for running the country—its ideas, reforms, initiatives to dig Peru out of its ruins and put it back on the road to recovery. The reason was simple: the three of us knew that the parties had very different points of view on what the plan for governing the country ought to be and we preferred to leave the discussion for a later time that never came round. We would talk about the political gossip of the moment, about what Alan García's next machination would be —what ambush, intrigue, or infamy he was cooking up this time— and we would discuss, whenever we could manage to keep Belaunde from wandering off the subject, the question of whether the Front would present joint candidates in the municipal elections in November 1989 or whether each party would go its own way with its own candidates.

Now that I had become involved, I made a depressing discovery in these tripartite meetings: that real politics, not the kind that one reads and writes about, thinks about and imagines (the only sort I was acquainted with), but politics as lived and practiced day by day, has little to do with ideas, values, and imagination, with teleological visions— the ideal society we would like to create—and, to put it bluntly, little to do with generosity, solidarity, and idealism. It consists almost exclusively of maneuvers, intrigues, plots, paranoias, betrayals, a great deal of calculation, no little cynicism, and every variety of con game. Because what really gets the professional politician, whether of the center, the left, or the right, moving, what excites him and keeps him going is *power*, attaining it, remaining in it, or returning to it as soon as possible. There are exceptions, of course, but they are just that: exceptions. Many politicians begin their careers impelled by altruistic sentiments—changing society, attaining justice, fostering development, bringing morality into public life. But along the way, in the petty, pedestrian practice of day-to-day politics, these fine objectives become, little by little, mere clichés of the speeches and statements of the public persona that they acquire, which in the end makes them all but indistinguishable from each other. What prevails in politicians, finally, is the gross and sometimes immeasurable appetite for power. Anyone who is not capable of feeling this obsessive, almost physical attraction to power finds it nearly impossible to be a successful politician.

That was my case. Power had always aroused my mistrust, even in my early years as a revolutionary, and one of the functions of my vocation, literature, that had always seemed to me to be most important was to be, precisely, a form of resistance to power, an activity thanks to which power—all powers—might be permanently questioned, since good literature always ends up showing those who read it the shortcomings of life, the inevitable limitation of all power to fulfill human aspirations and desires. It was this distrust of power, along with my biological allergy to any form of dictatorship, that had so attracted me, from the 1970s on, to liberal thought, that of an Aron, a Popper, or a Hayek, of Friedman or of Nozick, with its commitment to defending the individual against the state, to decentralizing power by pulverizing it into multiple private powers that counterbalance each other, and to transferring economic, social, and institutional responsibilities to the citizenry as a whole instead of concentrating them in the political elite that rules the country.

After nearly a year of negotiations we finally agreed on the official constitution of the Democratic Front. I was entrusted with drawing up the declaration of principles, and Belaunde, invariably shrewd when it came to gestures, suggested that we go sign it, in a public ceremony, in the cradle and bastion of Aprismo: Trujillo. We did so on October 29, 1988, after each of us led rallies separately throughout all of the North (I went to Chiclayo). The demonstration was a success, inasmuch as it covered nearly three-quarters of Trujillo's immense and orderly main square. But in the Declaration of Trujillo, an academic proceeding that took place prior to the rally, in which the delegates of AP, the PPC, and Libertad offered a diagnosis of the situation in Peru, the hidden quarrels and rivalries within the Front began to come to the surface. In what seemed like an ill omen at the very outset, minutes before the ceremony was to start in the main hall of the Santo Domingo de Guzmán cooperative, a heavy metal room divider fell down on top of the table that Belaunde, Bedoya and I were to occupy. Belaunde and I, who had already arrived, were still standing waiting for Bedoya, who was riding in a motorcade through the streets of

Trujillo. "You see," I said jokingly to the former president, "the Toucan's lack of punctuality has its positive side: he's saved our necks." But this first public act of the allies proved to be far from a cheerful occasion. Contrary to what had been agreed on—everyone crying out the same slogans at the same time so as to demonstrate the fraternal spirit of the alliance—when the three of us appeared together in public, each of the three contingents hailed only its own leader and shouted only its own rallying cries in chorus, so as to show that it was the largest one. And once the joint meeting was over, the three forces separated so that each of them could hold its own meeting that night for its local supporters. (Since Libertad did not have its own headquarters yet, we held our festivities in the street.)

The order of speakers proved to be a bone of contention. Bedoya and my friends in Libertad insisted that as the leader and future candidate of the Front I ought to close the ceremony. Belaunde objected, on the grounds of his age and his status as the former president of Peru; I would be the principal speaker only after my candidacy had been publicly announced. In the end, we did as he wished. I spoke first, then Bedoya, and Belaunde ended the meeting. Idiocies of this sort took up a great deal of our time, giving rise to suspicions, and everyone agreed that they were *important*.

The Democratic Front never came to be a coherent and integrated force, in which the common objective prevailed over the interests of the parties that constituted it. Only when it became clear that there would be a second round of voting, after the tremendous surprise of the first round—the very high percentage attained by Alberto Fujimori, an unknown, and the certainty that in the final round the vote of Apristas and leftists would go to him—did the shock that we had had bring militants and leaders together and induce them to cooperate without the partisan pettiness that had predominated until April 8, 1990.

This shortsighted view of politics became particularly evident where the municipal elections were concerned. Scheduled to be held on November 12, 1989, barely five months before the presidential election, they were going to be the dress rehearsals for the contest for the presidency, since they would serve as a measure of the relative strength of the contending forces. Before we had even discussed the subject, Belaunde announced that AP would put up its own candidates, since, in his view, the Democratic Front existed only for the presidential election.

For months it was hard to discuss the subject with him. Bedoya agreed with me that if each of the three political forces went its separate way in the municipal elections it would create an image of division and antagonism that would drastically reduce our chances of taking root as an alliance. When we were by ourselves, Belaunde told me that the populist rank and file of his party wouldn't stand for the idea of sharing the lists of municipal candidates with the PPC, which did not exist outside of Lima, and that he could not risk being the target of rebellion within his own party for that reason.

Since the whole problem appeared to be one of a bid for the most power, I proposed to the Freedom Movement that it give up the idea of putting up a single candidate for mayor or city councilor anywhere in Peru, so that AP and the PPC could share the candidacies between them. I thought that this gesture would make it easier for us allies to come to an agreement. But not even then would Belaunde let his arm be twisted. The matter finally attracted the attention of the communications media, and members of AP and the PPC, for the most part, but members of Libertad and supporters of SODE as well, got involved in a stupid debate that the media in thrall to the government and those on the left did their utmost to magnify in order to show the weakness and the groundswell of opposition that according to them was eating away at our alliance.

Finally, in mid-June of 1989, after innumerable and on occasion violent arguments, Belaunde gave in and accepted the idea of single candidacies. There then began another fight between AP and the PPC, this time over which of the two parties would put up the candidate for a given municipality. They never reached an agreement, and in addition, the provincial bases of each party contested the decisions of their national leaders, since all of them wanted nothing less than everything and neither party seemed prepared to make the slightest concession to its ally. The rank and file of Libertad too had cried to high heaven over our agreement not to put up any candidates, and there were a number of defections.

Alarmed by what this presaged for the future if the Front was elected, I managed to get Libertad to authorize me to offer the PPC and AP each 40 percent of the lists of candidates for Congress, instead of the

33 percent each that was their rightful share, in return for giving up any sort of ministerial quotas or reserved posts, something that, moreover, corresponded to a provision of the Constitution which regards the designation of the cabinet as the prerogative of the president. Belaunde and Bedoya agreed to this. My idea, naturally, was not to leave the allies out in the cold if we got into office, but to be free to be able to call upon as collaborators only those who were honest and capable, who believed in the reforms and were prepared to fight for them. That Libertad should have only 20 percent of the congressional candidates, and that the allies from SODE should also be included within this much-reduced percentage, demoralized many radical members of Libertad, to whom such altruism appeared to be both excessively generous and impolitic, because it barred many independents from competing and lent credence to those who said that I was a puppet of the traditional pols.

It had been Belaunde and Popular Action that had placed the most obstacles in the way of an agreement concerning the municipal elections, but it was Bedoya who brought on the crisis, with a statement on television, on the night of June 19, 1989, denying with a minimum of tact what I had just announced at a press conference: that AP and the PPC had finally reached an agreement concerning the municipal candidacies in Lima and Callao, the ones that up to that point had been the cause of the worst controversies between the two parties. I listened to Bedoya's statement on the late news broadcast on television, just after getting into bed. His loud disclaimer was a resounding demonstration of how disunited we were and the trivial reasons for our being at odds. I got up out of bed, went to my desk, and spent the rest of the night reflecting.

For the first time, I was overcome by the idea that I had been badly mistaken to embark upon this political adventure. Perhaps Patricia was right. Was it worthwhile to go on? The future looked at once dark and ludicrous. AP and the PPC would go on squabbling to see who would head the electoral lists and how many candidates for municipal councilman each party would get and what places the candidates of each party would have on the lists, until the Front had lost all the prestige it had. Was it in this spirit that we would achieve the great peaceful transformation? Was it possible with such an attitude to dismantle the macrocephalic state and transfer our immense public sector into the hands of the citizenry? The moment our own supporters were elected to office, wouldn't all of them immediately make a move—exactly as the Apristas had done—to divide up the administration into smaller units and demand that still more divisions be created so that there would be more public posts to fill?

The worst of all this was how blind we had been to what was going on around us. In mid-1989 armed attacks were becoming more and more frequent from one end of the country to the other; according to the government, they had already caused some eighteen thousand deaths. Whole regions—such as the Huallaga area, in the jungle, and nearly the whole of the central Andes—were little short of being completely under the control of Sendero Luminoso and the Túpac Amaru Revolutionary Movement. Alan García's policy had caused the country's hard currency reserves to vanish into thin air and the printing of paper money with no backing presaged an inflationary explosion. Companies were working at a half and in some instances a third of their proven capacity. Those Peruvians who were able to do so were taking their money out of the country and those who managed to find a job abroad left. Tax revenues had fallen to the point where we were suffering from a general collapse of public services. Every night the television screens showed heartbreaking scenes of hospitals without medicines or beds, of schools without desks, without blackboards, and sometimes without roofs or walls, of districts without water or light, of streets strewn with refuse, of production workers and office clerks on strike, in desperation over the dizzying fall in the standards of living of the population. And the Democratic Front was paralyzed—over which party would propose its list in each of the municipalities!

When dawn came, I drew up a stern letter* addressed to Belaunde and Bedoya, informing them that, in view of their inability to reach an agreement, I was withdrawing as a presidential candidate. I woke Patricia up to read her the text, and it surprised me that, instead of rejoicing, she had certain reservations regarding my resigning as a candidate. We made plans to go abroad immediately so as to avoid the predictable pressures. I had been invited to receive a literary prize in Italy—the Scanno, in the Abruzzi—so the next day we bought our

* Reprinted in Álvaro Vargas Llosa, *El diablo en campaña* (*The Devil on Campaign*). Madrid: El País/Aguilar, 1991, pp. 154–57.

tickets, in secret, for twenty-four hours later. That afternoon I sent the letter, via Álvaro, my older son, to Belaunde and to Bedoya, after informing the executive committee of Libertad of my decision. I saw some of my friends with sad faces—I remember Cruchaga's, paperwhite, and Freddy's, as red as a prawn's—but none of them attempted to dissuade me. The truth is that they too were tired of the absurd way in which the Front had bogged down. I gave instructions to the security guards not to allow anyone to enter the house and we unplugged the telephone. The news reached the communications media early that evening and had the effect of a bombshell. All the channels began their nightly news program with it. Dozens of reporters surrounded my house and immediately a parade of people from all the political camps of the Front began. But I received no one nor did I appear when, later on, a spontaneous demonstration of some hundreds of members of Libertad surrounded the house, with Enrique Chirinos Soto, Miguel Cruchaga, and Alfredo Barnechea as speakers.

Early in the morning on June 22, the security guards took us to the airport and managed to get us aboard the Air France flight immediately, thereby enabling us to dodge another demonstration of members of Libertad, headed by Miguel Cruchaga, Chino Urbina, and Pedro Guevara, whom I glimpsed in the distance from the little window of the plane.

When we arrived in Italy, two journalists were waiting there for me, both of whom, heaven only knows how, had discovered where I was headed: Juan Cruz, from *El País* in Madrid, and Paul Yule, from the BBC, who was making a documentary on my candidacy. My conversation with them surprised me, since both of them were convinced that my resignation was simply a tactic to force the intractable allies to give in.

In the end, that was what everyone would believe, and the practical result, when the episode was over, was that after all, contrary to what many people thought, I wasn't as bad a politician as I seemed to be. The truth of the matter is that my resignation was not planned with the intention of marshaling public opinion so as to put pressure on AP and the PPC. It was genuine, stemming from my loathing for the political maneuvering in which the Front was submerged, the conviction that the alliance was not going to work, that we would disappoint the expectations of many people, and that my effort was going to be useless. But Patricia, who never lets me get away with anything, says that that, too, is a debatable truth. For if I had really believed that there was no hope, I would have used the word *irrevocable* in my letter of resignation, something I had not done. So that perhaps, as she believes, in some secret compartment I harbored the illusion— the desire—that my letter would settle our differences.

It did settle them, temporarily. From the day I left the country, the independent communications media severely criticized the PPC and AP, and criticisms rained down on the heads of Bedoya and Belaunde in the form of editorials, articles, and statements. The number of people who announced their intention to vote for me suddenly rose impressively all over the country and in every social sector. Up until then public opinion polls had always shown me to be the leading candidate against the candidates of the APRA (Alva Castro) and the United Left (Alfonso Barrantes), but with a potential vote that never went beyond 35 percent of the total. At this point the figure rose to 50 percent, the highest I had attained at any point in the campaign. Libertad enrolled thousands of new members, to the point that membership cards gave out and more had to be printed in a great hurry. Our various local headquarters were filled to overflowing, day and night, by a multitude of supporters and members who urged us to break with AP and the PPC and go before the voters by ourselves. And on my return to Lima, I found 4,890 letters (according to Rosi and Lucía, who counted them) from all over Peru, congratulating me for having broken with the other parties (with Popular Action in particular, which had aroused more antagonisms).

Some months before, we had hired the Sawyer/Miller Group as advisers, an international firm with extensive experience in election campaigns, since they had worked with Cory Aquino in the Philippines and with a number of presidential candidates in Latin America, among them the Bolivian Sánchez de Lozada, who was the one who recommended the firm to us. This matter of asking a foreign company for advice concerning an electoral battle in Peru seemed to arouse in Belaunde, who had twice won the presidency without the need for this sort of help, a hilarity that his inbred sense of politeness kept under control with only the greatest difficulty. But the fact is that Mark Malloch Brown and his collaborators at the Sawyer/Miller Group were a great help with their opinion polls, which allowed me to keep close

track of the feelings, fears, hopes, and changing mood of that complicated mosaic that goes to make up Peru. Their predictions were
usually right on the mark. A great deal of Mark's advice was rejected
because it clashed with certain matters of principle—I wanted the
election to be won in a certain way and for a specific purpose—and
frequently the consequences were precisely the ones that he had predicted. One of these pieces of advice, from the first opinion survey in
depth taken at the beginning of 1988 down to the eve of the second
electoral round—in June 1990—was to break with the allies and present myself as an independent candidate, with no ties to the political
establishment, and to represent myself, rather, as coming to save Peru
from the state into which the politicians had plunged it—all of them,
regardless of their ideologies. His advice was based on a conclusion
that all the surveys had shown from the beginning of the campaign to
the end: that there was, in the heart of the country—the C and D
sectors, those poor and extremely poor Peruvians who represented two-
thirds of the electorate—a profound disillusionment with and great
rancor toward political parties, particularly those that had already enjoyed power. The surveys also showed that the positive feelings I had
been able to arouse in the heart of the country bore a direct relationship
to my image as someone who came from outside the political milieu,
of an independent with no ties to the established parties. The creation
of the Democratic Front and my constant presence in the media
alongside two such long-standing establishment figures as Bedoya and
Belaunde were inevitably going to erode that image during the long
campaign and support for me would shift toward one or another of
my adversaries (Mark thought that it would be Barrantes, the leftist
candidate).

When Mark Malloch Brown learned of my resignation he was
happy. He was not surprised by the instant shift of public opinion in
my favor, nor by my increase in popularity in the surveys. And he too
presumed that I had planned it that way. "Well, you're learning," he
must have thought—he who once assured me that I was the worst
candidate he had ever worked with.

All this news reached me by telephone, through Álvaro, Miguel
Cruchaga, and Alfredo Barnechea, a congressman who, because of the
nationalization, had given up his membership in the APRA and joined
Libertad. After Italy, I had gone with Patricia to take refuge in the

south of Spain, fleeing from being besieged by the press. It was already decided that I would stick with my determination to resign and remain for a time in Europe. I had a long-standing offer to spend a year at the Wissenschaftskolleg, in Berlin, and I proposed to Patricia that we go there, to learn German.

At this juncture the news reached us. AP and the PPC had come to an agreement on all the points of contention between them and had put together joint lists of candidates in even the most remote parts of the country. Their differences had vanished as if by magic and they were waiting for me to come back to lead the Front and resume the campaign.

My first reaction was to say: "I'm not coming. I'm no good at that sort of thing. I don't know how to carry it off, and what's more, I don't like it. These months have given me more than enough time to realize that. I'll stick to my books and my papers, which I should never have left." My wife and I then had yet another politico-conjugal argument. She, who had come close to threatening to divorce me if I were a candidate, now urged me to go back to Peru, marshaling both moral and patriotic arguments. Since Belaunde and Bedoya had backed down, there was no alternative. That had been the reason for my withdrawal, hadn't it? Well then, it no longer existed. Too many good, unselfish, decent people were working day and night for the Front, back there in Peru. They had believed my speeches and my exhortations. Was I going to let them down, now that AP and the PPC seemed to be beginning to behave decently? The sawtooth mountain ranges of the lovely Andalusian town of Mijas bear witness to her admonitions: "We've taken on a responsibility. We have to go back."

That is what we did. We went back and this time Patricia threw herself into working in the campaign as though she had politics in her blood. And I didn't break with the allied parties, as many friends in Libertad too would have liked me to do, and as I ought to have done had I followed the opinion surveys, for the reasons I have already mentioned, which impressed me as being more worthy of being taken into consideration than the others.

FIVE

The Cadet

IN the years that I lived with my father, before I entered Leoncio Prado in 1950, innocence, the ingenuous vision of the world that my mother, my grandparents, and my aunts and uncles had inculcated in me, vanished. In those three years I discovered cruelty, fear, bitterness, a tortuous and violent dimension that is continually, at times more and at times less, counterbalanced by the kind and generous side of every human destiny. And it is probable that without my progenitor's contempt for literature I would never have pursued so obstinately what at the time was a game, but was gradually to turn into an obsessive and pressing need: a vocation. If in those years I had not suffered so much when he was around and if I hadn't felt that it was the best way I could think of to pull the wool over his eyes, I probably wouldn't be a writer today.

That I would be entering the Leoncio Prado Military Academy had been on my father's mind ever since he brought me to live with him. He would announce it to me when he gave me a tongue-lashing and when he bewailed the fact that the Llosas had brought me up like a spoiled child. I don't know whether he was well aware of what sort of an education pupils at Leoncio Prado received. I imagine he wasn't, or else he wouldn't have placed such high hopes in it. His idea was the same as that of many middle-class fathers with sons who were disobedient, rebellious, inhibited, or suspected of being queer: that a military college, with instructors who were career officers, would make of them young men who were disciplined, brave, respectful of authority, and with their balls in the right place.

Since in those days the idea of someday being just a writer never entered my head, when I was asked what I would be when I was grown up, my answer was: a sailor. I liked the sea and adventure novels, and being a sailor seemed to me to be a good way to combine those two things I was so fond of. Entering a military academy whose pupils received the rank of officers in the reserves was an advantageous jumping-off place for someone who aspired to enter the Naval Academy.

So when, on my completing the second year of secondary school, my father enrolled me in an academy on the Jirón Lampa, in the heart of Lima, to prepare me for the entrance exam to Leoncio Prado, I was all for his plan for me. To be a boarding student, to wear a uniform, to parade on the twenty-eighth of July along with the air corps, navy, and army cadets, would be fun. And living far away from him, all week long, would be even better.

The entrance exam consisted of physical and academic tests that took three whole days, in the vast area occupied by the school, on the edge of the cliffs of La Perla, with the sea roaring at the foot of them. I passed the exams, and in March 1950, just a few days before my fourteenth birthday, I appeared at the Academy with a certain excitement over what I was going to find there, wondering if those months of being confined to the school grounds until the first leave wouldn't be a big hardship. (Third-year cadets—those who had completed two years of secondary school—got to leave for the first time on the seventh of June, Flag Day, after having learned the rudiments of military life.)

There were some three hundred of us *perros*—plebes in the third year of the class that would graduate three years later, divided into eleven or twelve sections, according to our height; I was among the tallest, so that I was placed in the second section. (In my fourth year, I would be transferred to the first one.) Three sections formed a company, under the command of a lieutenant and a sergeant major. The lieutenant of our company was named Olivera; our noncommissioned officer, Guardamino.

Lieutenant Olivera made us get into formation, took us up to our dormitories, and assigned us our beds and lockers—they were bunk beds and I was assigned the top of the second one from the entrance. He made us change out of our civilian clothes into our everyday uniforms—a shirt and trousers of green twill, a field cap, and coffee-colored half boots—and then, lining us up in formation again in the courtyard, he gave us the basic instructions concerning proper respect, the way to salute, and the way to behave toward our superiors. And then everyone in our year was lined up in company formation so that the head of the academy, Colonel Marcial Romero Pardo, could welcome us. I am sure that he spoke of "the supreme values of the spirit," a subject that continually cropped up in his speeches. Then we were taken to lunch, in the enormous pavilion on the other side of an esplanade covered with grass on which a vicuña was wandering about, and where we saw our superiors for the first time: the cadets of the fourth and fifth years. We all contemplated with curiosity and slight alarm the four-year cadets, since they would be the ones who would initiate us. We *perros* knew that the hazing was the bitter test that we had to go through. Now, once we'd finished this meal, the fourth-year cadets would take out on us what had been done to them, on a day like today, the year before.

When lunch was over, officers and noncommissioned officers disappeared, and the fourth-year cadets flung themselves on us like a flock of ravens. We "whities" were a small minority in the vast ocean of Indians, mestizos, blacks, and mulattos, and aroused the inventiveness of our hazers. A group of cadets took me and a boy from a section of "shorties" to a fourth-year dormitory. They made us go through a "right angle" contest. We had to kick each other in the backside as we doubled over alternately; the one who kicked more slowly than the other was in turn kicked, hard, by the hazers. Afterward, they made us open our trousers fly and take out our penis and masturbate: the one who came first would be let go and the other would stay behind to make our torturers' beds. But, however hard we tried, fear kept us from getting an erection, and finally, bored by our incompetence, they took us out to the soccer field. They asked me what sport I went in for: "Swimming, sir." "Swim on your back from one end of the athletic field to the other, then, *perro.*"

I still have a sinister memory of that hazing, a savage and irrational ceremony which, beneath the appearance of a virile game, of a rite of initiation into the rigors of military life, served to allow the resentments, envies, hatreds, and prejudices that we had inside us to turn, without inhibitions, into a sadomasochistic bash. On that very first day, in the hours that the hazing lasted—it went on during the days that followed, in a more moderate way—I discovered that the adventure at Leoncio Prado wasn't going to be what, led astray by novels,

I had imagined, but something more prosaic, and that I was going to detest boarding school and military life, with its mechanical hierarchies based on chronology, the authorized violence that they signified, and all the rites, symbols, rhetorical devices, and ceremonies that constitute it, and that we, young as we were—fourteen, fifteen, sixteen years old—only half understood and distorted by putting it at times to comic and at times to cruel and even monstrous uses.

My two years at Leoncio Prado were quite hard and I spent a number of horrible days there, above all on weekends when I was being punished—the hours became immeasurably long, the minutes endless—but, looking back from a distance, I think that that couple of years were more beneficial than harmful to me. Although not for the reason that had led my father to enroll me there. On the contrary. During 1950 and 1951, shut up behind those bars corroded by the dampness of La Perla, on those gray days and nights filled with the gloomiest fog imaginable, I read and wrote as I had never done before and began to be (even though at the time I didn't know it) a writer.

Moreover, I owe to Leoncio Prado the discovery of what the country where I had been born was like: a society very different from that tiny one, marked off by the boundaries of the middle class, in which I had lived up until then. The Leoncio Prado Academy was one of the few institutions—perhaps the only one—that reproduced on a small scale the ethnic and regional diversity of Peru. Enrolled there were youngsters from the jungle and from the highlands, from every *departamento*, every race, and every economic stratum. As it was a state school, the fees for room, board, and tuition we paid were minimal; moreover, there was an ample system of scholarships—a hundred or so a year—that made the school accessible to boys from humble families, of peasant origin, or from marginal city neighborhoods and towns. A large part of the tremendous violence—what seemed to me tremendous but for other cadets less fortunate than I was their natural way of life—stemmed precisely from that mixture of races, regions, and economic levels of the cadets. The majority of us brought to this cloistered space the prejudices, complexes, animosities, and social and racial rancors that we had sucked in with our mother's milk. All these found expression at Leoncio Prado in personal and official relations, and found ways of venting themselves in rites and activities, like the hazing or the military hierarchies among the students themselves, which legitimized the bullying and the abuse. The scale of values erected around the basic myths of machismo and virility served, moreover, as a moral coverup for that Darwinian philosophy or law of the jungle that ruled at the school. To be brave, that is to say, *loco*, was the supreme form of manliness, and to be a coward the most abject and base. Any boy who denounced a superior for the mistreatment of which he was a victim merited the generalized contempt of the cadets and exposed himself to reprisals. The lesson was soon learned. During the hazing, some fourth-year cadets made one of my section mates, named Valderrama, climb up to the top of a ladder and then moved it so as to make him tumble down. He had a bad fall and when the ladder itself fell it cut off one of his fingers against the edge of a washbasin. Valderrama never told on the guilty parties and we all respected him for it.

There were a number of ways of proving one's manhood. Being strong, daring, and aggressive, knowing how to fight—to "get one off" was the expression that summed up marvelously well that ideal, with its mixture of sex and violence—was one of them. Another, to dare to defy the rules, engaging in bold or wild exploits which, if they were discovered, meant being expelled. To bring off such feats gave one entry into the coveted category of *loco*. To be *loco* was a blessing, because then it was publicly recognized that one would never belong to the much-feared category of *huevón*, to be yellow-bellied, or *cojudo*, without balls.

To be *huevón* or *cojudo* was to be chicken: not daring to butt or punch out someone who came to *batirlo*—to rag you or do you harm; not to know how to fight, not to dare, out of timidity or lack of imagination, to *tirar contra*—to sneak out of school after retreat, so as to go to a movie or a party, or at least to hide out somewhere to smoke or play dice in the arbor or in the abandoned building by the pool instead of going to classes. All those who belonged to this category were the scapegoats, whom the locos mistreated by word and by deed for their amusement and that of the others, urinating on them when they were asleep, demanding a certain quota of cigarettes, short-sheeting them, and making them suffer all sorts of humiliations. A good part of these doings were the typical deviltry of adolescence, but the characteristics of the school—being kept shut up, the heterogeneous composition of the student body, the military philosophy—frequently exacerbated mere pranks, turning them into extremes of real cruelty. I remember a sad sack of a cadet whom we nicknamed Fish Eggs. He was skinny as a rail, pale, and very timid; worst of all, at the beginning of the year, one day when the fearful Bolognesi—he had been a classmate of mine at La Salle and when we entered Leoncio Prado he showed himself to be an unrestrained loco by nature—tormented him with his taunts, he burst into tears. From that day on, he became the laughingstock of the company, whom anyone could insult or mistreat to show everyone, himself included, how macho he was. Fish Eggs finally turned into a sluggard, with no initiative, voiceless and almost lifeless: one day I saw him spat on by a loco, and his only response was to wipe his face off with his handkerchief and continue on his way. Of him, and of all the *huevones*, it was said that "their will had been broken."

In order not to have one's will broken, it was necessary to do daring things, so as to earn the good feeling and the respect of the others. I began doing them from the start: from the masturbation contests— the one who ejaculated first or who shot his sperm the farthest—to the famous escapades at night, after lights out. *Tirar contra*—going over the wall—was the most daring thing you could do, since anyone who got caught was expelled from the academy, without appeal. There were places where the wall was lower and could be scaled without risk: near the stadium, near La Perlita—a refreshment stand whose owner, a man from the highlands, sold us cigarettes—and near the abandoned building. Before taking off, you had to make a deal with the student on dormitory guard duty so that, when he reported on how many were present, he always included you. This could be managed by paying him off in cigarettes. After the bugle sounded retreat and the lights went out in the dorms, stealing out, then hugging the wall like a shadow, you had to go across the courtyards and playing fields, at times on all fours or crawling, until you reached the wall you'd chosen. After jumping over it, you made a quick getaway by cutting through the small farms and the open country that surrounded the school in those days. You took off to go to the Bellavista movie theater, to one of those in Callao, to some mediocre party not worth mentioning in those lower-middle-class neighborhoods, inhabited by impoverished families that had once been middle class and were now almost proles, where being at Leoncio Prado had a certain prestige (it had none, on the other hand, in San Isidro or Miraflores, where it was considered a school for half-breeds), and, at times—although this was seldom because they were quite far away—to go prowl around the brothels down by the port. But many times you went over the wall because it was risky and exciting and because you felt good when you got back in without having been discovered.

The most dangerous part was getting back in. You could run into the patrols of soldiers who made the rounds of the school, or learn, after jumping back over the wall, that the officer on guard had discovered the *contra*—the escape—because of the bricks or the planks that we used to scale the wall, and was waiting, crouching in the dark, for those who'd gone over the wall to come back so as to aim his flashlight at them and order: "Halt right there, cadet!" During the trip back, your heart pounded and the least noise or shadow, until you were curled up back in bed in the dorm, made you panic.

Tirar contra had great prestige and the boldest *contras*, surrounded by a legendary aura, were the talk of the school. There were famous *contreros*, who knew every inch of the hundreds of meters of walls of the school, and to *tirar contra* with them gave you a sense of security.

Another important activity was stealing articles of clothing. We had review once a week, usually on Fridays, the night before we got out on leave for the weekend, and if the officer found cigarettes in a locker, or if one or another of the regulation articles of clothing—ties, shirts, trousers, field caps, boots, or the heavy woolen jacket that we wore in winter—was missing, the cadet was confined to quarters for the weekend. To lose an article of clothing was to lose one's freedom. When someone stole a piece of clothing from you, you had to steal another one or pay one of the locos to do the job for you. There were experts at it, with a picklock in their pocket that opened all the lockers.

Another way of being a real man was to have lots of balls, boast of being a "mad jock with a big cock," who made out with countless females, and who, moreover, could "fire three shots in a row." Sex was an obsessive subject, the object of jokes and affectations, of shared secrets and of the dreams and nightmares of the cadets. At Leoncio Prado, sex and sexuality gradually lost for me the disgusting, repellent aspect that they had had ever since I found out how babies were born, and while there I began to think and fantasize about women without displeasure or guilt feelings. And to feel ashamed of being fourteen years old and never having made love. I didn't tell this, of course, to my pals, to whom I boasted of being a "mad jock with a big cock" too.

I had a friend from Leoncio Prado, Víctor Flores, with whom I used to box for a while alongside the swimming pool, on Saturdays after maneuvers. We confessed to each other one day that we had never gone to bed with a woman, and we decided that the first day we had weekend passes we would go to Huatica. So we did, one Saturday in June or July of 1950.

The Jirón Huatica, in the working-class district of La Victoria, was the street where the whores were. The little rooms were lined up, one adjoining the other, on both sidewalks, for some seven or eight blocks below the Avenida Grau. The whores—*polillas*, they were called—were at the little windows, showing themselves to the crowd of presumed clients who were filing by, looking them over, stopping now and again to discuss the price. A strict hierarchy was the rule along the Jirón Huatica, according to the block the whores were located in. The most expensive block—where the French whores were—was the fourth one; on the third and the fifth block, the prices dropped, then dropped further, until on the first, old and miserable whores, human wrecks, could be had for two or three soles (the ones on the fourth charged twenty). I remember very well that Saturday when Víctor and I went, with our twenty soles in our pockets, nervous and excited, to have the great experience. Smoking like chimneys so as to look older, we went up and down the block where the French whores were several times, without being able to make up our minds to go in. Finally, we let ourselves be persuaded by a very talkative woman, with dyed hair, who leaned halfway out onto the street to charm us into it. Víctor went first, then I went in. The room was tiny, with a bed, a basin full of water, a little chamber pot, and a light bulb enveloped in red cellophane that shed a more or less blood-colored light. The woman did not undress. She raised her skirt and, seeing me so disconcerted, burst out laughing and asked me if this was the first time. When I said yes, she was delighted, because, she assured me, giving a boy his first fuck brought good luck. She had me come closer and murmured something like "You're very afraid now but afterwards how pleased you're going to be." Her Spanish was odd, and when it was all over she told me she was Brazilian. Feeling that we were real men, Víctor and I then went off to have a beer.

I returned to Huatica many times in those two years at Leoncio Prado, always on Saturday afternoons and always to the block with the French whores. (Years later, the poet and writer André Coyné would swear to me that their being "French" was slanderous, since they were really Belgian and Swiss.) And I went several times to a slender and pretty *polilla*—a vivacious little brunette, good-humored and able to make her transitory visitors feel that making love with her was something more than a mere business transaction—whom we had baptized "Goldifeet" because, as a matter of fact, hers were tiny, white, and well cared for. She became the mascot of the section. On Saturdays one found cadets in their third year—or in their fourth year—forming a line in front of the door of her little hole in the wall. The majority of the characters in my novel *La ciudad y los perros* (*The Time of the Hero*), written using memories of my years at Leoncio Prado as a basis, are very free, distorted versions of real models, while others are completely imaginary. But the elusive "Goldifeet" is there as my memory preserves her: self-assured, attractive, vulgar, facing up to her humiliating job with indomitable good humor and giving me, on those Saturdays, for twenty soles, ten minutes of bliss.

I know very well everything that lies behind prostitution, in social terms, and I do not defend it, except for those who engage in it of their own free choice, which was doubtless not the case with "Goldifeet," nor with the other *polillas* of the Jirón Huatica, driven there by hunger, ignorance, the lack of jobs, and the evil arts of the pimps who exploited them. But going to the Jirón Huatica, or later on to the brothels of Lima, is something that did not give me a guilty conscience, perhaps because paying the *polillas* gave me a sort of moral alibi in some way or other, disguising the filth and the cruelty of the rite with the mask of an aseptic contract that, on being fulfilled by both parties, freed the two of them of any ethical responsibility. And I believe that it would be a disloyalty to my memory and to my adolescence not to recognize, too, that in those years in which I was leaving my childhood behind, women like "Goldifeet" taught me the pleasures of the body and of the senses, taught me not to reject sex as something nasty and denigrating, but instead to experience it as a source of life and of pleasure and made me take the first steps inside the mysterious labyrinth of desire.

From time to time, I saw my friends of the *barrio*, in Miraflores, when I had a weekend pass, and I went with them to one party or another on Saturdays, or, on Sundays, to the matinee at the movie theaters and sometimes to soccer matches. But the military academy was imperceptibly separating me from them, to the point of converting the intimate fraternity of days gone by into a sporadic and distant relationship. It was no doubt my fault: they struck me as too childish, with their Sunday rites—matinee, an ice cream at the Crem Rica, the skating rink, sunset from the Salazar gardens—and their adolescent crushes, now that I was in a school for men who did cruel things and now that I was going to the Jirón Huatica. A fair number of my friends in the *barrio* were still virgins and were hoping to lose that status with the maids who worked at their houses. I remember a conversation, on one of those Saturday or Sunday afternoons, on the corner of Colón and Juan Fanning, in which, in a circle of kids from the *barrio*, one of them told us how he had "fucked the mestiza," after having tricked her into taking *yohimbina* (a fine powder that, so it was said, drove women crazy, which we talked about endlessly as some sort of magic substance, and which, moreover, I never saw). And I remember another afternoon when some boy cousins of mine told me of the Machiavellian strategy that they had conceived in order to "get inside the slit" of one of the maidservants, someday when their parents were gone. And I remember my profound malaise on both occasions and on all of the ones when my friends, from Miraflores or from school, boasted of fucking the mestizas who worked at their houses.

That is something I never did, that always made me indignant, and doubtless was one of the first manifestations of what would later be my rebellion against the injustices and the abuses that happened every day and everywhere, with complete impunity, in Peruvian life. As regards this subject of maidservants, moreover, what, in those years, manifested itself as a trauma in the Llosa family had made me very sensitive. I have recounted how my grandparents brought from Cochabamba to Peru a lad from Saipina, Joaquín, and a newborn baby boy, Orlando, that one of the cooks abandoned in their house. The two of them had gone on living with the family, in Piura, and then later in the apartment on the Dos de Mayo, in Lima, and finally in a bigger one that my grandparents rented in a group of townhouses on the Calle Porta, in Miraflores. My uncles found a job for Joaquín, who went off to live by himself. Orlando, who had always lived among the household servants and who at the time must have been going on ten, came to resemble, more and more as he grew older, the third of my uncles—more, even, than this uncle's legitimate children. Although the subject was never brought up in the family, it was always there and nobody dared to mention it, or, what is even worse, do anything to make up in some way for what had happened, or to lessen its consequences.

Nothing was done, or, rather, something was done that made things worse. Orlando came to have an intermediate status, a sort of limbo, that was no longer that of a servant but still not that of a member of the family. Auntie Mamaé, who had gone back to live with my grandparents on the Calle Porta, put down a mattress for him in her room, so that he could sleep there. And he ate at a little table set apart, in the same dining room but without sitting down at table with my grandparents and my uncles and the rest of us. He addressed my granny in the familiar form and called her, just as my cousins and I did, "Granny," and called our great-aunt "Mamaé." But he addressed my grandfather in the polite form and called him Don Pedro, and addressed my mama and my uncles with the same formal terms of address, including their father, whom he called Señor Jorge. The only ones with whom he used the familiar *tú* form were my girl and boy cousins and me. What that childhood must have been like, lived amid total confusion, a servant or little less for three-quarters of the family, and a relative of the rest, and the bitterness, humiliation, resentment, and pain that must have accumulated in him, like water stagnating in a well, is difficult to imagine. It is a paradox that people as generous and noble as my grandparents could, blinded by prejudices or taboos that were those of their milieu and had come to form part of their nature, aggravate, by that ambiguous status in which they caused him to live, the drama of his birth. Years later, I was one of the first of the family to treat Orlando as a relative, to present him as a cousin of mine, and I did my best to have a friendly relationship with him. But he never felt comfortable with me, nor with the rest of the family, save for Granny Carmen, to whom he was always close until the end.

Although I was never very studious at Leoncio Prado, there were certain classes I followed with great ardor. There were excellent teachers, like the one who taught world history, Aníbal Ismodes, to whose classes I lent an enthusiastic ear. And the physics teacher, a slender, elegant little highlander called Huarina, who was rumored to be a "brain." He had done his postgraduate studies in France, and in his classes he gave the impression that he knew everything; he was able to make the most obscure experiments and the most complex laws and tables enjoyable. Of all the science courses that I've taken, the one I had with Professor Huarina in my second year at Leoncio Prado is the only one that entertained, intrigued, and excited me in the way that until then only history courses had done. Literature courses were taught as part of Spanish, that is to say, of grammar, and were usually unbearably boring courses in which we were required to memorize, along with the rules of prosody, syntax, and spelling, the life and works of famous authors, but not to read their books. Never, in all my years as a student, was I made to read a book, apart from the assigned textbooks. The latter included a few poems or fragments of classic texts that were difficult to understand because of the rare words and the uncommon turns of phrase, so that my memory retained little or nothing of them. If I took to any classes in school, it was the ones in history, because of the good teachers I had. Literature was a vocation that came to light outside of the classroom, in an oblique and personal way.

It was only later that I discovered that one of my teachers from Leoncio Prado was a great Peruvian poet and an intellectual figure whom, in my years at the university, I would admire: César Moro. He was short and very thin, with sparse, fair hair and blue eyes that looked upon the world, on people, with an ironic little gleam deep down inside the pupils. He taught French, and gossip around the school had it that he was a poet and a fairy. His exaggeratedly polite manners and something affected about him and the rumors that circulated aroused our animosity against someone who appeared to be the negation incarnate of the morals and the philosophy of Leoncio Prado. In class we used to rag him, the way we ragged the *huevones*. We threw spitballs at him or subjected him to those concerts of razor blades stuck in the groove where the desktop opened and twanged with our fingers; the more daring among us asked him questions—transparent gibes and taunts—that the rest of the class guffawed at. I can still see Loco Bolognesi, walking after him one afternoon, wiggling his arm behind Moro's backside as though it were a gigantic cock. It was very easy to rag Professor César Moro because, unlike his colleagues, he never summoned the officer on guard to restore order, cursing us out or filling out forms to deprive us of weekend passes. Professor Moro put up with our deviltry and rudeness with stoicism, and, it might even be said, with a secret pleasure, as though it amused him that these little savages insulted him. For him, it must have been one of those risky games that the Surrealists were so inclined toward, a way of testing oneself and exploring the limits of one's own fortitude and those of human stupidity on a juvenile scale.

At any event, César Moro didn't teach classes in French at Leoncio Prado so as to get rich. Years later, on the occasion of his death, I discovered, from an impassioned text that André Coyné published about him,* that Moro had participated in the Surrealist movement in France, and I began to read that body of work of his that (as if to cut himself off even more from that country of which he said, in one of his marvelous aphorisms, that "in Peru they only cook broad beans"†) he had written for the most part in French. When I looked into the details of his life, I saw that his salary, at the school, had been pitifully meager. Anywhere else, he would have been less exposed and could have earned more. What must have attracted him about Leoncio Prado was no doubt the cruelty and irritation aroused among the cadets by his delicate appearance, his inquisitive and ironic attitude, and the fact that there had been rumors that he was a poet and made love like a woman.

To write, at school, was possible—tolerated and even applauded— if one wrote the way I did: professionally. I don't know how I began writing love letters for the cadets who had sweethearts and didn't know how to tell them that they loved them and missed them. In the beginning it must have been a game, a bet, with Víctor, or Quique or

* André Coyné, *César Moro* (Lima: Torres Aguirre, 1956).
† "En todas partes se cuecen habas, pero en el Perú sólo se cuecen habas." ("They cook broad beans everywhere, but in Peru they only cook broad beans.") (*Trans. note*)

Alberto or another of my friends in the dormitories. Then they probably passed the word on. The fact is that, at some time during my first year at the academy, they came to search me out and to ask me, invariably with prudence and a touch of embarrassment, to write love letters for them, and among my clients there were cadets from other sections and perhaps from other years. They paid me with cigarettes but I wrote them free of charge for my friends. I liked playing Cyrano, because, on the pretext of saying what was appropriate, I learned of the details of the love relations—complicated, guileless, transparent, ill-intentioned, chaste, sinful—of the cadets, and prying into that intimacy was as entertaining as reading novels.

I remember very well, on the other hand, how I wrote my first erotic novelette, a couple of pages scribbled in a rush so as to read them aloud to a group of cadets of the second section, in the dorm, before lights-out. The text was received with an outburst of approving obscenities (I have described a similar episode in *La ciudad y los perros*). Later on, as we were getting into our bunks, my neighbor, Vallejo the black, came to ask me how much I would sell him my novelette for. I wrote many others, afterward, for fun and on assignment, because I had fun doing it and because with them I paid for my vice of smoking (smoking was forbidden, of course, and a cadet who was caught smoking had his weekend pass taken away). And also, surely, because writing love letters and erotic novelettes was not looked down on or considered a shameful activity or something that only pansies did. Literature with the characteristics that mine possessed was quite acceptable in that temple of machismo and earned me a certain reputation as an oddball.

Even so, Loco wasn't among the nicknames I had. They called me Bugs Bunny, Rabbit's Foot, or Skinny (which I was), and, now and then, Poet, because I wrote and, above all, because I spent all day, and sometimes all night, reading. I believe I've never read as much and as passionately as in those years at Leoncio Prado. I read at recess and at hours when I was supposed to be studying, hiding the book during classes underneath my notebooks, and sneaked out of the classroom to go read in the arbor next to the swimming pool, and read, at night, when it was my turn to be on guard duty, sitting on the floor of chipped white tiles, in the dim light in the dormitory bathroom.

And I read every Saturday and Sunday that I was consigned to quarters, which added up to a goodly number. Immersing myself in fiction, escaping from the moldy, whitish dampness of the confines of the college and toiling in the depths of the underseas abyss in the *Nautilus* with Captain Nemo, or being Nostradamus, or the son of Nostradamus, or the Arab Ahmed Ben Hasan, who kidnaps the proud Diana Mayo and takes her to live with him in the Sahara, or sharing with d'Artagnan, Portos, Athos, and Aramis the adventures of the Queen's necklace, or those of the Man in the Iron Mask, or confronting the elements with Han d'Islande, or the rigors of Jack London's Alaska teeming with wolves, or, in Scottish castles, the knights errant of Sir Walter Scott, or spying on the gypsy girl from the twists and turns and the gargoyles of Notre Dame with Quasimodo, or, with Gavroche, being an amusing and daring street urchin in Paris in the middle of the insurrection, was more than entertainment: it was to live real life, exciting and magnificent life, so superior to that other one of routine, dirty tricks, and the tedium of being a boarding student. The books ended, but their intensely vivid worlds full of marvelous presences continued to whirl around in my brain, and I translated myself to them again and again in my imagination and spent hours there, even though to all appearances I was very quietly and seriously listening to the math lesson or our instructor's lecture on cleaning a Mauser rifle or the technique of a bayonet attack. From an early age, I had had that ability to take leave of everything around me to live in a world of fantasy, to re-create through imagination the make-believe stories that held me spellbound, and in those years of 1950 and 1951 it was converted into my defensive strategy against the bitterness of being shut in, far from my family, from Miraflores, from girls, from the *barrio*, from those beautiful things I enjoyed when I was free.

When I was allowed out on weekends, I bought books and my uncles always had a new supply ready for me to take back to school. When darkness began to fall on Sunday night and the time came to change out of civvies into my uniform to go back to the boarding school, everything began to turn bad: the movie became ugly, the soccer match dull, the houses, the parks, and the sky grew gloomy. I suffered a vague malaise all over. In those years I must have hated the late afternoon and evening on Sundays. I remember many books that

I read in those years—*Les Misérables*, for instance, with its imperishable effect on me—but the author to whom I am most grateful is Alexandre Dumas. Almost all of his books were in the yellow paperback editions put out by Tor or the Sopena edition in dark-colored hard covers with a paper jacket: *The Count of Monte Cristo, Memoirs of a Doctor, The Queen's Necklace, The Taking of the Bastille,* and the very long series that ended with the three volumes of *The Viscount of Bragelonne.* The great thing was that his novels had sequels; on finishing the book the reader knew that there was another, others, that continued the story. The saga of d'Artagnan, which begins with the young Gascon arriving in Paris as a forsaken provincial and ends many years later, at the siege of La Rochelle, when he dies, without having received the marshal's baton that the king is sending him via a postboy, is one of the most important things to have happened to me in my life. I have rarely identified more closely with works of fiction, or transubstantiated myself to a greater degree into the characters and milieus of a story, or found such intense pleasure and intense pain in what I read. One day Loco Cox, a pal of mine in the same year as I was, clowning around, snatched out of my hands one of the volumes of *The Viscount of Bragelonne,* which I was sitting out of doors reading in front of the dormitories. He started running and passing the book to others as though it were a basketball. That was one of the few times that I got into a fight at school, flinging myself on him in a blind rage, as though it was my life that was at stake. To Dumas, to the books of his that I read, I owe many things that I did and that I was afterward, that I still do and still am. From those days on, it was from the images that sprung from such reading that there stemmed my eagerness to learn French and to go off to live someday in France, a country that was, during the whole of my adolescence, my fondest dream, a country that was associated in my fantasies and desires with everything that (having been well taught by Dumas and other novelists) I would have liked life to offer: beauty, adventure, boldness, generosity, elegance, ardent passions, undisguised sentiment, extravagant gestures.

(I have never again reread any of the novels of Dumas that dazzled me when I was a youngster, books like *The Three Musketeers* or *The Count of Monte Cristo.* In my library I have the volumes of the Pléiade edition that contain them; but each time that I have begun to leaf through them, a reverential fear that they will no longer be what they once were, that they will not be able to give me what they gave me when I was fourteen and fifteen, stops me. A similar taboo kept me from rereading *Les Misérables* for many years. But when I did so, I discovered that it was also a masterpiece for an adult of today.)

In addition to the reading that changed my life, in addition to its opening my eyes to my own country and making me go through experiences that I used in writing my first novel, my two years at Leoncio Prado allowed me to practice the sport that I liked best: swimming. I was made a member of the school team and trained and participated in intramural competitions, although not in the inter-school championship, in which I was going to compete in the freestyle race, because, just as we were on our way to the National Stadium, the headmaster of Leoncio Prado decided for some reason to withdraw the school from competition. Belonging to the swimming team had its advantages: the members of it were given extra food (a fried egg at breakfast and a glass of milk in the middle of the afternoon) and, sometimes, instead of Saturday field maneuvers, we went to the pool to train.

Saturday was the happiest day of the week for those who had permission to leave for the weekend. Or, rather, the happiness began on Friday night, after the evening meal, with the movie in the improvised auditorium with wooden benches and a roof of corrugated iron. That movie was a foretaste of freedom. On Saturday the bugle blew reveille almost before it was light, since that was the day for field maneuvers. We went out into the wide-open spaces of La Perla and it was fun playing war games—setting up ambushes, taking a hill by assault, breaking a siege—especially if the lieutenant who was heading the company was Lieutenant Bringas, a model officer, who took maneuvers very seriously and sweated as much as we did. Other officers took things easier and confined themselves to intellectual leadership. The likable Lieutenant Anzieta, for instance, one of the most indulgent ones it fell to my lot to serve under. He had a grocery store; we could order packages of caramels and cookies from him, which he sold to us more cheaply than the price we paid for them on the street. I invented a little poem for him, which we sang to him while in formation:

Si quiere el cadete	If the cadet
ser un buen atleta	Wants to be a good athlete
que coma galleta	Let him buy cookies
del teniente Anzieta.	From Lieutenant Anzieta.

On finishing my first year at Leoncio Prado, I told my father I wanted to apply for admission to the Naval Academy. I don't know why I did that, since by that time I knew only too well that my temperament was incompatible with military life; perhaps so as to stick to my guns—a character trait that has got me into a lot of hot water —or because being a cadet at the Naval Academy would have meant my emancipation from my father's tutelage, something I dreamed of day and night. To my surprise, he replied that he did not approve of that decision and that, therefore, he would not give me the money that had to be put up as a fee in order to take the entrance examination. With the bitterness I felt toward him, I attributed this refusal to his stinginess—a defect, moreover, that he was not free of—for one of the reasons he put forward, also, was that, according to the regulations, if a cadet, after three or four years at the Naval Academy, asked for a discharge, he was obliged to reimburse the navy for everything that his education had cost. And my father was sure that I would not last at the Academy.

Despite his refusal, however, I went to La Punta to get the list of requirements for entering the Academy (I had thought that I would ask my uncles for the money to enroll), but at the Academy I discovered that in any case I would not have been able to request admission that year, since candidates had to be past fifteen before doing so and I wouldn't be fifteen until March 1951. I had to wait another year, then.

In that summer of 1951 my father took me to work with him in his office. The International News Service was in the first block of the Jirón Carabaya, in the Calle Pando, a few meters from the Plaza San Martín, on the first floor of an old building. The office, at the end of a long corridor with a floor covered in yellow tiles, consisted of two large rooms, the first of which was divided by partitions into two areas: in one, the radio operator received the news dispatches, and in the other, the editors translated them into Spanish and adapted them so as to send them on to *La Crónica*, which had exclusive rights to all the services of the International News Service. The room in the back was my father's office.

From January to March, I worked at the INS as a messenger, taking to *La Crónica* the cables and articles from the news service. I began at five o'clock in the afternoon and finished work at midnight on the dot, which left me a good part of the day free to go to the beach with my friends from the *barrio*. Most of the time we went to Miraflores–Los Baños, as people still called it—which, despite being a stony beach, had the best waves for bodysurfing. Bodysurfing was a marvelous sport. The waves at Miraflores broke far from shore and the experienced surfer could get carried along for fifty meters or more by tensing his body and giving the necessary arm strokes at just the right moment. On the beach at Miraflores was the Club Waikiki, the symbol of snobbery; its members rode waves on Hawaiian surfboards, at the time a very expensive sport, since the boards, made of balsa wood, were imported from the United States, and only a handful of Peruvians had the financial means to practice it. When fiberglass surfboards began to be manufactured, the sport became a more democratic one, and today it is practiced by Peruvians of all social classes. But in those days, middle-class people from Miraflores, such as I was, looked on those surfboards of the members of the Waikiki as something unattainable, cutting through the waves at Miraflores while we had to be content to bodysurf. We also went to La Herradura, with a fine sandy beach and fierce waves where the pleasure was not in letting oneself be carried along by them but in daring to ride down with them as they broke, and always placing one's body very far ahead of the crest so as not to be trapped by the underside and slammed against the bottom.

That summer was also the one of a frustrated romance with a girl from Miraflores, whose appearance in the mornings, atop the terrace of Los Baños, in her black bathing suit and little white slippers, her short hair and her honey-colored eyes, left me speechless. Her name was Flora Flores and I fell in love with her at first sight. But she never formally acknowledged my suit, although she allowed me to accompany her, after the beach, to her house, near the Colina movie theater, and sometimes came out for long walks with me, under the ficus trees of the Avenue Pardo. She was pretty and graceful, quick-witted too, and when I was with her I turned into a boy who was slow-witted and stammered. My timid advances to make her my sweetheart were rejected in such a subtly flirtatious way that I was always left with what seemed to be a lingering hope. Until, on one of our walks along the promenade lined with poplars, I introduced her to a handsome friend of mine, who, to top it all off, was a swimming champion: Rubén Mayer. Under my very nose he began to butter her up and shortly thereafter she fell for him, head over heels. To make a girl fall for you and formally declare that she is your sweetheart is a custom that was to decline little by little, until today it is something that to the younger generations, speedy and pragmatic when it comes to love, seems like prehistoric idiocy. I still have a tender memory of those rituals that love consisted of when I was an adolescent and it is to them that I owe the fact that that stage of my life has remained in my memory not only as violent and repressive but also as made up of delicate and intense moments that compensated me for all the rest.

I believe that it was in that summer of 1951 that my papa went on a trip to the United States for the first time. I am not quite certain, but it must have been in those months, since I remember having enjoyed during that period a freedom that would have been inconceivable if he had been in the house. The year before, we had moved, yet again. My father sold the little house in La Perla and rented an apartment in Miraflores, in the block of townhouses on the Calle Porta to which, at more or less the same time, my grandparents moved. Despite their being neighbors now, the relations of my father with the Llosas would continue to be nonexistent. If he met my grandparents on the street, he greeted them, but they never visited each other, and only my mama and I often dropped in at the houses of my aunts and uncles.

Going to the United States was a dream my father had long cherished. He admired that country, and one of the things he prided himself on was having learned English as a young man, something that had been of help to him in getting his jobs with Panagra and, later on, his position as representative of the INS in Peru. Ever since my brothers had moved there, he had been talking about that plan. But on that first trip he did not go to Los Angeles, where Ernesto and Enrique lived with their mother, but to New York. I remember going to say goodbye to him at the Limatambo airport with my mama and the INS employees. He was in the United States for several weeks, perhaps a couple of months, trying to set up a clothing business, which apparently turned out badly for him, since, later on, I heard him complain of having lost part of his savings in that New York venture.

The fact is that that summer I felt more free. My job kept me tied down from late afternoon until midnight, but that didn't bother me. It made me feel like an adult and it made me proud that my father paid me a salary at the end of the month, just like the editors and radio operators of the International News Service. My work was less important than theirs, naturally. It consisted of running from the office to *La Crónica*, which was on the sidewalk just across the street, the Calle Pando, bringing the news bulletins, every hour or every two hours, or whenever a news flash came in. I had the rest of the time free to read those novels that had become an addiction. At around 9 p.m., the editor, the radio operator on duty, and I went to have dinner at an inexpensive restaurant on the corner, full of motormen of the San Miguel streetcar line, whose terminal was just opposite.

In those months, as I ran between the editing tables of the office and *La Crónica*, the idea of becoming a newspaperman occurred to me. This profession, after all, wasn't all that far from what I liked— reading and writing—and seemed like a practical version of literature as a vocation. Why should my father object to the fact that I was a newspaperman? Wasn't he one, in a manner of speaking, by working at International News Service? And, as a matter of fact, the idea that I would become a newspaperman didn't strike him as a bad one.

In my second year at Leoncio Prado I don't believe I told anybody that I was going to be a navy officer, but instead repeated over and over, until I'd convinced myself of it, that, after finishing at Leoncio Prado, I would study journalism. And on one of those weekends, my father told me that he would speak with the editor-in-chief of *La Crónica* so that I might work there for the three months of the next summer. That way I would see from the inside what that profession was like.

In that year of 1951 I wrote a play: *La huida del inca (The Inca's Escape)*. I read one day, in *La Crónica*, that the Ministry of Education was soliciting entries for a contest of theatrical works for children, and that was what spurred me on. But the idea of writing drama haunted me from that time forward, as did that of being a poet or a novelist, and perhaps even more than these two latter. The theater was my first literary love. I have a very vivid memory of the first stage play I saw, when I was still just a little boy, in Cochabamba, in the Achá theater. The performance was at night and for grownups, and I don't know why my mama took me along with her. We took our seats in a box and suddenly the curtain rose and there, beneath a very strong light, some men and women didn't tell a story but *lived* it. As in the movies, but even better, because these weren't figures on a screen but beings of flesh and blood. At one point, during an argument, one of the gentlemen gave a lady a hard slap in the face. I burst out crying and my mama and my grandparents laughed: "But it's only make-believe, silly."

Apart from the evenings when there were little performances at school, I don't remember having gone to the theater, until the year I entered Leoncio Prado. That year, I do remember, I went on several Saturdays to the Teatro Segura, or to the Municipal, or to the little stage of the National School of Dramatic Art, in the vicinity of the Avenida Uruguay, generally in the first balcony or even in the peanut gallery, to see Spanish or Argentine companies—in those days, though today it seems unbelievable, such things happened in Lima—that put on plays by Alejandro Casona, Jacinto Grau, or Unamuno, and, sometimes, on rare occasions, a classic work by Lope de Vega or Calderón. I always went alone, because it was none of my neighborhood pals' idea of a good time to go to downtown Lima to take in a play, even though every once in a while Alberto Pool decided to go with me. Whether good or bad, the performance always filled my head with enough images for me to lose myself in dreams for days, and I came out of the theater each time with the secret ambition to be a playwright someday.

I don't know how many times I wrote, tore up, rewrote, and again tore up and rewrote *La huida del inca*. Since my activity as a scribe who penned love letters and erotic novelettes had won for me among my pals at Leoncio Prado the right to be a writer, I didn't work on my play in hiding, but during hours when I should have been studying, or after classes, or right in class and during my nights on guard duty. Grandpa Pedro had an old Underwood typewriter, which he had never parted with since the days in Bolivia, and on weekends I spent hours typing on it, with two fingers, the original and the copies for the contest. When I had finished it, I read it to my grandparents and to Uncle

Juan and Aunt Laura. Grandpa took it upon himself to deliver *La huida del inca* to the Ministry of Education.

That little work was, as far as I recall, the first text that I wrote in the same way in which I would later write all my novels: rewriting and correcting, redoing a thousand and one times a very confused draft that, little by little, after countless emendations, would assume definite form. Weeks and months passed without news of what sort of luck I had had in the contest, and when I finished my second year at Leoncio Prado, and at the end of December or the beginning of January of 1952 went to work at *La Crónica*, I scarcely ever thought about my play—with the forbidding subtitle of *An Inca drama in three acts, with a prologue and an epilogue in the contemporary era*—or of the literary competition for which I had submitted it.

SIX

Religion, Municipal Elections, and Backsides

O NCE the conflict with Popular Action and the Christian Popular Party over the municipal candidacies had been settled, I returned to Lima, on July 14, 1989, after having been gone twenty-two days. A motorcade of cars, trucks, and buses met me at the airport, headed by Chino and Gladys Urbina and the handful of boys and girls from the young people's section of the Freedom Movement, with whom Chino and Gladys were to organize all our campaign rallies throughout Peru. Speaking from the terrace of the house to those who had accompanied me to my home in Barranco, I made my peace with the allies and thanked AP and the PPC for having put an end to their municipal quarrels.

The next day I went to say hello to Belaunde and Bedoya and the three of us were completely reconciled. In my absence a committee of both their parties, made up of Eduardo Orrego and Ernesto Alayza Grundy—candidates for the first and second vice presidencies—had made a Solomon-like distribution of the offices of councilmen and mayors that would fall to each party throughout the country.

The problem was the mayoralty of Lima, the one that would have the greatest political effect on the presidential campaign. It fell to Popular Action to designate the candidate and it was taken for granted that it would be the architect Eduardo Orrego. Born in Chiclayo in 1933, and a disciple of Belaunde Terry's who shared his political beliefs from the start, Orrego was regarded as the natural heir to the populist throne. The AP congress, held at the end of April 1989 in Cuzco, had elected him as the party's candidate for the first vice presidency. After Belaunde, he was the leader with the best image in his party. He had been mayor of Lima between 1981 and 1983 and had experience on the municipal level. His administration had been spirited although not successful, because of the lack of funds, which the heads of Popular Action had cut down on for his office, dooming him to powerlessness. The most important thing he did was to obtain from the World Bank a credit of 85 million dollars for the mayor's office. But the bureaucracy saw to it that those funds would not materialize until after he had left office, so that only the mayor who succeeded him, the leader of the United Left, Alfonso Barrantes, the winner of the 1983 municipal election, could use them.

I was not at all intimately acquainted with Eduardo Orrego before the election campaign. I regarded him as one of the populists who had done the most to keep alive the romantic spirit of renewal that gave birth to Popular Action during Odría's dictatorship. I knew that Orrego had traveled far and wide in a sort of process of political self-instruction—he had worked in Algeria and traveled in Africa, Asia and, extensively, in the People's Republic of China—and I had a hunch that, unlike what had happened with others of his fellow party members, the years hadn't dulled the enterprising spirit of his youth. Thus, when, some time later, Belaunde asked me whom I preferred as first vice president among the three or four names that were being bruited about, I answered, without hesitation: Orrego. I knew that Eduardo had been in very delicate health, because of a heart operation, but I was assured that he had made a good recovery. I was pleased to have him as a running mate, although at that juncture—July 1989— I was still wondering, not without apprehension, what it would be like to deal and work on a day-to-day basis with the person called upon to replace me should the presidency become vacant.

He turned out to be likable, intelligent, and amusing, always prepared to intercede with Popular Action to smooth rough edges and expedite accords with the other allies, and his anecdotes and witticisms made the long trips and the wearisome social gatherings of the campaign enjoyable. I don't know how he managed it, but in every city and town he would invariably disappear for a few hours to explore the markets and craft workshops or visit hidden diggings, and would infallibly reappear with a handful of archaeological finds or handicrafts or with some little live animal underneath his arm (I understand that his passion and that of Carolina, his wife, for animals have turned their house into a zoo). I envied him that ability to preserve, in the middle of our absorbing and hectic public activities, his personal enthusiasms and sense of curiosity, since I had the feeling that, as far as I myself was concerned, politics had deprived me of mine forever. During the entire campaign we never had a single argument and I was convinced that he would loyally collaborate with me in governing the country.

But, although he never told me so, Eduardo struck me as a man disillusioned with politics and, deep down, completely skeptical as to the possibilities of changing Peru. Despite the fact that, in a very Peruvian way, he tempered it with jokes and cheerful anecdotes, something sour and sad, a bitter underside, showed through his words when he recalled how, during the time he spent in public office—in the mayoralty of Lima or in his brief term as head of the Ministry of Transport and Communications—he had discovered on every hand, among friends and among adversaries, and even on the part of persons above all suspicion, shady deals, influence peddling, and thefts. Hence, he did not seem to be at all surprised by the corruption in Alan García's administration, as though he had seen it coming and it was an inevitable culmination of inveterate practices. It was as if that experience, in addition to the gloomy evolution of Peruvian politics since his years of youthful populist enthusiasms, had put a damper on Eduardo's dynamism and his confidence in Peru.

At rallies he spoke ahead of me. He always did so briefly, with one or two jokes about the Aprista administration, and addressing me as "*President* Mario Vargas Llosa," which usually brought an ovation. The frantic, all-absorbing campaign never allowed me to have what I was often tempted to have with Orrego: a frank conversation, in which I would have perhaps come to learn the profound reasons for what seemed to me to be his irremediable disenchantment with politics, politicians and, perhaps, with Peru.

My other companion on the presidential list, Dr. Ernesto Alayza Grundy, was very different. Quite a bit older than we were—he was going on seventy-seven—Don Ernesto was named by the PPC as the candidate for the second vice presidency as a compromise between Senator Felipe Osterling and Representative Celso Sotomarino, when, at the congress of their party, held between April 28 and the first of May 1989, it looked as though Sotomarino would win the nomination in preference to Osterling, who, up until then, had been thought to be a sure thing. A very independent, combative, bad-tempered man, Sotomarino had been a stubborn opponent of the idea of the Front, had frequently attacked Popular Action and Belaunde, and harshly questioned my candidacy, so that naming him would have been inconsistent. With good judgment, Bedoya proposed to the congress a compromise candidate behind whom all the members of his party closed ranks: the venerable figure of Alayza Grundy.

Many people—including me, since I had a high opinion of him—regretted that Osterling, an attorney and a prestigious university professor with an excellent record in Congress, was not on the ticket, because of what his energy and good image would have contributed to it. But I soon discovered that, despite his advanced age, Don Ernesto Alayza Grundy was a splendid substitute.

We were friends, at a distance. At one time or another we had exchanged private letters, engaging affectionately in controversy on the subject of the state, which, in a lecture, I had characterized, following Karl Popper, as a "necessary evil." Don Ernesto, an orthodox follower of the social doctrine of the Church, and like the latter, suspicious of liberalism, reprimanded me in polite terms, setting forth to me his views on the matter. I answered him by giving him a detailed account of mine, and it is my opinion that from that interchange it was clear to both of us that despite their differences, a liberal and a follower of the Church's social doctrine such as he could understand each other, since they shared a broad ideological common denominator. On other occasions, and always with the same exquisite manners, Don Ernesto had sent me the Church encyclicals outlining its position in the social domain, and his own writings. Although the aforementioned texts usually aroused in me more hesitations than enthusiasm—the Christian social theory of "supplementarity," besides being a tongue twister, always seemed to me to be a door through which a state control of all economic life could secretly slip through—these overtures of Don Ernesto's made a gratifying impression on me. Here, among Peruvian politicians, was someone interested in ideas and doctrines, who understood politics as a cultural phenomenon.

My not being a believer was a reason for concern, and perhaps for anxiety, to the Catholics who backed me in Libertad and in the Christian Popular Party, in particular those who were not, as were the majority of those I knew, perfunctory, purely social believers out of habit, but sincere members of the Church who took great pains to live according to the dictates of their faith. I know few Catholics of this sort, and Don Ernesto Alayza Grundy is one of them—as is attested by his participation, always in the front ranks, in activities promoted by the Church in the educational or social field, his own exemplary professional and family life (he has eleven children), and his image of integrity and impeccable honesty, which had not suffered the slightest blemish, and that is saying a great deal, in over half a century of public life.

When I began my political activity, anticipating what my adversaries would obviously attempt to exploit to the limit in the coming months and years, I explained in an interview with César Hildebrandt that I was not a believer, nor was I an atheist either, but, rather, an agnostic, and that I would refuse to discuss religion during the campaign—for religious beliefs, like friendships, a person's sex life, and sentimental ties, belong to the realm of what is private, and this realm must be rigorously respected and never turned into a subject of public debate. I also stated forcefully that, as was evident, whoever governed Peru, whatever his convictions might be, ought to be aware that the great majority of Peruvians were Catholics and act with due respect for their concerns.

Throughout the entire campaign I abided by this rule and never again touched on the subject, nor did I respond when, in the final months, the administration sent its spokesmen to ask the people, their faces distorted by anxiety: "Do you want to have an *atheist* president? Do you know what an *atheist* president will mean for Peru?"

(For a fair number of my compatriots, it turned out to be impossible to differentiate atheism from agnosticism, however hard I tried, in that interview, to explain that an atheist is also a type of believer—someone who believes that God does not exist—whereas an agnostic affirms the same uncertainty about the nonexistence of a divine being and life beyond this earthly one as about their existence.)

But despite my refusal to discuss it again the subject pursued me like a shadow. Not only because the APRA and the administration made use of it unrestrictedly—there were innumerable articles in all the Aprista and Neoaprista pamphlets and scandal sheets, radio and television spots, fliers distributed in the streets, et cetera—but also because it tormented many of my supporters. I could write a book of anecdotes on the subject. I have hundreds of affectionate letters, especially from humble people, telling me that they were making novenas and vows and reciting prayers for my conversion, and many others from prying questioners, asking me what sort of religion the one I practiced—agnosticism—was, what its doctrine, its morality, and its principles were, and where one could find its churches and priests. At every rally, popular meeting, and tour of the streets, dozens of hands invariably slipped little holy images, medals, rosaries, talismans, written prayers, crosses, flagons of holy water into my pockets. And there arrived at my house anonymous gifts of religious images, lives of saints, manuals of piety—the most frequent one: *Camino (The Path)* by Monsignor Escrivá de Balaguer—or very pretty little boxes with Catholic relics, water from Lourdes or Fátima or soil from Jerusalem inside. On the day of the close of the campaign, in Arequipa, on April 5, 1990, after the rally in the Plaza de Armas there was a reception at the convent of Santa Catalina. A lady came over to me and with an air of mystery said to me that the mother superior wanted to see me. Taking me by the arm, she led me through the iron grille that partitions off the area where the cloistered nuns live. A door opened. A little nun in glasses, smiling and charmingly courteous, appeared. It was the mother superior. She invited me to cross the threshold and pointed out to me a little chapel where in the half-shadow I could make out white coifs and dark habits. "We're praying for you," she whispered to me. "And I don't need to tell you *why*."

Very early on, I brought up the subject in a closed meeting of Libertad. The political committee agreed with me that, in conformity with the rule of sincerity that we had established for ourselves, I could not hide my status as an agnostic for the sake of an easier win at the polls. At the same time, it was imperative for us, no matter how great the provocations, to avoid controversy over the religious question. None of us suspected at the time—toward the end of 1987—the importance that the subject of religion would take on between the first and the second round of voting, as a result of the successful mobilization of the evangelical churches in favor of Fujimori.

Among the leaders of the Freedom Movement there were a fair number of Catholics cut from the same cloth as Don Ernesto Alayza

Grundy: dedicated, consistent, and on very close terms with the hierarchy or with certain ecclesiastical orders or institutions, to the point that I once hinted that, surrounded by people like them, it was likely that the Holy Spirit would preside over the sessions of our political committee. In the 1960s, Miguel Cruchaga had been the organizer of the Catholic renewal movement in Peru. Lucho Bustamante kept up a very close friendship with the Jesuits, in whose school he had studied, and taught at the University of the Pacific, which had ties to the order. Our brand-new secretary of the *departamento* of Lima, Rafael Rey, was a member of Opus Dei, someone who had taken the vows of poverty, obedience, and chastity (the latter of which, let me say in passing, he defended like a besieged fortress against the disrespectful assaults of many female members of Libertad). And on the political committee there were several dyed-in-the-wool Catholics—"catholic, apostolic, Roman, and holier than thou," as one of them joked. (Among the best-known ones I shall mention Beatriz Merino, Pedro Cateriano, and Enrique Chirinos Soto.)

Even though, I am certain, my religious position perturbed all of them, I must thank them for never making me aware of it, not even in a veiled way, and not even at the times when the campaign against my "atheism" became more violent still. It is true that, in accordance with what we advocated with regard to privacy, we never discussed religion in the Freedom Movement. Nor did my Catholic friends come forth to make public use of their status to put a stop to the attacks: they were, as I have already said, believers who tried to live in accordance with their beliefs, for whom it was not conceivable to exploit their faith, either to attack the adversary or to promote themselves.

This was also how Don Ernesto Alayza Grundy comported himself. Throughout the entire campaign he maintained an absolute discretion regarding the subject of religion, which never turned up in our conversations, not even when thorny questions arose, such as birth control, which I explicitly defended and which he would have found it hard to approve of.

But apart from his being discreet and completely honest—I was happy with the image of moral purity that he brought with him to his candidacy for the office of second vice president—Don Ernesto was a marvelous fellow campaigner. He was tireless and invariably good-humored, and his physical resistance left all of us amazed, as did his tact and his spirit of solidarity: he never used his advanced age or his prestige to ask for or to accept the slightest privilege. I sometimes had to firmly demand that he not accompany me—when it was a question, for instance, of going to places such as Huancavelica or Cerro de Pasco, where it was necessary to go up to altitudes of more than twelve thousand feet—because he was always all set to climb steep slopes in the Andes, sweat bullets in the jungle, or shiver from the cold on high mountain plateaus in order to reach all the towns on the planned itinerary. His joyousness, his naturalness and straightforwardness, his ability to adapt to the rigors of the campaign, and his youthful enthusiasm for what we were doing helped to make the endless trips back and forth to towns, districts, and regions bearable. He was usually the first speaker at our rallies. He spoke slowly, his long arms stretched out and his ascetic silhouette towering over all of us on the speakers' platform. And with his little piping, slightly falsetto voice and a roguish twinkle in his eyes he would end his brief speech with a metaphor: "I have leaned over to listen to the pulse of the depths of Peru. And what did I hear? What did that deep throbbing say? *Fre-de-mo! Fre-de-mo! Fre-de-mo!*"

I had heard, since before my trip to Europe, that Eduardo Orrego refused to accept the candidacy for the mayoralty of Lima that Popular Action offered him. He left for France with his wife, Carolina, almost at the same time as I returned, and in the press there were many speculations about this. Belaunde confirmed to me that Orrego was hesitant, but he told me that he was confident that he could make him change his mind before the final date for candidates to register —August 14—and asked me to help persuade him.

I phoned him in Paris. Eduardo seemed to me to have his mind firmly made up. The reason he put forward was a tactical one. The opinion polls for the mayoralty predicted that he would win 20 percent, half of what I would receive in the two rounds of voting for the presidency. If he won fewer votes or lost the municipal election, he told me, his failure would be a millstone around my neck for my campaign. We ought not to take the risk of his losing. When judged from the perspective of what occurred in the municipal elections, his refusal to run proved that his intuition was correct. Had he had a presentiment that he'd be beaten?

Perhaps there was another, more secret, reason. At the time of my withdrawal as a presidential candidate and the uproar that followed, Congressman Francisco Belaunde Terry—the brother of the former president, the founder of Popular Action, and one of the populists who had suffered from the most harassment by Velasco's dictatorship—had held Orrego responsible for the intransigence of Popular Action concerning the lists of joint candidates, saying, if the newspapers weren't lying, very harsh things about him. Although I never heard Orrego make the slightest allusion to the incident, this episode may have influenced his decision.

(Let me say, between parentheses, that Francisco Belaunde Terry had always been one of the populists whom I respected most, one of those rare politicians who lend dignity to politics. Because of his independence, which sometimes made him stand up to his own party when his conscience so dictated, and because of that maniacal uprightness of his that led him, despite his meager financial means, never to accept the raises in salaries, bonuses, and reimbursements that the members of Congress continually passed to increase their incomes, and to give back his paychecks or donate them to the doormen and congressional employees when the APRA forced though a measure that *prohibited* a congressman or a senator from refusing the increases. Because of his utter scorn for the conventions and the calculations that rule the life of the politician, Francisco Belaunde—tall and gaunt, a living historical encyclopedia, a voracious reader and an elegant speaker, yet one who gave the impression of having stepped out of literature and the past—always struck me as being a man from another time or from another country, a lamb set down in the middle of a pack of wolves. He was capable of saying what he thought and believed, although that trait put him in prison and sent him into exile, as happened to him during the dictatorships of Odría and Velasco, and yet he persisted, even though it made enemies of the members of his own party or of the institutions which every good politician fears and fawns over: the communications media. In the 1985 election campaign, on the occasion when I announced on television that I would not vote for Alan García but for Bedoya Reyes for president, I added that, on the lists of congressional candidates, I would cast my ballot for two candidates whom, for the welfare of Peru, I would like to see in Congress: Miguel Cruchaga and Francisco Belaunde Terry.

(Ever since the demonstration in the Plaza San Martín—and perhaps even before that—Francisco Belaunde Terry had been a persistent advocate of the idea of the Front and of my candidacy. And he had said very clearly that he disagreed with the populists who insisted, violently at times, not hiding their hostility toward the Freedom Movement and toward me, that his brother Fernando be a candidate once again. This, as is only natural, had earned him the animosity of many of his fellow party members, in particular those nobodies whose only credential for occupying leadership posts in Popular Action and being its candidates for Congress was their adulation of its leader, and hence they had hindered, by every possible means, the creation of the alliance. This situation was made worse for Francisco Belaunde Terry when, on the night of my withdrawal in June 1989, he appeared at my house, in the very middle of a demonstration by members of the Freedom Movement, and immediately after went to the headquarters of Libertad to express his support for the movement. Moreover, his wife, Isabelita, was a devoted activist in Acción Solidaria—the Solidarity program—and worked for months with Patricia to promote social aid programs in the shantytowns of San Juan de Lurigancho.

(Those mediocrities who, as happens in every party and particularly in those most ridden with bossism, are the ones who usually take over the leadership posts, plotted together to keep Francisco Belaunde Terry—without the shadow of a doubt the most mainstream populist member of Congress—from being the candidate of his party on the lists of the Democratic Front. Libertad then proposed that he be one of our candidates for the congressman's seat for Lima and he accepted, honoring our quota with his name. But, to the misfortune of the Peruvian Congress, he was not elected.)

When I told Belaunde Terry of my conversation with Orrego, he resigned himself to finding a replacement for him. He asked me what I thought of Juan Incháustegui and I hastened to tell him that he seemed to me to be a magnificent choice. An engineer and a man from the provinces, he had been a good minister of energy and mines and had signed up as a member of AP not before but after having been minister, in the last days of Belaunde's second term in office. Although I knew him only by sight, I was very much aware of the laudatory terms in which Belaunde had referred to him in our conversations in the Presidential Palace, at the midpoint of his presidency.

After certain hesitations—he was a man of modest financial resources and the income for the mayor of Lima was minimal—Incháustegui agreed to represent the Front. The PPC, for its part, chose Lourdes Flores Nano as its candidate for representative mayor. A young attorney, Lourdes had become very popular because of her likable nature and her fine oratory during the mobilization against the nationalization of the banks.

The pair of them were magnificent and I breathed a sigh of relief, certain that we would win the municipal election in Lima. The affable presence of Incháustegui, his flashes of wit, his lack of cutting polemic, won the sympathies of voters. His status as a man from the provinces was another good credential. Although he had been born in Arequipa, he had studied and lived in Cuzco and considered himself a native of that city, so that this ought to win many people over in the city of provincials that the capital of Peru had become. And, there alongside him, the warmth, youth, and intelligence of Lourdes Flores Nano— a new face in Peruvian politics—was an excellent complement.

However, from September on the opinion polls began to predict that the most votes would go not to Incháustegui but to a newcomer, Ricardo Belmont Cassinelli. The owner of a radio station and of a small-scale television channel, on which for several years he had been the emcee of a very popular talk show—"Habla el Pueblo" ("The People Speak")—Belmont had never entered politics before, nor did he seem interested in doing so. His name was associated, rather, with sports, which he engaged in and promoted—he had been a boxing impresario—and in TV marathons to raise funds for the San Juan de Dios Clinic, which he had organized for several years. His image was that of a likable emcee and a favorite of the masses—because of his manner of speaking filled with "in" words, such as *manito*, for "pal," *patita*, for "getting the bounce," *chelita*, for "blondie," and all the picturesque expressions of the latest slang popular with teenagers— associated with the world of show business, of popular singers, comedians, and *vedettes*, and not with public affairs. However, in the preceding municipal election certain publications, among them *Caretas*, had mentioned his name as a possible independent candidate for the mayoralty of Lima.

In mid-June of 1989, Belmont suddenly sent out the call for a rally in the Plaza Grau, in the district of La Victoria, in which, backed by Augusto Polo Campos, the composer of traditional Peruvian music, he announced the creation of the civic movement Obras and his candidacy for mayor.

In the interviews on TV that he took part in during the weeks that followed, Belmont put forth very simple ideas, which he was to repeat all through his campaign. He was an independent disillusioned by political parties and by politicians, since they had never fulfilled their promises. It was time for professional experts and technicians to take over the solution of problems. He always added that his ideology could be expressed in just one formula: he was for private enterprise. He also said that he was going to vote for me in the presidential election, "because my ideas are the same as Vargas Llosa's," but that he didn't trust my allies: hadn't AP and the PPC already been in power? And what had they done?

(These are the things that Mark Malloch Brown would have liked for me to say; or better put, those that, according to his opinion polls, Peruvian voters wanted to hear. Among those who heeded this message, ranting against politics and parties, was someone who was as much of a novice in such contests as Belmont, an obscure former rector of a technical university named Alberto Fujimori, who must have pricked up his ears and picked up a goodly number of hints.)

Since the day Belmont announced his candidacy, I was sure that this call to independent voters and his attacks on the political establishment would make an impression on our electorate. But the one who foresaw events most accurately was Miguel Cruchaga. I recall a conversation with him in which he regretted that Belmont was not our candidate: a new face and yet a well-known one, which, beneath the apparent superficiality and tastelessness of his statements, represented the sort of candidate that we were eager to promote: a self-made young entrepreneur, in favor of private initiative and a market economy, without the stigma of a political past.

On July 27, I had a long meeting with Ricardo Belmont, at my house in Barranco, at which Miguel Vega Alvear was also present. Because of the agreements within the Front, I was not able to propose to him what, no doubt, he would have accepted—being our candidate for the mayoralty—but instead limited myself to making him see the danger that his candidacy, by dividing the independent and the democratic vote, would end up handing over, once again, the municipality of Lima to the APRA (its candidate was Mercedes Cabanillas) or to the United Left (whose internal crisis, which had long been brewing, exploded at that point and brought about its division).

Belmont was very confident. My alliance with the other parties struck him as a mistake, because in the most impoverished sector, whose sentiments he sounded out every day on his programs, there was a widespread rejection of them and above all of Popular Action. He shared this opinion. He was aggrieved, moreover, because Belaúnde's administration had discriminated against him, refusing to give him back the channel that the military dictatorship had expropriated from him, as it had done in the case of the other TV channels.

"The people who will vote for me will come above all from sectors C and D, from the poor and the very poor," he assured me, "and the party that I am going to take votes away from isn't going to be the Democratic Front but the United Left. My own class, the bourgeoisie, has nothing but contempt for me, because I talk slang and because they think I lack culture. However, even though I'm a whitie, mestizos and blacks from the shantytowns like me a lot and will vote for me."

It turned out the way he said it would. And what he promised me in that conversation was also true, expressed in terms of an allegory that he was to repeat many times: "The municipal elections are the preliminary bout and the Front and I must do our handkerchief dance in them. But the presidential election is the main bout and then I'll come out in favor of you. Because I share your ideas. And because I need you to be president in order to be a success as the mayor of Lima."

Belmont's campaign was very clever. He used fewer television commercials than we and the APRA did, he visited over and over again the humblest neighborhoods, he declared until we were fed up with hearing it that he was in favor of me but against "the parties that are all burned out," and to everyone's surprise, in the televised debate with Juan Incháustegui, when we were certain that Juan would steamroller him with his technical marshaling of facts, Belmonte came out very well, thanks to the advisers that he brought with him, and above all to his slangy impudence and his experience in front of the camera.

The municipal elections brought on the break between the factions of the left, held together up until then in a precarious coalition under the leadership of Alfonso Barrantes Lingán. This leadership had been disputed for some time by the most radical sectors of the United Left, who accused the former mayor of Lima of bossism, of having toned down his Marxism to the point of changing it into a social-democratic position and, even graver still, of having put up such a respectful opposition to Alan García's administration that the two of them gave the appearance of being hand in glove.

Despite inordinate efforts of the Communist Party to avoid the rupture, it took place nonetheless. The United Left presented as its candidate for the mayoralty of Lima a Catholic with leftist leanings, the sociologist and university professor Henry Pease García, who was also to be their candidate for the presidency of the Republic. The sector that supported Barrantes, for its part, under the label of Acuerdo Socialista (Socialist Alliance), put up another sociologist, Senator Enrique Bernales, as its candidate for the first vice presidency on the ticket with Barrantes.

The second anniversary of Libertad was approaching—we had designated the rally in the Plaza San Martín on August 21, 1987, as the event that marked its beginning—and those of us on the political committee thought that this was a good chance to show that, unlike the Communists and Socialists, we had really managed to achieve unity.

We had celebrated the first anniversary of Libertad on August 21, 1988, in the city of Tacna, with a demonstration on the Paseo Cívico. Until just a short while before the time announced for the rally, almost the only people about were a handful of curiosity seekers standing around by the rostrum. I was waiting in a nearby house that belonged to friends of my family, and a few minutes before 8 p.m., I went up to the roof to sneak a look around. On the platform was Pedro Cateriano, with his stentorian voice and assertive gestures, delivering his harangue to empty air. Or just about, since the Paseo Cívico could be seen to be deserted, while on the corners and the sidewalks leading to the Paseo, groups of bystanders were indifferently watching what was going on. But half an hour later, when the ceremony had already begun and we had started singing the de rigueur anthems, the people of Tacna began to congregate, and crowds of them continued to flock onto the Paseo until they filled several blocks. Finally, a crowd accompanied me through the streets and I had to speak again from the hotel balconies.

To celebrate the second anniversary we chose the Amauta Coliseum in Lima, which Genaro Delgado Parker allowed us to use without charge, because it was a vast space—there was room for 18,000 people—and because we believed that it would be a good opportunity to put forward a serious explanation of the aim of the Democratic Front, by bringing together all our candidates for mayors and councilmen in the various districts of Lima. We also invited the principal leaders of AP, the PPC, SODE, and the UCI (a small group, headed by Francisco Diez Canseco, at that time a congressman, which was later to withdraw from the alliance).

The program was in two parts. The first, made up of dances and songs, was entrusted to Luis Delgado Aparicio, who was, on the one hand, an attorney who specialized in labor questions and, on the other, a popular figure on radio and television thanks to his salsa programs, or, as he puts it in his inimitable style, programs of Afro-Latin-Caribbean-American music, as well as a famous professional dancer. The second part, the political one properly speaking, would consist of Miguel Cruchaga's speech and mine.

The group that we had named Movilización, the youth movement, the district committees, and Solidarity all made a great effort to fill the Amauta. The problem was transportation. The person responsible for it, Juan Checa, had hired a number of buses and trucks and given us the use, for nothing, of others that belonged to his company, but on the appointed day many of these vehicles failed to turn up at the meeting places agreed upon. Hence the men and women of Libertad in charge of mobilization found themselves, in many districts, with hundreds of people who had no way to get to the Coliseum. Charo Chocano, in Las Delicias de Villa, went out onto the highway and hired two buses that were passing by, and in Huaycán, the indefatigable Friedel Cillóniz and her helpers literally took a truck by storm and persuaded its driver to take them to the Amauta. But thousands of people were left hopping mad. Despite this, the stands of the Coliseum were full.

I had been there since seven that night, all ready, in the car, accompanied by the security guards, driving round and round the Amauta. But, over the radio, those inside who were responsible for the ceremony, Chino Urbina and Alberto Massa, held me back, telling me that people were still coming in and that the emcees—Pedro Cateriano, Enrique Ghersi, and Felipe Leno—had to be given time to warm up the crowd. So half an hour, an hour, an hour and a half went by. To control our impatience, we drove all around Lima several times and, whenever we mentioned the Coliseum, the answer was the same: "Just a little while longer."

When, finally, they gave me the green light and I entered the Amauta, there was a contagious, festive, euphoric atmosphere, with pennants and placards of the various committees waving on the stands, and the supporters from each district competing by way of songs and repeated refrains. But nearly two hours had gone by since the time that had been set! Roxana Valdivieso was singing, on the rostrum, a theme song of the Movement. Just a short time before, Juan Incháustegui and Lourdes Flores had made a triumphal entry that they topped off by dancing a *huaynito*. And Lucho Delgado Aparicio's show had long since ended. The daily papers and television channels hostile to Libertad were then enabled to create a scandal, because between the folklore numbers popular dancers in scanty costumes suddenly appeared, dancing a frenetic salsa. According to the press, the sight of those wildly wiggling hips, backsides, breasts, and thighs had caused many respectable members of Congress belonging to the PPC to feel embarrassed and their faces to turn beet-red, and someone said that Don Ernesto Alayza Grundy, the embodiment of probity, had been affronted by the performance. But Eduardo Orrego assured me afterwards that all that was false and that, as a matter of fact, Don Ernesto had contemplated the dancers with perfect stoicism. And it was obvious to me that Enrique Chirinos Soto was brimming over with pleasure at what he had seen.

In any event, when I began to speak, after a Proustian introduction by Miguel Cruchaga (because, in accordance with his fondness for allegories, this time Miguel used Proust to construct one of them), it was about 10 p.m. I hadn't taken five minutes developing the first subject—the changes in the national political panorama, in which, previously, the ruling ideas were those focused on state control, whereas now public debate was centered on a market economy, privatization, and popular capitalism—when I began noticing a stir in the stands. The spotlights blinded me and I couldn't see what was happening, but it seemed to me that the stands were emptying. As a matter of fact, people were leaving in a stampede. Only the section that I was facing directly, the two or three hundred municipal candidates, and leaders of the Democratic Front remained in their seats until the end of my speech, which I brought to a hasty close, wondering what the devil was going on. The buses and trucks had been hired till 10 p.m. and the audience, especially the people from distant "young towns"—the shantytowns that had grown up on the outskirts of Lima—didn't want to return home by walking five, ten, or twenty kilometers.

In short, our inexperience and lack of coordination turned the festivities of the second anniversary of the Movement into a disaster as far as publicity was concerned. *La República*, *La Crónica*, *El Nacional*, and other semiofficial government publications made particular mention of the half-empty stands of the Amauta as I was speaking and illustrated the news stories with the shapely backsides of Delgado Aparicio's salsa dancers. In order to counteract the bad effect, Lucho Llosa produced in the days that followed a TV spot showing another aspect of the celebration: stands jammed full of people, and ancient Inca princesses dancing a stately *huaynito*.

SEVEN

Journalism and Bohemia

THE three months that I worked at *La Crónica*, before my last year of secondary school, brought great upheavals in my life. While I was there, I learned what journalism actually was, and I became acquainted as well with a Lima that up until then had been unknown to me, and for the first and last time I lived a bohemian life. I hadn't yet reached the age of sixteen—my sixteenth birthday wasn't till the 28th of March of that year—but my wish to cease to be an adolescent, my impatience to reach adulthood, was fulfilled in that summer of 1952.

I have recalled that adventure in my novel *Conversation in The Cathedral*, with the inevitable cosmetic changes and additions. The excitement and the churning stomach with which I went up the stairs of the very old two-story building on the Calle Pando where *La Crónica* is located, in order to present myself that morning in the office of the managing editor, Señor Valverde, a very kindly gentleman who passed on to me certain notions about journalism and announced to me that I would earn five hundred soles a month. That day or the next I was given a press card, with my photo and seals and signatures that said "journalist."

The administrative offices and then, through a courtyard with ornamental grilles and tile flooring, the print shop were on the ground floor. On the second floor were the editorial room for the morning paper, a small room where the evening edition was put out, and the living quarters of the managing editor, whose two good-looking daughters we sometimes watched, in admiring silence, as they passed through the corridor just outside the editorial room.

The main editorial room was a vast space with some twenty desks, at the very back of which was the conductor who directed that orchestra: Gaston Aguirre Morales. The local news staff, the one for the international news, and the one for the crime page divided up the territory between them, separated like building lots by invisible frontiers that everyone respected (the staff that covered sports had its own office). Aguirre Morales—a man from Arequipa, tall, thin, likable, and extremely courteous—welcomed me, sat me down at an empty desk in front of a typewriter, and gave me my first assignment: writing up an item on the presentation of his credentials by the new Brazilian ambassador. And right there and then I received from his own lips my first lesson in modern journalism. I had to begin the news item with the lead, the main fact, summed up in a brief sentence, and develop it in the remainder of the news item in a direct and objective manner. "A reporter's success lies in knowing how to find the lead, my friend." When, in fear and trembling, I brought him the finished piece, he read it, struck out a number of useless words—"Conciseness, precision, total objectivity, my friend"—and sent it to the printers'. I must not have slept that night, waiting to see my very own writing in print. And the next morning, when I bought *La Crónica* and leafed through it, there was the box: "This morning the new Brazilian ambassador, Señor Don . . . presented his credentials." I was now a journalist.

Around five o'clock in the afternoon I would go to the editorial room to receive my assignments for the day and for the next morning: inaugurations, ceremonies, well-known public figures who were arriving or departing, parades, prizes, winners of lotteries or of the *polla* and the *pollón*—winning bets on horses that in those days amounted to very large sums—interviews with singers, circus managers, bullfighters, scholars, eccentrics, firemen, prophets, occultists, and all the activities, occupations, or human characters who for one reason or another deserved to be mentioned in the news. I had to go from one district of Lima to another, in a station wagon belonging to the paper, along with a photographer, sometimes the chief one himself, the great Ego Aguirre, if the subject warranted it. When I came back to write up the news items, the editorial room was just as it should have been. A thick cloud of smoke hovered above the desks and the typewriters were clacking away. It smelled of tobacco, ink, and paper. There was the sound of voices, of laughter, of the running footsteps of reporters bringing their copy to Aguirre Morales, who, red pencil in hand, read it, corrected it, and sent it down to the printers'.

The arrival of the chief editor of the crime page, Becerrita, was the high point of each night. If he came in sober, he went, wordless and ill-tempered, through the editorial room to his desk, followed by his assistant, the pale and ramrod-straight Marcoz. Becerrita was a short, husky man, with his hair slicked down with brilliantine and the square and angry face of a bulldog, in which there stood out, as straight as if drawn with a ruler, a little hairline mustache, which looked as though it had been traced with a charcoal pencil. He had created the "red page"—the one reporting major crimes and felonies—one of the greatest attractions of *La Crónica*, and it sufficed to see him and hear him, with his vitriolic little eyes, grainy from lack of sleep, perpetually watchful, his shiny suits, pressed countless times, reeking of tobacco and sweat, with lapels full of grease spots, and the microscopic knot in his filthy tie, to surmise that Becerrita was a citizen of Hell, that the underworld haunts of the city held no secrets for him. If he came in drunk, his fierce mineral laugh preceded him, loud guffaws, resounding from the stairway, that shook the grimy windows and the paint-chipped walls of the editorial room. Milton would begin to tremble, for he was Becerrita's favorite victim. Becerrita would go over to Milton's desk to make fun of him, cracking jokes that made the reporters on the staff hold their sides laughing, and sometimes, aiming his "piece" at him—because he always went about armed, the better to resemble his caricatural image—chased him about among the desks, his pistol at the ready. On one of those occasions, to everyone's terror, he accidentally got off a shot that ended up embedded in the spiderwebs on the ceiling of the editorial room.

But, despite the bad times he gave us, neither Milton, nor Carlos Ney, nor I, nor any of the other reporters felt any animosity toward Becerrita. We all felt a sort of fascination with him, because he had created in the journalism of Lima a distinct genre (which, with time, was to degenerate into something unimaginable), and because, despite his binges and his ugly face, he was a man whom nightfall in Lima turned into a prince.

Becerrita knew and frequented, in addition to the police stations, all the brothels in Lima, where he was feared and fawned upon because a scandalous news item in *La Crónica* meant a fine or having the place closed down. Sometimes he took Milton, Carlos, and me (we three became inseparable) with him, after the paper had been put to bed around midnight, to Nanette's, on the Avenida Grau, or to the brothels in Huatica, or to the more elegant ones on the Avenida Colonial, and almost the moment we crossed the threshold, there was the madam, in person, and the bouncers on duty, welcoming him with kisses and slaps on the back. He never smiled or returned their greetings. He confined himself to growling, without taking his cigar stump out of his mouth: "Beer for the boys."

Then, installed at a little table in the bar, with all of us sitting around him, he would drink one beer after another, raising the cigar stump to his lips every once in a while, indifferent to the hubbub all around him, to the couples dancing, or to the fights started by certain belligerent patrons whom the bouncers shoved out into the street. Sometimes Becerrita would start recalling, in a gravel voice, anecdotes about his adventures as a police reporter. He had known and seen from close up the worst hoods, the most hardened criminals of Lima's underworld, and remembered with pleasure their horrifying deeds, their rivalries, their knife fights, their heroic or ignoble deaths. Even though I felt a touch of the fear aroused by someone who has spent his years among the most pestilential low life, Becerrita dazzled me. He seemed to me to have stepped out of a disturbing novel about the lower depths. When it came time to pay the bill—on the rare occasions when he was charged anything—Becerrita used to grab his pistol and lay it on the table: "I'm the only one here who's going to take out his wallet."

When, after I had worked at *La Crónica* for two or three weeks, Aguirre Morales asked me if I wanted to substitute for one of the crime page reporters who was sick, I gladly accepted. Although Becerrita was terrifying because of his fearful temper, the reporters who worked with him were as devoted as dogs to him, and in the month that I worked under him I too came to feel proud of being part of his team. This consisted of three or four reporters, although sometimes it would have been more accurate to call them data gatherers, since a couple of them confined themselves to bringing us bare facts that Marcoz and I took charge of writing up. The most picturesque one of the bunch was a gaunt young man who appeared to have stepped out of a comic strip or a puppet show. I've forgotten his real name, but I remember the name he went by at the radio station—Paco Denegri—his wraith-like appearance, and the thick eyeglasses that enlarged his myopic eyes to a monstrous size. And his velvet voice as the male lead of a radio serial, an activity he engaged in at Radio Central during his hours off.

Becerrita was a tireless worker, with an unbridled passion, a fixation on his job. Nothing in the world seemed to interest him but those bloody feasts of violence—lovers' suicides, accounts settled by knife thrusts, rapes, deflorations, incest, filicides, holdups and fast getaways, arson, clandestine prostitution, corpses washed up by the sea or thrown off a cliff—that we, his peons, kept collecting night and day in our rounds of the police headquarters of the most ill-famed districts in Lima: La Victoria, El Porvenir, and Callao. He reviewed these happenings and a second was all it took for him to shuffle through them and identify the one that had the right amount of filth. "This one's news." His instructions were brief and categorical: "Interview this one, go and check that address, this one smells to me like a fake." And when a reporter came back with the news item, written up according to his instructions, he always knew—his little eyes gleamed and his jaws hung open as he crossed out or added—how to make the spectacular, terrible, cruel, base, or devious feature or detail of what had happened stand out. Sometimes, after the beers at the brothel, he would still drop by the print shop of *La Crónica* to make sure that his page—a page that in reality was two or three pages and sometimes even more—had come out intact, with the amounts of blood and filth that he had specified.

My tour of police headquarters began at around seven at night, but it was later, from ten or eleven o'clock on, that the patrol cars arrived back at the stations with their loads of thieves, bloodthirsty lovers, those badly injured from fights in bars and bordellos, or transvestites, who were cruelly hounded and who always merited the honors of the police-blotter page. Between PIPs (police detectives) and Civil Guards, Becerrita had a fine-meshed network of informers, whom he had done favors for—hiding facts or giving on his page the information that put them in the best light—and thanks to those sources we often scooped our rival, *Última Hora*. Becerrita's page had been the sovereign queen of violent death and scandal for many years. But this new daily, *Última Hora*, the evening edition of *La Prensa*, which had introduced slang and cant—local idioms and vulgar expressions—into their headlines and their news items, fought Becerrita for the scepter and on certain days snatched it away from him: that left him beside himself. Scooping *Última Hora*, outdoing it with bigger doses of death and pandering, on the other hand, made him growl with pleasure and let out those outlandish guffaws that seemed to come from the innermost depths of a tunnel or a stone quarry, and not from a human throat.

Despite the fierce competition that brought our two daily papers face to face in their fight for the sensationalist kingdom, I came to be a very good friend of the chief editor of the crime page of *Última Hora*, Norwin Sánchez Geny. He was a Nicaraguan and had come to study law at the Catholic University in Lima. He began to work as a journalist in his free time and thereby discovered his vocation. And his talent as well, if talent is the right name for what he and Becerrita had created (something that other journalists would later develop to criminal extremes). Norwin was young, skinny, an inveterate bohemian, generous, a tireless, lecherous whoremaster and beer drinker. After the third or fourth glass he would begin to recite the first chapter of the *Quijote*, which he knew by heart. His eyes would fill with tears: "What great prose, damn it all!" Very often, Carlos, Milton, and I would go by to get him at the *Última Hora* editorial room, upstairs at *La Prensa*, on the Jirón de La Unión, or he would pick us up on the Calle Pando, and we would go have a few beers, or on payday take off for a brothel. (Norwin, that likable fellow, returned some years later to Nicaragua, where he became a serious, upright man, according to what he wrote me in a letter that I unexpectedly received in 1969, while I was giving a series of lectures at the University of Puerto Rico. He gave up journalism, studied economics, graduated, and became a bureaucrat. But shortly thereafter he met the sort of end that *Última Hora* capitalized on: he was murdered, in a cheap bar in Managua, during a fight.) The places we went to most often were some little Chinese bars, on La Colmena and its environs, very old, smoke-filled, stinking, crowded places which stayed open all night, in some of which the tables were separated from each other by screens or thin wooden partitions—as in Chinese restaurants—covered with graffiti in pencil or carved with a knife and cigar burns. All of them had soot-stained, grimy ceilings, red-tiled floors on which the waiters, young mountain boys who could barely get out a few words in Spanish, threw bucketfuls of sawdust so as to sweep up the puke and gobs of spit of drunks more easily. In the dim light the night owls of downtown Lima, the dregs of humanity, could be seen: inveterate souses, bourgeois gays cruising for pickups, hookers, no-account pimps, office clerks winding up a bachelor dinner. Those of us from *La Crónica* would talk and smoke together, the others would recount their adventures as journalists, and I would listen to them, feeling very much older than my sixteen years—a birthday I had not yet reached—and yet I was a real bohemian, a real journalist. And I secretly thought that I was living the same life that had been lived, right here, when he came to the capital from his provincial Trujillo, by the great César Vallejo, whom I began to read for the first time—surely following the advice of Carlos Ney —during that summer. Hadn't he spent his nights in the bars and brothels of bohemian Lima? Didn't his poems, his short stories testify to it? This was the path, then, to literature and to genius.

Carlos Ney Barrionuevo was my literary mentor during those months. He was five or six years older than I and had read a great deal, modern literature in particular, and published poems in the cultural supplement of *La Crónica*. Sometimes, late at night, when beers took away his timidity—his nose already red and his greenish eyes gleaming feverishly—he took out of his pocket a poem scribbled in a page of his reporter's notebook and read it to us. He wrote poems that were hard to understand, full of strange words, that intrigued me as I listened to them, for they revealed to me a completely unknown world, that of modern poetry. It was from him that I learned of the existence of Martín Adán, many of whose sonnets from *Poesía de extramares (Poetry from Beyond the Sea)* he could recite from memory, and whose bohemian figure—shuttling back and forth between the madhouse and the tavern—Carlos would go religiously to spy on at the Cordano bar next to the Presidential Palace, headquarters of the poet Martín Adán on the days when he left the psychiatric clinic in which he had decided to live.

I am more in debt for my literary education to Carlitos Ney than to all my teachers at secondary school and most of the ones I had at the university. Thanks to him, I became acquainted with some of the books and authors that would brand my adolescence with fire—the Malraux of *Man's Fate* and *Man's Hope*, the American novelists of the Lost Generation, and above all Sartre, whose short stories, collected in *The Wall*, Ney gave me one afternoon, in the Losada edition with a prologue by Guillermo de Torre. Through this book there began a relationship with Sartre's work and thought that was to have a decisive effect on my vocation. And I am certain that it was also Carlitos Ney who first spoke to me of Eguren's poetry, of Surrealism and of Joyce, whose *Ulysses* he must have bought me, in the dreadful translation published by Santiago Rueda, which, let me say in passing, I was hardly able to get through, skipping whole pages and not understanding very much of what I read.

But, even more than what he had me read, I owe to my friend Carlos Ney his having taught me, on those bohemian nights, everything I didn't know about books and authors that were making the rounds in the vast outside world, without my even having heard that they existed, and having given me an intuition of the complexity and richness that went to make up that literature, which for me, up until then, had meant little more than adventure stories and a handful of classic or modernist poets.

Talking about books, about authors, about poetry with Carlitos Ney, in the filthy little rooms of downtown Lima, or in boisterous and promiscuous brothels, was exciting. Because Carlos was sensitive and intelligent and had an inordinate love of literature, which, I am convinced, must have represented for him something more profound and basic than the journalism to which he was to devote his whole life. I always believed that, at one time or another, Carlitos Ney would publish a book of poems which would reveal to the world that enormous talent he seemed to be hiding and which, in the wee hours, when alcohol and staying up all night had made all his timidity and sense of self-criticism disappear, he let us catch a glimpse or two of. That he didn't bring out such a book, and that his life was spent instead, I suspect, between the frustrating editorial rooms of Lima daily papers and his "nights of bohemian investigations," is not something that surprises me today. For the truth is that, as happened to Carlitos Ney, I have seen other friends of my youth who appeared to have been called to be the princes of our republic of letters gradually become inhibited and fade away, because of that lack of conviction, that premature and profound pessimism that is the sickness par excellence, in Peru, of the best and the brightest—a curious means, it would seem, adopted by those who are worth the most, to defend themselves from the mediocrity, the frauds, and the frustrations that intellectual and artistic life offers in such an unfavorable milieu.

When we had a bit of money, instead of going to the Chinese bars on La Colmena, we used to go to a chic bohemian place: the Negro-Negro. In that basement underneath the arcades of the Plaza San Martín I felt as though I were in the Paris I dreamed of, in one of the *caves* where Juliette Greco sang, with the existentialist writers listening. The Negro-Negro was a boîte with intellectual pretensions; in it theatrical performances and recitals were given and French music was played. In the wee hours, at its tiny tables and between its walls papered with covers from *The New Yorker*, an exquisite and eccentric fauna got together: painters such as Sérvulo Gutiérrez, who had been a boxer and who one night recounted there how he had challenged a member of the armed forces to a fistfight in a taxi; actors, actresses, or musicians who'd just finished their performances, or, simply, bohemians and night owls in suits and ties. It was there, one night after many beers, that a sophisticate from Arequipa named Velando had me try a "snort," assuring me that, if I breathed in those grains of white powder, they would make my dizziness from the alcohol disappear in one fell swoop and leave me fresh and ready to go on for the rest of the night. In fact, the "snort," because it was too big a dose or because I was constitutionally allergic to it, left me in a state of nervous overexcitement, an anxiety and a malaise worse that any "downer" from drinking too much, and took away all desire to repeat that experience with drugs. (That "sniff" of cocaine, the only one I ever took in my life, was to have a melodramatic resurrection, forty years later, during the 1990 electoral campaign.)

During that summer, and because of my job at *La Crónica*, I saw a corpse for the first time in my life. The image has lingered in my memory, which brings it back to me every so often to grieve me or depress me. One afternoon, when I arrived at the paper, Becerrita sent me off to El Porvenir in search of a scoop that a "data gatherer" had just phoned in to him. The San Pablo was a miserable cheap hotel, with rooms to take hookers to, on a street that crossed the Avenida 28 de Julio, in those days a neighborhood with a bad reputation for prostitution, robbery, and mayhem. The police let me past after I'd shown them my press card with my photograph, and at the end of several dark hallways, lined on each side with symmetrical little rooms, I suddenly came upon the naked corpse of a very young mestiza who had been stabbed to death with a knife. As he photographed her from different angles, the great Ego Aguirre joked with the PIPs. The atmosphere exuded squalor and grotesque depravity, in addition to the cruelty of the underground. For several days I filled whole pages of *La Crónica* with news stories on the mysterious murder of the "night moth" of the Hotel San Pablo, investigating her life, tracking down friends and relatives of hers, going and coming amid bars, bordellos, and miserable back streets, trying to dredge up facts about her, and then writing the sort of hair-raising pieces that were the specialty of *La Crónica*.

When I went back to the local news section, I had a certain nostalgia for those lower depths that work under Becerrita had given me a glimpse of. But I didn't have time to get bored. The editor-in-chief assigned me the job of chasing down the winners of the *polla* and the *pollón* and interviewing them. The first or the second week of this hunt, we were informed that the winner of several millions was in Trujillo. They put me into a station wagon belonging to the paper, along with a photographer, and the two of us started out to track him down. At Kilometer 70 or 71 along the highway, a truck coming in the opposite direction forced our driver off the road. The car turned over once or twice on the sandy ground and I was thrown out, breaking the windshield as my body went through it. When I came to, a red station wagon, with a compassionate driver, was taking me back to Lima. They put the photographer, who also had several slight injuries, and me in a private clinic and *La Crónica* published a little box with the news of the accident, picturing us as war heroes.

A moment of grave danger came about on one of those days when I was in the clinic, when there suddenly appeared, in the room I shared with the photographer, a night moth of the Avenida Colonial, who went by the name of Magda, with whom I had been having a romance for a time. She was young, with a pretty little face, dark chestnut hair and bangs, and one night, in that brothel, I had agreed to let her offer me her services on credit (I barely had enough money for the room). We saw each other later, in the daytime, in a Crem Rica that was next to La Cabaña in the Parque de la Exposición, and we went to the movies, holding hands and kissing each other in the dark. I had seen her two or three times after that, where she worked or on the street, before her sudden appearance in my hospital room. She was sitting on my bed, alongside me, when through the window I spied my father approaching, and such fear must have showed on my face that she immediately realized that something serious might happen, and quickly got to her feet and left the room, meeting my father on the threshold. He must have thought that the young lady with all the makeup was a visitor of the photographer's, because he didn't ask me anything about her. Despite the work and the great time I was having that summer as a grownup, when confronted with the figure of my father I was still a little boy.

I mention Magda—I don't know if that was her real name—because of this anecdote, and because I believe I fell in love with her, although at the time, doubtless, I wouldn't have confessed it to any of my bohemian friends, since what man in his right mind fell in love with a hooker? That day at the clinic was the last time I saw her. A number of events followed each other in rapid succession. A few days after being let out of the hospital I had to go to Piura, and the night I went looking for her, at that house on the Avenida Colonial, she hadn't come to work. And a year later, when I came back to Lima and went nosing around to see if I could find her, the house was no longer a bordello and (as had more or less happened to me) she had become respectable.

After a month or a month and a half of working at *La Crónica*, I had a conversation with my father about my future. Just for a change, we had moved yet again, from the apartment on the Calle Porta to a little house on Juan Fanning, also in Miraflores. Since I got home very late from work—just as dawn was breaking, as a matter of fact— my father had given me the key to the house. We talked together in the dining room for about an hour, with the melodramatic solemnity that he was so fond of. As always in his presence, I felt uncomfortable and mistrustful, and, with a slight stammer, I told him that journalism was my real vocation. I would devote myself to it after finishing school. But, now that I was working on *La Crónica*, why didn't I keep my job while I went through the final grade of secondary school? Instead of going through it at Leoncio Prado, I could enroll at some state school, such as Guadalupe or Melitón Carbajal, and work and study at the same time. After that, I would enter the University of San Marcos and continue my studies without giving up my job at *La Crónica*. That way, I would be practicing my profession at the same time that I was studying.

He heard me out and then agreed: it was a good idea. The one who wasn't at all pleased by this plan was my mother. That job that kept me out of the house all night worried her terribly and made her suspect the worst (that is to say, the truth). I knew that on many a night she stayed awake, waiting for me to come home, and sometimes, half asleep, I would hear her, early in the morning, tiptoeing into my room to fold and hang up the suit that I had thrown down on the bed any which way. (After her passion for my father, my mother's other ones were for cleanliness and order. I have inherited from her the first of these: dirt, in particular the literal sort, is intolerable to me; as for order, it has never been my strong point, except where writing is concerned.) But, even though the idea that I would go on working at night at *La Crónica* while I finished the last year of secondary school frightened her, she did not dare oppose my father's decision, something that, moreover, would have been of little avail.

And so, when the accident on the highway going north happened while I was on the job—in mid-March—I had already received the reports of my grades from Leoncio Prado, announced to the military academy that I wouldn't be back, and made vague inquiries at two or three state schools about enrolling for my final year. At all of them they put me on the waiting list, and trusting that one or another of them would accept me, I forgot all about the matter. I thought that at the last moment a recommendation would open for me the doors of Guadalupe, of Melitón Carbajal, or of some other state school. (It had to be a public high school because they were free and because I imagined that they would be more lenient about my working at the same time as a journalist.)

But all these plans fell through, without my knowing it, as the doctors at the private hospital were treating me for the contusions I had received when the car turned over. Besides my mother, my aunts and uncles too were alarmed about my nightly forays. They had heard gossip here and there about my having been seen in bars or boîtes and one night, to top it all off, I ran into the most happy-go-lucky and party-loving of my uncles, Jorge, in the Negro-Negro. I was sitting at a table with Carlitos Ney, Norwin Sánchez, and the sketch artist Paco Cisneros, and there were also two or three other individuals at the table whom I hardly knew. But Uncle Jorge knew them very well, and taking me aside to have a few words with me, he told me that they were shady characters, drunks and cocaine addicts, and what was I, a mere snot-nosed kid, doing in such company? My explanations, instead of re-assuring him, worried him even more.

There was a family council and the aunts and uncles decided that I was well on the road to perdition and that something had to be done. What they decided to do was bold: to talk to my father. They never saw him and knew that he detested them. They were of the opinion that my mother's marriage had been a great misfortune, but for her sake, they had made an effort to receive my father as a guest in their homes and behave cordially toward him when they happened to run into him. He, however, stuck to his guns and did not try to hide his feelings. He never visited them. He would come by to drop my mother off at Aunt Lala's, or Aunt Gaby's, or at my grandparents', but he didn't get out of the car to say hello to them, nor did he do so at night, when he came by to take her back home. The decision to have a talk with him was a bitter pill they swallowed for the sake of what they believed to be a major consideration.

Uncle Pedro, Uncle Juan, and Uncle Jorge went to his office. I never knew how the conversation went. But I can imagine what they told him. That if I went on working at La Crónica I would never finish high school or study for a career. And that, to have any sort of future, I must leave that night job immediately.

A few days after I got out of the hospital and went back to work, I entered the editorial room at La Crónica one afternoon, and Señor Aguirre Morales remarked to me in a friendly way: "What a shame that you're leaving us, my good friend. We're going to miss you; we already feel that you're one of the family." That was how I learned that my father had just quit my job for me.

I went to his office and had only to take one look at his face—that of critical moments: more or less livid, with lips that were a little dry and slightly parted, and a fixed stare, with that little yellow glint deep down in the pupils—to know what was coming. Without informing me of my uncles' visit, he began to read me the riot act, telling me that, instead of taking a job at La Crónica to work as a responsible employee, I had come there to wallow in vice and become a degenerate. He was bellowing with rage and I was sure he was about to beat me. But he didn't hit me. He confined himself to giving me a few days' time to show him the registration certificate from the school in which I was going to finish my last year of secondary school. And, naturally, I wasn't to get any bright ideas such as claiming that there was no vacancy for me in any state school.

And so, overnight, I went from a frequenter of saloons and dens of iniquity to a forlorn scholar in search of classrooms in which to finish high school. I had lost too much time. It was now the end of March and in none of the schools that I made the rounds of was there a vacancy. And then I had one of the best ideas in my life. I went to the main telephone office and called my Uncle Lucho, in Piura. I told him what was going on. Uncle Lucho, who, ever since I was a small boy, had been solving the family's problems, solved this one as well. He knew the head of the San Miguel state school, near his house, and would go have a word with him immediately. Two hours later, he called me back at the main telephone office to tell me that I had already been enrolled, that classes began on such and such a day, that Aunt Olga was happy that I was coming to live with them. Did I need money for a ticket to Piura?

I presented myself at my father's, swallowing hard, convinced that he would shout abuse at me and refuse to let me go to Piura. But, on the contrary, it struck him as a very good idea, and he even allowed himself to tell me something that whetted my appetite: "I can already see you working as a journalist in Piura at the same time that you're studying. Don't ever try to pull my leg."

So why not? Why not work on some newspaper in Piura at the same time that I was finishing school? I asked my friends on *La Crónica*, and the kindly headline writer, Alfonso Delboy, who knew the owner of *La Industria*, wrote a letter of recommendation to him for me. And Aguirre Morales another.

The last farewell was said as we celebrated my birthday, on the 28th of March 1952, over beers with Carlitos Ney, Milton von Hesse, and Norwin Sánchez Geny, in a restaurant on the Calle Capón, Lima's Chinatown. It was a gloomy farewell, because they were friends I had come to appreciate and perhaps because I had an intuition that I would never again share with them those feverish experiences with which I had brought my early youth to an end. And so it turned out. The following year, when I came back to Lima, I didn't hang out with them again or frequent the same places, which my memory would nonetheless preserve, with a bittersweet taste, and which I tried to re-create long afterwards with retouches dreamed up by my imagination, in *Conversation in The Cathedral*.

With my last paycheck from *La Crónica* I bought a ticket to Piura at the Cruz de Chalpón bus company. And my mama, her eyes filled with tears, packed my suitcase, in which I put all the books I owned and the manuscript of my little play.

I spent the twenty-four hours of the trip, through the endless deserts of the northern coast, in a rattletrap bus, torn between opposed feelings: a bit sad at having left that adventurous and somewhat literary job at *La Crónica* and the good friends it had brought me, but happy at the same time at the prospect of seeing my Uncle Lucho again, and curious and excited, imagining what this second stay in remote Piura would be like.

EIGHT

The Freedom Movement

THE Freedom Movement was organized in a painter's studio. At the end of September 1987, those of us who had planned the Meetings for Freedom were summoned to Fernando de Szyszlo's by Freddy Cooper. There, amid half-finished paintings and masks and pre-Hispanic feather cloaks, we exchanged ideas about the future. The success of the fight against Alan García's attempt to nationalize the banks had filled us with enthusiasm and hope. Peru was changing, then. Should we return to our usual occupations, telling ourselves that our task was fulfilled, or was it worth our while to make this nascent organization a permanent one, with an eye to the coming elections?

The dozen friends gathered together there agreed to continue our political activity. We would create something of broader scope and more flexible than a political party, a *movement*, to be known as the Movimiento Libertad, that would bring together those independents who had mobilized against state control and put down roots in the popular sectors, in particular among the tradesmen and small businessmen working within the so-called informal or parallel economy, a form of popular black market capitalism. They were an example of the fact that, despite the triumph of the ideology of state control among the elite of the country, an instinct for free enterprise existed among the Peruvian people. At the same time that it was attempting to organize these sectors, Libertad would draw up a thoroughgoing reform program and modernize Peru's political culture, opposing both socialist collectivism and mercantilist capitalism by putting forward a liberal policy.

Of the goals we set ourselves in that hours-long conversation under the bewitching spell of Szyszlo's paintings, the only one we completely achieved was the program. The Plan for Governing that the team headed by Luis Bustamante Belaunde had been doing the preliminary work on was what we came up with that morning: a realistic program for putting an end to privileges, government handouts, protectionism, and state control, opening up the country to the world and creating a free society in which everyone would have access to the market and live under the protection of the law. This Plan for Governing, full of ideas, with a firm determination to take advantage of the opportunities of our time so that Peruvians of every estate could attain a decent life, is one of the things that make me proud of those three years. The serious commitment to the work at hand on the part of Lucho Bustamante, of Raúl Salazar (who, despite the fact that he belonged to SODE and not to Libertad, was the head of the economics team of the Democratic Front), and of the dozens of men and women who, along with them, devoted countless days and nights to drafting the first rough outline for a new country, was a marvelous source of encouragement for me. Each time I attended the meetings of the executive committee for the Plan for Governing, or one of the specialized committees, even the most technical ones—such as those on reform in the mining sector, customs, the port authority, administration, or the judicial system—politics ceased to be that frantic, inane, and often sordid activity that took up most of my time and became instead a task requiring intellect, technical knowledge, the comparing of ideas, imagination, idealism, generosity.

Of all the social groups that we did our best to attract to the Freedom Movement, the one we had the most success with was the one which produced those engineers, architects, attorneys, physicians, entrepreneurs, economists who made up the committees of the Plan for Governing. Most of them had never been in politics before and had no intention of being politically active in the future. They loved their professions and wanted only to be able to practice them successfully, in a Peru different from the one that they could see falling apart before their eyes. Though they were hesitant at first, we eventually managed to persuade them that only with the cooperation of people like themselves could we make Peruvian politics more decent and more effective.

Between that meeting in Szyszlo's studio and March 15, 1988, when we opened the headquarters of the Freedom Movement, in Magdalena del Mar, there intervened five months of exhausting efforts to attract supporters. We worked long and hard, but unsystematically, feeling our way. Nobody in the original group had any experience as an activist or a gift for organization. And I to an even lesser degree than my friends. Having spent my life in a study, making up stories, was not the best possible preparation for founding a political movement. And my right arm in this task, a faithful and beloved friend, Miguel Cruchaga, the first secretary general of Libertad, who had lived shut up in his architect's studio and was most unsociable, was in no position to make up for my ineffectiveness. But not for lack of dedication: he was the first, in a gesture that deserves to be called heroic, to give up his profession in order to devote himself full time to the Movement. Later others would do the same, making out as best they could or living in near poverty, with only the small amount of financial help that Libertad managed to give them. From public squares, we moved on to private houses in those last months of 1987 and the early ones of 1988. Friends or sympathizers invited young people of their neighborhoods in and Miguel Cruchaga and I talked to them, answered their questions, and provoked discussions that went on till late at night. One of those meetings took place at the home of Gladys and Carlos Urbina, who would later be great guiding spirits of the mobilization campaign. And another one at the home of Bertha Vega Alvear, who, with a group of women, would found, shortly thereafter, Acción Solidaria, the Solidarity program sponsored by Libertad.

It was also one of our goals to recover—to bring back to life—those intellectuals, journalists, or politicians who, in the past, had defended liberal positions, arguing against socialists and populists and countering, by promoting the theory of the free market, the tide of paternalism and protectionism that had submerged Peru. In order to attain that goal we organized the Jornadas por la Libertad: Freedom Days. They lasted from nine in the morning till nine at night. There were talks whose purpose was to show, with statistics, how greatly the various nationalizations had impoverished the country and increased discrimination and injustice, and how the policy of government intervention, besides destroying industry, went against the interests of consumers and favored small-scale mafias which the system of quotas and preferential dollar exchange rates enriched without their having to compete or to serve the public. And there were talks devoted to explaining the "informal economy" as an answer on the part of the poor to the discrimination of which they were the object, since proper legal licensing for even the smallest enterprise or business activity was expensive and selective, available only to those who had money or political pull. And to defending those itinerant peddlers, artisans, tradesmen, and small-scale businessmen, of modest origins, working as *informales*, who in many fields—transportation and housing in particular—had proved to be more efficient than the state and sometimes even more so than the large-scale, full-time entrepreneurs who were legally licensed.

During the Freedom Days, the criticism of socialism and mercantilist capitalism endeavored to point out the deep-seated identity of two systems which, beneath their divergences, were related by virtue of the predominant role played in both by the state, the "planner" of economic activity and the dispenser of privileges. A recurrent theme was the necessity of reforming that state—by strengthening it, by streamlining and paring away its excesses, by opening it up to technology, and by making it moral—as a fundamental requirement for development.

There was always a talk too on those countries of the Third World to which market-oriented policies and the promotion of exports and of private enterprise had brought rapid growth, countries such as the four "Asian dragons"—South Korea, Taiwan, Hong Kong and Singapore—or Chile. In all those countries, the more or less liberal economic reforms were in flagrant contradiction to the repressive and dictatorial activity of their governments, and in the course of the Freedom Days we did our best to show that this contradiction was neither acceptable nor necessary. Freedom had to be understood as something indivisible, politically and economically. The Freedom Movement must win an electoral mandate for these ideas that would allow us to concretize them in a democratic civilian regime. A great liberal reform was possible under democratic rule, provided that a clear majority voted for it. To achieve this, it was indispensable to be open and aboveboard, explaining in detail what we wanted to do and the price that it would exact.

We held the first Freedom Day in the Hotel Crillón, in Lima, on February 6, 1988; the second, devoted to agrarian subjects, at the San José hacienda in Chincha on February 18; on February 26, in Arequipa; a Young People's Day, in Lima, on March 5; on March 12, a day in the young town of Huáscar, on the informal economy; and on March 14, a Women's Day, in which there participated for the first time an economist who became yet another of the leaders of Libertad: Beatriz Merino.

During these Freedom Days we managed to line up hundreds of supporters, but their greatest importance lay in the field of ideas. For many of those who attended them it was unheard of for a political organization in Peru to speak out, in the most straightforward terms, in favor of a free market, to defend capitalism as more efficient and fairer than socialism and as the only system capable of safeguarding people's freedoms, to see in private enterprise the driving force of development and call for a "culture based on success" instead of on resentment and the state handouts advocated by Marxists and conservatives alike, even though their rhetoric was different. The word *capitalism* had come to be taboo, except to denigrate it. (I received strong recommendations from leaders of AP and the PPC never to use it in speeches.)

Those who attended the Freedom Days were divided into study and discussion groups of eight or ten, and then, once the explanatory talks had been given, we held a general meeting. When it was over, Miguel Cruchaga, who was the one who worked out the format of the Freedom Days, gave me an enthusiastic introduction and I spoke, and we ended the Jornada by singing that song composed for the demonstration in the Plaza San Martín which had become the theme song of Libertad.

The distinction between "movement" and "party" that had taken up a great deal of our time in Szyszlo's studio turned out to be too subtle for our political habits. For despite its name, the Movimiento Libertad functioned from the start as something indistinguishable from a party. The vast majority of its members took it to be one and there was no way to disabuse them of this notion. Laughable situations came up, indicative of customs deeply rooted in the national psychology, owing to the tradition of *clientelismo*—party patronage. Since the mere idea of the *carnet*—the individual membership book carried by party members—was associated with this system, which both the AP and the APRA administrations had put into practice, giving their own adherents (who could show their *carnets*) preference when it came to government jobs and favors, we decided that the Movement would not have *carnets*. Recording one's name on a list written down on a plain sheet of paper was all that would be required to sign up as a member. It was impossible to get this idea across in the popular sectors, where the members of Libertad felt that their status was inferior to that of the Apristas, the Communists, the socialists, and so on, who were able to show off impressive-looking *carnets* full of seals and little flags. The pressure put on those of us on the executive committee to give out *carnets*—brought to bear by the section for young people, by Mobilization, by Solidarity, and by the committees in the provinces and the *departamentos*—was impossible to turn aside. We explained over and over again that we wanted to be different from other parties, that if we came to power we wanted to keep a Freedom Movement *carnet* from being used in the future as a symbol for abuses, but it was no use. Then I suddenly discovered that our committees in certain city districts and towns had begun to give out *carnets*, loaded with more and more signatures and bright-colored emblems, and some of them even bearing my photograph. Considerations of principle collided with the argument of activists: "If they aren't given a *carnet*, they won't sign up." So at the end of the campaign there was not just *one* Movimiento Libertad *carnet* but a whole heterogeneous collection of them, invented by various local headquarters to suit themselves.

The philosopher Francisco Miró Quesada, an old friend, who came to visit me every so often or wrote me long letters to offer me political suggestions, had been a member of Popular Action at one time. His experiences had led him to the depressing conclusion that in Peru it was highly unrealistic to give a political party a democratic structure. "Whether rightist or leftist, our parties fill up with scoundrels," he sighed. Libertad did not fill up with scoundrels, since, to our great good fortune, those persons whom we caught doing something dishonest—invariably something involving money—and whom we were obliged to ask to leave the Movement, were scarcely more than a handful in a group that, shortly before the first round of voting, had over a hundred thousand members. But it never became the modern, popular, democratic institution that I had dreamed of. From the very start it contracted the vices of Peruvian political parties: bossism, cliques, factionalism. There were groups that took over committees and encysted themselves in them, allowing no one else to participate. Or groups were paralyzed by internal squabbles over trivial matters, which drove away valuable people, who, although they sympathized with our ideas, did not care to waste their time in intrigues and petty rivalries.

There were *departamentos*, such as Arequipa, in which the organizing group, a tightly knit team of young men and women, managed to create an efficient infrastructure, which would produce members of Libertad like Óscar Urviola, who later was to become a first-class congressman. Or such as Ica, where thanks to the prestige and the decency of the farmer Alfredo Elías, Libertad attracted valuable people. And something similar happened in Piura, owing to the deeply committed idealism of José Tejero. But in other *departamentos*, such as La Libertad, the original group split into two and later on three rival factions that fought among themselves for three whole years over the leadership of the departmental committee, and this naturally kept the membership from increasing. And there were several others, such as Puno, where we made the mistake of entrusting the organization to people without ability or dependability. I will not forget the impression it made on me to note, on a visit to the communities of the Altiplano, that our departmental secretary in Puno treated the peasants with the arrogance of the old-time political bosses.

That Libertad relied in certain places on such unsuitable leaders has an explanation (although it does not constitute a justification). Support in the provinces came to us from groups or individuals who offered to help lay the foundations of the Movement; in our impatience to cover the entire country, we accepted those offers without screening them, sometimes making precisely the right choice and at others making monumental errors. That should have been corrected by having the national leaders make regular swings around the interior so as to perform on the spot that basic, unsung, often boring missionary work of the activist, indispensable if the goal is to build a solid political organization. We didn't do this, at least not in the first year of our existence, and it was owing to this that in many places Libertad was born crooked, and later on it proved to be difficult to twist it back into the proper shape. I was aware of what was going to happen but could do nothing about it. My admonitions, whether plaintive or enraged, in the executive and political committees, that the leaders must go out into the provinces had little effect. They traveled with me to appear at rallies, but lightning visits of that sort did not further the work of organization. The reason they resisted was not so much the fear of terrorist attack as it was the endless hardships which, owing to the near collapse of the country, they would be forced to endure wherever they went. I told my friends that their propensity for the sedentary life would have regrettable consequences. And that was how it turned out. With a few exceptions the organization of Libertad in the interior proved to be far from representative. And in our committees as well there reigned and handed down decisions in thundering tones that immortal figure: the cacique.

I met many of these political bosses in those three years, and whether they were from the coastal regions, the mountains, or the jungle, they all seemed to be cut from the same cloth by the same tailor. They were, or had been, or inevitably would become senators, representatives, mayors, prefects, subprefects. Their energy, their abilities, their Machiavellian machinations, and their imaginations were concentrated on just one goal: to attain, to hang on to, or to recover a modicum of power through every means, licit or illicit, at their disposal. They were all ardent followers of the moral philosophy summed up in the precept: "To live without money from the state is to live in error." All of them had a little court or retinue of relatives, friends, and protégés whom they made out to be popular leaders—of teachers, of peasants, of workers, of technicians—and placed on the committees they presided over. They had all changed ideologies and parties the way one changes one's shirt, and they had all been, or at some point would become, Apristas, populists, and Communists (the three principal sources of sinecures in the history of Peru). They were always there, waiting for me, on the roads, in the stations, at the airports, with bouquets of flowers, bands, and bags of herbs to throw for good luck, and theirs were the first arms to reach out and hug me wherever I arrived, with the same affection with which they had embraced General Velasco, Belaunde, Barrantes, Alan García, and they always managed things in such a way as to be at my side on the speakers' platform, microphone in hand, introducing me to the audience and offering to organize rallies and doing everything possible to be seen with me in photographs in the newspapers and on television. They were always the ones who, when a rally was over, tried to carry me about in triumph on their shoulders—a ridiculous custom of Peruvian politicians in imitation of bullfighters, and one that I always refused to allow, even if I occasionally had to defend myself with a good swift kick—and they were the ones who sponsored the inevitable receptions, banquets, dinners, lunches, barbecues, which they made into even grander occasions by delivering flowery speeches. Usually they were attorneys, but among them there were also owners of garages or transportation companies, or former policemen or ex-members of the military, and I would even go so far as to swear that they all looked alike, with their tight-fitting suits, their ridiculous little hairline mustaches of present, past, or future members of Congress, and their thunderous, saccharine, high-flown eloquence, ready to rain down in torrents at the slightest opportunity.

I remember one of them, a perfect specimen of the species, in Tumbes. Going a bit bald, in his fifties, with a cheerful smile, a gold tooth, he was introduced to me on the first political junket I made to that department, in December 1987. He climbed out of a car that was belching smoke, with an entourage of half a dozen people, whom he defined in these words: "The pioneers of the Freedom Movement in Tumbes, Doctor. And I, sir, am the helmsman, at your service." I found out later that at one time he had been a "helmsman" of the APRA, and after that of Popular Action, a party he deserted in order to serve the military dictatorship. And after going through our ranks, he contrived to become a leader of Francisco Diez Canseco's UCI (Unión Cívica Independiente: Independent Civic Union) and, finally, of our ally SODE, which put him up as a regional candidate of the Democratic Front.

Battling with political bosses, tolerating political bosses, using political bosses was something I never learned how to do. They doubtless read on my face the disgust and the impatience they aroused in me, representing as they did, at the provincial level, everything that I would have liked politics in Peru *not* to be. But this did not prevent the committees of Libertad in many provinces from falling into the hands of local bosses. How to change something that was so visceral a part of our political idiosyncrasy?

The organization of Libertad in Lima worked better. The first departmental secretary, Víctor Guevara, and his team whose guiding light was a brilliant young man who had just received his degree in architecture, Pedro Guevara, worked with all their might, bringing together the members of the Movement in each district of the city, using the best people to constitute the first nuclei and making plans for the elections. When Rafael Rey took Víctor Guevara's place, we had more than fifty thousand members in the capital, from almost every district in the city. The Movement had much deeper roots in the neighborhoods with high and middle incomes than in the poorer districts, but over the months that followed we managed to make rather impressive inroads in the latter as well.

I still have a very vivid image of our first attempt to organize in the young towns. A group of residents of Huáscar, one of the poorest shantytowns in San Juan de Lurigancho, wrote a letter to Miguel Cruchaga asking for information about the Movement, and we suggested to them that we organize a Freedom Day there where they lived. We went out one Saturday in March 1988. When we arrived at the soup kitchen, on the edge of a stretch of stony ground, there was no one there. Little by little, some hundred people showed up: barefoot women, suckling babes, curious onlookers, a rather tipsy man who kept cheering for the APRA, dogs that ran in and out between the legs of the people who were giving explanatory talks. And there too were María Prisca, Octavio Mendoza, and Juvencio Rojas, who a few weeks later would make up the first Libertad committee in Peru. Felipe Ortiz de Zevallos explained how, by debureaucratizing the state and by simplifying the burdensome legal system, tradesmen and craftsmen of the informal economy could work legally, with proper permits accessible to everyone, and spoke of the stimulus that this would be for people's welfare. We had also brought along a prosperous businessman, who had begun by doing his buying and selling in the informal economy, like many of those present, so that they, who knew everything there was to know about frustration and failure, would see that success too was possible.

A group of women who, from the days of the campaign against state ownership, had been working with tireless enthusiasm for Libertad, went out with us to San Juan de Lurigancho. These women had painted slogans and made banners, transported people to and from public squares, collected signatures, and in those days swept floors, scrubbed down walls, and nailed doors and windows in place so that the house that we had just rented on the Avenida Javier Prado would be in fit shape for the opening, on March 15. This building, the headquarters of the Movement, would fulfill its function thanks especially to women like them, all volunteers—Cecilia, María Rosa, Anita, Teche . . . —who stayed on there morning, noon, and night, signing up members, working the computer, writing letters, taking care of the secretarial work, the purchasing of supplies, the cleaning, the complex machinery of a political headquarters.

Six of them, headed by María Teresa Belaunde, decided, in those last days of the summer of 1988, to work in the new slum settlements and shantytowns on the outskirts of Lima. In that immense urban belt where émigrés from the Andes end up—peasants fleeing from drought, hunger, terror—a person can read, from the building material of the hovels—bricks, wood, sheets of tin, and straw mats—as though they were geological strata, the age of the migrations that are the best barometer of the great shift of the nation's population toward the capital and of the country's economic failure. It is in these *pueblos jóvenes*, the young towns, that the poor and the wretched who make up two-thirds of the population of Lima are to be found. And it is there that the problems faced by Peru are experienced in their starkest reality: the lack of housing, of potable water and proper sewage disposal, of work, of medical facilities, of food, of transportation, of education, of public order, of safety. But that world, so full of suffering and violence, is also ablaze with energy, with ingenuity and the will to survive: it was there in those shantytowns that the new popular capitalism, which came to be called the "informal," or "parallel," economy, had sprung up—a phenomenon that could be transformed, if one became politically aware of what it represented, into the driving force of a liberal revolution.

And so Acción Solidaria—the Solidarity program—was born, with my wife Patricia as president of it all through the campaign. At the beginning there were only six women who were members and two and a half years later there were three hundred of them, and in the whole of Peru some five hundred, since the example of the women members of Libertad spread to Arequipa, Trujillo, Cajamarca, Piura, and other cities. Theirs was not charity work but political militancy that translated into concrete facts the philosophy according to which the poor had to be given the means to emerge from their poverty by themselves. Acción Solidaria helped organize workshops, businesses, companies, gave technical training courses and instruction in arts and crafts, arranged for credit for public works projects chosen by popular vote of the people who lived in the neighborhood, and offered technical and administrative advice as these projects were under way. Thanks to its efforts, dozens of stores, artisans' workshops, and small industries appeared in the neediest districts of Lima, along with countless mothers' clubs and day-care centers. And schools and medical dispensaries were built, streets and avenues were opened up, water wells were put in, and an irrigation system was even installed in the peasant community of Ji-camarca. All with no official support whatsoever but, rather, with the undisguised hostility of that state which Alan García's administration had turned into a subsidiary of the APRA.

Just as in my meetings with the government planning committees, my visits to the workshops in cooking, mechanics, sewing, weaving, leather working, and so on, to the classes in reading and writing, nursing, running a business, or family planning, and to the construction projects sponsored by Acción Solidaria were a tonic to me that revived my enthusiasm. Such visits reassured me that I had done the right thing by entering politics.

I have been speaking of the *women* of Acción Solidaria, because for the most part it was women who took charge of that branch of the Movement, although many men worked hand in hand with them: Dr. José Draxl, for instance, who coordinated the basic courses on health, the engineer Carlos Hara, responsible for the community development projects, and tireless Pedro Guevara, who took over the work in the most remote and depressed areas as though they were a religious apostolate. The Solidarity program changed the life of many of the women members of Libertad, since before joining the Movement very few of them had had the same vocation for social service and the same practical experience in the field that the main leader of this part of the Movement, María Teresa Belaunde, did. The great majority of them were housewives, from families with moderate or high incomes, who up until then had lived a rather empty and even frivolous life, blind and deaf to the seething volcano that is the Peru of underdevelopment and wretched poverty. Beginning to rub elbows every day with people who lived amid ignorance, sickness, and unemployment, people who were the victims of multiple abuses—taking on a commitment that was ethical as well as political and social—transformed them in a short time into individuals who were clearheaded about the Peruvian drama and aroused in many of them the determination to do something concrete. I include my own wife among them. I saw Patricia transformed by working in Acción Solidaria and in what would be its best fruit, the PAS (Programa de Apoyo Social: Program for Social Aid), an ambitious project intended to counterbalance the sacrifices that the stabilization of the economy would call for among the poorest segments of society. Even though she so thoroughly detested politics, she became passionately devoted to work in the young towns, in which she spent many hours during those years, readying herself to help me in the task of governing our country.

The women of the Solidarity program lacked a political vocation, but I was hoping that at least some of them would assume public responsibilities later on. With individuals like that, the whole nature of Peruvian politics could be changed. Seeing what they were doing, discovering how quickly they became thoroughly familiar with the entire range of problems of marginality and transformed themselves into excellent social promoters of social change—without them the Movement would never have put down roots in the young towns— was a refreshing contrast to the shady dealings of provincial political bosses or the petty intrigues within the Democratic Front. When, at the beginning of 1990, we drew up the lists of congressional candidates, I did my best, using the authority granted me by the first Libertad Congress, to convince two of the most dedicated leaders of Acción Solidaria, Diana de Belmont and Nany Bonazzi, to be our candidates for seats representing Lima. But both refused to abandon their work in the southern districts of the city for a seat in Congress.

From the days of the Plaza San Martín on, the subject of money had come up. Organizing rallies, opening party headquarters, going on tours about the country, setting up a national infrastructure, and keeping a campaign going for three years costs a good deal of money. Traditionally, in Peru, election campaigns provide an opportunity to raise money, under cover of which part of it ends up in the pockets of those on the take, who abound in all parties, and in many cases frequent them with this end in view. There are no laws regulating the financing of parties or of political campaigns and even when there are such laws, they are a dead letter. In Peru, such laws do not even exist as yet. Individuals and companies make discreet contributions to various candidates—it is not unusual for them to give money to several different ones at the same time, according to the candidates' standing in public opinion polls—as an investment in the future, so as to assure themselves of the ensuing privileges that are the daily bread of mercantilism: import licenses, tax exemptions, concessions, monopolies, commissions, that entire discriminatory framework that keeps an economy that is under government control functioning. The entrepreneur or industrialist who does not collaborate knows that tomorrow the winning party can get even with him by administrative means and that he will be at a disadvantage in comparison with his competitors.

All this, like the shady deals under cover of the power of those who occupy the presidency, the ministries, and important posts in the administration, is something so widespread that public opinion has come to resign itself to it as though it were a decree of fate: is there any sense in protesting against the movement of heavenly bodies or the law of gravitation? Corruption, illegal dealings, using a public post to line one's pockets, have been congenital to Peruvian politics since time immemorial. And during Alan García's administration, all this beat every previous record.

I had promised myself to put an end to this epiphenomenon of Peruvian underdevelopment, because without a moralization of power and of politicians democracy would not survive in Peru or would go on being a caricature. And also for a more personal reason: the thieves and the thievery associated with politics make me sick to my stomach. It is a human weakness I am unable to tolerate. Stealing while occupying a government post in a poor country, where democracy is still in diapers, has always struck me as an aggravating circumstance of the crime thus committed. Nothing takes away the prestige of democracy and works so unrelentingly for its downfall as corruption. Something in me rebels, beyond all reason, when I am confronted with this criminal use of power that has been obtained thanks to the votes of naïve and hopeful people, in order to fatten one's own bank account and those of one's bosom buddies. It was one of the reasons why my opposition to Alan García was so unrelenting: because under his administration political graft became the general rule in Peru, to extremes that made a person's head swim.

The subject sometimes woke me up at night, in a fit of anxiety. If I were president, how could I keep thieves from doing as they pleased in my administration? I talked the matter over countless times with Patricia, with Miguel Cruchaga and other friends in Libertad. Doing away with state interventionism in the economy would, naturally, reduce graft. It would no longer be ministers or important officials in ministries who would decide, through decrees, the success or failure of businessmen, but consumers. It would no longer be bureaucrats who would fix the value of foreign currencies, but the market. There would be no more import or export quotas. And the privatization of state enterprises would drastically reduce the possibilities for graft and peculation on the part of bureaucrats and government officials. But until a genuine, functioning market economy existed, there would be any number of chances for underhanded deals. And even later on, power would always give the person who held it a chance to sell something under the table and enable him to reap a profit for himself from the privileged information that any government official possesses. An efficient and incorruptible judiciary is the best check against such excesses. But our system of justice had also been eaten away by venality, particularly in recent years, when the salary of judges had been reduced, in real terms, to a mere pittance. And President García, as a precaution against what the future might bring, had filled the judiciary with people devoted to him. In this field, too, we would have to be prepared, as in the fight to establish a free market economy, to wage a war without quarter. But winning this war would be more difficult than winning the other one, for in this one the enemy was not only on the side of our adversaries. It was crouching among our own followers.

I made a conscious decision not to find out who had given donations and contributions to Libertad and to the Democratic Front, nor how much the sums donated amounted to, so as not to find myself, later on, if I were president, unconsciously predisposed in favor of the donors. And I made it a rule that only one person would be authorized to receive financial contributions to the campaign: Felipe Thorndike Beltrán. Pipo Thorndike, a petroleum engineer, an entrepreneur, and an agricultural expert, had been one of the victims of General Velasco's dictatorship, which had expropriated all his holdings. He had been obliged to go into exile. While he was abroad he built his businesses and his fortune back up, and in 1980, with a stubbornness as great as his love for his native land, he returned to Peru with his money and his determination to work with a will. I had confidence in his honesty, which I knew to be as great as his generosity—he was another of those who, ever since the days of the Plaza San Martín, had devoted himself to working full time alongside me—and that was why I entrusted such a thankless and time-consuming task to him. And I set up a committee of people of unquestionable probity to supervise the expenditures of the campaign: Freddy Cooper, Miguel Cruchaga, Fernando de Szyszlo, Miguel Vega Alvear, who were sometimes given a helping hand by the administrative secretary of the Freedom Movement, Rocío Cillóniz. * I forbade all of them to give me any information whatsoever about what was received and what was spent, and laid down only the following rule: accept no money from foreign governments or from companies (all donations were to be made on a personal basis). These conditions of mine were fulfilled to the letter. I was very seldom consulted or informed about the subject. (One of the rare exceptions was the day that Pipo, deeply moved, could not keep himself from commenting to me that the head of government planning for the Front, Luis Bustamante Belaunde, had turned over to him the $40,000 that a group of businessmen had made certain he received so as to give him a helping hand in his campaign for a seat in the Senate.) The few times that, during an interview, someone mentioned the possibility of monetary aid being offered me, I interrupted him and explained that the financial circuits of Libertad and of the Democratic Front did not run through my house.

Between the first and second round of voting, one of the schemes thought up by the government to slander us consisted in having the Aprista and Communist majority in Congress appoint a committee that would summon the candidates before it to reveal how much their campaign expenditures amounted to and the sources of their financial funds. I remember the skeptical looks on the faces of the senators on that committee when I explained to them that I couldn't tell them how much we had spent on the campaign because I didn't know and gave them the reasons why I hadn't wanted to know. Once the second round was over, and despite the fact that no law existed that required us to do so, through Felipe Thorndike and the head of the campaign of the Front, Freddy Cooper, we informed that committee of the amount that we had spent. And that was how I too learned that in those three years we had received and spent the equivalent of some four and a half million dollars (three-quarters of which went for TV ads).

* Unlike the first four, whose loyalty I have no way of thanking them for, the moment we lost the elections Rocío Cillóniz hastened to put out a de luxe scandal sheet, whose goal, in the brief time that the disaffection of its readers enabled it to survive, was to serve as a mouthpiece for renegades from Libertad.

This figure, modest by comparison with other Latin American campaigns—if one thinks, for instance, of Venezuela or Brazil—is, of course, a high one for Peru. But it is far from the astronomical sums that, according to our adversaries, we squandered in our efforts to win. (One United Left congressman, reputed to be an honest man, Agustín Haya de la Torre, stated, without one hair of his mustache trembling: "The Front has already spent more than forty million dollars.")

We held the first congress of Libertad in the Colegio San Agustín in Lima, between April 14 and 16, 1989. It was organized by a committee headed by one of my most faithful friends, Luis Miró Quesada Garland, who, despite his formidable repugnance for politics, worked with me day and night for three years in a spirit of self-sacrifice. We elected him honorary president of the congress, to which delegates came from all over Peru. In the weeks before, there had been elections within the Movement to choose the members of the congress, and the Lima districts and neighborhoods participated enthusiastically. At the opening ceremonies, on the night of the 14th, the district committees arrived with orchestras and musical groups, and the gaiety of the young people turned the ceremony into a party. Instead of delivering my speech extemporaneously, it seemed to me that the occasion—in addition to the opening of this first congress, with Belaunde and Bedoya we had formally set up the Democratic Front, at Popular Action's Asociación Perú, and SODE had joined the alliance—demanded that I write it beforehand and read it aloud.

Aside from this speech, I wrote only three others beforehand, though I improvised and delivered hundreds of others. During tours of the interior and the various districts of Lima I spoke several times each day, in the morning and at night, and in the last weeks there were rallies that took place at the rate of three or four a day. In order to keep my throat in good condition, Bedoya advised me to chew whole cloves between one speech and the next, and the physician who accompanied me—there were two or three of them, who took turns on duty, along with a small emergency team in case there was an attempt on my life—kept stuffing lozenges down my gullet or handing me the throat spray. I tried not to talk between rallies, so as to give my throat irritation time to go away. But even so it was sometimes impossible to keep my voice from turning hoarse or getting clogged up with phlegm. (In the jungle, late one afternoon, I arrived at the town of

La Rioja with almost no voice left. And the moment I began speaking a stiff breeze came up that finished the job of ruining my vocal cords. In order to finish my speech, I had to beat myself on the chest, like Tarzan.)

Speaking in public squares was something I had never done before the Plaza San Martín. And it is something for which having given classes and lectures is of no help, and may even be a hindrance. For in Peru political oratory has remained at the romantic stage. The politician goes up onto the platform to charm, to seduce, to lull, to bill and coo. His musical phrasing is more important than his ideas, his gestures more important than his concepts. Form is everything: it can either make or destroy the content of what he says. The good orator may say absolutely nothing, but he says it with style. What matters to his audience is for him to sound good and look good. The logic, the rational order, the consistency, the critical acumen of what he is saying generally get in the way of his achieving that effect, which is attained above all through impressionistic images and metaphors, ham acting, fancy turns of phrase, and defiant remarks. The good Latin American political orator bears a much closer resemblance to a bullfighter or a rock singer than to a lecturer or a professor: his communication with the audience is achieved by way of instinct, emotion, sentiment, rather than by way of intelligence.

Michel Leiris compared the art of writing to bullfighting, a fine allegory for expressing the risk that the poet or the prose writer ought to be prepared to run when it comes time to confront the blank page before him. But the image is even more appropriate for the politician who, from atop a few boards, on a balcony, or in the atrium of a church, faces a crowd worked up to fever pitch. What he has before him is something as massive as a bull bred for the arena, an awesome creature and at the same time one so ingenuous and manipulable that it can be made to move in whatever direction he chooses, providing he makes skillful passes with the red cape of intonation and gesture.

That night in the Plaza San Martín I was surprised to discover how erratic, how fitful the attention of a crowd is and how elementary its psychology, the ease with which it can be made to pass from laughter to anger, be moved, be driven into a frenzy, be reduced to tears, in unison with the speaker. And how difficult it is to make contact with the reason, rather than with the passions, of those who attend a rally.

If the language of politics all over the world is made up of platitudes, this is even more the case where it is a custom centuries old for public speaking to be an incantatory art.

I did what I could not to perpetuate that custom and did my best to use the speakers' platforms to promote certain ideas and to disclose the program of the Front, avoiding demagoguery and clichés. To my way of thinking, those public squares were the ideal place to put across once and for all the fact that to vote for me was to vote for certain concrete reforms, so that there would be no misunderstandings concerning what I intended to do or the sacrifices that it would cost.

But I don't believe that I succeeded in putting across either of these two things. For Peruvians did not vote for *ideas* in the elections, and despite all my precautions I very often noted—especially when fatigue got the better of me—that all at once I too was resorting to ham acting or an unexpected remark to milk applause from the audience. In the two months of the campaign for the second round, I tried to sum up our proposed program in just a few ideas, which I repeated, again and again, in the most simple and direct way, enveloped in familiar popular imagery. But the weekly polls showed each time that the decision as to which candidate to vote for was made, in the overwhelming majority of cases, on the basis of the personalities of the people running for office and out of obscure impulses, and never on account of the programs the voters were offered.

Of all the speeches I gave, I remember as the best ones, or in any event the least bad ones, two that I was able to prepare in the hospitable garden of my friends Maggie and Carlos Ferreyros—with no body-guards, reporters, or telephones—for the launching of my candidacy, in the Plaza de Armas, the main square of Arequipa, on June 4, 1989, and the one closing the campaign, on the Paseo de la República, in Lima, on April 14, 1990, the most personal one of all. And also, perhaps, the brief address, on June 10, before the grief-stricken crowd that rushed to the doors of the headquarters of Libertad as soon as it became known that we had lost.

At the congress of the Movement there were speeches, but there was also an ideological debate which quite possibly did not interest all the delegates as much as it did me. Was the Freedom Movement going to promote a market economy or a *social* market economy? Enrique Ghersi defended the first thesis and Luis Bustamante Belaunde the second, in an intelligent interchange that caused a number of those attending to speak up in favor of one formula or the other. The discussion was more than a semantic itch. By way of the sympathy or the antipathy provoked by the adjective *social*, the heterogeneous composition of the Movement became clearly evident. Not only liberals had signed up as members of it, but also conservatives, Christian Socialists, Social Democrats, and a goodly number—the majority perhaps—without any ideological position, with an abstract loyalty to democracy or with no more than a negative definition: they were not Apristas or Communists and saw in us an alternative to whatever it was they detested or feared.

The most closely knit group and the one most closely identified with liberalism—or so it appeared at the time; things would change later —was one made up of young people between the ages of twenty and thirty, who had had their first passage at arms as journalists working together at *La Prensa* when that daily was released from state control by Belaunde in 1980, under the tutelage of two journalists who, for quite some time, had been defending the free market and combating government interventionism: Arturo Salazar Larraín and Enrique Chirinos Soto (both had joined Libertad). But these young people, among whom was my son Álvaro, had gone quite a bit further than their teachers. They were enthusiastic followers of Milton Friedman, of Ludwig von Mises, or of Friedrich Hayek, and the radicalism of one of them—Federico Salazar—bordered on anarchism. Several of them had worked or were still working at Hernando de Soto's Instituto Libertad y Democracia (Freedom and Democracy Institute) and two of them, Ghersi and Mario Ghibellini, were co-authors with him of *El otro sendero (The Other Path)*, for which I had written the foreword,* and in which it was shown, supported by exhaustive research, how the informal economy, set up just outside the law, was a creative response of the poor to the discriminatory barriers imposed by that mercantilist version of capitalism which was the only variety with which Peru was acquainted.

That investigation, made by a team directed by Hernando de Soto, was of great importance to the furthering of liberal ideas in Peru, and

* "La revolución silenciosa," in Hernando de Soto, *El otro sendero* (Lima: Editorial El Barranco, 1986), pp. xvii–xxix; reproduced in *Contra viento y marea, III*, pp. 333–48.

marked off a sort of borderline. De Soto had organized, in Lima, in 1979 and 1982, two international symposia to which he brought a roster of economists and thinkers—Hayek, Friedman, Jean-François Revel, and Hugh Thomas among others—whose ideas were a strong breath of modernizing fresh air in that Peru that was just emerging from so many years of populist demagoguery and military dictatorship. I had collaborated with Hernando in staging these events, speaking at both, helped him set up the Instituto Libertad y Democracia, closely followed his studies on the informal economy, and continued to be enthusiastic about his conclusions. I urged him to put them together in a book and when he did so, besides writing the foreword for it, I promoted *El otro sendero* in Peru and in the outside world as I have never done for a book of my own. (I even went so far as to insist, to the point of brazenness, that *The New York Times Magazine* accept an article that I had written about it, which finally appeared on February 22, 1987, and later was widely reprinted in many countries.) I did so because I thought that Hernando would be a good president of Peru. He too believed that and thus our relationship seemed to be an excellent one. Hernando was as vain and touchy as a prima donna, and when I first met him in 1979, just after his arrival from Europe, where he had lived for a good part of his life, he struck me as a slightly pompous and ridiculous figure, with his Spanish studded with Anglicisms and Gallicisms and his aristocratic, affected snobbishness (he had added a coquettish "de" to his father's name, and for that reason Belaunde sometimes referred to him as "that economist with the name of a conquistador"). But I soon had the impression that I had discovered, beneath his picturesque outward appearance, a more intelligent, more modern person than the ordinary run of our politicians, someone who could lead a liberal reform in Peru and who, despite his mania for publicity, was therefore worth all the support I could give him, both inside and outside the country. Support him I did, with great success and also, I confess, no little embarrassment, once I discovered that I was forging for him an image of an intellectual which, as my countrymen have it, wept when it was superimposed on the original.

At the time of the mobilization against nationalization, Hernando was on holiday, in the Dominican Republic. But I phoned him and he returned to Peru earlier than he had planned to. Although in the beginning he expressed reservations as to the rally in the Plaza San

Martín—as an alternative, he proposed a symposium on the informal economy in the Amauta Coliseum, an indoor stadium, but then later he and all the people from the Instituto Libertad y Democracia collaborated with enthusiasm in organizing the Plaza San Martín demonstration. His right-hand man in those days, Enrique Ghersi, was one of the organizers and de Soto one of the three speakers who preceded me. His presence on that platform had given rise to much covert pressure, which I resisted, convinced that those of my friends who were opposed to his speaking, maintaining that his odd words in English would make people burst out laughing, were behaving as they did out of jealousy and not, as they kept assuring me, because he seemed to them a man with more ambitions than principles and one whose loyalty was dubious.

His later conduct proved that my friends had been absolutely right. On the very eve of the rally on August 21, in which in theory he was to play an active part, de Soto had a discreet interview with Alan García at the Presidential Palace, which established the foundations of a close and advantageous collaboration between the administration and the Instituto Libertad y Democracia and which was to launch de Soto on a headlong career as an opportunist (one that was to reach new heights later under the administration and the dictatorship of Fujimori, the new president). That collaboration was cleverly contrived by Alan García in order to publicize himself, all of a sudden, after 1988, in one of those somersaults of which demagogues are capable, as a promoter of private property among Peruvians of scant means, a president who was fulfilling one of the fundamental aspirations of the Democratic Front: to make of Peru "a country of proprietors." To this end, he had himself photographed right and left, arm in arm with de Soto, Peru's "liberal," and sponsored sensational and above all inordinately expensive projects—because of the publicity costing millions that surrounded them—in the young towns, which Hernando and his Institute carried out for him, in what he maintained was open competition with the Front. The maneuver had no major political effect, though as far as I was personally concerned, it admittedly was of great help to me to learn of the unsuspected abilities of the star performer involved, whom, with my characteristic naïveté, I had at one time believed capable of cleaning up Peruvian politics and saving the country.

While—impelled by the spite toward which he was so easily inclined or for more practical reasons—de Soto turned out in Peru to be a sly and sneaky enemy of my candidacy, in the United States he showed, wherever and whenever he got the chance, the video of the rally in the Plaza San Martín as proof of his popularity.* But the person who in this barefaced way doubtless attracted more sympathy and support from liberal institutions and foundations in the United States for his Instituto Libertad y Democracia contrived, at the same time, to let slip out insinuations against the Democratic Front at the Department of State and various international agencies in the presence of individuals who sometimes came to me, all upset, to ask me what these Machiavellianisms meant. They simply meant that the person who had described the mercantilist system in Peru with such preciseness had ended up being its prototype. Those of us who aided and abetted him—and, in a manner of speaking, invented him—must admit frankly, without mincing words: we had not contributed to the cause of freedom or to that of Peru, but, rather, whetted the appetites of a homegrown Rastignac.

But his swift passage through the world of ideas and liberal values left behind a good book. And also, to a certain extent, that group of young radicals who, at the first congress of Libertad, so heatedly defended the deletion of an adjective.

The radicalism and the excitement of the young Turks headed by Ghersi—above all of the Jacobin Federico Salazar, always prompt to denounce any symptom of mercantilism or deviation tending toward state control—rather frightened Lucho Bustamante, a prudent man and, as the person responsible for the Plan for Governing, someone who was determined that our program should be realistic as well as radical (since liberal utopias also exist). Hence his insistence, with the backing of a number of the economists and professionals on his team, that the Movement should adopt as its own the formula that Ludwig Erhard (or rather, his adviser Alfred Müller-Armack) had used to label the economic policy which, after 1948, launched Germany's amazing economic takeoff: the social market economy.

* See, as an example of de Soto's cunning, the article in *The Wall Street Journal* for April 20, 1990, by David Asman, a journalist unwittingly taken in by his sly self-promotion, who attributes to him the organization of the Meeting for Freedom of August 21, 1987.

My own inclination was to drop the adjective "social." Not because I believe a market economy incompatible with any form of redistribution of wealth—a thesis to which no liberal would subscribe, although there are varying points of view on the scope that a policy of the redistribution of wealth should have in an open society—but because in Peru it is more closely associated with socialism than with the equality of opportunity that is a feature of liberal philosophy. My objection also had to do with conceptual clarity. The military dictatorship had applied the label "social" to everything that it collectivized and brought under state control and Alan García martyrized Peruvians by repeating it in every one of his speeches, explaining that he was nationalizing banking so that it would fulfill a "social function." The word used in that odd sense cropped up so often in political discourse that it had become more of a populist catchword than a concept. (I have always felt affection toward those young extremists, even though every so often one of them accused me of heterodoxy as well and, with the passage of time, two of them—Ghibellini and Salazar—turned out to be rather contemptible. But during the period to which I am referring, they appeared to be generous and idealistic. And their incorruptibility and their intransigence, I told myself, would be useful when the day came to undertake the arduous task of making the country moral.)

The congress did not come to any decision with regard to the adjective "social" and the debate remained an open-ended one, but the interchange marked the best intellectual moment of the meeting and served to set many members to thinking. The real conclusion came with the practical efforts of the two following months, in which Lucho Bustamante's team drew up the most advanced liberal project thus far proposed in Peru, and none of the "young Turks" found anything in it to object to.

To what point did we manage to make *ideas* put down roots among members of Libertad? To what degree did Peruvians who voted for me vote for liberal ideas? I don't know. This is a doubt that I would like very much to clear up. In any event, the effort we made to give ideas a primordial role in the life of the Freedom Movement was a many-sided one. The national committee on basic principles and culture was established, which the congress chose Enrique Ghersi to head, together with a school for party leaders that was Miguel Cruchaga's idea and enthusiastically conducted by Fernando Iwasaki and Carlos Zuzunaga.

Shortly after the congress Raúl Ferrero Costa, who had been dean of the Bar Association, and a group of professionals and students associated with him joined Libertad. His handling of affairs as dean had been magnificent, and had been the occasion for his traveling extensively throughout Peru. When Víctor Guevara gave up his position as head of the national committee for organization, I asked Raúl to take his place, and despite the fact that he knew how difficult a post it was, he agreed. At that time, the secretary general, Miguel Cruchaga, aided by his wife Cecilia, had taken on an almost overwhelming task: recruiting and training the sixty thousand election supervisors we needed in order to have a representative at every single one of the tables for registering voters in the entire country. (The election supervisor is the sole guarantee against fraud when voters register or cast their ballots.) All the work of organizing was thus left in Ferrero's hands.

Raúl made a tremendous effort to improve the status of Libertad in the provinces. Aided by some twenty co-workers, he traveled tirelessly throughout the interior, setting up committees where none existed as yet and reorganizing the ones that did. The infrastructure of Libertad was expanding. On my travels I was impressed to see that in remote provinces in Cajamarca, Ancash, San Martín, or Apurímac I was received by organized groups of members of Libertad on the front of whose headquarters there could be made out, from a long way away, that red and black emblem of Libertad whose calligraphy bore a family resemblance to Poland's Solidarność. (In 1981, when the repressive laws against the labor movement headed by Lech Walesa were made public, I had led, along with the journalist Luis Pásara, a protest demonstration, and I suppose that because of this precedent, many people believed that the similarity of the two symbols had been my idea. But in all truth, although the close resemblance struck me as a happy coincidence, I didn't plan it, nor do I know to this day whether it was devised by Jorge Salmón, who was responsible for publicity for Libertad, or Miguel Cruchaga or Fernando de Szyszlo, who, in order to help us raise funds, had designed a splendid lithograph with the Libertad insignia.)

We agreed to hold elections within the Movement before the national ones. This decision impressed many of our members as being an imprudent one, which was going to divert both our resources and our energies and serve as an excuse for squabbles inside the Movement, when what we ought to be doing was concentrate on fighting against our adversaries now that we were going into the final stretch of the campaign. I was one of those who defended the idea of these internal elections. It was my belief that they would serve to democratize many committees in the provinces, which thanks to these elections would free themselves of the entrenched local political bosses and emerge from them much stronger, with genuine representatives from the rank and file.

But I would venture the guess that in two-thirds of the provinces the caciques managed to rig the election procedures and get themselves elected handily. The clever tactics they used were technically unobjectionable. They published or spread word of the time limits for the registration of candidates or the date of the election in such a way that it was only their partisans who found out about them, or else they had the list of members drawn up in such a way that their potential adversaries were not registered to vote or were recorded as having registered after the date that had been set as the limit to participate in the elections. The head of our national committee on electoral affairs, Alberto Massa—an irresistibly humorous member of the political committee whom all the other members could hardly wait to hear ask for the floor because his remarks were always sparklingly witty and made us roar with laughter—on whose head there had rained down the condemnations, protests, and criticisms of the victims of such maneuvers, left us openmouthed with astonishment at the ruses and the cunning tricks that he had been learning of.

We did what we could to undo the chicanery. We declared null and void the elections in those provinces where the number of voters had been suspiciously low, and passed judgment on the internecine accusations wherever it was possible to do so. But in other cases—the national elections were already upon us—we were obliged to resign ourselves to recognizing certain committees of questionable legitimacy in the interior of the country.

In Lima it was different. The elections for the secretariat of the *departamento*, which Rafael Rey's list was to win, were carefully planned and it was possible to avoid or to stop any dirty tricks in time. I made the rounds of the districts on election day, and it was exciting to see the long lines of members of the Freedom Movement waiting outside on the street to vote. But the one who had been Rey's opposing candidate on our ticket—Enrique Fuster—could not bear having been defeated: he resigned from Libertad, attacked us in the government-controlled press and turned up a few months later as a candidate for a congressional seat on the list of a rival party.

The new departmental committee in Lima went on expanding the work of organizing all through the capital and, aided by the Solidarity program, in the young towns as well, from which, in the last months of 1989 and the first of 1990, Patricia and I had received invitations nearly every day to inaugurate new committees. We went every time we could. At this point my obligations began at seven or eight in the morning and ended after midnight.

In those inaugurations one rule was observed without exception: the more humble the neighborhood, the more elaborate the ceremony. Peru is an "old country," as the novelist José María Arguedas reminded his readers, and nothing betrays how far back in time the Peruvian psyche goes as does the people's love of ritual, form, ceremony. There was always a very colorful speakers' platform, with flowers, little flags, noisemakers, paper garlands hanging from the walls and ceilings, and a table with things to eat and drink after the official ceremony. There was invariably a group of musicians and sometimes folk dancers, from the mountains and the coast. The parish priest never failed to show up, to sprinkle holy water about and bless the local headquarters (which might well be a crude structure made of reeds and rush matting in the middle of nowhere) and a crowd dressed in vivid colors, wearing what were obviously their very best clothes, as for a wedding or a baptism. The national anthem had to be sung at the beginning and the theme song of Libertad at the end. And in between the crowd had to listen to a great many speeches. For every last member of the directorate—the district secretary general, along with the heads of the district committees on basic principles and culture, on women's initiatives, on youth programs, on voting registration, on social issues, et cetera, et cetera—had to speak, so that no one would feel left out. The ceremony went on and on—seemingly forever. And afterward a document in baroque legalese, complete with a great many seals, had to be signed, bearing witness to the fact that the ceremony had taken place, and anointing and sanctifying it. And then came the show, folk music and dances, *huaynitos* from the high country, *marineras* from Trujillo, black dances from Chincha, *pasillos* from Piura. Though I begged, ordered, pleaded—explaining that with such grand and glorious activities the whole campaign schedule went to hell—I very seldom managed to get them to make these inaugurations any shorter, or to beg off from the picture taking and the autograph sessions, or of course to get out of being the target of handfuls of *pica-pica*, a demoniacal powder that worked its way all over my body and into my most hidden recesses and made me itch like crazy. Despite all that, it was hard not to be won over by the extraordinary warmth and the unrestrained emotionalism of these popular sectors, so different in that respect from middle- and upper-class Peruvians, inhibited and emotionally undemonstrative.

Patricia, whom to my surprise I had already seen giving interviews on television—something she had always refused to do before—and delivering speeches in the young towns, used to ask me, when she saw me come back from these inaugurations covered from head to foot with confetti: "Do you still remember that *once upon a time* you were a writer?"

NINE

Uncle Lucho

I F, of the fifty-five years that I have lived, I were allowed to relive just one, I would choose the one I spent in Piura, at Uncle Lucho and Aunt Olga's, doing my final year of secondary studies at the Colegio San Miguel and working at *La Industria*. Everything that happened to me there, between April and December 1952, kept me in a state of intellectual enthusiasm and joie de vivre that I have always recalled with nostalgia. Of all those things, the main one was Uncle Lucho.

He was the oldest of my uncles, the one who, after Grandfather Pedro, had been the head of the Llosa tribe, the one to whom everybody went for help and the one whom I had secretly been fondest of, ever since I possessed the faculty of reason, there, in Cochabamba, when he made me the happiest creature in the world by taking me to swimming pools where I learned to swim.

The family was proud of Uncle Lucho. My grandparents and Auntie Mamaé told how, in Arequipa, he had won the prize for excellence, every year, at the Jesuit school, and Granny dug up his report cards to show us the outstanding grades he received when he graduated. But Uncle Lucho hadn't been able to pursue the career in which, with his talent, there was no doubt in anyone's mind that he would have achieved all sorts of triumphs, because his being such a good-looking young man and being such a success with the ladies was his downfall. When he was still a youth, about to enter the university, he got one of his girl cousins pregnant, and the scandal, in serene and straitlaced Arequipa, forced him to go off to Lima until the family calmed down. The mere fact of his return caused another scandal, when, while still scarcely past adolescence, he married Mary, a woman from Arequipa twenty years older than he was. The couple had to leave the horror-

stricken city and go off to Chile, where Uncle Lucho opened a bookstore and went on with his adventures as a Don Juan, which finally
ruined his precocious marriage.

Once separated from his wife, he journeyed to Cochabamba, to his
grandparents'. Among my early memories are those of his handsome
presence—like a movie actor's—and of the jokes and anecdotes that
were told at the big family dinner table on Sundays concerning the
conquests and gallantries of Uncle Lucho, who, from that time on,
helped me to do my homework and gave me extra classes in math.
Then he left to work in Santa Cruz, first with my grandfather on the
Saipina hacienda and then on his own as the representative for various
firms and products, among them Pommery, the champagne. Santa
Cruz has the reputation of being the place in Bolivia with the prettiest
women, and Uncle Lucho always said that he spent all the money he
made in his business dealings there on Pommery champagne, which
he sold to himself so as to court the beauties of Santa Cruz. He often
came to Cochabamba and his arrivals brought a great tidal wave of
energy into the house on Ladislao Cabrera. Of all the comings and
goings in that family, I was most delighted by his visits, because even
though I loved all my uncles dearly, Uncle Lucho was the one who
seemed to me to be my real papa.

He finally settled down and married Aunt Olga. They went off to
live in Santa Cruz, where legend has it that one of Uncle Lucho's
spiteful sweethearts from the town, a beautiful woman also named
Olga, came on horseback one afternoon to shoot five bullets at Aunt
Olga's windows for having monopolized—in theory at least—such a
choice catch. My predilection for Uncle Lucho was owed not only to
how affectionate he was with me, but also to the aura of adventure,
of life in perpetual renewal, that surrounded him. Ever since then I
have felt a fascination for people who appear to have stepped out of
novels, the ones who have made a reality of Chocano's line of verse:
"I want my life to be a torrential stream . . ."

Uncle Lucho spent his life changing jobs, trying his hand at all
sorts of businesses, always unsatisfied with what he was doing, and
although most of the time what he tried turned out badly, there is no
doubt that he was never bored. The last year we were in Bolivia, he
was smuggling rubber into Argentina. It was an undertaking that the
Bolivian government, outwardly, tried to wipe out but secretly en-

couraged, since it was a good source of foreign currency for the country. Argentina, the victim of an international embargo because of its favorable stance toward the Axis during the war, paid a price equal to its weight in gold for this product from the Amazon jungles—whether India or gum rubber. I remember having gone with Uncle Lucho to some warehouses in Cochabamba where the rubber, before being hidden in the trucks that would take it to the border, had to be sprinkled with talcum powder to mask its odor, and having felt a sinful excitement when I too was allowed to throw a few handfuls of talcum onto the forbidden product. Shortly before the end of the war, one of Uncle Lucho's convoys was confiscated at the border, and he and his partners lost their shirts. Just in time for him and Aunt Olga—and their two little daughters, Wanda and Patricia—to come settle in Piura with my grandparents.

Once arrived there, Uncle Lucho had worked for several years for the Romero Company, in a car distributorship, but in 1952, when I went to live with him, he was a farmer. He had rented the San José rural holding, on the banks of the Chira River, on which he grew cotton. San José was between Paita and Sullana, some two hours' journey from Piura by car, and I often went out there with him, in the two or three trips a week that he made, in a rickety black truck, to oversee the irrigation, the spraying of pesticides, or the clearing of the land. As he spoke with the farmhands, I rode horseback, swam in the irrigation ditch, and invented stories about earth-shaking passions between young landowners and peasant girls who picked cotton. (I remember having written a long story of this sort to which I gave the elegantly euphuistic title "La zagala" ["The Shepherdess"].)

Uncle Lucho was very fond of reading and as a young man had written poetry. (Later on, at the university, I learned through professors who had been his friends in his youth, in Arequipa—Augusto Tamayo Vargas, Emilio Champion, and Miguel Ángel Ugarte Chamorro, for instance—that in those days all his intimate friends were convinced that his vocation was to be an intellectual.) I still remember some of his verses, in particular a sonnet, in which he compared a lady's beautiful moral qualities to the beads of a necklace, and in our conversations during that year in Piura, when I spoke to him of my vocation and told him that I wanted to be a writer even if I starved to death, because literature was the best thing there was in the world, he used to recite that sonnet to me, as he encouraged me to follow my literary inclinations without giving a thought to the consequences, because— it is a lesson that I learned and have tried to transmit to my children—the worst misfortune that can befall a man is to spend his life doing things that he doesn't like to do instead of those that he would have liked to do.

Uncle Lucho listened to me read aloud to him *La huida del inca*, and many poems and short stories, offering me certain criticisms at times—exuberance was my major defect—but tactfully, so as not to hurt my feelings as a novice writer.

Aunt Olga had fixed up a room for me at the back of the little patio of their tiny house on the Calle Tacna, just a little way away from its intersection with the Avenida Sánchez Cerro, opposite the Plaza Merino, where my brand-new school, San Miguel, was located. The house occupied the lower floors of an old building, and consisted of a small living room, a dining room, a kitchen, and three bedrooms, plus the bathrooms and bedrooms for the household help. My arrival wrecked the orderly household, which had grown—besides Wanda and Patricia, nine and seven years old, Lucho had been born and was two years old by then—and the three cousins had to be jammed together in one bedroom so that I could have my own, all to myself. In it, on a couple of shelves, were Uncle Lucho's books, old volumes published by Espasa-Calpe, editions of classics put out by Ateneo, and, above all, the complete collection of the Biblioteca Contemporánea, published by Losada, some thirty or forty books of novels, essays, poetry, and theater that I am certain I read from beginning to end, in that year of voracious reading. Among Uncle Lucho's books, I found an autobiography, published by Diana, a Mexico City publishing house, that kept me awake for many nights and gave me a violent political jolt: *Out of the Night*, by Jan Valtin. Its author had been a German Communist, in the Nazi era, and his autobiography, full of episodes of clandestine militancy, of sacrifices of fates and fortunes to the cause of revolution, and of hideous abuses was, to me, a detonating device, something that for the first time gave me pause and made me think about justice, political action, revolution. Although, at the end of the book, Valtin severely criticized the Communist Party, which sacrificed his wife and dealt with him in the most cynical way, I remember having finished the book feeling great admiration for those lay saints who, despite the risk of being tortured, decapitated, or condemned to spend the rest of their lives in the underground cells of the Nazis, dedicated their lives to fighting for socialism.

Since the school was just a few meters from the house—all I had to do was cross the Plaza Merino to get to it—I got up out of bed as late as possible, dressed in a mad rush, and raced off when they were already blowing the whistle for the beginning of classes. But Aunt Olga refused to let me skip breakfast and would send the maid to San Miguel with a cup of milk and a slice of buttered bread for me. I don't know how many times I had to go through the embarrassing experience of seeing the head supervisor, "el Diablo"—"the Devil"—come into the classroom just after the first morning lesson had started, to summon me: "Vargas Llosa, Mario! To the door, to have his breakfast!" After my three months as a night-owl reporter on *La Crónica* and a steady customer of brothels, I had gone back to being a youngster with a family.

I didn't regret it. I felt happy that Aunt Olga and Uncle Lucho pampered me, and that at the same time they treated me like a grownup, giving me complete freedom to go out at night, or stay home reading until all hours, something that I often did. For that reason it took a superhuman effort on my part to get up in time for school. Aunt Olga signed blank cards for me, so that I could invent excuses myself for being late. But since I turned them in too often, Wanda and Patricia were given the responsibility for waking me up each morning. Wandita did so gently; her younger sister, Patricia, took advantage of this chance to give free rein to her wicked instincts and had no compunction about throwing a glass of water all over me. She was a little seven-year-old demon hidden behind a cute turned-up nose, flashing eyes, and curly hair. Those glasses of cold water she poured on top of me became a nightmare and I awaited them, still half asleep, with anticipated shivers. Stunned and startled by the sudden dash of cold water, I would throw the pillow at her in fury, but she would answer me with a great burst of laughter too big to have come out of her semi-skeletal little body. Her bad behavior beat all the records of family tradition, including my own. When something wasn't to her liking, Cousin Patricia was capable of crying and stamping her feet for hours on end, until her tantrums infuriated Uncle Lucho, whom I once observed putting her under the shower fully dressed, to see if that would make her stop screaming. At a certain period when she slept in my room, I took it into my head to write her a poem, and she learned it by heart and used to fill me with embarrassment by reciting it in front of Aunt Olga's friends, lingering over each word and giving it gelatinous accents so that it would sound even worse:

Duerme la niña	The little girl sleeps
cerquita de mí	right next to me
y su manecita	and her little hand
blanca y chiquitita	white and wee
apoyada tiene	she keeps folded tightly
muy junta de sí . . .	right next to her . . .

At times, I gave her a quick pinch or pulled her ears, whereupon she would kick up a fuss and begin howling as though she were being skinned alive, and in order that Uncle Lucho and Aunt Olga wouldn't believe I'd been mistreating her, I had to placate her by pleading with her or putting on a clown act. She used to exact a price for the deal: "Either you buy me a cup of chocolate or I'll go on screaming . . ."

San Miguel de Piura was opposite the Salesian school, but unlike it, it didn't have a roomy and comfortable building; it was in an old house made of reeds and clay with a corrugated zinc roof, not at all suited to its needs. But San Miguel, thanks to the efforts of its head-master—Dr. Marroquín, to whom I gave so many headaches—was a splendid school. In it many youngsters from humble Piura families— from La Mangachería, from La Gallinacera and other districts on the outskirts of the city—attended classes with youngsters from the middle class and even from the top families of Piura, who were enrolled there either because the priests of the Salesian school wouldn't put up with them any longer or because they were attracted by the good teachers at San Miguel. Dr. Marroquín had managed to persuade distinguished professionals of the city to come to the school to give classes—above all to pupils in my year, the last one before graduation—and thanks to this I had the good luck, for instance, to study political economy with Dr. Guillermo Gulman. It was this course, I believe, and also Uncle Lucho's advice, that made me make up my mind to study, later on at the university, for degrees in Letters and in Law. But in those classes of Dr. Gulman's, the law seemed much more profound and important than something that had to do merely with lawsuits: it was an open door to philosophy, to economics, to all the social sciences.

We also had an excellent history teacher, Néstor Martos, who wrote a daily column in *El Tiempo* entitled "Voto en Contra" ("A Vote Against") on local issues. Professor Martos, an impenitent bohemian with a debauched face, who seemed to arrive in class, every so often, directly from some little bar where he had spent the whole night drinking *chicha*, his hair uncombed, his chin stubbled, and with a muffler covering half his face—a muffler, in torrid Piura!—was transformed in the classroom into an Apollonian expositor, a painter of frescoes of the pre-Inca and Inca eras of American history. I listened to him spellbound, and my face turned beet-red one morning in that class, in which, without mentioning my name, he devoted himself to enumerating all the reasons why no true Peruvian could be a "Hispanist" or praise Spain (which I had done, that same day, in my column in *La Industria*, on the occasion of the visit to Piura of the ambassador of that country). One of his arguments was this: In the three hundred years of colonialism, had any ruler ever deigned to visit the American possessions of the Spanish Empire?

The literature teacher was a little less lofty—we had to memorize the adjectives that described the classics: San Juan de la Cruz, "profound and essential"; Góngora, "baroque and classicist"; Quevedo, "ornate, festive, and imperishable"; Garcilaso, "Italianizing, dead before his time, and a friend of Juan Boscán's"—but this blind teacher, José Robles Rázuri, was a very fine person. When he discovered my vocation, he held me in high esteem and used to lend me books—he had put pink paper covers on all of them and a little seal with his name—among which I remember the first two of Azorín's that I read: *Al margen de los clásicos* (*Marginal Notes to the Classics*) and *La ruta de Don Quijote* (*The Path of Don Quixote*).

In the second or third week of classes, in a daring gesture, I told Professor Robles in secret about my little work for the theater. He read it and proposed something to me that gave me heart palpitations. The school habitually put on one of the ceremonies commemorating Piura Week, in July. Why didn't we suggest to the head of San Miguel that the school put on my *La huida del inca* this year? Dr. Marroquín gave his approval of the project and, without further ado, I was put in charge of directing it, for its very first performance on July 17, in the Teatro Variedades. You can imagine how excited I was when I ran home to tell the news to Uncle Lucho: We were going to put on *La huida del inca*! And at the Teatro Variedades, no less!

If only because it allowed me to see, onstage, living with the fictitious life of the theater, something that I myself had invented, my debt to Piura can never be repaid. But I owe it other things. Good friends, some of whom I still have. Several of my old classmates of the Salesian school, such as Javier Silva and Manolo and Richard Artadi, had gone on to San Miguel, and among my new schoolmates there were others, the Temple twins, the León cousins, the Raygada brothers, who became my soulmates. This fifth year of secondary school turned out to be a pathbreaking one, since for the first time so-called mixed classes were tried out in a state school. In our class there were five girls; they sat in a row by themselves and our relations with them were formal and distant. One of them, Yolanda Vilela, was one of the three "vestals" in *La huida del inca*, according to the faded program of the performance that I've carried in my wallet, as a talisman, ever since.

Of all that group of friends, my closest pal was Javier Silva. He was already, at sixteen, what he would be later, many times over: fat, gluttonous, intelligent, tireless, unscrupulous, likable, loyal, always ready to embark on any and every adventure, and more generous than anybody else. He says that as long ago as that year I had convinced him that life far from Paris was impossible, that we had to go there as soon as we could, and that I dragged him with me to open a joint savings account, so as to be sure of having the money for the passage. (My memory tells me that that took place later in Lima, when we were university students.) He had a gigantic appetite and on the days when he was given pocket money—he lived around the corner from my house, in the Calle Arequipa—he would come by to invite me to El Reina, a restaurant on the Avenida Sánchez Cerro, where he ordered an appetizer and a beer for us to share. We used to go to the movies—to the Municipal, to the Variedades, or to the Castilla, the open-air movie theater with only one projector, so that at the end of each reel there was an intermission. We would go swimming at the Club Grau, and we would visit the Casa Verde, the Green House, on the road to Catacaos, to which I had to drag him the first time after getting him over the panic fear that his father, a much-loved doctor in Piura, had instilled in him, assuring him that if he went there he'd catch syphilis.

The Casa Verde was a big cabin, a building a bit more rustic than a house, a much happier and more sociable place than the brothels in Lima, which were usually sordid and frequently the scene of violent brawls. The bordello in Piura had retained the traditional function of a place to meet and hold get-togethers, and was not merely a house of prostitution. Piurans of all social classes went there. I remember being surprised one night to find the prefect, Don Jorge Checa, at one of the tables, moved by the *tonderos* and the *cumananas* of a trio from the Mangachería district. They went to listen to music, to eat the regional dishes—young goat, ceviche, or the stew of pork, corn, and bananas called *chifles*, and cream custards, along with light *chicha* and thick *chicha*—or to dance and to talk together, and not just for love-making. The atmosphere was easygoing, informal, cheery, and rarely spoiled by rows. Much later, when I discovered Maupassant, I couldn't help associating that Casa Verde with his beautifully portrayed Maison Tellier, just as La Mangachería, the joyful, violent, and marginal neighborhood on the outskirts of Piura, was always identified in my memory with the Court of Miracles of Alexandre Dumas's novels. Ever since I was a small boy, the real-life things and people that have moved me most have been the ones that most closely resembled literature.

My generation experienced the swan song of the brothel, buried that institution that was gradually to die out as sexual mores became more relaxed, the pill was discovered, the myth of virginity gradually became obsolete, and boys began to make love to their sweethearts. The banalization of sex that resulted is, according to psychologists and sexologists, a very salutary development for society, which, in this way, finds an outlet for its numerous neurotic repressions. Something very positive, doubtless. But it has also signified the trivialization of the sexual act and the disappearance of a privileged source of pleasure for contemporary humans. Stripped of mystery and of centuries-old religious and moral taboos, as well as of the elaborate rituals that surrounded the practice of it, physical love has come to be the most natural thing in the world for the younger generations, a gymnastic exercise, a temporary diversion, something very different from that central mystery of life, of the approach by way of it to the gates of heaven and hell that it still was for my generation. The brothel was the temple of that clandestine religion, where one went to celebrate an exciting and perilous rite, to live, for a few short hours, a life apart. A life founded on terrible social injustices, no doubt—from the next year on, I would be conscious of this and would be very much ashamed of having gone to brothels and having frequented whores like a contemptible bourgeois—but the truth is that it gave many of us a very intense, respectful, and almost mystical relationship to the world and the practices of sex, something inseparable from the intuition of the sacred and of ceremony, of the active unfolding of fantasy, of mystery and shame, of everything that Georges Bataille calls transgression. Perhaps it is a good thing that sex has come to seem something natural to most mortals. To me it never was, nor is it now. Seeing a naked woman in a bed has always been the most disquieting and most disturbing of experiences, something that never would have had for me that transcendental nature, deserving of so much tremulous respect and so much joyous expectation, if sex had not been, in my childhood and adolescence, surrounded by taboos, prohibitions, and prejudices, if in order to make love to a woman there had not been so many obstacles to overcome in those days.

Going to that house daubed with green paint, on the outskirts of Castilla, along the road to Catacaos, cost me my meager paycheck from *La Industria*, so I went only a few times a year. But each time I left there with my head full of impassioned images, and I am certain that from that time on I vaguely dreamed of one day making up a story, the scene of which would be that Casa Verde. It is possible for memory and nostalgia to embellish something that was wretched and sordid—what can one expect of a little bordello in a tiny city such as Piura?—but as I remember it, the atmosphere of the place was happy and poetic, and those who went there really had a good time, not only the johns but also the gay men who worked as waiters and bouncers, the whores, the musicians who played waltzes, *tonderos*, mambos, or *huarachas*, and the cook who prepared the food in sight of everyone, doing dance steps around the stove. There were only a few little rooms with rough beds for couples, so that often it was necessary to go out into the open among the sand dunes all about to make love, amid the mesquite and the goats. The lack of comfort was compensated for by the warm bluish atmosphere of Piuran nights, with the soft light of the moon when it was full and the sensual curves of dunes amid which one caught glimpses, on the other side of the river, of the twinkling lights of the city.

Just a few days after my arrival in Piura, I presented myself, with my letters of recommendation from Alfonso Delboy and Gastón Aguirre Morales, at the home of the owner of *La Industria*, Don Miguel F. Cerro Guerrero. He was a spindly little oldster, a little bit of a man with a weather-beaten face, covered with a thousand wrinkles, in which keen, restless eyes betrayed his indomitable energy. He had three daily provincial newspapers—issues of *La Industria* for Piura, Chiclayo, and Trujillo—which he ran from his little house in Piura with an energetic hand, and a cotton plantation, in the vicinity of Catacaos, which he rode out to on the back of a lazy mule as old as he was, so as to supervise things personally. He rode it matter-of-factly down the middle of the street, heading for the Old Bridge, paying no attention to pedestrians and to cars passing by. He made a stop at the main office of *La Industria*, in the Calle Lima, into whose patio surrounded by grillwork the mule would burst without warning, badly pitting the tiling with its hoofs, so that Don Miguel could have a look at the material in the editorial room. He was a man who never tired, who worked even when he was asleep, who was nobody's fool, stern and even hardhearted but possessed of a rectitude that made those of us who worked under him feel secure. Legend had it that one night somebody had asked him, at a dinner accompanied by a great deal to drink, at the Centro Piurano, if he was still able to make love. And that Don Miguel had invited the other guests to accompany him to the Casa Verde, where he had, to all intents and purposes, laid that doubt to rest.

He read the letters through very carefully, asked me how old I was, speculated about how it would be possible for me to combine a newspaper job with my classes at school, and finally made his mind up and hired me. He pegged my monthly salary at three hundred soles and outlined in the course of that conversation what my work would entail. I was to go to the newspaper office as soon as my morning classes were over, in order to look through the Lima papers and extract and write a roundup of the news that might be of interest to Piurans, and I was to come back at night, for another two or three hours, to write articles, do reporting, and be on hand for emergencies.

La Industria was a historic relic. One compositor, Señor Nieves, set its four pages by hand—I don't believe he ever progressed as far as using a Linotype. To watch him working, in the dark little room at the back, in that "print shop" where he was the sole printer, was a spectacle. Skinny, with thick-lensed glasses for his nearsightedness, always dressed in a short-sleeved undershirt and an apron that at one time had been white, Señor Nieves would place the original copy on a lectern, to his left. And with his right hand, at incredible speed, he would remove one by one the type characters from a bunch of little boxes laid out around him, and set the text in the form which he himself would then print, on a prehistoric press whose vibrations shook the walls and roof of the building. Señor Nieves seemed to me to have escaped from novels of the nineteenth century, those of Dickens especially; the craft, at which he was so skilled, an eccentric survival, was something already extinct in the rest of the world and something that would die out with him in Peru.

A new managing editor of *La Industria* had arrived in Piura at almost the same time that I did. Don Miguel F. Cerro Guerrero had brought from Lima Pedro del Pino Fajardo, a veteran journalist, to raise the circulation of the paper, in its cutthroat competition with *El Tiempo*, the other local paper (there was a third, *Ecos y Noticias*, that came out late, hardly ever, or never, on bright-colored paper, and was almost illegible because the print came off on the reader's hands). We had two reporters. Owed Castillo, whose regular job was to attend to the depth gauges for the Piura River, was in charge of the sports news—later on, in Lima in the days of the military dictatorship, he would have a distinguished career as a filthmongering journalist. And I wrote up the local and international news. In addition, there were outside collaborators, such as Dr. Luis Ginocchio Feijó, a physician whom journalism came to interest as passionately as his profession.

We hit it off well with Pedro del Pino Fajardo, who, at the beginning, tried to give a rather flamboyant slant to *La Industria*, which shocked certain Piuran ladies, who went so far as to send a letter of protest against the scandalous tone of a feature article by the editor-in-chief. Don Miguel Cerro demanded of del Pino Fajardo that he restore to the daily its traditional serious respectability.

I had great fun working there, writing about anything and everything, and permitting myself the luxury, every so often, thanks to the kindliness with which Pedro del Pino welcomed my literary enthusiasms, of publishing poems that occupied one entire page of the four that made up each issue of the paper. On one of these occasions, in which a poem of mine gloomily entitled "La noche de los desesperados" ("The Night of the Desperate") filled the page, Don Miguel, who had just dismounted from his mule, doffed his big sombrero of fine Catacaos straw and pronounced this sentence, which touched my heart: "Today's edition is sinfully *exuberant*."

Apart from the endless news items I wrote or the interviews I conducted, I put out two columns, "Buenos Días"—"Good Morning"— and "Campanario"—"The Bell Tower"—one under my own name and the other under a pseudonym, in which I made comments on current events and frequently spoke (ignorance is intrepid) of politics and of literature. I remember a couple of long articles on the revolution of 1952 waged by the MNR (Movimiento Nacionalista Revolucionario: Nationalist Revolutionary Movement) in Bolivia, which won Víctor Paz Estenssoro the presidency, and whose reforms—the nationalization of mining companies, agrarian reform—I praised until Don Miguel Cerro reminded me that we were living under the military dictatorship of General Odría, and that I should moderate my revolutionary enthusiasms, since he didn't want *La Industria* to be closed down.

The Bolivian revolution staged by the MNR greatly excited me. I learned certain details about it from a very direct source, since the family of my Aunt Olga, particularly her younger sister, Julia, who lived in La Paz, wrote her letters with many anecdotes and exact information about the events and the leaders of the uprising—such as the one who would become the vice president under Paz Estenssoro, Siles Suazo, and the leader of the miners, Juan Lechín—which I used for my articles in *La Industria*. And that revolution with strong leftist and socialist tendencies, so fiercely attacked in Peru by the daily papers, especially by Pedro Beltrán's *La Prensa*, helped, as much as my reading of that book by Jan Valtin, to fill my head and my heart with ideas

—perhaps it would be better to say images and emotions—that were socialist and revolutionary.

Pedro del Pino Fajardo had had a lung disease and had stayed for a time at the famous hospital for tuberculosis at Jauja (the one they used in order to scare me, at my grandparents', when I was a little boy, so as to force me to eat), about which he wrote a novel that fell somewhere between being festive and being macabre, which he gave me shortly after we met. And he also showed me several of his works for the theater. He looked kindly on my vocation and encouraged it, but the real help he gave me was of a negative sort, causing me to have a presentiment from that time on of the mortal danger that bohemia represented for literature. Because in his case, as in that of so many writers, living and dead, in my country, his literary vocation had foundered on disorder, a lack of discipline, and above all alcohol, before the creative light dawned in him. Pedro was an incorrigible bohemian; he could spend entire days—entire nights—in a bar, telling extremely funny stories, and absorbing immeasurable quantities of beer, pisco brandy or any other alcoholic drink. He soon reached a scintillating, overexcited state, and remained in it, for hours and hours, days and days, burning up, in dazzlingly brilliant and ephemeral soliloquies, what were no doubt, by that time, the last vestiges of a talent that never managed to take definite shape because of his dissolute life. He was married to a granddaughter of Ricardo Palma, a heroic young blonde, who, with the responsibility for the care of a child who was only a few years old, used to come to rescue Pedro from the little bars.

I have never learned how to drink; in my short bohemian life, in the summer in Lima that I worked on *La Crónica*, more out of mimicry than out of a liking for it, I had drunk a great deal of beer—though I could never go on pisco binges, for instance, with my colleagues— but even beer had a bad effect on me, since I soon began to have a headache and feel nauseated. And now that I was in Piura, I had so many things to do, what with classes, my job on the newspaper, the books and other things I was trying to write, that the whole business of spending hours in a café or a bar, talking endlessly, as around me people began to get plastered, bored me and exasperated me. I would invent any sort of pretext to escape. That allergy began there in Piura, I believe, and had to do with a physical intolerance for alcohol that I

no doubt inherited from my father—who was never able to drink—
and with the distaste I felt at the spectacle of the way my friend Pedro
del Pino Fajardo deteriorated, a distaste that gradually grew stronger
until it had become a phobia. Neither in my years at the university
nor afterward have I lived the bohemian life, not even in its most
pleasant and benign forms, those back-room gatherings at table, those
evenings in a coterie of like-minded friends, from which I have always
fled like a cat from water.

Pedro del Pino stayed for no more than a year and a half or two
years in Piura. He went back to Lima and there he became the editor-
in-chief of a publication touting the policies of Odría's dictatorship,
La Nación, in which, without my permission, he reprinted several of
my columns from *La Industria*. I sent him a furious letter of protest,
which he didn't publish, and I didn't see him again. When the dictatorship ended, in 1956, he emigrated to Venezuela and died shortly
afterward.

We began to rehearse *La huida del inca* at the end of April or the
beginning of May, in the afternoons, three or four times a week, after
classes let out, in the library of the school, a vast room on the top
floor lent to us by San Miguel's affable librarian, Carmela Garcés. In
the cast, the selection of which took several days, there were students
of the school, the Raygada brothers, Juan León and Yolanda Vilela
from my class, and Walter Palacios, who was later to become a professional actor as well as a revolutionary leader. But the stars were the
Rojas sisters, two girls from outside the school, very well known in
Piura—one of them, Lira, for her magnificent voice, and the other,
Ruth, for her dramatic talent (she had already played roles in several
plays). The lovely voice of Lira Rojas caused General Odría, who had
heard her sing while on an official visit to Piura, to offer her a scholarship and send her to Lima, to the National Music School.

I feel no need to remember the work (a soap opera with Incas,
as I have said), but I am touched when I recall what slowly brought
it to life, over a period of two months and a half, with the enthusiastic collaboration of the eight actors and the persons who helped
us with the stage sets and the lighting. I had never directed, or
ever seen anybody direct a play, and I spent entire nights without
a wink of sleep, taking notes on the staging. The rehearsals, the
atmosphere that was created, the camaraderie, and my dream of

seeing the little play finally taking shape, convinced me that year that I would be not a poet but a playwright: drama was the prince of genres and I would inundate the world with works for the theater like those of Lorca or Lenormand. (I have not reread nor have I seen the plays of the latter performed on the stage, but two works of his, which had been published in the Biblioteca Contemporánea series and which I read that year, left a profound impression on me.)

From the first rehearsal I fell in love with my female lead, the slender Ruth Rojas. She had wavy hair that kissed her shoulders, a long neck like the stem of a flower, very pretty legs, and a walk like a queen's. Hearing her speak was a pleasure fit for the gods, because as she did so she added to the warm, lingering, and musical cadence of Piuran speech a lilt of coquetry and gentle irony all her own that went straight to my heart. But the timidity that always came over me with the young women I fell in love with kept me from ever addressing a flirtatious remark to her or anything that might make her suspect what I felt for her. What was more, Ruth had a sweetheart, a young man who worked in a bank and who used to come to get her when rehearsals were over.

We could only run through a couple of rehearsals in the theater itself, in mid-July, just before the performance, when it seemed impossible that Maestro Aldana Ruiz would finish painting the stage sets in time; he didn't finish them until the very morning of July 17. The advertising for the work was tremendous, in *La Industria* and in *El Tiempo*, over the radio, and, finally, over loudspeakers going up and down the streets—I remember having seen Javier Silva go past the door of the newspaper office, shouting into a megaphone, from atop a truck: "Don't miss the event of the century, in an evening performance, at the Teatro Variedades . . . ," as a result of which all the seats were sold out. On the night of the performance, many people who hadn't been able to get tickets broke through the barriers and poured into the theater, filling the aisles and the orchestra. What with all the disorder, the prefect himself, Don Jorge Checa, lost his seat and had to witness the entire performance standing up.

The work proceeded without mishap—or almost—and there was loud applause when I came out onto the stage, along with the actors and actresses, to acknowledge my authorship of it. The one semi-mishap occurred at the romantic moment of the work, when the

Inca—Ricardo Raygada—kissed the heroine, who was supposed to be deeply in love with him. At just that point a look of disgust crossed Ruth's face and she began to screw up her face. Later she explained to us that it was not the Inca who had repelled her, but a live cockroach that had attached itself to his *mascaipacha*—his symbolic imperial tassel. The success of *La huida del inca* was responsible for our giving, the following week, two performances more, to one of which I managed to sneak in Wanda and Patricia, since the censorship board's classification of the work as one "suitable for minors over fifteen years of age" made it necessary to get them in on the sly.

In addition to *La huida del inca*, the show included some sung numbers, by Lira Rojas, and a performance by Joaquín Ramos Ríos, one of the most original characters in Piura. He was an outstanding exponent of an art that no longer exists today, or at any event, is considered obsolete and ridiculous, but at that time was a prestigious one: recitation. Joaquín had lived in Germany in his early years and had imported from there the German language, a monocle, a cape, a number of extravagant aristocratic mannerisms and an unbridled fondness for beer. He recited Lorca, Darío, Chocano marvelously well, and the Piuran bard Héctor Manrique—whose sonnet "Querellas del jardín" ("Quarrels in the Garden"), which began: "Era la agonía de una tarde rubia . . ." ("It was the death agony of a golden afternoon . . .") Uncle Lucho and I used to declaim at the top of our lungs as we crossed the desert on the way to his farm—and he was the star of all the literary-musical evenings in Piura. Apart from reciting, all he did was wander about the streets of Piura, with his monocle and his cape, dragging along after him a kid goat that he introduced as his gazelle. He always went around half drunk, mimicking—in the grimy holes-in-the-wall of the *chicherías*, in the bars, and at the liquor stands in the market—the turn-of-the-century extravagances of Oscar Wilde or of his imitators in Lima, the poet and short-story writer Abraham Valdelomar and the *colónidas*, the Parnassian and Symbolist poets of the late nineteenth century, before a public of Piuran mestizos who didn't pay the slightest attention to him and treated him with the contemptuous tolerance that one accords idiots. But Joaquín wasn't one, because, amid the alcoholic haze in which he spent his life, he would suddenly start talking about poetry and poets in a very intense way, which revealed a profound familiarity with them. In addition to respect, I felt tenderness for Joaquín Ramos and I was deeply grieved, years later, to run into him in the center of Lima, a total wreck and so drunk he was unable to recognize me.

For the vacation during national holiday week, my class wanted to organize a trip to Cuzco, but the money we raised—with the performances of *La huida del inca*, raffles, lotteries, fairs—wasn't enough and we got only as far as Lima, for a week. Although I slept at night with my classmates at a normal school on the Avenida Brasil, I spent the daytime hours with my grandparents and my aunts and uncles, in Miraflores. My parents were in the United States. It was the third trip my father had taken there, but my mother's first. They had gone to Los Angeles and this was to be another attempt on my father's part to set up a business or find a job that would allow him to leave Peru. Even though he never talked to me about his financial situation, I have the impression that it had begun to deteriorate, because of the money he had lost in his commercial experiment in New York, and because his income had dwindled. This time they stayed in the United States for several months and when they came back, instead of renting a house in Miraflores, they took a little apartment, with just one bedroom, in a very poor district, Rímac, an unmistakable sign of financial difficulties. And so, when, at the end of that year, I came back to Lima to enter the university, I didn't go to live with my father, but with my grandparents, on the Calle Porta. I was never again to live with him.

Shortly after returning to Piura, I received an unexpected piece of news (everything went well for me during that year in Piura): *La huida del inca* had won second place in the theatrical competition. The news, published in the Lima daily papers, was reprinted by *La Industria* on the first page. The prize consisted of a small amount of money, and many months were to go by before Grandpa Pedro—who took the trouble to go to the Ministry of Education every week to ask for it—could collect it and send it to me in Piura. I doubtless spent it on books, and perhaps on visits to the Casa Verde.

Uncle Lucho encouraged me to be a writer. He wasn't so naïve as to advise me to be *only* a writer, because what would I have lived on? He thought that practicing law would allow me to reconcile my literary vocation with keeping food on my table and urged me to put money aside from then on so as to get to Paris someday. From that time forward, the idea of traveling to Europe—to France—became a pole-star. And until I managed to get there, six years later, I lived with the eagerness to be off and the conviction that if I stayed in Peru I wouldn't ever attain my goal, because what Peruvian who had stayed here had ever managed to become a real writer?

I didn't know any Peruvian writers, except dead ones or ones I knew only by name. One of these latter, who had published poems and written works for the theater, passed through Piura around that time: Sebastián Salazar Bondy. He was the literary adviser of Pedro López Lagar's Argentine company, which had a brief run at the Teatro Variedades (it put on a work by Unamuno and another by Jacinto Grau, if memory serves me). At both performances I kept fighting against my shyness so as to approach Sebastián, whose tall, slender silhouette I saw strolling up and down the aisles of the theater. I wanted to talk to him about my vocation, to ask him for advice, or merely to have concrete verification that a Peruvian could manage to become a writer. But I couldn't work up my nerve, and years later, when we had become friends and I told him about my hesitation, Sebastián couldn't believe it.

I often went with my Uncle Lucho on trips to the interior of the *departamento* and one time to Tumbes, where he was exploring a business deal having to do with fish. We went to Sullana, Paita, Talara, Sechura, and also to the provinces in the highlands of Piura, such as Ayabaca and Huancabamba, but the landscape that lingered in my memory and conditioned, I feel, my relationship with nature was that Piuran desert that has nothing monotonous about it, that changes with the sun and with the wind, and in which, because of the vast horizon and the clear blue sky, one always has the sensation that, just on the other side of one sand dune or another, the sea will suddenly appear, with its silvery glints and its foamy waves.

Every time we went out of town in the creaking black station wagon and that nearly endless white or gray expanse stretched out before us, undulating, burning-hot, interrupted every so often by patches of mesquite, by little huts made of wild reeds and clay, and traversed by mysterious flocks of goats that seemed to be lost in the immensity that surrounded them, over which lizards suddenly zigzagged or iguanas toasted themselves in the sun, motionless and disquieting, I felt great excitement, a seething impulse. That vast space, that boundless horizon—every so often the lower ranges of the Andes appeared, like the shadows of giants—filled my head with adventurous ideas, with epic tales, and the number of stories and poems I planned to write using this setting, peopling it, was endless. When in 1958 I left for Europe, where I was to remain for many years, that landscape was one of the most frequently recurring images I preserved of Peru, and also the one that used to make me feel the most homesick.

When the semester was already well along, one fine day Dr. Marroquín announced to those of us in our last year that this time final exams would not be given in accordance with a preestablished schedule, but rather without prior notice. The reason for this experimental procedure was so as to be able to evaluate the student's knowledge with greater accuracy. Examinations announced beforehand, for which the students prepared by memorizing the material of the course in question the night before, gave an imprecise idea of what they had assimilated.

The whole class panicked. The fact that a student prepared for a chemistry exam could go to school only to be tested in geometry or logic left us with our hair standing on end. We began to imagine a cataract of classes that we'd flunk. And in our last year at school!

Javier Silva and I incited our classmates to rebel against the experiment (long afterward I found out that that project had been the subject of Dr. Marroquín's doctoral dissertation). We held meetings and an assembly in which a committee was named, with me as president, to speak with Dr. Marroquín. He received us in his office and politely listened to me ask him to post the examination schedules. But he told us that his decision was irrevocable.

We then planned a strike. We would refuse to go to classes until the measure was revoked. There were nights when, beside ourselves with overexcitement, we discussed the details of the operation with Javier and other classmates. On the morning agreed on, when the hour for classes to begin came round, we retreated to the Eguiguren embankment. But there, several boys, scared to death—in those days, a student strike was unheard of—began to murmur that they might expel us and that it would be better to go back and attend classes. The argument turned into a bitter one, and finally one group refused to go on with the strike. Demoralized by this desertion, the rest of us agreed to return for afternoon classes. When we went back inside the school, the head proctor took me to the principal's office. Dr. Marroquín's voice trembled as he told me that, as the one responsible for what had happened, I deserved, *ipso facto*, to be expelled from San Miguel. But instead, in order not to ruin my future, he would expel me only for seven days. And that I should tell Agricultural Engineer Llosa (he called Uncle Lucho that because he often saw him in the riding boots he wore when he went out to his farm) to come have a talk with him. Uncle Lucho had to listen to Dr. Marroquín's complaints.

My temporary expulsion caused something of a stir and even Don Jorge Checa, the prefect, dropped by the house to offer to act as intermediary so that the principal would reverse his decision. I don't remember if he shortened my expulsion or whether I was expelled for the entire week, but, once the punishment was over, I felt like Jan Valtin after he had survived the Nazis' prisons.

I mention the episode of the abortive strike because it was to become the subject of my first published short story, "Los jefes" ("The Leaders"), and because in it the first glimpses of a burgeoning concern on my part could be discerned. I don't believe I had thought much about politics before that year in Piura. I remember that when I was working as a messenger at International News Service, I was indignant when the editors received a warning that all information that arrived concerning Peru had to be discussed with the chief administrator of the Ministry of the Interior before being sent on to *La Crónica*. But even when I was working at the newspaper as a reporter, I didn't think about the fact that we were living under a military dictatorship, which had forbidden political parties and exiled many Apristas, as well as the former president, Bustamante y Rivero, and a number of his collaborators.

In that year in Piura, politics entered my life at a gallop and with the idealism and confusion with which it usually bursts upon a young man. Since what I read, in utter disorder, left me with more questions than answers, I pestered Uncle Lucho, and he explained to me what socialism, Communism, Aprism, Urrism, fascism were, and patiently listened to my revolutionary pronouncements. What did they consist of? In my becoming aware that Peru was a country of contrasts, of millions of poor people and barely a handful of Peruvians who had a comfortable, decent standard of living, and that the poor—Indians, mestizos, and blacks—were, in addition to being exploited, looked down on by the rich, a large part of whom were whites. And in my very keen feeling that that injustice had to change and that this change would come about through what was known as the left, socialism, revolution. From those last months in Piura on, I began to think, in secret, that at the university I would try to contact those who were revolutionaries and be one of them. And I also decided that I would take the entrance exams for the University of San Marcos and not for Católica, a university for well-off kids, "whities," and reactionaries. I would go to the national one, the one for mestizos, atheists, and Communists. Uncle Lucho wrote to a relative and a friend of his since childhood, a professor of literature at San Marcos—Augusto Tamayo Vargas—telling him about my plans. And Augusto wrote me a few encouraging lines, telling me that at San Marcos I would find fertile ground for my concerns.

I arrived at the final examinations with a certain anxiety, because of that strike, thinking that the school might take reprisals. But I passed all of them. The last two weeks were frantic ones. I stayed up all night, going over the year's notes and outlines, with Javier Silva, the Artadis, the Temple twins, and often, with as much irresponsibility as ignorance, we took amphetamines so as to stay awake. Amphetamines were sold at the pharmacy without a prescription, and nobody in my circle of friends realized that they were a drug. The artificial lucidity and nervous tension left me feeling weak and depressed the next day.

After the final exam, I had one of those literary encounters that, I suspect, have had a prolonged effect on my life. I came back home around noon, happy at having now left the school behind me, physically exhausted by the many nights in a row that I had forced myself to stay awake, determined to sleep for many long hours. And, already in bed, I picked up one of the books that belonged to Uncle Lucho, a big fat one whose title by itself didn't seem particularly striking: *The Brothers Karamazov*. I read it from cover to cover as fast as I could turn the pages, in a hypnotic state, getting up out of bed every so often like an automaton, not knowing who or where I was, until Aunt Olga came bustling in to remind me that I had to have lunch, and dinner, and breakfast. Between Dostoevsky's magic and the paroxysmal power of his story, with its hallucinatory characters, and my overwrought nervous state brought on by the sleepless nights and the amphetamines of the two weeks of exams, that uninterrupted reading jag of almost twenty-four hours was a real trip, in the sense that that benign word would take on in the 1960s, with the drug culture and the hippie revolution. I have since reread *The Brothers Karamazov*, appreciating it better, beyond a shadow of a doubt, in its infinite complexities, but without living it as intensely as I did on that day and that night in December, when I ended my life as a schoolboy with this tremendous novelistic crowning touch.

I stayed in Piura for a few weeks more, after the exams. Uncle Jorge was to drive out to the San Jacinto hacienda, near Chimbote, where Uncle Pedro was the doctor, and Uncle Lucho agreed to go out there to join them, so that the brothers could see each other, and the plans were that I would go back to Lima in my Uncle Jorge's car. To save me time in preparing for my enrollment at San Marcos, Grandpa had sent to me in Piura a guide for students preparing for the entrance examinations, the *cuestionarios desarrollados*—"models of ideal answers"—and I spent the mornings before my work began at *La Industria* going over the questions and the model answers.

I had high hopes at the prospect of entering the university and beginning adult life, but I felt sad at leaving Piura and Uncle Lucho. The help he gave me that year, during the stage that lies on the borderline between childhood and young adulthood, is one of the best things that ever happened to me. If the expression means anything, I was happy during that year, as I had never been in Lima in any of the previous years, although there had been splendid moments in the course of them. There in Piura, between April and December of 1952, with Uncle Lucho and Aunt Olga, I had enjoyed peace of mind, a way of life without chronic fear, without hiding what I thought, wanted, and dreamed, and this helped me organize my life in a way that harmonized my aptitudes and ineptitudes with my vocation. From Piura, during all of the following year, Uncle Lucho was to continue to help me with his advice and his encouragement, in long replies to the letters I wrote to him.

Perhaps for that reason, but not for that reason alone, Piura came to mean a great deal to me. Adding together the two times that I lived there, they amount to less than two years, and yet that place is more immediately real in what I have written than anywhere else in the world. Those novels, short stories and a play set in Piura do not exhaust these images of that region's people and landscapes that still hover round about me, battling to be turned into works of fiction. The fact that it was in Piura that I had the joy of seeing a work I'd written presented on the stage of a theater and that I made such fast friends there doesn't explain everything, because reason never can explain feelings, and the tie that one forms with a city is of the same sort as the one that suddenly binds one to a woman, a real love affair, with deep and mysterious roots. The fact is that, even if after those last days in 1952 I never lived in Piura again—though I visited it, very sporadically—in a manner of speaking I went on living there, taking the city with me wherever I went, all over the world, hearing Piurans speaking in that lilting, drawling way of theirs, with their typical *guás* and *churres* tacked on to the end of words and their super-superlatives—*lindisísima, carisísima, borrachisísimo*—contemplating their languorous desert landscapes and sometimes feeling on their skin the searing language of its sun.

At the time of the battle against the nationalization of the banks, in 1987, one of the three protest demonstrations we staged was in Piura, and Piura was the first city I went to on campaign, after the launching of my candidacy in Arequipa, on June 4, 1989. Piura was the *departamento* where I visited the most provinces and districts and to which I returned most often during the campaign. I am certain that my subconscious predilection for Piurans and for what was Piuran played a part in that. And, doubtless, for that very reason I was to experience such disappointment, in June of 1990, on discovering that the voters in Piura were not attuned to my feelings, since they voted by a large majority for my opponent in the final round on June 10,* despite the fact that Fujimori had made hardly more than a furtive visit to the city in the course of his campaign.

The trip to go meet Uncle Jorge was postponed several times, until finally we took to the road, at the end of December, very early in the morning. Our journey was marked by all sorts of mishaps—having to change a tire on the highway and confronting problems with the motor of the station wagon, which overheated. The meeting with the uncles coming from Lima took place in Chimbote, at that time still a quiet village of fishermen, with the very well-run Hotel de Turistas on the

---

* The tally of the second round of voting for the *departamento* of Piura was 56.5 percent (253,758 votes) for Cambio 90 and 32.5 percent (145,714 votes) for the Democratic Front.

shores of a beach with crystal-clear water. We had a dinner with the whole family—Uncle Jorge's wife, Aunt Gaby, and Uncle Pedro were there—and the next day, early in the morning, I said goodbye to Uncle Lucho, who was going back to Piura. When I gave him a hug, I burst into tears.

TEN

Public Life

EVER since the rally in the Plaza San Martín, my life had ceased to be private. Never again, until I left Peru after the second round of voting for the presidency, in June 1990, did I enjoy that privacy that I had always guarded so jealously (to the point of remarking that what attracted me about England was the fact that since nobody there ever picked a quarrel with anybody else, people turned into ghosts). Ever since that rally, at any hour of the day or night, there were people at my house, holding meetings, conducting interviews, organizing something or other, or else standing in line to talk with me, with Patricia, or with Álvaro. Reception rooms, hallways, stairways were always occupied by men and women whom I'd often never met and whose reason for being there was utterly unknown to me, reminding me of a line from a poem by Carlos Germán Belli: "This is not your house, you're a man of the wilds."

Since María del Carmen, my secretary, soon found herself swamped with work, others came to give her a hand, first Silvana, then Rosi and Lucía and later on two volunteers, Anita and Elena, and a room next to my study had to be built to lodge that woman's army and make room for paraphernalia that I (who have always written by hand) saw, as if in a dream, being brought into the house, being installed and beginning to work all around me: computers, faxes, photocopy machines, intercoms, typewriters, new telephone lines, rows of filing cabinets. That office, next to the library and a few steps away from our bedroom, operated from early in the morning till late at night, and till dawn in the weeks immediately preceding the election, so that I came to feel that everything about my life, including sleeping and even more intimate matters, had become public.

During the campaign against nationalization we had two bodyguards inside the house, till the day when, sick and tired of running at every turn into armed men with pistols that terrified my mother and Aunt Olga—who were both living with us then—Patricia decided that the security unit would stay outside the house.

The story of the bodyguards included a comic chapter on the night of the Plaza San Martín. With the sudden increase in terrorism and crime—kidnapping had become a flourishing industry—there began to be more and more private surveillance and protection agencies in Peru. One of them, known as "the Israelis," since its owners or directors came from Israel, was in charge of protecting Hernando de Soto. And he arranged, along with Miguel Cruchaga, to have "the Israelis" guard me at that time. Manuel and Alberto, two ex-Marines, came to my house. They accompanied me to the Plaza San Martín and stood at the foot of the speakers' platform on August 21. When I finished speaking, I invited the crowd to go with me to the Palace of Justice to hand over to the AP and the PPC members of Congress the list of signatures against nationalization. During the march, Manuel disappeared, swallowed up by the crowd. But Alberto stuck to me like glue amid all the chaos. A station wagon belonging to "the Israelis" was to pick me up on the steps of the neoclassic white building on the Paseo de la República. With Alberto there beside me as always, like my shadow, and the two of us nearly crushed to a pulp by the demonstrators, we went down the stairs. All of a sudden, a black car with the doors open appeared out of nowhere. I was lifted off my feet, shoved inside, and found myself surrounded by armed strangers. I took it for granted that they were "the Israelis." But then I heard Alberto shouting: "It's not them, it's not them!" and saw him struggling. He managed to dive into the car just as it was taking off and landed like a dead weight on top of me and the other occupants. "Is this a kidnapping?" I asked, half jokingly and half seriously. "Our job is to look after you," the bruiser who was driving answered. And immediately thereafter, he spoke a phrase straight out of a movie into the hand microphone he was holding: "The Jaguar is safe and we're going to the moon. *Over.*"

It was Óscar Balbi, the head agent of Prosegur, a company that was a competitor of "the Israelis." My friends Pipo Thorndike and Roberto Dañino had arranged for Prosegur to provide for my security that night, but had forgotten to tell me. They had spoken with Jorge Vega, the chairman of the board of directors of Prosegur, and the entrepreneur Luis Woolcot had paid the expenses (I learned this two years afterward).

A while later, and through arrangements made by Juan Jochamo-witz, Prosegur decided to take over the responsibility for the security of my house and my family for the three years of the campaign, without ever asking us for a fee (as a result, the government canceled the contracts it had with Prosegur to guard state enterprises). Óscar Balbi organized the security for all my trips and for the rallies of the Dem-ocratic Front and was invariably at my side in the planes, helicopters, trucks, light vans, motorboats, and on the horses that I used in those years to make two complete swings around the whole of Peru. Only once did I see a situation get the better of him: in the late afternoon of September 21, 1988, in the little rural community of Acchupata, in Cajamarca, in the Cumbe mountain range, where the 14,500-foot altitude made him fall off his horse and we had to resuscitate him by giving him oxygen.

I am grateful to him and to all his companions, because they lent me services that there would have been no way to pay for—and ones that are indispensable in a country where political violence has reached the extremes that it has in Peru. But I must say that living under permanent protection is like living in prison, a nightmare for anyone who enjoys his freedom as much as I do.

I could no longer do what I have always liked doing, ever since I was a youngster, in the afternoon after finishing writing: wander about through different parts of town, explore the streets, slip into matinees at those neighborhood movie houses so old they creak and where the fleas eventually drive a person out, climb into jitneys and public buses, with no fixed goal, so as to come to know, little by little, the innermost parts and the people of that heterogeneous labyrinth, so full of con-trasts, that is Lima. In recent years I had become known—more for a television program that I put on than for my books—so that it was no longer as easy for me to amble about without attracting attention. But from August 1987 on it was impossible for me to go anywhere without being immediately surrounded by people and applauded or booed. And going through life followed by reporters and in the middle of a ring of bodyguards—at first there were two of them, then four, and finally fifteen or so in the last months—was a spectacle somewhere between a clown act and an annoyance that took away all my pleasure. It is true that my killing schedules left me practically no time for anything unrelated to politics, but even so, in my rare free moments it was unthinkable, for example, for me to go into a bookstore—where I was so besieged I couldn't do what a person does in such places: browse about among the shelves, leaf through books, turn everything topsy-turvy in the hope of coming across some superb unexpected find—or to a theater, where my appearance gave rise to demonstrations, as happened at a recital by Alicia Maguiña, at the Teatro Municipal, when the audience, on seeing me come in with Patricia, divided into adherents who applauded and adversaries who jeered. In order for me to see a play, José Sanchís Sinisterra's *Ay, Carmela*, without incident, friends from the Ensayo group seated me, all by myself, in the balcony of the Teatro Británico. I mention these performances because, as I remember, they were the only ones I attended during those years. And as for the movies, something that I'm as fond of as I am of books and the theater, I went to two or three of them at most, and always more or less stealthily (entering after the film had begun and leaving before it was over). The last time—it was at the Cine San Antonio, in Miraflores—Óscar Balbi came to my seat halfway through the movie to get me because they had just thrown a bomb at one of the local headquarters of Libertad and left a watchman with a bullet wound. I went to soccer games two or three times and to a volleyball match too, as well as to bullfights, but these were appearances that were decided on by the campaign directors of the Democratic Front, for the obligatory sessions of "mingling with the crowd."

The diversions, then, that Patricia and I could allow ourselves consisted of going to the houses of friends for dinner and every once in a while to a restaurant, though we were well aware that this latter would make us feel spied on or like performers in a stage show. I often thought, with shivers running up and down my spine: "I've lost my freedom." If I were president, it would be like that for five more years. And I remember the sense of amazement and the happiness that came over me on June 14, 1990, when, after all that was over, I landed in Paris and even before unpacking any of the suitcases went for a walk down the Boulevard St.-Germain, feeling like an anonymous passerby once again, without escorts, without police details, without being recognized (or nearly so, since all of a sudden, as if by spontaneous generation, there appeared in front of me once more, blocking my way, the ubiquitous, omniscient Juan Cruz, of *El País*, to whom I found it impossible to deny an interview).

Once my political life began, I made a decision: "I'm not going to stop reading or writing for at least a couple of hours every day. Not even if I'm president." It was only partially a selfish decision. It was also dictated by the conviction that what I wanted to do, as a candidate and as head of the government, I would do better if I kept intact a private, personal space, walled in to keep out politics, a space consisting of ideas, reflections, dreams, and intellectual work.

I kept this promise I'd made to myself only insofar as reading was concerned, although not always the minimum of two hours a day that I'd set myself. As for writing, it was impossible for me. Writing fiction, that is to say. It wasn't only the lack of time. It was impossible for me to concentrate, to give myself over to the play of imagination, to attain that state of breaking completely away from and suspending everything around me, which is what is so marvelous about writing novels and works for the theater. Preoccupations of the moment, far removed from the realm of pure literature, kept interfering, and there was no way of escaping from the exhausting march of events. Moreover, I never managed to get used to the idea that I was alone, even though it was very early in the morning and the secretaries hadn't come in yet. It was as if my beloved demons had fled from my study, resentful at my lack of solitude during the rest of the day. It distressed me, and I gave up trying. In those three years, I wrote only a light erotic divertissement—*Elogio de la madrastra* (*In Praise of the Stepmother*) —along with speeches, articles, brief political essays, and a number of forewords for a collection of modern novels published under the Círculo de Lectores imprint.

Having a schedule that permitted so little time for reading made me very exacting: I couldn't offer myself the luxury of reading as anarchically as I have always been in the habit of doing, and I read only books that I knew were going to hypnotize me. And so I reread certain novels very close to my heart, among them Malraux's *La Condition humaine* (*Man's Fate*), Melville's *Moby Dick*, Faulkner's *Light in August*, and Borges's short stories. A bit unnerved at discovering how little intellect—how little intelligence—is involved in the daily round of political tasks, I also made myself read difficult works that forced me to think while I read and to take notes. Ever since *The Open Society and Its Enemies* fell into my hands in 1980, I had promised myself to study Karl Popper. I did so in these three years, every day, early in the morning, before going out for my daily run, when often it was just barely daylight and the quiet of the house reminded me of the prepolitical period of my life.

And at night, before going to sleep, I read poetry—always the classics of the Spanish Golden Age, and usually Góngora. Each time it was a purifying bath, if only for half an hour, to get away from arguments, plots, intrigues, invectives, and be the guest of a perfect world, freed of all contemporaneity, resplendently harmonious, inhabited by all the nymphs and literary villains anyone could wish for and by mythological monsters, who moved about in landscapes refined to quintessences, amid references to Greek and Roman fictions, subtle music, and pure, clean architecture. I had read Góngora since my university years, with rather distant admiration, because his very perfection struck me as just a touch inhuman and his world too cerebral and chimerical. But between 1987 and 1990 how grateful I was to him for being all of that, for having built that baroque enclave outside of time, suspended in the most illustrious heights of intellect and sensibility, emancipated from the ugly, the mean and petty, the mediocre, from all that sordid warp and woof of which daily life is woven for the majority of mortals.

Between the first and the second electoral round—between April 8 and June 10, 1990—I was unable to do my studious hour or hour and a half of reading in the mornings, even though I sat down in my study with a copy of Popper's *Conjectures and Refutations* or *Objective Knowledge* in my hands. My head was too immersed in the problems, in the tremendous tension of each day, in the news of attempts on people's lives and of murders—for over a hundred persons with ties to the Democratic Front, district leaders, candidates for national or regional offices, or sympathizers, were assassinated in those two months, humble people, beings no different from others who all over the world are the privileged victims of political terrorism (and also of counterterrorism)—and I had to give up. But not a single day, not even the day of the election, went by without my reading a sonnet of Góngora's, or a strophe of his *Polifemo* or his *Soledades* or one or another of his ballads or rondelets, and through these verses to feel that, if only for a few minutes, my life became purer. May these present lines stand as evidence of my gratitude toward the great man of Córdoba.

I had thought I knew Peru well, since I had made any number of trips to the interior, beginning when I was still a small boy, yet my constant travels over those three years revealed to me a profound aspect of my country, or rather, the many aspects, the many faces that constitute it, its impressive geographical, social, and ethnic diversity, the complexity of its problems, its tremendous contrasts, and the shocking levels of poverty and helplessness in which the majority of Peruvians lived.

Peru is not one country, but several, living together in mutual mistrust and ignorance, in resentment and prejudice, and in a maelstrom of violences. Violences *in the plural*, that of political terror and that of the drug traffic; that of common crime, which, with the country's impoverishment and the collapse of the (limited) rule of law was making daily life more and more barbarous; and then too, of course, the so-called structural violence: discrimination, the lack of opportunity, unemployment, and the starvation wages of vast sectors of the population.

I knew all this; I had heard it and read it and seen it, from a distance and in a few quick glances, the way we Peruvians who have the good fortune to belong to the tiny privileged segment that surveys call Sector A see the rest of our compatriots. But between 1987 and 1990 I came to know all that at close range, had it at my fingertips almost every day, and to a certain degree I can say that I lived it. The Peru of my childhood was a poor and backward country: in the last decades, mainly since the beginning of Velasco's dictatorship and in particular during Alan García's presidency, it had become poorer still and in many regions wretchedly poverty-stricken, a country that was going back to inhuman patterns of existence. The famous "lost decade" for Latin America—lost by the populist policies of domestic development, government control, and economic nationalism recommended by the Economic Commission for Latin America, imbued with the economic philosophy of its president, Raúl Prebisch—was particularly tragic for Peru, since our governments went much further than others when it came to "defending itself" against foreign investments and sacrificing the creation of wealth to its redistribution. *

An administrative district I knew well, in earlier days, was the *departamento* of Piura. And today I couldn't believe my eyes. The little towns of the province of Sullana—San Jacinto, Marcavelica, Salitral—or of Paita—Amotape, Arenal, and Tamarindo—not to mention those in the mountain country of Huancabamba and Ayabaca, or those in the desert—Catacaos, La Unión, La Arena, Sechura—seemed to have died a living death, to be languishing in hopeless apathy. It is admittedly true that, in my memory, the dwellings were as crude as they are today, made of clay and wild cane, and that people went barefoot and groused about the lack of roads, of medical dispensaries, of schools, of water, of electricity. But in these poor small towns of my childhood in Piura there was a powerful vitality, a visible light-heartedness and a hope that now seemed to have died out altogether. They had grown a good deal—some of them had tripled in size, they were full to overflowing with kids and with people without jobs, and an air of decay and decrepitude, if not of total despair, appeared to be swallowing them up. In my meetings with local townspeople, the same chorus was repeated over and over: "We're dying of starvation. There are no jobs."

The case of Piura is a good illustration of that phrase by the naturalist Antonio Raimondi, who, in the nineteenth century, defined Peru as "a beggar sitting on a bench made of gold." And also a good example of how a country *chooses* underdevelopment. The ocean off the coast of Piura has a wealth of fish that would suffice to give work to all the men in Piura. There is oil offshore, and in the desert the immense phosphate mines of Bayóvar that have not yet been worked. And the soil of Piura is very fertile and produces abundant crops, as shown in the past by its landed estates that grew cotton, rice, and fruit and were among the best-cultivated haciendas in Peru. Why should a *departamento* with resources such as that die of starvation and lack of jobs?

General Velasco confiscated those large landed estates from which, indeed, the workers received a very small percentage of the profits, and turned them into cooperatives and enterprises of so-called social

---

* In 1960, Peru occupied eighth place in Latin America; at the end of Alan García's administration it had dropped to fourteenth.

property, in which, in theory, the peasants replaced the former owners. In practice, the new owners were the boards of directors of these socialized enterprises, who bent their every effort to exploiting the peasants, as much as or more than the peasants' old bosses ever had. With an aggravating circumstance. The former owners knew how to work their lands, replaced worn-out machinery, reinvested. The heads of the cooperatives and social property enterprises devoted their efforts to administering them politically, and in many cases their one concern was to plunder them. The result was that soon there were no profits to share.*

When I began my campaign, all the farm cooperatives in Piura except one were technically bankrupt. But a social property enterprise never goes broke. The state releases it each year from the debts it has contracted with the Banco Agrario (in other words, it passes the losses on to the taxpayers), and President Alan García was in the habit of turning these releases from debt into public ceremonies, with glowing revolutionary rhetoric. This explained why rural Piura had grown poorer by the year ever since the agrarian reform that had been put into effect in order that, according to Velasco's oft-repeated slogan, "the owner will no longer feed on the poverty of the peasants." The owners had disappeared, but the peasants were eating less than they had before. The only beneficiaries had been the petty bureaucrats catapulted to the head of these enterprises through political power, boards of directors against whom, in our meetings, members of cooperatives continually came up with the same accusations.

As for the commercial fishing industry, what had happened was even more self-destructive. In the 1950s, thanks to the vision of a handful of entrepreneurs—of one from Tacna in particular, Luis Banchero Rossi—a pioneer industry sprang up on the Peruvian coast: the manufacture of fish meal. In a few years Peru became the number-one producer in the world. This created thousands of jobs, dozens of factories, turned the little port of Chimbote into a large commercial and industrial center, and developed commercial fishing to the point that Peru, in the 1970s, became a country with a larger fishing industry than Japan.

---

* In the 1960s, Peru's income per capita from agriculture and cattle raising was second in Latin America; in 1990, it was next to last, superior only to that of Haiti.

In 1972 Velasco's military dictatorship nationalized all the fisheries and made of them a gigantic conglomerate, Pesca Perú, which he put into the hands of a bureaucracy. The result: the ruin of the industry. When I began my travels around the country in 1987, the situation of that mammoth, Pesca Perú, was critical. Many fish meal factories had been closed—in La Libertad, in Chimbote, in Lima, in Ica, in Arequipa—and innumerable boats belonging to the conglomerate were rotting in the harbors, without the spare parts or replacements that would enable them to go out to sea to fish. This was one of the public sectors that drained off the most state subsidies, and was therefore one of the major causes of the nation's impoverishment. (A moving episode of my campaign was the surprising decision, in October 1988, of the inhabitants of a little town on the coast of Arequipa, Atico, to gather in a body, with their mayor at the head, to plead for the privatization of the fish meal factory which, in days gone by, had been the principal source of employment in the town. It had now been closed. The moment I heard the news, I flew there in a very small plane that made a bumpy landing on the beach at Atico, so as to show the townspeople that my sympathies lay with them and to explain to them why we proposed to return to private ownership not only "their" factory but all the public enterprises in the country.)

The fishing and fish meal manufacturing disaster had hit Piura hard. I was really taken aback when I saw the coast of Sechura overcome by inertia. I remembered the harbor bustling with fishing smacks and small seagoing boats and the streets jammed with *camareros*—refrigerator trucks—that had crossed the vast desert to go all the way up there to buy little anchovies and other fish needed to keep the factories of Chimbote and other ports in Peru working.

And as for the oil in the marine deposit off Piura and the phosphates of Sechura, there they were, with people hoping that someday the capital and the technology needed to exploit them might come to Peru. During his first year in office, Alan García had nationalized the Belco Oil Company, an American concern that operated offshore on the northern coast. Since then the country had been involved in international litigation with the company. This, on top of the declaration of war of the Aprista government against the International Monetary Fund and the entire world financial system, its hostile policy toward foreign investments, and the growing insecurity in Peru because of terrorist activities, had made the country a plague-ridden nation: nobody extended credit to it, nobody invested in it. After being an exporter of petroleum, Peru in these years became an importer. That was why the Piura region had that heartbreaking look of desolation. And it was a symbol of what had been happening all over Peru for the past thirty years.

But compared with other regions, impoverished Piura was enviable—prosperous, almost. In the central Andes, in Ayacucho, Huancavelica, Junín, Cerro de Pasco, Apurímac, as well as in the Altiplano bordering on Bolivia—the *departamento* of Puno—that zone referred to as one of critical poverty, which was also the one to which terrorism and counterterrorism had brought the most bloodshed, the situation was even worse. The few roads had been disappearing little by little because of lack of maintenance and in many places Sendero Luminoso had dynamited the bridges and blocked the trails with boulders. It had also destroyed experimental crops and livestock, wrecked the buildings and killed off hundreds of vicuñas in the Pampa Galeras Reserve, pillaged agricultural cooperatives—principally those of the Valle de Mantaro, the most dynamic ones in all the high country—assassinated local agents from the Ministry of Agriculture and foreign experts in rural development who had come to Peru on international cooperation projects, murdered small-scale farmers and miners or caused them to flee for their lives, blown up tractors, power plants, hydroelectric installations, and in many places killed the cattle and rubbed out the members of cooperatives and communes who tried to oppose their razed earth policy, whereby they intended to throttle the cities to death, Lima above all, by allowing no food to reach them.

Words do not offer a precise account of what expressions such as "subsistence economy" or "critical poverty" mean in terms of human suffering, of the bestialization of life through lack of jobs and any hope of change for the better, through the impoverishment of the environment. This was the state of affairs in the mountain country in the center of Peru. Life there had always been poor, but now, with the closing of so many mines, the abandonment of crop-bearing lands, the isolation, the lack of investment, the nearly total disappearance of interchange with other regions, and the sabotage of centers of production and public services, it had been reduced to horrifying levels.

Seeing those Andean villages, daubed with the hammer and sickle and the slogans of Sendero Luminoso, from which entire families were fleeing, abandoning everything, driven half mad with desperation because of the violence and the wretched poverty, to go off to swell the armies of unemployed in the cities—villages in which those who stayed appeared to be the survivors of some biblical catastrophe—I often thought: "A country can *always* be worse off. Underdevelopment is bottomless." And for the last thirty years Peru had done everything possible to ensure that there would be more and more poor people and that its poor would each day be more impoverished still. In the face of those millions of Peruvians who were literally dying of hunger, in that Andean Cordillera that has the richest mining potential on the continent—that Cordillera from which there came the gold and the silver that made the name of Peru ring out all over the world with a music of precious metals and become a synonym of munificence—wasn't it obvious that politics ought to be oriented toward attracting investments, starting up industries, stimulating trade, restoring land values, developing mining, agriculture, and cattle raising?

The principle of the redistribution of wealth has an unquestionable moral force, but it often blinds its advocates and keeps them from seeing that it does not promote social justice if the policies that it gives rise to paralyze production, discourage initiative, drive away investments: that is to say, if they result in an increase in poverty. And redistributing poverty, or in the case of the Andes, the severest privation, as Alan García was doing, does not feed those who confront the problem as a matter of life or death.

Ever since my disillusionment with Marxism and socialism—in theory on the one hand, but above all in reality, the kind I had become acquainted with in Cuba, in the Soviet Union, and in the so-called popular democracies—I suspected that the fascination of intellectuals with state control had to do not only with their vocation for seeking handouts or a regular income, a vocation nurtured by the patronage system that had caused them to live under the sheltering shadow of the Church and of princes and had been continued by the totalitarian regimes of the twentieth century, in which intellectuals, on condition that they proved docile, automatically formed part of the privileged elite, but also with their lack of economic knowledge. From that time on, I tried—in a very undisciplined way, unfortunately—to remedy in one way or another my ignorance in this field. After 1980, thanks to a year's fellowship at the Wilson Center, in Washington, I did so in a more orderly way and with growing interest, on discovering that despite appearances economics, far from being an exact science, was as open to creativity as the arts. When I entered the political arena, in 1987, two economists, Felipe Ortiz de Zevallos and Raúl Salazar, who was to become the head of the economic team of the Democratic Front, began to give me weekly lessons on the Peruvian economy. We met in a little room overlooking Freddy Cooper's garden, at night, for a couple of hours, and I learned many things there. I also learned to respect the talent and the decency of Raúl Salazar, the key figure in the detailed development of the program of the Front, the person who, had we won, would have been our minister of finance. I once asked Raúl and Felipe to figure out for me how much each Peruvian would get if an egalitarian-minded administration redistributed all the wealth that existed in the country at that time. The answer: approximately fifty dollars per capita.* In other words, Peru would go on being the same country of poor people that it was, with the aggravating circumstance that after even such a measure it would never cease to be just that.

In order for a country to emerge from poverty, redistributive policies don't work. Others do work, the ones which, since they take into account an inevitable inequality between those who produce more and those who produce less, lack the intellectual and ethical fascination that has always surrounded socialism, and have been condemned because they encourage the profit motive. But egalitarian-oriented economies based on solidarity have never raised a country out of poverty; they have impoverished it even further. And they have frequently limited freedoms or caused them to disappear altogether, since egalitarianism requires strict planning, which starts out by being economic and gradually spreads to the rest of life. From this there results inefficiency, corruption, and privileges for those in power that are a negation of the very concept of egalitarianism. The rare cases of the economic takeoff of countries of the Third World have all, without exception, followed the plan of a market economy.

* In 1990, the book value of Peru's one hundred largest private corporations was $1,232 million. This amount, divided equally among 22 million Peruvians, would give each person $56. (I am grateful to Felipe Ortiz de Zavallos and Raúl Salazar for these particulars.)

In each of my trips to the central mountain region between 1987 and 1990, and I made many of them, I felt a tremendous sadness on seeing what life there had become for at least a third of Peruvians. And I returned from each of these trips more convinced than ever of what had to be done. Reopen the mines that had been closed for lack of incentives to export, since the artificially low value of the dollar had caused small and medium-sized mining operations to come close to disappearing altogether, so that only large-scale mining had survived, in extremely precarious conditions. Attract capital and technology in order to open new companies. Put an end to the price controls on agricultural products whereby the Aprista administration condemned peasants to subsidize the cities, the pretext being to lower the price of food for the masses. Give title deeds to the hundreds of thousands of peasants whose land had been divided up by the cooperatives and do away with the regulations forbidding corporations to invest in rural holdings.

But in order to accomplish all this, it was imperative to put an end to the terror that had taken hold in the Andes, allowing the revolutionaries to do as they pleased.

Traveling in the Andes was arduous. In order to avoid ambushes, it had to be done suddenly and unexpectedly, with a small party, sending Mobilization activists ahead to alert the most reliable people no more than one or two days in advance. It was impossible to go overland to many provinces of the central mountain region—Junín, after Ayacucho, had been victimized by the most attacks. The journey had to be made in small planes that landed in unbelievable places— cemeteries, soccer fields, riverbeds—or in light helicopters which, if a storm suddenly overtook us, had to set down wherever they could —on top of a mountain sometimes—until the weather cleared. These acrobatics completely unnerved some of the friends of Libertad. Beatriz Merino took out crosses, rosaries, and holy medals she wore over her heart, and invoked the protection of the saints without self-consciousness. Pedro Cateriano intimidated the pilots into giving him reassuring explanations about the flight instruments, and kept pointing out to them the threatening thunderheads, the sharp peaks that suddenly loomed up, or the snaky rays of lightning that zigzagged all about us. The two of them were more afraid of flying than of terrorists, but never refused to go with me when I asked them to.

I remember the very young little soldier, practically a child, whom they brought to me at the abandoned airport of Jauja on September 8, 1989, so that we could take him back to Lima with us. He had survived an attack that noon in which two of his buddies had died—we had heard the bombs and the shots from the speakers' platform in the main square in Huancayo, where we were holding our rally—and he was losing a lot of blood. We made room for him in the very small craft by having one of the bodyguards stay behind. The boy was surely under the army's legal age limit of eighteen. He was holding a container of plasma above his head, but his strength gave out. We took turns holding it up. He didn't complain once during the flight. He stared blankly into space, with an astonished, wordless desperation, as though trying to understand what had happened to him.

I remember how, on February 14, 1990, as we were leaving the Milpo mine, in Cerro de Pasco, the triple glass of a side window of our light van shattered, turning into a spider web, as we were driving past a hostile group. "This was supposed to be an armored van," I said. "It is," Óscar Balbi assured me. "Against bullets. But that was a stone." It wasn't armored against cudgels either, because at a sugar mill in the North, a handful of Apristas had smashed all its window-panes to smithereens a few weeks before. The theoretical armor, more-over, turned the vehicle into an oven (the air conditioning never worked), so that, as a general rule, we jolted over the roads with a door held open by my security guard Professor Oshiro's foot.

I remember the members of the Libertad committee of Cerro de Pasco, who turned up at a regional meeting, some of them battered and bruised and others injured, since that morning a terrorist com-mando unit had attacked their headquarters. And I remember the members of the committee in Ayacucho, the capital of the Sendero Luminoso insurrection, where human life was worth less than any-where else in Peru. Every time I went to Ayacucho in those three years to meet with our committee, I had the feeling that I was with men and women who could die at any moment and was assailed by a sense of guilt. When the lists of candidates for national and regional legislative posts were agreed on, we knew that the risk for the men and women of Ayacucho whose names were on them would be even greater than before, and like other political organizations, we offered to get the candidates out of Ayacucho and hide them until after the election.

They didn't take us up on the offer. They asked me, rather, to see if I could arrange with the politico-military head of the region to allow them to go about armed. But Brigadier General Howard Rodríguez Málaga refused me permission for them to do so.

Shortly before that meeting, Julián Huamaní Yauli, a Freedom Movement candidate for a seat in the regional legislature, had heard people climbing up onto the roof of his house and ran out into the street for safety's sake. The second time, on March 4, 1990, he didn't have time to get out of the house. They surprised him at the front door, in broad daylight, and after gunning him down, the killers calmly walked off through a crowd which ten years of terror had taught not to see anything, hear anything, or lift a finger in such cases. I remember the badly mangled body of Julián Huamaní Yauli in his coffin, on that sunny morning in Ayacucho, and the weeping of his wife and his mother, a peasant woman who, with her arms around me, sobbed out words in Quechua that I was unable to understand.

The possibility of a terrorist attack on my life or my family was something that Patricia, my children, and I looked on from the start as a reality that we must be aware of. We agreed not to do things that were imprudent, but not to allow the danger to take our freedom of movement away from us. Gonzalo and Morgana were studying in London, so that the risk to them was confined to the months when they were on vacation from school. But Álvaro was in Peru; he was a journalist and the communications director of the Front and did not mince words when he attacked extremism and the government day and night; moreover, he kept giving the security service the slip, so that Patricia lived in constant fear that someone would come to announce to us that he had been murdered or kidnapped.

It was obvious that, as long as no one attempted to put an end to the insecurity that political violence was causing to reign in the country, the possibilities of an economic recovery were nil, even if inflation were brought under control. Who was going to come to open mines or drill oil wells or set up factories if he ran the risk of being kidnapped, assassinated, obliged to make regular payoffs to revolutionaries, and having his installations blown up? (The very next week after I had visited, in Huacho, in March 1990, the cannery for the export company Industrias Alimentarias, SA, whose owner, a courageous young entrepreneur, Julio Fabre Carranza, told us how he had escaped an attempt on his life, Sendero Luminoso reduced the cannery to rubble, leaving a thousand workers out of jobs.)

Bringing peace to the country was one of the first priorities, along with the fight against inflation. This was not a task for police and soldiers alone, but for civil society as a whole, since everyone would suffer the consequences if Sendero Luminoso turned Peru into the Cambodia of the Khmer Rouge or the Túpac Amaru revolutionaries turned it into another Cuba. Leaving the fight against terrorism in the hands of police and military forces had not produced positive results. On the contrary. The abuses of human rights, the disappearances, the extrajudicial executions had embittered the populace, which offered the forces of law and order no cooperation whatsoever. And without the aid of its citizens a democratic government cannot put down a subversive movement. The Aprista administration had aggravated the situation with its counterterrorist groups, such as the so-called Rodrigo Franco Commando Unit. These groups, as was common knowledge, were armed and directed from the Ministry of the Interior; they had assassinated attorneys and union leaders on close terms with Sendero Luminoso, placed bombs in print shops and institutions suspected of complicity with terrorism, and in addition hounded the president's most belligerent adversaries, such as Representative Fernando Olivera, who, in view of the fact that he persisted in denouncing in Congress the unlawful acquisition of property by Alan García, had been the target of terrorist threats.

My thesis was that terror should not be combated in an underhanded way, but openly and resolutely, mobilizing peasants, workers, students, and personally headed by the civil authorities. I had said that if I were elected, I would assume the leadership of the fight against terrorism in person, that I would replace the politico-military heads of the emergency area by civil authorities and arm the patrols formed by the peasants to confront the Sendero Luminoso detachments.

In Peru, in the *departamento* of Cajamarca, peasant patrols had shown how effective they could be. Working together with the authorities, they had cleared the countryside of cattle rustlers, and constituted an effective brake on terrorism, since thus far Sendero Luminoso and the MRTA (the Túpac Amaru Revolutionary Movement) had been unable to get a foothold in the countryside in Cajamarca. In all the indigenous communities, cooperatives, and villages of the Andes that I visited, I encountered an immense frustration on the part of the peasants, because they were unable to defend themselves against the terrorist detachments. They were obliged to feed, clothe, and lend logistical aid to the terrorists, and obey their sometimes absurd orders, such as to produce only enough for their own needs, not engage in commercial dealings, and not attend market fairs. Aid lent the cause of subversion exposed these people to often merciless reprisals on the part of the forces of order. Many communities had formed patrols that confronted the tommy guns and automatic rifles of the Sendero Luminoso and Túpac Amaru movements with clubs, knives, and hunting rifles.

I therefore asked Peruvians for a mandate to provide these patrols with arms that would allow them to defend themselves effectively against those who were killing them wholesale.* This proposal was severely criticized, especially outside Peru, where it was said that by arming the peasants I would open the gates to civil war (as though one didn't already exist) and that, in a democracy, it is the police and the military that are the institutions responsible for reestablishing public order. This criticism doesn't take into account the actual political conditions in underdeveloped countries. In a democracy that is taking its first steps, the introduction of free elections, independent political parties, and a free press does not mean that *all* of its institutions have become democratic. The democratization of the whole of society is a much slower process, and it is a long time before labor unions, political parties, the government, and business begin to act as they are expected to in a state ruled by law. And the institutions that are perhaps the slowest at learning how to function democratically, within the law and with respect for civil authority, are those which, in dictatorial systems, semidictatorial ones, and sometimes even apparently democratic ones, have long been accustomed to the authoritarian exercise of power: the police and the military.

The ineffectiveness demonstrated by the forces of order in the fight against the terror campaign in Peru had several causes. One of them: their inability to win over the civilian population and obtain active support from it, especially when it came to providing information,

---

* Of the 20,000 deaths caused by acts of terrorism up until mid-1990, 90 percent of those killed were peasants, the poorest of the poor in Peru.

which is indispensable in fighting an enemy that doesn't show its face, whose action is based on its successfully mingling with civil society, from which it emerges in order to make its attacks and to which it returns to conceal itself. And this inability was a result of the methods employed in the fight against subversion by institutions which had not been prepared for this sort of war, so different from a conventional one, and which often limited themselves to following the strategy of showing the villagers that they could be as cruel as the terrorists. The result was that, in many places, the forces of order aroused as much fear and hostility among the peasants as the guerrilla bands of Sendero Luminoso or the MRTA.

I remember a conversation with a bishop in one of the cities of the emergency area. He was a young man, with the look of someone who went in for sports, and very intelligent. He belonged to the so-called conservative sector of the Church, an adversary of liberation theology and hence above all suspicious of having been taken in, as have certain members of religious orders who are supporters of this tendency, by extremist propaganda. I asked him, a man who had traveled all over this martyrized land and spoken with so many people, to tell me how much truth there was in the stories of abuses of which the forces of order were accused. His testimony was overwhelming, above all with respect to the behavior of the PIPs: rapes, thefts, murders, horrendous assaults against the peasants, all committed with total impunity. I remember his words: "I feel safer traveling by myself through the backlands of Ayacucho than I do if protected by them." An incipient democracy cannot progress if it entrusts the defense of law and order to people who engage in such savagery.

Simplifications, however, must be avoided in this respect as well. The defense of human rights is one of the weapons that extremism makes most effective use of in order to paralyze governments that it wishes to overthrow, manipulating well-intentioned but ingenuous persons and institutions. In the course of the campaign I had several meetings with officers of the army and the navy, who informed me in detail about the state of the revolutionary war in Peru. And that was how I learned of the extremely difficult, not to say impossible, conditions in which soldiers and sailors are obliged to carry on that war, owing to the lack of adequate training and equipment, and owing to the demoralization that the economic crisis was causing in the ranks.

I remember a conversation, in Andahuaylas, with a young army lieutenant who had just come back from a scouting expedition in the area
of Cangallo and Vilcashuamán. His men, he explained to me, had
enough ammunition for just one engagement. In a second skirmish
with the insurgents, they no longer had the means to shoot back. As
for provisions, they had none with them at all. They had to hustle up
their own food as best they could. "You probably think we were obliged
to pay the peasants for that grub, right, Doctor Vargas? What with? I
haven't received my pay for two months now. And what I earn [less
than a hundred dollars a month] doesn't even go far enough to support
my mother back in Jaén. The extra money handed out to soldiers who
do really tough jobs gives them enough to buy smokes. Kindly explain
to me how we can get hold of enough cash to pay for what we eat
when we go out on patrol."

By 1989, the inflation of the past few years had reduced the real
pay of the military, as well as of all the other employees of the state,
to a third of what it had been in 1985. The detachments sent out to
fight subversion suffered a similar decrease. The dejection and the
frustration of officers and troops connected to the counterinsurgency
campaign were enormous. In the barracks, at the bases, the lack of
spare parts had put trucks, helicopters, jeeps, and armaments of every
sort out of service. There was, furthermore, a tacit rivalry between the
national police and the armed forces. The former considered themselves discriminated against by the latter, and soldiers and sailors accused the Civil Guard of selling their weapons to drug traffickers and
terrorists, who were allies in the valley of the Huallaga. And both
forces of order recognized that the terrible lack of resources had dramatically increased corruption in the military institutions, to neither
a greater nor a lesser degree than in public administration.

Only a determined participation of civil society alongside the forces
of order could reverse that tendency whereby, since the time it first
made its dramatic appearance in 1979 up until the present, it is subversion that is winning points and the democratic system of government
that is losing them. My idea was that, as in Israel, civilians should
organize to protect work centers, cooperatives and communes, public
services, and means of communication, and that all of this should be
done in collaboration with the armed forces, though under the direction of the civil authorities. This close collaboration would serve—as

had been the case in Israel, where there are doubtless many things to criticize but also others to imitate, among the latter the relationship that exists between their armed forces and civil society—not to militarize society but to "civilize" the police and the military, thereby closing the breach caused by their lack of acquaintance with each other, if not the outright antagonism, which in Peru, as in other countries of Latin America, characterizes the relationship between military and civilian life. In our program for civil peace, prepared by a committee headed by an attorney—Amalia Ortiz de Zevallos—and made up of psychologists, sociologists, anthropologists, social workers, jurists, and military officers, the activity of the patrols was regarded as part of a multiple process, aimed at the recovery by civil society of the emergency area placed under military control. At the same time that the exceptional emergency laws would be abrogated in the area and the patrols would begin to function, flying brigades of judges, doctors, social workers, organizers of agrarian programs, and teachers would go there, so that a peasant would have additional reasons to combat terrorism besides that of mere survival. I had decided, moreover, that in case I were elected, I would go to the emergency area to live, more or less permanently, in order to direct from there the civilian mobilization against terrorism.

At nightfall on January 19, 1989, a man who lived in Los Jazmines, a slum neighborhood adjoining the airport of the city of Pucallpa, saw two strangers come out of a patch of underbrush and run, carrying something, to the landing strip where the planes brake to a stop and make a turn to taxi to the disembarkation area. One of the two scheduled flights from Lima had just landed. The two strangers, seeing that the recent arrival was a commercial AeroPerú flight, went back to the thicket. The man who lived in Los Jazmines ran to alert the other people who lived in the area, whose residents had formed a patrol. A group of these civilian patrolmen, armed with clubs and machetes, went to check on what the two strangers were doing out there next to the runway. The patrol surrounded them, questioned them, and were about to take them to the police station when the two men drew revolvers and fired point-blank at the civilian patrolmen. They perforated Sergio Pasavi's intestines in six places; they shattered José Vásquez Dávila's femur; they fractured the collarbone of Humberto Jacobo the barber and wounded Víctor Ravello Cruz in the lumbar area. In the ensuing chaos, the strangers got away. But they left behind a bomb that weighed two kilos, a so-called Russian cheese, which contained dynamite, aluminum, nails, buckshot, bits of metal, and a short fuse. They were going to throw this bomb at the Faucett plane, which leaves Lima at the same time as the AeroPerú flight, but was two hours late that day. I was coming in on that plane, to set up the Libertad committee of Pucallpa, visit the Ucayali area, and preside over a political rally at the Teatro Rex in the city.

The civilian patrol brought their wounded to the regional hospital and made a deposition concerning the attempted bombing to the representative chief of police, a major in the Civil Guard (the chief of police had gone off to Lima), to whom they handed over the bomb. When they sought me out to tell me about what had happened, I rushed to the hospital to visit the wounded. What a horrible sight! Patients piled one atop the other, sharing beds, in rooms swarming with flies, and nurses and doctors working miracles to care for their patients, operate, heal, without medicine, without equipment, lacking the most basic sanitary conditions. After taking steps to see that the two civilian patrolmen in the most serious condition were transferred to Lima by Solidarity, I went to the police. One of the attackers, Hidalgo Soria, seventeen years old, had been captured, and according to the befuddled officer of the Civil Guard who took care of me, had confessed that he belonged to the Túpac Amaru Revolutionary Movement and admitted that the intended target of the bomb had been my plane. But like so many others, the suspect never got as far as the courts. Every time that the press tried to find out what had become of him, the authorities in Pucallpa put them off with evasive answers, and one day they announced that the judge had let him go free because he was a minor.

For Christmas 1989 the Solidarity program organized a show on December 23 in the Alianza Lima stadium, with the participation of film, radio, and TV artists, which was attended by some 35,000 people. Shortly after the performance had begun, it was announced over the radio that a bomb had been found in my house and that the bomb demolition squad of the Civil Guard had managed to defuse it and remove it, obliging my mother and my in-laws, the secretaries and the servants to leave the house. The fact that this bomb was found just as the show at the stadium began seemed suspect to us, a coincidence no doubt meant to spoil the celebration by forcing us to leave, and because we smelled a rat Patricia and my children and I deliberately remained on the platform until the Christmas festivities were over.* The suspicion that it was not a real attempted bombing but a psychological ploy was further confirmed that night, when we came back home to Barranco and the demolition squad of the Civil Guard assured us that the bomb—discovered by the watchman at a tourism school next door—wasn't filled with dynamite but with sand.

On November 26, a Sunday, a navy officer, dressed in civvies, came to my house, taking extraordinary precautions. Jorge Salmón, a mutual friend, had arranged for him to speak to me in private, face to face, since all my telephones had been bugged. The officer arrived in a car with one-way glass windows, which drove directly into the garage. He had come to tell me that the office of naval intelligence, to which he belonged, had learned of a secret meeting held in the National Museum, attended by President Alan García, his minister of the interior, Agustín Mantilla—widely held to be the organizer of the counterterrorist gangs—and the congressman Carlos Roca, together with Alberto Kitasono, head of the security units of the APRA, and a high-ranking official of the Túpac Amaru Revolutionary Movement. And that at this meeting it had been decided to rub me out, along with a group that included my son Álvaro, Enrique Ghersi, and Francisco Belaunde Terry. The assassinations were to take place in such a way that they would appear to be the work of Sendero Luminoso.

The officer had me read the report that the intelligence service had forwarded to the commander in chief of the navy. I asked him how seriously his institution took this report. He shrugged and said that if the river made a noise it was carrying stones along with it, as the saying had it. Through Álvaro, news of this fantastic conspiracy shortly thereafter reached the ears of Jaime Bayly, a young television reporter, who dared to make it public, causing a great furor. The navy denied the existence of such a report.

This was one of the many revelations that I received of attempts on my life and the lives of my family. Some of them were so absurd that

* The APRA is a specialist in this type of operation: on the eve of the launching of my candidacy, on June 3, 1989, anonymous voices phoned to warn me that there was a bomb on the plane that was taking me to Arequipa. After the emergency removal of the plane to an area of the airport far from the place where people were waiting for me to arrive, the aircraft was searched and nothing suspect was found.

they made us burst out laughing. Others were obvious fabrications of the informants, who used them as pretexts in an attempt to get to see me personally. Others, like the anonymous telephone calls, appeared to be psychological maneuvers by Alan García's followers, intended to demoralize us. And then there were the tips by well-wishers, by people of good will, who in reality knew nothing precise but suspected that I might be killed, and since they didn't want that to happen, came to talk to me about vague ambushes and mysterious planned attempts on my life because that was their way of begging me to take good care of myself. In the final stage of the campaign this reached such proportions that it became necessary to put a stop to it and I asked Patricia, María del Carmen, and Lucía, who were in charge of my agenda, not to give any more appointments to anyone who wished to discuss "a serious and secret subject having to do with Doctor Vargas's security."

I have often been asked whether I was afraid during the campaign. Apprehensive, yes, many times, but more of objects hurled at me, the kind that can be seen coming, than of bullets or bombs. As on that tense night of March 13, 1990, in Casma, when, as I was going up to the speakers' platform, a group of counterdemonstrators bombarded us from the shadows with stones and eggs, one of which hit Patricia on the forehead and broke. Or that morning in May 1990, in the Tacora district of Lima, when the good head (in both senses) of my friend Enrique Ghersi, who was walking along beside me, stopped the stone that had been hurled at me (all they managed to do to me was douse me in smelly red paint). But terrorism never robbed me of sleep in those three years, nor did it keep me from doing and saying what I wanted to.

ELEVEN

Comrade Alberto

I SPENT the summer of 1953 shut up in my grandparents' apartment, in the white townhouse on the Calle Porta, studying for the entrance exam to the University of San Marcos, writing a play (it took place on a desert island, with storms), and writing poems to a young neighbor, Madeleine, whose mother, who was French, was the owner of the house. It was another half-romance, not because of my timidity this time but due to the very strict watch kept by Madeleine's mother on her blond daughter. (Almost thirty years later, one night as I was going into the Teatro Marsano in Lima, where they were giving the first performance of a work of mine, a pretty lady whom I did not recognize blocked my path. With an indescribable smile she handed me one of those same love poems, whose first verse, the only one I dared read, made my face turn as red as a torch.)

We took the examination for admission to the Faculty of Letters in one of the old houses belonging to San Marcos scattered all through the downtown district of Lima, on the Calle de Padre Jerónimo, where a phantasmagoric Institute of Geography did its work. I made two new friends that day, Lea Barba and Rafael Merino, who were candidates for admission as I was, and also shared my passion for reading. Rafo had been enrolled at the Police Academy before deciding to study law. Lea was the daughter of one of the owners of the Negro-Negro, all of them descended from an anarcho-syndicalist leader of the famous workers' battles in the 1920s. Between one exam and the next, and during the days and weeks of waiting to be summoned to the oral exam, Rafo and Lea and I talked about literature and politics, and I felt rewarded for the long wait by being able to share my anxieties with people my own age. Lea talked so enthusiastically of César Vallejo, some of whose poems she knew by heart, that I began to read him attentively, trying my best to come to like him at least as much as I did Neruda, whom I had read since high school with constant admiration.

We occasionally went with Rafael Merino to the beach, we exchanged books, and I read him short stories that I'd written. But with Lea it was politics above all that we discussed, in a conspiratorial spirit. We confessed that we were enemies of the dictatorship and supporters of revolution and of Marxism. But could there possibly be any Communists left in Peru? Hadn't Esparza Zañartu killed, jailed, or deported all of them? At the time, Esparza Zañartu occupied the obscure post of administrative head of the Ministry of the Interior, but the whole country knew that that person without a history or a political past, whom General Odría had lured away from his modest wine business to bring him into the government, was the brain behind that security to which the dictatorship owed its power, the man behind the censorship of the press and radio broadcasts, and behind the detention and deportations, and also the one who had put together the network of spies and informers in labor unions, universities, public posts, and the communications media, the one who had kept any effective opposition against the regime from developing.

Nonetheless, the year before, 1952, the University of San Marcos, faithful to its tradition of rebellion, had defied Odría. On the pretext that they were reclaiming their rights as university students, those at San Marcos had demanded the resignation of the rector, Pedro Dulanto, gone out on strike, and occupied the university's traditionally inviolable inner grounds, which the police entered to drive them out. Almost all the leaders of the strike were in jail or had been deported. Lea knew many details about what had happened, about the debates in the San Marcos Federation and its allied chapters and the underground battles between Apristas and Communists (both of them groups persecuted by the government but each other's merciless enemies), to which I listened openmouthed.

Lea was the first girl whose fast friend I became who had not been brought up, as had my girlfriends from the *barrio* in Miraflores, to get married as soon as possible and be a good housewife. She had an intellectual background and was determined to get into San Marcos, to practice her profession, to stand on her own two feet. While she was intelligent and possessed of a strong personality, she was gentle at the same time, and could be so tenderhearted as to be moved to tears by a story about an incident in someone's life. I think she was the first one to talk to me about José Carlos Mariátegui, the Marxist ideologue, and the *Siete ensayos de interpretación de la realidad peruana* (*Seven Interpretative Essays on Peruvian Reality*). Even before classes started, we became inseparable. We went to exhibitions, to bookstores, and to the movies—to see French films, of course, in the two art houses downtown that showed them, Le Paris and Biarritz.

On the day I turned up on the Calle Fano to learn the results of the entrance exams, the minute they discovered my name on the list of those who had passed, a group lying in wait flung itself on me and baptized me. The San Marcos baptism was humane: they gave you a really short crew cut so as to oblige you to shave your head. From the Calle Fano I went with my close-cropped head to buy myself a beret and to a barbershop on La Colmena to get myself sheared almost to the scalp, so that my head looked like a coconut.

I had enrolled at the Alliance Française, so as to learn French. Two of us in my class were males: a young black who was studying chemistry and myself. The twenty or so females—all of them well-brought-up girls from Miraflores and San Isidro—amused themselves at our expense, making fun of our accent in French and playing pranks on us. After a few weeks, the black got fed up with their mockery and gave up coming to class. My shorn head as a San Marcos freshman was, of course, the object of the irreverence and hilarity of those fearsome girl classmates (among them was a Miss Peru). But I enjoyed the classes taught by the wonderful instructor, Madame del Solar, thanks to whom I was able within a few weeks to begin to read in French, with the aid of dictionaries. I spent many blissful hours in the little library of the Alliance, on the Avenida Wilson, peeking into magazines and reading such authors of transparent prose as Gide, Camus, or Saint-Exupéry, who gave me the illusion of having mastered the language of Montaigne.

In order to have a little money, I spoke with Uncle Jorge, the one in the family with the best job. He was the manager of a construction company and he gave me work by the hour to do—making bank deposits, writing letters and other documents, and taking them to government offices—which did not interfere with my classes. In that way I was able to buy cigarettes—I smoked like that proverbial bat, always dark tobacco, Incas at first and later on oval-shaped National Presidents—and to go to the movies. Shortly thereafter I got another, more intellectual job: a writer for *Turismo* magazine. The owner and managing editor was Jorge Holguín de Lavalle (1894–1973), a very fine sketch artist and cartoonist, who had been famous thirty years before, in the big magazines of the 1920s, *Variedades* and *Mundial*. An aristocrat and very poor, a Limeño to the bone, an indefatigable and charming raconteur of traditions, myths, and gossip about the city, Holguín de Lavalle was an absent-minded dreamer who brought out the magazine when he remembered to, or rather, when he had garnered enough ads to pay for printing an issue. The magazine was laid out by him and written from first page to last by him and by the current staff writer. Well-known intellectuals had passed by way of the magazine's very scanty editorial staff, among them Sebastián Salazar Bondy, and Señor Jorge Holguín de Lavalle, on the day that I went to talk with him, reminded me of this, thereby indicating that, even though the pay would be a paltry sum, my succeeding such illustrious individuals in the job would make up for that fact.

I accepted the job, and from then on, for two years, I wrote half or perhaps three-quarters of the magazine under different pseudonyms (among them the French-sounding Vincent Naxé, with which I signed the drama reviews). Of all that material I remember one text, "En torno a una escultura" ("Concerning a Statue"), written in protest against a barbarous deed committed during the dictatorship by the minister of education, General Zenón Noriega, who ordered the handsome statue of the hero withdrawn from the sculpture group of the monument to Bolognesi (created by the Spaniard Agustín Querol) because his pose did not strike General Zenón as heroic. And he had the original image of Bolognesi—shown at the moment he fell to the ground riddled with bullets—replaced by the grotesque puppet waving a flag that today makes what was once one of the fine monuments of Lima among its ugliest. Holguín de Lavalle was indignant at the mutilation but feared that my article would anger the government and the magazine would be closed down. In the end, he published it and nothing happened. With my salary from *Turismo*, four hundred soles per issue—and the magazine didn't come out every month, but only every second or even every third month—I could pay for (what days those were and how solid the Peruvian *sol* was!) subscriptions to two French periodicals, Sartre's *Les Temps Modernes* and Maurice Nadeau's *Les Lettres Modernes*, which I went to pick up, every month, at a little downtown office. I was able to live on this income—at my grandparents' I didn't pay for either my room or my board—and above all I had free time to read, for San Marcos and, in a very short time, for the revolution.

Classes began late, and with one exception, they were disappointing. San Marcos hadn't yet fallen into the decadence that in the 1960s and 1970s was little by little to turn it into the caricature of a university, and later on into a bastion of Maoism and even terrorism, but it was no longer even a shadow of what it had been in the 1920s, in the days of the famous generation of the 1919 Conversatorio, its high point as far as the humanities were concerned.

Of that famous generation of the Conversatorio two historians—Jorge Basadre and Raúl Porras Barrenechea—were still at San Marcos, and a few illustrious figures of a previous generation, such as Mariano Iberico in philosophy, or Luis Valcárcel in ethnology. And the Faculty of Medicine, in which Honorio Delgado taught, had as professors the best doctors in Lima. But the atmosphere and the way classes were conducted at the university were neither creative nor demanding. There was a breakdown both of morale and of intellectual standards, still not particularly noticeable, although widespread; professors skipped one class and turned up at the next, and along with some who were competent, others were of a mediocrity that put the students in their classes to sleep. Before entering the Faculty of Law and before becoming a candidate for a degree in literature, a student had to have had two years of general studies, among which there could be several electives. All the ones I chose were literature courses.

The majority of them were given without enthusiasm, by professors who did not know very much or who had lost all interest in teaching. But among these courses I remember one that ranks among the best intellectual experiences I have ever had: Sources of Peruvian History, given by Raúl Porras Barrenechea.

To me, that course, and what stemmed from it, justifies the years I spent at San Marcos. Its subject could not have been more limited or scholarly, since it was not about Peruvian history but about where to study it. But thanks to the wisdom and eloquence of the professor giving it, every lecture was a formidable display of knowledge about the past of Peru and the contradictory versions and interpretations of it that chroniclers, travelers, explorers, literati had offered, in the most diverse collections of correspondence and documents imaginable. Pint-sized, potbellied, dressed in mourning—for the death, that year, of his mother—with a very broad forehead, blue eyes boiling over with irony and lapels covered with dandruff, Porras Barrenechea turned into a giant on the little classroom dais and every last one of his words was followed by us with religious devotion. He lectured with consummate elegance, in a pungent and pure Spanish—he had begun his university career teaching the classics of the Golden Age, which he had thoroughly mastered, and traces of this mastery remained in his prose and in the precision and magnificence with which he expressed himself—yet he was not, even remotely, the garrulous professor, an empty-headed wordmonger who listens to himself talk. Porras was a fanatic when it came to exactitude and he was incapable of stating anything about anything that he hadn't thoroughly checked. His splen-did lectures were always documented by his reading from note cards in his minute handwriting, raising them up close to his eyes so as to decipher them. In each one of his classes we had the sensation that we were hearing something not to be found in any book, the result of personal research. The following year, when I began to work with him, I discovered that, in fact, Porras Barrenechea prepared that course, which he had been giving for so many years, with the rigor of someone about to face a class for the first time.

In my first two years at San Marcos I was someone I hadn't been in high school: a very diligent student. I studied all my courses thoroughly, even the ones I didn't like, handing in every one of the assignments given us, and in some cases asking the professor for a supplementary list of books, so as to go read them at the San Marcos library or at the National Library on the Avenida Abancay, in both of which I spent many hours during those first two years. Although they were far from being exemplary—at the National one had to share the reading room with very young schoolchildren who went there to do their homework and turned the place into a madhouse—I acquired there the habit of reading in libraries and I have frequented them ever since, in all the cities I have lived in, and in one of them, the beloved

Reading Room of the British Museum, I have even written a good part of my books.

But in none of the courses I took did I read and work as much as for Sources of Peruvian History, dazzled as I was by Porras Barrenechea's brilliance. After a masterly class on pre-Hispanic myths, I remember having rushed to the library in search of two books that he had cited, and although one of them, by Ernst Cassirer, defeated me almost immediately, the other was one of the most impressive of my readings of 1953: Frazer's *The Golden Bough*. Porras's course had such a great influence on me that during those first months at the university I often came to the point of asking myself whether I ought to specialize in history instead of literature, since the former, embodied in Porras Barrenechea, had all the color, the dramatic power, and the creativity of the latter, and seemed more deeply rooted in life.

I made good friends among my classmates and convinced a group of them that we should put on a play. We chose a comedy of manners, by Pardo y Aliaga, and even had copies of it made and cast the roles, but in the end the project came to nothing, through my own fault, I believe, since I had already begun to be active in politics, which started to absorb more and more of my time.

Of that whole group of friends, Nelly Alba was a special case. She had studied piano at the Conservatory since she'd been a little girl, and her vocation was music, but she had entered San Marcos to acquire an overall culture. From our first conversations under the palm trees of the courtyard of the Faculty of Letters, my lack of musical culture horrified her, and she took on the task of educating me, taking me to concerts at the Teatro Municipal, in the first row of the balcony, and passed on to me a somewhat hasty smattering of information about interpretative artists and composers. I gave her advice on what literary works she should read, and I remember how much the two of us liked the volumes of Romain Rolland's *Jean Christophe*, which we bought, a volume or two at a time, in Juan Mejía Baca's bookstore, on the Calle Azángaro. The kindly, effusive Don Juan gave us the books on credit and let us pay him in monthly installments. To pass by that bookstore once or twice a week, to have a look at what was new, was obligatory. And on days when we were lucky, Mejía Baca invited us to the tavern next door, to have a coffee and a hot meat pie, on him.

But the person I saw most often, every day in fact, inside and outside of classes, was Lea. Shortly after the beginning of the academic year, we had been joined by another student, Félix Arias Schreiber, with whom we were soon to constitute a triumvirate. Félix had entered San Marcos the year before, but had had to break off his studies because of illness, and therefore was in the freshman class with us. He belonged to a family of high social standing—one associated his surname with bankers, diplomats, and lawyers—but to a branch that was poor and perhaps even extremely poor. I don't know whether his mother was a widow or separated from her husband, but Félix lived alone with her, in one of a group of little townhouses with a common entrance on the Avenida Arequipa, and although he had studied in Santa María, the private high school for rich kids in Lima, he never had a cent and it was plain to see, from the way he acted and dressed, that he was having a hard time making ends meet. Félix's political vocation was much stronger—in his case excluding every other interest—than Lea's or mine. He already knew a bit about Marxism, he had a few books and pamphlets which he lent to us, and which I read in a state of bedazzlement at the forbidden nature of such fruits, which I had to carry around with paper covers concealing them so they would not be detected by the stool pigeons that Esparza Zañartu had infiltrated into San Marcos to flush out what *La Prensa* called "subversive elements" and "agitators." (All the daily papers of the period backed the dictatorship and, it goes without saying, were anti-Communist, but Pedro Beltrán's *La Prensa* was more so than all the others put together.) Once Félix joined us, other subjects were relegated to a secondary place and it was politics—or rather, socialism and revolution—that our conversations centered on. We chatted together in the patios of San Marcos—still located in the old mansion of the Parque Universitario, right in downtown Lima—or in little coffeehouses on La Colmena or Azángaro, and Lea sometimes took us to have coffee or a Coca-Cola on the downstairs floor of the Negro-Negro, in the arcades of the Plaza San Martín. By contrast to my earlier visits to the place, during my bohemian days on *La Crónica*, I didn't drink a drop of alcohol now and we talked about very serious things: the abuses committed by the dictatorship, the great ethical, political, economic, scientific, and cultural changes that were taking place in the U.S.S.R. ("in that country / where there exist / neither whores, thieves, nor priests," Paul

Éluard's poem said), or in the China of Mao Tse-tung that the French writer Claude Roy had visited and about which he had written so many marvelous things, in *Clefs pour la Chine* (*Into China*), a book whose every word we believed implicitly.

Our conversations went on till late at night. Often we walked back from downtown to Lea's house, on Petit Thouars, and then Félix and I went on to his house on the Avenida Arequipa, almost as far out as Angamos, and I then went on alone to the Calle Porta. The walk from the Plaza San Martín to my house took an hour and a half. Granny left me my dinner on the table and it didn't matter to me that it was cold (it was always the same, the only dish I could finish in those days: rice with breaded beef cutlets and fried potatoes). And if food didn't matter much to me ("For the poet, food is prose," my grandfather teased me), I didn't need much sleep either, for, even though I climbed into bed late at night, I read for hours before going to sleep. I indulged in friendship with my usual passionate enthusiasm and exclusivism, and Félix and Lea became a full-time occupation; when I wasn't with them, I was thinking how good it was to have friends like them, three of us who got along together so well and were planning a shared future. I also thought, although I was careful to keep it to myself, that I shouldn't fall in love with Lea, because it would be fatal for the trio we formed. What was more, wasn't the whole business of falling in love a typical bourgeois weakness, inconceivable in a revolutionary?

Around that time, we had made the longed-for contact. In one of the courtyards of San Marcos, someone had approached us, found out who we were, and, in a seemingly offhand way, asked what we thought of the students who were in jail, or questioned us about cultural subjects that, unfortunately, were not taught at the university—dialectical materialism, historical materialism, and scientific socialism, for example—subjects that anyone with an eye to the future ought to know about, as a matter of general information. And the second or third time, returning to the same subject, he had casually introduced into the discussion the question of whether it wouldn't interest us to form a study group, to investigate those problems that censorship, the fear of the dictatorship, or the fact that San Marcos was a bourgeois university kept from reaching it. Lea, Félix, and I said we'd be delighted. A month hadn't yet gone by since we entered the university and already we were in a study group, the first step that should be followed by militants of Cahuide, the name under which the Communist Party was trying to regroup in secret after repression and desertions and internal divisions had caused it nearly to disappear in previous years.

Our first instructor in that circle was Héctor Béjar, who in the 1970s was to be the head of a guerrilla group, the ELN (Ejército de Liberación Nacional: National Liberation Army), and spend several years in jail for that reason. He was a tall, likable lad, with a face as round as a wheel of cheese, with a voice that had a very fine timbre, which allowed him to earn his living as an announcer at Radio Central. He was a little older than we were—he was already in law school—and studying Marxism with him proved to be enjoyable, for he was intelligent and adept at conducting the circle's discussions. The first book we studied was Georges Politzer's *Beginning Lessons in Philosophy*, and then Marx's *Communist Manifesto* and *The Class Struggle in France*, and after that Engels's *Anti-Dühring* and Lenin's *What Is to Be Done?* We bought the books—and sometimes received in return, as a bonus, a back number of *Cultura Soviética*, on whose covers there were always smiling peasant lasses with robust cheeks, against a background of wheat fields and tractors—in a little bookstore on the Calle Pando, whose owner, a mustachioed Chilean always bundled up in a little scarf, kept a great deal of subversive literature hidden in a trunk in the back room of his shop. Later on, when I read Conrad's novels, full of shady conspirators, the mysterious, ashen face of that bookseller who purveyed clandestine books always came back to my mind.

We met in places that kept changing. In a miserable little room, at the back of an old building on the Avenida Abancay, where one of our comrades lived, or in a little house on Bajo el Puente, the home of a very pale girl whom we baptized the Bird, where one day we had a sudden scare, for in the middle of our discussion, a soldier showed up. He was the Bird's brother and wasn't surprised at seeing us; but we didn't go back there. Or in the rooming house in Barrios Altos, whose woman owner, a discreet sympathizer, lent us a room full of spider webs, at the far end of a garden. I belonged to at least four circles and the following year became the instructor and organizer of one of them, and I have forgotten the faces and the names of the comrades who taught me in them, of those who were taught along with me, and those whom I taught. But I remember very well those of the first circle, with the majority of whom we eventually formed a cell, when we began to take militant action in Cahuide. Besides Félix and Lea, there was a skinny young man with a voice as thin as a thread, in whom everything was small-sized: the knot in his tie, his tiny polite gestures, the little steps he took to get around in the world. His name was Podestá and he was the one who was nominally in charge of our cell. Martínez, on the other hand, a student studying for a degree in anthropology, was as hale and hearty as they come: he was an Indian, strong and warm, a dogged worker whose reports in the group were always interminable. His coppery, stony face never changed expression, and not even the most heated debates ever disturbed that impassivity. Antonio Muñoz, a highlander from Junín, on the other hand, had a sense of humor and allowed himself to break the mood of deadly seriousness of our meetings by making jokes now and again (I was to meet him once more, during the election campaign of 1989 and 1990, organizing committees of Libertad for the provinces of Junín). And there was also the Bird, that mysterious girl who made Félix, Lea, and me wonder at times whether she knew what the circle was all about, if she realized that she could be put in prison, that she was already a subversive militant. With her resplendent pallor and her delicate manners, the Bird dutifully did all the required reading and made reports, but she did not appear to absorb very much; one day she abruptly bade the circle goodbye, saying that she was going to be late for Mass . . .

After we'd been in the circle for a few weeks, Héctor Béjar decided that Lea, Félix, and I were ripe for a major commitment. Would we agree to an interview with a higher-up in the Party? We arranged to meet at nightfall, on the Avenida Pardo in Miraflores, and there was Washington Durán Abarca—at the time I was introduced to him only by his pseudonym—who surprised us by saying that the best way to dupe informers was to meet in bourgeois neighborhoods and out-of-doors. Sitting on a bench, under the ficus trees along the same promenade where I had tried without success to get the beautiful Flora Flores and other daughters of the bourgeoisie to fall for me, Washington gave us a synoptic picture of the history of the Communist Party, from its foundation in Peru by José Carlos Mariátegui, in 1928, up to our own day, when, under the name of Cahuide, it was being reborn from its ruins. After this historic beginning, under the inspiration of Mariátegui—whose *Siete ensayos de interpretación de la realidad peruana* we also studied in the group—the Party had fallen into the hands of Eudocio Ravines, who, after having been its secretary general and acting as an envoy of the Comintern in Chile, Argentina, and Spain during the Spanish Civil War, had become a turncoat, assuming the role of Peru's great anti-Communist and an ally of *La Prensa* and Pedro Beltrán. And, later on, the dictatorships and the severe repression had kept the Party outside the law and in hiding, surviving underground in more and more difficult conditions, with the brief exception of the three years of Bustamante y Rivero's administration, in which it was able to surface and act in plain sight. But then "liquidating and antiworker" currents had undermined the organization, separating it from the masses and leading it to make deals with the bourgeoisie: one former leader of the Party, Juan P. Luna, for example, had sold out to Odría and was now one of the senators of the fraudulent Congress of the military regime. The real leaders of the Party such as Jorge del Prado were in exile or in prison (as was the case with Raúl Acosta, the last secretary general).

Despite all this, the Party was still active behind the scenes and in the past year had played a decisive role in the strike at San Marcos. Many comrades who participated in it were in exile or in the penitentiary. Cahuide had been formed by combining the surviving cells, until a congress could be convoked. It consisted of a student section and a workers' section, and for reasons of security each cell knew only one responsible militant from the level immediately above. In no document or conversation were Party members' real names to be used, only pseudonyms. One could enter Cahuide as a sympathizer or as a militant.

Félix and I said that we wanted to be sympathizers, but Lea asked for full membership immediately. The oath administered to her by Washington Durán, in the murmur of an altar boy, was a solemn one—"Do you swear to fight for the working class, for the Party . . . ?"—and it impressed us. Then we had to choose our pseudonyms. Mine was Comrade Alberto.

Although we continued in the study circle, whose members and instructor changed every so often, the three of us began to work, at the same time, in a cell of the student section, which Podestá, Martínez and Muñoz also joined. The circumstances limited our militancy to handing out leaflets or selling, on the sly, a little clandestine periodical called *Cahuide*, for which several times I was called upon to write about international subjects from the "proletarian" and "dialectical" point of view. It cost fifty centavos and in it the two bêtes noires of the Party, the APRA and the Trotskyites, were attacked almost as severely as Odría's dictatorship.

This first target is understandable. In 1953, and despite having had to go underground, the APRA still had control of the majority of the labor unions and was the first, in fact the only Peruvian political party for which the word *popular* was appropriate. It was precisely the deep roots of the APRA in the popular sectors that had been an obstacle in the way of the development of the Communist Party, up until that time a small organization of intellectuals, students, and little workers' groups. At San Marcos then (and perhaps always), the vast majority of students were apolitical, with a vague preference for the left but without any party affiliation. Within the politicized sector, the majority of students were Apristas. And the Communists, a small minority, were concentrated above all in the Faculties of Letters, Economics, and Law.

What was practically nonexistent was Trotskyism, and it said a great deal about the ideological unreality in which Cahuide functioned that we dedicated so much time to denouncing a mere phantom in our leaflets or in our periodical. At that time there were no more than half a dozen Trotskyites at San Marcos, gathered around the person we thought of as their ideologue: Aníbal Quijano. The future sociologist held forth every morning in the courtyard of the Faculty of Letters, speaking in flowing words and devastatingly impressive statistics about the advances of Leon Davidovich Trotsky's partisans in the Soviet Union itself. "We have 22,000 Trotskyite comrades within the Soviet armed forces," I heard him announce, with a triumphant smile, in one of his perorations. And on another morning, one of Quijano's supposed supporters, who was later to be an AP representative—Raúl Peña Cabrera—left me dumbfounded: "I know you're studying Marxism. That's fine. But you should take a broad view of it, without sectarianism." And he presented me with a copy of Trotsky's *Revolution and Art*, which I read in secret, with a morbid feeling of transgression. Only two or three years later the picturesque Ismael Frías would arrive, bundled up in an outlandish gray overcoat totally unsuited to the

climate of Lima and with the appearance of an obese matron, to replace
Peña and Quijano as the Trotskyite ideologue of Peru. At the time,
in 1953, he was living in Mexico City, in Trotsky's house in Coyoacán,
where he officiated as the secretary of Trotsky's illustrious widow,
Natalia Sedova.

But just as it was very difficult, not to say impossible, to know who
was a Trotskyite, it was also hard to identify the Apristas and our
comrades. Outside of the people in our own cell and the leaders at
higher levels who came to give us talks or instruction—such as the
spirited Isaac Ahumala, who in his speeches invariably spoke of the
helots of Greece and of Spartacus's rebellion—only by divination or
sympathetic magic was it possible to identify the militants of the parties
that the military government had outlawed. Esparza Zañartu's informers and the fierce animosity between Apristas and Communists, and
between Communists and Trotskyites, all of whom suspected the others
of being informers, made the political atmosphere of the university
almost intolerable.

But finally it became possible for us to hold elections at the university
for the student committees in the several Faculties and then for the
University Federation of San Marcos (dismantled after the 1952 strike).
Among the candidates put up by Cahuide from the Faculty of Letters,
Félix and I were elected, and the two of us were also among the five
delegates that the committee in our Faculty elected for the Federation.
I don't know how we managed this latter, since in both the committee
and the Federation the majority were Apristas. And shortly thereafter
an episode occurred which, as far as I was concerned, was to have
literary consequences.

I have already said there were a fair number of students imprisoned.
The Internal Security Act allowed the government to send any "subversive" to jail and keep him or her there for an indefinite period,
without a court trial. The conditions in which those arrested found
themselves in the penitentiary—a red building in the downtown area
of Lima, where the Hotel Sheraton is also located, and which only
years later I would discover to be one of the rare panopticons* to have
been built according to the instructions of Jeremy Bentham, the British

---

* A building such as a prison, hospital, library, or the like so arranged that all parts
of the interior are visible from a single point. (*Trans. note*)

philosopher who invented them—were tough: they were obliged to sleep on the floor, without blankets or mattresses. We took up a collection to buy them blankets, but when we took them to the penitentiary, the warden informed us that those who had been arrested were incommunicado, because they were *political* prisoners—an infamous word during the dictatorship—and that only with the authorization of the administrative head of the Ministry of the Interior could the blankets be given to them.

Ought we, for humanitarian reasons, to ask for an interview with the brain of the repression under Odría? The subject gave rise to one of those discussions that leave everyone panting for breath, in the cell first, and then in the Federation. We were in the habit of discussing all questions beforehand in Cahuide, of planning a strategy and carrying it out in the student organizations, where we acted with a discipline and a coordination that very often allowed us to reach agreements despite our being a minority as compared to the Apristas. I don't know what position we defended with regard to the request for an audience with Esparza Zañartu, but I do know that the discussions were intensely bitter. Finally, the request for the interview was approved. The Federation named a committee, among whose members were Martínez and I.

The administrative head of the Ministry of the Interior gave us a midmorning appointment, in his office on the Plaza Italia. We were overcome with nervousness and excitement as we waited, amid grease-stained walls, police in uniform and in civvies, and office clerks crowded together in claustrophobic little cubicles. Finally we were ushered into his office. There was Esparza Zañartu, in the flesh. He did not get to his feet to greet us, nor did he ask us to sit down. He impassively scrutinized us from his desk. I have never forgotten that bored face with the look of parchment. He was a ludicrous little man, around forty or fifty, or rather, ageless, modestly dressed, with a scrawny, decrepit body, the incarnation of the harmless, of the man without qualities (at least physically speaking). He gave an almost imperceptible nod to indicate to us to say what we wanted to, and without uttering a word, listened to those of us who took the responsibility for speaking up—or rather, for stammering out an explanation of the matter of the mattresses and blankets. He didn't move a muscle and his mind appeared to be somewhere else, but he observed us as though we were insects. Finally, with the same expression of indifference, he opened a drawer, took out a pile of papers and waved them in our faces, murmuring "And what about this?" and shaking in his fist several issues of the clandestine *Cahuide*.

He said that he knew everything that was happening at San Marcos, including who it was who had written those articles. He thanked us for devoting our attention to him in every issue. But he warned us that we should be careful, because students went to the university to study and not to organize the Communist revolution. He spoke in a faint little voice without a cutting edge to it or subtle shadings, with the inexpressiveness and the mistakes in grammar of someone who has never read a book since leaving high school.

I don't remember what happened about the bedding, but I do remember my impression on discovering how completely out of proportion to the mediocrity we had before us was the idea Peru had of the shadowy figure responsible for so many exiles, crimes, censorship decrees, and imprisonments. On leaving after that interview I realized that sooner or later I was going to write what would eventually become my novel *Conversation in The Cathedral*. (When the book appeared, in 1969, and journalists went out to ask Esparza Zañartu, who in those days was living in Chosica, devoting his time to philanthropical causes and horticulture, what he thought of that novel, whose main character, Cayo Mierda, bore such a close resemblance to him, he answered [I can just imagine his bored gesture]: "Listen . . . if Vargas Llosa had consulted me, I'd have told him so many things . . .")

In the little more than a year that I was in Cahuide our epic revolutionary deeds were few and far between: an abortive attempt to get rid of a professor, a little periodical put out by the students' committee that had trouble surviving for even two or three issues, and a strike at San Marcos to demonstrate our solidarity with streetcar workers. And in addition, a free academy to prepare students seeking admission to San Marcos, in which I taught the literature course; this permitted us to recruit members for the study circles and Cahuide. The right to get bad professors fired (which became the right to get rid of reactionary ones) was one of those achieved by the university reform movement of the 1920s; it was abolished after the military coup of 1948. We tried to revive it in order to get rid of our professor of logic, Dr. Saberbein—for reasons I don't understand, since there were worse professors than he on the faculty—but we failed; in two tumultuous student assemblies, his defenders turned out to be more numerous than his attackers.

As for the periodical, my memory retains above all else the exhausting discussions in Cahuide concerning a trivial question: whether the articles should be signed or anonymous. Like everything we did, that too was the object of ideological analyses, in which the theses of all the participants were torn to pieces by dialectical and class arguments. The most serious accusation was: bourgeois subjectivism, idealism, lack of class consciousness. My readings of Sartre and *Les Temps Modernes* helped me to be less dogmatic than other comrades, and sometimes I dared to put forward certain Sartrean criticisms of Marxism, arousing the wrath of Félix, who, as he became more militant, had gradually become more and more inflexible and orthodox. The debate about signatures lasted for several days, and during one of these interchanges Félix lashed out at me with a devastating accusation: "You're a *subhombre*—a subhuman."

But, despite our disagreements in the internal debates of Cahuide (never in public), I went on being fond of him and of Lea, knowing full well that the business of being fond of one's friends was bourgeois. And it had pained me a great deal when we were separated, first in the circle and then in the cell, where Lea and Félix were to remain together. On both occasions it had seemed to me that Félix, in a way that would be imperceptible for anyone who didn't have very alert antennae, had slyly furthered that separation while at the same time giving every appearance of being resigned to it. Since I am by nature mistrustful and sensitive, I told myself that I was imagining conspiracies out of the envy I felt because they would be staying together. But I couldn't help thinking that, with that ultimate inflexibility of his, Félix had perhaps schemed to bring that separation about so as to toughen me, curing me of sentimentality, one of my most stubborn class defects . . .

Despite that, we three continued to see a great deal of each other. I sought them out whenever I could. One afternoon—six or eight months must have gone by since we had first met—Lea told me she wanted to talk to me. I went to her house, on Petit Thouars, and found her alone. We went out for a walk along the promenade that ran down the middle of the Avenida Arequipa, beneath the tall trees, between the double rows of cars that were going downtown or toward the ocean. Lea was nervous. I felt her trembling in her light dress, and although in the dim light I could barely see her eyes—night was beginning to fall—I knew that they must be gleaming and a little damp, as always when something was greatly troubling her. I was very nervous too, waiting to hear her tell me what was on her mind. Finally, after a long silence, in a very faint voice, but without searching for words, because she always knew how to choose them well, whether in a conversation or in an argument, she told me what Félix had confided to her the night before. That he had been in love with her for some time, that she was more important to him than anything else, including the Party . . . I felt cramps in my stomach and I cursed myself for having been so cowardly and for not having dared to do before what Félix had now done. But when Lea finished her account and confessed to me that, because of how close we were to each other, she had felt obliged to tell me what had happened, since she didn't know what to do, I, with the masochism that habitually takes possession of me at certain times, hastened to cheer her up: she should accept the situation, how could she doubt that Félix loved her? That turned out to be the most sleepless night I spent in my years at San Marcos.

I went on seeing Félix and Lea, but our relationship gradually grew chillier. Because of the strict propriety that revolutionaries observed in such personal affairs, the fact that both of them were now in love or engaged or living together (I don't know which, in fact) was invisible simply from watching how they behaved, except for their always going about together, since they were never seen to hold hands, or make any other gesture toward each other that would betray a sentimental relationship between them. But I knew that it existed, and even though they hid it very well whenever I was with them, I felt in my stomach that hollow, upset feeling experienced by resentful bourgeois.

Sometime afterward—perhaps one or two years later—I heard a story about them, told by someone who could not have suspected that I had been in love with Lea. It happened in the cell to which they belonged. They had had some sort of personal dispute, something more serious than a mere tiff. In the cell meeting, Lea all of a sudden accused Félix of acting like a bourgeois toward her and asked for a political analysis of his behavior. The subject took the others by surprise and the session ended in a psychodrama, with Félix engaging in the ritual of self-criticism. For a reason I am unable to explain, that episode, which I heard about long after the fact and perhaps in a distorted form, has been on my mind throughout the years and I have tried many times to reconstruct it and intuit its context and reverberations.

By the time I dropped out of Cahuide, in the middle of the following year, 1954, I hardly ever saw Lea and Félix, and from then on I practically never saw them. We didn't talk together or seek each other out in the remaining years at San Marcos, exchanging at most a brief hello when we ran into each other as classes were beginning or ending. When I lived in Europe, I had scarcely any news of them, except that they had gotten married and had children, and that both of them, or Félix at least, had followed the jagged trajectory of so many militants of his generation, leaving the Party and going back to it, being a leader of it or suffering from the divisions, ruptures, reconciliations, and new divisions of the Peruvian Communists in the 1950s and 1960s.

In 1972, on the occasion of President Salvador Allende's visit to Lima, I ran into both of them, at a reception at the Chilean embassy. There among the crowd of guests, we were barely able to exchange even a few words. But I still haven't forgotten Lea's joke about *Conversation in The Cathedral*—"Those demons of yours . . ." It is a novel in which several episodes of our years at San Marcos appear, transfigured.

Eighteen or twenty years went by without my hearing any more about them. And then one fine day, during the election campaign, on the eve of the launching of my candidacy in Arequipa, in May of 1989, my secretaries handed me the list of journalists who were requesting interviews with me, on which Félix's name appeared. I immediately granted him an interview, wondering whether it was the same person. It was. Almost four decades older, but still identical to the Félix I remembered: suave and conspiratorial, with the same modesty and the same carelessness in his dress and the same conscientiousness when it came time to ask questions, the ever-exclusive political perspective on the tip of his tongue, and writing for a little periodical as marginal and precarious as the one that we had put out together at San Marcos. I was moved, seeing him, and I imagine that he was too. But neither of us allowed the other to glimpse those embers of sentimentality.

Of my passage through Cahuide the one episode that gave me the feeling that I was working for the revolution was the strike at San Marcos to show our solidarity with the streetcar employees. Their union was controlled by militants from Cahuide. The student section threw itself wholeheartedly into seeing to it that the Federation of San Marcos joined the strike, and we succeeded. Those were exciting days because, for the first time, the members of my cell had the chance to take action outside the university—and with workers! We attended the meetings of the union and put out, with the strikers, in a little print shop in La Victoria, a daily bulletin that we handed out in the places where people who had been left without any means of transportation gathered. And in those days, too, in the meetings of the strike committee, I had the chance to discover several members of Cahuide I'd never known.

How many of us were there? I never found out, but I suspect that there were no more than a few dozen. Just as I never knew, either, who our secretary general was nor who the members of the central committee were. The harsh repression of those years—only after 1955 would the state security system be relaxed, after the fall of Esparza Zañartu—required secrecy with regard to our activities. But it also had to do with the nature of the Party, its conspiratorial predisposition, that vocation for the clandestine that had never permitted it—despite the fact that we talked so much about the prospect—to become a party of the masses.

It was this, in part, that made me fed up with Cahuide. When I stopped going to the meetings of my cell, around June or July of 1954, I had felt bored for some time by the inanity of what we were doing. And I no longer believed a word of our class analyses and our materialist interpretations which, although I wouldn't have said so straight out to my comrades, seemed puerile to me, a catechism of stereotypes and abstractions, of formulas—"petty bourgeois opportunism," "revisionism," "class interest," "class struggle"—which were used as all-purpose clichés, to explain and defend the most contradictory things. And, above all, because there was in my nature, in my individualism, in my growing vocation as a writer, and in my intractable temperament a visceral inability to embody that patient, tireless, docile revolutionary, a slave to the organization, who accepts and practices democratic centralism once a decision has been arrived at by the organization and all the militants adopt it as their own and apply it with fanatical discipline. Against this, even though I paid lip service to the fact that it was the price of being effective, my whole being rebelled. Ideological differences, which came to me, above all, from Sartre and *Les Temps Modernes*, of which I was a devoted reader, also played a role in my withdrawing from Cahuide. But I believe that this was a secondary factor. For, despite all that I read in the study circles, what I managed to learn about Marxism at the time was fragmentary and superficial. Only in the 1960s, in Europe, would I make a serious effort to read Marx, Lenin, Mao, and heterodox Marxists such as Lukács, Gramsci, and Goldmann or the superorthodox Althusser, spurred on by the enthusiasm awakened in me by the Cuban revolution, which, from 1960 on, revived that interest in Marxism-Leninism which, ever since I had parted company with Cahuide, I had thought no longer existed.

Although San Marcos, Cahuide, Lea, and Félix had been, for all that time, my all-absorbing preoccupation, I continued to see my aunts and uncles—I dropped by one or another of their houses in turn for lunch or dinner throughout the week—and wrote to Uncle Lucho, to whom I gave a detailed account of everything I was doing or dreaming of doing and from whom I always received letters full of encouraging words. I also saw a great deal of friends from Piura who had come to Lima to prepare for careers at the university, especially Javier Silva. Several of them lived with Javier in a boarding house on the Calle Schell, in Miraflores, a place they called Slow Death because of the terrible food they were served. Javier had decided to study architecture and went about disguised as an architect, with a little intellectual's beard and black turtlenecks, St.-Germain-des-Prés style. I had already convinced him that we had to go off to Paris, and I even encouraged him to write a short story, which I published for him in *Turismo*. His mysterious text began as follows: "My footsteps took on a larger surface area . . ." But the following year, he suddenly decided to be an economist and entered San Marcos, so that, from 1954 on, we were also fellow university students.

Thanks to Javier, who had joined it, I resumed contact with my Diego Ferré *barrio*. I did so a little furtively, because those boys and girls were bourgeois and I had ceased to be one. What would Lea, Félix, or the comrades from Cahuide have said if they saw me, on the corner of the Calle Colón, talking about those "terrific babes" who had just moved to the Calle Ocharán, or planning the Saturday night surprise party? And what would the boys and girls of the *barrio* have said of Cahuide, an organization which, in addition to being Communist, had Indians, mestizos, and blacks in it like the ones who were servants in their houses? They were two worlds, separated by an abyss. When I went from one to the other I felt I was changing countries.

The ones I saw least in all that time were my parents. They had spent several months in the United States—and then, soon after returning home, my father went back. These visits were yet other attempts to find some sort of job or set up a business that would allow him to move there permanently. My mother stayed with my grandparents, where there was barely room for us. My father's absence greatly distressed her and I suspected that she was afraid that, in a fit of rage, he would disappear, as he had the first time. But he came back, just as the year 1953 was coming to an end, and one day he summoned me to his office.

I went, feeling very apprehensive, because I never expected anything good to come of his summonses. He told me that my job at *Turismo* didn't involve real responsibility, that it was just one I did on the side, and that I should work at something that would allow me to go on building a career for myself at the same time that I was studying at the university, the way so many young people did in the United States. He had already spoken to a friend of his, from the Banco Popular, and a job was waiting for me there, beginning on January 1.

So I began 1954 as a bank clerk, at the Banco Popular branch in La Victoria. On the first day the manager asked me if I had any experience. I told him I had none at all. He gave a whistle, intrigued. "In other words, you got the job through pull?" Yes, I had. "You're in trouble," he announced. "Because what I need is a receiving teller. We'll see how you make out." It was a rough experience that went on after the eight hours I spent in the office, from Monday to Friday, and it was repeated in nightmares I had about it. I had to receive money from people for their savings passbooks or their current accounts. A great many of the customers were whores from the Jirón Huatica, which was around the corner from the bank branch, and who became impatient because it took me such a long time to count their money and give them a receipt. I dropped the banknotes or messed them all up as I fingered them, and sometimes, when I became completely flustered, I pretended to have finished counting them and gave them the receipt without carefully checking how much they had given me. On many afternoons, the balance didn't tally and I had to count the cash all over again in a state of real panic. One day I found I was a hundred soles short. Thoroughly downcast, I went to the manager and told him I'd make up the missing sum out of my salary. But with a mere glance at the balance, he found the error and laughed at my inexperience. He was a likable young man, determined that my colleagues appoint me as the branch's delegate to the union of bank employees, since I was a university student. But I refused to become a union delegate, and I didn't tell Cahuide about it, since I was certain that they would have asked me to accept. If I took on that responsibility I would have to remain a bank employee, and that was a most unpleasant prospect. I detested the work, the strict working hours, and looked forward to Saturdays the way I had when I was a boarding student at Leoncio Prado.

And then, in my second month at the bank, a chance to escape from making figures balance came my way unexpectedly. I had gone to San Marcos to get my grades and the secretary of the Faculty, Rosita Corpancho, told me that Dr. Porras Barrenechea, for whose course I had received an excellent grade, wanted to see me. I telephoned him, intrigued—I had never spoken alone with him before—and he asked me to come by his house, on the Calle Colina, in Miraflores.

I went there, filled with curiosity, delighted to be able to enter this redoubt whose library and collection of paintings and statues of *Don Quixote* was spoken of as something mythical. He ushered me into the little study where he usually worked and there, surrounded by a host of books of all sizes and shelves where little statues and portraits of Don Quixote and Sancho Panza were lined up, congratulated me on my final exam and the work that I had handed in to him—in which he had seen, with approval, that I had pointed out a historical error on the part of the archaeologist Tschudi—and proposed to me that I work with him. Juan Mejía Baca had commissioned the principal Peruvian historians to put together a collection on the history of Peru. Porras would be responsible for the volumes on the Conquest and the Emancipation. The publisher and chief editor of the series would pay him for two assistants to help him with the bibliography and the documentation. He already had one working with him: Carlos Araníbar, a student who was studying for his degree in history at San Marcos. Did I want to be the other one? My pay would be five hundred soles a month and I would work at his house, from two to five in the afternoon, from Monday to Friday.

I left his house in an indescribable state of euphoria, to write my letter of resignation to the Banco Popular, which I handed to the manager the following morning, without hiding from him the happiness I felt. He couldn't understand it. Did I realize that I was leaving a steady job for one that would be short-lived? My co-workers at the branch offered me a farewell dinner in a Chinese restaurant in La Victoria, during which they kept teasing me about my customers from the Jirón Huatica, who definitely weren't going to miss me.

Filled with apprehension, I told my father the news. Despite the fact that I was going on eighteen, my fear of him reappeared on such occasions—a paralyzing sensation that minimized and nullified my arguments even in my own eyes, even on subjects concerning which I was certain that I was right—as well as the malaise I felt whenever he was near at hand, even in the most harmless situations.

He heard me out, turning slightly pale and scrutinizing me with that glacial gaze that I have never seen in anyone else, and once I had finished he demanded that I prove to him that I was going to earn five hundred soles a month. I had to go back to Dr. Porras's to seek supporting evidence. He gave me the signed document, somewhat surprised, and my father confined himself to heaping scorn on me for a time, telling me that I hadn't left the bank because the other job was going to be more interesting, but because of my lack of ambition.

And at the same time that I obtained the job with Porras Barrenechea, another fine thing happened to me: Uncle Lucho moved to Lima. Not for the right reasons. A sudden flood of the Chira River, owing to diluvial rains in the Piura mountains, had caused the waters to break through the barriers of the San José farm and destroy all the cotton fields, in a year in which the cleared land had produced plants with very heavy bolls and an exceptional harvest was expected. The investment and efforts of many years were wiped out in a matter of minutes. Uncle Lucho turned the plantation back to its owners, sold his furniture, loaded Aunt Olga and my cousins Wanda, Patricia, and Lucho in his station wagon, and got ready to fight for survival yet again, this time in Lima.

His presence was going to be something wonderful, I thought. The truth was that we needed him. The family had begun to collapse. Grandpa suffered from bad health and had difficulty remembering things. The most alarming case was that of Uncle Juan. Since his arrival from Bolivia he had found a good job, in an industrial company, for he was content and, moreover, a family man, devoted to his wife and children. He had always been fond of drinking more than he should have, but this seemed to be something that he was able to control at will, just a few excesses on weekends, at parties, and at family reunions. However, ever since the death of his mother, a year and a half before, his drinking had been increasing. Uncle Juan's mother had come from Arequipa to live with him when it was discovered that she had cancer. She played the piano wonderfully well, and when I went to my cousins Nancy and Gladys's house, I always asked Señora Laura to play the "Melgar" waltz by Luis Duncker Lavalle and other compositions that reminded us of Arequipa. She was a very pious woman, who knew how to die with composure. Her death was Uncle Juan's downfall. He stayed shut up in the living room of his house, refusing to open the door, drinking until he passed out. From that time on, he used to go on drinking like that, hour after hour, day after day, until the kindly, good-natured person he was when he was sober turned into a violent being who sowed fear and destruction all around him. I suffered as much as Aunt Lala and my cousins because of his downfall, those crises during which he little by little destroyed all his furniture, and kept entering and leaving sanatoriums—cures that he tried over and over and that were always useless—and filling with bitterness and financial hardships a family that he nonetheless adored.

Uncle Pedro had married a very pretty girl, the daughter of the overseer of the San Jacinto hacienda, and after having spent a year in the United States, he and Aunt Rosi were now living on the Paramonga hacienda, whose hospital he was the head of. That family was getting along very well. But Uncle Jorge and Aunt Gaby were fighting like cats and dogs, and their marriage seemed to be on the rocks. Uncle Jorge had kept on getting better and better jobs. With prosperity, he had acquired an insatiable appetite for entertainment and women, and his dissipations were a source of continual marital quarrels.

The family's problems affected me deeply. I experienced them as though each one of those dramas in the different households of the

Llosas concerned me in the most intimate way. And with more than my share of naïveté, I believed that with Uncle Lucho's arrival everything was going to be all right again, that thanks to the great righter of wrongs the family would once again be that serene, indestructible tribe, sitting around the big table in Cochabamba for another boisterous Sunday dinner.

TWELVE

Schemers and Dragons

B ETWEEN the end of September and the middle of October of 1989, after registering my candidacy at the national election board, I made a lightning-quick trip through four countries which, ever since the beginning of the campaign, I had been referring to as an example of the development that any country on the periphery that chooses economic freedom and joins the world's markets can achieve: Japan, Taiwan, South Korea, and Singapore.

They lacked natural resources, they were overpopulated and had started from zero, because of their colonial status or backwardness or because of a war that left them devastated. And the four of them, opting for development outward, had succeeded in becoming countries that exported and, by promoting private enterprise, brought about industrialization and a very rapid modernization, which ended mass unemployment and noticeably raised their standard of living. The four of them—but Japan in particular—were now competing in world markets with the most advanced countries. Were they not an example for Peru?

The object of the trip was to show Peruvians that we were already getting under way something we were proposing, the opening up of our economy toward the Pacific—negotiating with authorities, companies, and financial institutions of those countries. And that I was well enough known on the international scene to be received in those milieus.* Álvaro managed to get Peruvian television to broadcast, each

---

* Before this trip, I had had interviews with other heads of state or of government, three of them European—the German chancellor, Helmut Kohl, in July 1988; the British prime minister, Margaret Thatcher, in May 1989; the president of the Spanish government, Felipe González, in July 1989—and three Latin Americans: the presi-

[255]

night of my tour through these four Asiatic countries, between September 27 and October 14, 1989, the images that the mustachioed cameraman who accompanied us, Paco Velázquez, sent to it via satellite.

Velázquez traveled with us thanks to Genaro Delgado Parker, one of the owners of TV Channel 5, who paid his expenses. At the time, Genaro, an old acquaintance of mine and a friend, was said to be an enthusiast of my candidacy. On the night that it was launched, in Arequipa, on June 4, 1989, he gave us a million dollars' worth of ad time for nothing, after a discussion with Lucho Llosa, in which the latter accused him of being ambiguous and opportunistic when it came to his political tactics. Genaro visited me every so often to make suggestions and pass on political gossip to me, and in order to explain that if I was attacked on Channel 5's news broadcasts and programs, it was the fault of his brother Héctor, an Aprista and an intimate friend and adviser to President Alan García during the latter's first year in office.

According to Genaro, Héctor had won over his younger brother, Manuel, to his cause, and between the two of them they had placed him in the minority in the running of the channel, so that he had found himself obliged to give up any sort of executive post and the directorship of the company. Genaro always made me feel that I had been the original cause of his breaking off with Héctor—which had even gone as far as a fistfight—but that he had preferred to go through this family crisis rather than renounce a view of economics and politics that coincided with my own. Ever since I had worked with him as a reporter when I was still an adolescent, at Radio Panamericana, I had felt an irresistible warmth of feeling toward Genaro, but I always took his declarations of political love with a grain of salt. For I think I know him well enough to be certain that his great success as an impresario has been due not only to his energy and to his talent (of which he has more than enough), but also to his gift as a chameleon, his skill as a

---

dents of Costa Rica, Óscar Arias, on October 22, 1988; of Venezuela, Carlos Andrés Pérez, in April 1989; and of Uruguay, Julio María Sanguinetti, on June 15, 1989. And I would do likewise later on with the president of Brazil, Collor de Mello, on February 20, 1990. In the publicity for the campaign we used photographs and films of these meetings to create for me the image of a statesman.

sharp businessman with a talent for swimming in both water and oil and for persuading both God and the Devil, at one and the same time, that he is their man.

His conduct, during the campaign against nationalization, was erratic. In the beginning, he placed himself in a position of headlong opposition to the measure, and Channel 5, which at the time he headed, opened its doors to us and was little short of being the spokesman for our mobilization. On the eve of the rally in the Plaza San Martín, he came to see me with suggestions, some of them very amusing, for my speech, which Channel 5 broadcast live. But in the days that followed, his position gradually changed from solidarity to neutrality, and then to hostility, with the rate of speed of an astronaut. The reason was a summons, at the most heated moment of the campaign, that he received from Alan García, who invited him to breakfast at the Presidential Palace. Once this interview was over, Genaro hurried out to my house, to tell me all about it. He recounted to me a version of his chat with the president, in which the latter, in addition to railing against me, had made veiled threats against him, which he did not tell me about in detail. I noted that he was quite upset by that meeting: half panic-stricken and half euphoric. The fact is that immediately thereafter Genaro left for Miami, where he disappeared into thin air. It was impossible to locate him. Manuel—the manager as well of a chain of radio stations—who took over the business, eliminated us from the news bulletins and placed many obstacles and difficulties in our way, even when it was a matter of getting our paid advertisements on the air.

After a few months, Genaro came back to Lima and, as though nothing had happened, renewed his contacts with me. He often visited me at my house in Barranco, offering me aid and counsel, while at the same time he pointed out to me that his influence with regard to the channel was limited now, since Héctor and Manuel had ganged up on him. Despite this, his offer of a million dollars' worth of free publicity was honored by the company even after Genaro was no longer the director of the channel. Through almost the whole of the campaign, Genaro posed as a man on our side. He was present at the launching of my candidacy in Arequipa, and in order to promote it brought together a small group of journalists who, working with Álvaro, distributed materials to the press that could be of help to us. That was how it happened that Paco Velázquez traveled through Asia with me.

Less intelligent and clever than Genaro, his brother Héctor chose to become involved with the APRA, assuming ticklish responsibilities in Alan García's administration. He was commissioned by the latter to negotiate with the French government a smaller-sized purchase than the twenty-six Mirage planes that the Belaunde administration had ordered, part of which Alan García had decided to send back. The long-drawn negotiation, whereby in the end Peru kept twelve and returned fourteen, led to an accord that was never completely clear. This was one of the matters in which, according to persistent rumors, there had been shady dealings and commissions amounting to millions. *

I was repeatedly counseled by advisers and allies of the Front to avoid all mention of the Mirages, because of the risk that Channel 5 would turn into a merciless enemy of my candidacy. I disregarded the advice for the reason already mentioned: so that nobody in Peru would have the wrong idea as to what I was intending to do if I were elected. I am not definitely accusing Alan García and Héctor Delgado Parker in connection with this affair. For, even though I made every effort to acquire detailed information concerning the negotiations having to do with the Mirages, I never managed to arrive at a definite opinion about it. But, for that very reason, it was necessary to determine if the accord had been an open and aboveboard negotiation or not.

In the middle of my trip through Asia, a fax from Álvaro arrived for me one night in the hotel in Seoul: Héctor Delgado Parker had been kidnapped, on October 4, 1989, in the vicinity of Panamericana Television, by a commando unit of the Túpac Amaru Revolutionary Movement, which, in the course of the operation, had killed his chauffeur and wounded Héctor. He remained a captive for 199 days, until April 20, 1990, when his kidnappers let him loose in the streets of Miraflores. During this time, the executive director of Channel 5

* In July 1991, at the time of the international scandal concerning BCCI, the District Attorney of New York County, Robert Morgenthau, accused Alan García's government of having caused his country to lose $100 million by ordering that it not intervene in BCCI's negotiations to repurchase its fourteen planes through a country in the Middle East, thereby implying that shady dealings were involved.

was the youngest of the brothers, Manuel, but Genaro again came to
have a certain hand in running the company. At a press conference
during the Economics and Agriculture Forum 1990–1995, organized
by the Universidad Nacional Agraria, on January 30, 1990 (at which,
let it be said in passing, exasperated by the ferocity of the slander of
me by officialdom, which was becoming even worse at that time, I
went too far, calling Alan García's administration "a government of
shitheads and thieves"), I mentioned, among the affairs that would be
the object of an investigation, the matter of the Mirages. Days later,
in one of the most mysterious episodes of the campaign, Héctor's
captors allowed him to answer me and proclaim his innocence, from
the "people's prison," by means of a videotape that was broadcast on
César Hildebrandt's program on Channel 4, on Sunday, February 11,
1990. The evening before, Manuel Delgado Parker had sought Álvaro
out, so as to inform him of the existence of this videotape and assure
him that the family would not authorize its being broadcast. The
Aprista press accused me of putting Héctor's life in danger by mentioning the Mirages while he was being held captive by his kidnappers.
After that episode, Channel 5 was to turn into a key element of the
campaign orchestrated by the government against us.

But all that took place a few months later, and during the trip to
the Orient, at the beginning of October 1989, thanks to the good
offices of Genaro and his cameraman, Álvaro was able to inundate
the TV channels and the daily papers with pictures in which I appeared
as little less than a head of state, conversing with the president of the
Republic of China, Lee Teng-hui, in Taiwan, or with the prime
minister of Japan, Toshiki Kaifu. The latter proved to be very cordial
toward me. On October 13, 1989, he postponed a meeting with Carla
Hills, the United States trade representative, in order to receive me,
and in our brief talk together he assured me that if I was elected Japan
would support my administration in its efforts to bring Peru back into
the financial community. He told me that he looked with favor on
our effort to attract Japanese investments. Prime Minister Kaifu had
been chairman of a Peruvian-Japanese friendship committee of the
Diet and was aware of the fact that I had frequently used the example
of Japan as proof that a country could rise from its ruins and that as
a presidential candidate I stood in favor of the economic opening of
Peru toward the Pacific. (In the second round of the election, Fujimori

made good use of my harangues on the subject, telling the voters: "I agree with what Doctor Vargas Llosa says about Japan. But don't all of you think that the son of Japanese parents can be more successful than he in pursuing that policy?")

The Keidanren, a federation of private companies in Japan, organized a meeting in Tokyo between representatives of Japanese industries and banks and the entrepreneurs who accompanied me on the tour: Juan Francisco Raffo, Patricio Barclay, Gonzalo de la Puente, Fernando Arias, Raymundo Morales, and Felipe Thorndike. I asked them to travel with me because in their respective branches—finance, exports, mining, fishing, textiles, metallurgy—they represented modern businesses, and because I considered them to be efficient entrepreneurs, eager to progress and capable of learning from the companies that we visited in the "four dragons." It was a good thing to show Asian governments and investors that our project for opening up trade could count on the support of the Peruvian private sector.

This was one of the few cases which involved a coordinated effort between groups of entrepreneurs and my campaign for the presidency. The positive feelings that, in the society we wanted to build, the private entrepreneur would be the driving force behind development, thanks to whose vision the jobs that we needed would be created, the foreign currency that was in such short supply would reach Peru, the standards of living of the populace would continually rise—someone recognized and approved of by a society without complexes, conscious of the fact that, in a country with a market economy, the success of businesses favors the entire community.

I never hid from entrepreneurs the fact that, during a first stage, they would be the ones who would have to make great sacrifices. Today I am less certain, but at the time it seemed to me that many, the majority perhaps, came around to admitting that they would have to pay that price if they wanted someday to be the peers of those entrepreneurs who, in Japan, Taiwan, South Korea, or Singapore, showed us their factories and made our heads swim with their figures on rates of growth and their worldwide sales. I managed to communicate to at least some of them my conviction that it depended solely on us whether, on a day in the not too distant future, that filthy and violent metropolis that the City of Kings (as Lima was called in the colonial period) had become would look in the eyes of tourists like the impeccable and wholly modern city-state of Singapore.

"When I arrived here thirty years ago, there, where you now see those skyscrapers, that avenue with boutiques that need not envy those in Zurich, New York, or Paris, and those five-star hotels, were swamps infested with crocodiles and mosquitoes." I can still see that figure, pointing, from his window at the Singapore Chamber of Commerce, of which he was the head, at the center of that city, of that tiny country, that left me with an unforgettable impression.

Like Peru, Singapore was a multiracial society—whites, Chinese, Malayans, Hindus—with different languages, traditions, customs, and religions. But they had as well a very small area of land, with barely room for the country's population, and suffered from an extreme tropical climate, with suffocating heat and torrential rains. Except for a good geographical situation, they lacked natural resources. That is to say, they were the victims of all those factors regarded as the worst obstacles to development. And yet they had become one of the most modern and most advanced societies in Asia, with a very high standard of living, the largest and most efficient port in the world—whose perfect, spanking-white cleanliness made it look like a sort of clinic, and where a ship unloaded and loaded again in barely eight hours— and high-technology industries.* (The growth rate of its gross domestic product between 1981 and 1990 had averaged 6.3 percent per year and the growth rate of its exports between 1981 and 1989 7.3 percent, according to the World Bank and the International Monetary Fund.) Its different races, religions, and customs coexisted in that financial mecca, with one of the most active stock exchanges on the globe and a banking system that had interlocking networks throughout the planet. All of this had been brought about in less than thirty years, thanks to economic freedom, the market, and internationalization. It

---

* I remember having had a discussion, in London, about Singapore with the writer Shiva Naipaul, who had just returned from there. According to him, that progress, the rapid modernization, represented a cultural crime against the Singaporeans, who were "losing their souls" because of it. Were they more authentic then, when they lived surrounded by swamps, crocodiles, and mosquitoes, than they are now, living amid skyscrapers? More picturesque, doubtless, but I am certain that all of them— all of the inhabitants of the Third World—would be ready to give up being picturesque in exchange for having work and living with a minimum of security and decency.

is true that Lee Kuan Yew had been authoritarian and repressive (only recently had he begun to tolerate opposition and criticism), something that I was not going to imitate. But why couldn't Peru attain a similar development, within a democratic system? It was possible, if a majority of Peruvians so chose. And at that point in the campaign, the signs were favorable: the polls always placed me very far ahead, with those intending to vote for me wavering between 40 and 45 percent.

It was not easy to obtain offers of aid and investments, since I was a mere candidate for president. However, we secured concrete promises for the Program for Social Aid of some four hundred million dollars (Taiwan, two hundred million, and South Korea and Japan, a hundred million each). On the tour, I could show the governments of those countries and many companies what we were going to do to change the self-destructive course that Peru had taken. The country's image had fallen to lamentable extremes: an insecure and violent place, quarantined by the financial community, which, since the declaration of war by the Aprista administration against the International Monetary Fund, had removed Peru from its agenda, excluding it from all programs for credit or aid and with no interest in its continued existence.

To my arguments that Peru was endowed with resources that the Asian countries of the Pacific needed—beginning with petroleum and minerals—and that it was therefore possible to make both economies complementary by converting the Pacific into a bridge for exchanges, the answers always tended to be the same ones. Yes, but before that, Peru had to get out of its impasse with the International Monetary Fund, without whose endorsement no country, bank, or business enterprise would trust commitments made by the Peruvian government. The second condition was to bring a definite end to terrorism.

In the case of Japan, the matter was a particularly delicate one. Government officials and entrepreneurs told us, without beating about the bush, of their annoyance at the lack of compliance with the commitments made by Peru regarding the North Peru pipeline, financed by Japan. Many years ago, Peruvian administrations had stopped amortizing this debt that had been contracted in the days of the military dictatorship, but more serious still for a country where formality is everything, the present administration did not even offer any explanation. The officials in charge of the project answered neither letters nor telexes. And the special envoys that had been sent had been received neither by the president nor by government ministers but by second-level bureaucrats whose instructions appeared to be to answer with excuses and evasive promises (the famous Peruvian institution of the *meceo*: to keep shilly-shallying until one's conversational partner gets tired of insisting). Was this any way to behave toward friendly countries?

I tirelessly repeated to bureaucrats and entrepreneurs that it was against this sort of procedure and political morality that I was fighting. And I explained to everyone that in our program renegotiation with the IMF and the fight against terrorism were absolute priorities. I don't know whether they believed me or not. But I did obtain a number of things. Among them, an accord with the Keidanren to hold in Lima, immediately following the election, a meeting of Peruvian and Japanese entrepreneurs charged with laying the foundations of a collaboration that would include everything from the thorny subject of unpaid debts to the way in which Japan could aid Peru to reenter the financial world and the sectors in which Japanese businesses could invest in the country. Tireless Miguel Vega Alvear, who had organized the trip through the Orient, was placed in charge of making preparations for this meeting, at the end of April or the beginning of May (the elections were to be held on April 10 and we did not reject the idea that we might win in the first round of voting).

The most spectacular reception given me on the entire tour was in Taiwan. And I left there convinced that important investments would be forthcoming from that country as soon as we won the election. Officials from the Ministry of Foreign Relations were waiting for me as I got off the plane, two cars with sirens escorted me wherever I went, President Lee Teng-hui received me at an official audience, as did the minister of foreign relations, and we had a long working session with the leaders of the Kuomintang and with private entrepreneurs. And also something that I had insistently requested: a detailed account of the agrarian reform that had transformed the island of great semi-feudal landholdings that Taiwan had been when Chiang Kai-shek arrived there into an archipelago of small and medium-sized farms in the hands of private owners. This reform was the driving force that led to the industrial takeoff that turned Taiwan into the economic power that it is today.

When I was a student, in the 1950s, Taiwan was a bad word in Latin America. The progressivist sectors considered that for a country to "Taiwanize itself" was the worst sort of opprobrium. For the ruling ideology—that confused mixture of socialism, nationalism, and populism that had ruined Latin America—the image of Taiwan was that of a semicolonial factory, a country that had sold its sovereignty for a mess of pottage: the U.S. investments that allowed the existence of manufacturing plants in which millions of miserably paid workers sewed trousers, shirts, and dresses for multinational corporations. In the middle of the 1950s, the Peruvian economy—whose export volume then amounted to as much as two billion dollars per year—was superior to Taiwan's and the income per capita of both countries was under a thousand dollars. When I visited the island, income per capita in Peru had gone down to around half of what it was in the 1950s and Taiwan's had increased more than 700 percent ($7,530 for 1990). And after having experienced an average annual growth rate of 8.5 percent between 1981 and 1989 (with its exports increasing at the rate of 12.1 percent over the same period),* Taiwan now had reserves of $75 billion, whereas when Alan García's tenure in office ended, Peruvian reserves were negative and the country was bearing the crushing burden of an external debt of $20 billion.

Unlike South Korea, whose development, no less impressive than Taiwan's, had had as a driving force seven enormous conglomerates, in Taiwan businesses of small and medium size, working at a very high technological level, had multiplied: in 1990 80 percent of its factories, the majority of them oriented toward exports and highly competitive, had less than twenty workers. This was a model that suited us. Officials and businessmen in Taiwan spared no effort to satisfy my curiosity and arranged a program of visits for me which, although it was a killing one, turned out to be very instructive. I remember in particular the impression of science fiction conveyed to me by the scientific industrial park of Hsin Chu, where the world's large corporations were invited to experiment with products and technologies for the future. In Taiwan I received the firmest promises of aid should the Democratic Front assume power.

Naturally, there was a political interest behind this. Peru broke off

* Data from the World Bank and the International Monetary Fund.

diplomatic relations with Taiwan in order to recognize the People's Republic of China, in the days of Velasco's dictatorship. Since that time, succeeding Peruvian administrations had reduced the country's commercial contacts and exchanges with Taiwan; under Alan García, they had dwindled to nothing. In order to maintain a presence in Peru, Taiwan still had a commercial office in Lima, the manager of which was the semiofficial representative of his government. But he was not even authorized to give out visas. Although in none of the interviews of me was I asked any concrete questions, I volunteered to government authorities the information that my administration would engage in consular and commercial relations, as other countries had done, without breaking off diplomatic relations with the People's Republic of China.

As I had done with Mrs. Thatcher and with Felipe González, prime ministers of countries with problems of the same sort, I asked government leaders in Taiwan for advice concerning antiterrorist activities. Like the others, they too promised to advise me. And they immediately made me an offer to set up two scholarships, for a short eight-week course in antisubversive strategy. The Freedom Movement sent Henry Bullard, a jurist who was a member of the Democratic Front's committee on civil peace and human rights, and another person, as enigmatic as he was efficient, about whom I never managed to find out very much, except that he was a karate black belt and a Nisei: Professor Oshiro. He was the trainer and technical director of the security personnel of Prosegur, and the person who replaced Óscar Balbi—or reinforced him—following me around like a shadow at rallies and on my trips around the country. Of an indefinable age—between forty and forty-five, perhaps—and slender and strong as a rock, invariably wearing a light sport shirt, his serene and peaceable air made me trust him. Professor Oshiro never opened his mouth, except to utter a few incomprehensible murmurs, and nothing appeared to irritate him or bring him out of his meditative mood: neither the attacks of the Aprista "buffaloes" at demonstrations nor the storms that, all of a sudden, would make the small plane in which we were flying shudder violently. But if need be, his reactions were extraordinarily fast. Like the time, in Puno, during the festivities to celebrate Candlemas. We had entered the stadium, where a performance of folk dances was being given, and were greeted by a hail of stones, thrown from one of the boxes. Before the thought of raising my arms to protect myself had even crossed my mind, Professor Oshiro had already spread out his big leather coat, like an umbrella—one against showers of stones—over me and stopped, or at least deadened, their impact. The antisubversive course in Taiwan did not greatly impress him, but he took the trouble to present me with a report on everything he had heard and learned in it.

Since the trip through Asia was political, and with an overloaded agenda, I had hardly any time in those weeks for cultural activities or for seeing writers. With two exceptions. In Taipei I had lunch with the leaders of the local PEN club and was able to have a brief conversation with the magnificent Nancy Ying, of whom I had become a very good friend when I was the international president of that organization. And, in Seoul, the Korean PEN center gave a reception for me, to which it invited those who had accompanied me on the tour. It was presided over by an imposing figure, dressed in a very beautiful silk kimono with a flower print and carrying painted paper fans. The banker and industrialist Gonzalo de la Puente, making a bow worthy of a Renaissance courtier, leaned over to kiss the figure's hand: "*Chère madame . . .*" We discreetly informed him that the person was a *cher monsieur*, a venerable poet, and apparently a very popular one.

Just after my return to Lima I gave a press conference reporting on my trip and the good prospects for the development of Peru's economic relations with the countries of the Pacific Rim. The tour received good reviews from the media. There seemed to be a unanimous feeling in favor of Peru's improving its interchanges with countries possessing enormous excess financial funds available for industrial investment. Wasn't it absurd not to have taken advantage of this opportunity which our neighbor, Chile, was already making such good use of?

Worried by the polls' prediction of a crushing victory for the Democratic Front, on November 27, 1989, Alan García broke what, by a provision of the Constitution and by custom, should be the president's attitude during the electoral process: a genuine or a feigned neutrality. And at a press conference, he appeared on the TV screens to say that if nobody "stands up to him" (by "him" meaning me), he would do so. By refuting, for example, the figures that I had given regarding the number of public employees in Peru. According to him. there were *only* 507,000 people on the state payrolls. This was a subject of capital importance for us, and we had investigated it as thoroughly as was possible. Several times I had attended meetings of our committee on a national system of budget control, and the person who headed it, Dr. María Reynafarje, had given us a very interesting description of the underhanded tricks and crooked dealings which successive administrations had used to swell the number of employees in public enterprises. Alan García had exaggerated this practice to the point of perversion. The Peruvian Institute of Social Security, for instance, had a system of contracts with supposed firms employing security guards, and funds whose existence was kept as closely guarded as though they were a sort of military secret—a dodge that allowed the government to pay the salaries of hundreds of thugs and gunmen who belonged to its paramilitary groups. It was not hard for me, then, to argue with García and demonstrate the very next day, with figures in hand, that the number of Peruvians who received pay and salaries from the state (officially or through the subterfuge of temporary contracts) was over a million. The opinion surveys made after this polemical exchange showed that out of every three Peruvians, two believed me and only one believed him.

After that, and as a reprisal against my well-publicized trip through Asia, Alan García announced that Peru was granting recognition to Kim Il Sung's regime and establishing diplomatic relations with North Korea. He hoped in this way to prevent or, at the least, put difficulties in the way of Peru's economic interchanges with South Korea, and, indirectly, with the other countries of the Pacific Rim, for which Kim Il Sung's dictatorship for life—under which North Korea was contending with Libya for the title of the state most actively promoting terrorism on a global scale—was an outcast regime.

But this was not the only reason. Through that gesture, Alan García was also repaying favors received by him and his party from that regime which, besides having been quarantined by the community of civilized countries, represented a survival of the most despotic form of Stalinist megalomania. During the 1985 presidential campaign, the communications media in Peru had pointed out with amazement the continual trips by Aprista leaders and by Alan García himself to Pyongyang, where, for instance, Representative Carlos Roca, dressed in a proletarian uniform, was in the habit of being photographed with North

Korean officials. That the government of Kim Il Sung had given financial aid to Alan García's campaign was something that went without saying, and there had even been a vitriolic denunciation in which a photographer from the periodical *Oiga** had chanced upon a secret reunion of Aprista leaders and the semiofficial delegation of North Korea in Peru, at which, supposedly, one of the deliveries of campaign funds had been made in a shoe box!

During Alan García's term in office the contacts had continued, in a more worrisome way. There was a strange purchase by the Ministry of the Interior of North Korean submachine guns and rifles to update the weaponry of the police and the Civil Guard. Nonetheless, only a part of that weaponry in fact reached those forces, and there were many reports concerning the final destination of the remainder—ten thousand firearms, apparently. It was another affair about which the government had never offered a convincing explanation. The alarm about the weapons imported from North Korea came not only from the press, but from the armed forces as well. The officers of the navy and the army with whom I talked in unbelievable meetings—in which it was necessary to change vehicles and places several times—had all referred to this subject. What had happened to those rifles? According to the most alarmist among them, they had ended up in the hands of the shock forces of the Aprista party and their paramilitary commando units, while according to others, they had been resold to drug traffickers, terrorists, or on the international market, to the profit of the few high-ranking officers and civilian bureaucrats closest to the president.

What benefit could bring Peru to legitimize a terrorist regime, which had trained and financed groups of Peruvian guerrilla fighters from the MIR and the FLN in the 1960s, and which was not in a position to be a market for our products nor a source of investment? The drawbacks, on the other hand, were going to be enormous, beginning with the obstacle that this would present for our obtaining credits and investments from the government of South Korea—which by contrast had abundant financial resources.

In accordance with the Front's committee on foreign policy, which was headed by a retired ambassador, Arturo García, and which (discreetly) advised various civil servants who were active in the admin-

* *Oiga*, Lima, February 11, 1985.

istration, I announced, on November 29, that once installed, my government would put an end to all relations with Kim Il Sung's regime. Several members of the consultative commission of the Ministry of Foreign Relations resigned from it in protest against Alan García's decision to recognize North Korea.

THIRTEEN

The Fierce Little
Sartrean

I WORKED with Raúl Porras Barrenechea from February 1954 until a few days before I left for Europe, in 1958. The three hours a day I spent there, in those four years and a half, from Monday to Friday, between two and five in the afternoon, taught me more about Peru and contributed more to my education than the classes at San Marcos.

Porras Barrenechea was a master in the old style, who liked being surrounded by disciples, from whom he demanded complete loyalty. An elderly bachelor, he had lived in that old house with his mother until she died the year before, and he now shared it with an aged black servant who had perhaps been his nursemaid. She addressed him with the familiar *tú* and scolded him like a little boy, prepared the delicious cups of chocolate with which the historian received the intellectual luminaries who came by on a pilgrimage to the Calle Colina. Of those, I remember as the most delightful conversationalists the Spaniard Don Pedro Laín Entralgo; the Venezuelan Mariano Picón-Salas, a historian, essayist, and sharp-witted humorist; the Mexican Alfonso Junco, whose timidity disappeared when the conversation turned to the two subjects that impassioned him, Spain and the faith, for he was a militant crusader for Hispanism and Catholicism; and our compatriots the poet José Gálvez, who spoke a very pure Spanish and had a mania for genealogy, and Víctor Andrés Belaunde—in those days Peru's ambassador to the United Nations—who often passed through Lima, and who, on one occasion I am thinking of, talked all night and didn't allow either Porras or any of the guests at the gathering over chocolate given in his honor to get a word in edgewise.

Víctor Andrés Belaunde (1883–1966), who belonged to the generation before Porras's, a philosopher and a Catholic essayist as well as a diplomat, had a celebrated controversy with José Carlos Mariátegui, whose theories on Peruvian society he refuted in his *La realidad nacional*,* in which he defended a Christian corporatism that was as artificial and unreal as the schematic—although a most novel approach for the time and widely influential—Marxist interpretation of Mariátegui's *Siete ensayos*. Porras esteemed Belaunde, although he did not share his ultramontane Catholicism, or that of José de la Riva Agüero (1885–1944), or the latter's crepuscular enthusiasms for fascism, although he did appreciate his erudite and all-inclusive vision of the Peruvian past, which Riva Agüero interpreted as a synthesis of the indigenous and the Spanish. Porras professed an admiration without reservation for Riva Agüero, whom he regarded as his master and with whom he had in common meticulousness, exactitude regarding facts and quotations, a love of Spain and of history understood in Michelet's romantic fashion, a certain ironic disdain for the new intellectual currents which held the individual and the anecdotal in contempt—anthropology and ethnohistory, for instance; while at the same time he stood apart from him by virtue of a much more flexible turn of mind with regard to religion and politics.

Diplomacy, to which Porras Barrenechea had devoted part of his life, had taken up a great deal of his time and energy, keeping him from crowning his career with what everyone expected of him, that masterwork on the history of the Discovery and the Conquest of Peru—or the biography of Pizarro—subjects on which he had been preparing to write the definitive work since his early years and on which he had managed to acquire so much information that it resembled omniscience. Up until then, Porras's wisdom had taken the form of a series of learned monographs on chroniclers, travelers, or ideologists and defenders of emancipation, as well as of beautiful anthologies on Lima and Cuzco or of essays, that were to appear over those years, on Ricardo Palma, Riva Agüero's *Paisajes peruanos (Peruvian Landscapes)*, or his textbook on *Fuentes históricas peruanas*.† But those of us who admired him, and he himself, knew that these were mere crumbs of the great overall work on that watershed era of Peruvian

---

* Written in exile, from 1929 to 1930, and published in several issues of the *Mercurio Peruano*. The first edition in book form appeared in Paris in 1930, with a second part on Leguía's eleven years of dictatorship (1919–1930).
† Lima: Editorial Mejía Baca, 1956.

history, that of its establishing close relations with Europe and the West, which he knew more about than anyone else. A fellow scholar of his generation, Jorge Basadre, had fulfilled an equivalent undertaking in his monumental *Historia de la República*, which Porras had annotated from beginning to end and on which he had passed judgment, an opinion at once respectful and severely critical, in his microscopic handwriting, at the end of the last volume. Another fellow scholar of his generation, Luis Alberto Sánchez, exiled at the time in Chile, had also crowned his career with a voluminous history of Peruvian literature, under the title *Literatura peruana*. Although he had certain reservations and differences of opinion with Basadre, Porras had intellectual respect for him; for Sánchez, a disdainful commiseration.

Unlike Basadre or Porras, that third musketeer of the celebrated generation of 1919, Luis Alberto Sánchez (the fourth, Jorge Guillermo Leguía, died very young, leaving only the bare outline of an *oeuvre*), who, as the leader of the APRA, had lived for many years in exile, was the most international and the most fecund of the trio, but also the most devil-may-care and the least rigorous when it came time to publish. That he should write entire books in one go, trusting in his memory alone (even if it was the impressive memory of Luis Alberto Sánchez), without verifying the data, citing books he hadn't read, making mistakes as to dates, titles, names, as frequently occurred in the flood of his publications, made Porras furious. Sánchez's inaccuracies and carelessness—even more than his ill-will and his retaliations against his political adversaries and his personal enemies that can be found in abundance in his books—exasperated Porras for a reason that from a distance I think I now understand better, a loftier reason than what, at the time, appeared to me to be a mere rivalry between scholars of the same generation. Because those liberties that Sánchez took in the practice of his profession took for granted the underdevelopment of his readers, the inability of his audience to identify them and condemn them. And Porras—like Basadre and Jorge Guillermo Leguía and, before them, Riva Agüero—even though he wrote and published little, always did so as though the country to which he belonged were the most cultivated and best-informed one in the world, demanding of himself an extreme rigor and perfection, as would be only proper for a historian whose research is going to be subjected to the examination of the most responsible scholars.

Those years also brought the polemic between Luis Alberto Sánchez and the Chilean critic Ricardo A. Latcham, who, reviewing the former's essay on the novel in Latin America—*Proceso y contenido de la novela hispanoamericana (History and Content of the Hispano-American Novel)*—pointed out a number of errors and omissions in the book. Sánchez answered with lively rejoinders and jokes. Latcham thereupon overwhelmed his adversary with an inexhaustible list of inaccuracies—dozens and dozens of them—which I remember seeing Porras read, in a Chilean publication, murmuring half to himself: "How shameful, how shameful."

Since Sánchez survived Leguía, Porras, and Basadre by many years, his version of the generation of '19—the intellectual quality of which would not be repeated again in Peru—has been enthroned in a manner little short of canonical. But, in all truth, it suffers from the same defects as the innumerable books of this good underdeveloped writer for underdeveloped readers that Sánchez represented. I am thinking, above all, of the prologue he wrote for Porras's posthumous book on Pizarro, published in Lima in 1978 by a group of Porras's disciples, and put together piecemeal, without giving the proper bibliographic information, jumbling together published and unpublished texts in a confused and uneven hodgepodge. I do not know to whom we owe the responsibility, or rather the irresponsibility, for this ugly edition —with commercial advertisements inserted in between the pages— which would have horrified that historian who was a perfectionist, but even today I understand still less the reason for entrusting the prologue to Luis Alberto Sánchez, who, faithful to his character and his habits, made of this introduction a subtle masterwork of malice, recalling amid saccharine manifestations of friendship for "Raúl" those episodes that had been especially embarrassing to Porras, such as his having supported General Ureta and not Bustamante y Rivero in the 1945 elections and not having resigned as ambassador to Spain, a post to which Bustamante had appointed him, at the time of Odría's military coup in 1948.

Porras Barrenechea's disciples and friends, of different generations and professions—among them were historians and professors and diplomats—all dropped by the Calle Colina, to visit him, to attend the chocolate gatherings as night fell, to pass on to him gossip about the university, politics, or the Ministry of Foreign Relations, which delighted him, or to ask him for advice and recommendations. The most frequent visitor of all was a close companion who belonged to his own generation, also a diplomat, a regional historian (of Piura) and a journalist, Ricardo Vegas García. Nearsighted, neat as a pin, impossibly ill-tempered, Don Ricardo had solitary fits of rage about which Porras told most amusing anecdotes, such as how he had seen him—or rather, heard him—smash to bits a toilet whose chain he'd had difficulty pulling, and pummeling to pieces with his fists a table on which he had begun by giving slaps of his hand to demand service. Don Ricardo Vegas García would enter the house on the Calle Colina like the waterspout of a tornado and invite everyone to have tea at the Tiendecita Blanca, where he always would order ladyfingers. And woe to anyone who resisted his invitations! Beneath his arrogance and his brusque remarks, Don Ricardo was a generous and likable man, whose friendship and loyalty Porras appreciated enormously and whom he later was to miss a great deal.

The university professors who dropped by most often were Jorge Puccinelli and Luis Jaime Cisneros, and César Vallejo's widow came by too—the fearsome Georgette, whom Porras protected following the death of her husband in Paris—and many culturally lionized poets, writers, or journalists, whose presence gave the house on the Calle Colina a warm and stimulating atmosphere, in which the intellectual discussions and dialogues were larded with gossip and ill-will—the great Peruvian sport of *raje*—bad-mouthing—of which Porras, an old Lima hand (even though he'd been born in Pisco), was an outstanding practitioner. The gatherings used to last till far into the night and end up in some café in Miraflores—El Violín Gitano or La Pizzería on the Diagonal—or in El Triunfo, in Surquillo, an ill-reputed little bar that Porras had renamed Montmartre.

My first task, at the historian's house, consisted of reading the chronicles of the Conquest, making note cards on the myths and legends of Peru. I have an exhilarating memory of those readings in search of data on the Seven Cities of Cíbola, the Kingdom of the Great Paititi, the marvels of El Dorado, the land of the Amazons, that of the Fountain of Youth and all the time-hallowed fantasies of utopian kingdoms, enchanted cities, continents that had disappeared, which the encounter with America brought back to life in the present among those migrating Europeans who ventured, dazzled by what they saw, into the lands of Tahuantinsuyo and resorted, in order to understand them, to the classical mythologies and the arsenal of medieval legends. Although very different in their composition and their aim, some of them written by rough, unlettered, uncultivated men induced by the sure sense that they were witnessing events of transcendent importance to leave behind testimony as to what they did, saw, and heard, these chronicles mark the appearance of a written literature in Spanish America, and already, through their most unusual mixture of fantasy and realism, of unbridled imagination and fierce verisimilitude, as well as through their abundance, their picturesqueness, their epic breadth, their descriptive itch, lay down the pattern for certain characteristics of the future literature of Latin America. Some accounts, above all those of monastic chroniclers, like Father Calancha, could be prolix and boring, but others, such as those of the Inca Garcilaso or Cieza de León, I read with genuine pleasure, as monuments of a new genre that combined the best of literature and history, for it had, like the latter, its feet immersed in lived experience and its head in fiction.

It was not only fun to spend those three hours consulting chronicles; in addition, if I had any sort of question of my own, there was the possibility of hearing a disquisition from Porras on persons and episodes having to do with the Conquest. I remember, one afternoon, because of some question or other that I don't recall which Aranibar or I put to him, a master class that he gave us on "the heresy of the sun," a deviation or heterodoxy from the point of view of the official religion of the Inca empire that he had reconstructed through the testimony of the chronicles, about which he was thinking of writing an article (a project which, like so many others, he never managed to get around to and actually finish). Porras had known the great figures of Peruvian literature, and many of Latin American and Spanish literature, and I listened to him, all ears, as he spoke of César Vallejo, with whom he had been on intimate terms before Vallejo died and the posthumous publication of whose *Poemas humanos* Porras was responsible for, or of José María Eguren, whose childish tender feelings and innocence he made fun of with the greatest irreverence, or of the apocalyptic end of Oquendo de Amat, a poet done in by tuberculosis and sheer rage, in a Spanish sanatorium to which he and the Marquesa de la Conquista—a descendant of Pizarro's—had had him transferred on the eve of the Spanish Civil War.

Although only Carlos Araníbar and I worked in the house on the Calle Colina on a regular schedule and with a salary (which the bookseller-editor Mejía Baca paid us at the end of each month), all Porras's old and new disciples—Félix Álvarez Brun, Raúl Rivera Serna, Pablo Macera, and, later on, Hugo Neyra and Waldemar Espinoza Soriano—often visited. Of all of them, the one in whom Porras had placed his greatest hopes, but also the one who managed to exasperate him and drive him almost out of his mind by the way he behaved, was Pablo Macera. Some five or six years older than I was, Pablo had already finished the courses for a degree in Letters but never presented his thesis, despite the exhortations and admonitions forthcoming from Porras, who could not foresee a time when Macera would subject his life to a little discipline and turn his talent toward doing solid, serious work. As for talent, Pablo had an abundance of it and it amused him to show it off and, above all, to waste it, in an oral exhibitionism that often was dazzling. He would drop into Porras's library all of a sudden, and without giving Araníbar and me time enough even to say hello to him, he would propose to us that we found the "Herren Club" of Peru, inspired by the geopolitical doctrines of Karl Haushofer, so that, in league with a group of industrialists, in five years we could take over the country and turn it into an aristocratic and enlightened dictatorship whose first step would be to reestablish the Inquisition and burn heretics in the main square once again. The following morning, having forgotten all about his delirious despotic scheme, he would perorate on the need to legitimize and promote bigamy, or to revive human sacrifices, or to call for a national plebiscite to determine democratically whether the earth was square or round. The worst foolishness, the most grotesque paradoxes became suggestive realities in Macera's mouth, since he had, as no one else did, that perverse faculty of the intellectual that Arthur Koestler speaks of: that of being able to demonstrate everything he believed in and of believing everything that he could demonstrate. Pablo believed in nothing, but he could demonstrate anything, eloquently and brilliantly, and he enjoyed noting the surprise that his maniacal theories, his paradoxes and puns, his sophisms and ukases aroused in us. His intellectual snobbery was blended with sparks of humor. He chain-smoked Lucky Strikes he threw away after having taken just one puff, so as to provoke a comment from the disconcerted spectator that allowed him to reply, voluptuously savoring each syllable: "I smoke nervously." That adverb, *nerviosamente*, which cost him many a sol, gave him shivers of pleasure.

Porras also succumbed at times to Macera's intellectual spell, and listened to him, amused by his verbal fireworks, but he very soon reacted and became furious at Macera's inner chaos, his snobbery and the complacency with which he gloried in his own neuroses, which Pablo cultivated the way others care for kittens or water their garden. During those years, Porras convinced Macera that he should enter a contest that International Petroleum was sponsoring for the best essay on history, and kept Pedro locked up in his library for several weeks until he finished the work. This book, which won the prize—*Tres etapas en el desarrollo de la conciencia nacional (Three Stages in the Development of the National Consciousness)*—was later to be disavowed by Macera himself, who has eliminated it from his bibliography and mentions it only to rail against it.

Although he later subjected himself to discipline and worked in a more or less orderly way at San Marcos, where, I believe, he is still teaching, and has published many works on travelers, historiography, and economic history, Macera still has not written that great comprehensive work that his teacher Porras was waiting for from him, and for which that intelligence with which he was endowed had, so to speak, predestined him. What Macera said—in the introduction to his *conversaciones* with Jorge Basadre—about Valcárcel, Porras, and Jorge Guillermo Leguía, now fits him like a ring on his own finger: "They have not completed their work and have done less than what their greatness asked of them."* Like Porras himself, his intellectual life appears to have been broken up into fragmentary efforts. Moreover, although it is many years since I have seen him or talked to him, judging by those interviews in which he allows himself to be exploited by a certain sort of publication, copies of which sometimes reach me, the old habit of the ukase and of tremendous absurdities

---

* Jorge Basadre and Pablo Macera, *Conversaciones* (Lima: Mosca Azul, 1974), p. 13.

has not disappeared with the passage of the years, although how moth-eaten and rusty it all sounds nowadays, what with everything that has happened in the world and, above all, in Peru.

In those years, in which we were quite close friends, it delighted me to get his goat and argue with him. Not so as to win the argument—a difficult task—but to enjoy his dialectical method, his feints and his traps, and the lighthearted nonchalance with which he could change his mind and refute himself with arguments as forceful as those that he had just used to defend precisely the opposite proposition.

My work at Porras's, and what I continually learned there, turned out to be a great incentive. In those years of 1954 and 1955 I threw myself into writing and reading, morning and night, more convinced than ever that my true vocation was literature. My mind was made up: I would devote my life to writing and to teaching. My university career was the ideal complement to my vocation, since there was a great deal of time free between classes at San Marcos.

I had stopped writing poems and plays, because I now felt more fascinated by fiction. I did not dare to embark on a novel, but I trained myself by writing short stories, of all lengths and on all possible subjects, almost always ending up by tearing them to bits.

Carlos Aranibar, whom I told that I was writing short stories, proposed to me one day that I read one of them in a group headed by Jorge Puccinelli, a professor of literature and the editor of a review that, although it came out late, came out erratically, or never came out at all, contained writing of quality and was one of the outlets that young writers counted on: *Letras Peruanas*. Dreaming of the prospect of passing this test, I searched through my texts, chose the short story that seemed to me to be the best one—it was called "La parda" ("The Woman with Dusky Skin"), and dealt with a vaguely described woman who wandered from one café to another telling stories about her life. I corrected it and on the appointed night presented myself where the literary circle was meeting that time: El Patio, a café frequented by bullfight fans, artists, and bohemians, in the little square in front of the Teatro Segura. The experience of that first reading in public of a text of mine was a disaster. There were at least a dozen people there, sitting around the large table on the second floor of El Patio, among whom I remember, besides Puccinelli and Aranibar, Julio Macera,

Pablo's brother, Carlos Zavaleta, the poet and critic Alberto Escobar, Sebastián Salazar Bondy, and perhaps Abelardo Oquendo, who was to become a close friend of mine a couple of years later. A bit intimidated, I read my story. An ominous silence followed the reading. No comments, no sign of approval or of disapproval: nothing but a depressing silence. After an interminable pause, various conversations started up again, on other subjects, as though nothing had happened. Much later in the evening, talking about something else, in order to emphasize his argument in favor of fiction that was realistic and national, Alberto referred disdainfully to what he called "abstract literature" and pointed to my story, which was still lying there in the middle of the table. When the gathering broke up and we'd all said goodbye to each other, once we were down on the street, Araníbar made amends by offering a few comments on my mistreated story. But once I arrived home, I tore it up and swore to myself never to go through an experience like that again.

The literary world in Lima in those days was rather mediocre, but I watched it enviously and tried to edge my way into it. There were two playwrights, Juan Ríos and Sebastián Salazar Bondy. The former lived the life of a recluse in his house in Miraflores, but the latter was often seen wandering about the courtyards of San Marcos, trailing after a good-looking classmate of mine, Rosita Zevallos, for whom he sometimes waited as classes let out, holding a romantic red rose in his hand. That courtyard of the Faculty of Letters at San Marcos was the general headquarters for the country's potential and virtual poets and writers of fiction. The majority of them had published at most one or two very slender volumes of poems and hence Alejandro Romualdo, who in those days had returned to Peru after a long stay in Europe, would make fun of them and say: "¿Poetas? ¡No! ¡Plaquetas!" ("Poets? No! Pamphleteers!"). The most mysterious of them was Washington Delgado, whose stubborn silence some interpreted as a sign of buried genius. "When that mouth opens—they said—Peruvian poetry will be filled with memorable arpeggios and trills." (The fact is that, when the mouth opened, years later, Peruvian poetry was filled with imitations of Bertolt Brecht.) Pablo Guevara, an intuitive poet, had just come out with a collection of verse entitled *Retorno de la creatura* (*Return of the Human Being*), whose exuberant poetry didn't seem to have anything to do with him, nor he to have anything to do with books—which, a little later on, he would abandon to devote himself to filmmaking. And poets in exile began to come back to Peru, a number of whom—Manuel Scorza, Gustavo Valcárcel, Juan Gonzalo Rose—had quit the APRA and turned into militant Communists (Valcárcel, for instance) or fellow travelers. The most sensational abandonment of the APRA was Scorza's, who from Mexico addressed a public letter to the leader of the Aprista party, accusing him of having sold out to imperialism—"Goodbye, Mr. Haya"—which circulated all over San Marcos.

Among the writers of fiction, the most respected, although he had not yet published a book, was Julio Ramón Ribeyro, who lived in Europe. *Dominical*, the Sunday supplement of *El Comercio*, and other publications occasionally printed his stories, ones like "Los gallinazos sin plumas" ("The Turkey Buzzards without Feathers"), which everyone commented on with respect. Of those in Peru, the most active was Carlos Zavaleta, who, in addition to publishing his first short stories in those years, had translated Joyce's *Chamber Music*, and was a great promoter of Faulkner's novels. It is to him, no doubt, that I owe my having discovered around this time the author of the saga of Yoknapatawpha County, which, from the first novel of his that I read —*The Wild Palms*—left me so bedazzled that I still haven't recovered. He was the first writer whom I studied with paper and pencil in hand, taking notes so as not to get lost in his genealogical labyrinths and shifts of time and points of view, and also trying to unearth the secrets of the baroque construction that each one of his stories was based on, the serpentine language, the fracturing of chronological sequence, the mystery and the profundity and the disturbing ambiguities and psychological subtleties which that form gave to his stories. Although I read a great many American novelists in those years— Erskine Caldwell, Steinbeck, Dos Passos, Hemingway, Waldo Frank —it was when I read *Sanctuary*, *As I Lay Dying*, *Absalom, Absalom!*, *Intruder in the Dust*, *These Thirteen*, *Knight's Gambit*, and other of Faulkner's works that I discovered the adaptability and the creativity of the narrative form and the marvels that could be wrought in a work of fiction when used by a novelist with Faulkner's skill. Along with Sartre, Faulkner was the author I most admired in my years at San Marcos; he made me feel that it was urgent for me to learn English so as to be able to read his books in their original language. Another writer, a somewhat elusive one, who appeared like a will-o'-the-wisp around San Marcos was Vargas Vicuña, whose subtle collection of stories, *Nahuín*, published in that period, aroused expectations of a body of work from him that, unfortunately, never was forthcoming.

But of all those poets and writers of fiction that I met every day in the courtyard of the Faculty of Letters at San Marcos, the flashiest figure was Alejandro Romualdo. A short little man, with mannerisms reminiscent of Tarzan and the legs of a flamenco dancer, he had been, before going off to Europe with a scholarship from Cultura Hispánica—the bridge to the outside world for penniless Peruvian writers—a sumptuous, musical poet, of the sort called a formalist (by contrast to socially oriented poets), who had written a beautiful book, *La torre de los alucinados (The Tower of the Hallucinated)*, that won the National Poetry Prize. At the same time, he had become famous for his political caricatures—in particular, hybrids of different persons—in Pedro Beltrán's *La Prensa*. Romualdo—Xano to his friends—came back from Europe converted to realism, to political commitment, to Marxism, and to revolution. But he had not lost his sense of humor or the wit and cleverness that came pouring out in the form of wordplay and jokes in the courtyard of San Marcos. "I *didn't hear* that abstract painting well," he would say, and also, puffing out his chest: "I believe in dialectical materialism and my wife supports me." He brought with him the originals of what was to be a magnificent book—*Poesía concreta (Concrete Poetry)*—politically committed poems animated by a spirit of justice, written with fine craftsmanship and a good ear, wordplay, disconcerting run-on lines, and moral and political defiance, in somewhat the same direction in which Blas de Otero, who had become a good friend of Romualdo's, had oriented his poetry in Spain. And in a reading that he gave at San Marcos, in which several poets participated, Romualdo was the star, milking his audience—above all with his flamboyant "Canto coral a Túpac Amaru, que es libertad" ("Choral Chant to Túpac Amaru, Who Is Freedom") of ovations that turned the reception room at San Marcos into the stage for what was practically a political rally.

In all truth, that was what that reading was. It must have taken place at the end of 1954 or the beginning of 1955 and at it all the poets read or recited something that could be interpreted as an attack on the dictatorship. It was one of the first manifestations of a progressive mobilization of the country against that regime which, since October of 1948, had governed with an iron hand, crushing every attempt to criticize it.

San Marcos was the focal point and amplifier of the protests. These often took the form of lightning demonstrations. Not very numerous groups of us—a hundred, two hundred people—would agree to meet in some very crowded place, the Jirón de la Unión, the Plaza San Martín, La Colmena, or the Parque Universitario, and at the hour when there were the most people there, we would gather in the middle of the street and begin to shout in chorus: "Freedom! Freedom!" Sometimes we paraded for one or two blocks, inviting passersby to join us, and then broke up as soon as the mounted Civil Guards or the antiriot vehicles equipped with high-pressure hoses that shot foul-smelling water at us appeared on the scene.

I went to all the lightning demonstrations with Javier Silva, who, with all his fat, had to exert superhuman efforts so as not to be left behind as we ran from the police. His political vocation was becoming more widely known in those days, as well as his unrestrained personality, which made him want to be in on everything and be everywhere at once, playing a major role in all the conspiracies. One afternoon I went with him to visit Luciano Castillo, the head of the minuscule Socialist Party, and a Piuran, like Javier, in his little office on the Jirón Lampa. After a few minutes Javier came out of his office, beaming. He showed me a card: in addition to signing him up as a member of the party, Luciano Castillo had promoted him to the post of secretary general of the Socialist Youth Movement. As such, a while later, on the stage of the Teatro Segura one night, he read a violent revolutionary speech against Odría's regime (which I wrote for him).

But, at the same time, he conspired with members of the APRA, which was springing up again, and with the new opposition groups that were organizing in Lima and in Arequipa. Of these groups, four would take definite shape in the following months, one of them with only an ephemeral existence—the National Coalition, guided by remote control by the daily *La Prensa* and Don Pedro Beltrán (who had gone over to the side in opposition to Odría), whose leader, Pedro Roselló, was also the organizer of an equally ephemeral group, the Owners' Association—and three others that turned out to be political organizations with a more prolonged future: Democracia Cristiana

(Christian Democracy), the Movimiento Social Progresista (the Social Progressivist Movement), and the Frente Nacional de Juventudes (National Youth Front), the seed of what was to become Popular Action, with Eduardo Orrego, at the time an architecture student, as one of the organizers.

By those years, 1954 and 1955, Odría's dictatorship had grown weak. The repressive laws remained intact—above all, the Law of Domestic Security, a juridical aberration under cover of which hundreds of Apristas, Communists, and democrats had been sent to prison or into exile since 1948—but the regime had lost its basis of support in broad sectors of the middle class and the traditional right which (primarily because of its opposition to the APRA) had supported Odría since his defeat of Bustamante y Rivero. Among these sectors, the principal one, and the one that after its break with Odría was to turn into the most battle-hardened opposition to the regime, was *La Prensa*. Its owner and editor-in-chief, Pedro Beltrán Espantoso (1897–1979), as I have already said, was the bête noire of the left in Peru. His was a case very much like that of José de la Riva Agüero. Like the latter, he belonged to a tradition-conscious, very prosperous family, and had received an excellent education, at the London School of Economics. There he imbibed the principles of classic economic liberalism, a cause he had supported in Peru since his youth. And like Riva Agüero, Beltrán tried to organize and to lead a political movement—the former conservative, the latter liberal—in the face of the indifference, not to say the contempt, of his own social class, the so-called ruling elite, too selfish and ignorant to see beyond their very petty interests. The intentions of both, in the years of their youth, to organize political parties that would take an active part in public life, ended in resounding failures. And the furious rage of Riva Agüero in his mature years—documented in his *Opúsculos por la verdad, la tradición y la Patria (Pamphlets in Favor of Truth, Tradition and the Fatherland)*—which poisoned his intellectual work and impelled him to defend fascism and withdraw into a ridiculous caste pride, doubtless had a great deal to do with the disappointment he felt because of his powerlessness to mobilize that national elite which, as such, possessed in all truth nothing except money that almost always had been inherited or ill-gotten.

Unlike Riva Agüero, Pedro Beltrán continued to be active in politics, but in a more or less indirect way, through *La Prensa*, which, in the

1950s, became, thanks to him, a modern newspaper, each of its editorial pages written by a very well-integrated and brilliant group of journalists, perhaps the best that any modern Peruvian publication has had (I shall cite the names of the best ones: Juan Zegarra Russo, Enrique Chirinos Soto, Luis Rey de Castro, Arturo Salazar Larraín, Patricio Ricketts, José María de Romaña, Sebastián Salazar Bondy, and Mario Miglio). With this team and perhaps thanks to it, Don Pedro Beltrán discovered in those years the virtues of political democracy, of which he had not previously been a convinced supporter. On the contrary, *La Prensa*—like the oldest Peruvian daily, *El Comercio*—had attacked Bustamante y Rivero's administration with great severity, conspired against it, and supported General Odría's barracks coup in 1948 and the electoral farce of 1950 in which the latter proclaimed himself president.

But beginning in the mid-1950s, Pedro Beltrán came to the defense not only of the market and private enterprise but also of political freedom and the democratization of Peru.* And he attacked censorship, for which he had lost respect, allowing himself more and more harsh criticisms of the regime's measures and its principal figures.

Esparza Zañartu, who was neither slow-witted nor dilatory, closed the paper, on which he mounted an assault with his informers and police, and Pedro Beltrán and his principal contributors ended up in the Frontón, the island prison just off Callao. He left it three weeks later—there had been strong international pressure for his release—as a hero of the freedom of the press (as he was proclaimed to be by the SIP (Sociedad Interamericana de Prensa: Inter-American Press Association) and with brand-new credentials as a democrat, which for the rest of his days would prove to be valid ones.

The climate changed as quickly as possible and Peruvians could once again engage in politics. Exiles from Chile, Argentina, Mexico returned, semiclandestine weeklies or biweeklies of just a few pages and of every ideological line began to appear, many of which disappeared after a few issues. One of the most picturesque of them was the mouthpiece of the Partido Obrero Revolucionario (T), the Workers'

* And for truth's sake, it must be admitted that he was to maintain that attitude until Velasco's dictatorship expropriated *La Prensa* and prostituted it by converting it into a mouthpiece of the regime. Pedro Beltrán would spend the last years of his life in exile, until his death in 1979.

Revolutionary Party (T)—T for Trotskyite, whose leader and perhaps only affiliate, Ismael Frías, recently back from exile, glided his sinuous humanity every noon all through San Marcos, predicting the imminent establishment of soviets of workers and soldiers throughout the length and breadth of Peru. Another, more serious publication, whose title changed each year—calling itself 1956, 1957, 1958—was put out by Genaro Carnero Checa, who, although expelled from the Communist Party for having supported Odría's coup d'état before being exiled by him, always maintained his ties with the U.S.S.R. and the socialist countries. In the Congress then in existence—a product of the fraudulent elections of 1950—a number of previously well-disciplined representatives and senators, sensing that the boat was shipping water, changed their old servility into independence and even, in the case of several of them, into open hostility toward the master. And in streets and public squares there circulated a hodgepodge of names and possibilities for the presidential election that, on paper at least, was scheduled to be held in 1956.

Of the new political groups that were emerging from the catacombs, the one that seemed to me to be the most interesting was the one that later coalesced into the movement that came to be known as Democracia Cristiana (the Christian Democrats). Many of its leaders in Arequipa, such as Mario Polar, Héctor Cornejo Chávez, Jaime Rey de Castro, and Roberto Ramírez del Villar—or their friends in Lima, Luis Bedoya Reyes, Ismael Bielich, and Ernesto Alayza Grundy—had worked with Bustamante y Rivero's administration, and because of this a number of them had been the victims of persecution and exile. They were young professionals still, without ties to the great upper-class economic interests, uncontaminated by political filth, present or past, who appeared to be bringing to Peruvian politics a democratic conviction and an unequivocal decency, what Bustamante y Rivero had so pristinely embodied during the three years of his administration. Like many others, as soon as that movement made its appearance, I thought it was being organized in such a way that Bustamante y Rivero would be its leader and guiding light and, perhaps, its candidate in the coming elections. This made it even more attractive to me, since my admiration for Bustamante—because of his honesty and his well-nigh religious worship of the rule of law, on which Aprismo heaped such ridicule, calling him the "limping legalist"—had remained intact during my militancy in Cahuide. That admiration, as I now see more clearly, had to do with the precise fact that the general public had fallen into the habit of commenting sympathetically on his failure with the cliché: "He was a president for Switzerland, not for Peru." In fact, during those "three years of struggle for democracy in Peru"—as the book of personal witness that he wrote in exile is entitled—Bustamante y Rivero governed as if the country that had elected him were not barbarous and violent, but a civilized nation of responsible citizens, respectful of the institutions and the norms that make social coexistence possible. From the fact that he had taken the trouble to write his speeches himself, in a clear and elegant prose with a turn-of-the-century cast, always addressing his compatriots without permitting himself the slightest demagoguery or shoddiness, as if taking as his point of departure the supposition that all of them formed an intellectually demanding audience, I saw in Bustamante y Rivero an exemplary man, a head of government that if Peru ever came to be that country which his governance aimed to make of it—a genuine democracy of free and cultivated individuals—Peruvians would remember with gratitude.

Javier Silva and I attended all the political gatherings at the Teatro Segura voicing opposition to Odría, meetings that the dictator gone soft now permitted: the one sponsored by the National Coalition, with Pedro Roselló as the main speaker, the one of the Socialist Party, with Luciano Castillo, and the one of the Christian Democrats, which was by far the best of all of them, by virtue of the quality of its backers and of its speakers. In a burst of enthusiasm, Javier and I signed the initial manifesto of the group, published in *La Prensa*.

And both of us were also present, of course, at the Córpac airport to receive Bustamante y Rivero, when he was able to return to Peru after seven years in exile. My friend Luis Loayza tells an anecdote about that arrival that I am not certain is true, but could well have been. A group of young people had organized to protect Bustamante when he got off the plane and escort him to the Hotel Bolívar, foreseeing that he might be attacked by thugs hired by the government or by Aprista "buffaloes" (who, with the liberalization of the dictatorship, had reappeared, launching attacks on Communist meetings). They had given us instructions to stand with our arms linked together, forming an unbreakable ring. But according to Loayza, who apparently was also part of that sui generis phalanx of bodyguards made up of two aspiring writers and a handful of good kids from Catholic Action, the moment Bustamante y Rivero appeared on the steps of the plane with his inevitable hat edged in ribbon—which he ceremoniously doffed to greet those who had come to welcome him—I broke the iron circle and ran to meet him, shouting feverishly: "Mr. President! Mr. President!" In short, the circle was broken, we were overrun, and Bustamante was pawed, pushed, and shoved by everyone—among them by my Uncle Lucho, a Bustamante fan whose suit coat and shirt were torn in the struggles of this encounter—before he reached the car that drove him to the Hotel Bolívar. Bustamante spoke, briefly, from one of the balconies of the hotel to express his gratitude for his reception, without giving the slightest hint of any intention of becoming active in politics again. And, in fact, in the months that followed, Bustamante was to refuse to enroll in the Christian Democratic Party or play any role whatsoever in active politics. Beginning at that time, he adopted the role that he kept up till his death: a wise patrician, above partisan squabbles, whose competence in international juridical questions would be frequently sought in the country and abroad (he was eventually named president of the International Court of Justice at The Hague), and who, in moments of crisis, was in the habit of sending a message to the country exhorting it to remain calm.

Although the climate in 1954 and 1955 was an improvement over the dense and oppressive atmosphere of preceding years, and the first public demonstrations tolerated, plus the new publications, created in the country a feeling of freedom in the air that stimulated political action, I nonetheless devoted quite a bit more time to intellectual work than to politics: attending classes at San Marcos, almost all of them in the morning, as well as those at the Alliance Française, and reading and writing nothing but short stories from that time on.

I believe that the bad time I had had with "La parda" in Jorge Puccinelli's coterie had the effect of unconsciously keeping me away from dealing with timeless cosmopolitan subjects, on which most of the stories that I wrote in those years had been based, and attracting me toward other, more realistic, ones, in which I deliberately made use of my own memories. Around that time there was a short story contest announced by the Faculty of Letters of San Marcos, to which I submitted two stories, both of them set in Piura, one of which, "Los jefes," was inspired by the abortive strike at the Colegio San Miguel, and the other, "La casa verde," by the brothel on the outskirts of the city, the warm haven of my adolescence. My stories didn't even receive honorable mention, and when I took the manuscript back, "La casa verde" struck me as a very bad piece of writing and I tore it up (I would return to the subject years later, in a novel), but the one of "Los jefes," with its bare hint of an epic air about it, in which my readings of Malraux and Hemingway were obvious, struck me as being recoverable, and in the months that followed I wrote it over several times, until it seemed to me to be worth publishing. It was very long for *Dominical*, the Sunday supplement of *El Comercio*, whose first page always had a story with a color illustration, so I proposed it instead to the historian César Pacheco Vélez, the editor-in-chief of *Mercurio Peruano*. He accepted it, published it (in February 1957), and made me fifty tear-sheet copies that I distributed among my friends. It was my first story to see print and was to furnish the title for my first book. That short story prefigures much of my later practice as a novelist: using a personal experience as a point of departure for the imaginary; employing a form that pretends to be realistic by virtue of its precise geographical and urban details; an objectivity arrived at through dialogues and descriptions observed from an impersonal point of view, effacing the author's tracks; and finally, a politically committed, critical attitude toward a certain set of problems that is the context or horizon of the story line.

In those years, an election was called for the rectorate of San Marcos. I don't remember who launched Porras Barrenechea's candidacy; he accepted with great hopes, and perhaps with a touch of self-congratulation—in those days being rector of San Marcos still meant something—but above all out of his enormous affection for his alma mater, to which he had devoted so many years and so much passionate enthusiasm. That candidacy was to be fatal for him and for his history of Peru. From the beginning, circumstances turned it into an anti-government candidacy. His rival, Aurelio Miró Quesada, one of the owners of *El Comercio*, regarded as one of the symbols of the aristocracy, the oligarchy, and opposition to the APRA (the Miró Quesada family had never forgiven the APRA for having murdered the former editor-in-chief of *El Comercio*, Don Antonio Miró Quesada, and his wife), assumed the character of an official candidacy. Student organizations, controlled by the APRA and the left, backed Porras, as did the Aprista professors (many of whom, such as Sánchez, were still in exile). Porras and Aurelio Miró Quesada, who up until then had had cordial relations, had a falling out, in a vitriolic polemic in the form of open letters and editorials, and *El Comercio* (whose building was stoned by demonstrators from San Marcos who came out in force to run through the downtown streets shouting in chorus the slogans "Freedom" and "Porras for rector") banished the name of Porras Barrenechea from its pages for some time (the famous "civil death" to which *El Comercio* condemned its adversaries was more feared, it was said, by those who belonged to Lima society than was political persecution).

Needless to say, those of us who worked with him and all his disciples engaged in brave efforts to ensure that Porras Barrenechea was elected. We divided up between us the professors who had the right to vote and the members of the University Council, and it fell to my lot and Pablo Macera's to visit those from Sciences, Medicine, and Veterinary Medicine at their homes. Except for just one of them, they all promised us their vote. When, on the eve of the election, in the dining room of the house on the Calle Colina, we totted up the probable results, Porras had two-thirds of the votes. But in the University Council, when the time came for the secret ballot, Aurelio Miró Quesada won handily.

In his speech in the courtyard of the Faculty of Law, after the election, standing before a crowd of students who tried to make up for his losing with their cheers and applause, Porras was indiscreet enough to say that, even though he had lost, he was happy to know that some of the most eminent professors of San Marcos had voted for him and mentioned by name some of those who had assured us of their vote. A number of them immediately sent letters to *El Comercio* denying that they had voted for him.

His victory did not offer Aurelio Miró Quesada any satisfaction whatsoever. The fierce—and very unjust—political hostility of the students toward him after his election, turning him into little less than the symbol of the dictatorial regime, something he never was, resulted in his almost never being able to set foot in the most important locales of San Marcos and forced him to attend to matters concerning the rectorate from an office on the periphery, the object of permanent harassment and the enmity of university cloisters where, thanks to the regime's increasing powerlessness, the heretofore clandestine forces of the APRA and the left were regaining the initiative and would soon be ready to take over the university. Shortly thereafter, this climate would lead the refined and elegant essayist that Aurelio Miró Quesada is to give up the rectorate and leave San Marcos.

Porras's defeat deeply affected him. I have the impression that the rectorate was the post he coveted the most—more than any political distinction—because of his close and long-standing relationship with the university, and not having attained it left in him a frustration and a bitterness that induced him, in the 1956 elections, to agree to be a candidate for a senatorial seat on a list of the Democratic Front (a creation of the Aprista party) and, during Prado's administration, to accept the post of minister of foreign relations, which he would occupy until a few days before his death, in 1960. It is true that he was a first-rate senator and minister, but that immersion in a political absorbent cut short his intellectual activities and kept him from writing that history of the Conquest which, when I began to work with him, he appeared to be determined to finish once and for all. He was occupied with it when the campaign for the rectorate intervened. I remember that, after keeping me busy making note cards on myths and legends for several months, Porras had me type out, in a single manuscript, all of his published monographs and articles and his unpublished chapters on Pizarro as well, to which he gradually added notes, corrected pages, and added more.

The fact that his candidacy for the rectorate of San Marcos had been supported by the APRA and the left—a curious paradox since Porras had never been an Aprista or a socialist, but rather a liberal inclined to be a conservative*—earned him the revenge of the regime, in whose publications he began to be attacked, at times in the basest of terms. A weekly that backed Odría, *Clarín*, brought out several articles against him, full of abominations. It occurred to me to write a manifesto of solidarity with him as a person and to collect signatures among intellectuals, professors, and students. We secured several

* Although, in his last public act as minister of foreign relations, he voted at the meeting of foreign ministers in Costa Rica in 1960 against the condemnation of Cuba, thereby disobeying instructions from Prado's government, and as a consequence found himself forced to resign. He died shortly thereafter.

hundred signatures, but there was nowhere to publish the manifesto, so we had to content ourselves with presenting it to Porras.

Thanks to this manifesto I met someone who was to be one of my best friends in those years and help me a great deal in my first efforts as a professional writer. We had given printed copies of the manifesto to various people to circulate and gather signatures for, and I was informed that a student at the Catholic University wanted to lend a helping hand. His name was Luis Loayza. I gave him one of the copies and a few days later we met in the Crem Rica on the Avenida Larco so that he could hand the signatures over to me. He had secured only one: his own. He was tall, seemingly absent-minded and aloof, two or three years older than I was, and although he was studying law, the only thing he cared about was literature. He had read everything and spoke of authors that I hadn't even known existed—men like Borges, whom he frequently quoted, and the Mexican writers Juan Rulfo and Juan José Arreola—and when I revealed my enthusiasm for Sartre and politically committed literature, his reaction was a crocodile-sized yawn.

We saw each other again soon thereafter, in his house on the Avenida Petit Thouars, where he read me some prose works that he was to publish, sometime later, in a private edition—*El avaro (The Miser)*, which came out in Lima in 1955—and where we had long, uninterrupted conversations in his library crammed full of books. Loayza, along with Abelardo Oquendo, with whom I didn't make friends until later, were to become my best pals of those years, and intellectually the most kindred spirits. We exchanged and discussed books and plans for our literary endeavors, and eventually constituted a warm and stimulating confraternity. Apart from our passion for literature, Lucho and I had great differences concerning many things, and for that reason we never got bored, for we always had something to have a heated argument about. Unlike me, always interested in politics and capable of becoming impassioned about almost any aspect of it and devoting myself entirely to it without thinking about it twice, politics bored Loayza stiff, and in general this and every other enthusiasm—except one for a good book—merited his subtle and sarcastic skepticism. He was against the dictatorship, of course, but more for aesthetic reasons than for political ones. Every once in a while I dragged him to lightning demonstrations and during one of them, in the Parque Universitario, he lost a shoe: I remember him running alongside me, never losing his composure, before a charge by the mounted Civil Guards, and asking me in a soft voice if doing such things was *absolutely indispensable*. My admiration for Sartre and his exhortations concerning social commitment sometimes bored him and sometimes irritated him—he preferred Camus, naturally, because he was more of an artist and wrote better prose than Sartre—and he dismissed both Sartre's ideas and my admiration for them with a sibylline irony that made me howl with indignation. I avenged myself by attacking Borges, whom he idolized, calling him a formalist, an antipurist, and even the *chien de garde* of the bourgeoisie. Our Sartre-versus-Borges arguments lasted for hours and sometimes made us stop seeing or speaking to each other for several days. It was surely Loayza—or perhaps it was Abelardo: I never found out which—who gave me the nickname they used to pull my leg: the fierce little Sartrean, *el sartrecillo valiante*.

It was because of Loayza that I read Borges, in the beginning with a certain reluctance—what is purely or excessively intellectual, what seems dissociated from a very direct experience of life, always arouses in me a refusal to let myself become involved in it—but with an amazement and a curiosity that always made me come back to him. Until little by little, down through the months and the years, that distance turned into admiration. And, in addition to Borges, I turned to many other Latin American authors who, before my friendship with Loayza, I knew nothing of, or out of sheer ignorance held in contempt. The list would be a very long one, but among them are Alfonso Reyes, Bioy Casares, Juan José Arreola, Juan Rulfo, and Octavio Paz, a thin volume of whose poetry Loayza discovered one day—*Piedra de sol (Sunstone)*—which we read aloud and which led us to eagerly seek out other books of his.

My lack of interest in the literature of Latin America—with the sole exception of Pablo Neruda, whom I always read devotedly—had been total before I met Lucho Loayza. Rather than lack of interest, perhaps I should say hostility. This was because the only modern Latin American literature studied at San Marcos or discussed in literary reviews and supplements was of the indigenist or folkloric and regionalist sort, that of novelists like Alcides Arguedas, author of *Raza de bronce (Race of Bronze)*; Jorge Icaza, author of *Huasipungo*; Eustasio Rivera, author of *La vorágine (The Vortex)*; Rómulo Gallegos, author of *Doña Bárbara*; Ricardo Güiraldes, author of *Don Segundo Sombra*; or even Miguel Ángel Asturias.

I had been forced to read that sort of narrative and its Peruvian equivalent in classes at San Marcos, and I detested it, since it appeared to me to be a provincial and demagogic caricature of what a good novel should be. Because in those books the background was more important than the flesh-and-blood characters (in two of them, *Don Segundo Sombra* and *La vorágine*, nature finally swallowed up the heroes) and because their authors apparently didn't know the first thing about how to put a story together, beginning with the ability to stay with the chosen point of view: in them the narrator was always butting in and offering his opinion, even when he was supposedly invisible, and furthermore, their ornate, bookish styles—especially in the dialogue—made stories that presumably took place among rude and primitive people so hard to believe that the illusion of reality never managed to break through the surface of them. All the so-called indigenist literature was a string of clichés about nature and of such great artistic poverty that one had the impression that for the authors writing good novels consisted in looking around for "good" subjects—weird and terrible events—and writing about them in unusual words taken straight out of dictionaries, as far removed as possible from everyday speech.

Lucho Loayza enabled me to discover another Latin American literature, more urbane and cosmopolitan, and more elegant as well, that had sprung up mainly in Mexico and in Argentina. And then, as he did, I began to read Victoria Ocampo's review, *Sur*, every month, a window opened out onto the world of culture, whose arrival in Lima seemed to set the pitifully provincial city to shaking with a mighty cascade of ideas, debates, poems, short stories, essays, from every language and every culture, and place those of us who devoured it in the middle of the contemporary culture of the entire planet. What Victoria Ocampo did through her *Sur*— and along with her, of course, all those who collaborated in this editorial adventure, beginning with José Bianco—is something for which we Hispano-American readers and writers can never be grateful enough, in the lifetimes of at least three generations. (That is what I told Victoria Ocampo when I met her, in 1966, at a Pen Club congress in New York. I always remember the happiness it gave me, many years after the ones that I am here recalling, to see a text of mine published in that review which each month made us experience the illusion of being in the intellectual avant-garde of the time.) In one of the recent or past issues of *Sur* that Loayza collected, I read the famous debate between Sartre and Camus concerning the existence of concentration camps in the Soviet Union.

My association with Lucho, which soon became an intimate one, did not depend solely on books or on our shared vocation. It also had to do with his generous friendship and how pleasant it was to spend time with him listening to him talk about jazz, which delighted him, or about films—we never liked the same ones—or compete with him in the great national sport of *raje*, or watch him compose his prose pieces of a languid, refined aesthete, *au-dessus de la mêlée*, with which he liked at times to entertain his friends. At a certain period he began having an amusing—but most bothersome—ethical and aesthetic reaction: everything that struck him as ugly or earned his scorn made him sick to his stomach. It was a real risk to go with him to an exhibit, a lecture, a recital, a movie, or simply to stop in the middle of the street to exchange a few words with someone, for if the person or the performance didn't meet his standards, he would begin retching right there on the spot.

Lucho had become acquainted with those Latin American authors thanks to a professor from the Catholic University, who had arrived not long before from Argentina: Luis Jaime Cisneros. He also taught a course in Spanish literature at San Marcos that I was enrolled in, but I became friends with him only later on, thanks to Loayza and Oquendo. Luis Jaime Cisneros also had a passion for teaching, and engaged in it outside the classroom, in a corner of his library—in a townhouse in Miraflores, on a street that crossed the Avenida Pardo —where he met with students who had a special liking for philology (his specialty) and literature, to whom he lent books (jotting the names of them down, with the date and the title, in a huge account book). Luis Jaime was thin, refined, polite, but he affected a slightly pedantic and bullying attitude toward his colleagues which earned him bitter enemies at the university. I myself had a mistaken impression of him until I began to visit him and form part of the little circle which was the recipient of Luis Jaime's culture and friendship.

Luis Jaime had signed the first manifesto of the Christian Democrats, and the latter, who were taking the first steps to form a party, had asked him to be the editor of the periodical of the group. He asked me if I would like to give him a hand and I told him I'd be delighted to. And thus there came into being *Democracia*, in theory a weekly, but which came out only when we had scared up enough money for the issue, sometimes twice a month and sometimes monthly. For the first issue I wrote a long article on Bustamante y Rivero and the coup that overthrew him. We got the review together in Luis Jaime's library, and had it printed in different shops each time, for they were all afraid that Esparza Zañartu—whom Odría had promoted to the post of minister of the interior, a political error that was providential for the reestablishment of democracy in Peru—would take reprisals against the printers. Since Luis Jaime, in order not to compromise his work at the university, did not want to appear as editor-in-chief on the masthead, I offered to let my name be used instead, and that was how *Democracia* appeared. On the first page there was an article, an unsigned one, as I remember, by Luis Bedoya Reyes, criticizing "Pradism," which was reorganizing in order to launch a second candidacy for the presidency by Manuel Prado, a former holder of that office.

Democracia had only just come out when I was summoned by my father to his office. I found him livid, waving about the weekly on which my name appeared on the masthead as editor-in-chief. Had I forgotten that *La Crónica* belonged to the Prado family? That *La Crónica* had exclusive rights to material that came from the International News Service? That he was the director of the INS? Did I want *La Crónica* to cancel his contract and leave him without a job? He ordered me to take my name off the masthead. So as a result, after the second or third issue, my friend and comrade from San Marcos, Guillermo Carrillo Marchand, succeeded me as the supposed editor-in-chief—the real one was Luis Jaime. And since after a few issues Guillermo also had problems because of his being on the masthead in that capacity, *Democracia* then came out with a fictitious editor-in-chief, whose name we filched from one of Borges's short stories.

The Christian Democrats played a major role in the downfall of Esparza Zañartu, which precipitated the death of the dictatorship. If he had continued to be in charge of the security forces of the dictatorship, the regime would perhaps have gone on beyond the elections of 1956, by faking the results, as it had done in 1950, in favor of Odría

himself or of some figurehead (there were several individuals lining
up to play that role). But the fall of the strongman of the regime
weakened it and plunged it into a state of disorder in which the opposition seized the opportunity to take over the streets.

Throughout the dictatorship Esparza Zañartu had occupied a relatively unimportant post—administrative head of the Ministry of the
Interior—which allowed him to remain in the background, for despite
the fact that he made all the decisions with respect to security, the
minister of the interior took public responsibility for them. The probable reason that led Odría to make Esparza Zañartu minister was that
nobody wanted to occupy that puppet post. Legend has it that when
General Odría summoned him to offer him the portfolio, Esparza
answered that he would accept it, out of loyalty, but that this measure
was the equivalent of suicide for the regime. And so it was. The
moment that Esparza Zañartu became a visible target, all the weapons
of the opposition were trained on him. The coup de grâce was the
demonstration by Pedro Roselló's National Coalition, in Arequipa,
which Esparza tried to break up by sending hired gunmen and police
in civvies as counterdemonstrators. The latter were routed by the Arequipans, and police began shooting at the dissidents, the result being
a large number of casualties. The drama of 1950 seemed to be repeating
itself, when, during the fraudulent elections, confronted with an attempted rebellion in the streets by the people of Arequipa, Odría had
resorted to a wholesale slaughter. But this time the regime did not
dare to bring tanks and soldiers out into the street to fire on the crowd,
as rumor has it that Esparza Zañartu wanted to do. Arequipa declared
a general strike, which the entire city took part in. At the same time,
in accordance with the long-standing custom that had earned it the
name of the caudillo city (since the majority of republican rebellions
and revolutions began there), the Arequipans tore up the paving stones
of the streets and set up barricades, where thousands upon thousands
of men and women of every social sector waited on the alert for the
regime's response to their list of demands: Esparza Zañartu's resignation, the abolition of the Law of Domestic Security, and a date set
for free elections. After three days of tremendous tension, the regime
sacrificed Esparza Zañartu, who, after resigning, hurriedly went
abroad. And although the dictatorship named a military cabinet, it
was evident to everyone, beginning with Odría himself, that the people

of Arequipa—the home territory of Bustamante y Rivero—had dealt him a fatal blow.

In that Arequipan epic, which, in Lima, we students at San Marcos supported with lightning demonstrations at which Javier Silva and I were always in the first row, the leaders at various times were Mario Polar, Roberto Ramírez del Villar, Héctor Cornejo Chávez, Jaime Rey de Castro, and other Arequipans of the nascent Christian Democratic movement. They were attorneys who had great prestige, friends and even relatives of the Llosa family, and one of them, Mario Polar, had been a suitor, or as my Granny Carmen put it, a "beau" of my mother's, to whom as a young man he had written some passionate poems that she kept hidden from my father, a man of retrospective fits of jealousy.

All these reasons finally aroused my wholehearted enthusiasm when the Christian Democratic movement organized itself as a party and I signed up as a member of it. I was immediately catapulted, I have no idea either how or by whom, to the departmental committee for Lima, of which Luis Jaime Cisneros, Guillermo Carrillo Marchand, and such respectable holders of academic chairs as the jurist Ismael Bielich and the psychiatrist Honorio Delgado were also members. The new party declared in its statutes that "it was not based on a creed," so that it was not necessary to be a believer in order to be militant in it, but in all truth the headquarters of the party—an old house with walls made of cane reeds and clay, with balconies—on the Avenida Guzmán Blanco, very near the Plaza Bolognesi, seemed like a church, or at least a sacristy, since all the well-known ultrapious believers in Lima were there, from Don Ernesto Alayza Grundy to the leaders of Catholic Action and of UNEC (Unión Nacional de Estudiantes Católicos: National Union of Catholic Students) and all the young people seemed to be students at the Catholic University. I wonder whether in those days there were any other students from San Marcos in the Christian Democratic Party except for myself and Guillermo Carrillo (Javier Silva was to sign up as a member sometime later).

What the devil was I doing there, among these people who were ultrarespectable, but light-years away from the Sartrean who ate priests alive, the leftist sympathizer not completely cured of the Marxist notions of the circle that I had belonged to, that I still felt myself to be? I wouldn't be able to explain it. My political enthusiasm was quite a

bit stronger than my ideological consistency. But I remember having
experienced a certain uneasiness whenever I was obliged to explain
intellectually my militancy in the Christian Democratic Party. And
things got worse when, thanks to Antonino Espinoza, I was able to
read material having to do with the social doctrine of the Church and
Leo XIII's famous encyclical *Rerum Novarum*, which the Christian
Democrats always cited as proof of their commitment to social justice
and their will to work for economic reform to favor the poor. The
famous encyclical fell from my hands as I read it, because of its
paternalistic rhetoric, its gassy sentiments and vague criticisms of the
excesses of capital. I recall having commented on the subject to Luis
Loayza—who, if I remember correctly, had also signed some Christian
Democratic text or other or had enrolled as a member of the party—
and having told him how ill at ease I felt after reading that celebrated
encyclical that struck me as being extremely conservative. He too had
tried to read it, and after a few pages had started retching.

Nonetheless, I did not part company with the Christian Democratic
Party (I would abandon it only years later, from Europe, because of
the lukewarmness of its defense of the Cuban revolution, when for
me the latter became an impassioned cause), because its fight against
dictatorship and for the democratization of Peru was impeccable and
because I continued to believe that Bustamante y Rivero would end
up being the leader of the party and perhaps its presidential candidate.
But, above all, because I, along with other more or less radical young
people, discovered among the leaders of the Christian Democratic
Party an attorney from Arequipa, who, although as devout a believer
as the others, seemed to us from the start to be a man of more advanced
and more progressive ideas than his colleagues, someone determined
not only to moralize and democratize Peruvian politics, but also to
bring about a profound reform so as to put an end to the iniquities of
which the poor were victims: Héctor Cornejo Chávez.

The fact that I speak of him in those terms today, in view of his
repulsive activities later as the adviser of Velasco's military dictatorship,
the author of the monstrous law confiscating all the communications
media, and the first editor-in-chief of *El Comercio* after the state had
taken it over, will make many people smile. But the fact is that, in
the middle of the 1950s, when he came to Lima from his native
Arequipa, this young attorney appeared to be a model of a politician

with clean hands, a man driven by his burning democratic zeal and an indignation that flared up on the slightest provocation against any and every form of injustice. He had been Bustamante y Rivero's secretary, and I was only too eager to see in him a rejuvenated and radicalized version of the former president, with the same moral integrity and the same unbreakable commitment to democracy and the rule of law.

Dr. Cornejo Chávez spoke of agrarian reform, of a reform of business enterprises based on profit sharing and a voice in their management by their workers, and he condemned oligarchy, large landowners, the "forty families," with Jacobin rhetoric. He was admittedly not a likable man, but, rather, cold and distant, with that ceremonious and rather pompous manner of speaking so frequent in Arequipans (especially those who had had experience before the bar), but his modest and almost frugal way of life made many of us think that, with him at the head, the Christian Democratic Party could accomplish the transformation of Peru.

Things turned out very differently. Cornejo Chávez eventually became the leader of the party—he was not its head in 1955 or 1956, when I was a militant in it—and was its candidate for the presidency in the election of 1962, in which he won an insignificant percentage of the vote. His authoritarianism and his personality little by little created tensions and factional quarrels within his own party, which culminated, in 1965, in the breakup of the Christian Democrats: a majority of the leaders and militants were to leave, with Luis Bedoya Reyes at their head, to form the Christian Popular Party, whereas Cornejo Chávez's party, reduced to its nadir, was barely to survive General Velasco's military coup in 1968. He then saw that his hour had come. What he was unable to secure by way of the ballot box, Dr. Cornejo Chávez obtained through the dictatorship: reaching power by virtue of the fact that the military entrusted him with tasks as undemocratic as gagging the communications media and gutting the power of the judiciary (since he was also to be responsible for the creation of the National Council of Justice, an institution through which the dictatorship placed judges in its service).

When Velasco fell from power—when he was replaced, after a palace coup led by General Morales Bermúdez, in 1975—Cornejo Chávez, after taking part in the Constituent Assembly (1978–1979), retired from politics, in which, surely, he had left behind him nothing but bad memories.

The nonexistent Christian Democratic Party—a handful of social climbers—figured, nonetheless, in the political life of Peru, allied to Alan García, who, in order to maintain the fiction of a liberalizing regime, always had a Christian Democrat in his administration. After Alan García Christian Democracy died out, or rather, its governing board went into hibernation to wait until circumstances would allow it to recover a few crumbs of power once it had become the parasite of another of the revolving heads of state.

But we are in 1955 and all that is still far in the future. After that summer, as I began classes in my third year at the university and discussed literature with Luis Loayza, was a militant in the Christian Democratic movement, wrote short stories, and made index cards from history books at Porras Barrenechea's, there arrived in Lima someone who would represent another earth tremor of my existence: "Aunt" Julia.

FOURTEEN

Cut-Rate Intellectuals

O N October 26, 1989, *El Diario*, the mouthpiece of Sendero Luminoso, published a communiqué in the name of a front organization, the MRDP (Movimiento Revolucionario en Defensa del
Pueblo: Revolutionary Movement in Defense of the People), calling
for a "class-based armed work stoppage" for November 3, "in support
of the war of the people."

The following morning, the United Left candidate for the mayoralty
of Lima and the presidency, Henry Pease García, announced that on
the day chosen by the Sendero Luminoso movement for the work
stoppage he would take to the streets with his supporters with the aim
of proving "that democracy [is] stronger than subversion." I was with
Álvaro, in my study—early each morning, before the meeting of the
"kitchen cabinet," we went over the program for the day—when I
heard the news on the radio. The idea instantly occurred to me to
join the demonstration and take to the streets too with my supporters
on November 3 in answer to the challenge of Sendero Luminoso.
Álvaro liked the idea, and to avoid its bogging down in complicated
consultations with the allies, I wasted no time and made my decision
public, in a telephone interview with "Radioprogramas." In it, I congratulated Henry Pease and proposed to him that we march together.

It caused a sensation that someone who for years had been a target
of native progressivist intellectuals, a group that included Pease, should
lend his support to an initiative of the Marxist left, and it struck some
of my friends as a political error. They feared that my gesture would
give Pease's candidacy a sort of backing (the opinion polls showed him
as having the support of less than 10 percent of those intending to
vote). But this was a typical case in which ethical considerations ought

to prevail over political ones. Sendero Luminoso was behaving more and more daringly and extending its area of activity; its attacks took place daily, as did its murders. In Lima, its presence had greatly increased in factories, schools, and the young towns, where its schools and indoctrination centers functioned in plain sight of everyone. Wasn't it a good idea for civil society to take to the streets to demonstrate in favor of peace on the same day that terrorism threatened to stage an armed work stoppage? The Peace March received a tidal wave of support, from political parties, unions, cultural and social institutions, and well-known figures. And it attracted a huge number of demonstrators, eager to show their repudiation of the horror into which Peru was gradually sinking through the messianic fanaticism of a minority.

Pressured by the prevailing mood, the candidates of the APRA (Alva Castro) and of the Socialist Alliance (Barrantes Lingán) joined the march too, although their lack of enthusiasm was evident. Both of them made a point of being present at the monument to Miguel Grau, on the Paseo de la República, and withdrew with their small delegations before the other contingents, the United Left column and that of the Democratic Front, which had begun the march, the former from the Plaza Dos de Mayo and ours from the monument to Jorge Chávez, had joined up together on the Avenida 28 de Julio.

After a slow, enthusiastic, and orderly march, the columns converged in front of the monument to Grau and there Henry Pease and I gave each other a friendly embrace. We laid bouquets of flowers at the foot of the monument and the national anthem was sung. The enormous crowd was made up not only of political militants but also of people who belonged to no party and had no interest in politics, who felt the need to express their condemnation of the murders, the kidnappings, the bombs, the disappearances, and other acts of violence that in recent years had so debased the value of life itself in Peru. There were many religious all round the monument to Grau—bishops, priests, nuns, lay Christians—who, amid the chorused slogans and locomotive cheers of the parties, let their own slogan be heard: "Se siente, se siente, Cristo está presente" ("We can feel it, we can feel it, Christ is here with us").

I wouldn't have joined the Peace March if the first move hadn't come from Henry Pease, an adversary who, as an intellectual and as a politician, seemed to me to be a respectable person. There are many ways of defining what is respectable. As far as I am concerned, the intellectual or the politician who says what he believes, does what he says, and does not use ideas and words as a mere device to further his ambition deserves respect.

Respectable intellectuals in this sense do not abound in my country. I say this with sadness, but I know what I'm talking about. The subject kept me awake nights for years, until one day I thought I understood why signs of moral dishonesty seemed greater among people in my profession than among Peruvians with other vocations. And why so many of them had contributed so effectively to Peru's political and cultural decadence. Before that, I had racked my brains trying to fathom why, among our intellectuals and above all the progressive-minded ones—the immense majority—there was such an abundance of rapscallions, scoundrels, impostors, con men. Why they could live so brazenly in a state of ethical schizophrenia, frequently belying by their actions in private what they promoted with such conviction in their writings and in their public conduct.

Anyone reading the manifestos, articles, and essays of these blustering anti-imperialists, anyone attending their classes or lectures, would have thought that hating the United States had become their apostolic mission. But almost all of them had applied for, received, and often literally *lived* on fellowships, aid funds, travel grants, special commissions, and assignments given them by U.S. foundations, and spent semesters and even entire academic years in the "entrails of the monster" (José Martí's expression), fed by the Guggenheim Foundation, the Tinker Foundation, the Mellon Foundation, the Rockefeller Foundation, et cetera, et cetera. All of them frantically pulled strings and many of them succeeded, it is certain, in grafting themselves as professors onto those universities of the country which they had taught their students, disciples, and readers to detest as the party responsible for all the calamities suffered by Peru. How to explain this masochism of the intellectual species? Why this eager race of so many of them toward the country whose insanities they spent their lives denouncing, denunciations thanks to which they had built, in large part, their academic careers and acquired their petty prestige as sociologists, literary critics, political scientists, ethnologists, anthropologists, economists, archaeologists or poets, journalists, and novelists?

Some full-blown flowers, chosen at random. Julio Ortega began his career as an "intellectual" working at a salaried job for the Congreso por la Libertad de la Cultura (the Congress for Cultural Freedom) in Lima in the 1960s, just at the time when it came out that this institution was receiving funds from the CIA, a revelation which led many writers who were there in good faith to withdraw from the Congress (he was not among their number). After that, he was avoided like the plague by progressives. With the advent of the revolutionary and socialist military dictatorship of General Juan Velasco Alvarado, he became a revolutionary and a socialist, thereby nailing down another salaried job. In the cultural supplement of one of the daily papers taken over by the dictatorship—*Correo*—of which he was named editor-in-chief, he devoted himself for several years to railing, in a "structuralist" jargon that combined intellectual ignorance with political baseness in symmetrical proportions, against those who did not accept as articles of faith the deportations, imprisonments, expropriations, censorship, and chicanery of Velasco-style socialism and to proposing, for instance, that diplomats who spoke up against the revolution be slapped in the face. When the dictator he was serving fell, because of an internal conspiracy by his own followers, many intellectuals were fired. Where did this pen pusher flee to earn his living? To the Cuba of his ideological affections? To North Korea? To Moscow? No. To Texas. To the university at Austin, for the time being, and when he was obliged to leave it, for the more tolerant Brown University, where, I suppose, he still is today, carrying on his battle in favor of an anti-imperialist revolution waged with tanks and drawn sabers. From there he sent articles during the election campaign to a Peruvian newspaper that fit him like a glove—*La República*—advising his far-distant compatriots not to waste this opportunity to vote for the "socialist choice."

Another case, demonstrating the same baroque morality. Dr. Antonio Cornejo Polar, a literary critic and a "socialist Catholic," as he was pleased to define himself—a way of reaching heaven without depriving himself of certain advantages of hell—had made himself a university career in that bastion of radicalism and of Sendero Luminoso sympathizers, San Marcos, which he managed to become rector of through the sole merits that, in his day and unfortunately even today, permit a candidate for the post to rise that high: his political ones. His "politically correct" progressivist line earned him the necessary votes, including those of the recalcitrant Maoists.

On March 18, 1987, in a talk in the United States, I spoke of the crisis in the national universities in Latin America and of how politicization and extremism had caused their academic levels to collapse and in some cases—such as that of my alma mater—had turned them into something that today scarcely deserved the name of university. In the predictable drumfire of protests that this caused in Peru, one of the most inflamed was that of the "socialist Catholic," who, around that time, had withdrawn from the rectorate, maintaining that the problems of the university had placed him in the highly unusual condition of a pre-heart attack victim. Indignant, my critic asked himself how someone could attack the Peruvian popular and revolutionary university from the Metropolitan Club in New York.* Up to that point everything appeared to be logically consistent. To my vast surprise, very shortly thereafter, the faculty advisory committee of a university of the imperialist monster asked me for a report on the intellectual competence of the person in question, a candidate for a lectureship in its Spanish department (a position which, naturally, he obtained). He is still there today, I presume, a living example of how one progresses in academic life by making the proper political choices at the proper moment.

I could mention a hundred other cases, all of them variants of this practice: create for yourself a public persona, convictions, ideas, and values for professional convenience, and at the same time, by your private conduct, belie them. The result of such inauthenticity is, in intellectual life, the devaluation of discourse, the triumph of clichés and empty rhetoric, of the dead language of slogans and platitudes over ideas and creativity. It is not by accident that, in the last thirty or forty years, Peru has produced almost nothing in the domain of thought worth remembering, while on the other hand it has built up a gigantic garbage dump of socialist, Marxist, and populist blather that has no contact with the reality of Peruvian problems.

In the realm of politics, the consequences have been even worse because those who had made a modus vivendi out of duplicity and ideological double-dealing won almost total control of the cultural life of Peru. And they produced almost everything that Peruvians studied or read, the ideological sustenance of the country, all that might satisfy

* "La fobia de un novelista," *Sí*, Lima, April 6, 1987.

the curiosity or appease the concerns of the young generations. Every-thing was in their hands: the universities and state schools and many private ones; the research institutes and centers; the magazines, the cultural supplements and publications, and, of course, the classroom textbooks. With their lack of culture and their contempt for any in-tellectual activity, the conservative sectors, which up until the 1940s or 1950s still had cultural hegemony over the country—with that brilliant generation of historians such as Raúl Porras Barrenechea and Jorge Basadre or philosophers such as Mariano Iberico and Honorio Delgado—had lost the battle sometime before and had not produced either individual talents or a concerted action capable of opposing the advance of the leftist intellectuals, who, once General Velasco took over as dictator, monopolized cultural life.

Yet leftist thought had an illustrious precursor in Peru: José Carlos Mariátegui (1894–1930). In his short lifetime, he produced an im-pressive number of essays and articles to further the spread of Marxism, of analyses of Peruvian reality, and works of literary criticism or political commentaries on current events notable for their intellectual acuity, and often for their originality. In them the reader can find a freshness of concept and an individual voice that were never to appear again among his avowed followers. Although they all call themselves Ma-riateguists, from the most moderate to the most extreme (Abimael Guzmán himself, the founder and leader of Sendero Luminoso, main-tains that he is a disciple of Mariátegui's), passing by way of the PUM (Partido Unificado Mariateguista: Unified Mariateguist Party), the truth of the matter is that after the brief apogee that Mariátegui represented for socialist thought, the latter entered a decline in Peru which touched bottom during the years of the military dictatorship (1968–1980), in which the opposing positions in intellectual debate appeared to be confined to two: the opportunism of the left or terrorism.

Intellectuals had as much responsibility as the military for what happened in Peru during those years, especially in the first seven—1968 to 1975, those of General Velasco's regime—in which all the wrong solutions for the nation's great problems were adopted, making them worse and plunging Peru into a state of ruin to which Alan García was to give the last turn of the screw. They applauded the destruction by force of the democratic system, which, however defec-tive and inefficient it may have been, permitted political pluralism, criticism, active unions, and the exercise of freedom. And with the argument that "formal" freedoms were the mask of exploitation, they justified the fact that political parties were forbidden, that no elections were held, that landed estates were confiscated and collectivized, that hundreds of businesses were nationalized and turned over to state control, that the freedom of the press and the right to criticize were suppressed, that censorship was institutionalized, that all the TV channels, the daily papers, and a large number of radio stations were expropriated, that a law was passed to subjugate the judicial power and place it in the service of the executive power, that hundreds of Peruvians were imprisoned and deported and a number of them assassinated. In all these years, having seized all the important communications media that existed in the country, they devoted themselves to harping on those slogans against democratic values and liberal democracy and to defending, in the name of socialism and the revolution, the abuses and iniquities of the dictatorship. And, of course, to raining down insults on those of us who did not share their enthusiasm for what Velasco's sycophants called "the socialist, participationist and libertarian revolution." And we lacked any forum for answering them.

Some of them, the fewest in number, acted in this fashion out of naïveté, truly believing that the longed-for reforms to put an end to poverty, injustice, and backwardness could come about by way of a military dictatorship which, unlike those of yesteryear, did not speak of "Western Christian civilization" but of "socialism and revolution."*

---

* I include among them Carlos Delgado, the civilian of greatest influence during the Velasco years and the one who wrote the majority of the speeches that the dictator delivered. A former Aprista and the ex-secretary of Haya de la Torre, the sociologist and political scientist Carlos Delgado resigned from the APRA when this party made a pact with the followers of Odría during Belaunde Terry's first term as president. He backed the military revolution and contributed greatly to giving it an ideological cover, at the same time that he was the driving force behind a large part of the economic reforms—industrial co-ownership, the agrarian reform, controls and subsidies, et cetera—many of which were modeled on what had been the program for governing of the Aprista party. Carlos Delgado believed in that "third position" and his support for the dictatorship was inspired by the illusion that the army could be the instrument for instituting in Peru the democratic socialism that he defended. In Sinamos (Sistema Nacional de Apoyo a la Movilización Social: National System of Support for Social Mobilization), Carlos Delgado gathered around himself a group of intellectuals— Carlos Franco, Héctor Béjar, Helan Jaworski, Jaime Llosa, and others—who shared his position and the majority of whom, with intentions as good as his own, actively collaborated with the regime in its nationalizations and the extension of state inter-

These ingenuous supporters of the dictatorship, people like Alfredo Barnechea or César Hildebrandt, soon lost their illusions and joined those who opposed the regime. But the majority were not partisans of the dictatorship out of naïveté or out of conviction, but, as their later behavior proved, out of opportunism. They had been *summoned*. It was the first time that a government of Peru had called on intellectuals and offered them a few crumbs of power. Without hesitating, they threw themselves into the arms of the dictatorship, displaying a zeal and a diligence that frequently went beyond what had been asked of them. This was the reason, no doubt, why General Velasco himself, a man without subtlety, had spoken of the intellectuals of the regime as of mastiffs he kept so as to scare the bourgeoisie.

And, in fact, that was the role to which the regime reduced them: to bark and bite from the vantage point of the newspapers, radios, television channels, ministries, and official agencies whose excesses we opposed. What happened to so many Peruvian intellectuals constituted for me a genuine trauma. From the time of my break with the Cuban regime, at the end of the 1960s, I had come to be the object of the attacks of many of them, but even so I had the feeling that they were acting as they did—defending what they were defending—guided by a faith and certain ideas. After having seen that sort of moral abdication by a generation of Peruvian intellectuals, in the years of Velasco's dictatorship, I discovered something that I still believe today: that for the great majority of them, those convictions were only a strategy to enable them to survive, build a career, get ahead. (In the days of the nationalization of the banks, the Aprista press published, with a great deal of ballyhoo, a number of irate

---

vention in the economy and in social life. But the criticisms that they deserve for this must be, especially in the case of Carlos Delgado, accompanied by a clarification: his good faith could not be doubted nor the consistency and openness with which he acted. He therefore always seemed "respectable" to me and I could disagree with him—and argue a great deal—without our friendship's being broken. Moreover, it is obvious to me that Carlos Delgado did as much as he could to prevent, with all the influence he had, the co-opting by the Communists and those closest to them of the institutions of the regime and that he also used that influence to mitigate insofar as possible the abuses of the dictatorship. When the magazine *Caretas* was closed down and its editor-in-chief, Enrique Zileri, was persecuted, he secured me an interview with General Velasco (the only one I ever asked the dictator for) and supported me when I protested against this closing down and the persecution of Zileri and urged him to end them.

statements by Julio Ramón Ribeyro, from Paris, accusing me of iden-
tifying myself "objectively with the conservative sectors of Peru" and
of opposing "the irresistible incursion of the popular classes." Ribeyro,
a very courteous and respectful writer and up until then a friend of
mine, had been given a diplomatic post at UNESCO by Velasco's
dictatorship and was retained in it by all the successive governments,
whether dictatorships or democracies, which he served obediently,
impartially, and discreetly. Shortly thereafter, José Rosas-Ribeyro, a
Peruvian ultraleftist from France, described him, in an article in *Cambio*,* trotting all over Paris with other bureaucrats of the Aprista regime
in search of signatures for a manifesto in favor of Alan García and the
nationalization of the banks signed by a group of "Peruvian intellectuals" established there. What had turned the apolitical and skeptical
Ribeyro into an untimely socialist militant? An ideological conversion?
The instinct of diplomatic survival. That was what he himself informed
me, in a message he sent me at the time—one that made a worse
impression on me than his statements—via his publisher, who was
also a friend of mine, Patricia Pinilla: "Tell Mario not to pay any
attention to the things that I am declaring against him, because they
represent only *favorable opportunities for me*.")

I then understood one of the most dramatic expressions of underdevelopment. There was practically no way in which an intellectual
of a country such as Peru was able to work, to earn his living, to
publish, in a manner of speaking to *live* as an intellectual, without
adopting revolutionary gestures, rendering homage to the socialist ideology, and demonstrating in his public acts—his writings and his civic
activities—that he belonged to the left. To get to be editor-in-chief of
a publication, to be promoted to higher academic rank, to obtain
fellowships, travel grants, invitations with expenses paid, it was necessary for him to prove that he was identified with the myths and
symbols of the revolutionary and socialist establishment. Anyone who
failed to heed the invisible watchword was condemned to the wilderness: marginalization and professional frustration. That was the explanation. Hence the inauthenticity, that "moral hemiplegia"—in
Jean-François Revel's phrase—in which Peruvian intellectuals lived,
repeating on the one hand, in public, an entire defensive logo-

* Supplement of *Unicornio*, Lima, October 25, 1987, p. 5.

machy—a sort of countersign in order to assure their posts within the establishment—which corresponded to no intimate conviction, a mere tactic of what the anglicism calls *posición amiento*, positioning oneself correctly. But when one lives in this way, the perversion of thought and language becomes inevitable. It was for that reason that a book such as the one brought out by Hernando de Soto and his team at the Freedom and Democracy Institute—*El otro sendero*—had aroused so much enthusiasm on my part: at last something was appearing in print in Peru that revealed an effort to think independently and originally on the underlying problems of Peru, breaking taboos and frozen ideological concepts. But, once more in the land of unfulfilled promises, that hope came to nothing almost the moment it was born.

When I thought I had found the explanation of what Sartre would call the *situation* of the writer in Peru in periods of dictatorship, I wrote a series of articles in the magazine *Caretas*, under the overall title of "El intelectual barato" ("The Cut-Rate Intellectual"),* which —this time for good reason—exacerbated the long-standing phobia against me on the part of those who knew very well that they had sold out. Alan García, with his infallible intuition for this sort of move, recruited several of them to be his mastiffs and let them loose on me, armed with the weapons that they wield so well. They played an important role during the campaign and spared no effort to bring it down to the level of mere mudslinging.

The first one hired was—a striking paradox—a journalist on the take who had faithfully served Velasco from his post as editor-in-chief of *La Crónica*, a figure of whom it can be said, without fear of being mistaken, that he is the most exquisite product that dung-collecting journalism in Peru has yet created and the one whose talent has contributed the most to beating even our recent records for pestilence: Guillermo Thorndike. From the pages of that daily, with a little band of collaborators recruited in the local literary pigsties (the exception was Abelardo Oquendo, one of the best friends of my youth, whose reasons for being there, surrounded by such resentful and scheming pen pushers as Mirko Lauer, Raúl Vargas, Tomás Escajadillo, and other even worse muckrakers, I was never able to understand), there

* Reproduced in *Contra viento y marea*, *II* (Barcelona: Seix Barral, 1990), pp. 143-55.

poured forth adulation of the dictator and a stubborn defense of his actions, alternating with infamous campaigns against their adversaries which censorship of the communications media prevented us from answering. One of the worst victims of these diatribes was the Aprista party, from which, at the same time that it stole from it a large part of its program for governing, the Velasco dictatorship attempted, through Sinamos (Sistema Nacional de Apoyo a la Movilización Social: National System of Support for Social Mobilization), to steal away the backing of the masses. At the time of the events of February 5, 1975, when a police strike degenerated into popular uprisings against the regime and in the burning down of the Círculo Militar and the daily *Correo*,* the newspaper, under Thorndike's editorship, blamed the Aprista party for the disorders and intoxicated public opinion with an anti-Aprista campaign compared to which the witch-hunts against Haya de la Torre's party by the ultraconservative press of the 1930s was mere child's play.

A few years later, however, from his position as editor-in-chief of the daily *La República*—another famous manifestation of a sewer metamorphosed into a paper—Thorndike would turn to serving the APRA and Alan García with the same enthusiasm and the identical vile means as when he was a toady of Velasco's. As a reward, following Alan García's victory in the election, he was sent to Washington at the taxpayers' expense (his likable wife, about whom nobody had ever known that she had even a casual relationship to culture, was named cultural attaché of Peru to the Organization of American States). Guillermo Thorndike was quickly summoned home from there by President Alan García in the days of the nationalization of the banks, so that he could apply his techniques of poisoning public opinion and wage one of his mudslinging campaigns against those of us who were opposed to the measure. A "hate office" was set up in a suite at the Hotel Crillón. From there, under Thorndike's direction and prepared by him, there came pouring forth, to daily papers, radio stations, and government-controlled TV channels, accusations, insinuations, and the most despicable attacks against my person and my family. (Among the lies—along the lines of the age-old ruse of committing a robbery

* See my article on the subject, "La revolución y los desmanes," *Caretas*, Lima, March 6, 1975; reproduced in *Contra viento y marea, I* (Barcelona: Seix Barral, 1990), pp. 311–16.

and then coming out into the street shouting "Thief!"—was that of my having been a Velasco supporter!) Thanks to unexpected allies, who, from the ranks of the Aprista administration itself, told us in secret how the "hate office" functioned, the daily *Expreso* revealed its existence and photographed Thorndike coming out of the Crillón, whereupon his operations diminished somewhat. Later, ever the diligent servant of the master of the day, Thorndike would publish a hagiographic biography of Alan García, and during the electoral campaign, García would once again bring him back to Peru to be editor-in-chief of a scandal sheet, *Página Libre*, which, in the final months before the elections, played a role that can easily be imagined. (A few days before the first round of balloting, a woman telephoned my house, many times, insisting on speaking to me or to Patricia, explaining that she would reveal her identity only to us. Patricia finally came to the phone to talk to her. The woman, Argentine by birth but Peruvian by marriage, was Guillermo Thorndike's mother. We had never met her. She was calling to say that she was so ashamed of what her son was up to in the pages of the newspaper of which he was the editor-in-chief that she had decided, for the first time in her life, to vote in the coming elections: she would vote for me, as a way of making amends, and we could make that fact public. We didn't do so at the time, but I am doing so now, with my thanks for an initiative which, in all truth, still amazes me.*

These are not mere anecdotes. They represent a general phenomenon, a state of affairs that affects the entire cultural life of Peru and that has repercussions on its political life. One of the contemporary myths concerning the Third World is that, in those countries frequently subjugated by despotic and corrupt dictatorships, intellectuals represent a moral reserve, which, although powerless in the face of the dominant brute force, constitutes a hope, a source from which, when things begin to change, the country will be able to draw ideas, values, and

---

* Since then, Guillermo Thorndike has enriched his dossier by performing new feats. In 1990 he was editor-in-chief of a scandal sheet, *Ayllu*, that sympathized with the MRTA terrorist movement. In it he fiercely attacked his former employer, Alan García, and presented sensationalist documents regarding his misdeeds while in power. Later he became editor-in-chief of *La Nación*, a daily paper in the service of the dictatorship of Alberto Fujimori.

persons that will allow it to promote freedom and justice. In reality, this is not how things are. Peru is a demonstration, rather, of how fragile the intellectual class is in the Third World—of the ease with which the lack of opportunities, the insecurity, the scarcity of means to carry out one's work, the absence of any accepted status in society, and the inability to exert any sort of effective influence make intellectuals vulnerable to corruption, to abandonment of their ideals, to cynicism and careerism.

When I first began to take an active part in Peruvian politics I was prepared for confrontations with my colleagues, whose techniques I was familiar with from the days when, at the end of the 1960s, I came into conflict with them by starting to criticize the Cuban revolution. From then on, I had been the target of their wrath, apparently for reasons having to do with ideological differences, although in truth, very often the real reason was rivalry and envy, which is also inevitable when someone has, or is perceived as having, recognition, of enjoying what goes by the name of success, by those who must confront all sorts of difficulties in order to practice their calling. I was, therefore, prepared to contend with those Peruvian intellectuals whom for some time I had promised myself only to read, and never again to keep company with.

And so it was a surprise to find, among my colleagues, a number of writers, professors, journalists, or artists who, knowing that they were exposing themselves to satanization in the milieu in which they worked, nonetheless made common cause with the Freedom Movement and helped me all through the campaign. I am not referring to friends like Luis Miró Quesada Garland or Fernando de Szyszlo, with whom I had waged political battles side by side for a long time now, but to persons such as the anthropologist Juan Ossio, the historian and publisher José Bonilla, the essayists Carlos Zuzunaga and Jorge Guillermo Llosa, the novelist Carlos Thorne, and a fair number of others who, like them, worked diligently for the victory of the Front, and to the several dozen university professors who joined our committees for government planning. Or to those who, though not members of Libertad, lent me invaluable aid with their writings and their pronouncements, such as the journalists Luis Rey de Castro, Francisco Igartua, César Hildebrandt, Mario Miglio, Jaime Bayly, Patricio Ricketts, and

Manuel d'Ornellas,* or the actor and stage director Ricardo Blume, whom I shall never be able to thank enough for the courage and generosity with which he staked everything, whenever necessary, in defense of what we both believed in. Or to intellectuals such as Fernando Rospigliosi and Luis Pásara and young writers such as Alfredo Pita, Alonso Cueto, and Guillermo Niño de Guzmán, who, from positions that were independent of and sometimes hostile to my own, made, amid the din of the electoral battle, the noblest of gestures toward me personally or toward what I was doing.

But among the adversaries too there were a number of intellectuals whose conduct attracted my attention, because, for the reasons that I have already mentioned, I didn't expect from them the propriety with which they acted, even in the most heated moments of the political debate. That was the case with Henry Pease García. A university professor, a sociologist, the director for a time of a well-known institute of social investigation, DESCO—financed by the German Social Democratic Party—Henry Pease was, with Alfonso Barrantes, representative mayor of Lima, and a close collaborator of the latter before the break that brought them both face to face as leaders of the two factions of the left in the battle for the presidency. Pease's conduct, as head of the most radical sector, in which, in point of fact, cut-rate intellectuals abounded, was exemplary. He made every effort to wage a campaign of ideas, promoting his program without ever having recourse to personal attacks or underhanded maneuvers, and acted at all times with a logical consistency and sobriety that was in sharp contrast to that of some of his followers. His personal life, moreover, had always likewise struck me as being consistent with what he wrote and defended as a public figure. This was a decisive reason for my accompanying him on the Peace March.

After this march, all of the public's attention and my own activity were focused on the municipal campaign. At the end of the week that followed the Peace March—on November 4 and 5—with Juan Incháustegui and Lourdes Flores I made the rounds of the shantytowns of Canto Chico, María Auxiliadora, San Hilarión, Huáscar, as well as many others in Chosica and Chaclacayo. And the following week

* These last two, to the distress of those of us who considered them to be exemplary democratic journalists, were to become, from April 5, 1992, on, militant defenders of Fujimori's coup d'état, which destroyed Peruvian democracy.

I toured various *departamentos* of the interior—Arequipa, Moquegua, Tacna, and Piura—participating in dozens of rallies, motorcades, interviews, marches, in favor of the candidates of the Democratic Front. In those final days of the municipal campaign, the internal tensions between the forces of the alliance seemed to disappear and we managed to present an image of understanding and union, which paved the way for a favorable result for our first ordeal by electoral fire, on November 12.

However, the municipal elections were not the overwhelming victory for us that the opinion polls had predicted. The Front won more than half the districts of the country, but this majority was clouded by the defeats suffered in key cities, such as Arequipa, where Luis Cáceres Velázquez, of the Frenatraca (Frente Nacional de Trabajadores y Campesinos: National Front of Workers and Peasants) was reelected; Cuzco, where the former leftist mayor, Daniel Estrada, won by a wide margin; Tacna, where Tito Chocano, a former member of the Christian Popular Party, came in first; and above all Lima, where Ricardo Belmont managed to win more than 45 percent of the vote, against the 27 percent for Incháustegui. *

Once the results were known, on the same night as the balloting, I went with Incháustegui to the Hotel Riviera, on the Avenida Wilson, which had been turned into the general headquarters of the OBRAS movement, to congratulate Belmont, and posed in front of the battery of photographers and television cameramen who filled the place to overflowing, between Belmont and Incháustegui, lifting up the arms of both of them to suggest subliminally that, in some way, the victory of the independent was also mine and that the defeat of Incháustegui had done me no harm. Álvaro did what he could to see that this image was widely publicized in the press and on television.

In my statements, I made prodigious efforts to emphasize the "overwhelming victory" of the Democratic Front, which had won thirty district mayoralties of greater Lima (against seven for the United Left, two from lists of independents, one for the Socialist Alliance and not a single one for the APRA).

But in private, the results of the municipal elections left us very

---

* Henry Pease, of the United Left, with 11.54 percent, the Aprista candidate Mercedes Cabanillas, with 11.53 percent, and the candidate of the Socialist Alliance, Enrique Bernales, who won barely 2.16 percent, straggled far behind.

worried: there was a coolness, bordering on antipathy, on the part of large popular sectors toward the established political forces, whether of the left or of the right, and a proclivity toward placing their trust and hopes in anyone representing something different from the establishment. There was no other explanation for the unusually heavy vote for Belmont, someone whose principal merit—aside from his popularity as a radio and television emcee—appeared to be that he was not a politician, that he came from outside politics. More serious still, the final opinion poll indicated that, although on a national scale those intending to vote for me were still hovering around 45 percent, there was a growing tendency, in the least privileged sectors, to see me as belonging to the unpopular political class.

I was aware of the need to do something to correct that image. But I still thought that the best way to do so would be by presenting my program for governing the country to the Peruvian people. This program would demonstrate that my candidacy represented a radical break with traditional politics. The campaign was almost over and we would very soon have a chance to explain what this program was: at the meeting of CADE (the Annual Conference of Executives).

Getting a little ahead of myself, I should like to note that Ricardo Belmont Cassinelli's winning of the office of mayor of Lima refuted those who, after June 10, interpreted my defeat in exclusively racial terms. If it were true, as any number of commentators have said, including Mark Malloch Brown,* that it was hatred of the whites and a sort of racial solidarity that led large popular sectors to vote for the "little Chinaman," since they were under the impression—as Fujimori persistently suggested in the course of his campaign during the second round—that the "yellow man" was closer to the Indian, the mestizo, and the black than to the "white man" (traditionally associated with the man enjoying privileges and the exploiter), then how were you to explain the resounding victory of that ginger-haired gringo with light green eyes, "Red" Belmont, whom, as he himself had predicted, the voters of sectors C and D, which included the immense majority of the mestizos, Indians, and blacks of Lima, voted into office by a landslide?

I do not deny that the racial factor—the obscure resentments and

* "The Consultant," *Granta*, no. 36, London, Summer 1991, pp. 87–95.

profound complexes associated with this subject exist in Peru, of course, and all the ethnic groups of the national mosaic are victims of it and responsible for it—played a role in the campaign. It did indeed, despite my efforts to avoid it or, once it was already there, to bring it out into the open. But the decisive factor in the election was not skin color—neither mine nor Fujimori's—but a sum total of reasons, of which racial prejudice was only one component.

FIFTEEN

Aunt Julia

AT the end of May 1955, Julia, a younger sister of Aunt Olga's, arrived in Lima to spend a few weeks' vacation. She had been
divorced not long before from her Bolivian husband, with whom she
had lived for several years on a hacienda in the Altiplano; since their
separation, she had been living in La Paz, with a woman friend from
Santa Cruz.

I had known Julia in my childhood in Cochabamba. She was a
friend of my mother's and often came to the house on Ladislao Cabrera;
once, she lent me a romantic novel in two volumes—E. M. Hull's
The Sheik and *Son of the Sheik*—which delighted me. I remember
the tall and graceful figure of that friend whom my mother and my
aunts and uncles called "the little Chilean" (because, although she
lived in Bolivia, she had been born in Chile, as had Aunt Olga) dancing
very vivaciously at Uncle Jorge and Aunt Gaby's wedding celebration,
a dance that my cousins Nancy and Gladys and I spied on from a
stairway until the wee hours of the night.

Uncle Lucho and Aunt Olga lived in an apartment on the Avenida
Armendáriz, in Miraflores, very near Quebrada, and from the windows
of the living room on the second floor you could catch a glimpse of
the Jesuit seminary. I used to go to their house to have lunch or dinner
very often, and I remember having happened to come by one noon,
on leaving the university, just after Julia had arrived and was still
unpacking. I recognized her hoarse voice and her hearty laugh, her
slender, long-legged silhouette. She made a few joking remarks as she
greeted me—"What! You're Dorita's little boy, that crybaby from
Cochabamba?" She asked me what I was doing these days and was
surprised when Uncle Lucho told her that besides being a student

working toward a degree in Letters and Law, I wrote for newspapers and magazines and had even won a literary prize. "So how old are you now?" "Nineteen." She was thirty-two, but didn't show her age because she looked young and pretty. When we said goodbye to each other, she said to me that if my *pololas*—my sweethearts—would let me, I should go to the movies with her some night. And that, of course, she'd be the one who paid for the tickets.

The truth was that I hadn't had a sweetheart for quite some time. Except for my platonic attachment to Lea, in recent years my life had been devoted to writing, reading, studying, and being active in politics. And my relationship with women had been friendly or as a fellow militant, not sentimental. I hadn't set foot in a brothel again since Piura, or had even one love affair. And I don't think that that austerity had weighed too heavily on me.

I am positive, though, that on this first meeting, I didn't fall in love with Julia, nor did I think very much about her after we said goodbye to each other, nor, probably, after the two or three times that I saw her next, always at Uncle Lucho and Aunt Olga's house. I'm sure of it because of something that happened a short while later. One night, after several hours at one of those conspiratorial meetings that we frequently held at Luis Jaime Cisneros's, on coming back to the town-house on the Calle Porta I found a note from my grandfather on my bed: "Your Uncle Lucho says you're a cad, who agreed to go to the movies with Julita and never showed up." And as a matter of fact, I had completely forgotten about it.

The next day I raced to a florist's shop on the Avenida Larco and sent Julia a bunch of red roses with a card that said: "Humble apologies." When I went to apologize in person that afternoon, after working at Dr. Porras's, Julia did not hold my having forgotten against me and teased me a lot about the red roses.

That same day, or very soon afterward, we began going to the movies together, to the evening performance. We almost always went on foot, often to the Barranco, crossing the Quebrada de Armendáriz and walking through the little zoo that existed in those days around the lagoon. Or to the Leuro, in Benavides, and sometimes even as far as the Colina, which meant nearly an hour's walk. We always got into an argument because I wouldn't let her pay for the tickets. We saw Mexican melodramas, American comedies, Westerns, and gangster movies. We talked about lots of things and I began to tell her how I wanted to be a writer and how, as soon as I could, I was going off to live in Paris. She no longer treated me like a little kid, but it doubtless never entered her head that I might someday become something more than the one who took her to the movies on nights when she was free.

Because, shortly after she arrived, pesky suitors started buzzing around Julia. Among them, Uncle Jorge. He had separated from Aunt Gaby, who went off to Bolivia with their two children. The divorce, which made me very sad, was the culmination of a period of dissipation and scandalous skirt-chasing on the part of the youngest of my uncles. He had become very well off after his return to Peru, when he had begun as a low-level employee with the Wiese organization. One day, after having been promoted to the position of manager of a construction company, he disappeared. And the next morning, on the society page of *El Comercio*, his name turned up among the first-class passengers on the *Reina del Mar*, which was sailing for Europe. Coupled with his name was that of a Spanish lady with whom he had been having a not at all secret love affair.

It was a great scandal in the family and gave Granny Carmen many a crying spell. Aunt Gaby left for Bolivia and Uncle Jorge stayed for several months in Europe, living like a king and squandering money he didn't have. Finally, he was left high and dry, in Madrid, unable to pay for his return passage. Uncle Lucho had to perform miracles to get him back to Peru. He returned with no job, no money, and no family, but still possessed of his drive and his skill, which, along with his likable nature, permitted him to get on his feet again. That was the point at which Julia arrived in Lima. He was one of the beaux who invited her out. But Aunt Olga, who was inflexible when it came to matters of manners and morals, forbade Uncle Jorge to date her sister Julia, because he was a scatterbrain and a carouser, and she subjected her sister to such close watch that it made Julia almost die laughing. "I've gone back to the days of having a chaperone and having to ask permission to go out," she told me. And she also told me that Aunt Olga breathed freely when, instead of accepting invitations from her pesky suitors, she went to the movies with Marito.

Since I was already in the habit of dropping by their house all the time, and Uncle Lucho and Aunt Olga often were going out some-where, they used to take me with them and circumstances turned me into Julita's partner. Uncle Lucho was a devotee of horse racing and sometimes we went to the racetrack, and the four of us celebrated Aunt Olga's birthday, on June 16, at the Bolívar grill, where one could dine and dance. During one of the pieces that we were dancing to, I kissed Julia on the cheek, and when she drew her face back to look at me, I kissed her again, on the lips this time. She didn't say anything to me but a look of stupefaction crossed her face, as though she'd seen a ghost. Later, as we were going back to Miraflores in Uncle Lucho's car, I held her hand in the dark and she didn't draw it away.

I went to see her the next day—we had agreed to go to the movies—and as chance would have it, nobody else was in the house. She received me, intrigued and at the same time tempted to laugh, looking at me as though it weren't me and I couldn't possibly have kissed her. In the living room, she said to me jokingly: "I don't dare offer you a Coca-Cola. Would you like a whisky?"

I told her that I was in love with her and would let her do anything she pleased, except to treat me ever again like a little kid. She told me that she'd done many mad things in her life, but that this was one she wasn't going to do. Fall in love with Lucho's nephew—with Dorita's son, no less! She wasn't a woman who seduced minors, after all. Then we kissed each other and went to the evening showing at the Cine Barranco, sitting in the last row of the orchestra, where we went on kissing each other from the beginning of the movie to the end.

An exciting period of secret rendezvous began, at different hours of the day, in little coffeehouses downtown or at neighborhood movie theaters, where we talked in whispers or remained silent for long intervals, holding hands and constantly worrying that a member of the family might suddenly turn up. The secrecy and having to dissemble in front of Uncle Lucho and Aunt Olga or the other relatives seasoned our love with a piquant pinch of risk and adventure that to an incorrigible sentimentalist like me made it all the more intense.

The first person to whom I revealed, in confidence, what was happening was the inseparable Javier Silva, my friend since we were young boys. He had always been my confidant in affairs of the heart and I his. He was permanently enamored of my cousin Nancy, whom he showered with invitations and presents, and she, as beautiful as she was flirtatious, played with him like a cat with a mouse. My friend till death, Javier racked his brain to make my amorous interludes with

Julia easier to arrange, organizing evenings at the movies and the theater, occasions on which, moreover, Nancy always accompanied us. On one such evening we went to the Teatro Segura, to see Molière's *L'Avare*, put on by Lucho Córdoba, and Javier, who could never get the better of his ostentatiousness, paid for a box, so that nobody who was in the theater could fail to see us.

Did the family suspect anything? Not yet. Their suspicions were aroused during a weekend outing at the end of June, at the Paramonga sugar plantation, where we went to visit Uncle Pedro. There was a party there, for some reason or other, and we all went out together in a motorcade: Uncle Lucho and Aunt Olga, Uncle Jorge, perhaps Uncle Juan and Aunt Laura too, though I'm not certain, and Julia and I. Uncle Pedro and Aunt Rosi put us up as best they could, in their house and in the guest house at the hacienda, and we spent several very enjoyable days, with walks through the cane fields, having a look at the sugar mills and refining equipment, and on Saturday night at the party, which lasted till breakfast time. While at the hacienda, Julia and I cast prudence to the winds and exchanged glances and whispers or danced in a way that aroused suspicion. I remember Uncle Jorge suddenly bursting into a little reception room where Julia and I had sat down to talk together, and on seeing us there, he raised his glass and cried: "Long live the fiancés!" The three of us laughed, but an electric current passed through the room. I felt uncomfortable and it seemed to me that Uncle Jorge had also become very uncomfortable. From that moment on I was certain that something was going to happen.

In Lima, we went on seeing each other in secret during the day, in coffeehouses downtown where we always felt on edge, and going to the movies at night. But Julia suspected that her sister and her brother-in-law smelled a rat, from the way they looked at her, especially when I came to get her to go to the movies. Or was all of that paranoia on our part, the result of our uneasy consciences?

No, it wasn't. I discovered that by chance one night when on the spur of the moment I decided to drop in at Uncle Juan and Aunt Lala's on Diego Ferré. From the street I saw the living room lights all on, and through the curtains, the whole family gathered together. All the aunts and uncles, but not my mother. I immediately presumed that Julia and I were the reason for this secret meeting. I went into the house, and when I appeared in the living room, they hurriedly dropped whatever subject it was that they had been talking about. Later on, my cousin Nancy, very frightened, confirmed that her parents had devoured her with questions so as to get her to tell them whether "Marito and Julita were in love." It alarmed them that "the beanpole" could be having a love affair with a divorcée, a woman thirteen years older than he was, and they had summoned the tribe together to see what ought to be done.

I immediately foresaw what would happen. Aunt Olga would send her sister back to Bolivia and tell my parents, so that they would remind me that I was still legally a minor. (In those days one reached one's majority at the age of twenty-one.) That same night I went to get Julia, on the pretext that we were going to the movies, and asked her to marry me.

We had been walking along the sea walls of Miraflores, between the Quebrada de Armendáriz and the Salazar gardens, which were always deserted at that hour. At the bottom of the cliff, the sea roared, and we walked along very slowly, in the damp darkness, hand in hand, stopping with every step to kiss each other. Julia started by telling me just what I expected she would: that this was madness, that I was still just a brat and she a grownup woman, that I hadn't yet finished my studies at the university or begun to live, that I didn't even have a real full-time job or a cent to my name and that, under those circumstances, marrying me was a crazy idea that no woman who had an ounce of sense would go along with. But that she loved me and that if I were that mad, she was too. And that we should get married right away so they wouldn't separate us.

We agreed to see each other as little as possible, as meanwhile I made arrangements for our elopement. I set to work the next morning, without hesitating for a moment as to what I was about to do, and without stopping to think about what we'd do once we had the marriage certificate in hand. I went to wake up Javier, who was now living just a few blocks from my house, in a boarding house on the corner of Porta and 28 de Julio. I told him the news and after the de rigueur question—wasn't this an utterly insane thing to do?—he asked me how he could help me. We had to get hold of a mayor, in a town not very far from Lima, who would agree to marry us despite my not being of age yet. Where? Who? I then remembered my university buddy and fellow Christian Democrat militant Guillermo Carrillo Marchand. He was from Chincha and spent every weekend there, with his family. I went to talk to him and he assured me that there would be no problems, since the mayor of Chincha was a friend of his; but he preferred to make inquiries first, so we'd know for certain before going there. A few days later he went to Chincha and came back very optimistic. The marriage ceremony would be performed by the mayor himself, who was delighted by the idea of the elopement. Guillermo brought me the list of papers that were required: certificates, photographs, requests on officially stamped paper. Since it was my mother who kept my birth certificate for me and it wasn't prudent to ask her for it, I asked my friend Rosita Corpancho, the secretary of the Faculty at San Marcos, to help me out, and she let me remove the pertinent part of my university record so as to have it photocopied and notarized. Julia had her papers with her in her handbag.

Those were feverish days, with endless rushing about and exciting talks, with Javier, with Guillermo, and with my cousin Nancy, whom I also turned into an accomplice, asking her to help me find a little furnished room or a boarding house. When I told her the news, Cousin Nancy opened her eyes as wide as saucers and began stammering something or other, but I put my hand over her mouth and told her that she had to get to work immediately so the plan wouldn't fall through, and she, who was very fond of me, immediately went about looking for a place for us to live. Efficiently: in two or three days' time she announced to me that a lady, a co-worker of hers in a social aid program, had a townhouse divided up into tiny little apartments, near the Diagonal, and that one of them would be empty at the end of the month. It cost six hundred soles, slightly more than the pay I received for my work at Porras Barrenechea's. Now all I had to worry about was how we were going to have enough money to eat!

Javier, Julia, and I left for Chincha in a jitney one Saturday morning. Guillermo had been waiting for us there since the night before. I had taken all my savings out of the bank and Javier had lent me his, which together ought to be enough for the twenty-four hours that we figured the adventure would last. It was our plan to go directly to the mayor's office, spend the night in Chincha, at the Hotel Sudamericano, near the main square, and go back to Lima the next day. A friend from

San Marcos, named Carcelén, had been entrusted with the task of calling Uncle Lucho that Saturday afternoon, with the simple message: "Mario and Julia have gotten married."

In Chincha, Guillermo told us that there was an unforeseen complication: the mayor had a lunch on his schedule, and since he had promised to marry us himself, we would have to wait for a few hours. But we were to go to the lunch as his guests. We went. The little restaurant looked out over the tall palm trees of Chincha's sunny main square. There were some ten or twelve people there, all men, who must have been drinking beer for quite a while already, since they were tipsy and some of them downright plastered, including the likable young mayor, who began by proposing a toast to the couple about to be wed and very shortly thereafter began to flirt with Julia. I was furious and ready to butt him with my head, but practical reasons held me back.

When the accursed lunch was over, and Javier and Guillermo and I were able to carry the mayor, dead drunk, to his office, another complication arose. The registrar, or representative mayor, who had been preparing the marriage certificates, said that if I couldn't present a notarized permit from my parents authorizing the wedding, he couldn't perform the ceremony, since I was a minor. We begged and threatened him, but he wouldn't give in, as meanwhile the mayor, in a semi-comatose state, followed our argument with glassy eyes, burping and completely out of it. Finally, the registrar advised us to go to Tambo de Mora. There wouldn't be any problem there. Such things could be done in a little town, but not in Chincha, the capital of the province.

We then began a pilgrimage from one town in the province to another, in search of an understanding mayor, which lasted all that afternoon, that night, and almost all of the following day. I remember it as something phantasmagoric and filled with anxiety: the ancient taxi that was taking us along dusty roads, full of potholes and stones, amid cotton fields and vineyards and stock farms, the sudden glimpses of the sea and the succession of squalid offices of mayors who inevitably slammed the door in our faces when they discovered how old I was. Of all the mayors or representative mayors of those hamlets, I remember the one in Tambo de Mora, a huge barefoot, potbellied black who burst out laughing fit to kill and exclaimed: "In other words you're kidnapping the girl!" But when he took a look at my birth certificate, he scratched his head: "No way!"

We went back to Chincha as it was getting dark, discouraged and worn out, but determined to go on with the search the next morning. That night Julia and I made love for the first time. It was a cramped little room, with a monastic-style window that caught the light from the roof and pink walls on which pornographic and religious images had been pasted up. All night long the shouting and singing of drunks reached our ears from the bar of the hotel or from some neighborhood tavern. But we paid no attention to them, happy as we were, making love to each other and vowing that even though all the mayors of the world refused to marry us, nothing could separate us now. When we finally fell asleep, full daylight was entering the room and morning sounds could be heard.

Javier came to wake us up around noon. Since very early that morning, he and Guillermo had gone on, in the rattletrap taxi, with their exploration of neighboring towns, without much success. But finally Javier found the solution in the course of a conversation with the mayor of Grocio Prado, who told him he didn't see any problem about marrying us if, on my birth certificate, we revised the date of the year in which I was born by changing 1936 to 1934. The two years' difference would make me legally of age. We looked closely at the certificate and it was easy: right there and then we added to the 6 the little mark that turned it into a 4. We then went immediately to Grocio Prado, by way of a trail buried in dust. The city hall was closed and we had to wait a while.

To pass the time, we visited the house of the person who had made the town famous and had turned it into a pilgrimage center: the Blessed Melchorita. She had died a few years before, in the same whitewashed hut with walls of wild reeds and mud in which she had always lived, caring for the poor, mortifying herself, and praying. She was reputed to have wrought miraculous cures, made prophecies, and in her saintly ecstasies communicated in foreign languages with the dead. Around a photograph of her, showing her face of a mestiza, framed by the hood of a crudely woven ankle-length habit, were dozens of little lighted candles and women praying. The town was a tiny one, on sandy ground, with a large stretch of open countryside that served both as a main square and as a soccer field, surrounded by farms and growing crops.

The mayor finally arrived, in the middle of the afternoon. The formalities were exceedingly, dishearteningly slow. When everything appeared to be ready, the mayor said that a witness was needed, since Javier, a minor, wouldn't do. We went out onto the street to talk the first passerby into being the witness. A farmer from thereabouts, he agreed but, after mulling it over, said that he couldn't be a witness to a marriage ceremony in which there was not one measly drop of alcohol so as to drink to the happiness of the bride and groom. So he left and after a few endless minutes came back again with his wedding present: a couple of bottles of Chincha wine. We drank a toast or two with him, after the mayor had reminded us of our rights and duties as man and wife.

We returned to Chincha as night was already falling, and Javier left at once for Lima, with the mission of seeking out Uncle Lucho, so as to reassure him. Julia and I spent the night at the Hotel Sudamericano. Before going to bed, we ate something in the little bar of the hotel and were overcome by a fit of laughter on discovering that we were talking in very low voices, like conspirators.

The next morning, the hotel desk clerk woke me up to announce that there was a phone call for me from Lima. It was Javier, in a panic. On the return trip, the minibus he was in had gone off the road so as to prevent a collision. His conversation with Uncle Lucho had been a good one, "under the circumstances." But he had had the scare of his life shortly thereafter, when my father suddenly turned up at his boarding house and shoved a revolver into his chest, demanding that he reveal my whereabouts. "He's turned into a madman," Javier said to me.

We got out of bed and went to the main square of Chincha, to take the minibus to Lima. We spent the two hours of the trip hand in hand, looking into each other's eyes, scared to death and happy. We went directly to Uncle Lucho's on Armendáriz. He received us at the top of the staircase. He kissed Julia and said to her, pointing to the bedroom: "Go confront your sister." He was sad, but he didn't upbraid me or tell me that I had done something quite insane. He made me promise him that I wouldn't give up going to the university, that I would finish my courses. I swore I would, and also that my marrying Julia wouldn't keep me from becoming a writer.

As we were talking together, I could hear Julia and Aunt Olga in the distance, behind the locked bedroom door, and it seemed to me that Olga had raised her voice and was crying.

I went from there to the apartment on the Calle Porta. My grandparents and Auntie Mamaé were a model of discretion. But the confrontation with my mother, who was there, was dramatic, with tears and outcries on her part. She said I'd ruined my life and didn't believe me when I swore to her that I'd be an attorney and even a diplomat (her great ambition for me). Finally, calming down a little, she told me that my father was beside himself and that I should keep out of his way, since he was capable of killing me. He was carrying his famous revolver in his pocket.

I bathed and dressed as hurriedly as I could to go see Javier, and just as I was leaving the house a summons came for me from the police. My father had had me summoned to police headquarters in Miraflores to declare there whether it was true that I had gotten married, and where and with whom. The policeman in civvies who questioned me made me spell out my answers as he typed them out, with two fingers, on a clattering old hulk of a machine. I told him that, as a matter of fact, I had married Doña Julia Urquidi Illanes, but that I wasn't going to declare in what mayor's office because I was afraid my father would try to annul the marriage and I didn't want to make the task any easier for him. "What he's going to do is denounce her as a corrupter of minors," the policeman warned me amiably. "He told me so when he swore out this complaint."

I left police headquarters in search of Javier and we went to consult an attorney from Piura who was a friend of his. He was very obliging, and didn't even charge me for the consultation. He told us that altering my birth certificate did not annul the marriage in and of itself, but that it might be a reason to declare it annulled if there was a court trial. If not, in two years, the marriage was automatically "legal." But my father could formally accuse Julia of corrupting minors, although, in view of my age, nineteen, in all likelihood no judge would take the accusation seriously.

Those were days of yearning bordering on the absurd. I continued to sleep at my grandparents' and Julia at Aunt Olga's, and I saw my brand-new wife only for a few hours at a time, when I went to visit her, as before the wedding. Aunt Olga treated me with her usual affection, but one night her face was grim. Through my mother, my father had sent me threatening messages: Julia was to leave the country or be prepared to suffer the consequences.

On the second or third day, I received a letter from him. It was ferocious, the ravings of a madman. He set a date just a few days away for Julia to leave the country on her own initiative. He had spoken with one of the ministers in Odría's government, who was a friend of his, and the friend had assured him that, if she didn't leave *motu proprio*, he would have her expelled as an undesirable. As it went on, the letter became more and more exasperating. He ended up by telling me, amid obscenities, that if I didn't obey him, he would kill me as if I were a rabid dog. After his signature, as a postscript, he added that I could go to the police to ask for help, but that that would not keep him from pumping five shots into me. And he signed his name a second time as proof of his determination.

I talked over with Julia what we should do. I had plans impossible to carry out, such as leaving the country (using what for a passport? using what for money?) or going to some province too far away for my father's long arm to reach (living on what? with what sort of job?). Finally, she was the one who proposed the most practical solution. She would leave and go to stay with her parents in Chile. Once my father had calmed down, she would come back. Meanwhile, I could arrange to secure other sources of income and find a boarding house or an apartment. Uncle Lucho argued in favor of this strategy. It was the only sensible one, in view of the circumstances. Filled with rage, with sorrow, with a feeling of powerlessness, after a fit of tears I had to resign myself to Julia's leaving.

In order to pay for her ticket to Antofagasta I sold almost all my clothes and took out a loan, at the pawnshop run by the Municipality of Lima, with my typewriter, my watch, and everything I owned that could be pawned as collateral. On the eve of her departure, feeling sorry for us, Aunt Olga and Uncle Lucho discreetly withdrew after dinner, and I was able to be alone with my wife. We made love and wept together and promised to write each other every day. We didn't sleep all night long. At dawn, Aunt Olga and Uncle Lucho and I went with her to the Limatambo airport to see her off. It was one of those

typical winter mornings in Lima, with the invisible mist making everything damp and that fog that turns the façades of the houses, the trees,
and the silhouettes of people into ghostly apparitions. My heart raged
with fury, and I could hardly hold back my tears as, from the terrace,
I saw Julia going off toward the gangplank of the plane taking her to
Chile. When would I see her again?

Beginning that very day, I entered a period of frantic activity to
secure work that would allow me to be independent. I had the research
for Porras Barrenechea and the small assignments on the side with
Turismo. Thanks to Lucho Loayza—who, on learning the story of my
incredible marriage, made an unpleasant remark on how superior those
silent and unreal English marriages were to Latin ones, so disorderly
and earthy—I got an assignment to write a weekly column in the
Sunday supplement of *El Comercio*, the editor-in-chief of whose literary section was Abelardo Oquendo. An intimate of Loayza's, Abelardo was to be a close friend of mine too from then on. Abelardo had
me write up weekly interviews I had with Peruvian writers, with magnificent sketches by Alejandro Romualdo to illustrate them, for which
I was paid some thousand soles a month. And Luis Jaime Cisneros
immediately got me another job: writing the volume on Civic Education in a series of textbooks that the Catholic University was preparing for its applicants for admission. Despite my not being a student
at Católica, Luis Jaime arranged matters so as to persuade the rector
of the university to entrust the writing of that book to me (the first
work of mine ever published, although it has never appeared in my
bibliography).

Porras Barrenechea for his part immediately secured for me a couple
of jobs that were easy and decently paid. My interview with him was
rather surprising. I began explaining to him why I had not showed up
for two or three days, when he interrupted me: "I know all about it.
Your father came to see me." He paused and elegantly skirted this
pitfall: "He was very nervous. A quick-tempered man, isn't that so?"
I tried to imagine what the interview would have been like. "I calmed
him down with an argument that may have impressed him," Porras
added, with that wicked gleam in his eyes that suddenly appeared when
he made sly remarks. "After all, getting married is an act of manhood,
Señor Vargas. An affirmation of virility. It's not all that terrible, then.
It would have been much worse if his boy had turned out to be a

homosexual or a drug addict, isn't that true?" He assured me that, on leaving the Calle Colina, my father appeared to have calmed down.

"You did the right thing by not coming to tell what you were planning to do," Porras said to me. "Because I would have tried to knock a nonsensical idea like that out of your head. But now that it's a fait accompli, we'll have to find you more decent sources of income."

He promptly did so, with the same generosity with which he poured forth his wisdom for his students. The first job was as a library assistant at the Club Nacional, the institution that symbolized the aristocracy and the oligarchy of Peru. The president of the club, a hunter of wild beasts and a collector of gold art objects, Miguel Mujica Gallo, had placed Porras on its directorate as head librarian, and my job consisted of spending a couple of hours every morning in the beautiful rooms of the library, with pieces of English furniture and coffered mahogany ceilings, cataloguing the new acquisitions. But since the library bought few books, I was able to devote those hours to reading, studying, or working on my articles. The fact is that between 1955 and 1958 I read a great deal in those few short hours in the morning, in the elegant solitude of the Club Nacional. The club's library was a fairly good one—or rather, it had been, since the time came when its budget gave out—and it had a splendid collection of erotic books and magazines, a good part of which I read or at least leafed through. I remember above all the volumes of the series *Les Maîtres de l'amour*, edited by Apollinaire and often with a foreword by him, thanks to which I became acquainted with Sade, Aretino, Andrea de Nerciat, John Cleland, and, among many others, the picturesque and monothematic Restif de la Bretonne, a freakish writer who laboriously reconstructed the world of his time, in his novels and in his autobiography, from the point of view of his fetishistic obsession for the feminine foot. Those readings were very important, and for a fair time I believed that eroticism was a synonym of rebellion and of freedom in the social and artistic realm, and a marvelous source of creativity. That is what it seems to have been, at least in the eighteenth century, in the works and the attitudes of the *libertins* (a word which, as Roger Vailland liked to recall, does not mean "pleasure-loving," but "a man who defies God").

But it did not take me long—that is to say, only a few years—to realize that, with modern permissiveness, in the open industrial society of our day, eroticism changed sign and content, and became a commercial, manufactured product, as conformist and conventional as it could possibly be, and almost always of a dreadful artistic indigence. The discovery of erotic literature of high quality, which I made unexpectedly on the shelves of the Club Nacional, has had an influence on my work and left its deposit on what I have written. Moreover, the prolix and prolific Restif de la Bretonne helped me to understand an essential characteristic of fiction: that it serves the novelist to re-create the world in his image and likeness, to subtly rearrange it in accordance with his most secret appetites.

The other job that Porras Barrenechea secured for me was a gloomy one: cataloguing the graves of the oldest sections of the colonial cemetery of Lima, the Presbítero Maestro, whose registers had been lost. (The running of the cemetery was the responsibility of the Public Welfare Office of Lima, at that time a private institution, of which Porras was a member of the board of directors.) The advantage of this job was that I could do it very early in the morning or late in the afternoon, on work days or on holidays, and for as many hours or minutes as I liked. The head administrator of the cemetery paid me by the number of dead I catalogued. I managed to make some five hundred soles a month from this minor job. Javier sometimes accompanied me on my scouting trips through the cemetery, with my notebook, my pencils, my ladder, my spatula (to remove the crust of dirt that covered some of the tombstones), and my flashlight in case we were still there after dark. As I counted my dead and totted up the hours I'd worked, the head administrator, a tubby, likable, talkative man, told me anecdotes about the first sessions of each presidential session of Congress, which he had never failed to attend, from the days when he'd been just a youngster.

Before only a couple of days had gone by, I had taken on six jobs (a year and a half later, there would be seven of them, when I began working for Radio Panamericana), multiplying my pay by five. With the three thousand or three thousand five hundred soles a month they brought in, it was now possible for Julia and me to survive, if we found some inexpensive place to live. Luckily, the little apartment that had been promised to Nancy was now empty. I went to see it, was delighted by it, took it, and Esperanza La Rosa, the landlady, waited a week until, with my first pay from the new jobs, I was able to put down the deposit and the first month's rent. It was in an ocher-colored townhouse, divided up into individual dwellings so tiny that they seemed like doll houses, at the end of the Calle Porta, where the street grew narrower and narrower and finally dwindled to nothing at the foot of a wall that in those days separated it from the Diagonal. Our apartment consisted of two bedrooms and a little kitchen and a bathroom, both of these so tiny that only one person at a time could fit into them and then only by sucking in his or her belly. But despite its diminutive dimensions and its spartan furnishings, there was something utterly charming about it, with its cheerful curtains and the little patio with old furniture and pots of geraniums that each of the apartments looked out upon. Nancy helped me clean the place and decorate it to receive the bride.

After her departure, Julia and I wrote to each other every day and I can still see Granny Carmen handing me the letters with a wicked smile and a joke: "Now who can this little letter be from, who can it be from? Who can be writing so many letters to my little grandson?" Four or five weeks after Julia's departure for Chile, when I had already secured all those jobs, I phoned my father and asked him for an appointment. I hadn't seen him since before the wedding, nor had I answered his homicidal letter.

I became very nervous that morning on my way to his office. I was determined, for the first time in my life, to tell him that he could fire his damned revolver once and for all, but, now that I was able to support her, I wasn't going to go on living apart from my wife. Nonetheless, deep down, I was afraid, once the moment was at hand, that I would again lose my courage and again feel paralyzed in the face of his wrath.

But I found him oddly serene and rational as we spoke together. And because of certain things he said and others he forbore to mention, I have always suspected that that conversation with Dr. Porras—to which neither he nor I made the slightest allusion—had had its effect and helped him to resign himself in the end to a marriage planned without his consent. Very pale, he listened to me without a word as I told him of the jobs I had gotten and what I was going to earn from all of them, then assured him that it would be enough to support myself. And how, moreover, despite those various jobs, some of which I could do at home at night, I could attend classes and take the exams at the university. Finally, swallowing hard, I told him that Julia was married to me and that we couldn't go on living with her alone, there in Chile, and me here in Lima.

He didn't voice the slightest reproach. Instead, he spoke to me as though he were a lawyer, using certain legal technicalities on which he had collected detailed information. He had a copy of my declaration to the police, which he showed me, marked in red pencil. I gave myself away by admitting that I had gotten married when I was only nineteen. That was enough to start legal proceedings to annul the marriage. But he wasn't going to try to do that. Because, even though I had made a stupid mistake, getting married, after all, was a manly thing to do, a virile act.

Then, making a visible effort to employ a conciliatory tone of voice that I didn't remember his ever having used with me before, he immediately began to advise me not to abandon my studies, not to ruin my career, on account of this marriage. He was sure that I could go a long way, as long as I didn't do any more crazy things. If he had always acted harshly toward me, it had been for my own good, to straighten out what, through a misguided affection, the Llosas had twisted. But contrary to what I had thought, he loved me, because I was his son, and how could a father help loving his son?

To my surprise, he opened his arms for me to embrace him. I did so, without kissing him, disconcerted by the denouement of the interview, and thanking him for his words, in a way that might strike him as the least hypocritical one possible.

(That interview, sometime in the latter part of August 1955, marked my definitive emancipation from my father. Although his shadow will doubtless accompany me to my grave, and although at times, even today, all at once the memory of some scene, of some image, of the years when he had complete authority over me gives me a sudden hollow feeling in the pit of my stomach, after that meeting we never had another fight. Not directly, that is to say. In all truth, we saw very little of each other. And, in the years when the two of us were still in Peru—until 1958, when I left for Europe and he went with my mother to Los Angeles—or on the rare occasions later when we both happened to be in Lima, or when I went to visit the two of them in the United States, he often made gestures and said things and took steps aimed at lessening the distance between us and erasing the bad memories, so that we could have that close and affectionate relationship that we never had. But I, my father's son after all, never knew how to answer these overtures on his part, and even though I always tried to be polite to him, I never showed him more affection than I felt—that is to say, none whatsoever. The terrible rancor, my burning hatred of him in my childhood, gradually disappeared in the course of those years, above all as I discovered little by little how hard it had been for him during his first days in the United States, where he and my mother held down jobs as factory workers—my mother, for thirteen years, was a weaver in a textile mill, and he was employed in a shoe factory—and then working as doorkeepers and caretakers in a synagogue in Los Angeles. Naturally, even in the worst periods of that difficult adaptation to his new country, his pride did not allow my father to ask me for help or permit my mother to do so, except to buy her plane tickets to Peru, where they spent their vacations—and I believe that it was only in the last days of his life that he accepted help from my brother Ernesto, who provided him with an apartment to live in, in Pasadena.

(When we saw each other—every two, sometimes every three years, always for just a few short days—our relationship was polite but frigid. To him it was always something incomprehensible that I should have become known thanks to my books, that my name and sometimes my photograph should appear in *Time* or in the *Los Angeles Times*; this pleased him, no doubt, but also disconcerted and puzzled him and so we never spoke about my novels, until our last quarrel, the one that put us completely out of touch with each other until his death, in January 1979.

(It was a quarrel we had without seeing each other and without exchanging a single word, when we were thousands of kilometers apart, about *La tía Julia y el escribidor* [*Aunt Julia and the Scriptwriter*], a novel in which there are autobiographical episodes in which the father of the narrator is shown acting in much the way mine did when I married Julia. Months after the book came out I was surprised to receive a curious letter from him—I was living in Cambridge, England—in which he thanked me for acknowledging in that novel that he had been severe with me but that when all was said and done he had acted as he did for my own good "since he had always loved me." I didn't answer his letter. Sometime later, during one of the phone calls that I made to my mother in Los Angeles, she surprised me by saying that my father wanted to talk to me about *La tía Julia y el escribidor*.

Foreseeing some sort of ukase, I said goodbye to her and hung up before he could get to the phone. Some days later, I received another card from him, a violent one this time, accusing me of being resentful and of slandering him in a book, without giving him a chance to defend himself, reproaching me for not being a believer and prophesying divine punishment for me. He warned me that he would circulate this letter among my acquaintances. And as a matter of fact, in the months and years that followed, I found out that he had sent dozens and perhaps hundreds of copies of it to relatives, friends, and acquaintances of mine in Peru.

(I never saw him alive again. In January of 1979 he came from Los Angeles with my mother, to spend a few weeks' summer vacation in Lima. One afternoon, my cousin Giannina—Uncle Pedro's daughter—phoned me to announce that my father, who had been having lunch at their house, had fallen unconscious. We called an ambulance and I took him to the Clínica Americana, where he was found to be dead on arrival. The only people who came to the wake in the funeral chapel that night to bid him a last farewell were the surviving aunts and uncles and many nieces and nephews of that Llosa family that he had so detested. In the last years of his life, he had finally made his peace with them, visiting them and accepting their invitations in the brief trips he made to Peru from time to time.)

I left my father's office in great excitement to send Julia a telegram telling her that her exile was over and that I'd be sending her money for her plane ticket back to Peru very soon. Then I rushed over to Uncle Lucho and Aunt Olga's to pass on the good news to them. Although I was very busy now, what with all the jobs I'd taken on, every time I had a free moment I would hurry over to their house on the Avenida Armendáriz to have lunch or dinner, because with them I could talk about my exiled wife, the only subject that interested me. Aunt Olga too had finally become accustomed to the idea that her sister's marriage was irreversible, and she was happy that my father had agreed to Julia's return.

I immediately began to think up ways I could buy her plane ticket. Even though I was earning more money now, renting the apartment and redeeming my typewriter and my watch, indispensable for fulfilling all my work assignments, had left me without a cent. I was looking into how I could buy the plane ticket in installments or get a loan from the bank, when a telegram from Julia arrived for me, announcing her arrival on the following day. She had stolen a march on me by selling her jewelry.

I went to the airport to meet her, along with Uncle Lucho and Aunt Olga, and when Aunt Olga spied her among the passengers on the plane from Santiago, she made a remark that delighted me, because it showed that the family situation was back to normal: "Look how pretty your wife has made herself for the reunion."

That was a very happy day, to be sure, for Julia and me. The little apartment in the townhouse on the Calle Porta was as tidy as could be and in it were fragrant flowers to welcome the bride. I had brought all my books and clothes there the evening before, with great expectations, moreover, at the prospect of finally beginning to live an independent life, in a house of my own (in a manner of speaking).

I had planned to finish my college courses and then my studies in the two Faculties—Letters and Law—that came after that, and not only because I had promised my family that I would, but also because I was certain that only those degrees would allow me to have the minimum financial security needed to devote myself to writing, and because I thought that without them I'd never get to Europe, to France, something that continued to be the main goal of my life. I was more determined than ever to try to be a writer and was convinced that I would never manage to be one if I didn't leave Peru, if I didn't live in Paris. I talked this over a thousand times with Julia and she, who was adventurous and fond of new things, egged me on: yes, yes, I should finish my studies and apply for the scholarship that the Banco Popular and San Marcos were awarding for postgraduate studies in Spain. Then we would go to Paris, where I would write all the novels I had in my head. She would help me.

She helped me a great deal, from the very first day. Without her aid, I would not have been able to hold down my seven jobs, to find the time to attend classes at San Marcos, to compose the essays the professors assigned and, as if all that weren't enough, to write a fair number of short stories.

When, today, I try to reconstruct my schedule during those three years—1955 to 1958—I'm amazed: how was I able to do so many things and, on top of everything else, read piles of books, and cultivate the friendship of several wonderful friends such as Lucho and Abelardo, and also go to the movies every so often and eat and sleep? On paper, there aren't enough hours in the day to do all that. But I found room to fit it all in, and despite the hectic rushing around and the need to stretch every penny, they were exciting years of hopes renewed and enhanced, years in which, to be sure, I did not regret my sudden marriage.

I believe Julia didn't either. We loved each other, enjoyed each other's company, and although we had the inevitable fights that married life brings with it, during those three years in Lima, before the trip to Europe, our relationship was productive and mutually stimulating. One source of our quarrels was my fits of retrospective jealousy, the absurd, anguished fury I felt when I discovered that Julia had had a love life, and most important of all, following her divorce and up until the eve of her coming to Lima, she had had an impassioned love affair with an Argentine singer, who came to La Paz and caused havoc among the women in the city. For some mysterious reason—the subject makes me laugh today, but at the time it made me suffer a great deal and I made Julia suffer too on account of it—my wife's affair with the Argentine singer, which she naïvely mentioned in passing shortly after we were married, kept me awake nights and made me feel that, even though it was over and done with, it represented a threat, a danger to our marriage, for it stole a part of Julia's life from me, a part that would always be out of my reach, and that therefore we would never be able to be completely happy. I demanded that she recount to me a plethora of details about this adventure, and for that reason we sometimes had violent arguments, which would end in tender reconciliations.

But we also had fine times together. When one almost never has time, or money, for diversions, these, however rare and modest they may be, take on a wondrous quality, produce a pleasure unknown to those who can enjoy them when and as they please. I remember the childlike excitement it caused us, at the end of the month sometimes, to go out to lunch in a German restaurant on the Calle La Esperanza, the Gambrinus, where they served a delicious Wiener schnitzel, for which we joyfully prepared ourselves, looking forward to it for days. Or on certain nights, going to eat a pizza with a little pitcher of wine at La Pizzería, which a nice Swiss couple had just opened up on the Diagonal, and which, from the modest garage where it first set up in business, would become over the years one of the best-known restaurants in Miraflores.

Where we went at least once a week was to the movies. They delighted both of us. Unlike what happens to me with books, which, when they're bad, not only bore me but irritate me as well, since they make me feel that I'm wasting my time, I can put up with bad films very easily, and as long as they aren't pretentious, they amuse me. So we used to go see whatever was playing, and above all Mexican melodramas, full of moaning and groaning, with María Félix, Arturo de Córdoba, Agustín Lara, Emilio Tuero, Mirta Aguirre, and all the others, for which Julia and I had a perverse predilection.

Julia was a very good typist, so that I could give her the list of dead in the Presbítero Maestro scribbled in my notebooks and she would turn them into luminously clear index cards. She also typed my feature stories and articles for *El Comercio*, *Turismo*, and the magazine *Cultura Peruana*, for which I began to write, soon after, a monthly column devoted to the most important Peruvian political thinkers of the nineteenth and twentieth centuries, with the title of "Hombres, libros y ideas" ("Men, Books and Ideas"). Preparing that column, for a little over two years, was very enjoyable, since, thanks to Porras Barrenechea's library and the one at the Club Nacional, I could read almost all of them, from Sánchez Carrión y Vigil to José Carlos Mariátegui and Riva Agüero, passing by way of González Prada, whose virulent anarchical diatribes against institutions and political leaders of all stripes, in an exquisitely sculptured prose with the bright polish of the Parnassian poets, naturally made a tremendous impression on me.

The weekly interviews that Abelardo assigned me for *El Comercio* were very instructive with regard to the situation of Peruvian literature, although frequently they were disappointing. The first writer I interviewed was José María Arguedas. He had not yet published *Los ríos profundos (Deep Rivers)*, but the author of *Yawar Fiesta* and *Diamantes y pedernales (Diamonds and Flints)*, published not long before by Mejía Baca, was already surrounded by a certain cult that thought highly of him as a delicately lyrical narrator possessed of intimate knowledge of the world of the Indian. I was surprised by how timid and modest he was, how little he knew about modern literature, and his fears and hesitations. He made me show him the interview once I had written it up, corrected a number of things, and then sent a letter to Abelardo, requesting that it not be published, since he didn't want anyone's feelings to be hurt by it (because in it he had mentioned the stepbrother who had tormented him in his childhood). The letter arrived after the interview had already been printed. Arguedas was not disturbed by this and immediately sent me an affectionate little note, thanking me for how well I had dealt with him and his work.

I think that for that column I interviewed every living Peruvian who had ever published a novel in Peru: from the very elderly Enrique López Albújar, a living relic, who, in his little house in San Miguel, mixed up names, dates, and titles and spoke of men now seventy years old as "boys," to the brand-new arrival on the literary scene, Vargas Vicuña, who was in the habit of interrupting his public readings by letting out a shout that was his motto ("Long live life, goddamn it!") and who, after the beautiful prose passages of *Nahuín*, mysteriously vanished, at least from the world of literature. And passing, of course, by way of the likable Piuran Vegas Seminario, or Arturo Hernández, the author of *Sangama*, and dozens of writers, both men and women, on any number of subjects, the authors of novels about Creoles, about aborigines, about mestizos, about local customs, about blacks, which always fell from my hands and seemed very old (not ancient, just very old) because of the way in which they were written and, above all, structured as narratives.

At that time, largely because of my bedazzlement by Faulkner's works, I was continually fascinated by novelistic technique, and all the novels that came my way I read with a clinical eye, observing the way in which point of view was handled, how the chronology was organized, whether the function of the narrator was consistent or whether the inconsistencies and technical infelicities—the use of adjectives, for example—destroyed (got in the way of) the work's verisimilitude. I questioned all the novelists and short story writers whom I interviewed about narrative form, about their technical preoccupations, and their answers, disdainful of such "formalisms," always dismayed me. Some of them added "formalisms borrowed from abroad, imitations of European trends," and others went so far as to use the loaded word "telluric": "To me, the important thing is not form, but life itself," "My literature receives its sustenance from Peruvian essences."

Ever since those days I have abhorred the word "telluric," flaunted by many writers and critics of the time as the greatest literary virtue and the obligatory theme of every Peruvian writer. To be telluric meant to write a literature with roots in the bowels of the earth, in local landscape and local customs, preferably Andean ones, and to denounce the bossism and feudalism of the highlands, the jungle, or the coast, with cruel episodes involving *mistis* (whites in positions of power) who raped peasant girls, drunken authorities who stole, and fanatical, corrupt priests who preached resignation to the Indians. Those who wrote and promoted telluric literature failed to realize that, despite their intentions, it was the most conformist and conventional literature in the world, the repetition of a series of clichés, put together mechanically, in which a folkloristic language, affected and caricatural, and the carelessness with which the narratives were constructed completely corrupted the historico-critical testimony meant to justify them. Unreadable as literature, they were also false social documents, in truth a picturesque, banal, and complaisant adulteration of a complex reality.

For me, the word *telluric* came to stand for provincialism and underdevelopment in the field of literature, the elementary and superficial version of the writer's vocation held by the ingenuous pen pusher who believes that good novels can be written by inventing good "subjects" and has yet to learn that a successful novel is a valiant intellectual effort, a struggle with language and the invention of a narrative order, of an organization of time, of movements, of an imparting of information alternating with silences on which it depends entirely whether a piece of fiction is true or false, moving or ridiculous, serious or stupid. I didn't know whether I would manage to become a writer someday, but I did know after those years that I would never be a *telluric* writer.

To be sure, not all the Peruvian writers whom I interviewed had that folkloristic scorn for form nor did they shield their laziness behind an adjective. One of the exceptions was Sebastián Salazar Bondy. He had not written novels, but he had written short stories—in addition to essays, works for the theater, and poetry—and thus had a place in the series. That was the first time I conversed at length with him. I sought him out in his little office at the daily *La Prensa*, and we went downstairs to have coffee together, at the Crem Rica on the Jirón de la Unión. He was tall and slender and sharp as a knife, tremendously likable and intelligent and, unlike the others, well acquainted with modern literature, about which he spoke with an assurance and a keenness of judgment that filled me with respect. Like every young person who aspired to be a writer, I was a parricide, and Salazar Bondy, because of how active and many-sided he was—he seemed at times to represent the entire cultural life of Peru—turned out to be the "father" whom my generation had to bury in order to take on a personality of our own, and it was very "in" to attack him. I had done so too, severely criticizing, in *Turismo*, his play *No hay isla feliz (There Is No Happy Island)*, which I didn't like. Although we came to be intimate friends only much later, I keep remembering that interview, because of the good impression it made on me. Talking with him was a healthy contrast to other authors whom I had interviewed: he was living proof that a Peruvian writer didn't have to be telluric, that one could have a firm footing in Peruvian life and at the same time a mind open to the good literature of the whole world.

But of all my interviewees, the most picturesque and original one was, by far, Enrique Congrains Martin, who at the time was at the height of his popularity. He was a few years older than I was, blond and fond of sports, but very serious, to the point, I believe, of being impermeable to humor. He had a somewhat disconcerting fixed stare and his whole person exuded energy and action. He had come to literature for purely practical reasons, although that seemed scarcely believable. From an early age he had been a salesman of various products, and rumor had it that he was also the inventor of a special soap to wash saucepans, and that one of the fantastic projects he'd thought up had been to organize a union of domestic cooks who worked in Lima, so as to require, through this entity (he would be pulling the strings), all the housewives of the city to have their kitchenware scrubbed with the soap that he'd invented. Everyone thinks up mad undertakings; Enrique Congrains Martin had the ability—unheard of in Peru—to invariably put into practice the crazy projects that he came up with. From being a soap salesman he went on to be a book salesman, and so one day he decided to write and publish the books he sold himself, convinced that no one would resist this argument: "Buy this book, of which I am the author, from me. Have a good time reading it and help the cause of Peruvian literature."

That was how he had come to write the collection of short stories *Lima, hora cero (Lima, Zero Hour), Kikuyo*, and most recently the novel *No una, sino muchas muertes (Not One, but Many Dead)*, with which he brought his career as a writer to an end. He published his books and sold them from office to office, from house to house. And nobody could say no to him, because to anyone who told him he didn't have any money, his reply would be that payment could be made in weekly installments of a few centavos. When I interviewed him, Enrique had dazzled all the Peruvian intellectuals who couldn't see how he could be, at one and the same time, all the things he was.

And this was only the beginning. As soon as he got to literature he left it behind and went on to become a designer and salesman of peculiar pieces of furniture with three legs, a grower and seller of miniature Japanese trees, and, finally, a clandestine Trotskyite and a conspirator, and therefore thrown in prison. He got out and fathered twins. One day he disappeared and I had no news of him for a long time. Years later I discovered that he was living in Venezuela, where he was the prosperous owner of a speed-reading school, where a method was used that he himself, naturally, had invented.

A couple of months after her return from Chile, Julia became pregnant. The news came as an indescribable shock to me, because I was convinced at the time (was this too an obvious proof of Sartre's influence on me?) that my vocation might possibly be compatible with marriage, but that it would irremediably founder if children who had to be fed, dressed, and educated entered the picture. Goodbye dreams of going off to France! Goodbye plans to write extra-long novels! How to devote oneself to an activity that didn't put food on the table and work at things that brought in money to support a family? But Julia was looking forward to having a baby with such high hopes that I was obliged to hide my deep distress, and even to simulate an enthusiasm I didn't feel at all at the prospect of being a father.

Julia hadn't had any children during her previous marriage and the doctors had told her that she couldn't have any, which was a great frustration in her life. This pregnancy was a surprise that overjoyed her. The German woman doctor who saw her gave her a very strict regimen to follow in the first months of her pregnancy, in which she was to move about as little as possible. She obeyed the doctor's orders with great self-discipline, but after several warning signs, she lost the baby. It was very soon after the beginning of her pregnancy and it did not take long for her to recover from her disappointment.

I believe it was around that time that someone gave us a puppy. He was a lovable mutt, although a bit neurotic, and we named him Batuque—Rumpus. Little and wiggly, he would leap all about to welcome me home and used to jump up onto my lap as I read. But at times he would suddenly be overcome by unexpected fits of bad temper and make a lunge at one of our neighbors in the townhouse on the Calle Porta, the poet and writer María Teresa Llona, who lived by herself, and whose calves, for some reason, attracted and infuriated Batuque. She put up with it graciously, but we often found ourselves very embarrassed.

One day, when I came home at noon, I found Julia bathed in tears. The dogcatchers had taken Batuque to the pound. The men in the van had practically grabbed him out of her arms.

I rushed off to get him at the pound, which was near the Puente del Ejército. I managed to get there in time and rescue poor Batuque, who, the minute they took him out of the cage and I picked him up, pissed and shat all over me and lay trembling in my arms. The spectacle at the pound left me as terrified as he was: two *zambos* (men half Indian and half black) who worked there were beating to death, right in plain sight of the dogs in cages, the animals who had not been reclaimed by their owners after several days had gone by. Driven half out of my mind by what I had seen, I went off with Batuque and sat down in the first cheap little coffeehouse I came across. It was called La Catedral. And it was there that the idea crossed my mind to begin with a scene like that the novel that I would write someday, inspired by Esparza Zañartu and Odría's dictatorship, which, then in 1956, was gasping its last.

SIXTEEN

The Great Change

IT is a custom that at CADE, the Annual Conference of Executives, the presidential candidates present their plans for governing. The meetings arouse great interest and the explanatory speeches are delivered before audiences full of entrepreneurs, political leaders, government officials, and many journalists.

Of the ten candidates, CADE invited those four of us who, according to the opinion polls, were the only ones in December 1989 who might possibly be elected: the candidates of the Democratic Front, of the APRA, of the United Left, and of the Socialist Alliance. Four months away from the elections, Alberto Fujimori's name did not turn up in the surveys, and when eventually it did, he was vying for last place with the Prophet Ezequiel Ataucusi Gamonal, the founder of the Israelite Church of the New Universal Pact.

I was impatiently awaiting the chance to present my program, showing the Peruvian people what was new about my candidacy and the drive for reform that inspired it. I was chosen to give the final speech ending the conference, on the afternoon of the second day, after the speeches by Alva Castro and Henry Pease, and the one by Barrantes, who set forth his ideas in the morning of the second day, Saturday, December 2. Speaking last seemed to me to be a good sign. Those chosen to be on the panel with me were a man who was for the Front, Salvador Majluf, the president of the National Association of Industries, and two dignified adversaries: the agrarian technician Manuel Lajo Lazo and the journalist César Lévano, one of the few judicious Marxists in Peru.

Although those in charge of our Plan for Governing had not finished drawing up the program, in the last week of November Lucho Bustamante handed me the draft of a speech setting forth its main features. Performing miracles as far as time was concerned, since those were the days of the public controversy with Alan García regarding the number of government employees, I managed to seclude myself for two whole mornings so as to write the text of my speech,* and on the eve of the CADE conference I met with the directorate of the Plan for Governing for a practice session in answering the predictable objections of the panel and the audience.

After describing the impoverishment of Peru in recent decades and the contribution of the Aprista government to the cataclysm ("Those who, taking Señor Alan García Pérez at his word, as set forth in his speech at this same forum in 1984, invested their entire savings, made a miserable deal: today they have less than 2 percent of their savings left"), I explained our proposal for "saving Peru from mediocrity, from demagoguery, from hunger, from underemployment, and from terror." From the very start, coming straight to the point, I made the aim of our reforms clear: "We already have political freedom. But Peru has never really tried to follow the path of economic freedom, without which any democracy is imperfect and condemned to poverty . . . All our efforts will be directed toward turning Peru from the country of proletarians, the unemployed, and the privileged elites that it is today into a country of entrepreneurs, property owners, and citizens equal before the law."

I promised to take on the task of leading the fight against terrorism and mobilizing civil society, arming peasant patrols and making every effort to have this example of self-defense be imitated in urban and rural centers of production. Civil authorities and institutions would again take control of the emergency zones that had been entrusted to the military.

This step would be a strong one, but one within the law. There must be an end to the violations of human rights committed by the forces of order in their antisubversive campaign: the legitimacy of democracy depended on it. Peasants and humble Peruvians would never aid the government in confronting the terrorists as long as they felt that police and soldiers were riding roughshod over them. In order

---

* *Acción para el cambio: el programa de gobierno del Frente Democrático* (Lima, December 1989).

to demonstrate my administration's resolve not to tolerate abuses of this sort, I had decided—as I outlined to Ian Martin, the secretary general of Amnesty International, who visited me on May 4, 1990—to appoint a commissioner of human rights, who would have an office in the Presidential Palace. In the following months, after shuffling through many names, I asked Lucho Bustamante to sound out Diego García Sayán, a young attorney who had founded the Andean Committee of Jurists and who, although he had ties to the United Left, seemed capable of carrying out the duties of this post impartially. This commissioner would not be appointed simply for show; he would have powers to follow up on complaints and accusations, to conduct investigations on his own, to initiate court proceedings, to draft projects for informing and educating public opinion, in schools, labor unions, agricultural communes, barracks, and police headquarters.

In addition to this commissioner, there would be another who would be responsible for the national program of privatization, a key reform of the program, that I too wanted to follow closely. Both commissioners would have ministerial rank. For this latter task I had designated Javier Silva Ruete, who at that time was the head of the program for privatization.

The first year would be the most difficult stage, owing to the inevitable recessionary nature of the anti-inflationary policy, the aim of which was to reduce the increase in prices to 10 percent per year. In the next two years—of liberalization and of major reforms—the increase in production, employment, and revenues would be moderate. But from the fourth year on, we would enter a very dynamic period, on a solid foundation, in which employment and revenues would increase. Peru would have begun the takeoff toward freedom accompanied by material well-being.

I explained all the reforms, beginning with the most controversial ones, from the privatization of public enterprises—it would begin with some seventy firms, among them the Banco Continental, the Society Paramonga, the Empresa Minera Tintaya, AeroPerú, Entel Perú, the Compañía de Teléfonos, the Banco Internacional, the Banco Popular, Entur Perú, Popular y Porvenir Compañía de Seguros, EPSEP, Laboratorios Unidos, and the Reaseguradora Peruana, and would continue until the whole of the public sector had been handed over to private hands—until the present number of ministries had been cut in half.

In education, I anticipated a thoroughgoing reform, so that equality of opportunity would at last be possible. Only if poor Peruvian children and young people received a high-level technical or professional education would they have equal status for getting ahead in life along with those children and young people from families with middle and high incomes who could attend private schools and universities. In order to raise the educational level of the poor, it was necessary to reform the programs of study so that they would take into account the cultural, regional, and linguistic heterogeneity of Peruvian society, modernize the training given teachers, pay them good salaries and give them well-equipped schools, with libraries, laboratories, and an adequate infrastructure. Did the impoverished Peruvian state have any way to finance this reform? Of course not. For that, we would have to put an end to the indiscriminate access to a free education. After the third year of secondary school, it would be replaced by a system of scholarships and grants, so that those who were in a position to do so would finance, in whole or in part, their own education. No student who lacked financial resources would be left without a secondary school or a university education; but middle and high income families would contribute to giving the poor the means to acquire an education that would prepare them to emerge from poverty. Parents would participate in the administration of the school centers and in determining the contributions made by each family.

Almost immediately, this proposal was used against us and became one of the most fiery warhorses sent into battle against the Front. Apristas, Socialists, and Communists proclaimed that they would defend "free education" with their lives, maintaining that we wanted to do away with it so that not only having enough to eat and having a job, but also getting an education would be a privilege of the rich alone. And a few days after my speech at CADE, Fernando Belaunde came to my house with a memorandum, reminding me that a free education was a firm plank in the Popular Action campaign platform. They would not abandon it. Populist leaders began to make statements along the same lines. The criticisms of the allied parties assumed such proportions that I called a meeting of all the parties of the Democratic Front in the Freedom Movement in order to discuss this measure. The meeting was a stormy one. In it, León Trahtenberg, the chairman of the committee on education, was relentlessly questioned by the populists Andrés Cardó Franco, Gastón Acurio, and others.

I myself intervened in the argument, on that and other occasions, as the defender of our proposal. It is demagoguery to uphold in principle universal free education, if the result of it is that three children out of four study in schools that lack libraries, laboratories, bathrooms, desks, and blackboards, and often even ceilings and walls, that teachers receive inadequate training and earn starvation wages, and that therefore only the young people of the middle and upper classes—who can afford to pay for good schools and good universities—receive an education that assures them of a successful professional career.

In my conversation with Belaunde I made myself very clear: I would not yield on this or any other point of our program. I had given in when it came to the municipal elections and the congressional lists, allowing Popular Action and the Christian Popular Party a great many advantages, but when it came to the Plan for Governing I would make no concessions. The one reason why I wanted to be president was to carry out *those* reforms. The educational one was among the most important, since it was aimed at putting an end to one of the most unjust forms of cultural discrimination: that stemming from differences in income.

Finally, although we were unable to keep dissident voices within the alliance from speaking out against this measure from time to time, we managed to get Popular Action, against their will, to put up with it. But our adversaries continued to attack us mercilessly on the subject, with advertising campaigns and pronunciamentos by teachers' unions and associations in defense of "popular education." The campaign was such that León Trahtenberg himself sent me his letter of resignation from the committee (I did not accept it) and came to me, at the beginning of January 1990, to propose that we retreat from our position, in view of the negative reactions. With the backing of Lucho Bustamante, I insisted that it was our duty, since the measure seemed to us to be necessary, to go on defending it. But despite my constant preaching about it—from that time on, in all my speeches I brought the subject up—this was one of the reforms that frightened the voters most and made a fair number of them decide to vote against me.

I am writing these lines in August 1991, and I see, by clippings from newspapers in Lima, that the teachers in state schools—380,000 of them—have been on strike for five months, in despair over their living conditions. Pupils in public schools risk missing out on the entire year of studies. And even if they don't, a person can easily imagine what, with the huge parenthesis of five months of no schooling, this year will mean for these students in academic terms. The bishop of Huaraz states in a magazine that it is a scandal that the average pay of a schoolteacher is scarcely more than a hundred dollars a month, which means that they and their families go hungry. For five months now, because of the strike, all the state schools have been closed, and since the new administration took office the state has not built a single classroom, because of a lack of funds. But education continues to be free and Peruvians should congratulate themselves that the great victory of the people was not cast aside!

This controversy taught me a great deal about the power of ideological myth, which is able to completely replace reality. Because the free public education that my adversaries defended so zealously was nonexistent, a dead letter. For some time, the well-nigh total bankruptcy of the nation's treasury kept the state from erecting schools, and the immense majority of classrooms that were constructed in marginal districts and young towns to meet the growing demand were built by the people of the neighborhood themselves. And the parents also took over the maintenance, the cleaning, and the repair of the national primary and secondary schools because of the inability of the state to cover these expenses.

Every time I toured a poor neighborhood, in Lima or in the provinces, I visited a number of schools. "Did the government build these classrooms?" "No! We did!" Owing to the economic crisis, it had been some time since the Peruvian state had contributed anything except the teachers' salaries. The parents had filled the vacuum by taking it upon themselves to build and maintain the schools in the poorest neighborhoods and districts in the country. In my speeches I always emphasized that, in just a couple of years, our Solidarity program had built, thanks to donations, volunteer work, and the collaboration of the local residents, more day-care centers and schoolrooms than the Peruvian state. Moreover, Enrique Ghersi discovered that that same Aprista government that harped day and night on the threat to free public education had passed measures that required parents who enrolled their children in state schools to pay "fees" to parents' associations which would go to a national education fund. Like many other unrealistic measures, making education free, which had served only to do further harm to the poor by increasing discrimination, had gradually been modified in practice, owing to the force of circumstances.

I placed great hopes in the reform of education. I was convinced that the most effective way to achieve justice in Peru was high-level public instruction. Sometimes I pointed out that I had studied in public schools, such as Leoncio Prado and San Miguel in Piura, and at the University of San Marcos, so that I knew the defects of the system (although they had grown worse since my days as a student). But these efforts to persuade my compatriots of the sound principles underlying our proposed reform of education were useless, and those who accused me of wanting to keep the people ignorant prevailed.

Two other reforms that I announced at the CADE were also the object of fierce attacks: that of the labor market and the new model for government employment. The former was made out by my adversaries to be a clever way of allowing entrepreneurs to fire their workers, and the latter to be a plan to turn out half a million public employees into the streets. (In a video against us that managed, in less than a minute, to pile up, one on top of the other, plagiarism [it repeated images from Pink Floyd's *The Wall*], distortion, and slander, the government pictured me, disfigured by fangs à la Dracula, as bringing on an apocalyptic shock, in which factories were closed, prices shot into the stratosphere, children were thrown out of schools, and workers out of their jobs, and the entire country blew up in a nuclear explosion.)

Like free education, job security is a false social victory, which, instead of protecting the good worker against arbitrary dismissal, has turned into a mechanism for protecting the inefficient worker, and an obstacle to the creation of jobs for those who need work—in Peru, at the end of 1989, seven out of every ten adults. Job security favored 11 percent of the economically active population. It was, then, a small minority that had job security and an income that ensured that the number of unemployed would remain constant. The laws protecting the worker meant that, after a trial period of three months, a worker turned into the owner of his job, from which it was practically impossible to remove him, since the "just cause" for his dismissal referred to in the Constitution had been reduced, by the laws in force at that time, to a "grave dereliction of duty," something almost impossible to prove. The result was that companies functioned with a minimum of personnel and hesitated before expanding for fear of finding themselves later on with the dead weight of a payroll that was too large. In a country where unemployment and underemployment affected two-thirds of the population and where creating work for the immense majority was an extremely urgent necessity, it was imperative to give the principle of job security a genuinely *social* meaning.

Explaining that I would respect rights already won—the reforms would affect only those newly hired—I enumerated at CADE the principal measures needed to mitigate the negative effects of job security: lack of productivity would be included among the just causes for dismissal, the trial period for evaluating the worker's ability would be extended, commercial enterprises would be offered a vast range of possibilities for hiring temporary workers that would allow them to adjust their work force to market variations, and to combat unemployment among young people, contracts for training and apprenticeship, part-time work, and contracts for rotating workers and early retirement would be drawn up. In addition, the worker would be allowed to set himself up as a private and autonomous business and negotiate with the employer for providing his services on a contract basis. Within this package of measures, the democratization of the right to strike was also included, which up to that time had been the monopoly of the highest levels of the union hierarchy, and which, in many cases, forced the rest of the workers to go out on strike through a sort of blackmail. Strikes would be decided on by secret, direct, and universal vote; strikes that affected vital public services and strikes in support of other unions or associations would be prohibited; the practice of taking hostages and occupying work sites, as an adjunct to union work stoppages, would be penalized.

(In March 1990, during our congress on "La revolución de la libertad"—"The Revolution of Freedom"—Sir Alan Walters, who had been one of Margaret Thatcher's advisers, assured me that these measures would have a favorable effect on the creation of jobs. He reproached me, I admit, for not having been as radical with regard to the minimum wage, which we were going to maintain. "It appears to be an act of justice," he said to me. "But it is one only for *those who are working*. The minimum wage is an injustice for those who have lost their job or enter the labor market and find all the doors shut. To benefit these latter, those most in need of social justice, the minimum wage is an injustice, an obstacle that blocks their path to employment. The countries where there are the most jobs are those in which the market is freest.")

I explained, particularly on visits to factories, that an efficient worker is too expensive for businesses to let him go, and that our reforms would not affect rights already won, but would apply only to *new* workers, those millions of Peruvians who were unemployed or who had miserable jobs, whom we had the duty to help by quickly creating work for them. I can see why workers alienated by populist preaching were bound to be hostile, because they didn't understand these reforms, or because they understood them and feared them. But the fact that the majority of the unemployed, in whose favor these reforms were conceived, should vote massively against *these* changes in particular says a great deal about the formidable dead weight of populist culture, which leads those who are most discriminated against and exploited to vote in favor of the system that keeps them in that condition.

As for the half million public employees, it is worth telling the entire story, because this subject, like that of free education, had a devastating effect in my disfavor among the humble sectors and because it shows how effective dirty tricks can be in politics. The news that, once I took office, I would throw 500,000 bureaucrats out into the streets appeared in that great orchestrator of out-and-out lies, *La República*,* as a statement that Enrique Ghersi, the "young Turk" of the Freedom Movement, had supposedly made in Chile, to a Chilean journalist.† In fact, Ghersi hadn't said any such thing and he hastened to deny this piece of information, once he returned to Peru, in the press§ and on television. A while later, the Chilean journalist himself, Fernando Villegas, came to Lima and denied this cock-and-bull story,** in the

---

* Lima, August 9, 1989, p. 3.
† The interview with Ghersi appeared in the Santiago *El Diario* (in the section Finance–Economy–Business) of August 4, 1989, and in it there is a discussion in general terms regarding whittling down the bureaucracy, but no specific figure is mentioned.
§ *Expreso*, Lima, August 10, 1989, p. 4.
** *Ojo*, Lima, December 22, 1989.

daily papers and on TV. But by this point the concerted lies regarding the 500,000 employees, organized by a cabal consisting of *La República*, *Hoy*, *La Crónica*, and the state-run radio stations and TV channels, had become an incontrovertible truth. Even leaders of the Democratic Front, my allies, were convinced of it, since some of them, such as the PPC leader Ricardo Amiel and the populist Javier Alva Orlandini, confirmed the falsehood in their statements to the press instead of denying it—by criticizing Ghersi for the slanderous untruth they attributed to him!*

What is certain is that neither Ghersi nor anyone in the Front could have said any such thing, because there was no way of determining how many public employees were superfluous, since there was no way of even knowing how many of them there were. The Democratic Front had a committee, headed by Dr. María Reynafarje, trying to determine the number, and it had tracked down more than a million (excluding the members of the armed forces), but the evaluation was still going on. Naturally, this bureaucratic inflation had to be drastically reduced, so that the state would have only those functionaries it needed. But the transference from the public sector to the private of the tens or hundreds of thousands of excess bureaucrats was not going to be accomplished through untimely dismissals. We were aware of the problem, and my administration, not only for legal and ethical reasons, but also for practical ones, was not going to make the stupid mistake of beginning its term in office by making this problem many times worse. Our plan was to painlessly relocate unneeded bureaucrats. This process of decanting would go on gradually as, with the reforms, economic growth started, new business concerns came into being, and the ones that already existed began to work at full capacity. This process would be speeded up by the government, through incentives to bring about voluntary resignations or early retirements. Without trampling anyone's rights underfoot, doing our best to encourage the market to carry out the relocation, a good part of the bureaucracy would pass over to the civil sector—a good part, although at this juncture the exact number could not be determined.

* See the statements by Ricardo Amiel in *La República* and in *La Crónica*, August 6, 1989, and that of Javier Alva Orlandini in *El Nacional*, November 30, 1989.

But fiction routed reality. In perfect synchronization, the moment the falsehood was printed in *La República* (with huge headlines on the front page), the government began its campaign, via the radio stations and the TV channels it controlled and via its fanatical followers, distributing millions of leaflets throughout the country, and repeating daily, in every possible form, through all its mouthpieces, from its leaders to its shadiest newsmongers, the rumor that I would begin my administration by firing half a million government employees. Declarations, denials, explanations, from me, from Ghersi, or from those in charge of the Plan for Governing, were of no use whatsoever.

From a very early age I have lived my life fascinated by fiction and the spell it casts, because my vocation has made me highly sensitive to that phenomenon. And I have long since realized how far the realm of fiction extends beyond the bounds of literature, cinema, and the arts, genres in which it is thought to be confined. Perhaps because it is an irresistible necessity that the human species tries to satisfy in one way or another, even by unimaginable ways of behaving, fiction makes its appearance everywhere, crops up in religion and in science and in activities more obviously vaccinated against it. Politics, particularly in countries where ignorance and passions play as important a role in it as they do in Peru, is one of those fields that has been well fertilized so that what is fictitious, what is imaginary, will take root. I had many chances to verify this during the campaign, above all with regard to the subject of the half a million bureaucrats threatened by my liberal ax.

The left immediately joined the campaign and there were union agreements, manifestoes in protest and repudiations, public demonstrations of government employees and workers at which they burned me in effigy or carried coffins about the streets with my name on them.

The apogee was a judicial proceeding against me, initiated by the CITE (Confederación Intersectorial de Trabajadores Estatales: Intersectorial Confederation of State Workers), a union group controlled by the left that had been seeking legal recognition for some time. Alan García hastened to grant it now, for that very purpose. The CITE initiated what, in legal jargon, is called "a proceeding preparatory to an admission of guilt" before the judiciary because of "the risk of losing their jobs confronted by its members." I was summoned before the

26th Civil Court of Lima. Besides being grotesque, the matter was a
legal absurdity, as even adversaries like the Socialist senator Enrique
Bernales, for instance, and the Aprista representative Héctor Vargas
Haya declared.

In the executive and political committees of Libertad we discussed
whether I should appear before the judge, or whether this was tantamount to collaborating with Alan García's Machiavellian tactics, permitting the hostile press to cause a great uproar over me, brought
before the bar in the Palace of Justice by workers threatened with
dismissal. We decided that only my attorney would appear. I entrusted
this mission to Enrique Chirinos Soto, a member of the political
committee of Libertad, which I had invited to advise me. Enrique,
an independent senator, journalist, historian, and an authority on the
Constitution, was one of those liberals of yesteryear, like Arturo Salazar
Larraín, educated alongside Don Pedro Beltrán. A journalist whose
opinion carried weight, a subtle political analyst, a conservative without
complexes, and a staunch Catholic, Enrique is one of the intelligent
politicians—despite being a little scatterbrained—that have appeared
in Peru, and a native Arequipan who has been able to maintain the
legal tradition of his home territory. He almost always attended the
meetings of the political committee, during which he was in the habit
of remaining completely silent and motionless, giving off an aroma
of good Scotch whisky, in a sort of voluntary catatonia. Every so often,
something would arouse him from his geologic torpor and impel him
to speak: his contributions to the discussion were wondrously clear-
sighted and helped us to surmount complicated problems. Every once
in a while, remembering his function as adviser, he sent me little
notes that I read with delight: descriptions of the political situation at
the moment, tactical advice, or simply comments on what was going
on at the time, written with great wit and humor. (None of his many
talents kept him, however, from making a monumental blunder between the first and the second round of voting.) Enrique was a brilliant
polemicist and easily proved to the court the legal impertinence of the
CITE's accusation.

On January 2, the judge of the 26th Civil Court of Lima backed
down on his decision to force me to appear, and declared the CITE's
request for a hearing null and void. CITE appealed and Chirinos Soto
made an outstanding impression with his oral report before the bar of

the Civil Superior Court of Lima, on January 16, 1990, which confirmed the lower court's decision.*

As a colophon to this episode, I shall point out a curious coincidence. During Alan García's administration, because of the inflation coupled with recession—so-called stagflation—analysts calculated that in Peru some half a million jobs were lost, the same figure that, according to his campaign, I was planning to eliminate from the government's payroll. The subject would provide material for an essay on the Freudian theory of transference and, surely, for a politics-fiction novel.

Another radical measure that I announced at the CADE conference did not, however, cause any significant repercussions: the reform of General Velasco's agrarian reform, which was still in force. Our adversaries' failure to mount a big campaign against this issue was due, perhaps, to the fact that the present arrangements in rural Peru—above all, in the state-run cooperatives and SAIS (Sociedades Agrarias de Interés Social)—were so clearly repudiated by the peasants that our adversaries would have had a hard time attempting to defend the status quo. Or, perhaps, because the peasant vote—thanks to the mass migration to the cities in recent decades—today represents barely 35 percent of the national electorate (and absenteeism at the polls is higher in the country than in the city).

In agriculture too we proposed to introduce a market economy, by privatizing it, so that the transference from enterprises under complete or partial state control to civil society would serve to create a large number of independent owners and entrepreneurs. Much of this reform was already under way, through the efforts of the peasants themselves, who, as I have said, had gradually been parceling out the cooperatives—dividing them up into individual private plots of land—despite the fact that this was forbidden by law. Their action had affected two-thirds of the rural areas of the country, but it had no legal validity. The movement of the *parceleros*, born independently, in opposition to the parties and the unions of the left, had for years represented a hopeful sign to me—like that of the *informales*, those earning their living from the parallel economy. The fact that the poorest of the poor had opted for private enterprise, for emancipation

* Chirinos Soto's report was published in *El Comercio*, Lima, January 23, 1990.

from state tutelage, was, even though they themselves didn't know it, a resounding demonstration that the doctrines of collectivism and state ownership had been repudiated by the Peruvian people and that, through this trying experience, they were discovering the advantages of liberal democracy. And so, on June 4, 1989, in the Plaza de Armas of Arequipa, on declaring my candidacy, the *parceleros* and the *informales* were the heroes of my speech; I referred to them by calling them the spearhead of the transformation for which I was seeking the vote of Peruvians.

(My campaign strategy was based, in large part, on the supposition that *parceleros* and *informales* would be the principal support for my candidacy. That is to say, I foresaw a campaign in which I would manage to persuade these sectors that what they were doing, in the cities and in the countryside, corresponded to the reforms that I wanted to carry out. I failed without question: the immense majority of *parceleros* and *informales* voted against me—rather than in favor of my adversary—having been frightened off by my antipopulist preaching; in other words, they voted in defense of the populism against which they had been the first to rebel.)

The reform of the agrarian reform was to be accomplished by giving title deeds to the members of cooperatives that had decided on the privatization of the collectivized landholdings and by creating legal procedures so that other cooperatives could imitate them. Privatization would not be obligatory. Those cooperatives that wanted to continue as such could do so, but without state subsidies. As for the large sugar refineries on the coast—Casagrande, Huando, Cayaltí, for instance —the government would offer them technical advice as to how to turn themselves into private companies, and their members into stockholders.

The run-down condition of these refineries—at one time the principal exporters and drawers of foreign capital to Peru—was the product of the inefficiency and the corruption that the system of government control had introduced into them. Under private and competitive management they could recover and serve to create jobs and foster rural development, since they owned the richest landed properties with the best intercommunications in the entire country.

The reform of the system of land ownership would create hundreds of thousands of new owners and entrepreneurs in the country, who could get ahead, thanks to an open system, without the obstacles and discrimination of which agricultural areas had always been a victim by comparison with the cities. There would no longer be the price controls on agricultural produce that had doomed entire regions to ruin, or impelled them to produce coca—regions where the peasants were obliged to sell their produce below cost, with the consequence that Peru now imported a large part of its food. (I repeat that this system permitted memorable chicanery: the privileged who had been granted import licenses, who received undervalued dollars, could, in just one of these operations, leave accounts abroad amounting to millions of dollars. As I write these lines, in fact, the magazine *Oiga** has just revealed that one of Alan García's ministers of agriculture, a member of his circle of intimates, Remigio Morales Bermúdez—the son of the ex-dictator—deposited in the Atlantic Security Bank, in Miami, more than twenty million dollars during his term in office!) With a market economy, farmers would receive fair prices for their produce, determined by supply and demand, and would have the necessary incentives to invest in agriculture, to modernize their techniques of cultivating crops, and pay taxes on their incomes sufficient to permit the state to improve the infrastructure of roads and highways that had deteriorated and nearly disappeared in certain regions. The familiar spectacle in the last years of the Aprista regime of tons of rice produced by the impoverished growers of the *departamento* of San Martín rotting in warehouses while Peru wasted tens of millions of dollars importing rice—and on the side, enriching a handful of bigwigs with political pull—would not be repeated. This was another constant subject of my speeches, especially to audiences of peasants: the reforms would immediately benefit millions of Peruvians who were barely scratching out a living; liberalization would bring rapid growth to agriculture, livestock raising, and agroindustry and a social restructuring that favored those who were poorest. But in my innumerable trips to the highlands and the mountains, I always noted the resistance of country people, above all the most primitive of them, to allowing themselves to be convinced. Because of centuries of mistrust and frustration, doubtless, and because of my own inability to formulate this message in a convincing way. Even in the periods of my candidacy's

* *Oiga*, Lima, August 12, 1991.

greatest popularity, the places where I noted the strongest rejection were the rural regions. Puno in particular, one of the most miserably poor *departamentos* (and one of those richest in history and in natural beauty) of the country. All my tours of Puno were the object of violent counterdemonstrations. On March 18, 1989, in the city of Puno, Beatriz Merino, after delivering her speech without letting herself be intimidated by a crowd that booed her and shouted "Get out of here, Aunt Julia!" at her (the scant applause we received came from a handful of members of the PPC, since AP had boycotted the rally), fainted from the shock and from the 12,000-foot altitude and had to be given oxygen right there on the spot, in one corner of the speakers' platform. On the following day, March 19, in Juliaca, Miguel Cruchaga and I were almost unable to give our speeches, because of the catcalls and the racist shouts ("Get out of here, you Spanish!"). On another tour, on February 10 and 11, 1990, our leaders had me suddenly appear in the stadium, during the celebration of Candlemas, and I have already recounted how we were greeted by a shower of stones thrown at us, which thanks to the reflexes of Professor Oshiro didn't harm me, but made me fall ignominiously to the ground. The rally to mark the close of the campaign, on March 26, 1990, in the main square, was very well attended, and the efforts by groups of troublemakers to break it up did not succeed. But our hopes because of the large crowd were sheer illusion, since in both the first and the second round my lowest percentage of votes in Peru was in that *departamento*.

At CADE I also put forward the plans to privatize the postal and customs services and to reform the tax system, but only mentioned in passing many other subjects because of the time limit. Among these subjects, the one that mattered most to me was privatization. I had been working for some time on it with Javier Silva Ruete.

Javier, whom the readers of my books are more or less acquainted with, since—with due regard for the distances that separate fiction and reality—he had served me as the model for the Javier of my first short stories and of *Aunt Julia and the Scriptwriter*, had had an outstanding career as an economist and had occupied important political posts. After graduating from San Marcos, he had honed his skills in Italy, and worked in the Central Reserve Bank. He was Belaunde Terry's youngest minister during his first term in office—at the time Javier was a member of the Christian Democratic Party—and, after that, secretary general of the Andean Pact. When General Velasco was overthrown by the coup hatched in the Presidential Palace, his successor, General Morales Bermúdez, named Silva Ruete minister of finance, and his direction of the ministry put an end to certain upheavals of the Velasco regime, such as inflation and the exclusion from international organizations. The group that, with Javier, managed the economy during that period had formed the nucleus of the small political association of technical experts and professionals, SODE, that formed part of the Democratic Front (Manuel Moreyra had been the president of the Central Bank at the same time that Silva Ruete was minister of finance). The people of SODE, such as Moreyra, Alonso Polar, Guillermo van Ordt, Raúl Salazar himself, and several others, had had a prime role in the drawing up of our Plan for Governing and I invariably found in them support for the reforms we proposed and allies against the resistances to the reforms on the part of AP or the PPC.

In order to get Popular Action to accept the incorporation of SODE as part of the Democratic Front I had had to perform miracles, since Belaunde Terry and the populists had strong prejudices against it because of SODE's collaboration with the military dictatorship and because of the extremely tough stand that SODE, particularly Manolo Moreyra and Javier Silva, had taken against Belaunde Terry's second term. There was the further fact that SODE had collaborated with Alan García during his electoral campaign, having been his ally for a time, and from whose congressional lists two members of SODE had been elected, Javier to the Senate and Aurelio Loret de Mola to the Chamber of Representatives. Silva Ruete, moreover, had been an adviser to Alan García in the latter's first year in office. But I made a point of emphasizing to Belaunde how SODE had broken with the APRA since the days of the nationalization of the banks, supporting our campaign very actively, and how indispensable it was to have in our administration a team of high-level technical experts. Belaunde and Bedoya finally reluctantly gave in, but never felt very happy with this ally.

It made both of them uneasy, moreover, that Javier Silva Ruete was one of the owners of La República, that loathsome monster of a daily paper. Born under the editorship of Guillermo Thorndike, that specialist in sleaze, as a yellow scandal sheet, tireless in the exploitation or fabrication of sensationalism—crimes, gossip, denunciations, gruesome stories, human smut frenetically exhibited—*La República*, without ceasing to exploit this sort of filth, at the same time immediately turned into the mouthpiece of the APRA and of the United Left, in a case of political schizophrenia improbable in any country but Peru. The explanation of this hybrid was, apparently, the fact that among the owners of *La República* there was a perfect balance between the power of Senator Gustavo Mohme (a Communist) and that of Carlos Maraví (a fervent nouveau-riche Aprista), who had arrived at the opera buffa formula of placing the news stories and editorials of the daily in the service of these two masters who were each other's enemies. Javier's role in this complicated situation and amid people of that sort—his name appeared on the masthead as chairman of the board of directors of the company that published *La República*—was always a mystery to me. I never asked him why he had done as he did nor did we speak of the subject, since both he and I wanted to maintain a friendship that had meant a great deal to both of us since we were youngsters and we tried not to put it to the test by subjecting it to the treacherous pressures of politics.

We had seen very little of each other when he was a minister during the military dictatorship and while he was an adviser to Alan García. But when we did occasionally run into each other, at some social get-together, our mutual affection was always there, stronger than anything else. At the time of the events at Uchuraccay, after the report of the commission which I wrote and defended publicly, *La República* carried out a campaign against me that lasted for many weeks, in which false testimony and lies were followed by insults, by extremes of monomania. The substance of the attack pained me less than the fact that all these insults appeared in a newspaper owned by one of my oldest friends. But our friendship survived even this experience. This was another argument that I used with Belaunde and Bedoya to win their approval for including SODE in the Democratic Front: *La República* had vented its fury on few people as mercilessly as it had on me. It was necessary, then, to cast suspicion aside and trust that Javier and his group would behave decently toward the Front.

SODE's change of attitude came about as a result of the campaign to nationalize banking. Manuel Moreyra was one of the first to condemn the step, from Arequipa, where he happened to be, and he devoted countless statements, lectures, and articles to the subject. His resolve caused all of his colleagues to follow his lead and precipitated the break between SODE and the APRA. SODE's two members of Congress, Silva Ruete and Loret de Mola, fought the measure in the two legislative bodies. From that time on, there had been close collaboration between SODE and the Freedom Movement.

The reasons why I asked Javier confidentially to lead the committee on privatization were his competence and his capacity for work. In the first months of 1989 we talked, in his study, and I asked him if he was ready to assume that task, keeping in mind the following: the privatization was to include the whole of the public sector and be planned in such a way as to permit the creation of new owners among the workers and employees of the privatized enterprises and the consumers of their services. He agreed. The main objective of the transference to civil society of public enterprises would not be technical—to reduce the fiscal deficit, to provide the state with revenue—but social: to multiply the number of private shareholders in the country, to give millions of Peruvians with small incomes access to ownership. With his characteristic enthusiasm, Javier told me that from that moment on he would abandon all his other activities to devote himself body and soul to that program.

With a small team, in a separate office, and with funds from the campaign budget, he worked for an entire year making a survey of the nearly two hundred public enterprises and setting up a system and a sequence for privatization, which was to begin on a precise date, July 28, 1990. Javier sought advice in all the countries with experience of privatization, such as Great Britain, Chile, Spain, and a number of others, and began negotiations with the International Monetary Fund, the World Bank, and the Inter-American Bank for Development. Every so often, he and his team gave me progress reports on their work, and when it was finished, I invited foreign economists—the Spaniard Pedro Schwartz and the Chilean José Piñera, for instance—to give us their opinion. The result was a solid and thoroughgoing program that combined technical rigor and the will to change on the one hand and creative boldness on the other. It gave me genuine satisfaction when I was able to read the thick volumes and verify that the plan was a marvelous instrument to break the back of one of the principal sources of corruption and injustice in Peru.

Javier, who had agreed to be the head of the committee on privatization, also agreed not to be a candidate for Congress, so as to devote himself full time to this reform.

The reaction of the media and of public opinion to my speech at CADE was one of consternation at the magnitude of the reforms and the frankness with which they were put forth, and widespread recognition that, among the four speakers, I had been the only one to present a complete plan for governing (the magazine *Caretas* spoke of the "Vargas Coup"). * On December 5, I had a working breakfast at the Hotel Sheraton with some hundred foreign journalists and correspondents, to whom I gave further details concerning the program.

My speech at the CADE conference was to be preceded and continued by a publicity campaign, in newspapers, on radio and on television, to disclose the reforms in the C and D sectors. This campaign, which began very well, in the first months of 1989, was then interrupted for various reasons, one of them being the quarrels and tensions within the Front, and another, an unfortunate spot on TV that showed a little monkey urinating.

José Salmón was responsible for the media campaign, and collaborated very well with Lucho Llosa, my brother-in-law, whom I had asked, because of his experience as a filmmaker and a television producer, to advise me in this field. During the campaign against nationalization and in the early days of Libertad, the two of them were in charge of all advertising and publicity. Then, when the Democratic Front was set up, the campaign manager, Freddy Cooper, who didn't get along well either with Salmón or with Lucho, began to call more and more for publicity on the company owned by the brothers Ricardo and Daniel Winitsky, who also prepared TV spots on their own. (I shall be more specific and add that, like Jorge Salmón, the Winitskys did so in order to lend the Front their support and without charging us any fees for their services.) From that time on, in this touchy field, there was a bifurcation or parallelism that, at one moment, led to chaos and caused serious harm to the "campaign of ideas" that we ought to have waged.

At the beginning of 1989 Daniel Winitsky planned a series of TV ads using animals to promote the ideas of Libertad. The first one, with

* "Vargas Llosa's speech at CADE was unquestionably impressive, but more than one of his listeners is already trembling." *Caretas*, Lima, December 4, 1989.

a tortoise, was amusing and everybody liked it. The second one, with a fish, in which Patricia, my children, and I were to participate, never got filmed: the fish died of asphyxiation, clouds hid the sun, sudden sandstorms thwarted the takes on the deserted beach at Villa where we tried to film it one morning. With the third ad, disaster overtook us, all because of a little monkey. Daniel had had an idea for a very brief spot, showing the damage wrought by the ever-increasing number of bureaucrats. In it a public employee, transformed into a monkey, was shown in his office, where, instead of working, he was reading the newspaper, yawning, loafing about, and even pissing on his desk. Freddy showed me the spot on a hectic afternoon packed tight with interviews and meetings, and I didn't see anything shocking about it, except for a certain vulgarity that, perhaps, wouldn't upset the audience it was aimed at, so I gave it my okay. This tactlessness would no doubt have been caught and corrected if the spot in question had been analyzed by the person responsible for media advertising, Jorge Salmón, or by Lucho Llosa, but because of his personal antipathies toward them which, at times, interfered with his work, Freddy went over both their heads, seeking only my approval for the spot ads. In this case, we paid the price for our indiscretion.

The little micturating monkey caused a major scandal, with both supporters and adversaries of Libertad finding it distasteful, and the Apristas made good use of the uproar. Upstanding ladies who were offended sent letters to newspapers and magazines or appeared on television protesting against the "vulgarity" of the ad, and government leaders appeared on the little screen, upset because self-sacrificing public employees were being ridiculed in that way, comparing them to animals. So that was how Vargas Llosa was going to treat them when he became president, like monkeys or dogs or rats or something even worse . . . There were editorials, apologies to government functionaries, and my house and the Freedom Movement received many calls from supporters urging us to take the spot in question off the TV channels. We had already done so, of course, once we realized how counterproductive it had turned out to be, but the administration saw to it that it continued to be shown on television for several days longer. And, up until the eve of the elections, the state-run channel kept bringing it back to the screen.

Criticisms of the little monkey were forthcoming from our allies as well, and even Lourdes Flores, the young attorney who had been our candidate for representative major of Lima, admonished us in a public speech for our lack of tact. The affair reached its peak when, in *Caretas*, Jorge Salmón was criticized for an ad that he hadn't even been consulted about. But Jorge, in this and in other unpleasant incidents of which he was the victim during the campaign, showed a gentlemanliness that equaled his loyalty to me.

A while later, when the time came to begin the "campaign of ideas," in order to prepare public opinion for our launching of the program, both Jorge Salmón and the Winitskys, with Daniel now recovered from the setback of the peeing monkey, presented me—each team on its own—with a plan. Jorge's was politic and prudent; it avoided polemics and confrontation, and avoided giving precise details about the reforms, emphasizing, above all, the "positive" aspects: the need for peace, work, modernization. I appeared as the restorer of collaboration and fraternity among Peruvians. The Winitskys' plan, on the other hand, was for a sequence in which each spot, in a very lively but also a very blatant way, focused on the evils that we were trying to face up to—inflation, state control, bureaucracy, international isolation, terrorism, discrimination against the poor, an ineffective educational system—and the remedies for them: fiscal discipline, restructuring of the state, privatization, reform of education, mobilization of the peasantry. I liked the Winitskys' project a lot and approved of it, something that Salmón accepted, with a fine sense of fair play. And Lucho Llosa directed the filming of the first two "educational" spots.

Both of them were excellent and the opinion polls we took to check on their impact on the C and D sectors were encouraging. The first one showed the damage caused by inflation suffered by those who lived on a fixed income and the only way to put an end to it—by drastically reducing the printing of money without backing—and the second one, the paralyzing effects that government intervention had on production, stifling private enterprises and preventing the emergence of other new ones, and how, with a free market, there would be incentives for the creation of jobs.

Why was this sequence interrupted, after my speech at CADE, when it was so necessary to publicize the reforms? I can give only a tentative explanation of something that, obviously, was a grave error.

I believe that, at first, we didn't go on filming the new spots planned by Winitsky because of the approach of the year-end holidays. We had special ads made for Christmas, and Patricia and I each recorded separate holiday greetings. Then, in January of 1990, when we should have gone on with the "campaign of ideas," we found ourselves confronted by the tremendous amount of publicity put out to discredit us, in which every effort was made to present our proposal in a false light by attacking me personally, by making me out to be an atheist, a pornographer, a practicer of incest, an accomplice of the murderers of Uchuraccay, a tax evader, and a number of other horrors.

It was a mistake to try to refute the lies of this campaign through ads on television, instead of sticking to publicizing our proposed reforms. In allowing ourselves to be dragged into an area of controversy in which we had everything to lose, all we accomplished was to see my image cheapened by petty political maneuvering. Mark Malloch Brown was right when he insisted that we shouldn't pay any attention to the mudslinging campaign. I thought so too, but after the first days in January, my hectic activities were such that I no longer had sense enough to mend the error. At that point, moreover, it was too late to do so, since something had begun that inflicted another grave blow on the Front: the chaotic and wasteful television campaign of our congressional candidates.

The directorate of the Movement had given me the authority to decide on the order in which our candidates would be listed, and also to designate a small number of the candidates for seats as representatives and senators. As for their place on the list, I put Miguel Cruchaga, the secretary general and jack-of-all-trades of Libertad from the very start, at the head of the candidates for senator, and at the head of the list of candidates for representative, Rafael Rey, who had been departmental secretary of Lima. They all accepted their position on the lists, which I had decided on, with few exceptions, by following the percentage of votes won by each of the congressional candidates in elections within Libertad. The only one who had his feelings hurt, because he had been put in fourth place—after Cruchaga, Miguel Vega, and Lucho Bustamante—was Raúl Ferrero, who, after I had read off the list of candidates, announced to the political committee that he was resigning as a candidate. But a few days later he reconsidered.

Among the individuals whom I invited to be candidates of ours were, as a representative, Francisco Belaunde Terry, and as a senator, the entrepreneur Ricardo Vega Llona, who had supported us since the days of the campaign against nationalization. Vega Llona represented that modern and liberal spirit in the businessman that we wanted to see spread among entrepreneurs in Peru—someone sick and tired of mercantilism, a determined supporter of a market economy, and without the social prejudices or the pseudoaristocratic, snobbish airs of many Peruvian businessmen. I also invited, as candidates for senator, Jorge Torres Vallejo, who had been forced out of the APRA because of his criticisms of Alan García and who, as the former mayor of Trujillo, we thought would be able to attract votes for the Front in that Aprista bastion, and a journalist who defended our ideas in his column in the daily *Expreso*: Patricio Ricketts Rey de Castro. And among our own militants, I gave in to the pleas of my friend Mario Roggero, who wanted to be a candidate for congressman despite his not having participated in the elections within the Freedom Movement. I included him on our list because of the good work that he had done as the Movement's national secretary for unions, organizing various sectors of professionals, technicians, and craftsmen, never imagining that, once elected, he would turn out to be disloyal to those who had been responsible for his winning his seat in the Chamber of Representatives, first of all by helping Alan García out by taking a trip abroad so as not to cast his vote in Congress when the possibility came up of trying García for responsibility for the slaughter of prisoners that took place in June 1986, and then, after that, playing footsie with the regime that his party and his colleagues opposed.*

But we are still in the last weeks of 1989 and on one of those days—December 15—I had a brief literary parenthesis in the endless political hustle and bustle: the presentation, at the Alliance Française,

---

* His case was not the only one. Of the fifteen Libertad senators and congressmen, four deserted the Movement, on various pretexts, in the first year and a half of the new administration: Senators Raúl Ferrero and Beatriz Merino and congressmen Luis Delgado Aparicio and Mario Roggero. But, unlike the first three, who after parting company with Libertad maintained a discreet and even friendly attitude toward the Movement, Roggero devoted himself to attacking it in public communiqués and declarations. That was his response to the generous decision of the political committee which, instead of declaring him no longer a member of Libertad because of his absence when that vote was taken in Congress, confined itself to a mild warning. Several months later, the representative Rafael Rey also was to resign, after being criticized by the leaders of Libertad because of his gestures and declarations in favor of the dictatorship instituted by Fujimori on April 5, 1992, which he has been faithfully serving since.

of a translation of Rimbaud's "Un Coeur sous une soutane" ("A Heart beneath a Cassock") that I had done thirty years before and that had remained unpublished until Guillermo Niño de Guzmán and the enthusiastic cultural attaché of the French embassy, Daniel Lefort, finally took it upon themselves to bring it out. I could scarcely believe it when, for a couple of hours, I heard talk of poetry and literature, and of a poet whose works had been part of my bedside reading when I was young, and talked of them myself.

In the last days of December I went on tour once again, to take part in the distribution of gifts and toys throughout Peru that had been organized by a committee headed by Gladys Urbina and Cecilia Castro, the wife of the secretary general of Libertad in Cajamarca, and by the young people of Libertad's Mobilization section. Hundreds of people participated in this operation, the object of which, besides bringing a little gift to several thousand poor children—a drop of water in the desert—was to test our ability to conduct mobilizations of this sort. We were thinking of the future: it would be imperative, in the hardest days of the fight against inflation, to make great efforts to bring aid to every corner of Peru in the form of food and medicine that would make the tremendous ordeal less of a hardship. Were we capable of organizing civil operations of major importance in cases of emergency such as natural catastrophes or for campaigns such as those for self-defense, literacy, and hygiene among the masses?

The results, from this point of view, were all that we could have asked for, thanks to the excellent work of Patricia, Gladys, Cecilia, Charo, and many other women members of Libertad. With the exception of Huancavelica, in all the other capitals of *departamentos* and in a great number of provinces, the boxes, bags, and packages full of the gifts we had gathered together thanks to factories, businesses, and private individuals, all arrived. Everything got done within the time limits we'd set: storing, packing, transporting, distributing. Shipments of them went out by truck, bus, plane, accompanied by young people from Mobilization, and in each city they were received by a committee of Libertad, which had also collected donations and gifts in the region. Everything was ready for starting the distribution of the gifts on December 21. During the final days, I went by the headquarters of the Solidarity program, on the Calle Bolívar, several times, and it was a swarm of activity, a hive of busy bees, with charts and time schedules on the walls, and vans and trucks filled to overflowing arriving and departing. On the morning we left for Ayacucho to start the distribution there, I said to Patricia, whom I scarcely saw during that time, since she devoted eighteen hours a day to that operation, that if all went that well for the Front, we already had victory in our pockets.

We left at dawn on the 21st, with my daughter Morgana, who was on vacation, and in Ayacucho we were welcomed, along with the departmental committee of Libertad, by the younger of my two sons, Gonzalo, who, for several years by then, had devoted his winter and summer vacations—he was attending London University—to lending a helping hand to the Andrés Vivanco Amorín children's center. This institution had sprung up as a result of the revolutionary war being waged by Sendero Luminoso, which broke out in 1980 in this region. Because of it, Ayacucho was filled with abandoned children, who begged in the streets and slept on the benches of the Plaza de Armas or under the arcades bordering it. An old secondary schoolteacher, as poor as a church mouse but with a heart like the sun of his native land, Don Andrés Vivanco got to work. By knocking on people's doors, by begging at public and private offices, he managed to secure a place to house many of those children and give them a mouthful of bread. That orphanage required heroic efforts on his part, and Violeta Correa, President Belaunde's wife, helped him a great deal at the beginning. Thanks to her, the children's center obtained a plot of land on the outskirts of the city. In 1983, I donated to Don Andrés Vivanco the $50,000 that I had received as the Ritz-Hemingway Prize for my novel *La guerra del fin del mundo* (*The War of the End of the World*), and Patricia had managed to get aid from the Ayacucho Emergency Association, which, through the initiative of Anabella Jourdan, the wife of the United States ambassador, she and a group of her friends had created at the beginning of the 1980s to bring help to the martyred region of Ayacucho.

Since then my younger son, Gonzalo, had conceived a passion for the orphanage. He collected money from his acquaintances and friends, and on each of his vacations he brought the nuns who had taken charge of the institution food, clothing, and little trinkets. Unlike his brother Álvaro, he was never interested in politics, and when I began the electoral campaign, he kept going to Ayacucho several times a year to bring provisions to the children's center as though nothing had changed.

The distribution of presents in Ayacucho was made at the children's center with an orderliness that did not cause us to foresee in any way what would happen in other cities, and afterward, I went to place flowers on Don Andrés Vivanco's grave, to visit the soup kitchen for the poor of San Francisco, the University of Huamanga, and to go through the Central Market. We lunched with the leaders of the Freedom Movement, in a little restaurant behind the Hotel de Turistas, and that was the last time I ever saw Julián Huamaní Yauli, who was murdered a few weeks thereafter.

From Ayacucho we went by plane to the jungle, to Puerto Maldonado, where, after the distribution of Christmas gifts, a street rally had been planned. The instructions to the committees of Libertad had been quite clear: the distribution was a celebration *within* the Movement, the object of which was to bring a little present to the children of militants, a ceremony not open to everyone, since we didn't have enough gifts for the millions of poor children in Peru. But in Puerto Maldonado the news of the distribution had spread throughout the city, and when I arrived at the fire station, the place selected for the ceremony, there were thousands of children and mothers with babies in their arms and on their shoulders, pushing and shoving desperately to get a place in line, since they had a presentiment of what in fact happened: the presents came to an end before the lines of people waiting did.

The sight was heartbreaking. Children and mothers had been there, roasting in the burning-hot sun of Amazonia, since very early that morning, four, five, six hours, to receive—if they managed to—a plastic sand bucket, a little wooden doll, a bit of chocolate, or a package of caramels. I was upset, hearing the mothers of Libertad trying to explain to that horde of children and barefoot mothers dressed in rags that the toys had given out, that they would have to go away empty-handed. The image of those sad or angry faces did not leave me for a single second, as I spoke at the rally and visited the local headquarters of Libertad, and as I held a discussion that night with our leaders, in the Hotel de Turistas, with the sounds of the jungle as a background, about our electoral strategy in Madre de Dios.

The next morning we flew to Cuzco, where the departmental committee of Libertad, headed by Gustavo Manrique Villalobos, had organized the distribution in a more sensible way, in the Movement's local headquarters itself, and for the families of enrolled members and active supporters. This was a committee of young people new to politics, in which I had great faith, since, unlike other committees, there seemed to exist an atmosphere of understanding and friendship among the men and women who constituted it. I discovered that morning that I was mistaken. As I left, two leaders of the Cuzco committee handed me, separately, letters that I read on the plane taking me to Andahuaylas. Both contained sulfuric accusations, with the usual charges against the other faction—disloyalty, opportunism, nepotism, intrigues—so that it did not surprise me to learn, shortly thereafter, that with regard to the candidacies for Congress, our Cuzco committee was also experiencing divisions and desertions.

In Andahuaylas, following the rally in the main square, Patricia and I were taken to the place where the Christmas presents were to be given out. My heart sank when I saw that, as in Puerto Maldonado, here too all the children and mothers of the city seemed to have crowded together in the lines that went around an entire block. I asked my friends from Andahuaylas who belonged to Libertad whether they hadn't been too optimistic by inviting the entire city to come receive presents when there wouldn't be enough for even a tenth of those lined up. But, gamboling about in high spirits because of the rally, which had filled the square, they laughed at my apprehensions. After the distribution began, Patricia and I went on our way, and as we left the place, we saw children and mothers flinging themselves, amid indescribable chaos, on the presents, knocking over barriers set up by the young people of Mobilization. The women and girls distributing the gifts saw a horde of eager hands advancing toward them. I don't believe that that Christmas won us a single voter in Andahuaylas.

In order to have a few days of complete rest, before the last stage of the campaign, Patricia and I, along with my brother- and sister-in-law and two couples who were friends of ours, went to an island in the Caribbean to spend the last four days of 1989. Shortly thereafter, back in Lima again, I came across a stern editorial in the magazine

Caretas,* criticizing me for having gone to spend the end of the year in Miami, since my trip would be interpreted as support of the U.S. military intervention in Panama to overthrow Noriega. (The Freedom Movement had expressed its disapproval of that intervention, in a communiqué that I wrote and that Álvaro read to the entire press corps. Our unequivocal rejection of military intervention included a severe condemnation of the dictatorship of General Noriega, which I had long criticized—and done so, even more pointedly, at the time when President García invited the Panamanian dictator to Lima and awarded him a decoration. Our solidarity with the democratic opposition to Noriega, moreover, had been made public, months before, on August 8, 1989, in a ceremony at the headquarters of the Freedom Movement, to which we invited Ricardo Arias Calderón and Guillermo Fort, the two vice presidents elected with Guillermo Endara in the elections that Noriega refused to recognize, an event at which Enrique Ghersi and I spoke. Furthermore, on that very short vacation, I did not visit Miami nor did I set foot on United States territory.) The little editorial combined factual errors and malevolence in a way that surprised me, coming from that magazine. I had been a contributor to *Caretas* for many years and considered its owner and editor-in-chief, Enrique Zileri, to be my friend. When the magazine was hounded and he himself was persecuted by the military dictatorship I made bold efforts to denounce the fact both inside and outside the country, even to the point, as I have said, that I asked to have an audience with General Velasco himself, despite the distaste I felt for him, in order to plead Zileri's cause, the most legitimate one in the world: the freedom of the press. When *Caretas* began to move closer to Alan García because such proximity brought the magazine profits in the form of paid state advertising or because, it was said, Zileri had been seduced by García's eloquence and flattery, I continued to figure among his contributors. Then, in May 1989, I agreed to speak in Berlin, at Zileri's insistence, at the congress of an international press institute that he was presiding over. At the time, *Caretas* had already given indications of its antipathy toward my political activity and toward Libertad, but without having recourse to methods that were incompatible with the tradition of the magazine.

* *Caretas*, Lima, January 8, 1990.

Hence, with a certain regret, I confess, since for many years the magazine had been my forum in Peru, I resigned myself to expecting no support whatsoever from *Caretas* in the months to come, but rather hostility that the approach of the elections would make even more stubborn. But I never imagined that the magazine—one of the few in the country with a certain intellectual standing,—would become one of Alan García's most docile instruments for turning public opinion against the Democratic Front, against the Freedom Movement, and against me personally. That editorial was like taking off the mask— the *careta*—of the *Caretas* that we were familiar with; since then and up until the end of the first round of voting—in the second, it changed its stance—its reporting was tendentious, aimed at aggravating the contention within the Front, at giving the appearance of respectability to many lies against me invented by the APRA or at making them public through the hypocritical device of repeating them so as to deny them, while at the same time it placed little value in, or ignored, any information that might be of benefit to us.

In the case of *Caretas* certain forms were respected, and it did not resort to the contemptible tactics of *La República* or of *Página Libre*; it specialized in sowing confusion and discouragement with regard to my candidacy in that middle class to which the readers of the magazine belonged, rightly supposing that they were inclined to favor me as a candidate and trying to manipulate them with more elegant subtleties than the journalistic swill eagerly consumed by readers of the scandal sheets.

Despite the fact that my advisers tried to persuade me not to do so, after that editorial appeared I had my name taken off the masthead of that weekly which, in the days of its founders—Doris Gibson and Francisco Igartua—surely would not have played the role that it did in the electoral campaign. My letter of resignation to Zileri, dated January 10, 1990,* contained only one sentence: "I request you to remove my name from the list of contributors to the magazine, since I am no longer one."

---

* *Caretas*, Lima, January 15, 1990.

SEVENTEEN

The Miter-Bird

S INCE my marriage, what with my classes at the university and the jobs to keep food on the table, I hadn't had much time left over for politics, although, every so often, I attended the meetings of the Christian Democratic Party and contributed to the sporadic issues of *Democracia*. (After the third year, I gave up going to the Alliance Française, but by then I read French easily; besides, for the degree in literature at San Marcos, I chose French for the foreign language requirement.) But politics would enter my life again in the summer of 1956 in the most unexpected way: as paid employment.

The electoral process that put an end to Odría's dictatorship was under way, and three candidates were coming to the fore as contenders for the presidency: Dr. Hernando de Lavalle, a wealthy man, an aristocrat, and a prestigious Lima attorney; the former president Manuel Prado, recently back from Paris, where he had lived since he left the presidency in 1945; and the one who appeared to be the minor candidate, because of a lack of financial resources and the air of youthful improvisation that marked his campaign: the architect and university professor Fernando Belaúnde Terry.

The election finally took place in a very questionable way, in legal terms, under the unconstitutional Law of Domestic Security, approved by the Congress that was a fruit of the dictatorship, which placed the APRA and the Communist Party outside the law—and kept them from presenting candidates. The votes that the Communist Party would have garnered were few and far between; those of the APRA, the party of the masses and with a disciplined organization that it had maintained during the time that it was an outlawed party, would have been decisive. From the beginning Lavalle, Prado, and Belaúnde sought, in secret negotiations and sometimes ones that were not so secret, an accord with the Apristas.

The APRA rejected Belaunde Terry from the start, with an instinctive certainty that in him Haya de la Torre, the founder of the APRA, would have not a cat's paw but, in a short time, a competitor. (Such a serious one that he was to win out over the Apristas in the elections of 1963 and 1980.) And its support of Manuel Prado, who during his presidency from 1939 to 1945 had outlawed the APRA and imprisoned, exiled, and persecuted many Apristas, was presumed to be impossible to secure.

Hence Hernando de Lavalle appeared to be the favorite. The APRA demanded to be made a legal party again and Lavalle promised the Aprista leaders to back a law defining the status of political parties that would allow the APRA to reenter civic life. In order to negotiate these accords a number of Aprista leaders had returned to Peru from exile, among them Ramiro Prialé, the great architect of what was to become the regime of coexistence (1956–1961).

Porras Barrenechea collaborated in establishing this rapprochement between Hernando de Lavalle and the APRA. Although he had never been an Aprista, nor a party outsider favorably inclined toward it—a status that included a fair number of the middle and even the upper bourgeoisie—Porras, who, as a member of the same generation as Haya de la Torre and Luis Alberto Sánchez, kept up a friendship with them, on the surface at least, had many contacts with the APRA during the electoral campaign, and agreed to be a candidate for a seat in the Senate on the list of friends of the APRA, headed by the poet José Gálvez, whom this party supported in the 1956 elections.

A close friend of Lavalle's, whose classmate he had also been at the university, Porras had actively supported the great alliance or civil coalition on which Lavalle wanted to base his candidacy. These forces included Luis A. Flores's old and almost extinct Revolutionary Union and the Christian Democratic Party, with whom he held conversations looking toward the future.

One afternoon, Porras Barrenechea summoned Pablo Macera and me and offered us jobs with Dr. Lavalle, who was looking for two "intellectuals" to write speeches and political reports for him. The pay was quite good and there were no fixed working hours. That night Porras took us to Lavalle's house—an elegant residence, surrounded

by gardens and tall trees, on the Avenida 28 de Julio in Miraflores—
to meet the candidate. Hernando de Lavalle was a kindly, elegant
man, extremely circumspect, timid almost, who received Pablo and
me most courteously and explained to us that a group of intellectuals,
headed by a young and distinguished professor of philosophy, Carlos
Cueto Fernandini, was preparing his program for governing, in which
he would place great emphasis on cultural activities. Pablo and I would
not be working with this group, however, but with the candidate alone.

Although I didn't vote for him in the 1956 elections, but for Fernando Belaunde Terry—I will explain why later—in those months
during which I worked alongside him I came to respect and esteem
Hernando de Lavalle. Ever since he had been a young man it was
said in Lima that someday he would be president of Peru. The descendant of an old family, Dr. Lavalle had been a brilliant student at
the university and after that was a very successful attorney. Only now,
when he was past sixty, had he decided—or rather, others had decided
for him—that he should enter politics, an activity for which, as became
clear during the electoral process, he was not well equipped.

He always believed what he told Pablo Macera and me on the night
we first met him: that the aim of his candidacy was to reestablish
democratic life and civil institutions in Peru after eight years under a
military regime, and that in order to achieve that goal what was needed
was a great coalition of Peruvians of all persuasions and a scrupulous
respect for the law.

"The harebrained Lavalle wanted to win the election *fair and
square*," I heard a friend of Porras Barrenechea's once say sarcastically,
at one of the historian's evening gatherings over cups of chocolate.
"The elections of 1956 were rigged so that he'd win them; but this
arrogantly proud, self-important candidate wanted to win *fair and
square*. And that's why he lost!" Something like that did in fact occur.
But Dr. Lavalle did not want to win that election fair and square out
of arrogant pride and self-importance, but because he was a decent
person, and naïve enough to believe that he could win with clean
hands an election which the existence of the dictatorship corrupted
from the very beginning.

Pablo and I were installed in an office as empty as a tomb—there
was never anybody in it except for the two of us—on the second floor
of a building on La Colmena, right in the downtown section of Lima.

Dr. Lavalle would drop in unexpectedly to ask us for drafts of speeches or proclamations. At our first meeting, Macera, in one of his typical outbursts, confronted Lavalle with this insolent remark: "The masses can be won over by contempt or by flattery. Which method should we use?"

I saw Dr. Lavalle's face of a sad tortoise pale behind his glasses. And I listened to him for some time, embarrassed and disconcerted, as he explained to Macera that there was another way, outside of those two extremes, of winning over public opinion. He preferred a more moderate one, one more in harmony with his temperament. Macera's brusque comments and wild remarks scared Lavalle—whom Macera wanted to have slip into his speeches every so often a quote from Freud or Georg Simmel or whoever else Pablo was reading at the time—but at the same time Lavalle was fascinated by him. He listened, enthralled, to his mad theories—Pablo expounded a great number of them every day, all of them contradictory, and then immediately forgot about them—and one day Lavalle said to me in confidence: "What an intelligent young man, but what an *unpredictable* one!"

An internal debate began within the Christian Democratic Party with regard to what its policy should be in the '56 election. The wing consisting of supporters of Bustamante, the most conservative one, proposed supporting Lavalle, whereas many others, above all among the young members, favored Belaunde Terry. When the subject was discussed in the departmental committee, I let it be known that I was working with Dr. Lavalle, but that if the party agreed to support Belaunde I would respect its decision and resign. At first, the idea of supporting Lavalle prevailed.

As the period for the registration of candidates for the presidential election was about to close, the rumor circulated all through Lima that the national board of elections would refuse to register Belaunde, on the pretext that he did not have the number of signatures required. Belaunde immediately called for a street demonstration, on June 1, 1956, which—a tactic that, in a manner of speaking, was to transform his small and enthusiastic candidacy into a great movement destined to give birth eventually to Popular Action—he wanted to lead to the very gates of the Presidential Palace. On the Jirón de la Unión he and the few thousand people who followed him (among them was Javier Silva, who never failed to show up at every demonstration) were stopped by the police with high-pressure water hoses and tear gas. Belaunde faced the police charge waving the Peruvian flag on high, a gesture that would make him famous.

That same night, with elegant circumspection, Dr. Hernando de Lavalle sent word to General Odría that if the national board of elections did not register Belaunde, he would give up his own candidacy and denounce the electoral process. "This idiot doesn't deserve to be president of Peru," it is said that Odría sighed when he received the message. The dictator and his advisers thought that Lavalle, with his idea of a grand coalition, in which there was room even for Odría's party—the name of which at the time was the Partido Restaurador (the Restoration Party)—was the one who would be their best rear guard if the future Congress was bent on investigating the crimes committed during the dictatorship. That gesture showed them that the timid conservative aristocrat was not the right person for that task. The fate of Hernando de Lavalle was sealed.

Odría ordered the national board of elections to allow the registration of Belaunde, who, in a large rally in the Plaza San Martín, thanked the "people of Lima" for entering his name on the list of candidates. After the famous incident of the flag and the police attack with water hoses, it began to appear that he could run for office on an equal footing with Prado and Lavalle, who, because of the costly publicity and the infrastructure on which they were counting, appeared to be the candidates with the greatest chances of winning.

Manuel Prado, meanwhile, negotiated behind the scenes to rally support for the APRA, to which he offered immediate legalization without going through the procedure of changing the status of political parties that Lavalle was proposing. Whether this was the decisive factor, or whether there were additional promises or gifts on Prado's part, as was rumored, was never proved one way or the other. The fact is that agreement was arrived at, a few days before the elections. The orders given by the Aprista party to its militants that, instead of voting for Lavalle, they were to vote for the ex-president who had outlawed them, jailed and persecuted them, were obeyed, in another demonstration of the APRA's iron discipline, and the votes of the Apristas won Manuel Prado the election.

In the end, Lavalle had been defeated by his public acceptance of the support of the Restoration Party, and by his statement, in the ceremony whereby the latter, through David Aguilar Cornejo, gave him its backing, that "he would continue the patriotic labors of General Odría." The Christian Democratic Party immediately withdrew its support from him and allowed its members to vote as they pleased. And many independents who would have voted for him, won over by his image as a capable and decent man, felt put off by a declaration implying that he sanctioned the dictatorship. Like the majority of Christian Democrats, I voted for Belaunde, who, although he ended up in third place, won an important percentage of the vote, and the necessary support to found Popular Action some months later.

When I lost my job with Dr. Lavalle, my income was reduced, but not for very long, since, almost immediately, I found two other jobs, one real and the other theoretical. The real job was the one on the magazine *Extra*, whose owner, Don Jorge Checa, the ex-prefect of Piura, had known me since I was a little boy. He took me on when the magazine was already on the verge of bankruptcy. At the end of each month, those of us on the editorial staff lived through moments of anxiety, because only the ones who arrived first at the head office received their pay; the others received vouchers for payment sometime in the future. Every week while I was there I wrote film reviews and articles on cultural subjects. Sometimes I too was left without a paycheck. But I didn't carry off *Extra*'s typewriters and even its office furniture, the way several of my colleagues did, because of my liking for Jorge Checa. I don't know how much money the prodigal Don Jorge lost in this publishing venture; but he lost it with the nonchalance of a great lord and a Maecenas, without complaining and without getting rid of the horde of journalists he kept on the payroll, a number of whom stole him blind in the most cynical way. He apparently realized what was going on but it didn't matter to him as long as he was having fun. And it was true that he was having a great time. He used to take the journalists from *Extra* to the house of his mistress, a good-looking woman whom he had set up in a house along Magdalena Vieja, where he organized lunches that ended up as orgies. The first jealous scene Julia ever made with me, after we'd been married a year and a half, must have been after one of those lunches, in what by now were the final weeks of existence of *Extra*, when I came back home in a rather unseemly state and with red stains on my handkerchief. The fight we had was a tooth-and-nail one and didn't leave me with much enthusiasm for going back to Don Jorge's hectic lunches. There wasn't much chance of that, moreover, because a few weeks later the editor-in-chief of the magazine, the intelligent and refined Pedro Álvarez del Villar, skipped the country with Don Jorge's mistress, and the staff of the weekly who hadn't been paid their salaries carried off the last remaining pieces of furniture and typewriters, so that *Extra* died of consumption. (I will always remember Don Jorge Checa, when he was prefect of Piura and I a senior at San Miguel, ordering me, one night at the Grau club: "Marito, you who are halfway toward being an intellectual, go up onstage and introduce The Andalusian gypsies from Spain to the audience." Don Jorge's idea of an intellectual was based, doubtless, on the intellectuals whom he had happened to meet and hire.)

Porras Barrenechea was elected senator representing Lima on the list presented by friends of the APRA, and in the first election held by Congress was chosen first vice president of the Senate. In that capacity he had a right to have two hired assistants, posts to which he appointed Carlos Araníbar and me. The job was a theoretical one, because, as Porras's aides, we went on working with him at his home, doing historical research, and dropped by Congress only at the end of each month to collect our modest salaries. After six months had gone by, Porras informed Carlos Araníbar and me that our posts had been done away with. That half year was my first and last experience as a civil servant.

Around that time, Julia and I moved from the minuscule little apartment in the townhouse on the Calle Porta to a roomier one, with two bedrooms—one of which I turned into a study—on Las Acacias, a few blocks away from Uncle Lucho and Aunt Olga's. It was in a modern building, very near the seawall and the ocean, in Miraflores, although it had only one window overlooking the street and so we had to keep the lights on all day long.

We lived there for more than two years, and I believe that, despite my exhausting daily routine, it was a time with many compensations, the best of which was, without a shadow of a doubt, my friendship with Luis Loayza and Abelardo Oquendo. I had met Luis sometime before, and Abelardo when I was a contributor to the Sunday supplement of *El Comercio*, whose literary section he was in charge of. From that period on, the three of us began seeing each other more and more often, until we constituted an inseparable triumvirate. We used to spend weekends together, at my place or at Abelardo and Pupi's, on the Avenida Angamos, or we would go out to eat at a Chinese restaurant, outings on which we were sometimes joined by other friends, such as Sebastián Salazar Bondy, José Miguel Oviedo (who was beginning to take up arms as a literary critic for the first time), a Spanish friend of Loayza's named José Manuel Muñoz, Pablo Macera, the actor Tachi Hilbck, or Baldomero Cáceres, the future psychologist, in those days more concerned with theology than with science and for that reason nicknamed Cristo Cáceres by Macera.

But Abelardo, Lucho, and I also saw each other during the week. We thought up all sorts of pretexts for meeting in downtown Lima to have coffee together and chat, between classes and our jobs, if only for a few minutes, because those meetings, in which we exchanged comments about one book or another, traded political, literary, or university gossip, stimulated us and compensated for the many boring and mechanical things involved in our daily routines.

Both Lucho and Abelardo had given up their literary studies at the university so as to devote all their time to their law studies. Abelardo had just received his law degree and was already a practicing attorney, in his father-in-law's office. Lucho was just finishing his last courses in the Faculty of Law and practicing in the office of a bigwig of Pradism: Carlos Ledgard. But simply knowing them was enough to be certain that what really mattered to them was literature, and that it would enter their lives again every time they tried to get away from it. I believe that in those days Abelardo wanted to get away from it. He had finished all his courses for a degree in Letters and had spent a year in Spain on a scholarship meant to enable him to write a doctoral dissertation on proverbs in the works of Ricardo Palma. I don't know whether it was this arid sort of research reminiscent of the dissection of cadavers—all the rage at the time in the field of stylistics, which exerted a dictatorship that had the effect of sterilizing university departments of literature—that made him sick and tired of the prospect of an academic career, or whether he left the field for practical reasons, telling himself that, having recently married and with a family in prospect, he had to think of more reliable ways of earning a living. The fact is that he had given up writing his dissertation and left the university. But not literature. He read a great deal and spoke with tremendous sensitivity about literary texts, poetry in particular, for which he had a surgeon's eye and exquisite taste. He sometimes wrote book reviews, always very penetrating ones, models of the genre, but he almost never signed them and at times I wondered whether Abelardo hadn't decided, because of his rigorous critical acumen, to give up writing so as to be the one person in whom he could attain that perfection he sought: a reader. He had studied the classics of the Golden Age intensively and I always provoked him into discussing them because hearing him express an opinion about *El Romancero*, Quevedo, or Góngora filled me with envy.

His genteel air and his repugnance for any sort of fakery, his maniacal concern for propriety—in his dress, his speech, his behavior toward his friends—called to mind an aristocrat of the spirit who, through an error of fate, was exiled in the body of a young man belonging to the middle class, in a hard practical world in which he was destined to have a difficult time surviving. When Lucho and I spoke of him, by ourselves, we called him the Dauphin.

In those days Lucho had, in addition to his passion for Borges, one for Henry James, which I failed to share. He was a cannibalistic reader of books in English, which he bought or ordered in a bookstore specializing in works in foreign languages, on the Calle Belén, and he continually surprised me with a new title or author he just discovered. I remember his great find, in an old bookstore downtown: a magnificent translation of Marcel Schwob's fine book, *Vies imaginaires*, which he was so enthusiastic about that he bought every copy of it in the store to distribute to his friends. Often our literary tastes differed, which gave us an excuse for stupendous arguments. Thanks to Lucho, I discovered exciting books, such as Paul Bowles's *The Sheltering Sky* and Truman Capote's *Other Voices, Other Rooms*, in Spanish translations. One of our violent literary arguments had a comical ending. The subject of it: Gide's *Les Nourritures terrestres*, which he admired and I detested. When I told him that the book seemed to me verbose, its prose affected and long-winded, he replied that the argument couldn't go on without Baldomero Cáceres, a fanatical fan of Gide's, taking part in it. We hunted Baldomero up, and Lucho asked me to repeat to his face what I thought of *Les Nourritures terrestres*. I did as he asked. Baldomero burst out laughing. He roared with laughter for a long time, doubled over, holding his sides, as though he were being tickled, as though he been told the funniest joke in the world. This line of argument shut me up.

We dreamed, naturally, of bringing out a literary review that would be our forum and the visible sign of our friendship. One fine day, Lucho announced to us that he would finance the first issue, with his salary from the Ledgard law office. There thus came into being *Literatura*, of which just three issues were to appear (the last of the three when Lucho and I were already in Europe). The first issue included a homage to César Moro—a teacher of mine at Leoncio Prado— whose poetry I had discovered a short time before and whose "inner exile" intrigued me and attracted me as much as his writings. On his return from France and Mexico, countries in which he lived for many years, Moro had lived in Peru a secret, marginal life, not mingling with writers, publishing practically nothing, writing texts, the majority of them in French, read by a small circle of friends. André Coyné gave us several of Moro's unpublished poems for that issue, which also contained contributions by Sebastián Salazar Bondy, José Durand, and a young Peruvian poet, the author of a number of very beautiful poems that Lucho had discovered in a lost issue of *Mercurio Peruano*: Carlos Germán Belli. The issue also contained a manifesto against the death penalty, signed by the three of us, occasioned by the execution in Lima by a firing squad of a convicted criminal (the "monster of Armendáriz") that had served as an excuse for a repellent public celebration: people had gathered at dawn on the Paseo de la República to listen, as day broke, to the fatal shots of the firing squad. The issue included as well Loayza's wonderful portrait of the Inca Garcilaso de la Vega. The publication of this little review, no more than a handful of pages, was an exciting adventure because this activity, like the conversations with Lucho and Abelardo, made me feel like a writer, an illusion that had little to do with the reality of how I spent my time, taken up as it was by all my jobs to earn our daily bread.

It seems to me that I was the one, with that inquisitiveness of mine that never left me—and still hasn't—who got us started, in the summer of 1957, holding spiritualistic séances. We usually held them at my place. A cousin of Julia's and Olguita's, whose name was also Olga and who was a medium, had arrived from Bolivia. She frequented the other world with the greatest of ease. In the sessions she played her role so well that it was impossible not to believe that spirits spoke through her mouth; or more precisely, through her hand, since they dictated their messages to her and she wrote them down. The problem was that all the spirits that obeyed her summons made the same spelling mistakes. Despite this, moments of ebullient nervous tension were created, and afterward I would stay awake all night long, tossing and turning in bed out of guilt at that contact with the world beyond.

In one of these spiritualistic sessions, Pablo Macera began pounding on the table: "Keep quiet, it's my grandmother." He was deathly pale, and there was no doubt about it; he believed it. "Ask her if I killed her from the fit of rage I caused her," he stammered. His grandmother's spirit refused to relieve his doubts and he held it against us for some time, telling us that our fooling around had deprived him of the chance to free himself of a distressing uncertainty.

In the library of the Club Nacional I also came across some books on satanism, but my friends categorically refused to have us conjure up the devil following the obscene recipes of those manuals. They would consent only to our going every so often, at midnight, to the romantic cemetery in Surco, where Baldomero, in a state of lyrical rapture, suddenly began to ballet dance in the moonlight, leaping about amid the graves . . .

The Saturday night meetings, at my house in Las Acacias, lasted till dawn and were usually very amusing. We sometimes played a terrific, semihysterical game: the laughing game. The one who lost had to make the others laugh by clowning around. I had a very effective trick. Imitating a duck's waddle, I rolled my eyes and cackled: "This is the miter-bird, the miter-bird, the miter-bird!" The self-important ones, such as Loayza and Macera, endured indescribable suffering when it was their turn to play the buffoon, and the only amusing gimmick that occurred to the latter was to pucker his mouth up like a baby and growl: brrrr, brrrr. A much more dangerous game was Truth or Consequences. In one of these sessions of collective exhibitionism, we listened, we heard, all of a sudden, from the timid Carlos Germán Belli—my admiration for his poems had led me to visit him in the very modest job as amanuensis that he had as a congressional clerk—a confession that amazed us: "I've slept with the ugliest women in Lima." Carlos Germán was a rigidly moral surrealist, much like César Moro, stuffed into the skeleton of a well-educated and inconspicuous young man, and one day he had decided to put an end to his inhibitions about women, posting himself at the exit of the building where he worked, on a corner of the Jirón de la Unión, and making provocative remarks to the women passing by. But his timidity made him tongue-tied with the pretty ones; his tongue would loosen only to proposition the ugly ones . . .

Someone else who often came to those gatherings was Fernando Hilbck, a classmate of Lucho's at the Faculty of Law and an actor. Loayza told how one day, in their last year, for the first time in seven years, Tachi became interested in a class: "How does it happen, Professor, that there are *several* codes? Aren't all of the laws in just one book?" The professor called him aside: "Tell your father to let you become an actor and don't waste any more time studying law." Tachi's father resigned himself and did just that, regretting that his son wouldn't be the star of the tribunals that he'd dreamed he'd be. He sent him to Italy and gave him two years to make himself famous in the movies. I saw Tachi in Rome, shortly before the fateful date came round. All he had managed to accomplish was to play the part of a furtive Roman centurion in a film, but he was happy. Then he went to Spain, where he had a brief career in the movies and the theater, and finally—yet another Peruvian to number among those who chose invisibility—he disappeared altogether. In the spiritualist séances or in the game of clowning around, Tachi Hilbck was unbeatable: his histrionic gifts transformed the gathering into a hilarious performance.

Chance brought Raúl and Teresa Deustua, just back from the United States, where Raúl had worked for many years as a translator at the United Nations, to live in the apartment next to ours on Las Acacias. Belonging to the same generation as Sebastián Salazar Bondy, Javier Sologuren, and Eduardo Eielson, Raúl was, like them, a poet, and the author of a play, *Judith*, that remained unpublished. A refined man who was very well read, especially in English and in French, he was one of those elusive figures of Peruvian culture who, after a brief appearance on the scene, disappear and become ghosts, because they go abroad and break all their ties to Peru, or because, like César Moro, they opt for inner exile, keeping their distance from everybody and everything that might remind them of their swift journey along the path of art, thought, or literature. I have always been fascinated by the case of those Peruvians who, because of a sort of tragic loyalty to a vocation difficult to reconcile with their milieu, break with the latter, and to all appearances with the better part of themselves—their sensitivity, their intelligence, their culture—so as not to make debasing concessions or compromises.

Raúl had stopped publishing his work (he had published very little, in all truth), but he hadn't stopped writing and his conversation was as literary as it could possibly be. We became friends, and he was very pleased to find a group of young men of letters that knew his writings, sought him out, and invited him to their gatherings. He had a fine collection of French books, which he generously lent us, and thanks to him I could read many Surrealist books and a number of wonderful issues of *Minotaure*. He had made a translation of Baudelaire's *Fusées* and *Mon Coeur mis à nu* and I spent many hours with him and Loayza, revising it. Like the majority of his poems and a *Chosica Diary*, a record of days spent in the pleasant old resort town in the mountains above Lima, which he used to read aloud to us, I believe that the Baudelaire translation never saw print.

I don't know why Raúl Deustua came back to Peru—out of nostalgia for the old country perhaps, and with the hope of finding a good job. He worked at different things, at Radio Panamericana and at the Ministry of Foreign Relations, to which Porras Barrenechea offered him entrée, but he never did find the comfortable position that he longed for. In a few months he gave up and left Peru once more, for Venezuela this time. Teresita, who had made friends with Julia, was pregnant and stayed behind in Lima to have the baby. She was very likable and being pregnant sometimes made her have sudden whims like this exquisite one: "I should like to nibble on the edges of wontons." Lucho Loayza and I went out to a *chifa*—a Chinese restaurant—to buy her some. When the baby was born, the Deustuas asked me to be his godfather, so that I had to take him in my arms to the baptismal font.

When Raúl left for Caracas he asked me if I wanted his job at Radio Panamericana. It was paid by the hour, like all the other ones I had, and I accepted. He took me to the rise on the Calle Belén from which the radio station broadcast, and that was how I first met the brothers Genaro and Héctor Delgado. At the time they were beginning the career that would take them to the very top, as I've already said. Their father, the founder of Radio Central, had given Radio Panamericana over to them, a station which, unlike Radio Central—whose appeal was popular, its specialties being soap operas and comedies—was aimed in those days at an elite audience, with programs of American or European music, more refined and a touch snobbish. Thanks to Genaro's drive and ambition, this little radio station for listeners of a certain cultural level was in a short time to become one of the most prestigious ones in the country, and he would be on the point of building what was to be a veritable audiovisual empire (on the Peruvian scale) over the years.

How did I manage, with the vast number of things that I was already doing, to add that job with the pompous title of news director of Radio Panamericana to the ones I already had? I don't know how, but I did. I suppose that some of my old jobs—the cemetery one, the one on *Extra*, the Senate one, the book on Civic Education for the Catholic University—had ended. But the one in the afternoons, at Porras Barrenechea's, and writing articles for *El Comercio* and *Cultura Peruana* went on. As did my studies in law and literature, although I attended few classes and confined myself to taking the exams. The work at Panamericana took up many hours of my time, so that in the next few months I dropped several of the jobs writing newspaper articles to concentrate on my programs at Radio Panamericana, which became more and more numerous while I was there, until they came to include "El Panamericano," the nightly news roundup.

I have used many of my memories of Radio Panamericana in my novel *Aunt Julia and the Scriptwriter*, where they are jumbled together with other memories and flights of fancy. Today I have doubts about what separates one sort from another, and it is possible that certain invented ones have crept in among the true ones here, but I suppose that too may go by the name of autobiography.

My office was in a wooden shack, on the roof, which I shared with a person so emaciated he was very nearly invisible—Samuel Pérez Barreto—who wrote, with amazing productivity, all the commercials that went out over the station. I was left openmouthed at seeing how Samuel, typing with two fingers, a cigarette dangling from his mouth, and talking to me nonstop about Hermann Hesse, was able, without pausing to think for one second, to spin out a whole series of witty comments on sausages or sanitary napkins, divinations about fruit juices or tailor shops, injunctions about cars, drinks, toys, or lotteries.

Advertising was the very air he breathed, something he did unconsciously with his fingers. His passion in life in those years was Hermann
Hesse. He kept reading or rereading him and talking about him with
a contagious enthusiasm, to the point that, for Samuel's sake, I dived
into *Steppenwolf*, where I almost drowned. His great friend, José León
Herrera, a student of Sanskrit, sometimes came to see him, and I
listened to them get involved in esoteric conversations as Samuel's
tireless fingers filled one sheet of paper after another with advertising
copy.

My work at Panamericana began very early in the morning, since
the first news bulletin was at 7 a.m. Then a five-minute one each
hour, until the noon one, which lasted fifteen minutes. The bulletins
began again at 6 p.m., and went on until "El Panamericano," the
10 p.m. news program, which was half an hour long. I spent the day
going back and forth between the station and the library of the Club
Nacional, or a class at San Marcos, or Porras's house. In the afternoon
and evening I stayed at the station for some four hours.

The truth is that I took a great liking to the work at Panamericana.
It began by being just another job to keep us alive, but as Genaro kept
pushing me to help him do new and different things and make the
programs better, and as our audience and influence kept growing, the
job turned into a commitment, something I tried to do creatively. I
became friends with Genaro, who, despite being the big boss, spoke
to everyone in an easygoing way and took an interest in everybody's
work, no matter how nondescript it was. He wanted Radio Panamericana to achieve a lasting prestige that went beyond mere entertainment
and to that end he had sponsored programs on movies, with Pepe
Ludmir, interviews and discussions of current events, on a program
of Pablo de Madalengoitia's, "Pablo y sus amigos"—and some excellent discussions of international politics by a Spanish Republican,
Benjamín Núñez Bravo, on a program called "Día y Noche."

I proposed to him that he put on the air a program on Congress,
in which we would rebroadcast part of the sessions, with brief commentaries that I would write. He agreed. Porras got permission for us
to record the sessions, and thus there came into being "El Parlamento
en síntesis" ("What's Going On in Congress"), a program that was
quite successful but wasn't on the air for long. Recording the sessions
meant that the tapes often contained not only the speeches of the

fathers of our country, but comments, exclamations, insults, whispers, and a thousand intimate interchanges which, when I edited the tapes, I was careful to cut out. But, one time, when I entrusted the task of editing them to Pascual Lucen, he allowed several salacious remarks by the Pradist senator from Puno, Torres Belón, the president of the Senate at the time, to go out over the air. The next day we were forbidden to record the sessions and the program died then and there.

By then, we had already launched "El Panamericano," which was to have a long career on the radio and, later on, on television. And the news service, which I was in charge of, allowed itself the luxury of having three or four staff writers, a first-class editorial writer—Luis Rey de Castro—and the star radio announcer Humberto Martínez Morosini.

When I began to work at Panamericana my only collaborator was the likable and loyal but very chancy character Pascual Lucen. He might very well turn up pickled in alcohol at seven in the morning and sit down at his typewriter to summarize the news items from the daily papers that I had pointed out to him, without moving a muscle of his face, letting out blasts of hiccups and belches that shook the windows. In a few minutes, the air in the shack reeked pestilentially of alcohol. He went on, nothing daunted, typing news summaries that I often had to do over from beginning to end, by hand, as I took them downstairs to the announcers. The minute my attention flagged, Pascual Lucen slipped a catastrophe into the news bulletin. For he had an almost sexual passion for floods, earthquakes, derailments; they excited him and his eyes gleamed as he longingly showed me a cable from France Presse or a newspaper clipping about them. And if I acceded and said to him, "Okay, give it a quarter of a page," he would thank me from the bottom of his heart.

Shortly thereafter, Demetrio Túpac Yupanqui arrived to give Pascual Lucen a helping hand. Demetrio was from Cuzco, a teacher of Quechua who had been a seminarian, and who for his part, whenever I let my guard down, filled the news bulletins with religious items. I never succeeded in getting the ceremonious Demetrio—whose photograph, in which he was dressed as an Inca on the heights of Machu Picchu and described as a direct descendant of the great Inca ruler Túpac Yupanqui, I had the surprise of seeing in a Spanish magazine not long ago—to call a bishop a bishop rather than a "purple-clad prelate." The third writer was a ballet dancer and an aficionado of Roman helmets—since it was difficult to come by them in Peru, a tinsmith friend of his made them for him—with whom I had literary conversations between one bulletin and the next.

Later on, Carlos Paz Cafferata came to work with me, a man who, over the years, was to have a distinguished career under Genaro. Back then, he was already a journalist who didn't seem to be a journalist (not a Peruvian one, at least) because of his frugality and his silences and a sort of metaphysical apathy toward the world and the afterworld. He was an excellent writer and editor, with a real instinct for differentiating between an important news item and a secondary one, for emphasizing and minimizing precisely the right aspects of an event, but I don't remember ever having seen him wax enthusiastic about anything or anybody. He was a sort of Zen Buddhist monk, someone who has attained Nirvana and is beyond emotions and beyond good and evil. Carlos Paz's silences and intellectual anorexia drove Samuel Pérez Barreto, a spirited and tireless conversationalist, out of his mind and he continually invented ruses to enliven, excite, and infuriate Paz. He never managed to.

Radio Panamericana reached the point of vying with Radio América for the title of best national radio station. The competition between the two was fierce and Genaro devoted his days and his nights to thinking up new programs and improvements to get the better of Panamericana's rival. During this period he bought a series of radio relays, which, installed at different locations within the country, would place Panamericana within reach of a large part of Peru. Obtaining permission from the government to install the relays was a real feat, in the process of which I saw Genaro begin to display his first talents as a politico. It is true that, without them, neither he nor any other entrepreneur would have been able to have the slightest success in Peru. The procedure was endless. He was blocked at every step through the influence of his competitors or by bureaucrats eager for bribes. And Genaro was forced to seek influence against those influences and make deals and promises right and left, over many long months, in order to obtain a mere permit that, moreover, would benefit communications and establish links between various parts of the country.

In the last two years that I was in Peru, as I wrote news bulletins for Panamericana, I managed to get one more job: a teaching assistant in the course on Peruvian literature at the University of San Marcos. Augusto Tamayo Vargas, the professor in charge of the course, who had been extremely kind to me since my first year at San Marcos, secured it for me. He was an old friend of my aunts and uncles (and as a young man, one of my mother's suitors, as I discovered one day by way of other love poems that she had also hidden at my grandparents') and I had attended his course, that first year, with great dedication. So much so that, shortly after I began it, Augusto, who was preparing an enlarged edition of his book *Literatura Peruana*, took me on to work with him, several afternoons a week. I helped him with the bibliography and typed chapters of the manuscript. Once in a while I gave him short stories of mine to read and he handed them back to me with encouraging comments.

Tamayo Vargas was in charge of several courses for foreigners at San Marcos, and since I was in the third year he had entrusted me with a short course on Peruvian authors in connection with the program, which I taught once a week and for which I earned a few soles. In 1957, when I started my last year in the Faculty of Letters, he asked me about my plans for the future. I told him that I wanted to be a writer, but that, as it was impossible to earn a living by writing, once I'd finished my studies at the university I would devote myself to journalism or teaching, since even though I was also going on, in theory, with my studies in the Faculty of Law—I was in my third year of law school—I was certain I would never practice law. Augusto advised me to get a university job. Teaching literature was compatible with writing, since it left more time free than other occupations. I had best begin right away. He had proposed to the Faculty that a post as teaching assistant be created for his chair in Peruvian literature. Might he propose my name?

Of the three hours of teaching that the chair entailed, Tamayo Vargas entrusted one to me, which I prepared, nervously and excitedly, at the library of the Club Nacional or between one news bulletin and the next in my shack at Panamericana. That one little hour a week obliged me to read or to reread certain Peruvian authors and, above all, to sum up my reactions to these readings in rational and coherent language, making notes and filling up note cards. I liked doing this and impatiently awaited the day for that class which Tamayo Vargas himself sometimes attended, sitting among the students, to see how I was doing. (Alfredo Bryce Echenique was one of my students.)

Even though my class attendance had fallen off badly ever since I had married, I had always felt warm ties to San Marcos, above all to the Faculty of Letters. My dislike of the courses at the Faculty of Law, on the other hand, was wholehearted. I went on with them out of inertia, so as to end something that I had begun, and with the vague hope that the title of attorney-at-law might serve me, later on, to earn at least enough to live on.

But I took several courses leading to a degree in literature out of sheer pleasure: the ones in Latin, for instance, by Professor Fernando Tola, one of the most interesting persons on the Faculty. He had begun, very early in his life, to study modern languages such as French, English, and German, which he then abandoned in favor of Greek and Latin. But when I was his student he had conceived a passion for Sanskrit, which he had learned by himself, and gave a course in it whose sole pupil was, I believe, José León Herrera, Samuel Pérez Barreto's friend. The irrepressible Porras Barrenechea joked: "They say that Doctor Tola knows Sanskrit. But who can tell?"

Tola, who belonged to what was known as high society, had caused what in those days was a tremendous scandal by abandoning his law-fully wedded wife and beginning to live with his secretary without trying to conceal the fact. He shared a little townhouse with her, on the Avenida Benavides, in Miraflores, crammed full of books, that he lent me without limit. He was a magnificent professor and his classes in Latin went on past the hour set for it on the official schedule. I greatly enjoyed them and remember having spent whole nights, wide awake and all excited, translating inscriptions on Roman funerary stelae for his course. I went to visit him at night sometimes in the little townhouse on Benavides, where I stayed for hours listening to him talk about the all-absorbing subject that obsessed him, Sanskrit. The three years that I studied Latin with him taught me quite a few more things than the language; and because of the many books on Roman civilization that Professor Tola had me read, I one day conceived the project of writing a novel about Heliogabalus, a project that, like so many others of those years, never came to anything more than a few short sketches.

In his Language Institute, Dr. Tola was publishing a little collection of bilingual texts, and I proposed to him that I translate Rimbaud's story "Un Coeur sous une soutane," which would not see print until thirty years later, right in the middle of the election campaign. I saw Dr. Tola years later, in Paris, where he stayed for some time perfecting his Sanskrit at the Sorbonne. Later on, he went to India, where he lived for many years and married for the third time—to an Indian woman, a professor of Sanskrit. I learned later that she chased after him all through Latin America, where this peripatetic and eternally young man had settled in Argentina (where he married for the fourth or perhaps the tenth time). By then he was an international authority on Vedic texts, the author of countless treatises and translations from Sanskrit and Hindi. I understand that for some years now he's lost interest in India, having become interested in Chinese and Japanese . . .

Other seminars that I enthusiastically attended in the Faculty of Letters were those given by Luis Alberto Sánchez, on his return from exile in 1956, on Peruvian and Hispano-American literature. I remember him above all because it was thanks to him that I discovered Rubén Darío, whom Dr. Sánchez explained in such a lively way and with such intimate knowledge that when classes let out I rushed to the library to ask for the books that he had discussed. Like many readers of Darío, I had regarded him, before that seminar, as a verbose poet, like other modernists, beneath whose verbal pyrotechnics, beautiful music, and affectedly French images, there was nothing profound, merely conventional thought borrowed from the Parnassian poets. But in that seminar I came to know the essential and unconventional Darío, the founder of modern poetry in Spanish, without whose powerful verbal revolution figures as disparate as Juan Ramón Jiménez and Antonio Machado in Spain, and Vallejo and Neruda in Hispano-America, would have been inconceivable.

Unlike Porras, Sánchez rarely prepared a class beforehand. He trusted in his powerful memory and improvised, but he had read a great deal and loved books, and he knew the innermost depths of Darío, for example, and was able to reveal him in all his secret grandeur hidden under the modernist tinsel of a fair part of his works.

Thanks to that course, I decided that my thesis in literature would deal with Darío, and in 1957 I began, in my free moments, to take notes and make file cards. I was going to need that degree if I wanted to pursue the career as a university professor toward which, thanks to Augusto Tamayo Vargas, I had taken the first step. And furthermore, I couldn't wait to finish my studies in Letters and present my thesis in order to become a candidate for the Javier Prado Fellowship, which would enable me to study for my doctorate in Spain.

The dream of that fellowship never left me. It was the only way I could make the trip to Europe, now that I was married. For the other literary fellowships, those in Hispanic Culture, hardly provided a living for just one person, let alone two. The Javier Prado, on the other hand, paid for a plane ticket to Madrid, which could be exchanged for two third-class boat tickets, and paid $120 a month for living expenses which, in the Spain of the 1950s, was a fortune.

The idea of going to Europe had stuck in my mind through all those years, even in those periods when, thanks to love or friendship, I lived intensely and felt happy. A worm kept gnawing at my conscience with the questions: "Weren't you going to be a writer? When are you going to start being one?" Because, even though the articles and the short stories of mine that were published in the Sunday supplement of *El Comercio*, in *Cultura Peruana*, or *Mercurio Peruano*, gave me for a moment the sensation that I had already begun to be a writer, I soon opened my eyes. No, I wasn't one. Those texts on the side, written by leaps and bounds, in the gaps of time that was devoted entirely to other work, were those of a simulacrum of a writer. I would be a writer only if I devoted myself to writing morning, noon, and night, putting into that undertaking all the energy that I was now wasting on so many things. And only if I felt myself surrounded by a stimulating milieu, an ambiance where writing did not seem to be such an odd, marginal activity, so lacking in harmony with the country in which I lived. To me, this ambiance had a name. Would I manage to live in Paris someday? Depression seeped down into my bones when I thought that if I didn't win that Javier Prado Fellowship that would catapult me to Europe, I would never get to France, and hence I would be as frustrated as so many other Peruvians whose literary vocation never got beyond the rudimentary stage.

This was, needless to say, a constant subject of conversation with Lucho and Abelardo. They used to drop by my shack at Panamericana after the 6 p.m. news bulletin and, until the next one, we could spend a little while together, having coffee in one of the old places

on the Plaza de Armas or La Colmena. I spurred them on to go to
Europe with me. We would face up to the problem of survival better
if we were together; we would write there the volumes we yearned to
write. The objective would be Paris, but if there was no way of getting
there, we would stop for a while in Monte Carlo, principality of
Monaco. This place, phrased as a name and surname, turned into
our trio's password, and sometimes, when we were with other friends,
one of the three of us would pronounce the emblematic formula—
Monte Carlo, principality of Monaco—leaving all the others puzzled.

Lucho was determined to leave. His law practice had convinced
him, I believe, that that profession repelled him as much as it did me,
and the idea of spending some time in Europe cheered him up. His
father had promised to help him financially, once he'd graduated. This
encouraged him to begin work on the thesis he needed to write so as
to get his degree.

Abelardo's trip was more complicated, since Pupi had just had a
little girl. And with a family, everything became risky and costly. But
Abelardo allowed himself to be infected at times by my enthusiasm
and also began to dream: he would try for the postgraduate fellowship
in law that got the winner to Italy. With that and some money he'd
saved he'd have enough for the trip. He too would get to the Europe
des anciens parapets and would show up at the rendezvous of literary
honor, in Monte Carlo, principality of Monaco.

In addition to our shared projects and fantasies, certain skirmishes
of the guerrilla warfare on the local literary scene contributed to rein-
forcing our friendship. I remember one episode in particular, because
I was the one who lit the fuse that set it off. From time to time I wrote
book reviews. Abelardo gave me an assignment to review an anthology
of Hispano-American poetry, compiled and translated into French by
the Hispanist Mathilde Pomès. In my review, a rather fierce one, I
wasn't content to limit myself to criticizing the book, but also slipped
in several very harsh sentences about Peruvian writers in general, the
"tellurics," the indigenists, regionalists, and local colorists in particular, and above all the modernist José Santos Chocano.

Several writers submitted a rebuttal—among them Alejandro Romualdo, with an article in the review 1957 entitled "No sólo los
gigantes hacen la historia" ("Not Only Giants Make History"), and
the poet Francisco Bendezú, a great exponent of bad taste in literature

and in life, who accused me of having offended the nation's honor by abusing the eminent bard Santos Chocano. I answered him in a long article and Lucho Loayza intervened with a lapidary volley. Augusto Tamayo Vargas himself wrote a text in defense of Peruvian literature, reminding me that "adolescence ought to be over soon." At that point I recalled that I was an assistant to the holder of the chair in that literature that I had just attacked (I believe that in my articles the only ones who were spared in the genocide were the poets César Vallejo, José María Eguren, and César Moro) and I was afraid that Augusto, in the face of such an incongruity, would take my job away from me. But he was too decent to do a thing like that, and no doubt thought that with the passage of time I would become more considerate and charitable toward native writers (and that is what has happened).

Although these petty controversies and literary and artistic fracases —they happened often—had very limited repercussions, they suggest that, however minor it might be, there was a certain cultural life in the Lima of that day. It was possible because Prado's administration brought an economic bonanza to the country, and for some time Peru opened up and had interchanges with the world. It happened, to be sure, despite the fact that the discriminatory mercantilist structure of institutions scarcely changed at all—the poor Peruvians of the C and D sectors continued to be hemmed in by poverty, with few opportunities to climb higher—but it brought the middle and upper classes a period of prosperity. It was owed, basically, to one of those bold and surprising initiatives of which that clever, cunning scoundrel of a politician (what in Peru they call a really foxy one!) whose name was Manuel Prado was capable. The severest critic his administration had was the owner of *La Prensa*, Pedro Beltrán, who in his newspaper mounted a daily attack on the economic policy of the regime. One fine day, Prado called Beltrán and offered him the Ministry of Finance and the premiership, with carte blanche to do what he thought best. Beltrán accepted and for two years applied the conservative monetarist policy that he had learned during his years as a student at the London School of Economics: fiscal austerity, balanced budgets, opening up the country to international competition, encouragement of private enterprise and investment. The economy responded admirably to this treatment: Peruvian currency became stronger—the country has never again had the solvency it did at that time—and domestic and foreign investment grew, employment increased, and the country lived for several years in a climate of optimism and security.

In the cultural domain, the effects were that books arrived in Peru from all over, and also musicians and theatrical companies and foreign art exhibitions—the Institute of Contemporary Art, founded by a private group and for a time directed by Sebastián Salazar Bondy, brought the most outstanding artists of Latin America to Peru, among them Matta and Wilfredo Lam, and many North American and European ones—and the publication of books and cultural periodicals (*Literatura* was one of them, but there were several others, and not only in Lima, but in cities such as Trujillo and Arequipa). The poet Manuel Scorza was to begin bringing out during those years popular editions of books that proved to be enormous successes and made him a small fortune. His bold socialist stance had lost its audaciousness and there were symptoms of the worst sort of capitalism in his conduct: he paid his authors—when he paid them at all—miserable royalties, with the argument that they ought to make sacrifices for the sake of culture, and he went around in a brand-new fire-engine-red Buick, with a biography of Onassis in his pocket. So as to irritate him, when we were together, I used to recite to him the least memorable of his verses: "Peru, I spit in vain on your name."

Nobody, however, outside of the little group of journalists who worked with him at *La Prensa*, appreciated Beltrán's work to orient economic policy in a different direction. Nor did anybody draw from what happened in those years conclusions favoring free market policies, private enterprise, and opening of the country to internationalism. Quite to the contrary. Beltrán's image continued to be fiercely attacked by the left. And socialism began in those years to break out of the catacomb in which it had been imprisoned and to win a place for itself in public opinion. Populist philosophy, in favor of economic nationalism, the growth of the state, and government interventionism as indispensable for development and social justice, which up until then had been the monopoly of the APRA and of the small Marxist left, multiplied and reproduced itself in other versions, thanks to the guiding hand of Belaunde Terry, who had founded Popular Action and in those years took its message from town to town throughout the whole of Peru; thanks to the Christian Democratic Party, in which Cornejo

Chávez's radical bent was growing stronger by the day; and thanks to a pressure group—the Movimiento Social Progresista (the Progressivist Social Movement)—formed by leftist intellectuals, which, although sorely lacking in mass support, was to have an important impact on the political culture of the era.

(After a little over two years in office in Prado's administration, believing that the success of his economic policy had made him politically popular, Pedro Beltrán resigned from the Ministry of Finance to try his hand at organizing a political movement, with his eye on the presidential election of 1962. His attempt was a resounding failure, the first time he took to the streets. A rally called for by Beltrán at the Colegio La Recoleta was broken up by the Aprista "buffaloes" and he wound up being laughed at. Beltrán would never again hold a single political post, until finally, with the advent of Velasco's dictatorship, *La Prensa* was taken from him, as was his hacienda, Montalbán, and his fine old colonial house in the downtown area of Lima was torn down, on the pretext of opening up a new street. He left the country to go into exile, where I met him, thanks to the journalist Elsa Arana Freyre, in Barcelona in the 1970s. He was by then an old man who spoke with pathetic nostalgia of that old colonial house in Lima demolished because of the pettiness and the stupidity of his political enemies.)

And with the same boldness with which he had appointed Beltrán his minister of finance, one fine day President Prado appointed Porras Barrenechea minister of foreign relations. The latter, since his election as senator, had had a distinguished career in Congress. With other independents and with the members of Congress belonging to the Christian Democratic Party and to Popular Action, he led a campaign to get Congress to investigate the illegal political and economic acts committed by Odría's dictatorship. The initiative did not get very far because the Pradist majority, along with its allies who were opposed to it (almost all of those on the list on which Porras had appeared as a candidate) and Odría's own supporters, blocked his efforts. This converted Porras Barrenechea into a senator who opposed Prado's administration, a role he played with great satisfaction and without thinking twice. Hence, his appointment as foreign minister came as a surprise to everyone, including Porras himself, who passed on the news, one afternoon, with stupefaction, to Carlos Araníbar and me: the president had just offered him the ministry, by telephone, in a two-minute conversation.

He accepted, out of a touch of vanity, I suppose, and also as another compensation for that rectorate that he had lost, a wound that went on bleeding as long as he lived. With his ministerial duties, his book on Pizarro came to a dead stop.

Shortly after this move, President Prado made another spectacular one, which brought Lima's fondness of gossip to white-hot heat: he managed to have his Catholic marriage to his wife of more than forty years (and the mother of his children) annulled, on the grounds of a "formal defect" (he convinced the Vatican that he had been forced to marry without his consent). And immediately thereafter—he was a man capable of anything, and what was more, like all the brazen rascals of this world, utterly charming—was wedded, in the Presidential Palace, to his mistress of many years. On the night of that wedding, I saw with my own eyes, strolling about the main square of Lima, in front of the Presidential Palace, as though observing one of the traditions at the time of the viceroyalty, in a novel by Ricardo Palma, a group of ladies from families in Lima of noble lineage, with elegant mantillas and rosaries, and a huge placard that read: "Long live the indissolubility of Catholic marriage."

EIGHTEEN

The Dirty War

O N January 8, 1990, the registration of candidates for the Senate and the Chamber of Representatives was closed. And the follow-ing day marked the start of a televised publicity campaign by our candidates for the two houses that had a devastating effect on everything that I had been saying since August 1987.

The Peruvian electoral system has what is known as the preferential vote. Candidates for the Senate and the Chamber of Representatives are not elected directly; their names appear on the ballot in a list made up by their party. Votes are cast for a party's list, not for individual candidates, and votes are not split between parties; all votes are for the straight ticket. But a voter can, in addition, mark on the ballot his or her preference for two candidates on each one of the lists. The number of senators and representatives on each list who win seats is proportional to the percentage of votes won by the list as a whole. The order in which candidates qualify to enter Congress is determined by the pref-erential vote.

The reason for this system was to allow voters to rectify the decision of the parties as to the order of preference on their lists. This, it was thought, would be a way to counteract the influence of the party hierarchies which draw up the lists, giving the voter the possibility of correcting the partisan processes at work in the selection of candidates. In practice, however, the preferential vote turned out to be a perverse system that transfers the electoral contest to within the congressional lists, since each candidate tries to win the voter's preference for himself rather than for his co-candidates.

In order to mitigate the bad effects of this practice, we drew up a little booklet with suggestions that set forth in didactic style the sore points in the system; it was distributed to our candidates in Libertad. In it, Lucho Bustamante, Jorge Salmón, Freddy Cooper, and I asked them not to promise anything in their publicity campaigns that I myself didn't promise and not to go in for lies and contradictions. Since the CADE conference, the entire election campaign had been a massive attack against our program by Apristas and Socialists and they shouldn't give our adversaries a chance to demolish what we had built up. It was also important to avoid wasting money. Jorge Salmón taught them about the risks of saturating TV screens with spot ads.

It was as if we'd been preaching to the deaf. A mere handful—less than ten, in any event—took the trouble to organize their campaign by coordinating what they said in their pitch to the voters with our Plan for Governing. I do not except from this charge the candidates of Libertad, several of whom shared responsibility for the excesses committed.

From January 9, when the Lima daily papers devoted an entire page to a full-face photo of Alberto Borea Odría, a PPC candidate for a Senate seat, until the end of March—that is to say, until a few days before the elections—the campaign for the preferential vote of our candidates kept growing, oppressively and anarchically, until it reached extremes that made me laugh and at the same time repelled me. "If what they are doing disgusts me all this much," I said over and over again to Patricia, "what must the reaction of the man in the street be to such a spectacle?"

All the private television channels spewed out images of the faces of our candidates from morning till night, in ads in which the squandering of money often went hand in hand with bad taste, and in which many of them offered everything imaginable and unimaginable, without its mattering to them that this was in flagrant contradiction to the most elementary principles of that liberal philosophy which, I kept saying, was the one that was ours, and even contradicted common sense. Some promised public works and others price controls and the creation of new public services, but most of them didn't offer any ideas whatsoever and limited themselves to promoting their face and their number on the list, in a strident voice, and as repetitively as a jackhammer. One senatorial candidate had his image enhanced by an aria from an operetta sung by a baritone, and a candidate for the Chamber of Representatives, to show his love for the people, appeared among the big backsides of mulattas dancing to Afro rhythms; another one was shown weeping, surrounded by elderly little men and women whose lot he sympathized with in a tremulous voice.

The propaganda of the Front's candidates made such a clean sweep of the audiovisual media that, in February and the beginning of March, they gave the impression that they were the only ones who existed, and that their opponents on the other lists had disappeared, or made such sporadic appearances that they looked like pygmies competing with giants or, more precisely, victims of starvation confronting millionaires.

Alan García appeared on TV to explain that he had made a calculation, according to which a number of Democratic Front candidates for seats in the Senate or in the Chamber of Representatives had now spent more money in TV spots than they would earn in their five years in office if they were elected. Were they subsidized, then, by oligarchic groups, whose interests they were going to defend in the National Congress against those of the Peruvian people? How were those members of Congress going to pay back their generous patrons?

Although President García didn't seem to be the ideal person to voice such scruples, it must have lingered in the minds of many people that all that excessive advertising concealed something shady. And other voters, those in the highlands, those who don't make analyses, those who follow their impulses, must simply have been indignant at that arrogant demonstration of economic power and suppressed the enthusiasm they had felt at the beginning for what appeared to be a proposal that was new and untouched by corruption. Many of those candidates were not new, but rather the cream of the crop of sharp political schemers, and of one or another of them it could not even be said that he had clean hands, since his passage through the previous administration had left behind him a wake that discredited him.

From the first opinion polls taken by the Sawyer/Miller Group it was evident that that extravagant publicity had had a negative impact on voters with small incomes, those into whose heads the official propaganda hammered the slogan that I was the candidate of the rich. What better parading of wealth than the ads that turned up on their television screens? All that might have been won in the previous year and a half with my preaching in favor of a liberal reform was lost in just days and weeks in the face of that assault of repeated appearances, ads, posters, which monopolized TV screens, radios, walls, news-papers, and magazines. In the midst of that vast and confusing over-abundance in which the emblem of the Democratic Front—a pre-Hispanic staircase shown in profile—was used to promote the most contradictory proposals and formulas, my message lost its air of re-form and of change. And my image as a person was confused with that of professional politicians and those who acted as though they were.

In February the opinion polls showed a decrease in the number of those intending to vote for me. One of only a few points, but one that brought me further away from the 50 percent necessary to win in the first round of balloting. Freddy Cooper summoned the congressional candidates of the Democratic Front to a meeting. He explained to them what was happening and suggested that they put a stop to the spots. Only a handful of candidates showed up. And Freddy had to confront a sort of mutiny; candidates of the Christian Popular Party and of Popular Action told him, without mincing words, that they refused to accept his request, since it would favor the candidates of Libertad, who had begun their campaigns before their allies in the Democratic Front. As this was happening I was touring the *departa-mento* of Lambayeque, in the North, so that it was only on my return to Lima that I was informed of the matter. I met with Belaunde and Bedoya, whom I assured that if we didn't put a stop to this extravagant publicity we would lose the elections. Both of them asked me to bring the subject up for discussion in the executive council of the Front, which meant losing several days.

In the meeting of the council the internal weakness of the alliance was evident. The explanations of the head of the campaign, with the results of the opinion surveys concerning the disastrous effect of the publicity on the preferential vote in hand, did not move the members, almost all of whom were candidates for the Senate or the Chamber of Representatives. In the name of the Christian Popular Party, Senator Felipe Osterling explained that many of the candidates of his party had waited until the final weeks of the campaign to launch their publicity and that to subject them to restrictions now would be unjust and discriminatory, and that, moreover, we ran the risk of being dis-obeyed. And in the name of Popular Action, Senator Gastón Acurio put forward similar reasons and another one, which many of those present agreed with: cutting down on our advertising meant leaving the field free for the list of independents headed by the banker Francisco Pardo Mesones, which, in fact, was also churning out a great deal. Those on the list headed by Pardo Mesones used the slogan "We're free," and Acurio made the executive council laugh by referring to it as "We're rich." Were we going to silence our candidates and hand the bankers of "We're rich" their seats in Congress on a platter? The upshot was that a utopian agreement was adopted that merely urged the candidates to cut down on their advertising.

That same Sunday, in an interview on television with César Hildebrandt, I said that the excesses of our candidates gave an impression of extravagance that the majority of Peruvians found offensive, in addition to causing confusion concerning our program, and I urged the candidates to correct these excesses. I did the same thing on three other occasions, but it was of little use, since not even the candidates of Libertad paid any attention to me. One of the exceptions was, of course, Miguel Cruchaga, who, on the same day as my declaration, drastically cut down on his advertising. And a few weeks later, at a press conference, Alberto Borea announced that, in obedience to my exhortations, he was winding up his campaign. But there were now very few days remaining before the elections and the damage was irreparable.

Not all the Libertad candidates committed excesses or had the financial means to do so. But a number of them did, and waged such extravagant campaigns that the bad impression did damage to the entire Front and to me in particular. It played a role in weakening the support of that 20 percent of the voters who, in the final weeks of the campaign, according to the opinion polls, changed their minds about voting for me and instead favored Alberto Fujimori, who, in January and February, and even in the first two weeks in March, remained at a standstill, with a projected vote of one percent in his favor. In that 20 percent, the least-well-off sector of the entire population of the country, the idea the APRA and the left were trying to drum into the heads of voters in that sector—that if I won the rich would come to power along with me to do as they pleased in my administration—was spectacularly confirmed by that costly advertising campaign that was possible only with powerful and well-organized financial backing.

In the middle of the hectic agenda that I was trying to get through every day, what had happened made me think, very often, about what this augured for the future, once the elections had been won. Our alliance was held together with safety pins, and the fidelity of our own leaders to the ideas, to the ethics, and to the proposals I made was subordinate to mere political interests. Nothing guaranteed me the support of the congressional majority—if we managed to secure it— for liberal reforms. This would come about only if there were enormous pressure from public opinion. From January on, therefore, all my effort was concentrated on winning those sectors of the provinces and regions of the interior where I had not yet been or to which I had had made only very brief trips.

In my travels through the *departamento* of Lambayeque I visited for the first time the agricultural cooperatives of Cayaltí and Pomalca, both considered solid bastions of Aprismo. In both of them, however, I was able to talk with no problems, explaining the implications of the privatization of communal land and the conversion of agrarian complexes into private enterprises, in which former members of a cooperative would become stockholders. I don't know whether I got my message across, but both in Cayaltí and in Pomalca there were warm smiles exchanged between the peasants and workers who were listening to me when I told them that they had the good fortune of working marvelously productive land and that, without price controls, without state monopolies, they would be the first social sector to benefit from liberalization. And even more than in the sugar mills, in Ferreñafe, and in Lambayeque, too, in Saña, in the huge rally in Chiclayo, or in the torrid little towns of the *departamento*, the campaign took on during those days the air of a lively fiesta, what with the inevitable dances and songs of the North opening and closing the rallies. The happiness and enthusiasm of the people was the best antidote against exhaustion. And it was something that made us forget at times the sinister side of the campaign: violence.

On January 9, the former minister of defense, Enrique López Albújar, an army general, was murdered in the streets of Lima by a terrorist commando unit; for a reason that never came to light, the general was not accompanied by an escort on the morning of the attack on his life. Since the sisters of General López Albújar were militants of Libertad in Tacna, I interrupted my tour of the North to return to Lima and attend the funeral rites. That assassination was the beginning of a sudden rise in political crimes in the country, whereby Sendero Luminoso and the Túpac Amaru revolutionaries tried to thwart the electoral process. Between January and February, more than six hundred persons died because of political violence and some three hundred attacks were put on record.

Also, as the elections approached, those who were acting within the law became extremely edgy. The APRA, returning to the weapons that made it famous in Peruvian history—stones, pistols, and cudgels— began to attack our rallies, with groups of "buffaloes" who did their best to break them up. There were frequent skirmishes that ended up with injured victims in the hospital. They never prevented us from holding our rallies, but in the course of a swing through the interior by Libertad, there were incidents that came very close to ending in tragedy.

In that northern *departamento*, an Aprista cradle and bulwark, the most important and most numerous cooperatives on the coast, such as Casagrande and Cartavio, are located, and I was determined to visit them. In Casagrande, although the counterdemonstration of "buffaloes" made an infernal racket—they were posted on the rooftops and in the narrow streets leading to the main square—the former Aprista senator Torres Vallejo and I were able to deliver our talks from the bed of a truck, and even take a turn on foot about the place, before leaving. But in Cartavio they had set up an ambush for us. The rally, attended by a fair number of people, took place without incident. Once it was over, as the motorcade was getting ready to leave, we were attacked by a horde armed with stones and knives and some with pistols, who hurled all sorts of things at us, even tires that they had set on fire. I was already in the supposedly armored van, one of whose windowpanes disintegrated from the stones being thrown at us, and despite the moments of chaos, I managed to grab the hand of one of my bodyguards when I noticed that, out of fear or rage, he was about to shoot point-blank at the attackers, headed by two Aprista leaders of the region: Benito Dioces Briceño and Silverio Silva. Four cars in our motorcade were smashed to pieces and burned, and among the injured was the English journalist Kevin Rafferty, who followed me all through the North and who, they told me, remained imperturbably calm as the blood streamed down his face. A similar cool-headedness was shown by my brother-in-law, who always stayed behind until the very end to make sure that the camera crews and sound technicians were protected, and Manolo Moreyra, the leader of SODE, who, in one of his usual streaks of inattention to what was going on, had stayed behind to inspect the place when the rally had already broken up. The attack did not give them time to reach their cars. So they then mingled with the assailants, who fortunately did not recognize them. Both of them escaped being thoroughly beaten up. The episode gave rise to many protests and President García made things worse by saying over television that there was no reason to make such a fuss "over a few little stones that landed on Vargas Llosa."

In point of fact, the stones were a secondary aspect of the "dirty war" against me prepared by García and his followers for this last stage. The essential part would be the maneuvers to discredit me, to which, from January on, the entire administration appeared to devote itself, under the baton of the minister of finance. They would gradually increase in number and intensity until the elections. It would be an almost infinite task to enumerate all of them, but it is worth giving an account of the most notorious ones, since they prove to what abysses of filth, and at times, of unintended humor, their backers reduced the electoral process.

On January 28, 1990, the minister of finance, César Vásquez Bazán—the most incompetent of the nobodies to whom Alan García gave that portfolio during his term in office—went on television, on the Channel 5 program "Panorama," to defy me to produce my annual sworn income tax returns since 1984 to prove that I had paid my taxes. And the following day a senator of the United Left, Javier Diez Canseco, showed those returns on television, assuring his audience that the figures that appeared on them were questionable "except for his income from author's royalties." He stated that I had undervalued my house in Barranco so as to get around paying the required amount of property tax on it.

There thus began a campaign which was to broaden by the day and on which two so-called adversaries—the Aprista administration and the extreme left represented by the PUM (the Unified Mariateguist Party) —collaborated to show the country that for the last five years I had filed false returns to avoid paying all the taxes I owed. I remember the insuperable feeling of disgust that came over me the few times I managed to see Vásquez Bazán (today a fugitive from Peruvian justice) on television screens, supposedly documenting this lie. Although it was sheer humbug from beginning to end, the massive synchronized propaganda that accompanied it for several long months, and the use of state agencies to distort the truth, were such that they managed to give this falsehood a sort of reality and a main role in the final round of the elections.

It is very difficult, if not impossible, for a writer to avoid paying taxes on the author's royalties he has received. These are deducted from the profit made from his books by the publisher himself, in the country where his books are published. It is rare for a Peruvian to live on his author's royalties, and therefore I had held consultations about my particular case, for many years before the election campaign, with one of the most outstanding tax lawyers in the country, a close friend of mine: Roberto Dañino. He—or, rather, his staff, and, above all, Dr. Julio Gallo—had for some time taken care of my sworn declarations. And, knowing very well that should I one day enter politics, everything about my life would be gone over with a fine-tooth comb in search of my vulnerable points, I had been particularly scrupulous about my annual income tax returns.

My books were not published in Peru and my taxes on the royalties they earned me were therefore paid in the countries where they were published and translated. Peruvian laws allow the sums paid by a Peruvian taxpayer on income earned abroad to be deducted from taxes owed in Peru. But, instead of going through this procedure, in Peru —where I earned no taxable income—I took advantage of a law exempting from taxation works considered to be of artistic value, a law that had been introduced in Congress by the APRA in 1965,* and approved by the congressional majority made up of members of the alliance between the APRA and Odría's supporters. (I will mention, in parentheses, that my program for governing contemplated the elimination of *all* tax exemptions, beginning with this very one.) In order for my books to be included within that category, I had to follow for each one of them a procedure before the National Institute of Culture and the Ministry of Education, which, eventually, handed down the applicable decision. Alan García's Aprista administration had done this with my last three books. Where, then, did my supposed tax evasion lie?

* Law 15792, of December 14, 1965.

Surrounded by journalists and cameramen, an Aprista attorney, Luis Alberto Salgado, hastened to the main offices of the National Tax Authority to ask that a tax hearing be opened to determine the amount of taxes I had cheated the Peruvian state out of. Obediently, the tax authorities opened not just one hearing but several dozen. In that way, there was always some sort of trouble brewing for me. Each of the items questioned by the Supervisory Board, which constitute supposedly private information, reached the Aprista and Communist press before they reached me and were publicized in the most scandalous way, so as to give the impression that I had already been found guilty and that my house in Barranco would very soon be seized.

Each item questioned—I repeat that there were several dozen of them—required an enormous amount of work by the secretaries, in order to hunt up documented justification for them, and the cost of transportation for this or that trip that I made to this or that university, to give this or that lecture, and letters and telexes to these universities to have them confirm that I had been paid the $1,000 or $1,500 recorded on my tax return for that year. The law firm to which Roberto Dañino belongs hadn't yet completed the dossier in answer to one questioned item when it received another one, or several at the same time, with the most outlandish requests for information and proof with regard to my travels, my lectures, my articles of the last five years, to verify that I hadn't concealed a single source of income. They were all answered to the tax authorities' complete satisfaction, with no proof whatsoever of a single irregularity on my part.

How much work did it represent for those in Roberto Dañino's law firm to help me confront that flood of investigations by the tax authorities ordered by President García as part of the dirty campaign against me? If they had charged me legal fees, I probably wouldn't have been able to pay them, for another of the consequences of those three years of immersion in active politics was the fact that my income dwindled away to almost nothing and I had to live on my savings. But Bobby and his colleagues refused any honorarium whatsoever for the effort that they had had to expend to show that I had not violated that "legality" that the Aprista administration used so shamelessly.

One day, Óscar Balbi brought me a recording of a telephone conversation between the editor-in-chief of *Página Libre*, Guillermo Thorndike, and the tax commissioner, in which the two of them discussed the next steps to take in the campaign with regard to my tax returns, because each step in those proceedings against me was planned in accordance with a strategy for getting the most publicity possible from the scandal sheets. Huge headlines announced that the tax investigators had left for Europe because the authorities had been informed that I was the principal stockholder in Seix Barral, the major Barcelona publishing house, the owner of the Carmen Balcells Literary Agency in the same city, and of real estate in Barcelona and on the Costa Azul. And one morning, when I was going from one meeting to another, in different rooms in the house, I saw my mother and my mother-in-law, leaning over the radio, listening to an announcer on Radio Nacional reporting that officials of the judiciary were on their way to Barranco to carry out the seizure of my house and of everything in it, as surety against the sum I owed the government for fraud, as had already been announced.

The leaders of the extreme left were diligent collaborators with the government in this campaign, in particular Senator Diez Canseco, who kept waving about on the little screen my sworn income tax returns, passed on to him by the APRA, as evidence against me. And one day I heard over the radio Ricardo Letts, another leader of the PUM, call me a thief. Up until then Letts, whom I have known for many years, and with whom I had maintained a firm friendship all that time despite our ideological differences, hadn't struck me as being capable of slandering a friend in the belief that it would gain him political benefits. But at this point in the campaign I already knew that, in Peru, there are few politicians whom politics, that Circe, doesn't turn into pigs.

The tax affair was just one of several maneuvers to discredit me which the García administration used in its attempt to prevent what at this juncture still appeared to be an overwhelming victory by the Democratic Front.* One of them made me out to be a pervert and a pornographer, as was proved by my novel *Elogio de la madrastra* (*In Praise of the Stepmother*), which was read in its entirety during peak listening hours, at the rate of a chapter a day, on Channel 7, which was controlled by the state. In a dramatic voice, the woman announcer

---

* In March, an opinion poll by the CIP (Centro de Investigaciones del Perú—Peruvian Center for Research) gave me 43 percent nationwide, against 14.5 percent for Alva Castro, 11.5 percent for Alfonso Barrantes, and 6.8 percent for Henry Pease.

who introduced each episode warned housewives and mothers to keep their children away from the TV set because they were going to hear nefarious things. But the people had the right to know everything about the person who aspired to preside over the country's destiny. Another announcer, a man this time, then proceeded to read the chapter, in melodramatic tones when there was an erotic passage. Afterward, a round table was held, in which Aprista psychologists, sexologists, and sociologists analyzed me. I was leading such a hectic life that I was unable, naturally, to allow myself the luxury of seeing those programs, but on one occasion I managed to watch part of one of them and was so amused that I remained glued to the TV set, listening to the Aprista general Germán Parra elaborate on the following thought: "According to Freud, Doctor Vargas Llosa ought to be under treatment for a mental disorder."

Another of the APRA's warhorses was my "atheism." "Peruvian! Do you want an atheist in the office of president of Peru?" was the question put to viewers in a televised spot in which there appeared a semi-monstrous face—mine—that looked like the incarnation and the prelude of every sort of iniquity. The "hate office" researchers found, in an article of mine on *huachafería*—a form of bad taste that is a national propensity—entitled "A Bit of Bubbly, Old Buddy?" a mocking phrase referring to the procession of the Lord of Miracles. Alan García, who, in order to show the Peruvian people how devout he was, dressed in purple in October and helped carry the platform of the Lord of Miracles on his shoulders with the expression of a contrite sinner on his face, hastened to declare to the press that I had gravely offended the Church and the most heartfelt act of devotion of the Peruvian people.* The strongest of García's supporters joined in the chorus, and for several days people were treated to the spectacle, in newspapers, over the radio, and on TV, of high Aprista officials and members of Congress suddenly converted into crusaders for the faith, making amends to the Lord of Miracles. I remember the fiery Mercedes Cabanillas, her face

---

* During the month of October many people in Lima dress in purple or wear something purple to show their devotion to the Lord of Miracles, a painting of the crucified Christ said to have been done on the wall of slaves' quarters in the seventeenth century, which has survived all of Lima's great earthquakes and is an object of veneration. On three days in October, the icon, which weighs three tons, is borne through the streets by teams of men in a spectacular procession that includes incense bearers and a choir. (*Trans. note*)

trembling with indignation, talking like a Joan of Arc prepared to go to the stake in defense of her religion. (It was amusing that all of this should be staged under the auspices of the party founded by Haya de la Torre, who had begun his political career, in May 1923, opposing the dedication of Lima to the Sacred Heart of Jesus, and who was accused, for a good part of his life, of being an enemy of the Church, an atheist, and a Freemason.)

I was overcome with a curious sensation in the face of these mud-slinging capers. I don't know if it was exhaustion brought on by the tremendous mental and physical effort required day after day to get through meetings, trips, rallies, interviews, and arguments, or whether I had developed a psychological defense mechanism, but I noted all that as though the person being invented by the negative campaign which was increasingly replacing any kind of rational debate were someone other than myself. But in the face of these extremes reminiscent of a one-act farce and the many violences of the electoral process, I began to be assailed by the thought that I had made a great mistake by focusing my strategy on telling the truth and outlining a program of reforms. Because ideas, intelligence, consistency, and above all decency seemed to have less place in the campaign with each passing day.

What was the attitude of the Church, on the eve of the first round of balloting? One of consummate prudence. Until April 8, it forbore to take part in the debate, not allowing itself to be dragged into the campaign issue of my "atheism" and my affronts to the Christ clad in purple, but at the same time not showing the slightest sign of approval of my candidacy. At the beginning of 1990, Cardinal Juan Landázuri Ricketts, the archbishop and primate of the Church in Peru, had retired because he had reached the age limit—he was seventy-six years old at the time—and had been replaced by a prelate ten years younger, the Jesuit Augusto Vargas Alzamora. I paid both of them the visits called for by protocol, not suspecting the extremely important role that the Church would play in the second round of voting. I had seen Cardinal Landázuri, an Arequipan who was related to my mother's family, a number of times at reunions of relatives on my mother's side. He had granted the dispensation that enabled me to marry my cousin Patricia in 1965 (since Uncle Lucho and Aunt Olga demanded that we be married in church), though I had not been the one who went to request it of him; my mother and my Aunt Laura did. Cardinal Landázuri had been assigned the mission of leading the Peruvian Church from May 1955 on, perhaps the most difficult period in its entire history, what with the division that liberation theology brought with it and the Communist and revolutionary militancy of a considerable number of nuns and priests, together with the process of secularization of Peruvian society, which made greater advances in those decades than in all the preceding centuries. A very prudent man, not given to impressive moves in new directions or bold intellectual advances, but a scrupulous and painstaking arbitrator and a most astute diplomat, Cardinal Landázuri had managed to maintain the unity of an institution undermined by tremendous dissensions. I went to see him at his home in La Victoria on January 18, with Miguel Cruchaga, and we talked for some time, about Arequipa, about my family—he remembered having been a schoolmate of Uncle Lucho's and told me anecdotes about my mother when she was a little girl—though he avoided the subject of politics and, of course, didn't say a word about the campaign regarding my atheism, at its height at the time. But as he was bidding me goodbye he whispered to me, with a wink, pointing to the priest who was with him: "This Father is a fan of the Democratic Front."

I didn't know Monsignor Vargas Alzamora. Accompanied by Álvaro and Lucho Bustamante, who, as I have already said, is a sort of Jesuit *ad honorem*, I went to congratulate him on his being named Primate of Peru. He received us in a little study at the Colegio La Inmaculada and from the first moment of the conversation between us I was impressed by his lively intelligence and his clearsightedness with regard to the problems confronting Peru. Although we did not mention the electoral campaign, we spoke at length of the backwardness, the poverty, the violence, the anarchy, the lack of stability, and the inequalities in Peru, and his information about all those subjects was as solid as his opinion was judicious. Slender and delicate, most circumspect in his speech, Monsignor Vargas Alzamora nonetheless betrayed signs of great strength of character. He seemed to me to be a modern man, sure of his mission and possessed of great fortitude beneath his courteous manners, surely the best helmsman for the Peruvian Church in the difficult times that it was going through. After I had bidden him goodbye, I said as much to Lucho Bustamante. I couldn't have imagined that the next time I saw the new archbishop of Lima it would be under spectacular circumstances.

Meanwhile, my trips throughout Peru followed one after the other without a letup, at a rate of visits to four, six, and sometimes more places a day, trying to cover for one last time the twenty-four *departamentos*, and in each one of them the greatest possible number of provinces and districts. The schedule set up by Freddy Cooper and his team—the efficient Pier Fontanot from the campaign's command headquarters was in charge—was met perfectly, and I must say that the logistics of the rallies, transportation from place to place, connections, food and lodging, rarely broke down, which, in view of the state of the country and the national idiosyncrasy, was a real feat. The planes, helicopters, motorboats, minivans, or horses were there, and in all the villages or hamlets there was always a little platform and two or three young people from Mobilization who had arrived there beforehand to make sure that the microphones and loudspeakers were working, and that a minimum of security measures were in place. Freddy had several aides whose time was devoted exclusively to giving him a hand at this task, and one of them, Carlos Lozada, whom we called Woody Allen because he looked like him, and also like Groucho Marx, intrigued me by his gift for being everywhere at once. He looked as though he were disguised as something or other, though we couldn't figure out what, with a strange headpiece, at once a cap and a helmet equipped with earflaps that reminded me of Charles Bovary's headgear, and a loose jacket with a big backpack from which he took out sandwiches when it was time to eat, portable radios for communications, soft drinks to allay people's thirst, revolvers for the bodyguards, batteries for the minivans, and even that day's papers so we wouldn't lose touch with the latest news. He was always on the run, and continually talking into a little microphone hanging from around his neck, with which he was constantly in communication with some mysterious control center to which he reported what was going on or from which he received instructions. I had the sensation that that eternal monologue of Woody Allen's was organizing my destiny, that he was deciding where I would speak, sleep, travel, and whom I would see or fail to see in the course of my junkets. But I never managed to exchange a single word with him. Later on I learned that he was a public relations man who, having begun to work for the campaign in a professional capacity, discovered his real vocation and secret genius: that of a political organizer. In all truth, he did a magnificent job, solved any and every problem and never created a one. Glimpsing, wherever I arrived, whether in the midst of the underbrush of the jungle or amid the crags of the Andes or in the little towns along the sandy coast, his bizarre outfit—the thick glasses of someone very nearsighted, a colored shirt, and that sort of article of furniture with slipcovers that he carried around on his back, that Pandora's box from which he took out unimaginable things—gave me a feeling of relief, the reassuring presentiment that, in that particular place, everything would come off as planned. One morning, in Ilo, immediately after we arrived, and before going to the rally in the main square where people were waiting for me, I decided to go down to the port, where a boat was being unloaded. I went up to it to speak with the stevedores, who, leaning on the gangplank of the vessel, were supervising the loading and unloading being done by the *puntos* (workers to whom they hire out their work), and all of a sudden, as though he were simply one more of those in the group, hidden underneath his combination cap and helmet and portable trunk of a backpack, talking into his microphone, I spied Woody Allen . . .

Amid these whirlwind tours all over Peru, I still arranged things so as to go to Brazil for a day, in answer to an invitation from the recently elected president, Fernando Collor de Mello. His triumph seemed to represent the victory of a radical liberal program, similar to mine, over Lula da Silva's ideas in favor of mercantilism, state control, and interventionism, and for this reason, as well as because of the importance of Brazil to Peru—its neighbor with more than three thousand kilometers of common borders—it was decided by the directorate of the Democratic Front that I should make the trip. I took Lucho Bustamante, the head of the Plan for Governing, with me so that he could meet with Collor's already appointed minister of finance—the instantly famous Zelia Cardoso—and Miguel Vega Alvear, whose Pro-Desarrollo (Association for Development) had drawn up a series of projects of economic cooperation with Brazil. One of these projects had aroused a great deal of enthusiasm on my part when it was described to me, and since that time I had encouraged its being worked out in detail. It had to do with linking the Pacific and Atlantic coasts through joining the highway systems of the two countries, following the Río

Branco–Asís–Ipanaro–Ilo–Matarani axis, which, at the same time that it satisfied a long-cherished Brazilian ambition—having a commercial outlet to the Pacific and its emerging Asian economies—would act as a powerful economic stimulus for the development of all the southern region of Peru, particularly Moquegua, Puno, and Arequipa. The likable Collor—who could have imagined in those days that he would be impeached, having been accused of misappropriating state funds? —received me in Brasília, in a house surrounded with gardens straight out of a Hollywood movie (herons and swans strolled about all around us as we lunched together), with an encouraging sentence: "Eu estou torcendo por vocé, Mario" ("I'm pulling for you, Mario") and the surprise of meeting an old friend, whom I had not expected to see there: José Guillermo Melquior, at that time the ambassador of Brazil to UNESCO. Melquior, an essayist and a liberal philosopher, a disciple of Raymond Aron and of Isaiah Berlin, with whom he had studied at the Sorbonne and at Oxford, was one of the thinkers who had defended with the greatest rigor and consistency the theses of a market economy and of the sovereignty of the individual in Latin America at a time when the collectivist and nationalist tide seemed to be monopolizing the culture of the continent. His presence at Collor's side struck me as a magnificent sign of what the administration of the latter gave promise of being (an assumption not confirmed by reality, unfortunately). Melquior was already seriously ill, with the disease that would take his life a short time later, but he didn't tell me so. On the contrary, I found him in an optimistic mood, joking with me about how times had changed since the days when, ten years before, in London, our countries seemed to us to be irredeemably immunized against the culture of freedom.

The meeting with Collor de Mello was extremely cordial but not very productive, because a large part of the conversation during the luncheon was monopolized by Pedro Pablo Kuczynski, one of my economic advisers, with jokes and pieces of advice that at times gave the impression of being orders to the brand-new president of Brazil as to what he should and shouldn't do. Pedro Pablo, the former minister of energy and mines in Belaunde's second term in office—the best minister the latter had—had been persecuted by Velasco's military dictatorship, to his good fortune. For living in exile allowed him to go from being a modest bureaucrat in the Central Reserve Bank of

Peru to an executive of First Boston, in New York, where, after his experience as a minister of Belaunde's, he was promoted to the office of president. In recent years he had traveled all over the world—he always specified a private jet, and if that couldn't possibly be arranged, the Concorde—privatizing state-owned companies and advising governments of every ideology and geographical location that wanted to know what a market economy was and what steps to take to attain one. Pedro Pablo's talent at handling economic matters was enormous (as was his talent for jogging and playing the piano, the flute, and the lute and telling jokes); but his vanity was even greater, and at that luncheon he displayed the latter above all, talking even with his elbows, giving us a professorial lecture and offering his services if there was need of them. At dessert, Collor de Mello took me by the arm and led me to an adjoining room where we could talk to each other alone for a moment. To my surprise, he told me that the project of integrating the Atlantic and Pacific coasts was bound to be confronted by the resistance and perhaps the open opposition of the United States, for that country feared that if the project were carried out, its commercial exchanges with the Asian countries of the Pacific Rim would suffer.

With the passage of time, I would often remember something that Collor said to me during the luncheon, at a moment when Kuczynski allowed him to get a word in edgewise: "I hope you win in the first round and don't have to go through what I did." And he explained that the second round of balloting in Brazil had been unbearably tense, so much so that for the first time in his life he had had doubts about his vocation for politics.

I was very grateful to Collor de Mello—as I was to President Sanguinetti of Uruguay—for inviting me in the thick of the election campaign, knowing that that would greatly displease President Alan García, and might displease the future Peruvian head of state, if I were not the winner. And I am sorry that this young and energetic president, who seemed so well prepared to carry out a liberal revolution in his country, failed to do so, except in a very partial and contradictory way, and, worst of all, did nothing to prevent corruption, with the consequent disastrous result.

On my return to Lima I found an invitation from the CGTP (Central General de Trabajadores del Perú: General Confederation of Workers of Peru), the Communist labor union, to set forth my Plan for Governing to the Fourth National Conference of Workers, which was being held in the Lima Centro Cívico. The debate had been organized to give the CGTP's blessing to the candidacy of Henry Pease García, of the United Left, as "the workers' candidate" and as a counterweight to the CADE conference. Only the four candidates who appeared to have any possibility of being elected were invited to this conference, as to the one held by CADE, but Alfonso Barrantes had invented an excuse for not attending, fearing that he would be humiliated by those who looked on him as having turned into a bourgeois and a revisionist. The APRA candidate, Alva Castro, on the other hand, turned up and ignored the jeers and catcalls. It seemed to me that I ought to attend too, precisely because the leaders of the Communist union were certain that I wouldn't have the courage to put my head in the lion's mouth. Moreover, I was curious to know the reaction to my proposals of those union delegates, steeped in Marxism-Leninism.

I hastily called together the leaders of the committees on labor and privatization—the obligatory subjects at the CGTP conference were the labor reform and popular capitalism—and, accompanied by Álvaro, we presented ourselves at the Civic Center on the afternoon of February 22. The place was packed with hundreds of delegates, and a group of extremists from Sendero Luminoso, barricading themselves in one corner, greeted me with cries of "Uchuraccay! Uchuraccay!" But it was the CGTP's own service in charge of keeping order that shut them up and I could explain my program, for more than an hour, without interruptions and I was listened to with the attention that an audience of seminarians would pay to the devil. I hope that some of them discovered that Satan wasn't as ugly as they made him out to be.

I told them that labor unions were indispensable in a democracy and that only in a democracy did they function as genuine defenders of workers, since in totalitarian countries unions were nothing but political bureaucracies and transmission belts for the watchwords of those in power. And that, for that reason, in Poland a labor union, Solidarity, in defense of which I had organized a march in the streets in Lima in 1981, headed the struggles for the democratization of the country.

As for Peru, I assured them that, even though it was against their firmest beliefs, our country was much closer to their ideal of state control and collectivization, with its swarm of public enterprises and generalized interventionism, than it was to the capitalist system, which it was acquainted with only in its most ignoble version: mercantilism. The reform that I was proposing had as its objective the removal of all the agencies of discrimination and exploitation of the poor by a handful of privileged individuals, thus assuring that justice would be accompanied by prosperity. The latter did not come about through the redistribution of existing wealth—which meant merely more wide-spread poverty—but with the establishment of a system in which every-one could have access to the market, to owning and running a business, and to private property. In order to bring this about, we had drawn up, in broad outline, the plans for large-scale "structural" reforms, such as property deeds for the *parceleros*, the removal of the barriers that restricted so many small businessmen and craftsmen to the in-formal economy, and, finally, the privatization of public enterprises. In this way there would come into being in Peru the popular capitalism whose principal beneficiaries would be those workers whose incomes populist policies had reduced so dramatically in the last five years.

With the help of Javier Silva Ruete, who had come with me, we explained that the privatization of public enterprises would be brought about in such a way that workers and employees could become stock-holders—providing concrete examples by citing the cases of companies such as PetroPerú, the big banks, or Minero Perú—and also explained that defending, in the name of social justice, state-controlled enter-prises such as SiderPerú, which was being kept alive artificially at enormous expense to the country, was an illogical argument, since the sums wasted in this way, from which only a handful of bureaucrats and politicians benefited, could be used to build the schools and hospitals that the poor were so badly in need of.

I was also very explicit with regard to job security. The first obligation of a government in Peru was to put an end to the poverty of so many millions of Peruvians, and to do so it was necessary to attract investment and stimulate the creation of new businesses and the growth of the ones that already existed, removing the obstacles that prevented this. "Job security" was one of them. The workers who benefited from it were a tiny minority, while it was the majority of Peruvians who needed jobs. It was not a happenstance that the countries with the best job opportunities in the world, such as Switzerland or Hong Kong or Taiwan, had the most flexible labor laws. And Víctor Ferro, of the committee on labor, explained why doing away with job security could not serve as an alibi for abuses.

I don't know if we convinced anyone, but I for one found satisfaction in speaking of these subjects before an audience such as that. I had few possibilities to win them over to our cause, naturally, but I trust that some of them at least understood that our program for governing was proposing an unprecedented reform of Peruvian society and that the situation of workers, of jobholders in the informal economy, of those on the margins of society, and in general, of those strata with the lowest incomes, constituted the main focus of my efforts. When the meeting was over, there was polite applause, and an exchange with the secretary general of the CGTP and a member of the central committee of the Communist Party, Valentín Pacho, that Álvaro has recorded in *El diablo en campaña*: "You see, Doctor Vargas Llosa, there was no reason to fear workers." "You see, Señor Pacho, workers have nothing to fear from freedom." In the communications media, news of my presence at the CGTP conference was passed over in silence by the organs controlled by the state, but friendly media made much of it and even *Caretas* and *Sí* conceded that I had been courageous.

The next day Álvaro, very excited, interrupted a meeting at my house with Mark Malloch Brown to tell me the results of the elections in Nicaragua: against all predictions, Violeta Chamorro beat Daniel Ortega at the polls and put an end to ten years of rule by the Sandinistas. After what had happened in Brazil, Violeta's victory confirmed the change in direction of the ideological winds in Latin America. I called her to congratulate her—I had known her since 1982, when she was resisting what seemed an unstoppable Sandinista mob which had covered the walls of her house with insults—and among the campaign leaders of the Democratic Front there were those who thought that I ought to make a lightning trip to Nicaragua, so as to have my photo taken with her as I had done with Collor de Mello. Miguel Vega Alvear even found a way to carry out the entire operation in twenty-four hours. But I refused, since in these last weeks it seemed imprudent

to me, and since on February 26 I had a meeting scheduled with
Peruvian military leaders at the CAEM (Centro de Altos Estudios
Militares: Center for Advanced Military Studies).

An important weapon in the "dirty war" waged against me was my
"antimilitarism" and "antinationalism." The APRA, in particular, but
also part of the left—which since the days of Velasco's dictatorship
had become militaristic—reminded voters that in a public ceremony,
in 1963, the army had burned my novel *La ciudad y los perros* (*The
Time of the Hero*) because it was regarded as being an insult to the
armed forces. The "hate office," digging around in my bibliography,
found many statements of mine and quotations I had cited in articles
and interviews attacking nationalism as one of the "human aberrations
that has caused the most bloodshed in history"—a sentence that, in
fact, I still stand behind—whereupon it disseminated them far and
wide, in huge quantities, in leaflets that were anonymous but had
been printed on the presses of the state-run Editora Nacional. In one
of them, voters were warned that the army would not allow "its enemy"
to take office and that, consequently, if I won the elections there would
be a military coup.

This was also something feared by the leaders of the Democratic
Front, who advised me to make public gestures and hold private meetings with high-ranking officers in the military so as to reassure them
with respect to the "antimilitarism" of my books and certain positions
I had taken some twenty or thirty years back (in favor of the Cuban
Revolution, for example, and of the MIR's guerrilla attack, led by Luis
de la Puente and Guillermo Lobatón, in 1965).

The armed forces were to play a decisive role in the elections, since,
because they were in charge of guaranteeing the legality of the electoral
process, it would depend on them whether Alan García got away with
it if he attempted to falsify the results. Ensuring their impartiality was
indispensable, as was holding an open dialogue with the military institutions along with which we would be governing the country on the
morrow. But holding an interview with the highest echelons was no
easy matter; they were afraid of reprisals by the president if he noted
a tendency on their part toward supporting the candidate of the Democratic Front. And they had every reason to do so, inasmuch as, ever
since assuming power, Alan García had caused tremendous upheavals
within the armed forces, transferring, retiring, and promoting officers

so as to make certain that adherents of his occupied the key posts. The navy had resisted these encroachments, holding to a certain institutional line with regard to promotions and the rotation of postings, but the air force, and above all the army, had been traumatized by the appointments that had been forthcoming from the Presidential Palace.

We had a committee of defense and internal order in the Front, headed by Johnny Jochamovitch, made up of half a dozen generals and admirals, which worked more or less secretly so as to protect the lives of its members from terrorist attacks and reprisals by the president's office. Every time I met with them I had the feeling of having gone underground because of the precautions that had to be taken—changing cars, drivers, houses we met in—but I must say that in every overall review of the situation they passed on to me—usually with General Sinesio Jarama, an expert in revolutionary warfare, as their spokesman—I noted that they were working very hard. From the first meeting I told them that the objective of our defense policy ought to be, at the institutional level, the depoliticization of the armed forces, their reconversion with an eye to the defense of civil society and democracy, and their modernization. The reform ought to guarantee that there would be no more political interference in the organization of the military and no more military interference in the political life of the country. There was friction at first between this committee and the one on human rights and civil peace, headed by Amalia Ortiz de Zevallos, with whom a number of military officers also collaborated, but they were finally able to coordinate their work, particularly with regard to the subject of subversion.

Through the members of these committees, or through friends, and at times at their own request, I had several interviews with military leaders on active duty concerning the operations of Sendero Luminoso and the MRTA. The most official meeting of all took place on September 18, 1989, at the Institute for Development, with the minister of the interior and Alan García's factotum, Agustín Mantilla, who, accompanied by a handful of generals and colonels of the police under the command of the military, gave me and a little group from Libertad a very frank exposition on Sendero Luminoso, the way it had taken root in the countryside and in the cities, and the difficulties involved in infiltrating spies into it and in obtaining information about such a hermetic and pyramidal organization which used such relentless methods. Minister Mantilla, who, let me say in passing, seemed to me to be more intelligent and articulate than could be expected of a man who had spent his life giving orders to hoodlums and gunmen, gave us a detailed account of a very recent operation, in a village in the highlands of the *departamento* of Lima, where Sendero, following its usual pattern, had "executed" all the authorities and taken over control of the place, through political commissars, turning it into a base of support for its guerrillas. An antisubversive commando unit had reached the village, after a night march amid the crags of the Andes, and captured and "executed" the commissars in turn, but the military detachment of Sendero had managed to escape. Minister Mantilla didn't beat about the bush and coldly told us that this was the only possible way to act in the war to the death that Sendero had unleashed and in which, he admitted, subversion was gaining ground. When he finished he took me aside, to tell me that the president sent me his greetings. (I asked him to give the president mine in return.)

Sometime before that, on June 7, 1989, the Naval Intelligence Service, which has the reputation of being the best-organized one of all the armed forces (institutional rivalries had prevented the integration of all the intelligence services), had given Belaunde, Bedoya, me, and a small group from the Democratic Front an explanatory talk several hours long on the same subject, in one of its buildings. The officers who presented the reports were very forthcoming and had a wealth of information at hand that appeared to be well-founded. They had photographs taken in Paris of the visitors to the center of operations set up there by Sendero Luminoso for their propaganda campaigns and the collecting of funds throughout Europe. Why, then, was the fight against subversion so ineffective? According to them, because of the lack of training and equipment for this type of war being fought by armed forces that continued to ready themselves and equip themselves for conventional warfare, and because of the meager support from the civilian population, which acted as though this were a fight between terrorists and the military that was no concern of theirs.

Despite the discretion they requested of us, news of that meeting leaked out and had serious consequences, since President García asked that punitive measures be taken against those responsible for its having been held. From then on, I met with officers on active duty all by myself, after journeys straight out of a movie, in which both the place we were to meet and the car I was to use were changed several times, as though the persons with whom I was going to converse were criminals with a price on their head and not highly respectable superior officers in the armed forces. The most absurd thing about these meetings, in almost every instance, was that they were useless, since nothing of any importance was discussed in them, and all we did was exchange political gossip or talk about vague schemes that Alan García might have up his sleeve to keep me from winning the election. I believe that, in many cases, these exaggeratedly complicated meetings were organized by military officers curious to see me in person and get an idea of the sort of man they would have to deal with if I were to become president of Peru.

The impressions I received from these meetings were rather disappointing. Because of the economic crisis and the general national decline, military careers had ceased to attract young men of talent and standards had been lowered to a dangerous degree. Some of the officers with whom I talked were arrogantly uncultured and looked on me as though I were an odd specimen when I explained to them what, in my opinion, the function of the army ought to be in a modern democratic society. Some of them were likable and congenial—the artillery colonel, for instance, who asked me point-blank, almost the moment we were introduced: "How good are you at drinking?" I told him that I was very bad at it. "Well then, you're screwed," he assured me. According to him, Alan García had won the affection and the respect of his colleagues by winning the "obstacle courses" that he organized in the Presidential Palace for high-ranking officers after the military parade on the national holiday. What kind of obstacle race was it? Rows of glasses and goblets alternately filled with beer, whisky, pisco, wine, champagne, and every sort of alcoholic drink imaginable. The president designated the contenders and took part in the competition himself. The one who cleared the most "obstacles" without toppling over onto the floor dead drunk was the winner. I assured the colonel that, since I drink very little and am allergic to drunkards, the celebration of the national holiday held at the Presidential Palace would be somewhat more sober during my term in office.

Of all those meetings the one that left me with a better impression was a conversation I had with General Jaime Salinas Sedó, at that time the head of the Second Sector whose armored division has almost always been the source of military coups in Peru. With him in that post democracy seemed assured. Cultivated, well-spoken, with elegant manners, he appeared to be very concerned about the traditional lack of communication between civil society and the military sphere in Peru, which, he said, was a continual danger for the rule of law. He spoke to me of the necessity of modernizing the armed forces and bringing them up to date technically, of eradicating politics from them, and of severely punishing cases of corruption, frequent in recent years, so that the military institutions in our country would have the prestige that they had in France or Great Britain. * Both he and Admiral Panizo, at the time chairman of the Joint Command, with whom I had a couple of private meetings, assured me emphatically that the armed forces would not permit any electoral fraud.

The speech I gave at the CAEM was one of three that I wrote and published during the campaign. † It seemed important to me to speak in depth, before the cream of the crop from the various military branches, about subjects which were central to the liberal reform of Peru and which involved the armed forces.

Unlike the situation that obtains in modern democracies, in Peru there has never been a deep solidarity between the armed forces and civil society, because of the military coups and the almost total lack of communication between civilians and the military. In order to achieve that solidarity and professionalism, the total independence and impartiality of the armed forces in the face of political factionalism and contention were necessary. And it was necessary that military officers be aware of the fact that, in the economic situation in which Peru found itself, military expenditures would be nonexistent in the immediate future, except for giving the armed forces adequate equipment for the battle against terrorism. This battle would be won only if civilians and military personnel fought shoulder to shoulder

---

* Faithful to these ideas, General Salinas Sedó, who had already retired, tried to start a movement, based on constitutional provisions, to restore democracy in Peru, on November 13, 1992, seven months after the authoritarian coup on April 5. But the attempt was a failure, and he and the group of officers who backed him are, as of the time when I am correcting the proofs for this book, currently in prison.

† "Civiles y militares en el Perú de la Libertad." Speech explaining the background of the current situation, delivered before officers of the Peruvian army, navy, and air force at CAEM (Centro de Altos Estudios Militares: Center for Advanced Military Studies), on February 26, 1990. Lima, 1990.

against those who had already caused damages amounting to ten billion dollars. As president, I would assume the leadership of this fight, to wage which peasants and workers would be called upon to join together in armed patrols, advised by the military. And I would not tolerate abuses of human rights, for such tactics were incompatible with a state under the rule of law and counterproductive if the aim was to win the support of the people.

It is an error to confuse nationalism and patriotism. The latter is a legitimate feeling of love for the land where one was born; the former, a nineteenth-century doctrine, restrictive and antiquated, which in Latin America had brought on fratricidal wars between countries and ruined our economies. Following the example of Europe, we had to put an end to that nationalistic tradition and work toward integration with our neighbors, the disappearance of borders, and continental disarmament. My government would make every effort, from the very first day, to remove all economic and political barriers that hindered close collaboration and friendship with other Latin American countries, and with our neighbors in particular. I ended my speech with an anecdote that went back to the days when I was teaching at King's College at London University. I discovered there one day that two of my most diligent students were young officers in the British Army, which had awarded them scholarships so that they could earn a master's degree in Latin American studies: "I learned from them that in Great Britain entering Sandhurst or the Naval Academy or the Air Corps was a privilege reserved for the most capable and hardworking young men—neither more nor less so than entering the most prestigious universities—and that the training that they received there prepared them not only for the din of battle (though naturally it also prepared them for that), but also for peace: that is to say, for serving their country effectively as scientists, as researchers, as technical experts, as humanists." The reorganization of the armed forces in Peru would be oriented toward that goal.

Two or three days after the CAEM meeting, the Sawyer/Miller Group had the results of a new national opinion poll, the most important one that had been taken up until then because of the number of people interviewed and the places included in the sample. I was first overall, with 41 or 42 percent of those in the sample intending to vote for me. Alva Castro had managed to climb to 20 percent, while

Barrantes was at a standstill with 15 percent and Henry Pease at 8 percent. The results didn't seem bad to me, since I was expecting a sharp drop because of the excessive propaganda put out for the preferential vote. But I didn't accept Mark Malloch Brown's proposal that I cancel the tours of the interior and concentrate on a media campaign and on visits to the marginal districts of Lima. My person and my program were well known in the capital, whereas in many places in the interior they still were not.

That same week, as, in the short breaks between meetings that I had in planes or minivans, I was scribbling the speech that I would deliver in a meeting with liberal intellectuals of different countries that Libertad had organized for March 7 to 9, the news of the assassination of our leader in Ayacucho, Julián Huamaní Yauli, reached me. I immediately flew to Ayacucho to attend his funeral and arrived as they were enshrouding his remains, in a little mortuary chapel that had been set up on the second floor of an ancient, dark building that had once been a private dwelling and was now the School of Public Accounting. I had a strange feeling as I stood there contemplating the head of this modest Ayacuchan, shattered to bits by Sendero bullets, remembering how, on each one of my trips to his homeland, he had accompanied me in my travels, formal and reserved, as the people in that part of the country usually are. His murder was a good example of the irrationality and stupid cruelty of the terrorist strategy, since it was not intended to punish any violence, exploitation, or abuse committed by the extremely modest and previously apolitical Julián Huamaní, but simply to terrify through the crime those who believed that elections could change things in Peru. He was the first leader of Libertad who had been killed. How many others would there be, I asked myself as we were taking his remains to the church, through the streets of Ayacucho, experiencing for the first time that feeling of guilt that, especially during the runoff vote, would overcome me every time I learned that the lives of militants or candidates of ours had been cut short by the terrorists.

Very shortly after the assassination of Julián Huamaní Yauli, on March 23, another of the Front's candidates for a seat in the Chamber of Representatives, the populist José Gálvez Fernández, was murdered as he left the school that he was the head of, in Comas, one of the popular districts in Lima. Unaffected, simple and straightforward, likable, he was one of the local leaders of Popular Action who had worked the hardest for the close collaboration between the allied parties of the Front. When I went to the headquarters of Popular Action that night, where they were holding a wake for him, I found Belaunde and his wife Violeta badly shaken by the assassination of their colleague.

But amid bloody events such as these, in the final days of the campaign there was also a stimulating contrast: the Freedom Revolution meeting. For many months, we had been planning to bring together in Lima intellectuals of various countries whose ideas had contributed to the extraordinary political and cultural changes in the world, in order to show that what we wanted to do in Peru was part of a process of the reappraisal of democracy, in which more and more peoples around the globe were participating, and in order to show our compatriots that the most modern thought was liberal.

The meeting lasted for three days, in El Pueblo, on the outskirts of Lima, where conferences, round-table discussions, debates took place, and at night, serenades and fiestas to which the presence en masse of young people who belonged to Libertad lent a great deal of color. We had hopes that Lech Walesa would attend. The leader of Solidarity had promised Miguel Vega, who went to see him in Gdansk, that he would do his best to come, but at the last minute the internal problems of his country kept him from attending, and he sent us a message, through two leaders of the Polish labor movement, Stefan Jurczak and Jacek Chwedoruk, whose presence on the speakers' platform, the night that they read the message aloud, gave rise to a great outburst of enthusiasm. (I remember Álvaro, more excited than usual, shouting Walesa's name at the top of his lungs, in chorus with everyone else, with his arms upraised.)

Cultural meetings are usually boring, but this one wasn't, not to me at any rate, nor, it seems to me, to the young people we brought from all over the country so that they could hear about the liberal offensive that was traversing the world. Many of them heard for the first time the things that were said there. Perhaps because of my total immersion in the stereotyped language of the electoral campaign, in those three days it seemed to me that I was tasting an exquisite forbidden fruit by hearing words without political cunning behind them or servitude to the immediate situation, used in a personal way, to explain the great changes that were taking place or that could suddenly occur in countries willing to reform themselves by staking everything on political and economic freedom—that was the subject dealt with by Javier Tusell—or simply to describe in the abstract, as Israel Kirzner did, the nature of the market. I remember the splendid explanatory speeches by Jean-François Revel and Sir Alan Walters as the high points of the meeting, and the explanation given by José Piñera of the economic reforms that brought Chile development and democratization. It was very stimulating, above all, thanks to the speeches by the Colombian Plinio Apuleyo Mendoza, the Mexicans Enrique Krause and Gabriel Zaid, the Guatemalan Armando de la Torre, and others, to realize that all over Latin America there were intellectuals attuned to our ideas, who looked on our campaign with the hope that, if it was carried through successfully in Peru, the liberal revolution would spread to their countries.

Among those who attended were two front-line Cuban freedom fighters: Carlos Franqui and Carlos Alberto Montaner. In the name of unequivocal democratic convictions, both of them had been fighting against Castro's dictatorship for many years now, ever since they first felt that the revolution for which they had fought had been betrayed. It seemed to me that, as the meeting came to an end, I ought to make a public declaration of my solidarity with their cause, to say that the freedom of Cuba was also a flag we rallied round, and that, if we won the election, free Cubans would have in Peru an ally in their fight against one of the last vestiges of totalitarianism in the world. I did so, before reading my speech, * provoking the predictable wrath of the Cuban dictator who, two or three days later, answered from Havana with his usual vituperations.

Octavio Paz, who was unable to come, sent a videotape with a recorded message, explaining why he now supported the candidacy which, two years before in London, he had tried to talk me out of, and Miguel Vega Alvear had trouble rounding up enough television sets so that everyone in the audience could hear the message. But he managed, and so Octavio Paz was there with us, through his image and his voice, during those days of the congress. His encouragement came at an opportune moment for me, for to tell the truth, every so

---

* "El país que vendrá." Closing speech of the Freedom Revolution meeting. Lima, March 9, 1990.

often I could hear, still pounding in my ears, the reasons he'd given me, two years before, in a conversation in his London hotel on Sloane Street, as we were having the orthodox tea and scones, for not going into politics: incompatibility with intellectual work, loss of independence, being manipulated by professional politicians, and, in the long run, frustration and the feeling of years of one's life wasted. In his message, Octavio, with that subtlety in developing a line of reasoning which, along with the elegance of his prose, is his best intellectual attribute, retracted those arguments and replaced them with other, more up-to-date ones, justifying my determination and connecting it with the great liberal and democratic mobilization in Eastern Europe. At that moment, it was invigorating for me to hear, from the lips of someone whom I had admired since my youth, the arguments in favor of my going into politics which I had put to myself sometime before. Not long afterward, however, I would have a chance to see how right his first reaction had been and how Peruvian reality hastened to prove this second one wrong.

But still more than for intellectual reasons, the three days of the congress were a real vacation for me, since I could hobnob with friends I hadn't seen for some time and meet wonderful people who came to the meeting bringing ideas and testimony that were like a breath of fresh air to this country with a marginal culture at a dead end that poverty and violence had turned Peru into. Except for the heavy security surrounding the meeting place, the foreign participants had no indication of the violence amid which the country was living, and they could even enjoy a spectacle of Peruvian music and folk dances to which, on the spur of the moment, Ana and Pedro Schwartz contributed several lively Sevillian dances. (I record this fact for history, for every time I have told people about it, nobody has believed me that the eminent Spanish economist was capable of such a feat.)

These three days of relative relaxation gave me energy, moreover, for the last month, which was dizzying. I began campaigning again on Sunday, March 11, with rallies in Huaral, Huacho, Barranca, Huarmey, and Casma, and from that time on, up until the ceremony closing the campaign, on April 5 in Arequipa, I visited half a dozen cities and towns every day, talking, leading motorcades, and giving press conferences in all of them and flying back to Lima almost every night to meet with the Front's national campaign leaders, with the team drawing up the Plan for Governing, and with the little group of advisers in the "kitchen cabinet," meetings that Patricia, the coordinator of my agenda, also attended.

Since the rallies almost always drew huge crowds and, in the final weeks, the internal rivalries seemed to have disappeared and the Front presented an image of cohesion and solidity, victory seemed certain to me. The opinion polls also predicted the same thing, although all of them discounted the possibility of a resounding victory in the first round. There would be a weeding out of the weaker candidates, and I preferred running against the APRA candidate in the second round, since I imagined that the anti-Aprismo of certain forces of the left would allow me to capture votes from that constituency. But, deep down inside, I didn't lose hope that, at the last moment, the Peruvian people would agree to give me the mandate I was seeking as early as April 8.

On March 28, my birthday, the reception given me in Iquitos was an apotheosis. A huge crowd accompanied me from the airport to the city, and Patricia, who was with me in the open-roofed touring car, and I were impressed to see that from all the houses and street corners more and more groups of enthusiasts came to join the dense procession that never stopped, not even for a moment, chanting in chorus the slogans of the Front and singing and dancing with indescribable happiness and fervor. (Every event in Amazonia turns into a fiesta.) A giant birthday cake awaited me on the speakers' platform, with fifty-four little candles, and even though the lights kept going out and the microphones didn't work well, the rally was so huge that Patricia and I were electrified.

I slept in Iquitos that night, for the three or four hours that had become my sleep ration, and on the following morning, very early, I flew to Cuzco, where, beginning with Sicuani, Urcos, Urubamba, and Calca, I set out on a tour that was to end, two days later at five o'clock in the afternoon, in the main square of the ancient capital of the Inca empire. For historical and also political reasons, Cuzco, the traditional bastion of the left, has symbolic value in Peru. The Plaza de Armas, its main square, where the stones of the ancient Inca palaces serve as a foundation for the churches and dwellings built in the colonial era, is one of the most beautiful and imposing ones I know, as well as one of the largest. The Libertad committee in Cuzco had promised me that, on that afternoon, it would be full to overflowing, and that neither Apristas nor Communists would manage to spoil the rally. (They had tried to attack us on all my previous tours of the *departamento*.)

I was getting ready to leave for the rally when Álvaro called me from Lima. I could tell that he was very upset. He was at the campaign headquarters, with Mark Malloch Brown, Jorge Salmón, Luis Llosa, Pablo Bustamante, and the analysts of the opinion polls. They had just received the final one before the election and had had a major surprise: in the marginal districts and young towns of Lima—60 percent of the capital—Alberto Fujimori had taken off in the last few days at a dizzying rate, displacing both the candidate of the APRA and that of the United Left as the one that voters intended to cast their ballot for, and there was every indication that his popularity was rising, "like foam, by the minute." According to the analysts it was a phenomenon restricted to the poorest districts of Lima and the C and D sectors; in the other districts, and in the remainder of Peru, the proportion of forces was still the same as before. Mark considered the danger a very serious one and advised me to suspend the tour, including the rally in Cuzco, and return to Lima immediately, in order to concentrate all our efforts, from that day on until the election, on the districts and neighborhoods on the periphery of the capital so as to halt that phenomenon.

I answered Álvaro that they were crazy if they thought I was going to leave my followers in Cuzco in the lurch, and told him that I would return to Lima the next day, after the rallies in Quillabamba and Puerto Maldonado. I left for the Plaza de Armas in Cuzco, and the spectacle there made me forget all the apprehensions of the campaign directors. It was late afternoon and a torrid sun was scorching the foothills of the Cordillera and the coast of Carmenca. The roofs of San Blas and the pre-Hispanic stones of churches and convents gave off flames. In the pure indigo-blue sky there were no clouds and a few stars were already out. The dense crowd that covered the enormous square seemed to be on the point of bursting with enthusiasm and in the transparent mountain air the weathered faces of the men and the bright colors of the women's wide skirts and the placards and flags which that forest of hands was waving were sharp and clear and seemed to be within reach of anyone who, from the speakers' platform erected in the atrium of the cathedral, stretched out an arm to touch them. During the entire campaign I have never been as moved as I was that late afternoon in Cuzco, in that ancient and beautiful Plaza de Armas where the ill-starred country in which I was born experienced its most sublime moments of glory and where, in days long gone, it was civilized and prosperous. I said as much, with a lump in my throat, to the architect Gustavo Manrique Villalobos of the Libertad committee, when, his eyes damp, he whispered to me, pointing to the impressive crowd: "We've kept our promise, Mario."

That night, at dinnertime, at the Hotel de Turistas, I asked who this Alberto Fujimori was, who now, only ten days before the election, seemed to begin to exist as a candidate, and where he came from. Up until then I don't believe I'd given a single thought to him, or ever heard anyone mention him in the analyses and projected results of the election made within the Front and the Freedom Movement. On rare occasions I had seen, in passing, the few sparse placards of the ghostlike organization that registered him as its candidate, the name of which, Cambio 90, was plagiarized from a slogan of ours, "El gran cambio, en libertad"—"The great change, in freedom"—and pictur-esque photos of this figure whose campaign strategy consisted of riding around on a tractor, sometimes with an Indian cap with earflaps above his Oriental face, repeating a slogan—Honesty, Technology, and Work—which represented his entire proposal for governing the coun-try. But not even as a folkloric eccentricity did this fifty-two-year-old agricultural engineer, the son of Japanese parents, with a twice-repeated surname—Fujimori Fujimori—reign supreme among the ten candidates for the presidency registered by the National Board of Elec-tions, since in that domain he was bested by one even more bizarre: Señor Ataucusi Gamonal, also known as the prophet Ezequiel.

The prophet Ezequiel was the founder of a new religion, the Israelite Church of the New Universal Covenant, which had sprung up in the mountain fastnesses of the Andes, and to a certain extent had taken root in rural communities and marginal neighborhoods of the cities. A humble man, born in the little town of La Unión (in the *depar-tamento* of Arequipa), educated by an evangelical sect in the central highlands, he had left that sect after having had a "revelation" in Tarma and founded his own. His faithful could be easily recognized because the women went around dressed in severe tunics and wore kerchiefs on their heads and the men had inordinately long hair and fingernails, since one of the precepts of their creed was not to interfere with the development of the natural order. They lived in communes, working the land and sharing everything, and had had confrontations with Sendero Luminoso. At the beginning of the campaign, Juan Ossio, an anthropologist who was studying the "Israelites" and had a good relationship with them, had invited me to have lunch at his house with the prophet Ezequiel and his chief apostle, Brother Jeremías Ortiz Arcos, since he thought that the support of the sect might win us votes among peasants. That lunch lingers in my mind as an amusing memory, in which all conversation with me was carried on by Brother Jeremías, a sturdy, astute mestizo who wore his hair in tangled braided dreadlocks and affected studied poses, as the prophet remained silent, lost in a sort of mystic rapture. Only over dessert, after having eaten like a Heliogabalus, did he return to this world. His eyes sought mine, and seizing my arm with his black talons, he uttered this definitive pronouncement: "I shall put you on the throne, Doctor." Encouraged by what we took to be a promise of aid in the election, Juan Ossio and Freddy Cooper went to have lunch with the prophet Ezequiel and his apostles in an "Israelite" tent, in a slum district of Lima, and Freddy remembered that love-feast as one of the least digestible ordeals of his ephemeral political career. And a useless one, moreover, since a short time thereafter the prophet Ezequiel decided to place himself on the throne in my stead, by launching his own candidacy. Although he had never reached even one percent in the opinion surveys, the analysts of the Front sometimes speculated on the possibility of a shift in the rural vote toward the prophet, thereby destabilizing the political panorama. But none of them had any inkling that the surprise would come from agricultural engineer Fujimori.

On my return to Lima, on the afternoon of March 30, I was confronted with a curious piece of news. Our security unit had gotten wind of an order given the evening before by President García to all the regional development corporations to the effect that, henceforth, they were to redirect their logistic support—transportation, communications, and advertising—withdrawing it from Alva Castro's Aprista candidacy and giving it instead to Cambio 90. At the same time, from that day on, all the communications media dependent on the government and with ties to García—especially Channel 5, "Radioprogramas," *La República*, *Página Libre*, and *La Crónica*—began to extol systematically a candidacy that, up until then, they had scarcely mentioned. The only person who didn't appear to be surprised at the news was Fernando Belaunde, with whom I met on the night of my return to Lima. "Fujimori's candidacy is a typical Aprista maneuver to take votes away from us," the ex-president assured me. "They did the same thing to me, in 1963, inventing the candidacy of engineer Mario Samamé Boggio, who said the same things I did, was a professor at the same university as I was, and who, in the end, received even fewer votes than the number of signatures that got him on the official list of candidates." Was the candidate in the cap with earflaps and the tractor an epiphenomenon invented by Alan García? In any event, Mark Malloch Brown was worried. The flash polls—we took one every day in Lima—confirmed that in the shantytowns the popularity of the "little Chinaman" was rapidly increasing.

Who was he? Where did he come from? He had been a professor of mathematics and rector of the Agrarian University, and in that capacity headed for a time the CONUP (Asamblea Nacional de Rectores: National Assembly of University Rectors). But his candidacy couldn't be weaker. He hadn't even been able to fill the quotas for senators and congressmen on his list. Among his candidates there were many pastors of evangelical churches, and all of them, without exception, were unknowns. We discovered later that he had included on his list of candidates his own gardener and a prophetess and palmist, implicated in a trial having to do with drugs, named Madame Carmelí. But the best proof of the lack of seriousness of his candidacy was that Fujimori himself was also a candidate for a Senate seat. The Peruvian Constitution allows this duplication, which is taken advantage of by many aspirants to seats in Congress who, in order to garner more publicity, register at the same time as presidential candidates. Nobody with a real possibility of being elected president runs for a senatorship at the same time, since according to the Constitution the two offices create a conflict of interest.

Although I did not cancel all the remainder of the tours scheduled for the last days before the election—Huancayo, Jauja, Trujillo, Huaraz, Chimbote, Cajamarca, Tumbes, Piura, and Callao—I made lightning visits, almost every morning before leaving for the provinces, to the young towns in Lima where Fujimori seemed to have the firmest support, and I also made a series of TV spots, talking with people from the C and D sectors who asked me questions about the points in my program under heaviest attack. With the brand-new support of planes and minivans belonging to the government, Fujimori began a series of junkets in the provinces, and news programs showed large audiences of humble Peruvians at all his meetings, people whom the "little Chinaman" with the poncho, the cap with earflaps, and the tractor who attacked all politicians in his speeches seemed to have bewitched overnight.

On Friday, March 30, the new mayor of Lima, Ricardo Belmont, endorsed my candidacy. He did so from my house in Barranco, after a conversation that proved to be very instructive to me. Fujimori's takeoff had greatly disturbed him, because not only had he repeated everything that Belmont had said in his municipal campaign—"I am not a politician," "All politicians have been failures," "The time for independent candidates has come"—but in addition the committees of Belmont's own organization, OBRAS, were being cannibalized by Cambio 90 in the marginal districts of Lima. His local offices were switching banners and the posters with his face were being replaced by others with the face of the "little Chinaman." In Ricardo's opinion, there wasn't the slightest doubt about it: Fujimori was a creation of the APRA. And he told me that the former Aprista mayor of Lima, Jorge del Castillo, had tried to get him to include Fujimori on his list of city councilmen, something he hadn't gone along with since Fujimori, though a university professor, was an absolute political unknown. Six months back, the presidential candidate of Cambio 90 had aspired to no higher office than that of municipal councilman.

As he had told Álvaro, with whom he had had several meetings prior to this one with me and with whom he had made friends, in the talk we had together Ricardo Belmont assured me: "I'm going to stop Fujimori." And in those last eight days of the campaign he did everything in his power to back my candidacy, in a press conference, on a television program he planned with that very purpose in mind, and by coming up onto the speakers' platform to offer me his support at the rally on April 4, on the Paseo de la República, with which we ended the campaign in Lima. None of this helped to hold back what reporters were soon to baptize as "the tsunami," but it left me with an image of Belmont as a likable person, who, predictably, was made to pay dearly for that display of loyalty to me by the future Peruvian government, which asphyxiated the mayoralty of Lima by depriving it of financial resources and condemning Belmont to a city administration that could accomplish next to nothing.*

On April 3 two good things happened. The attractive Gisella Valcárcel, who, after being a music hall performer, had gone on to host one of the most popular shows on television, after interviewing Fujimori on it announced to her audience, in his presence, that she was going to vote for me. It was a brave gesture, because Channel 5 had previously tried to keep Gisella from participating in the festivities that Acción Solidaria organized for Christmas. Nonetheless, she went to the stadium and emceed the show—even getting me to dance a *huayno*—and now, on the eve of the election, she had given me a public endorsement, trying to persuade her viewers to vote for me. I called to thank her, and to swear to her that this would not bring her reprisals; fortunately, none took place.

The second piece of good news was the results of the last nationwide opinion poll that Mark and his analysts, Paul, Ed, and Bill, brought to the house late that Wednesday afternoon: I had maintained my average of some 40 percent of the electorate intending to vote for me, and Fujimori's offensive, which included not only Lima but also the remainder of Peru—with the sole exception of the Amazon region— was taking votes away from the APRA and the United Left for the most part, causing them to drop down to third and fourth place respectively in almost all of the *departamentos*. Fujimori's advance in the marginal sections of the capital appeared to have been halted; and in districts such as San Juan de Lurigancho and Comas I had regained several percentage points.

Hundreds of reporters from all over the world were in Lima for the election on Sunday, April 8, and the campaign directors feared that the 1,500-seat capacity of the auditorium of the Sheraton would not provide enough room for them all. My house in Barranco was surrounded by photographers and cameramen night and day and the security guards had trouble holding off those who tried to scale the walls or leap into the garden. In order to maintain some privacy we

---

* Following the "self-coup" of April 5, 1992, the rivalry between Mayor Belmont and the brand-new dictator was to turn into an impassioned romance.

had to close the blinds and draw the curtains and have visitors drive their cars inside the garage if they didn't want to be hounded by the hordes of reporters. The election law didn't allow polls to be published for the two weeks preceding an election, but the daily papers abroad had already printed news stories about the surprising appearance at the last minute of a dark horse of Japanese origin in the Peruvian presidential election.

I didn't feel alarmed, as I had been at the time of the excessive ad campaign of our congressional candidates—which, in these two final weeks, was reduced to less extravagant dimensions—although I couldn't help thinking that between that campaign and the "Fujimori phenomenon" there was a reciprocal relation. That spectacle of economic immodesty presented by our candidates had suited the purpose of someone who made himself out to poor Peruvians to be just one more "poor man," disgusted with a "political class" that had never solved the country's problems. I thought, however, that the vote for Fujimori—the vote meant to castigate us—couldn't possibly amount to more than 10 percent or so of the electorate, the most uninformed and uncultured voters. Who else would vote for an unknown, without a program, without a team for governing, without any political credentials whatsoever, who had hardly campaigned outside of Lima, who had been jury-rigged overnight to serve as a candidate? No matter what the opinion polls said, it never entered my head that a candidacy so devoid of ideas and with no planning staff could carry weight in the face of the monumental effort we had put in over a period of almost three years of work. And secretly, without saying as much to Patricia, I was still cherishing the hope that Peruvians would give me a mandate for the "great change, in freedom" that Sunday.

A dream like that was nurtured, in large part, by a misinterpretation of the last rallies, all of which, beginning with the one in the Plaza de Armas of Cuzco, were most impressive. So was the one on April 4, on the Paseo de la República, in Lima, when I spoke of myself and my family in a very intimate way, explaining, against the propaganda that presented me as one of the privileged, that I owed everything I was and everything I possessed to my own work, and the one in Arequipa, the last one, on April 5, when I promised my countrymen that I would be "a rebellious and obstreperous president," just as the part of the country that I was born in had been in the history of Peru.

Those very well organized ceremonies, those public squares and avenues teeming with overexcited people hoarse from shouting our slogans in chorus—so many young people, above all—gave the impression of an overwhelming mobilization, of a country dazzled by the Front. Before the final rally, Patricia and my three children and I went through the streets of the city in an open touring car, in a motorcade that lasted for several hours, joined at every street corner in Arequipa by more and more people, with bunches of flowers or confetti, in an atmosphere of real delirium. During one of those tours of Arequipa, I had one of the most unexpected and nicest experiences of those years. A young woman approached the car, held up a baby just a few months old for me to kiss him, and shouted to me: "If you win, I'll have another baby, Mario!"

But anyone who had sat down with a cool head to add and subtract and attentively observe the sort of people who attended those marches and rallies would have had reservations: those who took part in them represented almost exclusively the third of Peruvians with the largest incomes. Although a minority, there were enough of them to fill the main squares of Peruvian cities, above all now that, for one of the few times in our history, those middle and upper classes had backed, en bloc, a political plan. But there were the remaining two-thirds, all those Peruvians who had been most impoverished and most frustrated by the national decline of recent decades—including those who had once been interested by my proposals only to have their interest flag out of fear, confusion, and displeasure at the manifestation, in the last months of the campaign, of what appeared to be the old elitist, arrogant Peru of the whites and the rich, something that our advertising contributed as much to as did the campaign of our adversaries—and as I presided over those grandiose rallies that left me with the impression that I was retaining the very nearly absolute majority that the opinion polls said I enjoyed, these Peruvians, the other two-thirds, had already begun to change their minds in a way that would make the election results turn out quite differently.

A number of friends had arrived in Peru from abroad, among them Carmen Balcells, my literary agent from Barcelona who had kept me company in any number of my ups and downs, my English publisher, Robert McCrum, and the Colombian writer and journalist Plinio Apuleyo Mendoza, all of whom I had a chance to see on the eve of election day, in the midst of the killing series of interviews with foreign correspondents that figured on my schedule. I had another surprise when my Finnish publisher, Erkki Reenpaa, and Sulamita, his wife, also showed up in Barranco. Their snow-white Scandinavian faces had suddenly appeared as though by magic amid the crowd at the rally in Piura, without my being able to figure out how it was possible for those two friends from Helsinki to have turned up in that remote corner of Peru. I learned later that they had followed me, all during that last week, from one city to another, accomplishing miracles so that, by renting cars and taking planes, they could be present at all my final rallies. And that night, I found at home a telegram that had been sent to me from Geneva by the close friend of my youth, Luis Loayza, whom I hadn't seen for years. It read: "An embrace, fierce little Sartrean," and I was deeply touched.

On Sunday the 8th, Patricia, Álvaro, Gonzalo, and I went to vote early in the morning at the Colegio Mercedes Indacochea, in Barranco, and Morgana came with us, dying with envy because her brothers could already vote. Then, before leaving for the Hotel Sheraton, I checked to see how those tens of thousands of representatives of our alliance, which a team headed by Miguel and Cecilia Cruchaga had been training for this day for months, were doing at the electoral tables in polling places all over the country. Everything was in good order; the transportation arrangements had worked and our representatives had been at their posts since dawn.

We had reserved several floors of the Sheraton for election day. On the first floor were the press offices of the Front, with Álvaro and his team, and on the second floor fax machines, telephones, and desks for correspondents had been installed and the conference room where I was to speak after the results were in had been made ready. On the eighteenth floor there was a computer network office, where Mark Malloch Brown and his team received projections of how the vote was going, reports from our representatives, and the results of exit polls that came in via the computers that Miguel Cruchaga had installed, in semisecrecy, in San Antonio. They handed me the first projection around noon.

The nineteenth floor was reserved for my family and close friends, and the security service had orders to allow no one else to set foot on it. I had a suite in which I shut myself up around eleven in the morning, all by myself. I was watching on television as the leaders of the various political parties, or famous sports stars and singers, came to the polling places to vote, and all of a sudden I was tormented by the idea that for five years it was more than likely that I wouldn't read or write anything literary again. Then I sat down and in a little book that I always carry around with me in my pocket I wrote this poem which, ever since I had read a book by Alfonso Reyes on Greece, I had been mulling over in my mind in my free moments:

ALCIDES

Pienso en el poderoso Alcides,
llamado también Hércules.
Era muy fuerte. Aún en la cuna
Aplastó a dos serpientes, una
por una. Y, adolescente,
mató a un león, gallardamente.
Cubierto con su piel, peregrino
audaz, fue por el mundo. Lo imagino
musculoso y bruñido, dando caza
al león de Nemea. Y, en la plaza
calcinada de Lidia, sirviendo
como esclavo y entreteniendo
a la reina Onfale. Vestido
de mujer, el venido
de Grecia hilaba y tejía
y, en su gentil disfraz, divertía
a la corte.
Allí lo dejo
al invicto joven trejo:
en el ridículo sumido
y, paf, lo olvido.

ALCIDES

I think of the powerful Alcides,
also called Hercules.
He was very strong. In his cradle still
he was known to have killed
two serpents, crushed to death,
one by one. And before reaching maturity
he killed a lion, valiantly.
Wearing its pelt, a fearless pilgrim,
he roamed the world. An image I can't
erase:
Muscular, burnished, giving chase
to the lion of Nemea. And in the torrid
public square in Lydia, serving
as a slave and entertaining
the Queen, Omphale. Dressed
as a woman, the man arrived
from Greece spun and wove
and, in his charming disguise,
amused the court.
There I leave
the young man, unbeaten yet,
neck deep in ridicule:
whom, just like that, I forget.

Around one o'clock in the afternoon, Mark, Lucho, and Álvaro came up to see me with the first projection: I had close to 40 percent and Fujimori 25 percent. The dark horse was giving further proof of the remarkably solid base he had established everywhere in the country.

Mark explained to me that my percentage would tend to go on in-creasing, but, seeking the look on his face, I could tell that he was lying. If these figures proved to be correct, the electorate hadn't given me a mandate and there would be a congressional majority hostile to our program.

I went downstairs to talk to my mother and my aunts, uncles, cousins, and friends, and ate a couple of sandwiches with them without telling them what I knew. Even Uncle Lucho, despite his stroke and paralysis, was there, smiling behind his immobility and silence, keep-ing me company on the great day. I went back up to the suite on the nineteenth floor, where at two-thirty they brought me a second and more complete nationwide projection. I immediately saw that it was disastrous: I had lost three points—I now had 36 percent—Fujimori was maintaining his 25 percent, the APRA had just under 20 percent and the two parties of the left, taken together, 10 percent. It didn't require gifts of prophecy to see into the future: there would be a second round in which Apristas, Socialists, and Communists would do an about-face and vote en bloc for Fujimori, making him the winner by a comfortable margin.

Álvaro stayed alone with me for a moment. He was very pale, with those dark blue circles underneath his eyes that, when he was a little boy, presaged a temper tantrum. Of my three children, he is the one who is most like me, in his passionate outbursts and in his enthusiasms, in his excessive surrender, without reserve or calculation, to his loves and his hates. He was twenty-four, and this campaign had been an extraordinary experience in his life. It was not my idea but Freddy Cooper's to make him our communications director, because he was a journalist, because he was continually obsessed by Peru, because he was so close to me and so closely identified with liberal ideas. It had been hard work to get him to accept. He said no to Freddy and me, but finally Patricia, who is even more stubborn than he is, persuaded him. Because of this, we have been accused of nepotism and baptized by the Aprista press as "the royal family." He had done his job very well, having fights with many people, of course, because he refused to make the slightest concession when it came to matters of principle or agree to anything that we might regret later, just as I had asked him to do. In all these months he had learned a great deal more than he had in his three years at the London School of Economics, about his

country, about people, and about politics, a passion that he acquired
in his adolescence and that had absorbed him ever since, just as in
his childhood religion had absorbed him. (I still have the surprising
letter he sent me, from boarding school, when he was twelve, informing me of his decision to leave the Catholic Church to be confirmed
by the Church of England.) "Everything's turned to shit," he said,
livid. "There won't be any liberal reform. Peru won't change and it'll
go on the way it always has. The worst thing that can happen to you
now is to win." But I knew that there was no longer any danger of
that.

I asked him to locate our representative at the National Board of
Elections, and when Enrique Elías Laroza came up to the nineteenth
floor, I asked him if it were legally possible for one of the two candidates
who had been finalists in the first round to give up competing in the
second one, handing over the presidency to the other candidate once
and for all. He assured me emphatically that this was possible.* And
still he egged me on: "Sure, offer Fujimori one or two ministries and
let him give up the second round." But what I was thinking of offering
my rival was something more appetizing than a few ministerial port-
folios: the presidential flag, in exchange for adopting key points of our
economic program and getting himself teams capable of putting it into
practice. My fear, from that moment on, was that, through an intermediary, Alan García and the APRA would go on governing Peru and
the disaster of the last five years would continue, until Peruvian society
broke down completely.

From that second projection on, I never had the slightest doubt
about the outcome nor did I have the slightest illusion as to my chances
of winning in the second round. In the previous months and years I
had been able to feel physically the hatred borne me by the Apristas
and the Communists, who found that my sudden appearance in Peruvian political life, defending liberal theses, filling public squares,
mobilizing middle classes which they had previously kept constantly
intimidated or bewildered, preventing the nationalization of the financial system, and demanding things that they had turned into

---

* This had happened in the 1985 elections, in which Alan García won a little less
than 50 percent, beating Alfonso Barrantes, who came in second. There ought therefore to have been a second electoral round, which was avoided because of the withdrawal of the candidate of the United Left.

taboos—"formal" democracy, private property and enterprise, capitalism, a market economy—had ruined what they took to be their unassailable monopoly of political power and of the future of Peru. The sensation, supported by opinion polls for almost three years, that there was no legal way of stopping that intruder who was bringing the "right" back to life, who would come to power with the enthusiastic backing of millions upon millions, had rendered their enmity even more poisonous, and with their ill-will further exacerbated by the intrigues orchestrated from the Presidential Palace by Alan García, their rancor toward me had been increased to the point of insanity. The appearance of Fujimori at the last minute was a gift of the gods for the APRA and the left, and it was obvious that both would devote themselves body and soul to working for his victory, without stopping for one minute to think of how dangerous it was to bring to power someone so ill-prepared to exercise it. Common sense, reason, are exotic flowers in Peruvian political life and I am sure that, even if they had known that, twenty months after he was elected, Fujimori was going to put an end to democracy, close down Congress, proclaim himself dictator, and begin to repress Apristas and Communists, they would have voted for him just the same, in order to keep a person whom they called enemy number one from taking office as president.

I reflected on all this after talking with Elías Laroza and, as the polling places closed and the television networks began broadcasting the first projections of the results, before I knew that they were still worse than what we had had hints of: between 28 and 29 percent for me and Fujimori a bare five points behind me with 24 percent. The APRA and the United Left won, between them, a third of the votes.

I mulled over in my mind what I ought to do. Negotiating with Fujimori as soon as possible, handing the presidency over to him there and then in return for his consenting to economic reform: putting an end to inflation, lowering tariffs, opening up the economy to competition, renegotiating with the International Monetary Fund and the World Bank to allow Peru to participate once again in the global financial system, and perhaps the privatization of certain public enterprises. We had the technical experts and the key personnel he lacked to put those measures into effect. My principal argument would be: "More than 50 percent of Peruvians have voted for a change. It is clear that there is not a majority in favor of the radical change that I am proposing; the results show a majority inclined toward moderate, gradual change—for that government by consensus which I have always said would be tantamount to paralysis and inconsistent with our principles. It is crystal clear that I am not the right person to carry out this policy. But it would be a mockery of the decision of the majority for Cambio 90 to serve for one purpose only—to allow the APRA to continue to govern Peru—when it is also obvious that only some 19 percent of Peruvians want to go on exactly as before."

At 6:30 p.m. I went down to the second floor to talk to the press. The atmosphere in the hotel was funereal. In the corridors, on the stairs, in the elevators, all that I saw were long faces, eyes brimming with tears, expressions of indescribable surprise, and a few, also, of utter rage. The conference room was jam-packed with journalists, cameras, and spotlights, and people from the Democratic Front who even in their dejection marshaled the strength to applaud me. When I could finally speak, I thanked the voters for my "victory" and congratulated Fujimori for the high percentage of votes he had received. I said that the results indicated a clear-cut decision in favor of change on the part of the majority of Peruvians, and that therefore it should be possible to spare the country the risks and tensions of a second round of voting and negotiate a formula that would give rise once and for all to an administration that would put its shoulder to the wheel.

At that point, Miguel Vega interrupted me to whisper in my ear that Fujimori had turned up at the hotel. Could he come in? I said yes, and suddenly there he was on the platform alongside me. He was shorter than he looked in photographs of him and Japanese through and through, down to his slight Japanese accent in Spanish. I learned afterward that, when he appeared at the door of the Sheraton, a group of supporters of the Front had tried to attack him, but that another group had held them back and helped his bodyguards protect him and escort him to the auditorium. We gave each other a friendly embrace for the photographers and I told him that we must talk together, the very next morning.

The nineteenth floor had filled with friends and supporters who, once they had learned the results, had rushed to the hotel and overflowed the security barrier set up to isolate me. The suite had the air of a wake and, at times, of a madhouse. People's faces reflected surprise, consternation, and great bitterness over the unforeseen results. The radio and television stations had begun to broadcast rumors that I was going to give up my candidacy, and the leaders of the APRA and the United Left were beginning to hint that in the runoff round they would throw their support to Fujimori's "popular candidacy." The owners of *El Comercio*, Alejandro and Aurelio Miró Quesada, the first to arrive, were adamant, insisting that there was no reason whatsoever for me to refuse to run in a second round since I still had every possibility of winning. Shortly thereafter, Belaunde Terry and Violeta arrived, and Lucho and Laura Bedoya and campaign directors of the Front. I stayed there until almost ten that night, saying and hearing the conventional things with which my friends, relatives, supporters, and I tried to hide the disappointment we felt.

As we left the Sheraton, Patricia firmly insisted that I get out of the car and say a few words to several hundred young people of Libertad who had been there since dusk, shouting slogans in chorus and singing. I recognized Johnny Palacios and Felipe Leno, the fervent secretary general of the young people's section of Libertad, who had been at my side on all the speakers' platforms everywhere in Peru, raising rallies to a fever pitch with his thundering voice. His eyes were damp, but he forced himself to smile. And on reaching home, despite its being almost midnight, I found myself again in the midst of a crowd of young people who had surrounded the house, whom I felt it my duty to thank for their loyalty.

When I was alone at last with Patricia and the children, dawn was breaking. Nonetheless, before going to bed, I made a first draft of the letter explaining to Peruvians why I would give up running for the presidency in the second round and urging those who had voted for the Front to support Fujimori's administration. I was hoping to show it to my opponent the following day as an enticement that would encourage him to accept an agreement that would allow certain points of the program to "change Peru, in freedom" to be saved.

NINETEEN

The Trip to Paris

O NE day in September or October 1957, Luis Loayza brought me a piece of unbelievable news: a short story contest, organized by a French magazine, the prize for which was—a two-week trip to Paris!

La Revue Française, a deluxe publication devoted to art and edited by Monsieur Prouverelle, was bringing out a series of issues, each of which was a monograph on a different country. The short story contest, with its coveted prize, was a feature of that series of monographs. An opportunity like that catapulted me to my typewriter, as was the case with every living Peruvian who knew how to write, and that was how I came to pen "El desafío" ("The Challenge"), a story about an old man who sees his son die in a knife duel, in the dry riverbed of the Piura, that is included in my first book, *Los jefes*, a collection of short stories published in 1959. (In English, the book's title is *The Cubs and Other Stories*.) I entered the short story in the contest, the winner of which was to be decided by a jury headed by Jorge Basadre and on which there were critics and writers—Héctor Velarde, Luis Jaime Cisneros, André Coyné, and Sebastián Salazar Bondy—and tried to think of something else, so that the disappointment wouldn't be as great if anyone else turned out to be the winner. Some weeks later, one afternoon when I was beginning to prepare the 6 p.m. news bulletin, Luis Loayza appeared in the doorway of my shack at Radio Panamericana, elated: "You're going to France!" He was as overjoyed as though he'd won the prize himself.

I doubt whether, either before or since then, any piece of news has excited me as much as that one. I was going to set foot in the city I'd dreamed of, in the mythical country where the writers I most admired had been born. "I'm going to meet Sartre, I'm going to shake hands with Sartre," I kept repeating that night to Julia and to Uncle Lucho and Aunt Olga, with whom Julia and I went out to celebrate the occasion. I was so overexcited I must not have slept a wink all night, bouncing in the bed out of sheer joy.

The official announcement of the winner of the prize took place at the Alliance Française and my beloved French teacher, Madame del Solar, was also there, very pleased that her former pupil had won the contest sponsored by *La Revue Française*. I met Monsieur Prouverelle, and we came to an agreement whereby I would take the trip after the final examinations at the university and the year-end holidays. These last days of 1957 were hectic ones, in which there were interviews of me published in the newspapers and my friends came by to congratulate me. Dr. Porras organized a chocolate party to celebrate my winning the prize.

I went to thank the members of the jury one by one, and that was how I met Jorge Basadre, the last great nonprovincial intellectual figure that Peru has produced. I had never spoken with him before. He was less given to recounting anecdotes and less scintillating than Porras Barrenechea, but much more interested in ideas, doctrines, and philosophy than Porras was, with a vast literary culture and a broad view of Peru's historical problems. The neatness and the discreet elegance of his home seemed to be a reflection of the organized intelligence of the historian, his mental clarity. He lacked vanity and did not make the slightest effort to show off his brilliance; he was earnest and formal, but very levelheaded. I spent two hours with him, listening to him talk about the great novels that had moved him deeply, and he spoke of Thomas Mann's *The Magic Mountain* in such a way that, when I left his house in San Isidro, I hurried to a bookstore to buy it. Sebastián Salazar Bondy, who had been in France for a few months not long before, said to me, enviously: "The best thing that can happen to anyone in the world is happening to you: going to Paris!" He drew up a list for me of indispensable things to do and see in the capital of France.

André Coyné translated *El desafío* into French, but it was Georgette Vallejo who revised the translation and polished it, working with me. I knew César Vallejo's widow because she often used to come to visit Porras, but it was only in those days when I was helping her with the translation, in her apartment in the Calle Dos de Mayo, that we became friends. She could be a fascinating person when she told anecdotes about famous writers she had known, although her stories were always weighted down by a secret passion. All Vallejo scholars habitually turned into her mortal enemies. She detested them, as though by coming to be on close terms with Vallejo they took something away from her. She was as thin and wiry as a fakir and had an awesome temper. At a famous lecture at San Marcos, in which the subtle poet Gerardo Diego recounted as a mild joke how Vallejo had died owing him a few pesetas, the shadow of the illustrious widow rose to her feet in the auditorium and coins sailed over the audience's heads toward the lecturer, as the air was deafened by the exclamation: "Vallejo always paid his debts, you wretch!" Neruda, who detested her as much as she detested him, swore that Vallejo was so afraid of Georgette that he used to make his escape over the rooftops or through the windows of their Paris apartment so as to be alone with his friends. Georgette lived in near penury in the days when I first knew her, giving private French classes, and cultivated her neuroses without the least embarrassment. She put out little spoonfuls of sugar for the ants in her apartment, she never took off the black turban she was invariably wearing every time I saw her, in dramatic accents she lamented the fate of the ducks doomed to decapitation at a Chinese restaurant next to the building where she lived, and she fought tooth and nail—by means of devastatingly cruel open letters—with all the publishers who had brought out or tried to bring out Vallejo's poetry. She lived extremely frugally, and I remember how one time, when Julia and I invited her to have lunch with us at La Pizzería on the Diagonal, she scolded us, with tears in her eyes, for having left food on our plates when there were so many hungry people in the world. Though her behavior was outrageous, she was generous: she was eager to help Communist poets who had financial or political problems, and on occasion, in times of repression, she hid them in her apartment. Being friends with her was arduous, like walking across burning coals, since the most trivial and unexpected thing might offend her and unleash one of her fits of fury. Despite this, she became a very good friend of ours and we used to go fetch her, bring her to our place, and sometimes take her out on Saturdays. Then, when I went off to live in Europe, she made me run errands for her—collect royalties owed her, mail her certain homeopathic medicines from a pharmacy at the Carrefour de l'Odéon, of which she had been a customer ever since the days of her youth—until, because of one of these errands, we too had a quarrel by letter. And even though we made up later on, we no longer saw each other very often. The last time I spoke with her, in Mejía Baca's bookstore, shortly before the beginning of that terrible last stage of her life that was to keep her in a clinic for years, turned into a vegetable, I asked her how things were going with her: "How do you expect they're going for a woman in this country where every day people are more evil, uglier, and crueler?" she answered, rasping her r's with obvious delight.

At Radio Panamericana they gave me a month's vacation, and Uncle Lucho secured me a loan of a thousand dollars from his bank, so as to enable me to stay in Paris, at my own expense, for two additional weeks. Uncle Jorge dug up an old gray overcoat which he'd kept around since the days of his youth and which the moths in Lima hadn't done too much damage to, and one morning in January 1958 I started out on the great adventure. Besides Julia, Uncle Lucho, Abelardo and Pupi, and Luis Loayza came to the airport to say goodbye to me. With great self-importance, I took along in my suitcase several copies of the very first issue of *Literatura*, just off the presses, so as to acquaint French writers with our review.

I have made many journeys in my life and have forgotten almost all of them, but I remember that two-day Avianca flight with a wealth of details, such as the magical thought that never left me: "I'm going to get to know Paris." There was a Peruvian medical student who was going back to Madrid on the plane, and two young Colombian girls, who had come aboard at the stop in Barranquilla, whom the two of us photographed each other with in the Azores. (A year later, in a bar in Madrid, the Peruvian Lucho Garrido Lecca showed that photo to Julia, sparking a monumental jealous scene.) The plane remained for hours at each stopover—Bogotá, Barranquilla, the Azores, Lisbon— and finally, early in the morning on a rainy winter day, it arrived at Orly, in those days a smaller and more modest airport than the one in Lima. And waiting there was Monsieur Prouverelle, yawning.

As his Dauphine went up the Champs-Élysées toward the Arc de Triomphe, it all seemed like a miracle to me. A cold dawn was breaking and there were no cars or pedestrians on the great broad avenue, but how imposing everything looked, how harmonious the façades and the show windows were, how majestic and magnificent the Arc de Triomphe. Monsieur Prouverelle drove around the Étoile so that I could enjoy the view before taking me to the Hôtel Napoléon on the Avenue de Friedland, where I would spend the two weeks of my prize. It was a luxurious hotel and Lucho Loayza was later to say that I described my entrance into the Napoléon the way the "savages" whom Columbus brought to Spain described their entrance into the court of Castile and Aragon.

During that month in Paris I lived a life that was to have nothing to do with the one I would lead during my stay of almost seven years in France later on, when I was almost always confined to the world of the *rive gauche*. In those four weeks at the beginning of 1958, on the other hand, I was a resident of the eighth arrondissement, on the *rive droite*, and to all appearances, anyone would have taken me for a South American dandy come to Paris to have myself a fling. In the Hôtel Napoléon I was given a room with a little balcony overlooking the street, from which I could glimpse the Arc de Triomphe. Across from my room someone who had also won a prize was staying: Miss France 1958, part of whose prize also consisted of a stay at the Napoléon. Her name was Annie Simplon and she was a girl with golden tresses and a wasp waist, to whom the manager of the hotel, Monsieur Makovsky, introduced me and with whom he invited me to dine and dance one night in a fashionable nightclub, L'Éléphant Blanc. Nice Annie Simplon took me on a tour of Paris in the Dauphine that she'd won along with her kingdom and my ears still ache from the bursts of laughter I sent her into, on the afternoon of that outing, with the French that I thought I'd learned not only to read but to speak.

The Hôtel Napoléon had a restaurant, Chez Pescadou, whose elegance intimidated me so much that I crossed it on tiptoe. My French did not allow me to decipher all the exquisite names of the dishes on the menu, and perturbed by the presence of that maître d'hôtel, who looked like a royal chamberlain in ceremonial dress standing alongside me, I chose them at random, pointing with my finger. And so I was surprised at lunch one day to find that I had been brought a little fishing net. I had ordered a trout and had to go get it myself, out of a tank in one corner of the restaurant. "This is Proust's world," I thought, bowled over, despite the fact that at the time I hadn't yet read even one line of *Remembrance of Things Past*.

On the morning after my arrival, almost the minute I woke up, around noon, I went out for a stroll along the Champs-Élysées. It was now crowded with people and vehicles and, behind the glass partitions, the terraces of the bistros were jam-packed with men and women, smoking, talking together. Everything looked beautiful, incomparable, dazzling to me. I was nothing but a *métèque*, a cheeky spic. I felt that this was my city: I would live here, write here, put down roots here and stay forever. In those days, Syrians and Lebanese prowled the streets of the center of the city, buying and selling dollars—the inevitable result of currency controls—and I didn't understand what those characters who approached me every so often, with furtive gestures, were offering me, until finally one of them, who spoke a sort of Spanuguese, explained to me what he was after. He changed some dollars for me, at a better rate than the one I got at the bank, and I made the mistake of telling him what hotel I was staying at. Later on, he phoned me several times, offering me diversions of all sorts, with *"mushashas muito bonitas"*—his Spanuguese for "very pretty girls."

Monsieur Prouverelle had prepared a program for me, which included a visit to the Hôtel de Ville, where they gave me a citation. We were accompanied by the Peruvian cultural attaché, an elderly gentleman who a while later would attain a moment of fame at a general conference of UNESCO during which he gave a speech attacking Picasso—making it clear that his criticisms were "of a painter by a painter," since he himself turned out landscape paintings in his time off from his diplomatic duties. He had become so refined (or was so absent-minded) that he kissed the hands of all the women doorkeepers at the Hôtel de Ville, to the astonishment of Monsieur Prouverelle, who asked me if this was a Peruvian custom. Our cultural attaché had lived in Europe for an eternity and the Peru of his memories was already long dead and gone, or had perhaps never existed. I remember how surprised I was, on the afternoon I met him—we had gone to have coffee together, after the visit to the Hôtel de Ville, at a bistro near the Châtelet—when I heard him say: "People in Lima are so frivolous, strolling up and down the Paseo Colón every Sunday." When were Limeños in the habit of going for Sunday strolls along that run-down Paseo in the downtown area of the city? Thirty or forty years before, no doubt. But, in all truth, that gentleman could have been a thousand years old.

Monsieur Prouverelle got *Le Figaro* to interview me and gave a cocktail party in my honor at the Hôtel Napoléon, at which he presented the issue of *La Revue Française* in which my short story appeared. He was, as he put it, *"un chauvin raisonné"*—a reasonable chauvinist—and he was amused and delighted by my unbridled enthusiasm for everything I saw round about me and my fascination for French books and authors. He was amazed that I went all about Paris continually associating its monuments, streets, and various sites with novels and poems that I knew by heart.

He made valiant efforts to arrange for me to meet Sartre, but he couldn't manage it. We got as far as Sartre's secretary at the time, Jean Cau, who, doing his job conscientiously, kept putting us off until we got tired of insisting. But I did manage to see Albert Camus, shake his hand, and exchange a few words with him. Monsieur Prouverelle found out that he was directing the revival of one of his plays, in a theater on the *grands boulevards*, and I posted myself there one morning, with my cheekiness of a twenty-one-year-old. After I'd waited for just a short time, Camus appeared, accompanied by the actress Maria Casares. (I recognized her at once, from a film I'd seen twice and liked as much as Lucho Loayza disliked it: Marcel Carné's *Les Enfants du paradis*.) I went over to him, stammering, in my bad French, that I admired him very much and that I wanted to give him a copy of a literary review, and to my surprise, he answered me in a few kindly sentences in good Spanish (his mother was a Spaniard from Oran). He was wearing the same raincoat as in all the photographs of him, and holding the usual cigarette between his fingers. He and she said something, immediately after that, about "le Pérou," a word that in those days was still associated in France with ideas of prosperity (*"Ce n'est pas le Pérou!"*—"This isn't Peru!").

The day after my arrival Monsieur Prouverelle invited me to have an aperitif with him at the Rhumerie Martiniquaise, in St.-Germain-des-Prés, and have dinner at Le Fiacre, warning me that he was taking me there because it was an excellent restaurant, but that the bar on the ground floor might shock me. I thought I had freed myself of any sort of prejudice, but it is true that as I went through that bar, where lustful elderly gentlemen were making out with boys, lavishing kisses on them and joyously fondling them in full view of everyone,

I was disconcerted. It was one thing to read that such things existed and another to see them.

The restaurant Le Fiacre, on the other hand, was most proper, and I learned there that Monsieur Prouverelle, before being editor of *La Revue Française,* had been in the military. He had hung up his uniform because of a great disappointment; I don't know whether it was a political or a personal one, but he spoke to me about it in a tone that impressed me, for it appeared to be a drama that had turned his life upside down. Dumbfounded, I heard him speak well of Salazar's regime, which, according to him, had put an end to the anarchy that had previously held sway in Portugal, a thesis I hastened to refute, shocked that anyone could believe that dictators such as Salazar or Franco had done anything good for their countries. He didn't insist, and instead changed the subject, telling me that he would introduce me the next day to a young lady, the daughter of friends of his, who could accompany me to visit museums and tour Paris.

And that was how I met Bernadette, whom I saw, from that time on, for many hours every day, until the eve of my return to Lima. And thanks to her I knew that something even better could happen to me than all the good things that had already come my way: being twenty-one years old and knowing a pretty, likable young French girl with whom to discover the marvels of Paris.

Bernadette had chestnut-colored bobbed hair, bright blue eyes with a penetrating gaze, and a pale complexion that, when her face grew flushed with laughter or embarrassment, set her person aglow with radiant charm. She must have been about eighteen and was a perfect *demoiselle du seizième,* a girl comme il faut, thanks to her invariably neat and tidy appearance, her excellent manners, and her very proper behavior. But she was also intelligent, amusing, possessed of an elegant and worldly-wise flirtatiousness, and seeing her and hearing her and being aware of her graceful silhouette at my side made shivers run up and down my spine. She was studying at an art school, and knew the Louvre, Versailles, L'Orangerie, Le Jeu de Paume like the palm of her hand, so that visiting museums with her doubled my pleasure.

We met each other very early each morning and began our tour of churches, art galleries, and bookstores, following a carefully thought-out plan. Early in the evening we would go to the theater or the movies, and on some nights, after dinner, to some *cave* on the *rive gauche* to listen to music and to dance. She lived on a street that crossed the Avenue Victor Hugo, in an apartment with her parents and an older sister, and she took me to her place a number of times to have lunch or dinner, something that was not to happen to me again in the many years I lived in France, even with my best French friends.

On going back to Paris again, to live there for some time a couple of years later, especially in the beginning, when I was having financial difficulties, I always remember as something fabulous that month in which, with pretty Bernadette, I went to all sorts of performances and to restaurants every night, and my days were spent visiting art galleries and out-of-the-way places in Paris and buying books. Monsieur Prouverelle got us complimentary tickets to the Comédie Française and the Théâtre National de Paris, directed by Jean Vilar, on the stage of which I saw Gérard Philippe, in Kleist's *The Prince of Homburg*. Another memorable theatrical performance was the staging of a play of Shakespeare's in which one of the roles was played by Pierre Brasseur, whose films I was continually trying to find a showing of. We also saw, I'm certain, Ionesco's *La Cantatrice chauve* (*The Bald Soprano*) and *La Leçon* (*The Lesson*), in the little theater on the Rue de la Huchette (where performances of both are still given today, after a run of nearly forty years), and that night, after the theater, we took a very long walk along the quays, on the banks of the Seine, during which I tried out a few flirtatious remarks in my imperfect French, making grammatical mistakes that Bernadette corrected. I also became acquainted with the Cinémathèque on the Rue d'Ulm, where we immured ourselves for an entire day, seeing four of Max Ophuls's films, among them *The Earrings of Madame de . . .* , with that great beauty Danielle Darrieux.

Since my prize paid me for only fifteen days at the Napoléon, for the last two weeks of my stay I had reserved a room in the Hôtel de Seine, in the Latin Quarter, recommended to me by Salazar Bondy. But when I went to say goodbye to the manager of the Hôtel Napoléon, Monsieur Makovsky told me that I should stay on, paying what I would be paying at the Hôtel de Seine. So I continued to enjoy the Arc de Triomphe until the end of my stay.

To me, another of the marvels of Paris was the bookstalls along the Seine and the little bargain bookstores in the Latin Quarter, where I laid in a good supply of books that later on I had no idea how to fit into my suitcase. I managed, in this way, to complete my collection of *Les Temps Modernes*, from the first issue on, with that initial manifesto of Sartre's in favor of political commitment which I knew almost by heart.

Years later, settled now in France, I had a long conversation about Paris one night with Julio Cortázar, who also loved the city and who once declared that he had chosen it "because being nobody in a city that was everything was a thousand times preferable to having things the other way around." I told him of that precocious passion in my life for a mythical city, which I knew only through literary fantasies and gossip, and how, by comparing it to the real version, in that month straight out of the *Thousand and One Nights*, instead of my being disappointed by it, the spell had grown even greater. (It lasted until 1966.)

He too felt that Paris had given something profound to his life that could never be repaid: a perception of what was best in human experience; a certain tangible sense of beauty. A mysterious association of history, literary invention, technical skill, scientific knowledge, architectonic and plastic wisdom, and also, in large doses, sheer chance had created that city where going out for a stroll along the bridges and the quays of the Seine, or observing at certain hours the volutes of the gargoyles of Notre Dame or venturing into certain little squares or the labyrinth of dark, narrow streets in the Marais, was a moving spiritual and aesthetic experience, like burying oneself in a great book. "Just as one chooses a woman and is or is not chosen by her, the same thing happens with cities," Cortázar said. "We chose Paris and Paris chose us."

At that time Cortázar had already settled in France, but in that month of January 1958 I hadn't yet met him, nor do I believe I knew of any of the many Latin American painters or writers there (*Pobre gente de Paris*—"Poor wretches in Paris"—Sebastián Salazar Bondy was to call them in a book of short stories inspired by them), with the exception of the Peruvian poet Leopoldo Chariarse, about whom I had heard Abelardo Oquendo tell very amusing anecdotes (such as having declared, in public, that his vocation as a poet was born "the day that, as a child, a black woman raped me"). Chariarse, who was later to become a flute player, an Orientalist, a guru and the spiritual father of a sect and the director of an ashram in Germany, at that time was a Surrealist, and he had great prestige within the little sect to which André Breton's movement had been reduced. The French Surrealists presumed that he was a revolutionary persecuted by the dictatorial regime in Peru (governed at the time by a most peace-loving Manuel Prado), and didn't suspect in the least that he was the sole poet in the history of Peru to be given a scholarship to Europe through an Act of Congress.

I learned all this through the poet Benjamin Péret, whom I went to visit in the very modest apartment where he lived, with the hope that he would give me certain information about César Moro, since one of my projects at the time was to write an essay on him. In France, Moro belonged to the Surrealist group for a number of years—he contributed to *Le Surréalisme au service de la Révolution* and the *Hommage à Violette Nozière*, and then organized, with Péret and Breton, an International Exposition of Surrealism in Mexico. However, in the official history of the group, he was rarely referred to. Péret proved to be very evasive, either because he scarcely remembered Moro or for some other reason, and told me almost nothing about the most authentic Surrealist born in Peru, and perhaps in all of Latin America. The person who gave me a clue to the reasons for this ostracism to which Moro had been condemned by Breton and his friends was Maurice Nadeau, whom I went to see, on an errand for Georgette Vallejo, to receive royalties from him for several of Vallejo's poems that had appeared in *Les Lettres Nouvelles*. Nadeau, whose *Histoire du Surréalisme* I was acquainted with, introduced me to a young French novelist who was with him—Michel Butor—and when I asked him why the Surrealists appeared to have "purged" Moro, told me that probably it was because of his homosexuality. Breton tolerated and encouraged every "vice" except for that one, ever since, in the 1920s, the Surrealists had been accused of being fairies. This was the incredible reason why Moro had come to be an inner exile too, even within the very movement whose morality and philosophy he himself embodied—someone whose integrity and talent alike were more genuine than that of the majority of those recognized and hallowed by Papa Breton.

In this month in Paris, I began for the first time, very secretly, to wonder whether I hadn't been overly hasty and made a mistake by getting married. Not because Julia and I didn't get along together, for we had no more quarrels than the usual married couple, and I am the first to admit that Julia helped me in my work, and instead of putting obstacles in the way of my literary vocation encouraged it. But, rather, because that initial passion for her had died out and been replaced by a domestic routine and an obligation that, at times, I began to feel as an enslavement. Could this marriage last? Time, rather than lessening our difference in age, would little by little make it more dramatic, until it turned our relationship into something artificial. The family's predictions would come true, sooner or later, and that romantic marriage would perhaps end up foundering.

These gloomy thoughts arose indirectly, during those days, as my tours of Paris and my flirtation with Bernadette went on. She devoured me with questions about Julia—her feminine curiosity was stronger than her polite upbringing—and she kept after me to show her a photograph of my wife. With this young girl I felt young myself, and in a certain way I relived, in those weeks, my early years in Miraflores and my amorous skirmishes in Diego Ferré. For not since I was thirteen or fourteen had I had a "sweetheart" or whiled away my time in such a marvelous way, wandering about and having fun, as I did during those four weeks in Paris. In the last few days, when my return to Peru was imminent, I was overcome by a tremendous anxiety attack and the temptation to stay in France, to break with Peru, break with my family, and immediately begin a new life, in that city, in that country, where being a writer appeared to be possible, where everything gave me the impression of having conspired to favor it.

The night I bade Bernadette goodbye was very tender. It was late, it was drizzling, and we kept endlessly saying goodbye to each other in the doorway of the building where she lived. I kept kissing her hands and tears glistened in her pretty eyes. The next morning, as I was about to leave for the airport, we had one last conversation over the phone. Then after that, we wrote to each other several times, but I never saw her again. (Thirty years later, at the most crucial moment of the election campaign, someone whom I was never able to identify slipped a letter from her under the door of my house.)

The trip to Lima, which was scheduled to take a couple of days, lasted all that week. We flew the first leg, from Paris to Lisbon, without problems, and took off from there exactly on time. But almost as soon as we started flying over the Atlantic, the pilot of the Avianca Super Constellation announced to us that one of the engines wasn't working properly. We went back to Lisbon. We stayed two days in that city, at Avianca's expense, waiting for the plane that was coming to our rescue, a delay that enabled me to have a glimpse of that pretty, melancholy capital. My money was all gone and I was dependent on the coupons that the airline gave us for lunches and dinners, but on one of those days a fellow passenger from Colombia invited me to a picturesque Lisbon restaurant to sample the cod *à la Gomes de Sá*. He was a young man who was a member of the Conservative Party. I looked on him as a strange creature—he wore a big broad-brimmed sombrero wherever he went and pronounced his words with the pretentiously and perversely precise accent of people from Bogotá—and I irritated him by asking him a number of times: "How can anyone be young and *conservative*?"

Finally, after two days, we boarded the replacement plane. We reached the Azores, but there bad weather kept it from landing. We were diverted to an island whose name I've forgotten, where, in the course of the terrifying landing, the pilot managed to damage one of the plane's wheels and put us through several moments of panic. When I arrived in Bogotá, my flight to Lima had left three days before, and hapless Avianca had to lodge me and feed me in Bogotá for several more days. The moment I was installed in the Hotel Tequendama, I went out for a stroll down one of the main downtown streets. I was looking into the show windows of a bookstore when I saw people running toward me, in the midst of a skirmish of some sort. Before I understood what was going on, I heard shots and saw policemen and soldiers dealing out blows right and left with their truncheons, so I too started to run, knowing neither where to nor why, and wondering what sort of city this was, where I had just landed and already they were trying to kill me.

I finally arrived in Lima, full of energy, determined to finish my thesis as soon as possible and perform miracles to win the Javier Prado Fellowship. I told Julia, Lucho and Abelardo, my aunts and uncles about my trip to Paris with unbridled enthusiasm, and my memory relived with vast delight everything I had seen and done there. But I didn't have much time for nostalgia, since, in fact, I set to work on my thesis on Rubén Darío's short stories, in all my free moments, at the library of the Club Nacional, between news bulletins at Pan-americana, and at night, at home, until sometimes I fell asleep over my typewriter.

A mishap occurred that interrupted that work pace. One morning my groin began to hurt—what I thought was my groin, that is, and turned out to be my appendix. I went to San Marcos to have a doctor see me. He prescribed several medicines for me to take, which didn't have the slightest effect on me, and shortly thereafter, Genaro Delgado Parker, who saw me limping, put me in his car and drove me to the Clínica Internacional, with which Panamericana had some sort of a deal. I had to have an emergency operation, since my appendix was now badly inflamed. According to Lucho Loayza, when I came out from under the anesthesia, I was shouting swear words, my mother was shocked and covered my mouth with her hand and Julia was protesting: "You're smothering him, Dorita." Although Radio Pan-americana paid for half the expenses of my operation, the part I had to pay for plus paying back the thousand-dollar loan I owed to the bank left me nearly broke. I compensated for those expenditures by churning out extra articles in the supplement of *El Comercio*, in the form of book reviews, and writing for the magazine *Cultura Peruana*, whose kindly editor-in-chief, José Flórez Aráoz, let me have two signed columns in each issue and publish notes or articles without a byline.

I finished my thesis before half a year had gone by, giving it a title that sounded scholarly—"Bases para una interpretación de Rubén Darío"—and began to harass my professors who were evaluating it— Augusto Tamayo Vargas and Jorge Puccinelli—to get them to write their reports as soon as possible so I could get my degree. One morning in June or July 1958, I was summoned by the historian Luis E. Valcárcel, at that time the dean of the Faculty of Letters, to defend my thesis in the auditorium at San Marcos, where degrees are awarded. My whole family attended this academic ceremony and the observa-tions and questions put to me by the professors who constituted the jury were kindly. My thesis was approved cum laude, and it was suggested that it be published in the review of the Faculty of Letters. But I kept putting off having it published, having in mind the idea of making improvements on it first, something I never got around to. Written in fits and starts, in the gaps of a life taken up almost entirely by jobs to keep food on the table, it was worthless, and the grade I received is better explained by the good will of the professors on the jury and the declining academic standards of San Marcos than by its merits. But my work on that thesis gave me the opportunity to read a great deal of the writings of a poet gifted with a fabulous verbal richness, to whose inspiration and skill the Castilian language owes one of the seminal revolutions in its history. For with Rubén Darío—the starting point of all the avant-garde movements of the future—poetry in Spain and Latin America began to be modern.

In my application for the Javier Prado scholarship, to earn a doctorate from the Complutense University in Madrid, I expressed my intention of continuing the same studies in Spain, taking advantage of the Rubén Darío archives that a professor from the University of Madrid, Antonio Oliver Belmas, had discovered not long before—something that, had circumstances permitted, I would have been more than happy to do. But there were insuperable obstacles standing in the way of my consulting those archives, and once my thesis was approved at San Marcos my involvement as a Darío scholar was interrupted. But not my devotion as a reader of his, for ever since then, after long parentheses sometimes, I reread him and I always experience the same amazement and admiration that his poetry occasioned in me on first reading it. (Unlike what happens to me in the case of the novel, a genre in which I have an invincible weakness for so-called realism, in poetry I have always preferred a luxuriant unreality, above all if a spark of flashiness and fine music accompanies it.)

Loayza graduated a little before or a little after I did, he too being determined to take off for Europe. In order to make concrete plans for the journey, we were both waiting for the decision of the jury for the Javier Prado scholarship. On the morning of the day that the winner was to be announced, my heart was in my throat when I arrived at San Marcos. But Rosita Corpancho, who enjoyed passing on good news, got up from her desk the moment she saw me appear: "They gave it to you!" I staggered out of her office to tell Julia that we were going to Madrid. My happiness, as we walked along La Colmena to the Plaza San Martín to take the minibus to Miraflores, was so great that I felt like giving out with a yell like Tarzan's.

We immediately began making preparations for the journey. We sold the furniture we had, so as to take a bit of money with us, and packed all my books in boxes and cartons, tossing inside them little balls of naphthalene and spreading packages of black tobacco around in them, since we had been assured that that was a good preventative against bookworms. It wasn't. In 1974, when I came back to Peru to live, after sixteen years abroad—during which time I returned only for short stays, with one exception, in 1972, a stay that lasted six months—and reopened those boxes and cartons that up until then had been stored at my grandparents' and at the houses of various aunts and uncles, a number of them offered a frightful spectacle: a green layer of mold covered the books, in which there could be glimpsed, as though it were a colander, the little holes through which the bookworms had bored their way inside to wreak their damage. Many of those boxes were now nothing but dust, bits and scraps, and vermin and had to be thrown into the trash. Less than a third of that first library of mine survived Lima's uncultured bad weather.

At the same time, I went on working at all my jobs and Lucho and Abelardo and I prepared the second issue of *Literatura*, in which an article of mine on César Moro appeared, and in which we rendered a brief homage to the Cubans of the 26th of July, who, with a romantic guerrilla fighter as their leader—that was what Fidel Castro seemed to us to be—fought against Batista's tyranny. There were a few Cubans in exile in Lima and one of them, active in the resistance, worked at Radio Panamericana. He kept me informed about the *barbudos* with whom, needless to say, I sentimentally identified myself. But in that last year in Lima, except for that emotional loyalty to the resistance movement against Batista, I did not engage in the slightest political activity and I had drawn apart from the Christian Democratic Party, in which, however, I remained enrolled as a member for several months more until, following Fidel's victory and in view of the luke-warm support that the Peruvian Christian Democrats gave him, I formally resigned from the party, in a letter that I wrote them from Europe.

All my energy and time, in those last months in Lima, were devoted to working so as to get a little money together, and to preparing for my stay abroad. Although the latter, in theory, was to last a year—the time limit of the scholarship—I had resolved that it would be forever. After Spain, I would find a way to get to France and would stay there for good. In Paris I would become a writer and if I returned to Peru, it would be for a visit, since in Lima I would never get past being that protowriter that I had become and the Peruvian writers whom I knew seemed to me to be. I had talked it over very seriously with Julia and she agreed to our uprooting ourselves. She too had high hopes for our European adventure and was completely confident that I would succeed in becoming a novelist and promised to help me reach that goal by making whatever sacrifices were necessary. When I heard her talk to me like that, I was assailed by bitter remorse for having allowed myself to be overcome, in Paris, by the bad thoughts I had had. (I have never been good at the widespread sport of cheating on one's wife, which I have seen being engaged in all around me, by the majority of my friends, with self-confident offhandedness; I fall passionately in love and my infidelities have always brought me moral and emotional traumas.)

The one person to whom I confided my intention of never returning to Peru was Uncle Lucho, who, as always, encouraged me to do what I thought best for my vocation. To the others, this represented a postgraduate stay abroad, and at San Marcos, Augusto Tamayo Vargas managed to get me a leave of absence, which assured me of having classes to teach in the Faculty of Letters on my return. Porras Barrenechea helped me secure two free passages on the Brazilian mail plane, from Lima to Rio de Janeiro (the flight took three days, since the plane made overnight stops in Santa Cruz and in Campo Grande), so that all Julia and I had to pay for was our passage by boat, in third class, from Rio to Barcelona. Lucho Loayza would travel to Brazil on his own and from there we would go on together. The only trouble was that Abelardo wouldn't be going along with us, but he assured Lucho and me that he would pull all the strings he could to get the scholarship from the Faculty of Law to go to Italy. Within a few months he was to surprise us by suddenly turning up in Europe.

When our preparations were already well under way, at the Faculty of Letters one day, Rosita Corpancho asked me if I wouldn't be tempted by the prospect of taking a trip to Amazonia. A Mexican anthropologist born in Spain, Juan Comas, was about to arrive in Peru, and for this reason the Summer Institute of Linguistics and San Marcos had organized an expedition to the Alto Marañón region, the homeland of the Aguaruna and Huambisa tribes, in which he was interested. I accepted, and thanks to this brief journey I became acquainted with the Peruvian jungle area and saw landscapes and people and heard stories that, later on, would be the raw material for at least three of my novels: *The Green House*, *Captain Pantoja and the Special Service*, and *The Storyteller*.

Never in my life, and I can assure my reader that I've been to quite a few places in the world, have I taken a more fruitful journey, one that afterward would arouse such stimulating memories and images for inventing stories. Thirty-five years later, every so often I still remember certain anecdotes and moments of that expedition by way of territories nearly virgin at that time and remote villages, where existence was very different from the other regions of Peru that I was acquainted with, and where, in the little settlements of Huambisas, Shapras, and Aguarunas that we reached, prehistory was still alive, they still shrank heads and still practiced animism. But, precisely because of how important it turned out to be for my work as a writer and how greatly I have profited from it, I feel more diffident about referring to that experience than I do about any other, since in no other has imagination, which jumbles everything together, become so intermingled with the experience itself. Moreover, I have written and spoken so much about that first journey I made to the jungle that I am certain that if someone were to take the trouble to verify all those eyewitness accounts and personal interviews that I have told about, he or she would notice the subtle changes, which are doubtless abrupt ones as well, that my unconscious and my imagination have continually incorporated into the memory of that expedition.*

What I am sure of is this: discovering the awesome power of the still untamed landscape of Amazonia, and its adventure-filled, primitive, fierce world, with a freedom unknown in urban Peru, left me filled with amazement. It also enlightened me in an unforgettable way with regard to the extremes of savagery and total impunity to which injustice might lead for certain Peruvians. But at the same time, it unfolded before my eyes a world in which, as in great novels, life could be an adventure with no frontiers, where there was room for the most inconceivable feats of daring, where living almost always

---

* I wrote about it for the first time in an article entitled "Crónica de un viaje a la selva" in the magazine *Cultura Peruana* (Lima: September 1958); then in a lecture published as *La historia secreta de una novela* (Barcelona: Tusquets, 1971); in Chapter IV of my novel *El hablador* (Barcelona: Seix Barral, 1987); and in countless reportages and articles as well.

meant risk, boldness, permanent change—all within the framework of forests, rivers, and lakes that seemed like those of Paradise on Earth. It would come back to my mind a thousand and one times in years to come and would be an inexhaustible source of inspiration for my writing.

We went first to Yarinacocha, near Pucallpa, where the base of the Summer Institute of Linguistics was located, and there met its founder, Dr. Townsend, who had created it for a purpose that was at once scientific and religious: so that his linguists—who at the same time were also Protestant missionaries—could learn languages and primitive dialects in order to translate the Bible into them. We then took off to visit the Alto Marañon tribes and were in Urakusa, Chicais, Santa María de Nieva, and many villages and settlements where we slept in hammocks or on makeshift cots; in order to reach some of them, after disembarking from the seaplane, we had to be taken to them in the frail canoes of native ferrymen. In one of the Shapra villages, the tribal chief, Tariri, explained to us the technique used to shrink heads, which his people still practiced; they had a prisoner there from a neighboring tribe with which they were at war; the man roamed about freely among his captors, but they kept his dog in a cage. In Urakusa, I met the tribal chief Jum, recently tortured by some soldiers and "bosses" from Santa María de Nieva, whom we also met, and whom I was later to try to bring to life in *The Green House*. In all the places we visited I learned of unbelievable things and met extraordinary people.

Besides Juan Comas, there traveled with us in the little seaplane the anthropologist Matos Mar, with whom I have been friends ever since, the editor-in-chief of *Cultura Peruana*, José Flórez Aráoz, and Efraín Morote Best, an anthropologist and folklorist from Ayacucho, whom we had to lift off the ground, literally, so that the seaplane could take off. Morote Best had visited bilingual schools and traveled among the tribes, under heroic conditions, bombarding Lima with denunciations of the abuses and iniquities suffered by the indigenous peoples. These latter received him in their villages with great affection and passed their complaints on to him and told him about their problems. The idea I formed of him was that of a very honest and generous man, who had profoundly identified himself with the victims of that country of victims known as Peru. I never imagined that the gentle, timid Dr. Morote Best would, as the years went by be won over by

Maoism, during his rectorate at Ayacucho University, and open the doors of that institution to the fundamentalist Maoism of Sendero Luminoso—whose mentor, Abimael Guzmán, he brought there as a professor—and be regarded as something like the spiritual father of the most bloody extremist movement in the history of Peru.

When I returned to Lima, I didn't even have time left to write the account of the expedition that I had promised Flórez Aráoz (I sent it to him from Rio de Janeiro, on my way to Europe). I spent my last days in Peru saying goodbye to friends and relatives and selecting the papers and notebooks that I would take with me. I felt very sad in the early morning of the day on which I bade my grandparents and Auntie Mamaé farewell, since I didn't know if I would ever see those three elderly people again. Uncle Lucho and Aunt Olga arrived at the Córpac airport to say goodbye to us after Julia and I were already aboard the Brazilian military plane, which, instead of seats, had parachutists' benches. We spied the two of them from the little window and waved goodbye to them, knowing that they couldn't see us. I was sure that I would see the two of *them* again, and that by that time I would at last be a writer.

TWENTY

Period

O N the day following the first round of voting, Wednesday, April 9, 1990, I phoned Alberto Fujimori early in the morning at the Hotel Crillón, his headquarters, and told him I needed to talk with him that same day, without witnesses. He agreed to inform me of the time and place for our meeting, and did so shortly thereafter: an address in the vicinity of the San Juan de Dios clinic, a house next door to a gas station and auto body shop.

The surprising results at the polls on the day before had created an atmosphere of consternation and Lima was a wasp's nest of rumors, among them one about an imminent coup d'état. The frustration and stupefaction of the supporters of the Front had been succeeded by anger, and during the day the radio stations broadcast news bulletins of incidents, in Miraflores and San Isidro, in which Japanese were insulted on the street or thrown out of restaurants. Such a reaction, besides being stupid, was terribly unjust, since the small Japanese community of Peru had given me many proofs of their support ever since the beginning of the campaign. A group of businessmen and professionals of Japanese origin met every so often with Pipo Thorndike to make financial contributions to the Front. I had held talks with them on three occasions, so as to explain our program to them and listen to their suggestions. And the Freedom Movement had chosen a Nisei agriculturalist, from Chancay, as its candidate for representative for the *departamento* of Lima. (He lost his life, shortly before the elections, when the firearm that he was cleaning went off accidentally.)

I had a great liking for the Peruvian–Japanese community, because of its industriousness and productivity—it had developed the agriculture of the northern section of the *departamento* of Lima in the 1920s and 1930s—and great sympathy for the dispossessions and abuses of which it had been the victim during Manuel Prado's first administration (1939–1945), which, after declaring war on Japan, expropriated the property of Japanese and expelled from the country a number of them who were second- or third-generation Peruvians. During Odría's dictatorship as well, Peruvians of Asian origin had been persecuted, by having their passports taken away from many of them and being forced to go into exile. In the beginning, I thought that those news reports concerning insults and attacks directed against the Japanese were the handiwork of the Aprista propaganda machine, that it signaled the beginning of the campaign to ensure Fujimori's victory in the second round of voting. But those news broadcasts had a basis in fact. Racial prejudice—an explosive factor that up until then had never been brazenly exploited in our elections, although it had always been present in Peruvian life—would come to play a primary role in the weeks that followed.

The results of the election had caused real trauma in the Democratic Front and in Libertad, whose leaders, in those first hours after our disastrous showing, had not hit on the proper reaction and fled from the press or answered the questions of correspondents with evasive and confused analyses. Nobody could explain the outcome of the election. The rumors that I was going to withdraw from a second round—which radio and television stations kept repeating—brought on a torrent of phone calls to my house, as well as an endless line of visitors, none of whom I received. Unable to understand what was happening, many friends also called from abroad—Jean-François Revel among them. Beginning shortly before noon, crowds of supporters gathered on the Barranco embankment, in front of my house. With others taking their place every so often, the horde of supporters stayed there all day, till nightfall. They remained silent and sad-faced, or else cried out catchphrases that betrayed their disappointment and anger.

Since I knew that the interview with my adversary would come to nothing if it took place under the siege to which the press had subjected me, Lucho Llosa and I organized a clandestine getaway from my house, in his station wagon, that fooled even the team in charge of security. He parked in the garage, I hunched down in the seat and the only thing that demonstrators, photographers, and security guards saw come out of the garage was Lucho, at the wheel of the station wagon. When, a block farther on, I was able to sit up straight again and saw that nobody was following us, I felt greatly relieved. I had forgotten what it was like to go about Lima without an escort and a wake of reporters.

Fujimori's house was near the exit ramp of the main highway, hidden behind a wall and the gas station and body shop. Fujimori himself appeared at the door to receive me, and it came as a surprise to me to discover, in that modest district, a Japanese garden, bonsai, ponds with little wooden bridges and small lamps, and an elegant residence furnished in the way an Oriental house would be, the whole secluded by high walls. I felt as though I were in a *chifa* or in a traditional dwelling in Kyoto or Osaka, rather than in Lima.

There was no one there except for the two of us, at least no one visible. Fujimori led me to a little reception room, with a large window overlooking the garden, and invited me to sit down at a table on which there was a bottle of whisky and two glasses, each of us directly facing the other, as though for a duel. He was a slender, rather rigid man, a little younger than I am, whose small eyes subjected me to such close scrutiny from behind his glasses that it made me feel ill at ease. He expressed himself in hesitant Spanish, making grammatical errors, and with the defensive mildness and formality of those who are not entirely comfortable with the language.

I told him that I wanted to share with him my interpretation of the outcome of the first round. Two-thirds of Peruvians had voted for change—the "gran cambio" of the Front and his Cambio 90, that is to say, against "politics as usual" and populist policies. If, in order to win the second round, he turned into a prisoner of the APRA and the United Left, he would do the country enormous harm and betray the majority of voters, who wanted something different from what they had had for the last five years.

The one-third of the total votes cast that I had received was not enough for the radical program of reforms that, in my judgment, Peru needed. The majority of Peruvians appeared to be inclined toward gradualism, consensus, compromises made on the basis of mutual concessions, a policy which, in my opinion, was incapable of ending inflation, of giving Peru a place in world affairs again, and of reorganizing Peruvian society on modern foundations. He seemed better qualified for furthering such a national accord; I felt that I was incapable of backing policies in which I didn't believe. In order to be consistent with the voters' message, Fujimori should try to seek the support of all the forces that in one way or another represented "change," that is to say, the forces of Cambio 90, those of the Democratic Front, and the most moderate ones of the United Left. I agreed that we should spare Peru the tension and waste of energy of a second round. With this aim in view, at the same time that I made public my decision not to take part in it, I would urge those who had supported me to respond in a positive way to a summons from him to collaborate. This collaboration was indispensable if his administration was not to be a failure, and would be possible if he accepted certain basic ideas of my proposal, particularly in the field of economics. There was a very tense atmosphere, dangerous for the safeguarding of democracy, so that it was indispensable for the new team to begin work immediately, restoring the country's confidence after such a long and violent election campaign.

He looked at me for quite some time as though he didn't believe me, or as though in what I had just told him there were some sort of hidden trap. Finally, once he had recovered from his surprise, he began, in a hesitant tone of voice, to speak of my patriotism and my generosity, but I interrupted him by saying to him that we should have a drink and speak of practical matters. He poured a finger of whisky in each of the glasses and asked me when I was going to make my decision public. The next morning, I said. It would be a good thing if we kept in contact so that, once my letter had been publicly disclosed, Fujimori could reinforce its message and call on the parties to collaborate. We agreed to proceed in this way.

We went on talking for a little while longer, in a less general way. He asked me if I had made this decision on my own or after consulting with someone, since, he assured me, he always made all important decisions all by himself, without discussing them even with his wife. He asked me who was the best economist among those who were my advisers and I replied that it was Raúl Salazar, and that of everything that had happened what I perhaps most regretted was the fact that Peruvians, by voting as they had, would be left without a minister of finance equal to Salazar, but that Fujimori could repair that damage by calling him. From his questions I noted that he didn't understand what I meant by the *mandate* that I had sought from the voters; he seemed to believe that it meant carte blanche to govern in whatever way a head of state with a mandate pleased, with no restraints. I told him that, on the contrary, it implied a very precise pact between a president and the majority of voters who had elected him in order to carry out a specific program for governing the country, something indispensable if thoroughgoing reforms in a democracy were the goal. We went on talking for a moment about several leaders of the moderate left, such as Senator Enrique Bernales, whom he told me he would include in the agreement we had arrived at.

Three-quarters of an hour had not yet gone by when I rose to my feet. He accompanied me to the front door and as we reached it I made a little joke by bidding him goodbye in the traditional Japanese way, with a bow and murmuring *"Arigato gosai ma su."* But he held his hand out to me without so much as a smile.

I went home hunched down in Lucho's station wagon, and once there, in my study, with all the "royal family" present—Patricia, Álvaro, Lucho and Roxana—we held a conclave during which I described to them my meeting with Fujimori and read them my letter withdrawing as a presidential candidate in a second round of voting. Outside on Malecón, the number of demonstrators had grown. There were now several hundred of them. They kept shouting for me to come outside and were chanting Libertad and Democratic Front slogans in chorus. With that din as background music, we had an argument— I believe it was the first time we had had such a heated one—since only Álvaro agreed with my decision to resign; Lucho and Patricia thought that the forces of the Front wouldn't go along with collaborating with Fujimori and that the latter was already too deeply committed to Alan García and the APRA for my gesture to destroy their alliance. Moreover, it was their belief that we could win the second round.

We were in the midst of the argument when I heard that outside the house the demonstrators had begun to shout slogans in chorus that had a racist and nationalist ring to them—"Mario is a real Peruvian," "We want a Peruvian," in addition to others that were downright insulting—and in indignation I went out to talk to them from the terrace of my house, with the aid of a megaphone. It was inconceivable that those who supported me should discriminate between Peruvians on the basis of the color of their skin. Having so many races and cultures was our greatest source of wealth, the phenomenon that created ties between Peru and the four cardinal points of the globe. It was possible to be a Peruvian whether a person was white, Indian, Chinese, black, or Japanese. Agricultural engineer Fujimori was as Peruvian as I was. The cameramen from Channel 2 were there and managed to broadcast this part of my talk on the news program "Ninety Seconds."

Early the following morning, Tuesday, April 10, I had the usual work session with Álvaro, during which we planned how we should disclose the news of my letter of resignation. We decided to do so through Jaime Bayly, who had never wavered in his support for me throughout the entire campaign and whose programs had a large audience. As soon as I had informed the political committee of Libertad, with which I had an appointment at 11 a.m, in Barranco, we would go with Bayly to Channel 4.

When, shortly before ten in the morning on that memorable day, the candidates for the first and second vice presidencies, Eduardo Orrego and Ernesto Alayza Grundy, arrived, there was already a horde of reporters on Malecón, struggling with my security forces, and the first of those groups which by noon had turned the grounds around my house into a rally were beginning to arrive. There was already a blazing sun and the morning was clear and bright, and very hot.

I gave Eduardo and Don Ernesto my reasons for not taking part in the second round and read them my letter. I had foreseen that both of them would try to dissuade me, as in fact they did. But I was disconcerted by the categorical statement made by Alayza Grundy, who, as a legal scholar, assured me that the step I was about to take was unconstitutional. A candidate could not refuse to compete in a second round. I told him that I had consulted Elías Laroza, who represented us before the National Election Board, and that he had assured me that there was no legal obstacle. In the present circumstances, my refusal to run a second time was the one thing that could keep Fujimori from becoming a prisoner of the APRA and ensure even a partial change of the policies that were destroying Peru. Wasn't that a stronger reason than any other? Hadn't a legal technicality been found to support Barrantes's refusal to run against Alan García in a second round in 1985? Eduardo Orrego had been informed early that morning of my intention to give up my candidacy by a call from

Fernando Belaunde, telephoning from Moscow, where he was attending a congress. The ex-president told Orrego that Alan García had phoned him from Lima, "all upset, since it had been learned that Vargas Llosa was thinking of giving up running as a candidate in a second round, which would invalidate the entire electoral process." How had President García come by the news of my resignation? Through the one and only possible source: Fujimori. The latter, after his talk with me, had hastened to discuss our conversation with the president and ask for his advice. Wasn't this the best proof that Fujimori was acting in collusion with Alan García? My resignation would be useless. On the contrary, if we went ahead and proved that Fujimori represented the continuation of the present government, we could reverse what appeared to be a desertion by so many independent voters who had turned to someone whom they believed, out of naïveté and ignorance, to be a candidate without ties to the APRA.

We were in the midst of this discussion when an uproar outside the front door drowned out our voices. Fujimori had unexpectedly turned up there, and our security force was trying to protect him from the avalanche of reporters who were questioning him as to his reasons for coming, and from supporters of mine who were jeering at him and catcalling. I showed him into the living room, as Don Ernesto and Eduardo went off to inform Popular Action and the Christian Popular Party of our talk.

Unlike the day before, when he struck me as being calm and serene, I noted that Fujimori was extremely tense, owing either to the hubbub at the front door or to what he had come to tell me. He began by thanking me for having expressed my strong disapproval of the racist slogans the night before (he had seen the telecast of my talk on Channel 2), and without hiding how upset he was, he added that constitutional problems might arise if I gave up my candidacy. This was unconstitutional and would invalidate the election process. I told him that it was my belief that this was not the case, but that, in any event, I would make certain that it would not bring about a crisis that would lead to a coup d'état. I saw him to the door, but I did not go out onto the street with him.

At the time the inside of my house was full to overflowing, as were the grounds outside. Every last member of the political committee of Libertad had arrived—the one time, it seems to me, that not one of them failed to show up—along with several of my closest advisers such as Raúl Salazar, and Jaime Bayly having been alerted by Álvaro. Patricia was holding a meeting in the patio with a fair number of the leaders of Acción Solidaria. We found room as best we could for some thirty people in the living room on the ground floor, and despite the heat, we closed the windows and drew the curtains so that the reporters and supporters gathered in the street wouldn't hear us.

I explained the reasons why a second round impressed me as useless and dangerous, and given the outcome on Sunday, the advantage if the forces of the Front reached some sort of agreement with Fujimori. Keeping Alan García's policy from continuing any longer was now the top priority. The Peruvian people had refused to give us the mandate that we had sought from them and there was no longer any possibility of carrying out our reforms—not even in the hypothetical case of winning in the second round, since we would have a majority against us in Congress—and therefore we should spare the country another campaign the result of which we already knew, since it was obvious that the APRA and the United Left would make common cause with my adversary. I then read them my letter.

I believe that all of those present spoke, a number of them in dramatic terms, all of them, with the exception of Enrique Ghersi, urging me not to drop out. Only Ghersi pointed out that, in principle, he did not reject the idea of negotiating with Fujimori if that would allow us to salvage certain key points of our program; but Enrique too had his doubts about the independence of the Cambio 90 candidate to make decisions about anything on his own, since, like all the other advisers, he believed him to be a vassal of Alan García's.

One of the most lively contributions to the discussion was the one made by Enrique Chirinos Soto, whom the monumental surprise of the election had pulled out of his lethargy and driven into a state of lucid paroxysm. He abounded with technical reasons proving that resigning from the second round went against the letter and the spirit of the Constitution; but it seemed to him even graver still to abandon the fight and offer a free field to a candidate who had been made up out of whole cloth, without a program or ideas or a team—to a political adventurer who, once in power, might well mean the collapse of democratic rule. He did not believe in my thesis that in the second round there would be a holy APRA-Socialist-Communist alliance backing Fujimori; he was certain that the Peruvian people would not vote for a "first-generation Peruvian, who did not have a single one of his dead kinfolk buried in Peru."* This was the first time that I had heard such an argument, but not the last. I was frequently to hear it from partisans of mine as cultivated and intelligent as Enrique: because Fujimori was the son of Japanese parents, because he didn't have roots in Peruvian soil, because his mother was a foreigner who still hadn't learned Spanish, he was less Peruvian than I was, less Peruvian than those who—whether Indians or whites—had shared Peruvian life for many generations.

Many times in the course of the next two months, I had to come out and say that arguments of that sort made me want Fujimori to win, since they betrayed two aberrations against which I have written and spoken throughout my life: nationalism and racism (two aberrations that, in fact, are one and the same).

Alfredo Barnechea delivered a long historical disquisition on Peruvian crises and decadence, which, according to him, had in recent years reached a critical point, which could be the source of an irreparable catastrophe, not only for the survival of democracy, but for the fate of the nation. The governing of the country could not be entrusted to someone who represented sheer dyed-in-the-wool knavery or was very probably a front for Alan García; my resignation was not going to appear to be a generous gesture to facilitate a change in the current situation. It would appear to be the haughty flight of a vain man whose self-esteem had been wounded. Moreover, it could lead to a ridiculous outcome. For, since it was constitutionally illegal, the National Election Board could call for a second round and allow my name to remain on the ballot, even though I wanted it removed.

At that point, Patricia interrupted our meeting to whisper in my ear that the archbishop of Lima had come to see me, in secret. He was upstairs in my study. I apologized to those present for leaving the meeting and, thunderstruck, went upstairs to see my illustrious visitor. How had he managed to get into the house? How had he been able to get past the barrier of reporters and demonstrators without being discovered?

* After April 5, 1992, Chirinos Soto was to arm himself with "constitutional" reasons to justify agricultural engineer Fujimori's coup d'état and attack those of us who condemn it. He now accuses me of being—a Marxist!

Many versions of this visit have made the rounds, and I admit that it was a determining factor in my reversing my decision not to participate in the second round. I have only now learned the true version, through Patricia, who, in order that this book might be a true account, finally made up her mind to tell me what had really happened. On the day after the elections, several calls had come from the archbishop's office, saying that Monsignor Vargas Alzamora would like to see me. In all the confusion, no one passed the message on to me. That morning, as we were holding our discussion in the meeting of the political committee, Lucho Bustamante, Pedro Cateriano, and Álvaro had left several times so as to keep Patricia and the leaders of Solidaridad, gathered together in the garden, informed about our heated discussion: "There is no way to convince him. Mario is going to give up running as a candidate in the second round." At that point, it was Patricia, who remembered the splendid impression that Monsignor Vargas Alzamora had made on me the day I met him, who suddenly had an idea. "Have the archbishop come here to talk with him. He can convince him." She conspired with Lucho Bustamante, and he telephoned to Monsignor Vargas Alzamora, explained to him what was happening, and the archbishop agreed to come out to my house. In order to get inside without being recognized, the car with reflecting plate-glass windows that I myself used when I went out and about was sent to fetch him, and brought him straight into the garage.

When I went upstairs to my study, which also had the blinds down so as to keep people from peering in from the street—there the archbishop was, taking a look at the books on the shelves. The half- or three-quarters of an hour that we talked together has become confused in my memory with certain of the most unusual episodes of the good novels that I have read. Although the conversation had the political situation of the moment as its only reason for being, subtle person that he is, Monsignor Vargas Alzamora managed to transform it into an interchange having to do with high culture, sociology, history, and lofty spirituality.

With a cheerful laugh, he remarked on his fantastic trip to my house, crouching down in the car, and like someone who is talking in order to while away the time, he told me that every morning, as soon as he got up, he always read a few pages of the Bible, opened at random. What chance had placed before his eyes that morning amazed him: it seemed to be a commentary on current events in Peru. Did I have a Bible at hand? I fetched the Jerusalem version and he told me which chapter and verses he was referring to. I read them aloud and the two of us burst out laughing. Yes, it was true, the intrigues and misdeeds ablaze with the fires of hell committed by that Evil One of the holy book were reminiscent of those of yet another one, more terrestrial and closer at hand.

Had it come as a surprise to him that, in the elections two days before, some fifteen evangelical representatives and senators on agricultural engineer Fujimori's lists had won? Well, yes, just as it had surprised all of Peru, although the archbishop had had advance notice, through parish priests, of a very resolute mobilization on the part of pastors of evangelical sects, in the urban slum settlements and in the villages and small towns in the mountains, to further Fujimori's candidacy. These sects had become more and more deeply involved with the marginal sectors of Peruvian society, filling the vacuum left by the Catholic Church because of the scarcity of priests. Naturally, nobody wanted to revive the wars of religion, altogether dead and buried now. In these days of tolerance and ecumenism, the Church got along quite harmoniously with the historic religious institutions that had come into existence at the time of the Reformation. But weren't these sects, frequently small and sometimes given to extravagant practices and doctrines, whose mother houses were located in Tampa and Orlando, going to add yet another factor leading to factionalism and division in a society already as fragmented and divided as our Peruvian one was? Above all if, as appeared to be the case, judging from the belligerent declarations of some of the brand-new evangelical representatives and senators, the aim of these sects in coming to our country was to make war on Catholics. (One of the evangelicals just elected had declared that there would now be a Protestant church alongside every temple of popery in Peru.) Despite all the commentaries and criticisms that could be made against it, the Catholic Church was one of the most widespread bonds of kinship between Peruvians of different ethnic groups, languages, regions, or economic levels. One of the few ties that had resisted the centrifugal forces that had increasingly been separating one group from another, furthering their enmities and stirring up trouble between them. It would be a shame for religion to be turned into another factor of division and controversy among Peruvians. Didn't it seem so to me?

Since so many things had been lost or were going badly, it was necessary to try to preserve, as precious objects, the good ones that still remained. Democracy, for instance. It was indispensable for it not to disappear, yet again, from our history. Not to offer pretexts to those who were endeavoring to put an end to it. This was a subject which, even though it was not officially within his sphere of responsibilities, he took very seriously. There were alarming rumors that had been circulating in the last few hours, and the archbishop believed that it was his duty to inform me of them. Rumors of a coup d'état, even. If a vacuum and a state of confusion came about, as would happen, for instance, if I withdrew from the electoral contest, that could be the pretext for those who were nostalgic for a dictatorship to strike their blow, maintaining that the interruption of the electoral process was giving rise to instability, anarchy.

The evening before, he had held a meeting with certain bishops and they had exchanged ideas concerning such subjects and they had all agreed that he should tell me the things he had just spoken of. He had also seen Father Gustavo Gutiérrez, a friend of mine, and he too advised me to go on with the runoff round.

I thanked Monsignor Vargas Alzamora for his visit and assured him that I would bear firmly in mind everything that I had heard him tell me. And I did just that. Until his arrival at my house I was convinced that the best thing I could do was to create, through the withdrawal of my candidacy in the runoff round, a de facto situation in which there were enormous possibilities that Fujimori would eventually form an alliance with the Democratic Front, which would give the future government solidity and prevent its becoming a mere continuation of Alan García's populism. But his warning that my decision might well unleash a coup d'état—"I have sufficient facts at my disposal for judging the situation to enable me to say such a thing"—made me hesitate. Among all the catastrophes that might suddenly happen to Peru, the worst would be to return once again to the era of barracks coups.

I saw Monsignor Vargas Alzamora to the car in the garage, from which he emerged once again in secret. I went upstairs to my study to get a notebook and at that point I saw robust María Amelia Fort de

Cooper emerge from the little adjoining bathroom, as though she were levitating. The archbishop's arrival had caught her by surprise in the bathroom and she remained there, bashful and silent, listening to our conversation. She had heard every word. She appeared to be in a trance. "You've read the Bible with the archbishop," she murmured in ecstasy. "I heard him and I could swear that the dove of the Holy Spirit has passed this way." María Amelia, who has four passions in life—theology, the theater, and psychoanalysis, but above all else waffles with chocolate syrup, and whipped cream—had climbed up, the night of the rally in the Plaza San Martín in 1987, onto the roof of the building alongside the speakers' platform, with sacks of *pica-pica*, whose contents she kept throwing down onto my head as I was delivering my speech. At the rally in Arequipa, the bottle-hurling by Apristas and Maoists saved me from new doses of that concoction, which causes a person to itch like mad, since she had to take refuge, with Patricia, underneath the shield of a policeman, but at the rally in Piura she perfected her technique and secured a sort of bazooka with which, from a strategic point of the platform, she cannonaded me with *pica-pica*, one blast of which, as the last cheers were ringing out, hit me square in the mouth and almost smothered me. I had persuaded her to forget *pica-pica* for the remainder of the campaign and work instead on the cultural committee of Libertad, which in fact she did, rounding up in it a fine group of intellectuals and cultural celebrities. Like other Catholic militants of Libertad, she always clung to the hope that I would come back to the religious fold. Hence the scene in my study enraptured her.

I went back down to the living room and informed my friends on the political committee of Libertad of the interview with the archbishop, asking them to keep the news of it strictly confidential, joking with them, to relieve the tension a little, about what incredible occurrences took place in this incredible country in which, all of a sudden, the hopes of the Catholic Church of facing up to the offensive of the evangelicals appeared to have been placed square on the shoulders of an agnostic.

We went on exchanging ideas for a good while and finally I agreed to postpone my decision. I would take a couple of days off to rest, outside Lima. Meanwhile, I would avoid the press. In order to placate the reporters at the door, I asked Enrique Chirinos Soto to go talk to them. He was to limit himself to telling them that we had made an evaluation of the results of the election. But Enrique interpreted this as meaning that I had made him one of my permanent spokesmen, and both when I left my house and in New York, and then in Spain, he made foolish statements in the name of the Democratic Front—not even the most intelligent man is one for twenty-four hours out of twenty-four—such as the one in which he declared that in Peru there had never been a president who was a first-generation Peruvian, which cables relayed to Peru and which made me out to be endorsing antediluvian racist ideas. Álvaro hastened to deny it, regretting having to do so, because of the appreciation and gratitude he felt toward Enrique, who had been his mentor when he was a novice journalist at *La Prensa*, and I did so too, on this occasion and on all the others when I heard a similar argument in circles close to me.

But in those suffocating sixty days between April 8 and June 10, this did not prevent the two subjects that came up that morning in the meetings at my house from being turned into the two principal issues of the elections: racism and religion. From that time on, the electoral process was to assume an aspect that made me feel as though I had been trapped in a spider web of misunderstandings.

That same afternoon I went with Patricia—Álvaro, indignant at my having yielded under pressure, refused to go with us—to a beach in the South, to the house of some friends, hoping to have a couple of days by ourselves. But despite the complicated tactics we tried, the press discovered that very same afternoon that we were in Los Pulpos and laid siege to the house where I was staying. I was unable to go out onto the terrace to get a little sun without being besieged by TV cameramen, photographers, and reporters who attracted curiosity seekers and turned the place into a circus. I therefore confined myself to talking with friends who came to see me, and to taking a number of notes with an eye to the second round, in which I had to try to correct those errors that had contributed the most, in the final weeks, to the nosedive of our popular support.

The next morning Genaro Delgado Parker turned up on the beach, looking for me. Suspecting why he'd come, I didn't receive him personally. Lucho talked with him, and as I had suspected, he was bringing a message to me from Alan García, proposing that we meet together in secret. I refused, nor did I accept that same proposal when it was later made to me twice by the president through other intermediaries. What could the aim of such a meeting be? Making a deal for securing the vote of the Apristas in the second round? Their backing had a price that I was unwilling to pay; and my mistrust of the man himself and his unlimited capacity for intrigue was such that, from the very start, it reduced to zero any possibility of coming to an understanding. Nonetheless, when a formal proposal of the Aprista party to begin a dialogue came, I named as my representatives Pipo Thorndike and Miguel Vega Alvear, who held several meetings with Abel Salinas and the former mayor of Lima, Jorge del Castillo (both of them very close to García). The dialogue led nowhere.

As soon as I returned to Lima, on the weekend of the 14th and 15th of April, I began making preparations for the second round. At the beach, I had reached the conclusion that there was no other alternative, since my withdrawal, besides creating a constitutional impasse that might serve as an alibi for a coup d'état, would be useless: all the forces of the Democratic Front were reluctant to make any agreement with Fujimori, whom they considered too involved with the APRA. It was necessary to put a good face on the bad times we were going through and try to raise the morale of my supporters, which, since April 8, had hit bottom, so that at least they would be good losers.

Criticisms and the search for those responsible for the results of the first round became more stubborn within our ranks; in the communications media accusations against various scapegoats proliferated. Opposing factions vented their fury on Freddy Cooper, as the campaign director, and also on Álvaro, Patricia—whom they accused of being the power behind the throne and of abusing her influence on me— and on Lucho Llosa and Jorge Salmón for the way in which they had managed the campaign publicity. There was no lack of criticism of me, for having permitted the extravagant advertising campaign by our candidates for seats in Congress, and for many other things, some of them quite justified and others motivated by downright racism in reverse: why had we brought to the fore so many white leaders and candidates in the Front, instead of balancing them with Indians, blacks, and mestizos? Why had it been a blond singer with blue eyes —Roxana Valdivieso—who got the rallies off to a lively start by singing the theme song of the Democratic Front, instead of a little mestiza from the coast or an Indian from the mountains with whom the dark-skinned masses of the nation could have better identified themselves? Although they became milder later on, these attacks of paranoia and masochism continued to be heard in our ranks all during the two months of the campaign for the second round.

Freddy Cooper handed me his resignation but I did not accept it. I also persuaded Álvaro to stay on as communications director, even though he still thought I'd made a mistake by going on with my candidacy. To placate those who were touchy about it, Roxana didn't sing at our meetings again and although Patricia went on working hard with Solidaridad and the Program for Social Aid (PAS), she did not give any more interviews or attend any more of the Front's public ceremonies or accompany me on my travels throughout the interior (this was her decision, not mine).

That weekend I called a meeting of the "kitchen cabinet," reduced now to those responsible for the campaign, for finances, for the media, and to the communications director, with the addition of a new member, Beatriz Merino, who had an excellent public image and had made a strong showing in the preferential voting, and we drew up a plan for the new strategy. Not the slightest modification would be made in the Plan for Governing, naturally. But we would talk less about sacrifices and more about the range of activities of the PAS and other social programs that we had begun to set up. My campaign would now be oriented toward demonstrating the activities to further solidarity and the social aspect of the reforms, and its efforts would be concentrated on the young towns and the marginal sectors of Lima and the principal urban centers of the country. Publicity would be reduced to a minimum and the amount of the campaign budget thus saved would be channeled toward the PAS. Since Mark Malloch Brown and his advisers insisted in no uncertain terms that it was indispensable to wage a negative campaign against Fujimori, whose image had to be exposed as a false one in the eyes of the general public, by demanding that he present his program for governing and thus reveal his weak points, I said that I would approve of such a strategy if it were based on the revelation of verifiable information. But after that meeting I could sense the scandalous levels of mudslinging in which both my supporters and my adversaries would indulge during the coming weeks. On Monday, April 16, on the Calle Tiziano, where it had its general headquarters, I met with the directors of the Plan for Governing and the heads of the principal committees. I urged them to go on working, as though in any event we were going to take over the presidency on July 28, and I asked Lucho Bustamante and Raúl Salazar to present me with a proposal for my ministerial cabinet. Lucho would be prime minister and Raúl would be in charge of the Ministry of Finance. It was indispensable for the teams of each branch of the administration to be ready for the changing of the guard. Moreover, it was advisable to evaluate the interrelationship between the forces in the Congress that had been elected on April 8 and to outline a policy for dealing with the legislative branch from July 28 on, so as to be able to carry out the most essential part of our program at least.

That same afternoon, at Pro-Desarrollo, I attended a meeting of the executive council of the Democratic Front, at which Bedoya and Belaunde Terry, as well as Orrego and Alayza, were present. It was a meeting marked by long faces, buried resentment, and visible apprehension. At that point not even the most experienced of those old pols could understand the Fujimori phenomenon. Like Chirinos Soto, Belaunde, with his deep-rooted idea of a mestizo, Indian-Hispanic Peru, was alarmed at the thought that someone with all his dead kin buried in Japan would get to be president. How could someone who was practically a foreigner have a profound commitment to the country? These arguments, which I heard from many of my supporters, among them a group of retired navy officers who visited me, made me feel that I was in the midst of a totally absurd situation, and left me wishing that Fujimori would win, just to see whether by his victory that ethnically biased vision of what was genuinely Peruvian had been expunged forever.

Yet something positive resulted from this meeting: a collaboration of the forces of the Democratic Front, in a fraternal spirit that had not existed before. From then on, until June 10, populists, members of the PPC, Libertad, and SODE worked together, without the quarrels, low blows, and pettiness of previous years, presenting a very different image from the one that they had previously offered. Because of the tremendous setback that the low number of votes they received signified for all of them, or because they sensed how risky it could be for Peru if there came to power someone who had come from nowhere and represented a leap in the dark or the continuation of García's administration through a straw man, or because of an uneasy conscience resulting from the selfish factionalism that often characterized our coalition, or simply because there were no longer any seats in Congress at stake, the enmities, jealousies, envy, rancor disappeared during this second stage. On the part both of leaders and of militants of the various parties comprising the Front there was a will to collaborate, which, although it was almost too late to change the final result, allowed me to focus all my efforts on the adversary and not be distracted by the internal problems that had given me such headaches during the first round.

Freddy Cooper set up a small campaign commando team with leaders of Popular Action, the Christian Popular Party, the Freedom Movement, and SODE, and composite teams left for various areas to breathe life into mobilizing the forces of the Front. Almost none of those called on refused to travel and many leaders spent days or weeks at a time going back and forth throughout the provinces and districts of the interior, trying to win back the votes that had been lost. Eduardo Orrego stayed in Puno, Manolo Moreyra in Tacna, Alberto Borea of the PPC, Raúl Ferrero of Libertad, and Edmundo del Águila of Popular Action in the emergency zone, and I believe that there was not a single *departamento* or region where they failed to raise the spirits of our downcast political partners, all this in an atmosphere of increasing violence, for ever since the day after the elections, Sendero Luminoso and the MRTA had unleashed another terrorist offensive that left dozens of people injured and dead all over the country.

It had been with Popular Action that the leaders and activists of the Freedom Movement had had the most difficulties coordinating the campaign in the first stage. Now, however, it was from Popular Action that I received the strongest backing, especially from its young and diligent secretary for the *departamento* of Lima, Raúl Diez Canseco, who, from mid-April on, devoted himself day and night until election day to working side by side with me, organizing daily trips around the shantytowns and slum settlements on the outskirts of Lima. I scarcely knew Raúl, and the only thing I had heard about him concerned the squabbles that he inevitably became involved in with the Libertad activists at rallies—he was the man Belaunde relied on for mobilizing members of Popular Action—but in those two months I really came to appreciate him for the way in which he committed himself to the second-round campaign when in all truth he no longer had any personal reason for doing so, since he was already assured of his seat in the Chamber of Representatives. He was one of the most enthusiastic and dedicated people in the Front, sparing no effort to help get things organized, solving problems, raising the morale of those who were losing heart, and infecting everyone with his own enthusiasm and his conviction with regard to the possibilities of winning which, whether they were genuine or feigned, were a tonic to ward off the defeatism and exhaustion that surrounded all of us. He came out to my house each morning, very early, with a detailed list of the public squares, corners, markets, schools, cooperatives, projects of the PAS under way which we would be visiting, and during the many hours of the day's tour he was never without a smile on his lips, making kindly remarks, and sticking very close to me in case I was attacked.

In order to demolish that image of a "haughty man," someone "aloof" from the people, which, according to Mark Malloch Brown's surveys, I had acquired in the eyes of humble voters, it was decided that, in this second stage, I would not tour the streets with my body-guards. They would accompany me at a distance, melting into the crowd, which would be able to approach me, shake hands with me, touch me and embrace me, and also, at times, tear off bits of my clothes or push me to the ground and mangle me if they felt like it. I went along with these arrangements, but I readily admit that it cost me a heroic effort. I didn't have—I don't have—any appetite for mingling with crowds and I had to accomplish miracles to conceal my dislike for that sort of semihysterical pushing and pulling, kissing, pinching and pawing, and smile even when I felt that those demon-strations of affection were crushing my bones or tearing a muscle. Since, moreover, there was always the danger of an attack—on many occasions we were forced to confront groups of Fujimoristas, and I have already recounted how the good head of my friend Enrique Ghersi, who also was in the habit of accompanying me, stopped a stone hurled straight at my face on one of these tours—Raúl Diez Canseco always arranged things so that, if Ghersi wasn't on hand, he himself would be close by to confront the aggressor. As darkness was falling, I would go back home, exhausted and aching all over, to bathe and change clothes, for at night I had meetings with those in charge of the Plan for Governing or the campaign commando team, and sometimes I had so many bruises that I had to rub myself all over with arnica as well before meeting with them. Every once in a while I recalled those terrific pages of Konrad Lorenz's study *On Aggression*, where he recounts how wild ducks, in their impassioned amorous flights, suddenly become infuriated and kill each other. For, engulfed in a multitude of overexcited people who were tugging at me and embracing me, I often felt that I was only one step away from immolation.

When I officially opened the runoff contest, on April 28, with a TV message entitled "De nuevo en campaña"—"On the Campaign Trail Again"—I already had two weeks of arduous work touring the marginal districts of Lima behind me. In that message I promised that I would do "everything in my power to get through not only to the intelligence but also to the heart of Peruvians."

In line with the new strategy, I was to inform the public of the work being accomplished by Solidaridad and, in particular, by the PAS, which by that time had dozens of work projects under construction in the districts on the periphery of Lima. Shown viewing the classrooms, playgrounds, day-care centers, soup kitchens, wells, irrigation ditches large and small, or roads built by the organization headed by Patricia, I explained that my plan for government included a vast, concerted aid program so that those Peruvians with the lowest incomes would be the least affected by the sacrifice required to get out of the trap set by state controls and inflation. The PAS was not a move to garner publicity. I didn't wish to talk about it before its basic infrastructure was in place and I had the ironclad guarantee of the two men responsible for getting it started—Jaime Crosby and Ramón Barúa—that the sum of $1.6 billion needed in order to keep the twenty thousand small-scale public works projects in the marginal towns and villages in Peru going over a period of three years would be definitely forthcoming, thanks to international organizations, friendly countries, and the Peruvian business class. The PAS was a reality already taking shape in April and May of 1990, and despite the fact that aid still reached us in minuscule amounts, as though doled out with an eyedropper—it was dependent on the implementation of our program by the administration in power, especially with regard to funds from the World Bank—it was impressive to see so many technicians and engineers and hundreds of workers turning these projects, chosen by local residents themselves as those most urgently needed for their community, into concrete realities. In all my speeches I devoted half the time allotted me to demonstrating that what we were doing gave the lie to those who accused me of lacking a sensitivity to social problems. That sensitivity ought to be measured in terms of accomplishments, not rhetorical promises.

To many leaders of the Front and friends of Libertad, the new strategy, more modest and popular, less ideological and polemical, seemed a timely rectification, and they thought that in this way we would win back the voters we had lost, the ones who had voted for Fujimori. For no one had any illusions about the Aprista vote or that of its Socialist and Communist variations. We were also encouraged by the increasingly resolute support of the Church. Wasn't Peru a Catholic country to its very marrow?

The last thing I had imagined was finding myself converted, overnight, into a defender of the Catholic Church in an electoral battle. But that is what began to happen, once the campaign was renewed, when it was evident that among the senators and representatives elected from the Cambio 90 list, there were at least fifteen evangelical pastors (among them Fujimori's second vice president, Carlos García y García, who had been president of the National Evangelical Council of Peru). The nervousness of the Catholic hierarchy over this sudden political rise of organizations that had previously been marginal was exacerbated by imprudent statements by several of the pastors who had been elected, Guillermo Yoshikawa for instance (the congressman for Arequipa), who had had a letter circulated among his faithful urging them to vote for Fujimori, with the argument that, when the latter became president, evangelical schools and churches would receive the same recognition and the same state subsidies as Catholic ones. The archbishop of Arequipa, Monsignor Fernando Vargas Ruiz de Somocurcio, appeared on TV on April 18 and reproached Señor Yoshikawa for using religious arguments in the campaign and for his defiant attitude toward the religion practiced by the majority of the Peruvian people.

Two days later, on April 20, the bishops of Peru issued a statement declaring that "it is not honest to employ religion to serve partisan political ends," along with the assurance that, as an institution, the Church was not supporting any candidacy. This pastoral letter from Peru's bishops was an attempt to calm the storm of criticisms that had been caused, in media with close ties to the government—where there were a large number of progressive-minded Catholics—by an interview granted to the program "Panorama," on Channel 5, on Easter Sunday (April 15, 1990) by the archbishop of Lima. When the interviewer confronted the prelate with a question concerning my agnosticism, Monsignor Vargas Alzamora, in a polemical theological interpretation, expatiated on the question to demonstrate that an agnostic was not a man without God, but, rather, someone seeking God, and a man who does not believe but would like to believe, a being in prey to an agonizing search not unlike Unamuno's, at the end of which lay a return to religious faith. The Aprista media and those on the left, already embarked on a battle-hardened campaign for Fujimori, reproached the archbishop for his bare-faced backing of the "agnostic" candidate, and a "leftist intellectual," Carlos Iván Degregori, stated in an article that with that definition of an agnostic, Monsignor Vargas Alzamora "wouldn't pass a theology exam."

On April 19, early in the afternoon, who should arrive at my house but the archbishop of Arequipa, he too hidden in a car that entered directly into the garage, for the reporters' siege of the place didn't let up until June 10. A short little man with a great booming voice, brimming over with congeniality and homespun charm, Monsignor Vargas Ruiz de Somocurcio had such good humor that we spent a very entertaining brief interlude—one of the few, if not the only one, in all those two months—as he told me that it was best for me to forget about "all that nonsense about having declared me an agnostic," because as the son of Catholic parents, baptized and married in the Church and the father of children who had also been baptized, I was Catholic *for all practical purposes*, whether I admitted it or not. And that, if I wanted to win the election, I shouldn't insist on continuing to tell the whole truth about the necessary economic adjustment, since that was tantamount to working for the adversary, especially since the latter said only the things that would win him votes. Not lying was a very good thing, of course; but revealing *everything* in an election campaign was to commit hara-kiri.

Joking aside, the archbishop of Arequipa was greatly alarmed by the offensive mounted by the evangelical sects in the young towns and marginal districts of Arequipa in favor of Fujimori, a campaign that had an obvious religious and sometimes anti-Catholic slant, because of the sectarianism of certain pastors who didn't spare their criticisms of the Church and even attacked the Pope, the saints, and the Virgin Mary in their harangues. Like Monsignor Vargas Alzamora, he too was of the opinion that this religious war could contribute to the social disintegration of Peru. Although the Catholic Church could not explicitly come out in my favor, he told me that, in his own diocese, he had encouraged those faithful who, in answer to the challenge from the evangelical sects, had decided to campaign for me.

From that time on, the electoral battle little by little came to resemble a religious war, in which naïve fears, prejudices, and clean weapons clashed with the dirty ones and the low blows and most treacherous maneuvers on both sides, to extremes that bordered on farce and surrealism. Very early in the campaign, three years previously, an activist of Solidaridad, Regina de Palacios, who worked in the young town of San Pedro de Choque, had shut me up in a room at the headquarters of the Freedom Movement, with some twenty men and women of that shantytown, without telling me who they were. Once we were alone, one of them began to speak as though inspired and to quote from the Bible from memory, and all of a sudden the others, getting to their feet and raising their hands on high, began to accompany that sermon with exclamations of "Hallelujah! Hallelujah!" At the same time, they urged me to do likewise, since the Holy Spirit had just made its appearance in the room, and to get down on my knees as a sign of humble submission to the newcomer. Completely taken aback and not knowing how I ought to react to this unexpected "happening"—some of those present had burst into tears, others were on their knees praying, with their eyes closed and their arms upraised—I could foresee the impression that would be made on those committees that constantly wandered about the corridors of the Libertad headquarters looking for a place to hold a meeting, if they chanced to open the door and come across such a spectacle. The evangelicals finally calmed down, composed themselves, and left, assuring me that I was the Anointed One and that I would win the election.

I believe that this was my first personal experience of the way in which evangelical sects had penetrated the marginalized sectors of the country. But even though I had many other such experiences later on, a number of them as surprising as that one, and I became accustomed to seeing, on all my visits to outlying urban districts, in the doorways of flimsy shacks and huts the ever-present emblem of Pentecostalists, Baptists, the Christian Missionary Alliance, the People of God, or dozens of other churches with names sometimes possessed of a picturesque syncretism, it was only during the campaign for the second round that I realized the magnitude of the phenomenon. It was true: in many poor parts of Peru where Catholic parishes were no longer served by the Church, either because the campaign of terrorist violence against parish priests (many had been assassinated by Sendero Luminoso) had led to the departure of those who remained or because there were no new priests to be assigned, the vacuum had been filled by Protestant preachers. These latter, men and women almost always of very humble origin, armed with the tireless and fervent zeal of pioneers, lived there on the spot, amid the same primitive conditions as the settlers of these towns, and had succeeded in making converts to those churches that required total surrender and permanent apostleship—so different from the lax and sometimes merely social commitment required by Catholicism—which proved, paradoxically, to attract those who, because of the precariousness of their lives, found in the sects an order and a feeling of security to which to cling. With Catholicism, by tradition and custom, the official—the formal—religion of Peru, the evangelical churches came to represent the informal religion, a phenomenon perhaps as widespread as, in the economic sphere, that of the tradesmen and "informal" businessmen of the parallel economy—whom Fujimori had been clever enough to enroll as allies of his candidacy, by proposing as his first vice president Máximo San Román, a humble "informal" businessman from Cuzco, the president of Fenapi Perú (Federación de Asociaciones de Pequeñas Empresas Industriales del Perú: Federated Associations of Small Industrial Enterprises in Peru), which since 1988 had brought together the principal provincial organizations of the parallel economy, and the APEMEPE (Asociación de Pequeños y Medianos Empresarios del Perú: Association of the Owners of Small and Medium-Sized Businesses in Peru).

I had no antipathy whatsoever against the evangelicals, and on the contrary, a great deal of sympathy for the way in which its sects' pastors had risked their lives in the highlands and in city shantytowns (where they were victims both of terrorists and of military repression) and for the way in which throughout the world the evangelical position had been, almost always, in favor of liberal democracy and a market economy. But the fanaticism and the intolerance with which some of them assumed their apostleship annoyed me as much as when such attitudes appeared among Catholics or politicians. Throughout the campaign, I held a number of meetings with pastors and leaders of Protestant churches, but I never wanted to establish any sort of organic relationship between them and my candidacy nor did I make them any promise other than that, during my administration, the freedom of religious worship in Peru would be respected to the letter. Precisely because I had declared myself to be an agnostic, I was careful to keep the religious question from rearing its head during the three years of the campaign, although I never refused to receive men of the cloth, whatever their religion, who wanted to see me. I received dozens of them, from the most diverse denominations, confirming to my own satisfaction yet again in those interviews that nothing attracts madness as surely (or exacerbates it as much) as does religion. One afternoon, my son Gonzalo came into the room, in a panic, to get me to leave a meeting: "What's happening to my mother? I've just opened a door and seen her, with her eyes closed and her hands joined, with a fellow leaping all around her like a redskin and giving her little blows on the head." It was a sorcerer, pastor, and layer-on of hands, Jesús Linares, a protégé of Senator Roger Cáceres, of the Frenatraca, who had urged me to receive him, assuring me that Linares was a man with spiritual powers and a seer, who had always been of help to him in his electoral battles. I didn't have time to see him and he was received in my place by Patricia, whom the pastor convinced that she should submit to that strange rite which, he said, would assure our spiritual welfare and victory at the polls. * This was one of the most eccentric, though not the only person with "occult powers" who tried to work in favor of my candidacy. Another one was a female soothsayer who, shortly before the second election, sent me a card proposing to me that, in order to win, she, Patricia, and I should take an "astral bath" together (without specifying what this consisted of).

* This individual also visited Álvaro, who, like Patricia, agreed to submit to the ritual of the laying-on of hands and has left a personal account of the episode in *El diablo en campaña*, pp. 180–81.

With precedents such as these it did not appear to be impossible, then, that emboldened by the high percentage of the vote obtained by Fujimori in the first round and the number of evangelicals elected to Congress, some of the most overexcited or delirious of those pastors should attack the Church or say and write things that the latter regarded as offensive. And that was indeed what happened. At the same time a famous evangelical preacher, a "Hispanic" from the United States, Brother Pablo—whose radio programs were heard throughout Latin America—was brought from California and filled a number of provincial stadiums in Peru, openly campaigning for Fujimori. In Arequipa, in Chimbote, in Huancayo, in Huancavelica, leaflets began to circulate in which Christians were urged to vote for my adversary; it was stated in them, moreover, that with the presidency of the latter the papist monopoly would come to an end, and the Church was accused of being in collusion with the exploiters of the people and the rich and of being the cause of many of Peru's misfortunes. And as though that were not enough, graffiti insulting Catholicism, the saints, and the Virgin Mary suddenly appeared on the façades and walls of Catholic churches.

I had given explicit instructions to the campaign commando team and to the leaders of Libertad not to employ such tricks, and forbade our militants to engage in the tactics of a dirty campaign, because in the first place they were immoral and also because unleashing a religious war could turn out to be counterproductive. But there was no way to avoid it. I learned later that members of the Libertad section for young people, passing themselves off as evangelicals who were for Fujimori, had gone through towns and markets slandering Catholics, and they were no doubt responsible for defacing some of the walls, but not all of them. For, incredible as it may seem—though nothing is incredible when it comes to fanaticism—some of the evangelical organizations, above all the most bizarre of them, believed, following the success attained by their candidates for seats in Congress, that the time had come to declare open war on the "papists." In Ancash, for instance, the Sons of Jehovah (not to be confused with Jehovah's Witnesses, also active pro-Fujimori militants) circulated a leaflet which, to the outrage of the local bishop, Monsignor Ramón Gurruchaga, they even distributed to nuns in a convent, saying that the moment had come for the Peruvian people to free themselves from servitude to a "pagan and fetishistic Church," and to emancipate children from the Church-run schools that "teach them to adore idols." Leaflets of a similar or even more aggressive tenor circulated in Huayanco, Tacna, Huancavelica, Huánuco, and above all in Chimbote, where the implantation of evangelical churches in neighborhoods inhabited by fishermen and workers in the fish-meal factories went back many years.* The evangelical mobilization in Chimbote had such sharp-honed anti-Catholic connotations that the bishop, Monsignor Luis Bambarén—a distinguished "progressivist" of the Peruvian Church—intervened in the polemic with forceful denunciations against sects that "hurl epithets at the Catholic faith" and with expressions of firm support for the archbishop. †

Religion was the main subject of the electoral debate. Ill-will, chicanery, spectacular moves, or comic misunderstandings entered into it, in a way that had no precedent in the history of Peru, where, unlike Colombia or Venezuela, countries in which there had been religious wars, the nineteenth-century rivalries between the Church and liberalism had never led to bloodshed. In the third week in May, the archbishop and primate of the Church in Peru, Monsignor Vargas Alzamora, published a pastoral letter to the Catholics of Lima, stating that "charity moves us to be silent no longer" and that he felt obliged to condemn "the insidious campaign against our faith" initiated by the evangelical sects "because of the political power they attained in the last legislative elections."

Without allowing himself to be scared off by the storm of criticism that this letter brought on in Aprista and leftist publications, which accused him of "having adopted the headband" (the militants of Libertad wore headbands at rallies), Monsignor Vargas Alzamora gave a press conference on May 23, declaring that he could not remain silent—"because silence means admission"—when confronted with publications that offended the Virgin Mary and the Pope and called the Church "pagan, iniquitous and fetishistic." He said that he did not hold all evangelical groups responsible for those attacks, only those few whose insults "ought to have a limit." And he announced that on

* See the vivid description of this process in José María Arguedas's posthumous novel *El zorro de arriba y el zorro de abajo* (*The Fox Below and the Fox Above*) (Buenos Aires: Editorial Losada, 1971).
† The Lima daily *Expreso*, May 28, 1990.

May 31 the effigy of the Lord of Miracles, Lima's most popular object of devotion, would leave its shrine and be carried in procession through the downtown section of the city, in order to accompany the image of the Virgin Mary, in amends for the insults heaped upon her and as a demonstration that the Peruvian people were Catholic. A short time before, in Arequipa, Archbishop Vargas Ruiz de Somocurcio had called upon the faithful, for the same reasons, to hold a procession on May 26 with the most highly venerated image of the southern region: that of the Virgin of Chapi.

In one of those early-morning balance sheets that I was in the habit of drawing up with Álvaro, in my study, I remember having said to him, around that time, as I began to put more stock in the whole business of "magic realism" because of the hallucinatory proportions that the religious quarrel was taking on, that my supporters who, without my either wanting or seeking it, were creating an image of me as the "defender of Catholicism against the evangelical sects" were mistaken if they believed that that was going to bring me victory at the polls. The Catholic Church in Peru had been deeply divided since the years of liberation theology, and I was well acquainted with enough progressive middle-class Catholics to know that they were much more progressive than they were Catholic. Irritated by the attitude of the hierarchy favoring my candidacy, they would resolutely turn, with holy zeal and in the name of their status as believers, which they were not at all embarrassed about turning into political capital, to exhorting the faithful not to allow themselves to be manipulated by the "reactionary hierarchy" and to vote for Fujimori in the name of "the popular Church." In this way, I would not only lose the election in any event, but would lose it in the worst possible way, in ideological confusion, religious misunderstanding, and political absurdity.

That is what happened. The bishop of Cajamarca, Monsignor José Dammert, a progressive in the Church, turned up on May 28 in *La República*, the daily paper capable of any imaginable calumny, to criticize the archbishop of Lima, who, according to him, "had fallen into the trap" and allowed himself to be used as a tool by the Front, and to condemn him for seeking to revive "the Catholicism of the Crusades, the Catholicism of the Conquest—what used to be called in Spain national Catholicism." That was how this prelate interpreted the archbishop's decision to bring out for the procession, along with the Lord of Miracles, an image brought to Peru by the conquistadors: the Virgin of Evangelization. (Other "progressives" would wonder whether this meant that Monsignor Vargas Alzamora wanted to bring the Inquisition back to life.) While many personalities and institutions of the sector of the Church regarded as being "conservative," such as Catholic Action, the CCEC (Consorcio de Centros Educativos Católicos: Association of Catholic Educational Centers), Opus Dei, Sodalitium, the Legion of Mary, closed ranks around the primate of the Peruvian Church, in the media controlled by the government and those of the left criticisms of the hierarchy by well-known "progressive" Catholics proliferated, such as the one by Senator Rolando Ames (in *La República*, May 30, 1990), protesting against the political pressure the episcopate was trying to bring to bear in my favor and against the conspiracy on the part of "certain bishops who are opposed to one of the presidential candidacies." In *Página Libre* there appeared daily lists of "progressive Catholics" urging voters to cast their ballots for Fujimori, and announcements that thousands of humble women who were members of clubs for mothers, "belonging to the Catholic, Apostolic, and Roman Church," had sent to the Pope a protest—with 120 pages of signatures!—against those Church authorities who were inducing the faithful to vote against Fujimori, "the candidate of the people" (June 1, 1990).

Going himself one better in this clown act, President García announced that he would attend the procession to amend the insult to the Virgin Mary, because for ten years he had been a member of the "Ninth Company of the Brotherhood of the Christ Clad in Purple," and that "those who believe that it is an act in bad taste and proclaim themselves to be agnostics" did not have the right to attend. Comparable to the unwitting humor of these declarations was a proposal, put forward in all seriousness, which I received at a meeting of the Democratic Front's campaign command, for me to give my permission for a miracle to take place in the course of that procession. Through clever electronic devices, the mouth of the Lord of Miracles could be made to open at a peak moment of the procession and utter my name. "If the Christ Clad in Purple speaks we win," Pipo Thorndike stammered excitedly.

Naturally, neither Patricia nor Álvaro nor I had planned to attend the procession (though my mother went to join it, sincerely alarmed that evangelical demons were about to take over Peru), but neither did the most militant of the Catholics among the leaders of the Freedom Movement attend, heeding Monsignor Vargas Alzamora's request that political leaders refrain from "altering the nature" of the ceremony. A great multitude covered the Plaza de Armas that day, just as the crowd that escorted the Virgin of Chapi, in Arequipa, had been huge.

Ever since the beginning of this campaign, Fujimori handled the religious question deftly, thanking the archbishop and the bishops for their good offices, proclaiming himself a convinced and avowed Catholic—his children were studying with the Augustinian Fathers—and promising that during his administration the relations between the Catholic Church and the state would not be modified one iota and expressing his pleasure at the appearance of "our highly venerated Lord of Miracles . . . something that an agnostic would not be able to say,"* on the streets out of season—for this procession is traditionally held in October. From then on, he never missed an opportunity to be photographed and filmed in churches or proudly showing the photograph of his son Kenji on the occasion of his first communion. He did not appear to have the slightest memory of the efforts made in his behalf by his allies, the evangelicals, whom, moreover, he hastened to dump the moment he assumed office. †

In the midst of this religious imbroglio, in which I felt completely lost, not knowing how to act so as not to make a faux pas, not to appear to be an opportunist and a cynic, and not to retract what I had said I believed and did not believe, I received a discreet request from the apostolic nuncio for us to have a talk together. We met in Alfredo Barnechea's apartment, and there the purple-clad prelate (as my long-ago staff writer Demetrio Túpac Yupanqui would have put it), a refined Italian diplomat, informed me, without spelling it out word by word, of the concern on the part of the Church because of the rise to political power of evangelical sects in a traditionally Catholic country such as Peru. Couldn't something be done? I told him jokingly that I was

---

*Television message to the Peruvian people, May 30, 1990.
† It must be said that the evangelical congressmen and senators behaved discreetly and respectfully toward the Catholic Church during their short period in office. And when Fujimori, after twenty months of his term as president, closed down Congress and proclaimed himself dictator, almost all of them, beginning with the second vice president, Carlos García, condemned what had occurred and made common cause with the democratic resistance against the coup d'état.

doing everything possible to prevent it, but that winning the second round did not depend on me alone. A few days later, Freddy Cooper came out to my house to announce to me that Pope John Paul II would receive me at a special private audience in Rome in three days' time. I could go, meet with the Pope, and be back in just over forty-eight hours, so that the timetable of the campaign wouldn't be affected. Such an interview would banish the last scruples that certain Peruvian Catholics of the old school might still have, despite what was happening, about voting for an agnostic. This opinion was also shared by several members of the campaign commando team and of the "kitchen cabinet." But even though there was a moment when I was tempted —more out of curiosity about the person of the Pope than because I placed any confidence in the beneficial effect of the meeting on the election—I decided not to make the trip. It would have been a move so obviously opportunistic that it would have made us all feel ashamed.

And along with religion, another equally unexpected, and more sinister, subject suddenly made its appearance: racism, ethnic prejudice, social resentment. All that has existed in Peru since before the arrival of Europeans, when the civilized Quechuas of the mountain regions had had the most profound contempt for the small and primitive cultures of the Yungas on the coast, and it has been a factor making for violence and an important obstacle to the integration of Peruvian society throughout the entire history of the Republic. But in no previous election campaign has it appeared as openly as in the second round of voting, placing in full public view one of the worst of our national flaws.

When racial prejudice is mentioned, one immediately thinks of the sort harbored by the person who is in a privileged position against the person who finds himself or herself discriminated against and exploited, that is to say, in the case of Peru, the prejudice of the white against the Indian, the black, and the different types of mestizos (all the possible combinations of Spanish, Indian, black, or Chinese blood, et cetera), since, to simplify—and, as far as the last few decades are concerned, to simplify a great deal—it is true that economic power has ordinarily been concentrated in the small minority with European ancestors, and poverty and wretchedness (this without exception) in aboriginal Peruvians or those of African origin. That minuscule minority which is white or can pass for white, thanks to money or their climb up the social ladder, has never concealed its scorn for Peruvians of another color and another culture, to the point that expressions such as *cholo, mulato, zambo, chinocholo* have in the mouth of this minority a pejorative connotation. Although nowhere written down, nor favored by any piece of legislation, there has always been among this small white elite a tacit discriminatory attitude against other Peruvians, which at times caused fleeting scandals, such as a famous one in the 1950s, for instance, when the Club Nacional blackballed a distinguished agriculturalist and entrepreneur from Ica, Emilio Guimoye, because of his Asian origin, or when in the puppet Congress of Odría's dictatorship, a legislator by the name of Faura tried to get a law passed whereby highlanders (meaning Indians) would have to ask for a safe-conduct pass in order to come to Lima. (In my own family, when I was a child, Aunt Eliana was discreetly ostracized for having married an Oriental.)

Furthermore, parallel and reciprocal to these sentiments and complexes, there exist the prejudices and rancors of other ethnic or social groups against whites and among each other, with disparaging attitudes inspired by geographic and local loyalties superimposing themselves on them and commingling with them. (Since the time that, following the Conquest, the axis of Peruvian economic and political life shifted from the highlands to the coast, the people from the coast have come to despise the highlander and to look on him as an inferior.) It is not an exaggeration to say that, if one took a penetrating X-ray of Peruvian society, setting aside those "proper forms" that cover them over and that are so deeply rooted in almost all the inhabitants of this "ancient realm" of ours—being "ancient" always involves formality and ritual, that is to say pretense and fiction—what appears is a veritable cauldron of hatreds, resentments, and prejudices, in which the white despises the black and the Indian, the Indian the black and the white, and in which each Peruvian, from his little social, ethnic, racial, and economic segment of the whole, asserts himself by holding in contempt the person he believes to be beneath him and by turning his envious resentment against the person he feels is above him. This phenomenon, which occurs to a greater or lesser degree in all the countries of Latin America with different races and cultures, is aggravated in Peru because, unlike in Mexico or Paraguay, for instance, racial crossbreeding among us has been slow, and social and economic differences have been maintained to a degree that is above the average in Latin America. That great social leveler, the middle class, which up until the mid-1950s had gradually been growing, began to come to a standstill in the 1960s and since then has been gradually decreasing. By 1990 it was very small, fragile, and incapable of slackening and lessening the tremendous tension between the few who were at the top economically—the immense majority of whom were white—and the millions of dark-skinned, poor, poverty-stricken, and wretched Peruvians.

Those subterranean tensions and divisions were aggravated in Peru with the advent of Velasco's dictatorship, which used racial prejudice and ethnic resentment in a quite explicit way in its propaganda campaigns to put a good face on the Velasco rule: his regime was that of mestizo and Indian Peruvians. He never managed to bring this off, since it never reached the point of taking root among the most underprivileged sectors, not even at the times when he carried out those populist reforms that aroused expectations in this part of the population—the nationalization of haciendas and businesses and state control of the oil industry—but some of that contentiousness, until then more or less repressed, surfaced and began to make its weight felt in public life in a more visible way than in days gone by, and to become tenser and more oppressive as, in large part because of those mistaken reforms, Peru became more impoverished still and fell even farther behind, and the economic imbalances between Peruvians increased. In the months of April and May 1990, all that suddenly overflowed, like a stream of mud, into the electoral contest.

Certain of my supporters, as I have already said, were the first to commit the error of openly giving proof of racist attitudes, and therefore I had been obliged, on the night of April 9, to remind those who shouted racist slogans in chorus at the doors to my house that Fujimori was as Peruvian as I was. When Fujimori, during his unexpected visit on the following morning, thanked me for having done so, I told him that we ought to try to make the subject of race disappear from the campaign, inasmuch as it was an explosive one in a country as violent as Peru. He assured me that he shared that belief. But in the weeks to come he resorted to the subject of race, to his benefit.

Since, on reopening the campaign, there were still reports of incidents in which Asians were the object of mistreatment or insults, in the second half of April I engaged in many gestures meant to demonstrate my rapprochement and solidarity with the Nisei community. I met with leaders of it, within the Freedom Movement, on April 20 and 25, and summoned the press on both occasions in order to condemn every sort of discrimination in a country that was lucky enough to be a crossroads of races and cultures. On that same April 20, I spoke with all the reporters and correspondents hastily sent from Tokyo to cover the second runoff election, in which, for the first time in history, a Nisei might become the head of state of a country outside Japan.

The Japanese colony published a communiqué on May 16, protesting against the racist incidents and emphatically stating that it had not sided as a group with either of the two candidates, and the Japanese ambassador, Masaki Seo—who had proved to be extremely cordial to me and to the Democratic Front—also made a statement denying that his country had made promises to any candidate. (Fujimori had been hinting that if he were elected gifts and credits from Japan would rain down on Peru.)

I believed that, in the light of all this, the subject of race would gradually fade away and that the electoral debate could focus on the two subjects in which I held an advantage: the Plan for Governing and the Program for Social Aid.

But the racial subject had poked only its head out. Soon its whole body would take part in the wrestling match, now pushed into the arena through the main entry by my adversary. On the pretext of protesting against racial discrimination, beginning with his first public rally, Fujimori began to repeat what would be the leitmotif of his campaign from that time on: that of *"el chinito y los quatro cholitos,"* the little Oriental and the four little mestizos. That is what the Vargasllosistas thought his candidacy represented; but they were not ashamed of being the same thing as millions and millions of Peruvians: *chinitos, cholitos, indiecitos, negritos.* Was it fair that Peru should belong only to *blanquitos*? Peru belonged to *chinitos* like him and to *cholitos* like the first vice president on his ticket. And then he introduced the likable Máximo San Román, who with his arms upraised showed the audience his strong Indian face of a *cholo* from Cuzco. When I was shown the video of a rally in Villa El Salvador on May 9, in which Fujimori used the racial subject in this undisguised way—he had already done the same thing before, in Tacna—defining the electoral contest before a crowd of impoverished Indians and *cholos* from the city's squatter slums as a confrontation between whites and coloreds, I greatly regretted it, for stirring up racial prejudice in that way meant playing with fire, but I thought that it was going to bring him good results at the polls. Rancor, resentment, frustration of people exploited and marginalized for centuries, who saw the white man as someone who was powerful and an exploiter, could be wondrously well manipulated by a demagogue, if he continually repeated something that, moreover, had an apparent basis in fact: my candidacy had seemed to enjoy the support of the "whites" of Peru en bloc.

In this way, the racial theme assumed a central place in the campaign. That racist tactic managed to make my own partisans feel out of place and cause them to experience some very uncomfortable moments. I remember having seen an interview on TV with one of the leaders of Popular Action, Jaime de Althaus, who was working on the committee for the Plan for Governing and was minister of agriculture in the cabinet proposed by Lucho Bustamante and Raúl Salazar, defending himself from the charge of a Channel 5 journalist that my candidacy was that of the whites, and pointing out that various leaders of ours were mestizos, of very humble origins, and with skin as dark as that of any Fujimorista. Jaime seemed to be trying to apologize for his having fair hair and blue eyes.

If we followed that route, we were lost. It goes without saying that, if it was a question of that, we could have shown that not only were there whites in the Front but hundreds of thousands of dark-skinned Peruvians, of every racial background imaginable. But *it was not a question of that*, and to me prejudices against a Japanese or an Indian Peruvian were as repugnant as those against a white Peruvian, and I said as much every time that I found myself forced to mention the subject. It could not be brushed to one side of the campaign now and an undetermined number—though I think it was a high percentage —of voters were sensitive to it, feeling that, by voting for a yellow man against a white one (that is what it appears that I am, in the mosaic of Peruvian races), they were engaging in an act of ethnic solidarity and retaliation.

If the electoral campaign had been a dirty one in the first round, it was now an obscene one. Thanks to spontaneous reports that reached us from different sources, and to verifications made by the people of the Democratic Front themselves or by reporters and media that backed my candidacy, such as the daily papers *Expreso*, *El Comercio*, and *Ojo*, Channel 4, the magazine *Oiga*, and above all César Hildebrandt's television program "En Persona" ("In Person"), the mystery surrounding the person of agricultural engineer Fujimori Fujimori began to fade. A reality quite different from the mythological one with which he had been invested by the communications media controlled by the APRA and the left began to emerge. For one thing, the "candidate of the poor" was not at all poor and enjoyed an estate considerably more substantial than mine, judging from the dozens of houses and buildings he owned, had bought, sold, and resold in the last few years, in different districts of Lima, understating their worth in the Property Registry so as to lower his income tax payments, as had been proved by the independent congressman Fernando Olivera, who had made the fight for morality in politics the warhorse of his entire term in office and who for that reason instituted criminal proceedings against the candidate of Cambio 90 before the 32nd District Tax Court for "tax fraud and betraying public faith," which, naturally, didn't get anywhere. *

Moreover, it was discovered that Fujimori was the owner of a farm of some thirty-five acres—Pampa Bonita—that had been given to him gratis by the Aprista government, on extremely rich land, in Sayán, not too far north of Lima, using, in order to justify that land grant, a provision of the Agrarian Reform Law that provided for the free distribution of land—to poor peasants! Nor was this his only tie to the Aprista administration. For a year Fujimori had had a weekly program on the state television channel, given to him by order of President García; he had been the head of a governmental committee on ecology; he had been the adviser on agriculture of the Aprista candidate in the 1985 campaign; and the APRA had frequently made use of him in various capacities in the course of their five-year administration. (President García had sent him, for instance, as the government delegate to a regional convention in the *departamento* of San Martín.) If not an Aprista militant, agricultural engineer Fujimori had been assigned missions and been granted privileges by the Aprista government that were conceivable only if he were someone who enjoyed the admin-

* Congressman Olivera, the leader of the FIM (Frente Independiente Moralizador: Independent Front for Morality), did not belong to the Democratic Front nor did he support my candidacy.

istration's confidence. His allegations against "traditional parties" and his persistence in presenting himself as someone undefiled by political service rendered was an electoral pose.

All this appeared in the press as information coming from us, but the one who beat the record for revelations was César Hildebrandt, in his Sunday TV program "En Persona." A splendid journalist because of his qualities as a tenacious bloodhound, a diligent and tireless investigator, quite a bit more cultivated than the general run of his colleagues, and courageous to the point of rashness, Hildebrandt is also a man with a touchy, surly disposition that makes him very hard to get along with, one whose independence has made him many an enemy and involved him in all sorts of quarrels with the owners or editorial directors of the magazines, newspapers, and TV channels on which he has chanced to work, with all of whom he broke off relations (although very often he made up with them later, only to invariably break off with them once again) whenever he felt that his freedom had been limited or was endangered. This sort of behavior had made him many enemies, of course, to the point that in the end he was even obliged to leave Peru. But it also earned him a prestige and a guarantee of independence and a moral reliability that enabled him to pass judgment and to criticize that no TV journalist had had before (nor, I fear, will have again for a long time to come) in Peru. Though a friend of several sectors of the left and rather close to them, always giving them a platform from which to speak on his programs, Hildebrandt gave clear evidence of a sympathy for my candidacy throughout the primary campaign, without that stopping him, naturally, from criticizing me and my collaborators whenever he thought it necessary.

But in the runoff election campaign Hildebrandt took it upon himself as a moral duty to do whatever was in his power to prevent what he called "the leap into the dark," for it seemed to him that a victory at the polls by someone who combined improvisation with cunning, plus a lack of scruples, could be like the final, fatal kick for a country which the politics of the last few years had left in ruins and more divided and violent than ever before in its history. Each Sunday "En Persona" presented both more and more attestations and the most severe denunciations concerning Fujimori's personal business deals— whether open and aboveboard or suspect—together with his hidden ties to Alan García and his authoritarian and manipulative character, of which he had shown signs during his term in office as rector of the National Agrarian University of La Molina. Many of Fujimori's colleagues in this research center campaigned actively as well, out of fear that he would be elected. Two delegations of professors and employees of the Agrarian University came to see me (on May 19 and June 4) in a public act of support, headed by the new rector, Alfonso Flores Mere (at that time I had a chance to see once again a friend of my early years, Baldomero Cáceres, now a professor at that research center and a stubborn defender of the growing of coca leaves as a crop, for historical and ethnic reasons), and in those meetings the professors from La Molina put forth any number of arguments, which some of them made public on Hildebrandt's program, concerning the risks that the country could incur by electing as president someone who, as rector of that university, had given obvious signs of an authoritarian personality.

Would those humble Peruvians who, in the first round, had voted for Fujimori because of his image as a person who was independent, with clean hands, poor, politically and racially discriminated against, a David confronting the Goliath of millionaires and powerful whites, become disillusioned with him? I had had indications that that was not going to be how it was one day, around the end of May, when Mark Malloch Brown and Freddy Cooper took me to an advertising agency to watch unseen, thanks to a one-way observation window, one of the periodic explorations that they were making of the mood of the voters of the C and D sectors. It was becoming clear then and it became increasingly clear that, however aggrieved Chirinos Soto or former President Belaunde might feel, humble Peruvians did not have the slightest misgivings about finding themselves to be more closely identified with a "first-generation" compatriot than with one who had had deep roots in the country for centuries. The elections were two or three weeks away and I had already been making tours through the young towns of the capital, inaugurating hundreds of public works projects of the PAS. To judge from what I saw and heard through the observation window during that session, the effort had not borne the slightest fruit. The people who had been asked to come to the agency, some twelve of them, were men and women chosen from among the poorest of Lima's slum dwellers. The session was being directed by a woman who, with an ease that was proof of long practice, turned those interviewed into veritable chatterboxes. Their identification with Fujimori was unconditional and, if I may use the expression, irrational. They attributed no importance whatsoever to the revelations about his real estate deals and the farm he'd been given and, instead, approved of them as something to be chalked up to his credit: "He's a really clever rascal, in a word," one of them said, opening his eyes wide with admiration. Another man confessed that, if it were proved that Fujimori was a tool of Alan García's, he would feel troubled. But he said that he would vote for him anyway. When the woman interviewing the group asked what impressed them most about Fujimori's "program," the only one to come up with an answer was a pregnant woman. The others looked at each other in surprise, as though they were being asked something incomprehensible; she mentioned that the "*chinito*" would give $5,000 to all students who graduated from school so as to be able to set up their own business. When they were asked why they wouldn't vote for me, it was noticeable that they were disconcerted at having to offer an explanation of something that they hadn't thought about. Finally, someone mentioned the stands we had taken that were most often criticized: the economic "shock treatment" and education for the poor. But the answer that appeared to sum up best the feeling of all of them was: "Rich people are for him, right?"

In the midst of the "dirty war," there were comical episodes reminiscent of the days of Pataphysics.* The winner's laurels went to a news report that appeared on May 30 in the Aprista daily *Hoy*. It assured readers that it was a word-for-word transcription of a secret report by the CIA concerning the election campaign, in which I was attacked with arguments that bore a noticeably close resemblance to those of Peru's indigenous left. Because of my friendly attitude toward the United States and my criticisms of Cuba and Communist regimes, on taking over the presidency I might well create a dangerous polarization in the country and stir up anti-American sentiments. The United States should not support my candidacy, since it did not further Washington's interests in the region. I barely glanced at the article, presented with the scare headline "U.S. Fears MVL's Arrogance and Obstinacy," taking it for granted that it was one of those hoaxes thought up by the

---

* An absurdist literary movement, contemporary with existentialism, which flourished in Paris in the 1950s. Many of its efforts to deflate pretentiousness of all sorts depended on outrageous parody. (*Trans. note*)

government-controlled press. To my vast surprise, on June 4, the U.S. ambassador, obviously ill at ease, came to offer me explanations concerning that text. So it wasn't a hoax, then? The ambassador, Anthony Quainton, confessed to me that it was authentic. It was the opinion of the CIA alone, not that of the embassy or of the State Department, and he had come to so inform me. I remarked to him that the good side of the matter was that the Communists could no longer accuse me of being an agent of that world-renowned agency.

I didn't have many contacts with the United States government during the campaign. Information in that country concerning what I was proposing was abundant and I took it for granted that, both at the State Department and at the White House, as well as in the political and economic organizations having to do with Latin America, there would be a positive attitude toward someone who defended a model of liberal democratic society and close and friendly ties with Western countries. Contacts with financial and economic organizations based in Washington—the World Bank, the International Monetary Fund, the Inter-American Bank for Development, in which the U.S. government had a decisive influence—were handled by Raúl Salazar and Lucho Bustamante and their collaborators and they kept me up to date on what appeared to be a good relationship. Before the campaign, on the basis of an article I wrote on Nicaragua for *The New York Times*, the secretary of state, George Shultz, had invited me to lunch in his office in Washington, a meeting at which we spoke of the relations between the United States and Latin America, as well as the specific problems of Peru, and in conjunction with that trip, thanks to the White House director of protocol, Selwa Roosevelt, an old friend, I had received an invitation to the White House, to a dinner dance, at which she introduced me, very briefly, to President Reagan. (My conversation with him didn't deal with politics but with the writer Louis L'Amour, whom he admired.) On another occasion, I was invited to the State Department by Elliott Abrams, the under-secretary of state for Inter-American Affairs, to exchange ideas, with him and with other officials who dealt with that subregion, about Latin American problems. During the campaign itself I went to the United States on three occasions, on very short visits, to address the Peruvian communities in Miami, Los Angeles, and Washington, but only on the last of these trips did I pay a call on the leaders of both parties in Congress, to explain to them what I was attempting to do in Peru and what we hoped would be forthcoming from the United States should we win. Senator Edward Kennedy, who was not in the capital at the time, telephoned me to inform me that he was following my campaign closely and that he wished me luck. That was the sum total of my relations with the United States in those three years. The Democratic Front did not receive one cent of economic aid disbursed at the request of the United States, where, as is revealed by that CIA document, there were agencies which, because of my overly explicit defense of liberal democracy, were of the opinion that I represented a danger to the interests of the United States in the hemisphere.

Not all of the other episodes of the "dirty war" were as amusing as this one. Aside from the daily news of assassinations of activists of the Front in various places throughout the country, which sent the campaign into a state of shock, the government, in order to counteract the campaign of accusations concerning Fujimori's real estate holdings and his business dealings, had relaunched its own campaign regarding my supposed income tax evasions, through the director of the Tax Office at the time, the diligent Major General Jorge Torres Aciego (whom Fujimori was later to reward for his services by appointing him minister of defense and later on ambassador to Israel), who kept sending his bureaucrats to the Tax Office daily with fantastic marginal annotations questioning my sworn tax declarations from previous years, amid stupendous publicity. Leaflets with the most absurd denunciations proliferated beyond measure throughout the streets of Lima and the provinces, and Álvaro found it impossible to take the time to deny all the lies or even read those dozens or hundreds of leaflets and pamphlets distributed to intoxicate public opinion, a campaign tactic employed by Hugo Otero, Guillermo Thorndike, and other of Alan García's public relations amanuenses, who, in those final weeks, beat all previous records in the fabrication of printed shit. Álvaro selected a few pearls from that proliferating dung heap for our meetings together early each morning, and sometimes we exchanged ironic comments about my angelical intention of waging a campaign of ideas. One of the tracts dealt with my drug addiction; another showed me surrounded with naked women, along with a doctored version of an interview of me that had appeared in *Playboy*, and mused: "Could this be why he's an atheist?"; another invented a declaration by a National Committee of Women Catholics exhorting believers to "close ranks against the atheist"; and another reproduced a news item from *La República*, with the dateline "La Paz, Bolivia," in which "Aunt Julia," my first wife, urged Peruvians not to vote for me but for Fujimori, something that she too promised to do (Lucho Llosa telephoned her to ask her if that statement was true, and she sent back a letter full of indignation at such slander). Another of the leaflets was a supposed letter from me to the militants of Libertad, in which, making a show of that brutal frankness I boasted of, I told them that, yes, we had to take jobs away from a million employees for the shock (the economic reform) to be a success, and that, without doubt, many thousands of Peruvians would die of hunger during the early days of the reforms, but after that there would be prosperous times, and that if, with the reform of education, hundreds of thousands of poor never learned how to read and write, things would be better for their children or their grandchildren, and that it was also true that I'd married one of my aunts and then a first cousin of mine and later on I might possibly marry a niece, and that I wasn't ashamed of it because that was what freedom was for. That campaign ended with a masterstroke, two days before the election, a date when, according to the law, no more electoral propaganda was allowed, with an invention of the state-controlled TV channel, which announced that in Huancayo children had begun to die, "infected by food from the PAS, which is headed by Señora Patricia."

Naturally, there were also a goodly number of fliers that attacked my adversary, some of them in such a base way that I wondered whether they'd come from us or whether they'd been conceived by the APRA to justify through such barefaced lies their accusations that we were racists. They almost invariably mentioned Fujimori's Japanese origin, supposed brothels that he owned from which his father-in-law had made a fortune, accusations that he raped minors, and other such outrageous nonsense. Álvaro and Freddy Cooper assured me that those fliers had not come from our press office or from the campaign commando team, but I am certain that more than a few of them originated in one or another of the numerous—and at this juncture frenetic—authorities or offices of the Front.

The high point of the second campaign stage was to be my public debate with Fujimori. It was something we had been looking forward to and methodically preparing for. I had announced from the start of the campaign that I would not participate in a debate during the first round—a pointless waste of time for someone who was many points ahead in the polls—but that, if there were a second round, I would. Ever since I resumed campaigning, in mid-April, we had carefully placed a share of our hopes in that public debate in which I would strive to demonstrate conclusively the superiority of the Front's proposal, with its Plan for Governing, its model of development, and its team of technicians, over Fujimori's. The latter, aware of the weakness of his position in a public debate in which it would be impossible for him to avoid discussing concrete plans, tried to diminish that risk by challenging me not to one, but to several debates—four at first, and then six—on various subjects, and in different places around the country, while at the same time he thought up all sorts of subterfuges to get out of what had been his own proposal. But, in this regard, we were helped along by stories on the subject in the press and the impatience of public opinion, which demanded that the spectacle be shown on the TV screen. I said I would agree to no more than a single, thoroughgoing debate, on all the subjects of the program, and named a committee, made up of Álvaro, Luis Bustamante, and Alberto Borea, the aggressive leader of the Christian Popular Party, to negotiate the details. Álvaro has amusingly recounted the details of the negotiation,* in which Fujimori's representatives went to unimaginable lengths to put obstacles in the way of the debate, and since they were given a great deal of daily coverage in the media, they contributed to creating what we were seeking: an enormous audience. The atmosphere of intensive preparation was such that almost all the television channels and radio networks in the country broadcast the debate live.

It was held under the auspices of the University of the Pacific, and the Jesuit Juan Julio Wicht performed veritable epic feats so as to make the whole thing come off impeccably. It took place on the night of June 3, in the Civic Center of Lima, filled to overflowing with three hundred journalists who had to be accredited beforehand, and twenty invited guests per candidate. It was directed by the journalist Guido Lombardi, who had very little to do, since, practically speaking, the debate never even got off the ground. Aware of the vulnerability of his situation once he would be obliged to refer specifically to a program

* *El diablo en campaña*, pp. 195–204.

for governing which he lacked entirely, Fujimori had brought along
with him, written out, his speeches (each of them six minutes long)
on all the subjects agreed on—Civil Peace, the Economic Program,
Agricultural Development, Education, Work and the Informal Economy, and the Role of the State—and unbelievable as it may seem,
he also had, all written out, the three-minute replies and one-minute
rebuttals to which each of us had a right. As a result, during the so-
called debate I felt, I imagine, like one of those chess players who
match skills with robots or computers. I would speak and then Fujimori
would read, although not even then did he fail to make mistakes in
gender and number in Spanish now and again. Whoever had written
those cards for him had tried to make up for the vacuousness of Cambio
90's proposal by repeating ad nauseam all the clichés of the "dirty
war": the terrible economic shock, the million Peruvians who would
lose their jobs (the average figure of half a million in the first round
had become twice as many in the second), the disappearance of education for the poor, and the usual personal attacks (pornography, drug
addiction, Uchuraccay). The spectacle of that tense man, frowning in
concentration, reading in a monotone, without daring to depart from
the libretto that he had brought with him on the little white cards,
written out in large letters, despite my efforts to get him to answer
concrete questions or specific charges having to do with his proposal
for governing, had something about it that was half comic and half
pathetic, and at times he made me feel ashamed, for him and for me
as well. (He used up the five minutes allotted each one of us to say a
few last words to the Peruvian people to wave a copy of the latest
edition of the daily paper *Ojo* around and denounce the fact that it
was already claiming that I had won the debate.)

What was owed to a people readying itself to exercise the most
important right in a democracy—electing its leaders—was, surely, not
this caricature of a debate. Or was it? Was it perhaps inevitable in a
country with the characteristics of Peru? Nevertheless the practice of
democracy in other poor countries with great economic and cultural
inequalities does not descend to the depths it did in Peru, where every
effort to elevate the campaign to a certain level of intellectual decorum
was swept away by an uncontainable wave of demagoguery, lack of
culture, shoddiness, and baseness. I learned many things in this election campaign, and the worst one of all was the discovery that the

Peruvian crisis should not be measured only in terms of impoverishment, the decrease in standards of living, the aggravation of contrasts,
the collapse of institutions, the acceleration of the rate of violence,
but that all of that together had created conditions in which the functioning of democracy became a sort of parody, in which the most
cynical and crafty always came up with the winning hand.

This said, if I must choose one episode of all the three years that
the campaign lasted that leaves me with a feeling of satisfaction, it is
my performance in that debate. For even though I went to it with no
illusions as to the result of the election, I was then able, despite my
adversary, or rather, thanks to him, to show to the Peruvian people,
in those two and a half hours, the seriousness of our program of reforms
and the preponderant role played in it by the fight against poverty, the
gigantic effort that we had made to remove all those privileges that
Peru had seen accumulating to ensure the prosperity of a privileged
elite while the majority fell farther and farther behind.

The preparations were meticulous and amusing. During several
days' retreat, in Chosica, I had a number of training sessions with journalists who were friends of mine, such as Alfonso Baella, Fernando
Viaña, and César Hildebrandt, who (the latter in particular) turned out
to be better grounded and more incisive than the combatant I was preparing myself to confront. Moreover, taking time I really didn't have, I
had prepared a number of syntheses, as didactic as possible, of what we
wanted to do in the domain of agriculture, in education, in the economy, in employment, and to restore civil peace. I kept to these subjects,
despite the fact that, from time to time, I was obliged to allow myself to
be distracted for a few moments so as to respond to the personal attacks,
as when I asked him, since he boasted of his superiority as a technocrat,
what had been done to the cows at the Agrarian University to make their
production mysteriously decrease from 2,400 liters of milk per day to a
mere 400 during the time that he was rector, or when, confronted with
his concern because I had had an experience with drugs when I was
fourteen years old, I advised him that he should worry, instead, about
something more contemporary that concerned him more directly—
like Madame Carmelí, the astrologist and candidate for a representative's seat in the list of Cambio 90, who had been sentenced to ten
years in prison for trafficking in drugs.

That night a great many people from the Front gathered at my house—there were members of the PPC, populists, members of SODE, mingling with the members of Libertad in an atmosphere that would have seemed impossible just a few weeks before—to watch with me the result of the opinion polls on the debate. Since all of them reported that I was the winner, and some of them gave me fifteen or twenty points' advantage, many of the people gathered together there thought that thanks to the debate we had ensured our victory on June 10.

Even though, as I have already pointed out, almost all my efforts in the campaign for the second round of voting were concentrated on making tours around the periphery of Lima—the shantytowns and marginal districts that had crept across the deserts and the mountains until they had turned into a gigantic belt of poverty and misery that squeezed the old part of Lima more and more tightly—I also made two trips to the interior, to the two *departamentos* which I visited most often in those three years and to which I felt the closest ties: Arequipa and Piura. The results of the first round, in both cities, had saddened me, since, because of the affection that I had always felt for both and because of the dedication that I bestowed on both during the campaign, I took it for granted that there would be a sort of reciprocity and that the vote of the people of Piura and Arequipa would favor me. But we won only in Arequipa with 32.53 percent against a very high 31.68 percent for Cambio 90; in Piura the APRA won the first round with 26.09 percent compared to 25.91 for us. Considering the high demographic density of both regions, the Front decided that I should make one last tour of them, above all to explain to Piurans and Arequipans the range of activities of the PAS, which had begun work in both places. During my trip to Arequipa I was present at the signing of an accord between the Municipality of Cayma and the PAS of Arequipa for the installation of medical dispensaries and first-aid centers, thanks to the financing and professional support received by that program. (In April and May close to five hundred dispensaries were installed by the PAS in marginal sectors of Lima and the interior.)

Both were very different trips from the ones I had made in the first campaign; instead of the multicolor rallies in the town squares and the dinners and receptions at night, there were only visits to markets, cooperatives, associations of *informales*, itinerant peddlers, and dialogues and meetings with labor unions, members of communes, leaders of neighborhoods, and communities and associations of all sorts, which began at dawn and ended after the stars had come out—held usually out of doors, by candlelight, and during which dozens of times, hundreds of times, I lost my voice and even my sense of discernment, as I tried to disprove the lies concerning the economic shock, education, and the million unemployed. I was so exhausted that, in order to preserve the little energy I had left, I remained silent as we moved about from place to place, and even when the trips lasted only a few minutes, I usually fell fast asleep. Despite such efforts to overcome my fatigue, I was unable, amid an endless interchange of questions and answers, in the Central Market of Arequipa, to keep myself from losing consciousness for a few minutes. The amusing thing is that when I came to, in a daze, the same leader was still perorating, not realizing what had happened to me.

I noticed the tension and the paroxysm reached by the electoral confrontation within Piura, in particular—a part of the country considered relatively peaceful—where I was obliged to tour the towns and villages that separate Sullana from San Lorenzo Colony amid great violence, and where my speeches frequently had as their audio background the jeers and catcalls of counterdemonstrators or the insults and punches my supporters and my adversaries were exchanging round about me. My grimmest memory of those days is that of my arrival, one torrid morning, in a little settlement between Ignacio Escudero and Cruceta, in the valley of Chira. Armed with sticks and stones and all sorts of weapons to bruise and batter, an infuriated horde of men and women came to meet me, their faces distorted by hatred, who appeared to have emerged from the depths of time, a prehistory in which human beings and animals were indistinguishable, since for both life was a blind struggle for survival. Half naked, with very long hair and fingernails never touched by a pair of scissors, surrounded by emaciated children with huge swollen bellies, bellowing and shouting to keep their courage up, they hurled themselves on the caravan of vehicles as though fighting to save their lives or seeking to immolate themselves, with a rashness and a savagery that said everything about the almost inconceivable levels of deterioration to which life for millions of Peruvians had sunk. What were they attacking? What were they defending themselves from? What phantoms were behind those threatening clubs and knives? In the wretched village there was no water, no light, no work, no medical post, and the little school hadn't been open for years because it had no teacher. What harm could I have done them, when they no longer had anything to lose, even if the famous "shock" had proved to be as apocalyptic as propaganda made it out to be? Of what free education could those poor creatures have been deprived, when their only school had already long since been closed by national poverty? With their tremendous defenselessness, they were the best possible living proof that Peru could not continue to exist any longer in the populist delirium, in the demagogic lie of the redistribution of a wealth decreasing by the day, providing instead dramatic evidence of the need for changing direction, for creating work and wealth through forced marches, for rectifying policies that were each day driving more new masses of Peruvians into a state of precariousness and primitivism that (with the exception of Haiti) no longer had any equivalent in Latin America. There was no way even to try to explain this to them. Despite the shower of stones, which Professor Oshiro and his colleagues tried to ward off with their coats spread out like an awning over my head, I made several attempts to talk to them over a loudspeaker, from the flatbed of a truck, but the outcries and the contention made such a din that I was forced to give up. That night, in the Hotel de Turistas in Piura, those faces and fists of exacerbated Piurans, who would have given anything to lynch me, made me reflect for a good while, before falling into my usual troubled sleep, on the incongruousness of my political adventure, and wish even more impatiently than on other days for June 10, liberation day, to arrive.

On May 29, 1990, shortly after 9 p.m., an earthquake shook the northeastern area of the country, causing large-scale damage in the Amazon *departamentos* of San Martín and Amazonas. One hundred fifty people were killed and at least a thousand were injured in localities in the *departamento* of San Martín: Moyobamba, Rioja, Soritor, and Nueva Cajamarca, as well as in Rodríguez de Mendoza in Amazonas, where more than half the dwellings had collapsed or were damaged. This tragedy allowed me to confirm the good work that had been done by Ramón Barúa and Jaime Crosby with the PAS, which, the moment the news of the earthquake reached us, we put to work mobilizing all possible aid. On the morning after the catastrophe, Patricia and former president Fernando Belaunde left for the devastated areas on a plane loaded with fifteen tons of medicine, clothing, and food supplies. It was the first help to arrive there, and I believe the only help, for a week later, when I visited the region on June 6, on another plane loaded with field tents, boxes of serum and medicine kits, the few doctors, nurses, and medical assistants who were doing their best to aid the survivors and the injured had only the resources of the PAS to count on. This program, organized with the limited resources of an opposition party, which the government harassed, was capable under those circumstances of accomplishing all by itself something that the Peruvian government was unable to do. The images in Soritor, Rioja, and Rodríguez de Mendoza were monstrous: hundreds of families were sleeping in the open, under the trees, after having lost everything, and men and women were continuing to dig in the rubble, in search of people who were still missing. In Soritor there was practically not a single habitable dwelling left, for the ones that had not entirely collapsed had lost their roofs and walls and risked tumbling down from one moment to the next. As though terrorism and political raving had not been enough, nature too was venting its fury on the Peruvian people.

A cheerful and pleasant note during the second round of campaigning—sunbeams amid a sky almost always covered with dark clouds or jarred by thunder and rent by lightning—was provided by popular celebrities from the world of radio, TV, and sports who, in the last weeks, came out in favor of my candidacy, and accompanied me on my visits to the squatter settlements of the young towns and the popular districts of Lima, where their presence gave rise to touching scenes. The famous women's volleyball team selected to represent Peru, which won the world semifinals—Cecilia Tait, Lucha Fuentes, and Irma Cordero in particular—couldn't get out of giving demonstrations with the volleyball in each place we visited, and Gisela Valcárcel's admirers besieged her to the point that our bodyguards had to rush to her rescue. From May 10 on, when the soccer star Teófilo Cubillas came to Barranco to offer me his public support, until the eve of the election, this was my routine each morning: receiving delegations of singers, composers, sports stars, actors, comedians, commentators, folklorists, ballerinas, whom, after a brief chat, I accompanied to the front door opening onto the street, where, before the press, they urged their colleagues to vote for me. Lucho Llosa was the one who had the idea of making these shows of support public and the one who thought up and orchestrated the first of them; others then sprang up spontaneously, and there were so many of them that I found myself obliged, for lack of time, to receive only those that could have a contagious effect on the voters.

The great majority of these shows of support had no ulterior motives, since they happened when, unlike what had gone on before the first round, I wasn't leading in the opinion surveys and sheer logic indicated that I was going to lose the second round. Those who decided to take that step knew that they risked reprisals in their occupations and in their professional future, since in Peru those who assume power usually tend to be resentful and for their revenge count on the far-reaching hand of the state, which Octavio Paz has rightfully called "the philanthropic ogre"—incapable of providing help to the victims of an earthquake but quite capable of enriching its friends and impoverishing its adversaries.

But not all those professions of support were as honestly motivated as those of a Cecilia Tait or a Gisela Valcárcel. There were others who tried to turn a profit out of their public backing of me, and I fear that, in more than one case, money was involved, despite my having asked those who were financially responsible for the campaign not to spend any funds for that purpose.

One of the most popular TV emcees, Augusto Ferrando, publicly invited me, on one of his series of programs called "Trampolín a la fama"—"Trampoline to Fame"—to join forces and take a gift of food supplies to the prisoners of Lurigancho, who had written him protesting the inhuman conditions of existence in this penitentiary. I agreed to do so, and the PAS readied a truckful of provisions that we took to Lurigancho on May 29, early in the afternoon. I had a gloomy memory of a visit to this prison that I had made several years before,* but now conditions appeared to have become even worse, since in this penitentiary built to hold 1,500 prisoners there were now around 6,000, and among them a fair number accused of terrorism. The visit was therefore frenzied, no more and no less so than society on the outside; the prison was divided between Fujimoristas and Vargasllosistas, who,

---

* "Una visita a Lurigancho," in Contra viento y marea, II (Barcelona: Seix Barral, 1983).

during the hour that Ferrando and I were there, as the food supplies were being unloaded, insulted each other and tried to drown each other out by shouting refrains and slogans at the top of their lungs. The prison authorities had allowed supporters of the Front to approach the courtyard, which we entered, while our adversaries stayed on the rooftops and against the walls of the prison wings, waving banners and insulting placards. As I spoke, aided by a loudspeaker, I saw the Civil Guards, with their rifles at the ready, aimed at the Fujimoristas on the rooftops, in case there were any shots fired from there or stones thrown our way. Ferrando, who had worn an old watch in case anyone tried to steal it, felt frustrated when none of the Vargasllosistas with whom we mingled tried their luck, and he ended up giving it to the last prisoner who gave him a friendly embrace.

Augusto Ferrando came to see me one night, shortly after that visit to the prison, to tell me that he was prepared, on his program, which had millions of TV viewers in the young towns, to announce that he would leave television and Peru if I didn't win the election. He was certain that, with a threat like that, countless humble Peruvians, for whom "Trampolín a la fama" was manna from heaven each Saturday, would make me the winner. I gave him my heartfelt thanks, of course, but I remained silent when, in a very vague way, he led me to understand that, by doing a thing like that, he would find himself in a very vulnerable position in the future. When Augusto left, I earnestly entreated Pipo Thorndike not to come to any agreement, for any reason, with the famous TV emcee that might involve any sort of economic reward. And I hope he paid attention to me. The fact is that, on the next Saturday, or the one after that, Ferrando announced, as a matter of fact, that he would end his weekly program and leave Peru if I lost the election. (After June 10, he was as good as his word and moved to Miami. But with his audience clamoring for him, he came back and resumed "Trampolín a la fama," a turn of events that made me happy: I would not have liked to be the cause of the disappearance of such a popular program.)

The declarations of popular support that most impressed me were the ones of two persons unknown to the general public, who had both suffered a personal tragedy and who, by publicly lending me their support, placed their peace of mind and even their lives in danger: Cecilia Martínez de Franco, the widow of the Aprista martyr Rodrigo

Franco, and Alicia de Sedano, the widow of Jorge Sedano, one of the journalists murdered in Uchuraccay.

When my secretaries told me that the widow of Rodrigo Franco had asked for a meeting with me in order to offer me her support, I was dumbfounded. Her husband, a young Aprista leader on very intimate terms with Alan García, had occupied highly important posts within the administration, and when he was murdered by a terrorist commando unit, on August 29, 1987, he was president of ENCI (Empresa Nacional de Comercialización de Insumos: National Enterprise for the Commercialization of Raw Materials), one of the large state corporations. His murder greatly upset the country, because of the cruelty with which it was carried out—his wife and a little son of his very nearly died in the fierce hail of bullets that raked his little house in Naña—and because of the personal qualities of the victim, who, despite being a party politician, was universally respected. I didn't know him, but I knew about him, through a leader of Libertad, Rafael Rey, a friend and companion of his in Opus Dei. As though his tragic death had not been enough, after his death Rodrigo Franco was subjected to the ignominy of having his name adopted by a paramilitary force of the Aprista administration, which committed numerous murders and attacks against persons and local headquarters of the extreme left, claiming responsibility in the name of the Rodrigo Franco Commando Unit.

On the morning of June 5, Cecilia Martínez de Franco came to see me. I had not met her before either, and I needed only to see her to be aware of the tremendous pressures that she must have had to overcome in order to take that step. Her own family had tried to dissuade her, warning her of what she was exposing herself to. But, making great efforts to control her emotion, she told me that she believed it to be her duty to make such a public statement, since she was certain that, in the present circumstances, that was what her husband would have done. She asked me to summon the press. With great composure, she made her declaration of support for me to the horde of reporters and cameramen who filled the living room; it predictably brought her threats of death, calumny in the press under government control, and even personal insults from President García, who called her a "dealer in corpses." Despite all this, two days later, on one of César Hildebrandt's programs, with a dignity that, for a few moments, seemed suddenly to ennoble the regrettable farce that the campaign had turned into, she explained her gesture once again, and again asked the Peruvian people to vote for me.

Alicia Sedano's public declaration of support for me took place on June 8, two days before the election, without prior announcement. Her unexpected arrival at my house, with two of her children, took both the journalists and me by surprise, inasmuch as since the tragedy of January 1983, when her husband, the photographer for *La República*, Jorge Sedano, was murdered with seven other of his colleagues by a mob of communal landholders in Ica, in the highlands of Huanta, in a place called Uchuraccay, like all the widows or parents of the victims she had frequently been exploited by the leftist press to attack me, accusing me of having deliberately falsified the facts, in the report of the investigating commission of which I was a part, so as to exonerate the armed forces from being in any way responsible for the crime. The indescribable levels of fraud and filth reached by that long campaign, in the writings of Mirko Lauer, Guillermo Thorndike, and other professional purveyors of intellectual trash, were what had convinced Patricia of how useless political commitment was, in a country like ours, and the reason why she had tried to dissuade me from mounting the speakers' platform on the night of August 21, 1987, in the Plaza San Martín. The "widows of the martyrs of Uchuraccay" had signed public letters against me, had appeared, always dressed from head to foot in black, at all the demonstrations of the United Left, had been unmercifully exploited by the Communist press, and, during the campaign for the second round, had been made the most of to further his campaign by Fujimori, who seated them in the first row at the Civic Center on the night of our "debate."

What had caused Sedano's widow to change her mind and back my candidacy? The fact that she suddenly felt revolted by the way she had been used by the real dealers in corpses. That was what she told me, in front of Patricia and her children, weeping, her voice trembling with indignation. The night of the debate at the Civic Center had been the last straw, for, in addition to demanding that they be present, they had obliged her and the other widows and relatives of the eight journalists to dress all in black so that the press would find their appearance more striking. I didn't ask her about the names or the faces of the "they" to whom she had referred, but I could well imagine who they were. I thanked her for her gesture and her support and took advantage of the occasion to tell her that, if I had reached the situation in which I now found myself, fighting to be elected to the presidency of Peru, something that had never before been an ambition of mine, it had been, in large part, because of the tremendous experience represented in my life by that tragedy of which Jorge Sedano (one of the two journalists killed in Uchuraccay whom I had known personally) had been a victim. While investigating it, so that the truth would come out, amid all the deception and lying that surrounded what had happened in those mountain fastnesses of Ayacucho, I had been able to see from close up—to hear and touch, literally—the depths of violence and injustice in Peru, the savagery amid which so many Peruvians lived their lives, and that had convinced me of the need to do something concrete and urgent so that our unfortunate country would change direction at last.

I passed the eve of election day at home, packing suitcases, since we had tickets to fly to France on Wednesday. I had promised Bernard Pivot to appear on his program "Apostrophes"—the next to the last in a series that had appeared on French TV for fifteen years—and was determined to keep that promise whether I won or lost the election. I was quite certain that the latter would be the case and that, therefore, this trip abroad would be a long one, so I spent several hours selecting the papers and file cards I needed in order to work in the future, a long way away from Peru. I felt completely exhausted, but at the same time happy that everything was nearly over. That afternoon, Freddy, Mark Malloch Brown, and Álvaro brought me the last-minute opinion surveys, from various agencies, and they all agreed that Fujimori and I were so evenly matched that either of the two of us could win. That evening Patricia, Lucho and Roxana, and Álvaro and his girlfriend and I went out to eat at a Miraflores restaurant, and the people at the other tables were uncommonly discreet all evening long, forbearing to engage in the usual demonstrations. It was as if they too had been overcome with fatigue and were anxious for the seemingly endless campaign to be over and done with.

On the morning of June 10, I went once again with my family to vote in Barranco, very early in the morning, and then I received a mission of foreign observers come to act as witnesses of the election procedures. We had decided that this time, instead of meeting the press at a hotel as I had done after the first round, I would go, as soon as the results were in, to the headquarters of Libertad. Shortly before noon, the results of the absentee balloting in European and Asian countries began to come in, on a computer set up in my study. I had won in all of them—even in Japan—with the one exception of France, where Fujimori had obtained a slight advantage. In my room, I was watching on television the last or the next to the last of the soccer matches for the world championship, when around one in the afternoon Mark and Freddy arrived with the first projections of the vote in Peru. The surveys had been wrong again, for Fujimori was ten points ahead of me throughout the country, with the exception of Loreto. This difference had increased when the first results were announced on television, at three that afternoon, and some days later the official computation count, by the National Election Board, would certify that he had won by 23 points (57 percent to my 34 percent).

At five in the afternoon I went to the headquarters of Libertad, at whose doors a great crowd of downhearted supporters had gathered together. I conceded that I had lost, congratulated the winner, and thanked the activists of Libertad. There were people who were openly shedding tears, and as we shook hands or embraced, a number of men and women friends of Libertad made a superhuman effort to hold back their tears. When I embraced Miguel Cruchaga, I saw that he was so moved he could barely speak. From there I went to the Hotel Crillón, accompanied by Álvaro, to greet my adversary. I was surprised at how small the demonstration by his partisans was, a thin crowd of rather apathetic people, who came to life only when they recognized me, some of them shouting, "Get out of here, gringo!" I wished Fujimori luck and went back home, where, for many hours, a parade of friends and leaders of all the political forces of the Front came by. Outside in the street, young people staging a spontaneous demonstration stayed until midnight, singing refrains in chorus. They came back the next afternoon and the one after that and stayed till far into the night, even after we had turned out all the lights in the house.

But only a very small group of friends of Libertad and of Solidarity found out the hour of our departure and came to the plane in which Patricia and I were embarking for Europe, on the morning of June 13, 1990. When the plane took off and the infallible clouds of

Lima blotted the city from sight and we were surrounded only by blue sky, the thought crossed my mind that this departure resembled the one in 1958, which had so clearly marked the end of one stage of my life and the beginning of another, in which literature came to occupy the central place.

Colophon

A LARGE part of this book was written in Berlin, where, thanks to the generosity of Dr. Wolf Lepenies, I spent a year as a fellow of the Wissenschaftskolleg. It was a salutary contrast with the preceding years to devote my entire time to reading, writing, conversing with my colleagues at the Kolleg, and struggling with the hieroglyphic syntax of German.

Early in the morning on April 6, 1992, I was awakened by a phone call from Lima. It was from Luis Bustamante Belaunde and Miguel Vega Alvear, who, at the second congress of Libertad, in August 1991, had taken my place as president and Miguel Cruchaga's as secretary general. Alberto Fujimori had just announced on television, to everyone's surprise, his decision to close Congress, the lower courts, the Tribunal for Constitutional Rights, and the National Judicial Council, to suspend the Constitution, and to govern by decrees. The armed forces immediately supported these measures.

In this way, the democratic system reestablished in Peru in 1980, after twelve years of military dictatorship, had its very foundations destroyed yet again, by someone whom, two years before, the Peruvian people had elected president and who, on July 28, 1990, on taking office, had sworn to respect the Constitution and the rule of law.

The twenty months of Fujimori's administration were very different from what his improvisation and his conduct during the campaign had made Peruvians fearful of. Once elected, he soon divested himself of the economic advisers whom, between the first and second rounds of voting, he had recruited within the precincts of the moderate left, and sought new collaborators within the sectors of entrepreneurs and the right. The portfolio of minister of finance was entrusted to a turncoat from Popular Action—Juan Carlos Hurtado Miller—and advisers and collaborators of mine in the Democratic Front were placed in important public offices. The man who had made of the rejection of the economic shock treatment his warhorse in the electoral battle inaugurated his government with a monumental decontrol of prices, while at the same time reducing at one stroke import tariffs and public expenditures. This process would then be accelerated by Hurtado Miller's successor, Carlos Boloña, who imposed on the country's political economy a clearly anti-populist, pro-private enterprise, pro-foreign investment, and pro-market bias, and initiated a program of privatizations and a reduction in the state bureaucracy. All this with the approval of the International Monetary Fund and the World Bank, with whom the government began to negotiate the return of Peru to the international community, renegotiating the payment of its debts and their financing.

Thereupon, in Peru and in many other places it began to be said that, even though defeated at the ballot box, I had vicariously won the election—one of those famous "moral triumphs" that conceal Peruvian failures—because President Fujimori had appropriated my ideas and put my program for governing into practice. His brand-new critics from within, the APRA and the parties of the left, said as much, as did the right, and the entrepreneurial sector in particular, which, relieved by the new president's change of direction, finally felt free of the insecurity of the Alan García era. The result was that this thesis —this fiction—in the end became the incontrovertible truth.

This has been, I believe, my real defeat, not the superficial one of June 10, because it perverts a good part of what I did and everything I tried to do for Peru. That thesis was already untrue before April 5, and is much more so since the power play whereby Fujimori deposed senators and congressmen who had a legitimacy as unquestionable as his own, and restored, with a new mask—as in those Kabuki melodramas where, beneath the masks of many characters, there is always the same actor—the authoritarian tradition, the reason behind our backwardness and barbarism.

The program for which I had sought a mandate and which the Peruvian people refused to give me proposed placing public finances on a sound footing, putting an end to inflation, and opening the Peruvian economy to the world, as part of an integral plan to dismantle

the discriminatory structure of society, removing its systems of privilege, so that the millions of impoverished and marginalized Peruvians
could finally accede to what Hayek calls the inseparable trinity of
civilization: legality, freedom, and property.* And to do so with the
acquiescence and the participation of Peruvians, not under cover of
darkness and treachery, that is to say, by fortifying, instead of under-
mining and prostituting, in the process of economic reforms, the newborn democratic culture of the country. That project contemplated
privatization not merely as a recourse for doing away with the fiscal
deficit and endowing the state's depleted coffers with funds, but as the
swiftest way in which to create a mass of new shareholders and a
capitalism with popular roots, to open the market and the production
of wealth to those millions of Peruvians which the mercantilist system
excludes and discriminates against. The present reforms have put the
economy on a sounder footing, but they have failed to further justice,
because they have not broadened in the slightest the opportunities of
those who have less, so as to enable them to compete on equal terms
with those who have more. The distance between what Fujimori's
administration has accomplished and my proposal is an abysmal one,
whose measure, in economic terms, is that between a conservative and
a liberal policy, and between dictatorship and democracy.

Nonetheless, having put a stop to runaway inflation and imposed
order where the demagoguery of the Aprista government had created
anarchy and a terrible uncertainty in the face of the future earned
President Fujimori considerable popularity, kept alive by communications media that supported with a sense of relief his unexpected
somersault. This enthusiasm went hand in hand with an increasing
loss of prestige suffered by political parties, all of which, commingled
in an irrational amalgam, began to be attacked by the new leader of
the country, from the first day of his administration, as responsible for
all the nation's ills, the economic crisis, the administrative corruption,
the inefficiency of institutions, the trivial and paralyzing maneuvering
in Congress.

This campaign, preparatory to the self-coup of April 5, had been
conceived, apparently, even before the new administration took office,

---

* Friedrich Hayek, *Law, Legislation and Liberty* (Chicago: University of Chicago
Press, 1973), vol. 1, p. 107.

by a small circle of Fujimori's advisers, and orchestrated under the direction of a curious individual, with a dossier straight out of a novel, someone the equivalent, in the present regime, to what Esparza Zañartu had been for Odría's dictatorship: a former army captain, a former spy, a former criminal, a former lawyer for drug dealers, and an expert in special operations named Vladimiro Montesinos. His meteoric (but secret) political career began, it would appear, between the first and second rounds of voting, when, thanks to his influence and contacts, he caused every trace of the suspicious deals involving the buying and selling of real estate of which Fujimori was accused to disappear from the public registers and judicial archives. From then on, he was to be Fujimori's adviser and right-hand man, and his contact with the Army Intelligence Service, an agency which, long before, but above all after the abortive attempt at a constitutionalist uprising led by General Salinas Sedó, on November 11, 1992, was to become the backbone of power in Peru.

Instead of a popular rejection in defense of democracy, the April 5 coup earned broad backing, from a social spectrum that went from the most depressed strata—the lumpenproletariat and the new migrants from the mountains—to the very top, and also included the middle class, which appeared to mobilize en masse in favor of the "strongman." According to the opinion surveys, Fujimori's popularity increased at a dizzying rate, and reached new heights (above 90 percent) with the capture of the leader of Sendero Luminoso, Abimael Guzmán, in which many naïvely believed they saw a direct consequence of the replacement of the inefficiencies and shiftiness of democracy by the swift and efficacious methods of the recently instituted regime of "national emergency and reconstruction." Other cut-rate intellectuals, with good syntax and this time with a liberal or conservative background—at the head of them my old supporters Enrique Chirinos Soto, Manuel d'Ornellas, and Patricio Ricketts—hastened to produce the proper ethical and juridical justifications for the coup d'état and to turn into the new journalistic mastiffs of the de facto government.

Those who condemned what had happened, in the name of democracy, soon found themselves political orphans and victims of a campaign of vituperation that was articulated by the hack journalists of the regime but had the endorsement of a substantial part of public opinion.

This was my case. Once I had left Peru, on June 13, 1990, I had decided not to participate further in professional politics, as I had between 1987 and 1990, and to abstain from criticizing the new government. I held to that, with the one exception of the brief speech I gave, on a lightning trip to Lima, in August 1991, to turn the presidency of Libertad over to Lucho Bustamante. But after April 5, 1992, I felt myself obliged, once again, plucking up my courage so as to overcome the visceral disgust that political action had left in my memory, to condemn, in articles and interviews, what seemed to me to be a tragedy for Peru: the disappearance of legality and the return of the era of strongmen, of governments whose legitimacy is founded on military force and public opinion surveys. Consistent with what, during the campaign, I had said would be the policy of my administration toward any dictatorship or coup d'état in Latin America, I asked the democratic countries and international organizations to penalize the de facto government by applying diplomatic and economic sanctions— as had been done in the case of Haiti, when the army overthrew the legal government—in order, in this way, to aid Peruvian democrats and discourage potential planners of coups d'état in other Latin American countries which (as has already been seen in Venezuela) might feel encouraged to follow Fujimori's example.

This position has, naturally, been the object of strident recriminations in Peru, and not only by the regime, the traitorous military leaders, and the journalists in their hire but also by many well-intentioned citizens, among them any number of former allies of the Democratic Front, to whom seeking economic sanctions against the regime appears to them to be an act of treason against Peru. They find themselves unable to accept the clearest lesson of our history: that a dictatorship, no matter what form it adopts, is always the worst of evils and must be fought by every available means, for the shorter the time that it remains in power the less damage and suffering will be inflicted on the country. Even in circles and persons I thought would be the least inclined to act by way of mere conditioned reflexes, I perceive a shocked stupefaction at what seems to them to be my lack of patriotism, an attitude dictated not by convictions and principles but by the bitterness of having suffered a defeat.

This is not something that I lose sleep over. And perhaps being so unpopular will enable me in the future to dedicate all my time and energy to writing, something at which—I touch wood—I trust that I am less inept than I am at undesirable (yet indispensable) political action.

My last reflection, in this book that has been difficult to write, is not optimistic. I do not share the broad consensus that appears to exist among Peruvians, that through the two electoral processes held in Peru after April 5—one for a Constituent Congress and one for a new role for town councils—legality has been reestablished and the government has recovered its democratic credentials. On the contrary, I think that these measures have served, rather, to make Peru go backward politically and that, with the blessing of the Organization of American States and many Western foreign offices, there has been restored in the country, with just a slight touch of makeup, the very old authoritarian tradition: that of caudillos, that of military power over civilian society, that of force and the intrigues of a coterie over institutions and the law.

Since April 5, 1992, an era of confusion and of notable paradoxes has begun in Peru, one that is very instructive as regards the unpredictability of history, its slippery nature and its surprising zigzags. A new antistate and anticollectivist mentality has spread in vast sectors, infecting many who, in 1987, courageously fought for the nationalization of the financial system and now enthusiastically support privatizations and the opening up of the economy. But how can one not deplore that this advance is weighed down by a simultaneous popular repudiation of political parties, of institutions, of the system of representative government and its autonomous powers that supervise and balance each other, and worse still, by the enthusiasm of vast sectors for authoritarianism and the providential caudillo? What purpose is served by the salutary reaction of the citizenry against the moth-eaten traditional political parties, if it tolerates the enthronement of that aggressive lack of culture that goes by the name of *chicha* culture, that is to say a contempt for ideas and morality and its replacement by shoddiness, vulgarity, con games, cynicism, jargon, and gibberish, which, to judge by the municipal elections of January 1993, appear to be the attributes most appreciated by the "new Peru"?

The support for the regime is based on a tissue of contradictions. The entrepreneurial sector and the right hail in President Fujimori the Pinochet that they were secretly yearning for, the military officers nostalgic for barracks coups have him as their transitory straw man, while the most depressed and frustrated sectors, which racist and anti-establishment demagoguery has penetrated, feel that their phobias and complexes have somehow been explained, through Fujimori's deliberate insults of the "corrupt" politicians and "homosexual" diplomats, and through a crudeness and vulgarity that gives these sectors the illusion that it is, at last, "the people" who govern.

The rhapsodies of the regime—grouped, above all, on the newspaper *Expreso* and the TV channels—speak of a new stage in the history of Peru, of a social renewal, of the end of political parties made up of bureaucratized and encysted hierarchies, blind and deaf to the "real country," and of the refreshing leading role being played in civic life by the people, who now communicate directly with the leader, without the distorting mediation of the corrupt political class. Isn't this the old refrain, the eternal monotonous singsong of all the antidemocratic currents of modern history? In Peru, wasn't it the argument of General Sánchez Cerro, the caudillo who, like Fujimori, also captured the fervor of "decent people" and "the plebs"? Wasn't it the argument of General Odría, who suppressed political parties so that there would be an authentic democracy? And is it any different from the ideological justification of General Velasco, who wanted to replace the rotten "partidocracy" with a participatory society, freed from that trash, the politicians? There is nothing new under the sun, except, perhaps, the fact that the reborn authoritarian harangue is now closer to fascism than to Communism, and can count on more ears and hearts than the old dictatorships. Is this something that should make us rejoice, or instead feel terrified as we face the future?

In the new political jigsaw puzzle, after April 5, 1992, many of yesterday's adversaries suddenly found themselves in the same trenches, and confronting the same losses. The APRA and the left, who opened the doors of the Presidential Palace to Fujimori, then became his principal victims, and their principal sources of strength, even when combined, did not amount to 10 percent of the vote in the municipal elections in Lima in January 1993. The great architect of the intrigues and maneuvers that paved the way for Fujimori's triumph, Alan García, after half destroying Peru and depriving his party of all prestige for the remainder of its life, is now in exile, like a number of his friends and collaborators, being prosecuted in various court trials for theft and corruption. The United Left fell apart, broke into fragments, and in the last election seemed to be reduced to dust.

But the weakening of the political forces that between them made up the Democratic Front, among them the Freedom Movement, having been harshly punished for their resolute defense of the Constitution and their refusal to recognize the legitimacy of the April 5 coup, has been no less dramatic.

Subjected to arduous trials and tribulations when it first began to exist on its own, Libertad, born under the auspices of that multitude of August 21, 1987, and the spell of Szyszlo's paintings, finds itself at a critical moment of its existence. Not only because the defeat of June 1990 reduced its ranks, but because the evolution of Peruvian politics since then has little by little confined it to a more or less eccentric function, like the other remaining political parties. Harassed or silenced by communications media which, with a few—admirable— exceptions, are tied hand and foot to the regime that they are serving, without resources and with a diminished militancy, it has nonetheless survived, thanks to the self-sacrifice of a handful of idealists who, against all odds, continue to defend, in these inhospitable times, the ideas and the moral values that brought us to the Plaza San Martín six years ago, never suspecting the great upheavals that would result for the country and for so many private lives.

Princeton, New Jersey
February 1993